This wonderful book is must reading for those who want to keep abreast of current thought on atonement theory. The essays in this work consider whether the suffering servant of Isaiah was truly "stricken by God." Michael Hardin writes, "Atonement is above all about violence and how we perceive God's relation to violence." One of the problems that is most alive today — caricatured by current "anti-religionists" and held by some traditional Christian theology — is the view of the Crucifixion as the vengeance of a wrathful God. The writers counter with a rich variety of analyses whose common thread is that violence comes from man and not from God.

— RENÉ GIRARD
Anthropological philosopher,
founder of mimetic theory

Satisfaction theories of atonement have had the negative results of isolating Jesus' death from his life and resurrection. We are therefore fortunate to have this book of essays that hopefully challenges that isolation by connecting Jesus' death with the restoration of God's peace, making possible a new reality in the world. I hope this book will be widely read and used.

— STANLEY HAUERWAS
Gilbert T. Rowe Professor of Theological
Ethics, Duke Divinity School

Stricken by God? undertakes a radical rethinking of the Christian doctrine of Atonement. Moving beyond a God who forgives us only if the divine sense of honor or justice, offended by sin, is satisfied by the violence of the crucifixion, this collection asks, Is that the ultimate Christian message? Is that the image of the God of love taught by Jesus? Or is it the product of feudal and juridical ways of thinking that are foreign to the Gospel? Was not Jesus killed by human malice and does not Jesus teach us to meet malice with love and to answer offense with forgiveness? Starting out from the Jesus of the New Testament, and not from entrenched theological traditions that go back to Anselm, the present volume is a major contribution to a new movement in theology that deserves the attention of everyone interested in Christianity's central teaching.

— JOHN D. CAPUTO
mas J. Watson Professor of Religion and
1anities and Professor of Philosophy,
.cuse University

Stricken by God? comes at a time when atonement theology has been experiencing a resurgence of interest and in some quarters controversy. To some degree this resurgence is explainable by the daily news and the global political issue of religion and violence, rooted deeply in divergent visions of God as a violent or non-violent being. This resurgence also flows from our reframing of Jesus in his historical and political context, and equally important, it is fuelled by our rediscovery of the radical nature of Jesus' gospel of the kingdom. For all of these reasons and more, *Stricken by God?* is a highly important contribution at a critical time, bringing together a range of thoughtful voices who raise important questions and pose needed and well-defended answers. This is a work I will refer back to often and recommend widely.

— **BRIAN D. MCLAREN**
Author/Activist

This impressive, ecumenical and eclectic volume casts light on atonement theory and its relation to violence from many angles. It illuminates necessary connections between the scholarly discussion of atonement theory within biblical studies and theology and the implications it holds for contemporary faith practice and spirituality. While the critique of linking necessary violence to redemption has often been associated with feminist theology, the sheer variety of contributors here illustrates that a wide array of Christians are seeking to interpret the cross and atonement in ways that do not continue to sanction and perpetuate violence today. These essays provide a wide variety of alternative interpretations of atonement which will greatly further the growing conversation on this topic.

— **MARIT TRELSTAD**
Associate Professor of Lutheran and
Constructive Theology, Pacific Lutheran
University; Editor: *Cross Examinations:
Readings on the Meaning of the Cross Today*

I wish that every defender of the penal substitution view of the atonement would read this book. *Stricken by God?* is as fine a collection of scholarly essays on the atonement as one can find in print. This book offers insightful, compelling and refreshing alternatives to penal substitution and is a must-read for all who care deeply about how Jesus' death saves us.

— **GREGORY A. BOYD**
(Ph.D. Princeton Theological Seminary)
Pastor and author of *Repenting of Religion* and *Cynic, Sage or Son of God? Recovering the Real Jesus in an Age of Revisionist Replies*

In *Stricken by God?* we encounter truthful Christian writing that seeks to liberate the gospel from its enslavement to the powers of this world. Here, the good news is offered boldly and freely: God loves us and wants us to be at peace with God and one another. Many centuries of accumulated and compromised Christian dogma are skillfully separated from the gospel truth that God was in Christ reconciling the world. The cloud of witnesses found in this book reminds us that God prefers mercy to sacrifice. The result is a renewal of the radical reformation commitment to the Word of God and to the people who are constituted by that Word — the Word who was with God from the beginning and without whom nothing was made that was made.

— **GERALD J. MAST**
Associate Professor of Communication, Bluffton University

In the search for constructive rethinking of the cross, this book is a mother lode of resources. The stature of the contributors, the focused clarity of the conversation and the urgency of the topic make *Stricken by God?* a work that will be accessible and transforming for a wide audience.

— **S. MARK HEIM**
Samuel Abbot Professor of Christian Theology, Andover Newton Theological School

It is difficult to overstate the importance of this collection. For way too long Christian atonement theology has underwritten violence in the name of retributive justice. However, now we have in one place essays from a wide variety of Christian traditions and perspectives that make a persuasive case for salvation theologies that have peace rather than violence at their core. A good part of the power of *Stricken by God?* comes from the impressive diversity of its authors. These essays prove that crucial work in articulating peaceable approaches to atonement is being done across the theological spectrum — and they further that work in powerful ways.

— **TED GRIMSRUD**

Professor of Theology and Peace Studies, Eastern Mennonite University, and author of *Embodying the Way of Jesus: Anabaptist Convictions for the 21st Century*

Stricken by God? is a volume representing both an important new movement of nonviolence that is beginning to find its way into churches in America and a theology of atonement that offers alternative perspectives and models to any form of the penal satisfaction theory associated with the name of Anselm. Influenced particularly by René Girard's anthropology of the cross and John Howard Yoder's ethical vision centered in the cross and the new community gathered around Jesus, the contributors offer bold and powerful new insights concerning the intrinsic connection of the cross of Christ, discipleship, and peacemaking.

— **JAMES WILLIAMS**

Professor Emeritus of Religion, Syracuse University, author of *The Bible, Violence, and the Sacred* and editor of *The Girard Reader*

Anyone who has ever preached, taught, heard or wondered about a "theology of the cross" needs to read this book. The authors collectively offer startling biblical, theological, historical and cultural insights that can help turn Christians away from violence and toward peacemaking.

— **JON PAHL**

Professor of the History of Christianity in North America, The Lutheran Theological Seminary at Philadelphia; Visiting Professor, Princeton University Department of Religion

STRICKEN BY GOD?

Nonviolent Identification
and the Victory of Christ

Edited by

Brad Jersak *and* Michael Hardin

WILLIAM B. EERDMANS PUBLISHING COMPANY
GRAND RAPIDS, MICHIGAN / CAMBRIDGE, U.K.

First published 2007
in Canada by
Fresh Wind Press
2170 Maywood Ct., Abbotsford, BC V2S 4Z1
www.freshwindpress.com

This edition published 2007
in the United States of America by
Wm. B. Eerdmans Publishing Company
2140 Oak Industrial Drive NE, Grand Rapids, Michigan 49505 /
P.O. Box 163 Cambridge P.O. Box 163, Cambridge CB3 9PU U.K.
www.eerdmans.com

Printed in the United States of America

12 11 10 09 08 07   7 6 5 4 3 2 1

ISBN 978-0-8028-6287-7

All articles contributed with permission from the authors and/or their publishers, who shall retain
copyrights. Authors' language, formatting and style preferences, including referencing and abbre-
viations, have been retained throughout. The editors have chosen to maintain internal consistency
within each chapter without insisting authors to be entirely consistent with each other (especially
since a number of chapters are reprints).

CONTENTS

CONTRIBUTORS

The Editors

Brad Jersak is a teacher with Fresh Wind Canada and the Listening Prayer Community. He is the author of *Can You Hear Me? Tuning In to the God Who Speaks,* and co-publisher of Fresh Wind Press and the *Clarion Journal of Spirituality and Justice* (www.clarion-journal.ca).

Michael Hardin is the Director of Preaching Peace, LLC, the founder of The Institute for Peace Theology and a member of the Colloquium on Violence and Religion. He has also published in the *Scottish Journal of Theology, St. Vladimir's Theological Quarterly, Brethren Life and Thought,* and the *Covenant Quarterly.*

The Authors

Willard Swartley is Professor Emeritus of New Testament at the Associated Mennonite Biblical Seminary, Elkhart, Indiana.

N. T. Wright is a New Testament scholar and the Bishop of Durham.

Marcus Borg teaches Religion and Culture at Oregon State University and is active in the Jesus Seminar.

James Alison is a Catholic theologian, priest, and Girardian author.

E. Robert Ekblad is Executive Director of Tierra Nueva and The People's Seminary in Burlington, Washington.

Richard Rohr is a Franciscan priest and director of the Centre for Contemplation and Action in Albuquerque, New Mexico.

Rowan Williams is the Archbishop of Canterbury.

Sharon Baker is Assistant Professor of Theology at Messiah College and author of *By Grace? (An) Economy of Atonement.*

Brita Miko is a novelist from Calgary, Alberta. Her first book, *Nailed,* tells the story of Hosea in present-day East Vancouver.

C. F. D. Moule is a specialist in N.T. Greek and Professor Emeritus of Divinity at Cambridge University.

Miroslav Volf is Director of the Yale Center for Faith and Culture and is Henry B. Wright Professor of Theology at Yale Divinity School.

Mark D. Baker is Associate Professor of Mission and Theology at Mennonite Brethren Biblical Seminary (Fresno, CA) and author of *Proclaiming the Scandal of the Cross.*

J. Denny Weaver is a retired professor at Bluffton College and author of *The Nonviolent Atonement.*

Wayne Northey is Co-Director of M2/W2 Association in British Columbia, Canada, and scholar in residence at St. Paul University in Ottawa, Canada.

Nathan Rieger is pastoring at the Winnipeg Centre Vineyard.

Anthony Bartlett is the author of *Cross Purposes* and Assistant Professor of Theology, Bexley Hall Episcopal Seminary, Rochester, NY.

Andrew P. Klager is a Ph.D. candidate in Ecclesiastical History at the University of Glasgow and specializes in Gregory of Nyssa.

Kharalambos Anstall was a Greek Orthodox theologian. Before his passing in 1998, he was also head of the Department of Transfusion Technology at the University of Utah Medical Center.

Ronald S. Dart teaches religious studies and political science at the University College of the Fraser Valley in Abbotsford, BC.

It could have been me put the thorns in your crown
Rooted as I am in a violent ground . . .
Still you pour out your love, pour out your love . . .

BRUCE COCKBURN

FOREWORD

Willard Swartley

The distinctive niche this book fills within the huge spate of recent publications on atonement (see Hardin's chapter) is its wide panorama of perspectives. This volume of twenty chapters excels not only in scope but also in its conceptual presentation, with seven topical parts: setting the table (Part 1); historical Jesus studies (Wright and Borg, Part 2); essays that connect atonement to sacrifice (Part 3), to forgiveness (Part 4) to justice (Part 5), and to nonviolence (Part 6, permeating explicitly or implicitly the entire volume); and to rebirth and deification (Part 7). The whole contributes a rich variety of biblical-exegetical, theological-philosophical, theological-political perspectives. The bookends, by Jersak and Dart, are fine alpha and omega contributions, setting the stage and inviting us to climb to a higher mountain.

Both Jersak's opening essay and the first part of Northey's (354-55) provide a helpful biblical database of the variety of Scriptural images describing Jesus' saving work—and to this belongs also Dart's all too brief commentary on the Beatitudes beside 2 Peter 1:4. Essays by Ekblad, Moule and Rieger contribute more exacting exegesis.

Dismayed by the dominance of the penal satisfaction theory in popular Christian thought, attributing its genesis to Anselm, the essays of this book provide alternative perceptions of atonement that depict God as loving, redeeming, defeating evil, forgiving, reconciling and empowering those redeemed to know restored *shalom* and to share life with/in God through Christ. Rather than portraying God as (or allowing the) punishing (of) his Son by requiring him to die on the cross for fallen humanity's sin, these essays form a kaleidoscope of alternative models: the cross as mirror that exposes human alienation and empowers transformation (M. Baker), experiencing atonement through ritual-liturgy (Alison), forgiveness-reconciliation models (Williams, S. Baker, Miko), through lenses of rectification, justice and embrace (Moule, Volf, M. Baker), and the "sanctifying action of divine grace" leading to *theosis* (Anstall, with complementing contributions by Klager and Dart).

Both Boersma's (*Violence, Hospitality, and the Cross*) and Weaver's (*Nonviolent Atonement* with its "narrative Christus Victor") books are frequently mentioned and also critiqued, from a variety of angles. Bartlett hears divine violence in both Boersma and Weaver, yes, in "narrative Christus Victor." Building on Girardian theory that deconstructs modern metaphysics and understands the problem of violence anthropologically, Bartlett presents Jesus' atoning work as God's sheer forgiveness of human violence and sin, freed from ransom, juridical, or moral influence theories. Disagreeing with Weaver and Boersma for mishandling violence—opposites in balance— Bartlett affirms divine intentionality in the cross, manifesting God's abysmal compassion. Hardin notes this difference between Weaver and Bartlett. He also clarifies a crucial distinction between divine and human violence, observing that human violence and Jesus' nonviolent response on the cross are inextricably linked. Sharon Baker's "anti-violence" is even more to the point, for it highlights the human violence of Jesus' crucifixion. She stresses, however, God's redeeming and forgiving purposes in Jesus' death on the cross motivated by love, not wrath or punishment.

I join the voice of John Howard Yoder to this engaging conversation. Evaluating Girard's contribution, Yoder speaks to the inextricable link between violence and atonement, accentuating God's/Jesus' way of dealing with violence. Yoder observes that how one interprets the meaning of Jesus' death depends on whether one draws on sacrificial, juridical, political or psychodynamic worldviews. The common baseline for understanding the cross in all these, however, "is that the thing to do with violence is not to understand it *but to undergo it.*"[1]

> The response that is needed is then not a new way to *think* about it—what we might properly call a "theological critique"—but something to be done about it. The response is divine judgment, not an explanation, not an evaluation, but an intervention.... The name of that intervention is "Jesus."[2]

Yoder correlates violence, the cross and salvation in this memorable expression:

> Every major strand of the New Testament, each in its own way, interprets the acceptance by Jesus of the violence of the cross as the means, necessary and sufficient, of God's victory over the rebellious powers. Violence is not merely a problem to solve, a temptation to resist, a mystery to penetrate, or a challenge to resolve with a theodicy. It is all of that, but that is not yet the good news. The good news is that the violence with which we heirs of Cain respond to our brothers' differentness is the occasion of our salvation. *Were it not for that primeval destructive reflex, there would have been no suffering servant, and no wisdom and power of God in the Cross.*[3]

---

1. For my use of Yoder and treatment of the topic of violence, see Swartley, *Covenant of Peace* (Eerdmans, 2006) 380-81, quoting Yoder's "Theological Critique of Violence," *New Conversations* 16 (1994): 5.

2. Yoder, "Theological Critique," 5.

3. *Ibid*, 6.

Yoder's perceptive comments disallow the notion that the cross is super-fluous to atonement. Indeed, might "nonviolent atonement" be an oxymo-ron? Both the human violence and God's redeeming purpose is evident in Regier's exegetical study of Acts 3 (cf. 4:27-28[4]). He speaks of "the intrinsic necessity of what redemption entailed for Jesus, living under the powers" in collusion with Satan. He notes also that atonement calls for action, not only explanation. In this collision between claimants to authority and Lordship, the crucified, risen Jesus is Lord, releasing humanity from Satan's grip in its many guises (indeed, a strong accent in Luke's two-volumes). Marvel of marvels, I add, in this cross-collision between Jesus and the powers—fueled by human rebellion and sin—we behold the love of the Father and the Son in ultimate self-donation "for the life of the world" (John 6:51; cf. Heb 2:9-10; 1 Pet 1:18-20).

To the many quests here to understand atonement, I commend *peacemak-ing* as an over-arching trope. God was in Christ (echo Donald Baillie's classic work) making peace; restoring relationship between humans and God; and through the cross, breaking down walls alienating humans from humans (Eph 2:14-18); and recreating the divine image in humanity (Eph 4:23-24) to partake of the divine nature (2 Pet 1:4; cf. 2 Cor 3:18). Volf uses the poetic motif of "embrace" for peacemaking and rightly describes the role of justice on the path to forgiveness, reconciliation and embrace. Klager too, analyzing Irenaeus, privileges the restoration of *shalom* and the reclaiming of the divine as the goal of Christ's cross-gift, though much attention to *nonviolence* blunts the peace-restoring accent—the two are not the same.[5] Atonement, for which there is not an unambiguous NT Greek word in the strict sense, is not free-standing.

What might yet be done on this topic? Perhaps enough ink has already been spilt. But the integration of the wealth of these perspectives into one coherent model beckons. At the same time, we need to simplify so that alter-native models can be grasped by those who know only the satisfaction-penal model (M. Baker has begun, partially, in his two books).

I am reminded of Karl Barth's summation of his multi-volume Systematic Theology, "Jesus loves me, this I know." After wading through these contri-butions, I also sum atonement simply: Jesus died for our sins, making peace, this I know!

Willard Swartley
Ascension Day, 2007

---

4. Including this text opens the door to a key issue: whether Acts really does put Rome in favorable light. See my discussion in *Covenant of Peace*, 164-73.

5. See *Covenant of Peace*, 6-7, 420-21.

PREFACE

Michael Hardin

In January 2007, seventy or so folks joined in Akron, PA for a two-day conference on the "Nonviolent Atonement" organized by Preaching Peace. There were eight featured speakers. I had hoped to be able to publish my contribution in a journal, as did several others. In the meantime, I wanted to make it available for readers of my website (www.preachingpeace.org) and so "Out of the Fog" went online for two weeks. Willard Swartley passed it on to Brad Jersak, co-editor of Fresh Wind Press.

Now, Brad is a kindred spirit with a clear sense of what makes the good news really, really good. Brad contacted me as he was putting together a collection of essays that he hoped would benefit those who were seeking an alternative to the encoded sacrificial paradigm of the Christian doctrine of the atonement and wanted to include my essay. In turn I recommended to Brad several other contributions from the NVA Conference in January.

Preaching Peace has created the Nonviolent Atonement Seminar featuring Tony Bartlett, Denny Weaver, Sharon Baker and myself. We will be traveling the US and Canada over the next few years bringing this new paradigm to churches, clergy and laity alike. A current schedule of seminars and information on how to book a Nonviolent Atonement Seminar in your area are available at www.preachingpeace.org.

What makes *Stricken by God?* a fun book to edit and a remarkable book to read are the many types of issues correlated to atonement and the various voices that have been assembled here. There are not only theologians here, but everyone is doing theology and opening up the manifold ways in which the wondrous work of God in Jesus Christ can be seen and understood.

There is more than just a conversation here; there is a movement. A movement of clergy and laity, theologians and bishops, united around a common theme: there is a need to construct a new paradigm of the atonement in the 21st century; the sacrificial model is flawed.

Marit Trelstad has a great line in her book *Cross Examinations*. She says, "All categories in Christian theology collide in the discussion of the Cross." More so, belief and behavior collide in the cross. Indeed, the flurry of writing on Nonviolent Atonement and its implications this past decade has demonstrated to some, at least, a direct correlation between belief and behavior. And one thing this collision in the cross has produced is the demise of the power of sacrificial theories of atonement and justifications for actions that are determined by the logic of violence.

Unlike sacrificial models of the atonement oriented to the Self and the assuaging of guilt, nonviolent models of atonement speak to the whole person so that both one's personal spirituality and one's ethics reflect congruency and that congruency looks a lot like Jesus. All the authors in this volume spell this out in one way or another.

The most current defense of a sacrificial theory of atonement belongs to Hans Boersma whose 2004 publication *Violence, Hospitality and the Cross* brought to the fore many of the problems when discussing violence in relation to God. Many authors in this volume respectfully engage Boersma but demur from his conclusions. Bartlett queries Boersma's use of Derrida, Klager his use and understanding of Irenaeus, Weaver his definition of violence, Northey his conjunction of theology and *Realpolitik*, and Hardin his dualism and misunderstanding of the mimetic theory proposed by Rene Girard. If this book seems overly preoccupied with Boersma, it is because he has set the problem of a sacrificial theory of the atonement clearly before us and it cannot be ignored. We look forward to further conversations with Dr. Boersma.

There is also bountiful use made of the mimetic theory. The reconfiguration of the anthropological categories of ritual, religion, sacrifice and scapegoating by Rene Girard and members of *The Colloquium on Violence and Religion* has had significant impact on studies of the atonement. Hardin, Bartlett, Alison, Sharon Baker, Mark Baker, Denny Weaver and Wayne Northey each comment on the heuristic power of the mimetic theory for the doctrine of the atonement. (Worth mentioning also is S. Mark Heim's *Saved from Sacrifice*, whose inquiry into the atonement utilizing the mimetic theory illumines many a dark corner).

The contributions by N.T. Wright, Miroslav Volf, Marcus Borg, Rowan Williams and C.F.D. Moule bring significant credibility to the discussion of this issue; it is no small thing we are engaged in when we seek to understand how God was reconciling the world in Christ.

This book is an ecumenical work and intends to show that the broad Christian tradition is a tradition that can focus on reconciliation and forgiveness. Some will note the paucity of women's voices in this volume. Last fall, Marit Trelstad produced her very important collection on the atonement (Cross Examinations) and most of the feminist and womanist theologians writing on atonement had contributed an essay to that volume. *Cross Examinations* is a powerful book of theological reasoning and an ally in deconstructing the false power of the logic of sacrificial theology.

Stricken by God? is a book that seeks to come at this business of nonviolent atonement from all kinds of angles, perspectives and traditions. It paints a comprehensive portrait of what is wrong in sacrificial ideologies and theories and presents an alternative paradigm of God's work for us, in us and with us in Jesus Christ. As I read these essays over and over I find myself smiling at the generosity of the Loving God borne witness to in Jesus Christ.

We would like to thank all of the contributors and publishers that make a book like this possible. We would also like to thank our proofreaders: Ed Strauss, Bryce Rich, Brita Miko, Ron Dart and Lorie Martin.

From the bottom of my heart, I thank my wife Lorri for sticking by my side and for modeling the deep, deep love of Jesus; to my daughters Galadriel, Arwen and Melian and my granddaughters Quelebrian and Laurelin for their love and support without whom I would have led an empty life. I am also grateful for my mentors, particularly Edwin A. Hallsten (emeritus North Park Theological Seminary) and Rene Girard. Finally, a special thanks to my ecclesial family at Akron Mennonite Church, their love for and support of our work is a daily blessing.

Brad thanks his natural family (Eden and the boys) and his faith family (Fresh Wind) for showing him the love of the Father. Thanks also to his mentors, soul-friends and the Agora newsgroup for granting both freedom and wise counsel when it is time to color outside the conventional lines.

Our prayer is that *Stricken by God?* might serve the Church as she seeks to faithfully follow Jesus Christ in all her words and ways.

Michael Hardin
Eastertide 2007

PART ONE

SETTING THE TABLE

Chapter One

NONVIOLENT IDENTIFICATION
AND THE VICTORY OF CHRIST

by Brad Jersak

INTRODUCTORY CONCERNS

I. Why gather?

Across virtually every stream of Christian faith, the doctrinal ground is shifting under our theology of the Cross and the atonement. Tectonic plates of understanding are sliding and grinding—long-standing assumptions concerning sin, wrath, judgement, salvation and the very nature of God are triggering theological tremors in every quarter.

Some perceive a dreadful crisis surrounding "the faith once delivered." Others feel a deep resonance to a fresh revelation of our first truths. Such core issues as why Christ died and how Christ saves are begging new questions. The current theological earthquake did not arise from mere boredom in seminary ivory towers. Experts and lay people alike are digging deep to such bedrock queries as, "Who is God?" and "What is the Gospel?" Very few givens remain. We might wonder, "Is nothing sacred?" That is exactly the question.

More specifically, a recent surge of literature, conferences and debates has re-opened the question of the meaning of Christ's death at varying depths of strata. What do these shifts say about God? About God's love? About God's justice? What is the "good news" and how do we proclaim it? What is the preaching of the Cross? In fact, what is the Cross? What is "the blood"? One might wonder whether this buckling, holy ground will once again yawn and swallow those who dare trespass.

In the midst of our wondering, we run into the relatively recent[1] dogmatization of penal substitution as *the* evangelical atonement creed. No longer content to call it a theory, many preach it as the required content of belief

---

1. By "relatively recent," I refer first to the birth of "satisfaction theory" in 1097 (Anselm, *Cur Deus Homo*) and formalized as Protestant dogma in Calvin's *Institutes 2.16.2* in 1559 and the Westminster Catechism (Question 49) in 1643. We might also see it finally embedded in the New World via the theological works of Charles Hodge at Princeton through the mid-1800s.

prescriptions for "salvation" — & what is salvation

in order to be "saved." Yet in these days, penal substitution is being reconsidered. Some are carefully cleansing it of misrepresentative accretions and defending its central position. Others feel it should be nuanced and relativized as one among a cluster of metaphors. Still others feel it needs to be renounced and bid good riddance. In the latter case, what alternatives do the dissenting voices propose? Are common themes rising to the surface that are truly rooted in the Scriptures and church tradition? That is the major question this book seeks to answer.

II. Who is at this table?

Included in this discussion are representatives of Anglican, Orthodox, Roman Catholic, Anabaptist and Evangelical traditions. They range from bishops to prison chaplains to novelists, all of whom have given significant thought to the meaning of the Cross of Christ.

While the members of these many traditions offer alternative readings of the atonement—even disagreeing sharply on a number of points—they have gathered around this table with a number of shared convictions.

A. They recognize that a shift in our understanding of the atonement is both necessary and well under way. A sense of urgency and inspiration is developing around our proclamation of the Cross.

B. Each author presents an alternative to the dominant theory of the atonement known as penal substitution. Most do not believe that the Cross saves us through the satisfaction of God's wrath by the punishment of Jesus Christ.

C. While these authors bring a variety of approaches to "Cross-talk," three common themes serve as an umbrella under which we might all gather:

> 1. God's **nonviolence** in Christ at the cross. I.e. While the Cross was a violent episode, we are not witnessing God's violence; the atonement is non-penal. Good Friday was not the outpouring of God's violence upon Christ to assuage his own wrath. That day was God's "No!" to wrath and "Yes!" to love and forgiveness in the face of *our* violence and wrath.

> 2. Christ's total **identification** with humanity in his incarnation and his call for us to identify with him in his life, death, resurrection and glorification. His solidarity with us draws us into the new humanity he is creating.

> 3. The **victory** of Christ over Satan, sin and death as he confronts and defeats them through his resistance, obedience, and resurrection.

III. Speaking of the Atonement

Historically, the question to which theories of the atonement addressed themselves was, "How does the Cross save us?" This question assumes that it is specifically the Cross (i.e. the death of Christ) that saves—a fair assumption based on Paul's commitment to preaching nothing but "Christ and him crucified" (1 Corinthians 2:2). He referred to the gospel as "the message of the Cross" (1 Corinthians 1:18) or "preaching salvation through the Cross" (Galatians 5:11). We're said to be "saved by his blood" or "by his death" (Romans 5). Indeed, the Cross seems to be the focus of Christ's mission and the central symbol of his incarnation.

The significance of the Cross raises further questions. Our authors will investigate the following:

- Why did Jesus die? (Both historically and theologically speaking. From the Jews' and Romans' perspective? From the apostles' perspective? From God's point of view? And specifically, from Jesus of Nazareth's point of view?)

- Did Christ have to die? (I.e. Did he have to be killed? Was it inevitable? Was it necessary?)

- Did he intend to die? (Or did he simply intend to *obey*, even unto death? In either case, why? What was he attempting to do? How did Christ understand his path to the Cross?)

Yet we mustn't collapse the whole Gospel narrative nor our entire soteriology into Good Friday. 1 Corinthians 15 tells us that apart from the resurrection, we would be of all people most pitied. Further, we ought not to divorce the events of Passion Week and Easter weekend from the life and ministry of Christ. The incarnation of Christ—the sending of God's Son *in toto*—is what makes our salvation possible.

Chris Hoke, a member of the Tierra Nueva (an international faith and justice community), put it to me this way:

> The key to my own thesis is that atonement precedes the Cross. The Cross is not the key *event* that saves us, but the *portrait par excellence* of the God we believe in. The Cross is God's climax—the living out of *his* type of power and love.

For a careful theology of atonement, we might more precisely ask, How does *Christ* save us? From who or what does he save us? And what does "save" mean? Secondarily, "What part did his death play in that salvation?" From there, we ask in what sense Jesus' death was (i.) necessary, (ii.) inevitable, and (iii.) intentional.

According to the apostolic tradition, Jesus knew that he would die,[2] and that it was *necessary*[3] in that it was the *inevitable* result of ultimate obedience to his Father and the wickedness of mankind. Anselm rightly identifies the atonement question as, "Why did God become man?" One reason the Word became flesh was in order to die.[4] In becoming fully human, Christ gained access to death so that he could confront death on our behalf and defeat the tyranny of death through his own death and resurrection.

In the physical realm, his death proves *inevitable* as he confronts imperial and religious systems with the nonviolent message of God. In the spiritual realm, his death is *intentional* in that he confronts the forces of death and hades and defeats them through his resurrection.

IV. My journey

I grew up believing that one must believe in penal substitution to be a Christian. I fully gave myself to the doctrine out of gratitude and love for Christ. In seminary, I fed my passion for the Cross by writing as my thesis, "The Nature of Christ's Substitution and Suffering." Assuming penal substitution, my question was this: If Christ paid in full the penalty for all humankind's sin, and if the penalty for humanity's sin is eternity in hell, then how can one person's relatively brief suffering and temporary death be considered full payment? Especially if the punishment should be eternal in duration and universal in scope? So many assumptions! I proposed that both the nature of the person (Christ) and the nature of the suffering (God-forsakenness) were eternal, amounting to just payment... something to that effect.

I had read my theology back through early church history and into the Bible as if the apostles and church fathers had authored my views. I confess to proof-texting in ways that did not allow Scripture to speak for itself. I imported the premises of penal substitution back into phrases like "Christ died *for* (*anti*) us" and words such as "propitiation" (the *hilasmos* and *hilasterion* word group). I read the theory retrospectively into the Old Testament sacrificial system and "Servant songs" like Isaiah 53.

However, I did learn along the way that penal substitution was just one of many atonement theories. I saw its initial development from Anselm's "satisfaction" theory[5] in the 11th century to its codification as "penal substitution"

---

2. Cf. Mark 8:31-32; 9:31; 10:33-34.

3. Cf. "must suffer" in Matt. 16:21; Luke 24:25-27 and the above texts.

4. Other reasons include: (i.) to give us a revelation of the Father and his love; (ii.) to model the ways of God and his kingdom; (iii.) to offer us salvation through belief in his name and his way; and (iv.) to destroy the works of the devil.

5. Greg Richards, *Agora newsgroup* (November. 7, 2006): I re-examined Anselm's *Curs Deus*

in the 1500s under the Reformers. But there were a number of other, earlier theories: Irenaeus's "recapitulation theory," the "moral influence theory," and "the ransom-paid-to-Satan theory." Then I read of modern expressions like Gustaf Aulen's "Christus Victor," René Girard's "mimetic theory" and the "nonviolent atonement" espoused by the Anabaptists.[6] This was a revelation: admitting that penal substitution in its modern form represents the Reformed theory and not the Christian dogma of the atonement. The so-called doctrine was really a debate.

THE ATONEMENT DEBATE

I. Charges against penal substitution

For those who subscribe to penal substitution, some very wise and influential authors remain in that court. The best essay that I've read from this point of view is J.I. Packer's *"What Did the Cross Achieve? The Logic of Penal Substitution."*[7] Packer believes that penal substitution is "at the very heart of the

Homo, since he either tends to get blamed or praised in discussions on the atonement. The picture of God as wrathful or vengeful is not incredibly strong, but the picture of God as wronged (or "injusticed") came out very clearly. The Cross is still all about justice—not as wrath or vengeance but rather as a gift. This comes out most clearly in Anselm's strong Trinitarian language, in which he couches his whole discussion. Anselm argues that all men were created to live lives of ceaseless praise to God, but through our lack of praise (or thanksgiving), we incur a considerable debt before God. Thus, if one were to live a life of ceaseless praise to God one would do no more than was required of all humans. This raises the question of how one pays off the debt owed to God, and for Anselm this requires "an extraordinary gift." Thus Anselm's famous statement: "This debt was so great that, while none but man must solve the debt, none but God was able to do it; so that he who does it must be both God and man." In one sense then, the Cross is not a necessity, because Jesus did not have to die, [the Reformers deny this] but chose to die as this amazing gift, amazing precisely because of his innocence. For a fuller picture: "Since he [Jesus] is very God, the Son of God, he offered himself for his own honor, as well as for that of the Father and the Holy Spirit. That is, he gave his humanity to his divinity, which is one person of the Triune God... For thus we plainly affirm that in speaking of one person we understand the whole Deity to whom as man he offered himself."

Not much talk of wrath or vengeance, but it is quite telling that the Cross is gift, from God for humanity to God. This also sounds like eschatology to me. Christ creates a spotless bride (humanity, his church) and hands them over to the Father to sing ceaseless praise to God forever. The Cross is the place where humans are liberated to praise.

6. Willard Swartley, in reviewing this essay, made this important point: "You tend to associate the left wing of the Reformation, Anabaptism, with 'nonviolent atonement.' This is certainly eisegesis into sixteenth century writings. Cf. *The Complete Writings of Menno Simons*, pp. 428-30 and 581-82. Menno is rich in his description of God's compassion and love shown in the cross, but he is also quite forthright about the violence of the cross—not God's, but ours as humans. He does use the term 'satisfy the guilt' on p. 430, but there is no signal of God's violence—hence, far from a penal theory. Nor is there ever any separation between God and Jesus during 'cross time.'" (Email from Willard Swartley, May 17, 2007)

7. J.I. Packer, "What Did the Cross Achieve? The Logic of Penal Substitution," *The Tyndale Bulletin* 25 (1974) 3-45.

Christian gospel" and "a distinguishing mark of the world-wide evangelical fraternity." The essay attempts to clarify the doctrine in order to avoid needless caricatures. Packer argues from logic and exegesis that the atonement is both penal and substitutionary while acknowledging and explicating the aspects of faith-knowledge and mystery with respect to the Cross.

More recently, Hans Boersma's *Violence, Hospitality and the Cross* attempts to integrate the major theories (including penal substitution) by minimizing our tendency to overextend atonement metaphors (e.g. ransom). I have written a review[8] that explains why, in the end, I wasn't sold.

These fine examples notwithstanding, some common charges against penal substitution through the centuries have included the following:

- **It pits Father against Son**—or the Father's wrath against the Son's forgiveness, even though behind this there is a pact rooted in love's search for a solution that honours justice (so that God can both justify and be just—Romans 3:26).

- **It makes God beholden**—to his own sense of honour (Anselm), law and/or justice (the Reformers), anger and wrath. In effect, God is under the law. To be more charitable, we might say that he must act consistently with his perfectly just character, which cannot minimize the seriousness of sin by letting it go unpunished.

- **It requires the debt of sin to be paid back**—there is no free gift. This type of God must be reimbursed—even if by proxy and with consent—before he can forgive or show mercy. Technically, the debt of sin must be paid back in full rather than cancelled or forgiven.

- **It says sin must be paid back by punishment**—the torment of the sinner satisfies God's need for wrath. The justice he requires is specifically retributive. Since no one can ever satisfy such wrath or repay the eternal debt for themselves—let alone for third parties—the punishment for mankind's collective sin-debt could only be extracted by someone of eternal nature and divine purity. Hence, the incarnation.

- **It paints God as retributive**—the picture of God derived from penal substitution looks vindictive and untrustworthy, repulsed by sinners and rather different than the Father's heart as portrayed perfectly by Jesus. For some, it reflects an angry and unbending facet of God's character that is inconsistent with the compassionate Father of the prodigal son who exacts no fee for re-entry into the family.

---

8. Brad Jersak, "Review of *Violence, Hospitality and the Cross* by Hans Boersma," *Clarion Journal of Spirituality and Justice* (http://clarionjournal.typepad.com).

- **It distorts divine justice**—such a God shows us a form of justice that requires an eye for an eye and spawns a retributive penal system, incites domestic violence, and failed experiments in parental "tough love" (nothing like the prodigal father).

- **It creates atheists**—authors like Steve Chalke[9] see in penal substitution a caricature of God who would be guilty of "cosmic child abuse." Orthodox Archbishop Lazar Puhalo explained it to me this way: "A god who demands the child-sacrifice of his own son to satiate his own wrath? That is *not* Jehovah; that is Molech. God was not punishing Christ on the Cross; he was IN Christ, reconciling the world to Himself."

II. The Rebuttal

Some very fine theologians have debated many of these difficulties throughout the centuries. To mention just a few spikes in the controversy, we have Abelard's "moral theory" versus Anselm's "satisfaction theory" (11th century), the Socinians's attempt to rebuff the Reformers (16th century), John Owen's answer to Hugo Grotius's "governmental theory" (17th century) and a host of alternatives that arise in the 20th century (most notably Gustaf Aulen's *"Christus Victor"* and René Girard's mimetic theory).

Finding such challenges to penal substitution unpersuasive, Edwin Tay, writing after the *Westminster Conference 2006* claims, "The history of criticism with respect to the penal doctrine is, interestingly, a history of the degeneration of criticism."[10]

For a fresh defence of penal theory, Garry Williams' essay *"Justice, Law, and Guilt"* was presented at the *EA* (Evangelical Alliance) *Symposium on Penal Substitution*. He addresses many of the charges against penal theory thoughtfully and succinctly. While Williams' responses may provide an adequate defence for those who want to hold that ground, those who have already abandoned penal territory will not likely be compelled to return home.

Earlier, I mentioned "alleged refutations," because even after listening to the proffered answers from Owen to Williams, not all of us are as convinced in our minds or satisfied in our hearts that their counter-arguments are valid. The best theological syllogisms complete with cross-referencing simply do not ring true to the God that Christ made known in the Gospels through word and deed and continues to make known in our experience of him today.

---

9. Steve Chalk, *The Lost Message of Jesus* (Grand Rapids, MI: Zondervan, 2003), 182.

10. Edwin Tay, *"Westminster Conference 2006: Some Reflections"* (http://theconventicle. blogspot.com/search/label/Trinity).

However, Williams' essay reminded me that when we speak of the Cross of Christ, we are on holy ground. We stand in a place of mystery that requires humility. We ought not violate the very love that Christ demonstrated by firing cannon balls over Golgotha at one another. We do well to present our proposals with genuine meekness, with generosity for our rival theorists, renouncing contempt wherever it lurks. Let us not tread, through lack of charity, upon the very Cross we proclaim.

Above all, while I feel it is time to wrestle again with our understanding of Christ's death, I would grieve the irony of breaking fellowship over it. Williams, in terms that evoke despair, warns that this might be called for:

> It is no escalation to say that proponents of penal substitution are charged with advocating a biblically unfounded, systematically misleading, and pastorally lethal doctrine. If the attack is simply on a caricature of the doctrine, all well and good. Then the way forward is simple: the critics need to say that they do believe in penal substitution itself and just not in warped forms of it. But if the accusation is indeed an accusation against penal substitution itself, as I suspect it is, then I fear that we cannot carry on as we are. As much as I would like to, and mindful of the injunctions of the Lord Jesus Christ himself to seek peace, I find it impossible to agree that this is just an intramural, within-the-family dispute, when it has been acknowledged by all parties that we are arguing about who God is, about the creedal doctrine of the Trinity, about the consequences of sin, about how we are saved, and about views which are held to encourage the abuse of women and children. So long as these issues *are* the issues, and I believe that they have been rightly identified, then I cannot see how we can remain allied together without placing unity above these truths which are undeniably central to the Christian faith. I say this with a heavy heart.[11]

If I hear Williams aright, then he is saying that he must break fellowship with all those who knowingly reject penal substitution as their doctrine of the atonement. I hope that I am misreading him. For my part, I believe we kneel in the shadow of the same Cross, allied not by doctrinal agreement but by the same blood that makes us siblings of God's grace.

Yet Williams is at least right that this is a central issue concerning the very nature of the God we claim to worship. What does it mean to disagree about the nature of God and the Gospel on such a fundamental level? This issue will divide us if it essentially creates two very separate and distinct faiths that worship two quite different gods. I'm hoping for better things as we keeping listening to each other.

III. Unanswered questions

Having nearly drowned in the depths of written theological debate—having pored over the Scriptures, the doctrinal treatises, the charges, the rebuttals

---

11. Garry Williams, *"Justice, Law, and Guilt,"* EA Symposium on Penal Substitution, 2005.

and the counter-arguments umpteen-hundred times—and having said my prayers—I lay down my weary head. And I'm still left with unanswered questions. Oh, I've read the "answers," but in the night-watch, before sleep overtakes me, I ask myself and God:

- Does sin separate us from God? If so, how?

- Must sin be punished? And does punishment really restore justice?

- Does punishment of a sinner truly satisfy God's wrath? Does sin agitate God in a way that is only rectified through violence and retribution?

- Does punishment pay for forgiveness? How? Why?

- Can or must God's wrath against sin be satisfied by punishment *before* he can forgive what he otherwise could not? Can't he forgive without it? Would that truly make him unjust?

- Is a guilty person's offence really erased by the punishment of yet another substitute victim? Rather than eye for an eye, why would taking the perfect eye of an innocent third party absolve me of sin?

- If it was God's will that Christ should die, did Christ endure suffering as punishment for God's sake or was it, rather, out of costly love for our sake?

- "Father, forgive them…" Was it God's will that we sacrifice Jesus for him? Were we being forgiven by sacrificing Jesus so that we could be forgiven for killing him? (This is dizzying.)

- Are the guilty agents of their own atonement as God allows them to commit the very act of sin for which they are being punished *and* by which they are being saved? If my sin crucified Jesus, then didn't my sin pay for my sin? This seems like circular reasoning to me… or simply nonsensical.

IV. Jesus' take

Aside from these compulsive nocturnal questions, a more straightforward, stubborn fact niggled away at my system. As a penal theorist, I unconsciously ignored or evaded Jesus' own understanding of the Cross. Since we acknowledge all atonement theories as metaphorical, why dismiss Jesus' parabolic take on His coming crucifixion?

I hear Jesus Christ quietly challenging us, "I appreciate your efforts to understand my death, to explain its meaning and significance. I really do. Quite clever, too. But since I'm the one who came, who suffered and died—since it was *my* mission that led to the Cross—might I offer my views on what happened? Would my perspective be welcome at the table of atonement talk?"[12]

Jesus' version of his mission included the Father sending and anointing him to:

- Announce the good news of the kingdom (Luke 4);
- Demonstrate God's compassionate love for the world (John 3); and
- Seek, find and save us, ultimately giving his life as a ransom for many (Mark 10:45).

A ransom implies that we are being set free from someone or something that is holding us in bondage. Our rescue, salvation and redemption are from captors and prisons. Question: Who is the captor, prison warden or slave owner? Is it God? He is never treated as such in Jesus' message. Instead, God-in-Christ is the Redeemer, the Rescuer, the Saviour.

Further, Jesus proclaims the Father and prays to the Father as the one sending him on this love mission, *never* as the one crucifying or punishing him. Jesus' references to radical service and his missionary martyrdom are extended in the parable of the wicked tenants of Matthew 20. He presents himself as the final prophet in a series of missionary attempts by a loving God to deliver his message of salvation. The King sends his Son, the tenants reject and kill him, and the Father-King is furious at their violent response (there's the wrath we might expect). In explaining the parable, Christ says,

> We are going up to Jerusalem, and the Son of Man will be betrayed to the chief priests and the teachers of the law. They will condemn him to death and will turn him over to the Gentiles to be mocked and flogged and crucified. On the third day he will be raised to life! (Matthew 20:18-19)

In this scheme, where does the Father fit in? Is he behind it? Inspiring them? No, Jesus and the Gospel writers point to Satan and wicked men as those who inspired the betrayal and murder of Jesus. What is the Father's role? He commissions Jesus to endure in love and then raises him up, thus conquering Satan, sin and death. Christ calls us to love, trust and obey his Father as he did, even unto death. He urges us to unite with him through death, resurrection and ultimate fellowship with God. *In Jesus' own understanding of the Cross, the element of substitution appears when Jesus humbly endures the wrath of mankind instead of invoking the wrath of God upon us.* He says as much to Peter[13] and to Pilate.[14]

---

12. Marcus Borg and N.T. Wright will share more in their chapters on why Jesus came and died from the perspective of the Gospels and of Jesus himself.

13. Matthew 26:52-54.

14. John 18:36.

This is not the whole story, but it illustrates how the Gospel text itself challenges satisfaction theology by sheer omission. The satisfaction of the Father is in his Son's obedience and faithfulness to the mission, expressing God's love and forgiveness to the uttermost. *The Father's foreknowledge and willingness to overturn our wicked intentions through forgiveness and resurrection is neither an endorsement of our murderous act nor divine complicity in it.* Rather, it testifies to God's power to redeem.[15]

Only by stretching its meaning to encompass God's "giving over (*paradidomi*[16]) of the Son" (in whom he dwelt bodily!) to our defiant "No!" could we speak of the Cross as God's wrath. But in that case, wrath has nothing to do with penal satisfaction. Andre Harden, a member of the Agora newsgroup, explains:

> While there is a lot of talk about God's wrath in the Bible, I see no evidence of it on Good Friday. There was no lightning bolt to strike the Son, no pestilence descended to harrow him, no plague of boils.
>
> As I just look at what really happened in the physical realm on Good Friday, I don't see God's anger. If police were called to the scene, they would have found no evidence to suggest a "second shooter." There was a loud and clear series of events that led to the death of Jesus. People were threatened by him. People betrayed him. People crucified him. Even most non-believers can agree that Jesus was mistreated and wrongly killed under Pontius Pilate.
>
> People killed him out of hate, spite and fear—plain and simple—really. Whatever theological theory we overlay, we must remember that the historical act was plain and simple and that humanity is fully responsible for it.

15. In asserting that God was neither punishing Jesus, nor in need of a wrathful death, I may appear to absolve God of any responsibility for Christ's death. When the evangelists of the early church preached the Gospel, they repeatedly laid the *blame* squarely on Jesus' crucifiers (Acts 2:23; 3:14-15; 4:10; 7:52; 10:39; 13:27-28; etc.), while asserting "but God raised him up" (Acts 2:24; 2:32; 3:15; 4:10; 10:40; etc.). However, as Dr. Robert Seale reminded me, the Scriptures also reveal that this all happened according to God's sovereign plan and foreknowledge (Acts 2:23, 3:18). This is a mystery that stalls us by design into a posture of repentance, wonder and gratitude.

Ultimately, God "delivered up/handed over" Christ and Christ "gave/delivered" himself (*paradidomi*) to and for us. Christ himself stated boldly, "The reason my Father loves me is that I lay down my life—only to take it up again. No one takes it from me, but I lay it down of my own accord. I have authority to lay it down and authority to take it up again" (John 10:17-18). God did indeed purpose to offer his Son in love to us for our salvation, and this included the foreknowledge of our violent rejection of him. God did this, not because he required penal satisfaction, but because our redemption would require Jesus' journey through the valley of suffering and death (at the hands of wicked men) that he might emerge in resurrection and victory (by God's power).

16. *paradidomi* - "[He] was *delivered up* because of our transgressions, and was raised because of our justification" (Romans 4:25 NASB); "He who did not spare His own Son, but *delivered* Him up for us all" (Romans 8:32 NASB); "*Delivered* Himself up for me" (Galatians 2:20 NASB); "Christ also loved you, and gave Himself up for us" (Ephesians 5:32 NASB); "Christ also loved the church and gave Himself up for her" (Ephesians 5:25 NASB). Cf. Isaiah 53:12 (LXX) - "delivered because of their iniquities." The pattern in Acts (every time) is (i) God delivered him, (ii) you/they killed/crucified him, (iii) God raised him to life.

I don't sense any affinity with the Father when I look at Good Friday. I see myself holding a smoking gun. I see the Father holding a weeping virgin.[17]

According to Jesus of the Gospels and the Gospel writers themselves, God sent his Son with good news of love, and then we responded by killing him. Something about giving his life (which includes more than dying) in this cause sets us free and gives us life. How so and from what, *according to Jesus*? I hear three answers from his mouth:

- We are set free through his death, because rather than replying to our vengeance and violence in kind, Jesus lives out his own message of love by forgiving us for his murder.

- He sets us free from death and the fear of death when we join him in a kind of death that nullifies death. The *first time* Jesus talks about the Cross, he does not yet reveal that he would be crucified, but uses it as a symbol of ultimate commitment to following his Way. It is a call to lose our lives (i.e. death to self) for his sake (cf. Matthew 10:38-39).

- Jesus sees his death as an hour of glory for the Son of Man (fulfilling Daniel 7), a cup of suffering leading to glorification (Luke 24:25; John 12:31-32). He becomes the first seed of many in a harvest movement that finds eternal life by giving our lives to God's kingdom-dream:

Jesus replied, "The hour has come for the Son of Man to be glorified. I tell you the truth, unless a kernel of wheat falls to the ground and dies, it remains only a single seed. But if it dies, it produces many seeds. The man who loves his life will lose it, while the man who hates his life in this world will keep it for eternal life" (John 12:23-25).

As with Jesus, "giving our lives" includes but exceeds the hour of our death. It is dedicating our whole lives to love (Matthew 13:31).

V. Therapeutic versus juridical theories

As the Gospel texts begin to sink in, we see that penal atonement is derived more from rational arguments and assumptions than from Jesus' own understanding. The doctrinal context is medieval feudalism and Reformation-era juridical metaphors, leading to these inherited tenets:

- Sin is primarily law-breaking, and God judges sin with death.

17. Andre Harden, *Agora newsgroup* (Nov. 2, 2006).

- Sin separates us from God, creating a great chasm of broken fellow-ship (cf. Isaiah 59:2 with Psalm 139 and Romans 5:20-21).

- God cannot look on sin or overlook it or simply forgive it. For God's wrath to be satisfied, it must be punished.

- Jesus bore the wrath of God on the Cross in my place to bridge the gulf between sinful man and holy God.

When we submit these basic assumptions to the biblical text, we find that they are not givens. While the Father loved us enough to pursue the human race for many millennia and offers us true fellowship whenever we draw near (and this included all the Old Testament saints), the death of the second Adam was necessary to remove sin and guilt and death and Satan's chains. We needed that, and *that* is why the Father needed it. Satisfaction theories say, "God needed it to assuage his wrath." I would say, "God needed it to make us whole to satisfy his love."

God need not say, "I just can't get over my children's sin. I am so incensed with them. They are repulsive to me and trigger my wrath and need for ven-geance. My hand is armed for their destruction. *Somebody* must pay me, and it has to be with punishment; with blood."[18]

But what if, alternatively, we imagine him saying, "I just can't get over *my children*. I'm so in love. I need to save them—even if it kills me." And so the wounds of Christ represent something far better than the satisfied wrath of an offended God. They speak of the power of God's great mercy and love for us. So Bernard says,

> And in fact where can be found safe and solid rest and security for the weak, but in the wounds of the Saviour? There I dwell with the greater security, in proportion to his power to save. The world rages, the body oppresses, the devil lies in wait to destroy. I do not fall, because my foundation is on a firm rock. I have committed a heinous sin. My conscience is disturbed, but shall not fall into despair, because I shall recall to remembrance the wounds of the Lord... My merit, therefore, is in the compassion of the Lord... This is the whole merit of man—to fix all his hope on him who saves the whole man.[19]

So it was for *our* sakes that he died—for salvation, deliverance, healing and restoration from the ravages of Fall that curse and chain us, rot us and kill us. We ate the poison fruit and succumbed to the serpent's venom in spite of our Father's gracious warnings. But now God has given us someone upon whom we can fix our hope for healing and wholeness—a *serpent on a pole!*

---

18. This is no caricature. I have drawn directly from John Calvin's *Institutes* and Jonathan Edwards' sermon, "Sinners in the Hands of an Angry God."

19. Bernard, cited in, of all places, Calvin's *Institutes* 3.7.3!

Then the LORD said to Moses, "Make a fiery *serpent,* and set it on a pole; and it shall be that everyone who is bitten, when he looks at it, shall live." So Moses made a bronze serpent, and put it on a pole; and so it was, if a serpent had bitten anyone, when he looked at the bronze serpent, he lived (Numbers 21:8-9 NKJV).

And as Moses lifted up the serpent in the wilderness, even so must the Son of Man be lifted up, that whoever believes in Him should not perish but have eternal life. For God so loved the world that He gave His only begotten Son, that whoever believes in Him should not perish but have everlasting life. For God did not send His Son into the world to condemn the world, but that the world through Him might be saved (John 3:14-17 NKJV).

Christ comes not as avenging judge but as great physician and grand antivenin for what happened in Eden. I am suggesting that the atonement becomes clear when we shift from juridical models over to a healing model of the Cross (as per Jesus very specifically in John 3). Or to recall Isaiah 53:5 (KJV), "by his stripes, we are *healed.*" But when we make this shift, everything needs double-checking: What is sin? What is wrath? What is justice?

VI. The Father's Heart

More than that, my own experience of God's love and grace in the context of "vile sinners" suggests some new thoughts. For example,

- What if the Fall of Genesis is not about the violation of a law, neces-sitating punishment. Perhaps it is about the venom of deception con-cerning God's nature and this led (and leads) humankind to partake of the poison fruit (anything from hedonism to moralism), requiring healing?

- What if, rather than separating us from the love of God, the Fall trig-gered God's great quest to descend into the chasm to seek and find the lost where they had stumbled? What if where sin abounds, grace abounds much more?

- What if forgiveness is not something that is earned through sacrifices or punishment but is freely offered as antivenin to all who will look to the Crucified One after the pattern of the bronze serpent?

- What if God was not punishing Jesus on the Cross, but rather, God was in Christ reconciling the world to himself?

This final step has become my central premise. Decades of active wrestling at the Cross and circling its many "what ifs" and "what abouts" have led me to this one core belief: **On the Cross, God was not punishing Jesus.** Rather, the very God from whose presence in Eden we had collectively fled—as if he were some kind of vindictive monster—came to seek and save his lost and now highly volatile children. It cost him everything, but the crucified God of love forgave us and saved us from spiritual captivity, sickness and death. We shall now unpack this thesis in the remainder of this chapter.

MY THESIS: NONVIOLENT
IDENTIFICATION AND VICTORY

Identification is a theme that crops up throughout the flow of the Gospel narratives and Paul's epistles, and appears repeatedly in both early and recent atonement literature. The call to mutual identification with Christ also parallels the language of "union" everywhere in the Catholic mystics. Identification/union creates an umbrella for other related themes like solidarity and recapitulation. Further, we perceive a necessary coupling of Christ's identification with man to the victory of Christ over Satan, sin and death.

Christus Victor (from Aulen to Weaver) is the fruit of this identification. Or conversely, identification is the "how" of the victory.

Identification is a unifying theme for the New Testament writers and the patristics, just as it is a unifying theme that brings together the modern writers herein, regardless of their various nuances. It seems to me that evangelicals need and HAVE an alternative to penal satisfaction theories that is more comprehensive than *Christus Victor* (but which includes it) and which is more objective than the moral influence theory (which still makes God the primary agent of the crucifixion) and which takes seriously Jesus' own understanding of his upcoming death (which is anything but penal. It's a human crime and a divine victory).

From there, identification unfolds as follows:

- At the Cross, Christ identifies and unites with all humanity in his incarnation and identifies with every victim (crying, "My God, my God" with all who have experienced abandonment) *and* perpetrator ("he numbered himself with the transgressors").

- We begin appropriately by identifying with those who crucified him. We put him there. Isaiah 53—we thought he was smitten by God, but it was our sins that put him there!

- We repent by choosing to identify instead with Christ in his commitment to actively resist the powers, but in his way (nonviolently and with forgiveness). Not the substitution of him dying instead of us or experiencing God's active punishment for us, but rather, dying with him (Romans 6) so that we might also live with him.

- We identify with him in his resurrection. We live eschatologically, as those upon whom the end of the ages has come (1 Corinthians 10:11), not only saved from something but unto something: the restoration of our true self. But even more, we are welcomed into the glory planned for us from the beginning (mystical union).

- I also emphasize the identification of the Father with the Son—but as God IN Christ—Yahweh himself as the One who is pierced (Zech. 12) or "Jesus as God crucified" as we'll see in Rowan Williams' essay.

Thus, Good Friday is about the end of God's wrath, not because it was satiated through an ultimate outpouring of God's anger at sin upon the Son, but because when Christ said, "Father, forgive them," he did. Not because the Father abandoned the Son (Psalm 22:1) but because the Father heard his cries and answered them (Psalm 22:24). The Father and Son, in perfect union, say "No!" to wrath[20] in a way with which we are to identify—which is why at least in part, all these writers believe in nonviolence and restorative justice.

In this chapter, I am not offering new ideas so much as a specific label that might function as a counterpoint to the category we call "penal substitution." I use *"nonviolent identification"* as an umbrella-phrase to cover the breadth of emerging ideas in atonement theology. I believe that even where the contributors to this compendium disagree with one another, they generally assent to the double-descriptor I am proposing: I.e. "Nonviolent Identification and Victory." Let us take each of these points in turn.

I. Nonviolent love versus redemptive violence (punishment)

First, I would suggest that the atonement is *nonviolent* as opposed to *penal*. At ground level, my conviction is that on the Cross, God the Father was *not* punishing Jesus Christ. This has enormous implications for our theology of the Cross, raising a number of core questions. If God was not punishing Jesus for our sins, in what sense is Christ a sacrificial lamb? What becomes of God's wrath needing to be satisfied? Do we still maintain that Christ paid in full the debt or endured the penalty of sin? My sense is that each of the esteemed authors herein questions whether the crucifixion of Christ secured our salvation through the satisfaction of God's wrath upon sin through the punishment of Jesus.

In each of the chapters, we'll see a direct challenge to penal satisfaction or an alternative proposal that emphasizes the nonviolence, forgiveness and

---

20. Some say that in Christ, the wrath of God is completely expunged (cf. James Alison). Others like Volf defer it to the end, reminding us that in this age, we follow the slain Lamb of Revelation 5 and 14 as opposed to the conquering Rider on the white horse of Revelation 19.

victory of God in Christ on Good Friday. Each of the authors sees the life and teachings of Christ as the way of nonviolence ("taking up your cross") to the nth degree in his death. Instead of God's wrath being poured out on and satiated in his own Son that day, we see God choosing to reject wrath, violence and vengeance as his rightful response to the wicked tenants who enacted his murder. We see God in Christ modeling perfectly his own call to love one's enemies and to pray for them, forgiving them from the heart. This is why we see the Cross as a manifestation of God's love rather than his wrath.

In *The Lost Message of Jesus*, Steve Chalke puts it this way (and has taken considerable heat for it, as you can imagine):

> The fact is that the cross isn't a form of cosmic child abuse—a vengeful Father, punishing his Son for an offence he has not even committed. Understandably, both people inside and outside of the Church have found this twisted version of events morally dubious and a huge barrier to faith. Deeper than that, however, is that such a concept stands in total contradiction to the statement, "God is love." If the cross is a personal act of violence perpetuated by God towards humankind but borne by his Son, then it makes a mockery of Jesus' own teaching to love your enemies and to refuse to pay evil with evil.
>
> The truth is, the cross is a symbol of love. It is a demonstration of just how far God as Father and Jesus as his Son are prepared to go to prove that love.[21]

Long ago, Irenaeus,[22] who abhorred attributing our violence against Christ to the agency of God, sums up his theory of the atonement this way:

> [We] have received, in the times known beforehand, [the blessings of salvation] according to the ministration of the Word, who is perfect in all things, as the mighty Word, and very man, who, redeeming us by His own blood in a manner consonant to reason, gave Himself as a redemption for those who had been led into captivity. And since the apostasy tyrannized over us unjustly, and, though we were by nature the property of the omnipotent God, alienated us contrary to nature, rendering us its own disciples, the Word of God, powerful in all things, and not defective with regard to His own justice, did righteously turn against that apostasy, and redeem from it His own property, *not by violent means*, as the [apostasy] had obtained dominion over us at the beginning, when it insatiably snatched away what was not its own, but by means of persuasion, as became a God of counsel, *who does not use violent means to obtain what He desires; so that neither should justice be infringed upon,* nor the ancient handiwork of God go to destruction. (Irenaeus of Lyons, *Adversus Haereses*, 5.1.1)[23]

Far from being the grand appeasement of God's anger, the Cross, then, is truly the ultimate demonstration of love's power to overcome evil through

---

21. Chalke, *The Lost Message of Jesus,* 182-183.

22. Bishop of Lyons, but thoroughly Eastern in origin and theology, was grand-disciple of the Apostle John via Polycarp. Beyond the N.T., we might see him as the father of atonement theology. Cf. Andrew P. Klager's chapter below.

23. Cf. Andrew Klager's thorough review of Irenaeus in this book.

forgiveness and nonviolence. That God sent Jesus to establish his kingdom of love, even knowing that he would be rejected and killed, and knowing that the kingdom depended on Jesus' willingness to face death—a step both necessary and intentional—is light years from saying that God satisfied his wrath by punishing his Son. Sending *my* son on a mission to preach love in a hostile, foreign place, knowing that his martyrdom was inevitable but also the seed from which a great harvest would come, is seriously different than actively killing him instead of and through those to whom he was sent.

A. Why did we think God was punishing Jesus?

Three of the building blocks of Evangelical penal theory are catch phrases inferred from our reading of Scripture (at least I must plead guilty to this charge) and then aligned in a simple syllogism:

1. God cannot look on sin.
2. God laid our sin(s) on Jesus (from Isaiah 53, 1 Peter 2:24, etc.).
3. God forsook Jesus, turning his face from him.[24]

These, taken together, lead us to a fourth premise, seldom questioned because it is based in a particular understanding of the biblical text:

4. God sacrificed Jesus for our sins and in our place (as substitutionary ram, lamb and/or scapegoat).

Responding to each point,

1. God cannot look on sin: Both reason and revelation tell me that a God who relates to humanity can, does and must continually look on sin or else he could not dwell with humankind at all. Our idea that God's holiness prevents him from looking on sin, as if it would somehow despoil his eyes, is an objection that was brought before God long ago. In Habakkuk 1:13, the prophet complains,

> You are of purer eyes than to behold evil,
> And cannot look on wickedness.
> Why do You look on those who deal treacherously,
> And hold Your tongue when the wicked devours
> A person more righteous than he? (NKJV)

Why is a holy God with pure eyes looking on sin and forcing Habakkuk to do so as well? And why is God allowing it? In effect, Habakkuk says, "You

---

24. This "God-forsakenness" was thus understood as the punishment which Christ endured for sin. Thus, Calvin (et al) reallocate the creeds' "descent into hell" from Jesus' victorious harrowing of hell to his torment on the Cross at the Father's hand (a radical and very late revision).

are a holy God and you cannot look on sin. So why are you? Why are you stalling with wrath?"

According to this first premise—that God cannot look on sin—is not "the conviction of sin by the Holy Spirit" (John 16) an oxymoron? Moreover, Psalm 139 completely precludes this premise as impossible.

2. God laid our sin(s) on Jesus: Isaiah 53 may be read as if God were actively heaping humanity's collective sin upon Jesus so that he would have a centralized target to personally direct his fatal punishment.[25] But the biblical picture is more subtle and wonderful. It is a word of hope to God's suffering people in exile (Israel). He compares their suffering to the sin offerings and scapegoats that bore the sins of the people through either sacrifice or exile (Lev. 4:29; 16:10). In the midst of this, God's prophetic Servant comes to stand in complete solidarity with his people, suffering in exile as a consequence of their disobedience. He so completely identifies with their suffering at the hands of their oppressors that they might *wrongly* be tempted to think that he has been "stricken by God, smitten and afflicted," as if he was also under God's wrath. The prophet warns that to think so would be a mistake (3-5).

> He was despised and rejected by men, *[Who rejected him? God? No, men did.]*
>> a man of sorrows, and familiar with suffering.
>> Like one from whom men hide their faces *[Who hid their face(s)? God? No, us.]*
> he was despised, and we esteemed him not.
>
> Surely he took up our infirmities
>> and carried our sorrows,
>> yet we considered him stricken by God, *[Who thought this? We did.]*
>> smitten by him, and afflicted. *[And was he?]*
>
> But he was pierced for our transgressions, *[No, our sins pierced him.]*
>> he was crushed for our iniquities; *[It was our iniquities that crushed him.]*
>> the punishment that brought us peace was upon him, *[Who punished him? We did. And his response? Peace, forgiveness, and reconciliation.]*
> and by his wounds we are healed. *[We wounded him, but he healed us.]*

As Christ identifies himself with the suffering servant and the slain lamb, we find out that his torment is not truly at the hands of Yahweh or even only our oppressors, but also ourselves! He ends up suffering with us *and* by us. It is our sin that he bears. Don't imagine him carrying a backpack-burden of our sins for us. *Bearing* here is more like enduring the brunt of our violence against him with patience and forgiveness.

---

25. But cf. Bob Ekblad's chapter in this book.

And Christ does this as the Father stays his hand of wrath against us. Why? Why would he withhold vengeance to such a degree that he seems like a conspirator? Why would he allow us to inflict suffering and crushing such that Isaiah says, "the Lord laid on him the iniquities of us all" (6) and "Yet it pleased the LORD to bruise him; he hath put *him* to grief: when thou shalt make his soul an offering for sin" (10 – KJV)?

We know that God finds *no pleasure* in the punishment of the wicked (Ezekiel 33:11), much less his suffering servant. What is going on here? The answer is that there is a bigger picture. Penal substitution is one attempt to paint it. But it overstates things when it makes God the wrathful punisher and his appeasement the purpose.

We need to flip perspectives. God's pleasure is found in the suffering servant's heart of humility, his willingness to identify with the exiles, the joy of the foreknown outcome and good fruit of Christ's suffering:

> He shall see *his* seed, he shall prolong *his* days, and the pleasure of the LORD shall prosper in his hand. He shall see of the travail of his soul, *and* shall be satisfied: by his knowledge shall my righteous servant justify many; for he shall bear their iniquities. Therefore will I divide him *a portion* with the great, and he shall divide the spoil with the strong; because he hath poured out his soul unto death: and he was numbered with the transgressors; and he bare the sin of many, and made intercession for the transgressors (Isaiah 53:10-12 KJV).

The pleasure comes not from God's relief as wrath is satisfied through punishment. Rather, it comes from the joy (our freedom) set before them (Father in Son) having endured the Cross (Hebrews 12:2, cf. Zechariah 12:8-10).

3. God turned his face from Jesus: Finally, one need not read between the biblical lines as to whether God turned his face from his Son on the Cross (his so-called "God-forsakenness"). Psalm 22 is the textual source of Christ's cry of dereliction (vs. 1). When read as a whole, in context, the very clear message is that God *did not* forsake Jesus; he *never* turned his face.

Psalm 22 is one of those Psalms (like Psalm 6 and 13) in which David cries out to God with a complaint, and then without telling us God's specific answer, has a shift in perspective that is evident later in the Psalm. We need to exercise spiritual ears to hear God's response through the silence between the first prayers of desperation and later prayers of thanksgiving.

In verse 1, we read prophetically about Christ's cry of dereliction: "My God, my God, why have you forsaken me?" Unfortunately, rather than reading on carefully, theologians often race ahead to develop a doctrine around this verse. Many of them conclude that while Christ was being crucified, this cry was evidence that Christ bore the wrath of God as the Father turned his face away.

But if we read the Psalm again, looking and listening for the Father's answer to Christ, much to our surprise we come to verse 24:

> For he has *not* despised or disdained
> the suffering of the afflicted one;
> he has *not* hidden his face from him
> but has listened to his cry for help.

What did David and then Christ himself hear, see or feel from the Father that would bring them to the revelation of verse 24? The initial cry was a cry of identification with every man, woman and child who has felt forsaken and abandoned, but an answer was forthcoming!

> During the days of Jesus' life on earth, he offered up prayers and petitions with loud cries and tears to the one who could save him from death, and *he was heard* because of his reverent submission. Although he was a son, he learned obedience from what he suffered and, once made perfect, he became the source of eternal salvation for all who obey him and was designated by God to be high priest in the order of Melchizedek (Heb. 5:7-10).

Let us be dialogical with this text. According to this passage, when did Christ offer prayers with loud cries and tears? "During the days of his life on earth," and particularly in Gethsemane and Golgotha (cf. Luke 22:42-44; Mark 15:34, 37). What did he cry? *To be saved from death.* Why was he heard? Because through fear of the Lord, he was obedient to the Father. How was he heard? In his resurrection and ascension, he was not abandoned to death, (cf. Acts 2:27-28) but was made our perfect high priest and source of salvation.

Christ's cry of dereliction was not his last word. While on the Cross, Jesus made the journey of faith from the darkness of God-forsakenness to the light of ultimate surrender and trust. He draws his last words, "Father, into your hands I commit my spirit," from Psalm 31, which should have clarified for us God's role at the Cross from the beginning. Some highlights from this messianic psalm:

> 1 In you, O LORD, I have taken refuge; let me never be put to shame;
>   deliver me in your righteousness.
> 2 Turn your ear to me, come quickly to my rescue;
>   be my rock of refuge, a strong fortress to save me.
> 4 Free me from the trap that is set for me, for you are my refuge.
> 5 *Into your hands I commit my spirit; redeem me, O LORD, the God of truth.*
> 7 *I will be glad and rejoice in your love, for you saw my affliction*
>   *and knew the anguish of my soul. [saw/knew versus caused/inflicted]*
> 8 You have not handed me over to the enemy
>   but have set my feet in a spacious place.
> 9 Be merciful to me, O LORD, for I am in distress;
>   my eyes grow weak with sorrow, my soul and my body with grief.

10 My life is consumed by anguish and my years by groaning;
    my strength fails because of my affliction, and my bones grow weak.
13 For I hear the slander of many; there is terror on every side;
    they conspire against me and plot to take my life.
14 But I trust in you, O LORD; I say, "You are my God."
15 My times are in your hands;
    deliver me from my enemies and from those who pursue me.
16 Let your face shine on your servant; save me in your unfailing love.
17 Let me not be put to shame, O LORD, for I have cried out to you;
    but let the wicked be put to shame and lie silent in the grave.
21 Praise be to the LORD, for *he showed his wonderful love to me*
    when I was in a besieged city.
22 In my alarm I said, "I am cut off from your sight!"
    Yet you heard my cry for mercy when I called to you for help.

4. God sacrificed his Son for us: This statement is completely true or false depending on one's definition and picture of sacrifice. What do we mean by sacrifice? Who sacrificed what or whom?[26] Why was he sacrificed? Was he a lamb slaughtered to pay back the debt to God for all the sins of the world? Was he the ram offered by God to replace Isaac (and you and I)? Or the Passover lamb that averted God's wrath through his blood? Is the sacrifice Christ's own living faith and obedience to God? Or was God sacrificing his son as a martyr-missionary to this world? Many Christians agree that Christ's sacrifice was to end all sacrifices, but why? Was it because Jesus was the perfect lamb that would finally satisfy God's need for the shedding of blood? Or was Christ exposing and annulling that very fallacy?[27] On the other hand, perhaps Christ's sacrifice is the first-fruits of a whole movement who would take up the Cross and become living sacrifices of co-suffering love for the world.

If this is so, we need to revisit the Old Testament history of sacrifice[28] and how Jesus of Nazareth relates to that history. Chronologically, we might recall briefly Isaac's ram, the Passover lamb of the Exodus, and the Levitical sacrifices.

a. Isaac's Ram: Frankly, the story of Yahweh's last-second provisional ram when Abraham was about to sacrifice Isaac preaches well for those who proclaim Christ as God's substitute (though the penal element is missing entirely). But is that the true meaning of the Isaac incident? I see two alternatives. First, we have in this story a dramatic refutation of child-sacrifice.

---

26. Did we sacrifice Jesus to God? Did God sacrifice to Jesus to us? Or to himself? Did Jesus sacrifice his corruptible human body in exchange for an incorruptible body? (Irenaeus)

27. Cf. the various works of anthropologist René Girard and the "Girardians" in his wake.

28. Cf. J. Denny Weaver's chapter and his book, *The Nonviolent Atonement.*

Listening to a skeptical BBC commentator's interview with Chief Rabbi Sir Jonathan Sacks is instructive:[29]

> **John Humphrys:** Why would a merciful God have done to Abraham what he did to Abraham—faced him with that agonizing dilemma, "Sacrifice your child if you believe in me"? Why would God have faced a human being with that wicked choice?
>
> **Jonathan Sacks:** We know that child sacrifice was incredibly widespread in the ancient world; we know that from every kind of archaeological evidence. Child sacrifice—which is referred to many times in the Hebrew bible as the most abominable of all acts—was the kind of thing you expected a god to ask of you. It's what gods regularly asked from their devotees. The essence of the story of Abraham is that at the critical moment, God says "Stop—I am not that kind of god"... He was teaching him, "I did that just so you should learn exactly what would happen if you don't listen carefully." So God slammed on the brakes; it was the most effective way of all of history.

Second, rather than identifying Christ as the ram in the story, the New Testament draws the parallel between God and Abraham (as fathers), who were willing to sacrifice (did not spare or withhold) Isaac and Jesus (as promised sons)[30] because of their confidence in a resurrection. In the end, all four characters are vindicated.

b. The Passover Lamb: Again, the Passover sacrifice of lambs might be seen as substitutionary in the sense that the death of the lamb averted the wrath of God from the homes covered by the blood—a death for a death to divert judgement. The problem is that the lambs were not being punished for the Jews' sins nor receiving the brunt of God's wrath in their place. Rather, this was a God-given covenant meal that identified his people as exempt from judgement and ready for deliverance.

Jesus, reflecting on and recreating a new Passover covenant describes the offering of his life for our release from slavery, *protection from the destroyer* (Exodus 12:23), exemption from judgement and the safety of a house where we eat the Lamb (Exodus 12:7) *getting it inside of us.*[31]

There is a forgiveness element to be sure, but it comes by sharing in the new Passover—entering covenant by *participation* in his meal, drinking from his cup. In Matthew 26:27-28, we read, "Then he took the cup, gave thanks and offered it to them, saying, 'Drink from it, all of you. This is my blood of the covenant, which is poured out for many for the forgiveness of sins.'"

29. *"Humphrys in Search of God"* (http://www.bbc.co.uk/religion/programmes/misc/scripts/humphryssacks.html).
30. Compare Gen. 22:12 with Rom. 8:32. Thanks to Nadine Bergen for pointing this out.
31. Conversation with Merie Vermeij at Appleseed Lodge, Westbank, BC, February, 2007.

Christ is the new Passover feast which brings liberation as we opt in to the New Covenant.[32] "For Christ our Passover also has been sacrificed. Therefore let us celebrate the feast" (1 Corinthians 5:7-8).

c. The Levitical Lamb: Crossan and Borg remind us that the roots of ancient animal sacrifice were not in punishment and substitution, but rather, based in protocols for human reconciliation: the proffered gift and the shared meal.

> How, then, did people create, maintain, or restore good relations with a divine being? What visible acts could they do to reach an Invisible Being? Again, they could give a gift or a meal... In a sacrifice the animal is *made sacred* and is given to God as a *sacred gift* or returned to the offerer as a *sacred meal.* That sense of sacrifice should never be confused with *suffering* or *substitution*... Offerers never thought that the point of the sacrifice was to make the animal suffer, or that the greatest sacrifice was one in which the animal suffered lengthily or terribly. For a human meal or a divine meal an animal had to be slain, but that was done swiftly and efficiently—ancient priests were also excellent butchers.[33]

Sacrificial gifts and meals were the basis of the Levitical system. These were festivals that brought community together to offer thanksgiving, receive forgiveness and enjoy reconciliation. To Jesus, reconciliation with God involves partaking in the sacrificial meal of his (Christ's) life, death and resurrection.

> Jesus said to them, "I tell you the truth, unless you eat the flesh of the Son of Man and drink his blood, you have no life in you. Whoever eats my flesh and drinks my blood has eternal life, and I will raise him up at the last day. For my flesh is real food and my blood is real drink. Whoever eats my flesh and drinks my blood remains in me, and I in him. Just as the living Father sent me and I live because of the Father, so the one who feeds on me will live because of me" (John 6:53-57).

d. Sacrifice versus Scapegoat: René Girard also sees Christ's death as sacrificial in the sense of giving one's life for the sake of another. Much of Girard's writing is given to showing how the Cross refutes the "scapegoat" mechanism in human culture.[34] But he goes on to define genuine sacrifice "on the basis of faith in a God of love who does not make a secret pact with his Son that calls for his murder in order to satisfy God's wrath."[35] "The suffering and death of the Son, the Word, are inevitable because of the inability of the world to receive God or his Son, not because God's justice demands

---

32. Cf. N.T. Wright's chapter herein.

33. Marcus Borg and John Dominic Crossan, *The Last Week* (San Francisco, CA: HarperSanFrancisco, 2006), 37.

34. So in John 11:47-52, Caiaphas exemplifies the wickedness behind scapegoating, but John sees a prophetic layer to his words in terms of the universal benefits of Christ's sacrifice.

35. Cf. René Girard, *Things Hidden from the Foundation of the Earth* (Stanford, CA: Stanford Univ. Press, 1978), 184.

violence."[36] Walter Wink, critiquing Girard in *Engaging the Powers*, agrees on this point:

> The God whom Jesus revealed as no longer our rival, no longer threatening and vengeful, but unconditionally loving and forgiving, who needed no satisfaction by blood—this God of infinite mercy was metamorphosed by the church into the image of a wrathful God of unequalled violence, since God not only allegedly demands the blood of the victim who is closest and most precious to him, but also holds the whole of humanity accountable for a death that God both anticipated and required. Against such an image of God, the revolt of atheism is an act of pure religion.[37]

The sacrifice is then one of God towards mankind as love confronts hatred with forgiveness. Jesus offers his Father the lifelong sacrifice of obedience and faith as he fulfills his calling even to the point of death at our hands. That mission would inevitably require the shedding of blood, because we are that violent, not because God is.

Far from being penal or a manifestation of God's wrath or the Father turning his face from his Son, the Cross is a manifestation of God-in-Christ's love and forgiveness—his nonviolent response to our wrath-filled rejection of him. But it is more than this. We move now to our second term: identification.

II. IDENTIFICATION VERSUS SUBSTITUTION

If our term, "identification," does not entirely negate "substitution," then I would argue that at the very least, it enfolds and eclipses it. We read throughout the Scriptures that Jesus died *for* us. For centuries, debate has continued as to whether the word translated "for" is best rendered "instead of" (as our substitute) or "on behalf of" (or "for the benefit of"). A nuanced sense of substitution is certainly in order if we focus on Christ experiencing the horrors of Satan, sin and death in such a way that we are rescued from their bondage. In other words, he does for me what I could never accomplish for myself. He does on my behalf and for my benefit what I was powerless to do.

But this is not how substitution is usually used in our pulpits. We generally hear that Jesus endured the wrath of God in our place. He suffered at the hands of his Father instead of us, paying the penalty for our sins so that we don't have to. In my opinion, this is to say too much (by making God the agent in Christ's torment) and not enough (by rescuing us from the call to take up our own cross and be crucified with Christ).

Christ did die for us—not merely instead of us—to bring about *mutual identification* with him: *union* with Christ in which an *exchange* happens. As

---

36. *The Girard Reader,* ed. by J.G. Williams (New York. NY: Crossroad Herder, 1996) 179.
37. Walter Wink, *Engaging the Powers* (Minneapolis, MN: Fortress Press, 1992) 149.

I become one with him in his death and resurrection—as he dies for me and I with him—he takes my sin and death in exchange for his life and righteousness. It is too simple to say that he dies in my place. No, we are grafted together—united—for a journey through Christ's life and mission, his death and resurrection, and his ascension and glorification with the Father. Let's pay attention to how this works out in 2 Corinthians 5:

> For Christ's love compels us, because we are convinced that one died *for all,* and therefore *all died.* And he died *for all,* that those who live should no longer live *for themselves* but for him who died *for them* and was raised again [for them]…
>
> Therefore, if anyone is *in Christ* [union], he is a new creation; the old has gone, the new has come! All this is from God, who reconciled us to himself through Christ and gave us the ministry of reconciliation: that God was reconciling the world to himself *in Christ,* not counting men's sins against them. And he has committed to us the message of reconciliation. We are therefore Christ's ambassadors, as though God were making his appeal through us. We implore you on Christ's behalf: Be reconciled to God. God made him who had no sin to be sin *for us,* so that *in him* we might become the righteousness of God (2 Corinthians 5:14-15, 17-21).

We see more than a substitution in this passage. Paul is preaching what I am calling "identification," but it actually encapsulates three concepts:

- Solidarity
- Union
- Exchange

A. Identification and Solidarity

Upon reading the various essays to follow, the reader will note that all of the authors move beyond substitution into at least one of the following examples of identification.

1. Christ identifies fully with us.

> The crucifixion of Jesus is not to be understood simply in good liberal fashion as the sacrifice of a noble man, nor should we too quickly assign a cultic, priestly theory of atonement to the event. Rather, we might see in the crucifixion of Jesus the ultimate act of prophetic criticism in which Jesus announces the end of a world of death (the same announcement as that of Jeremiah) and takes the death into his own person. Therefore, we say that the ultimate criticism is that God embraces the death that God's people must die. The criticism consists not in standing over against but in standing with.[38]

---

38. Walter Brueggemann, *The Prophetic Imagination* (Minneapolis, MN: Augsburg Fortress Publishers, 1978) 94.

- He identifies fully with humanity through the incarnation. He stands in solidarity with us from birth to death. The atonement does not begin or end with the Cross. Christ's reconciling work is initiated throughout his life and ministry, declaring that God's table is open to fellowship for all who will come (even before the Cross) and that forgiveness, healing and deliverance (not just provisionally pending his death, but actually as we come) are available to all who believe.

- He identifies fully with sinners.

- He is numbered with criminals.

- He stands with every innocent victim who has felt abandoned.

- He embraces the role of the Suffering Servant.

- He identifies with the history, calling, suffering and destiny of Israel.[39]

2. God identifies with and in Christ.

Whereas penal substitution presents God as superintending the death of Jesus and using wicked agents to pour out his wrath against sin in Jesus, pleased to punish him as payment for sin, the Scriptures locate God in Christ—Moltmann's "Crucified God"—Yahweh in solidarity with the suffering Servant:

a. 2 Corinthians 5:18-19

Now all these things are from God, who reconciled us to Himself through Christ and gave us the ministry of reconciliation, namely, that God was in Christ reconciling the world to Himself, not counting their trespasses against them, and He has committed to us the word of reconciliation (NASB).

b. Zechariah 12:1,10

This is the word of the LORD concerning Israel. The LORD, who stretches out the heavens, who lays the foundation of the earth, and who forms the spirit of man within him, declares: "And I will pour out on the house of David and the inhabitants of Jerusalem a spirit of grace and supplication. They will look on me, the one they have pierced, and they will mourn for him as one mourns for an only child, and grieve bitterly for him as one grieves for a firstborn son."

B. Identification and Union

As Christ identifies with us, so he calls us to identify with him. We are called to follow, participate and unite in Christ's "way" (the journey, the road, the

---

39. Cf. N.T. Wright's chapter.

path) of life, death and resurrection. Before jumping ahead to "take up your cross and follow me" as pure metaphor, we ought to remember that Jesus initial call to take up the cross was in the context of his path to literal crucifixion. In Mark 8:31-38, Jesus explicitly foretells his death and resurrection then immediately tells the crowd and the disciples that coming after him means taking up a cross and losing one's life in order to find it. Identification is central—substitution is absent. Beyond this immediate literal challenge, salvation through participation in Christ's journey extends to every generation.

Borg and Crossan[40] contrast atonement as substitution with atonement as *participation:*

> The basic and controlling metaphor for that [substitutionary atonement] understanding of God's design is our own experience of a responsible human judge who, no matter how loving, cannot legitimately or validly walk into her courtroom and clear the docket of all offenders by anticipatory forgiveness. The doctrine of vicarious, or substitutionary, atonement begs the question whether God must or should be seen as a human judge writ large and absolute. That is surely not the only and maybe not the best metaphor for God. What about the metaphor, for example, in which God is fundamentally Parent (Father, if you prefer) rather than Judge? As such, and as the Bible repeatedly asserts, God's unpunishing forgiveness has always been, is now, and ever will be freely available to any repentant sinner at any place at any time.

> But how then do you move beyond forgiveness to establish a positive union with God as loving Parent? Since for Christians Jesus is the revelation, the image, and the best vision possible of that God, it is only by participation in the life, death and resurrection of Jesus that such a salvific "at-one-ment" is possible.

Initially, identification with Christ requires that I identify with those who crucified him; my sin identifies me with the perpetrators.[41] We see our culpability, and mourning, we renounce our allegiance to the powers and align ourselves with the Crucified One (Romans 6, Galatians 2). We must ultimately identify either with those who crucified or the one who was crucified—penal substitution (at its worst) allows us to escape this great either/or. The message of the Cross is not, "I died so that you don't need to," but "Die with me so that you might rise with me."[42] Disciples of Christ live, die, rise and are glorified with him.

Four classic texts proclaim that Christ did not merely die in our place, as substitution asserts. Rather, we are called to union with Christ in his life, his mission, his ministry, his Way of co-suffering, sacrificial love and in his

---

40. Borg and Crossan, *The Last Week,* 101-102.
41. Zechariah 12:10 above: "The one whom *we* have pierced." Cf. Mark D. Baker's chapter in this book.
42. Cf. Brita Miko's chapter.

death. Thus we also unite with him in resurrection, ascension and glorification (all of which begin in this life and carry over to the next).

1. We unite with the crucified Christ

a. Romans 6:1-8

What shall we say, then? Shall we go on sinning so that grace may increase? By no means! We died to sin; how can we live in it any longer? Or don't you know that all of us who were baptized into Christ Jesus were baptized into his death? We were therefore buried with him through baptism into death in order that, just as Christ was raised from the dead through the glory of the Father, we too may live a new life.

If we have been united with him like this in his death, we will certainly also be united with him in his resurrection. For we know that our old self was crucified with him so that the body of sin might be done away with, that we should no longer be slaves to sin—because anyone who has died has been freed from sin.

Now if we died with Christ, we believe that we will also live with him.

In this passage, Paul includes three aspects of union: (i.) Union with Christ in his death; (ii.) union with Christ in his resurrection life (future); (iii.) and union with him in resurrection life (now), which is to say, freedom from sin and obedience to God. This calls into question both substitutionary death (he died so I don't have to) but also substitutionary obedience (he obeyed the Father so I don't need to). How did Christ explain this?

b. Matthew 10:37-40

Anyone who loves his father or mother more than me is not worthy of me; anyone who loves his son or daughter more than me is not worthy of me; and anyone who does not take his cross and follow me is not worthy of me. Whoever finds his life will lose it, and whoever loses his life for my sake will find it.

He who receives you receives me, and he who receives me receives the one who sent me.

Here, Christ is calling for us to identify with him—to unite with him—in the type of life and ministry that may well lead to a Cross. Moreover, we have Christ explicitly describing the Way of the Cross, defining discipleship in terms of those who unite with him in co-suffering love, which also ultimately leads to identification with his vindication:

c. Matthew 16:21, 24-28

From that time on Jesus began to explain to his disciples that he must go to Jerusalem and suffer many things at the hands of the elders, chief priests and teachers of the law, and that he must be killed and on the third day be raised to life....

Then Jesus said to his disciples, "If anyone would come after me, he must deny himself and take up his cross and follow me. For whoever wants to save his life will lose it, but whoever loses his life for me will find it. What good will it be for a man if he gains the whole world, yet forfeits his soul? Or what can a man give in exchange for his soul? For the Son of Man is going to come in his Father's glory with his angels, and then he will reward each person according to what he has done. I tell you the truth, some who are standing here will not taste death before they see the Son of Man coming in his kingdom.

d. Galatians 2:17-21

A fourth illustration of union vis-à-vis substitution is Paul's famous claim in Galatians 2:17-21.

> If, while we seek to be justified *in Christ,* it becomes evident that we ourselves are sinners, does that mean that Christ promotes sin? Absolutely not! If I rebuild what I destroyed, I prove that I am a lawbreaker. For through the law I died to the law so that I might *live for God.* I have been *crucified with Christ* and I no longer live, but Christ lives in me. The life I live in the body, I live by faith in the Son of God, who loved me and gave himself *for me.* I do not set aside the grace of God, for if righteousness could be gained through the law, Christ died for nothing!

Paul's mutual union with Christ includes his death with Christ (to sin and to the law), and Christ's life within him (for God by faith). When Paul says here that Christ gave himself *for me,* we cannot interpret that as *instead of* me (since he's just said, he was crucified *with* Christ) any more than saying that "I might live instead of God." "For me" and "for him" here has more to do with "in service of." He humbled himself for me and became a servant for me and endured death for me (Philippians 2:8). As I join myself to him as his servant, I die with him and live for him.

2. We unite with the resurrected and glorified Christ

a. Love Union—Catholic Mysticism

A thorough atonement theology ought also to engage with the Catholic mystical theologians from St. John of the Cross to William Johnston. The Roman Catholic theology of the Cross must be given space if we are to find a truly unifying theory of the atonement. Johnston, in *Mystical Theology: The Science of Love*[43] uses John of the Cross to treat the atonement as a revelation of love for the purpose of uniting God and his people. He also forwards Vatican II as a model for this type of unitive atonement. He quotes the council as saying:

> For by his incarnation the Son of God has united himself in some fashion with every man and woman. He worked with human hands, He thought with a human mind, acted by human choice, and loved with a human heart.

---

43. William Johnston, *Mystical Theology: The Science of Love* (United Kingdom: HarperCollins Pub. Ltd., 1995).

> For since Christ died for all, and since the ultimate vocation of everyone is in fact one and divine, we ought to believe that the Holy Spirit in a manner known only to God offers to everyone the possibility of being associated with this paschal mystery.

Whether we can embrace Vatican II or not, the long Catholic history of mystical union in the Cross exceeds the boundaries of the three theories[44] that Boersma treats as comprehensive. Penal atonement treats the Cross as an outpouring of divine wrath (for the sake of love), whereas mystics from the Apostle John to John of the Cross present it as a revelation of divine love for the sake of union/communion with Him:

> At the beginning it was love for the crucified Jesus; for John of the Cross was of the cross. And then love for Jesus crucified leads to identification with Jesus in accordance with the Pauline words, "I live, now not I, but Christ lives in me."[45]

Union, therefore, does not end with the Cross. The soul's journey is about consummation or love union with God.[46] Perhaps the language of God's hospitality is partially to blame for this oversight. Boersma's beautiful picture of the Father standing with open arms at the threshold is accurate and compelling. But again, we have a metaphor, this time underplayed. Beyond the open, hospitable arms of a Father, Scripture and the mystics take us into the embrace of the Bridegroom and the intimacy of the bridal chamber.

b. Deification/Divinization—The Orthodox Tradition

Another omission in most western surveys of atonement theory is the Orthodox theology of union with God through Christ via the Spirit resulting in our *deification* (or *divinization*, which Irenaeus defines carefully as the attainment of our *immortality* and *incorruptibility*). This union was initiated in the incarnation, climaxed in Jesus' death and resurrection, and is continually fulfilled by the Holy Spirit.[47] It was at the core of Irenaeus' soteriology:

> "We could not otherwise attain to incorruption and immortality except we had been united with incorruption and immortality" (*Against Heresies* IV 33:4).

> "For this is why the Word became man, and the Son of God became the Son of man: so that man, by entering into communion with the Word and thus receiving divine sonship, might become a son of God."

> "If the Word has been made man, it is so that men may be made gods" (*Against Heresies* V, Pref.).

---

44. Moral influence, satisfaction/penal substitution and *Christus Victor.*
45. Johnston, *Mystical Theology*, 70.
46. Cf. John of the Cross, *Spiritual Canticle* and *Dark Night of the Soul*, Teresa of Avila, *Interior Castles* and *The Way of Perfection*, Richard Rolle, *The Fire of Love,* Madame Guyon, *The Song of the Bride.*
47. Cf. our chapters by Anstall and Dart.

Strong statements, but this type of divinizing union was widely held among the church fathers:

Clement of Alexandria: "The Logos of God had become man so that you might learn from a man how a man may become God."[48]

Origen: "From [Christ] there began the *union* of the divine with the human nature, in order that the human, by communion with the divine, might rise to be divine."[49]

Athanasius: "[The Word] was made man so that we might be made God."[50]

"Man, being *united* to Him, may be able to partake... gifts which come from God."[51]

These church fathers draw us into the reality of Peter's doctrine of our "participation in the divine nature" (2 Peter 1:4): that salvation extends beyond forgiveness of sin and redemption from bondage to include union with God through our identification with Christ. I.e. they defined salvation as deification through union.[52] To the church fathers, and to this day in the Eastern Church, this is the essence and fruit of "at-one-ment."

C. Identification and Exchange

At the Cross, we find Jesus enacting a powerful dynamic of exchange. Of course, this began before Good Friday throughout Jesus' entire ministry and continues to this day by the ministry of his Spirit through the church. Jesus takes up Isaiah's description of this ministry as his own Great Commission in Luke 4. Isaiah talks in terms of trading our brokenness for his wholeness:

> The Spirit of the Sovereign LORD is on me,
>> because the LORD has anointed me
>> to preach good news to the poor.
>> He has sent me to bind up the brokenhearted,
>> to proclaim freedom for the captives
>> and release from darkness for the prisoners,
> to proclaim the year of the LORD's favor
>> and the day of vengeance of our God,
>> to comfort all who mourn,
> and provide for those who grieve in Zion—
>> to bestow on them a crown of beauty instead of ashes,
>> the oil of gladness instead of mourning,
>> and a garment of praise instead of a spirit of despair.

48. *Prot.* 1.8.4.
49. *Cels.* 3.28, cf. *Orat.* 27.13; *Cels.* 3.28.
50. *De Inc.* 54.3.
51. *Orat.* 4.6.
52. Cf. Jaroslav Pelikan, *The Christian Tradition: A History of the Development of Doctrine. Volume 1 & 2* (Chicago: University of Chicago, 1974); Adolph Harnack, *History of Dogma*, Tr. by Neil Buchanan (New York: Dover, cir. 1900); Michael Morrison, *"The Theological Legacy of Athanasius"* (http://www.angelfire.com/md/mdmorrison/hist).

They will be called oaks of righteousness,
    a planting of the LORD for the display of his splendor.[53]

Irenaeus picks up on the theme of exchange (which exceeds substitution) as Word and flesh, God and man, Christ and humankind are united—grafted together—in mutual communion.

> Since the Lord thus has redeemed us through His own blood, giving His soul for our souls, and His flesh for our flesh, and has also poured out the Spirit of the Father for the *union and communion* of God and man, imparting indeed God to men by means of the Spirit, and, on the other hand, *attaching man to God* by His own incarnation, and bestowing upon us at His coming immortality durably and truly, by means of *communion* with God—all the doctrines of the heretics fall to ruin.[54]

This is a powerful theory of the atonement that incorporates identification, union and exchange metaphors while at the same time evading the juridical issues of penal satisfaction.

Later, Athanasius clearly depends on and then expands on Irenaeus' theory. Note his use of union, solidarity and exchange and how these provide a context for sacrifice and substitution quite different from Anselm or Calvin.

> He assumed a body capable of death, in order that it, through belonging to the Word Who is above all, might become in dying a sufficient *exchange* for all, and, itself remaining incorruptible through His indwelling, might thereafter put an end to corruption for all others as well, by the grace of the resurrection. It was by surrendering to death the body which He had taken, as an offering and sacrifice free from every stain, that He forthwith abolished death for His human brethren by the offering of the equivalent. For naturally, since the Word of God was above all, when He offered His own temple and bodily instrument as a *substitute* for the life of all, He fulfilled in death all that was required. Naturally also, through this *union* of the immortal Son of God with our human nature, all men were clothed with incorruption in the promise of the resurrection. For the *solidarity* of mankind is such that, by virtue of the Word's indwelling in a single human body, the corruption which goes with death has lost its power over all... What, then, was God to do? What else could he possibly do, being God, but renew His Image in mankind, so that through it men might once more come to know Him? And how could this be done save by the coming of the very Image Himself, our Savior Jesus Christ? (Athanasius, *On the Incarnation,* 9)

> The words of Saint John: "The Word was made flesh," bear the same meaning, as we may see from a similar turn of phrase in Saint Paul: "Christ was made a curse for our sake." Man's body has acquired something great through its *communion and union* with the Word. From being mortal it has been made immortal; though it was a living body it has become a spiritual one; though it was made from the earth it has passed through the gates of heaven (Athanasius, *Epist. Ad Epictetum,* 5-9).

---

53. Isaiah 61:1-3.
54. Irenaeus of Lyons, *Adversus Haereses,* 5.1.1.

The active ingredient in the Cross event and the entire incarnation is thus (i.) the complete identification of Christ with mankind in every way, and (ii.) the participation of mankind in the death and resurrection of Christ. As Paul said, "He who knew no sin became sin for us that we might become the righteousness of God" (2 Corinthians 5:21). And from our side, "I am crucified with Christ... Christ lives within me" (Galatians 2:20). In other words, the Cross saves us because Christ unites Himself to our fallen humanity and unites us to Himself in His divine victory.

III. The Victory of Christ

Finally, most Christians have always agreed that a major aspect of the Cross is the victory of Christ. What appeared to the world as a colossal failure turns out to be a great conquest as Christ conquers Satan, sin and death. Some key Scriptures that demonstrate this intent:

- "The Son of God appeared for this purpose: to destroy the works of the devil" (1 John 3:8).
- "Now is the time for judgment on this world; now the prince of this world will be driven out" (John 12:31).
- "The prince of this world is coming. He has no hold on me, but the world must learn that I love the Father and that I do exactly what my Father has commanded me" (John 14:30-31).
- "The prince of this world now stands condemned" (John 16:11).
- "And having disarmed the powers and authorities, he made a public spectacle of them, triumphing over them by the cross" (Colossians 3:15).
- "Since the children have flesh and blood, he too shared in their humanity so that by his death he might destroy him who holds the power of death—that is, the devil—and free those who all their lives were held in slavery by their fear of death" (Hebrews 2:14-15).

Irenaeus picked up on this theme, preaching salvation through incarnation and especially the Cross as accomplishing freedom from sin, the destruction of death, and the defeat of the enemy:

> "The Word of God was made flesh in order that he might destroy death and bring man to life; for we were tied and bound in sin, we were born in sin and live under the power of death" (Irenaeus, *Epideixis,* 37).

So, when we speak of "the Cross," we are really using a two-layered symbol. First, the Cross is a picture of everything that Christ conquered in his death. It represents sin and shame, condemnation and judgement, the political and religious powers, and the great enemies of humanity: the devil and death.

But then, second, the Cross also represents Jesus' conquest over all of the above. I.e. *The Cross is our picture of Jesus' victory over the cross: the cross* (small-c and all it symbolized) *could not hold him.* It represents God's forgiving love that cleanses sin and shame, breaks the curse of the law, disarms the temporal and spiritual powers, and unlocks the gates of death and hell.

Thus, both pictures considered, the Cross is first a manifestation of the sin of man AND of the love of God which trumps it in victory. This victory includes but exceeds what the Cross accomplished. There is a whole series of victories to be pondered:

- Victory over temptation in the wilderness.

- Victory over sickness and demons (every kind of sickness and disease and over all the power of the evil one).

- Victory over Satan, sin and death through both Cross AND resurrection.

- Victory of Christ's ascension / glorification to the right hand of the God's throne (Daniel 7) where he now holds the keys of death and hades (Revelation 1) and where every knee will bow and every tongue confess that he is Lord (i.e. victorious king – Philippians 2:10-11).

These victories are to be our victories—real salvation and empowerment for those who believe.

> The Lord, through his passion ascended up on high, led captivity captive, and gave gifts to men, and gave power to them that believe in Him to tread upon serpents and scorpions and upon all the power of the enemy - that is, the prince of the apostasy. The Lord through his passion destroyed death, brought error to an end, abolished corruption, banished ignorance, manifested life, declared truth and bestowed incorruption. (Irenaeus, *Against Heresies* 2.20.3).

St. John Chrysostom (circa 400 AD) proclaimed the victory of Christ with such passion and anointing that his Easter homily was permanently imbedded in the annual liturgy of the Eastern churches' Holy Pascha celebration. The following excerpt highlights the "harrowing of hell" as preached in the early church and illustrates how the descent into hell and exodus from the grave are essential to the atoning work of Christ.

> Let no one grieve at his poverty,
> for the universal kingdom has been revealed.
>
> Let no one mourn that he has fallen again and again;
> for forgiveness has risen from the grave.
>
> Let no one fear death, for the Death of our Savior has set us free.
> He has destroyed it by enduring it.
> He destroyed Hell when He descended into it.

He put it into an uproar even as it tasted of His flesh.

Isaiah foretold this when he said,
"You, O Hell, have been troubled by encountering Him below."
Hell was in an uproar because it was done away with.
It was in an uproar because it is mocked.
It was in an uproar, for it is destroyed.
It is in an uproar, for it is annihilated.
It is in an uproar, for it is now made captive.

Hell took a body, and discovered God.
It took earth, and encountered Heaven.
It took what it saw, and was overcome by what it did not see.

O death, where is thy sting?
O Hell, where is thy victory?

Christ is Risen, and you, o death, are annihilated!
Christ is Risen, and the evil ones are cast down!
Christ is Risen, and the angels rejoice!
Christ is Risen, and life is liberated!

Christ is Risen, and the tomb is emptied of its dead;
for Christ having risen from the dead,
is become the first-fruits of those who have fallen asleep.

To Him be Glory and Power forever and ever. Amen!

CONCLUSION

To conclude, we have gathered voices, past and present, to suggest that we see nonviolent identification and victory as a table around which Orthodox, Catholic, Anglican, Anabaptist, Evangelical and Mainline theologians can rally. The work of Christ on the Cross, enfolded in the entire drama of his incarnation, calls the church and the world to identify with him who identified with them in every way. And I believe he calls us to know his Father apart from such misrepresentations as offended lord or punishing judge. He would show us that even the Cross is a manifestation of God's love and forgiveness as over against his wrath and punitive justice.

Christ taught us that the final resort in the face of human violence is to take up the cross and lay down one's life, not with defiant battle cries but as sheep to be slaughtered. Sacrificial, co-suffering love truly is a more powerful force. The Cross was not God's violent solution to sin—it was an act of love in which God destroyed the power of violence by refusing to be drawn into it. And yet, in opting for love over judgement and mercy over wrath, Christ is proven Victor in his resurrection. With significant breadth and depth of perspective, our authors unite now in inviting the reader to follow Christ into that same victory.

Chapter Two

OUT OF THE FOG:
NEW HORIZONS FOR ATONEMENT THEORY

by Michael Hardin

The Cross of Jesus Christ represents simultaneously a high estimate of the human creature, a grave realism concerning human alienation, and the compassionate determination of God to bring humankind to the realization of its potentiality for authenticity.[1]

Divine forgiveness is a perfect gift, a gift of justice that mirrors mercy, that triumphs over retribution and human notions of balanced books and just payment. Divine forgiveness is justice that triumphs in mercy. Divine justice is justice infected with mercy.[2]

The Nonviolence Atonement Conference Project has an existential context. I had mentioned to Tony Bartlett all of the books published on atonement since August 2006. He replied, "the explosion of atonement writing, indicating a crisis in Christian thought and existence, [is] stumbling on the issue of violence. And this I think is part of a wider human crisis."[3] This past autumn 2006, just a few miles from here, a gunman entered an Amish schoolhouse and killed five little girls. Five more are struggling for their lives. Violence had come to a community that did not know violence.

In the same week that the Amish school shootings occurred, I received in the mail a flyer from the Conestoga Valley Church of Christ. The front page carried the title "When the Omnipresent God Was Absent."[4] The author argues that God "was absent from Calvary." Why was this so? "The holiness of God was repulsed by the world's sin." God's holiness "was repelled" by human sin. "God's holiness may be his chief attribute. It is referred to in Scripture more than any other trait. 'Holiness is the central nature of the being of God from which such attributes as love, justice and mercy emanate.'"[5]

The author continues: "The justice of God inflicted upon Jesus the penalty

---

1. Douglas John Hall, *The Cross in Our Context: Jesus and the Suffering World* (Minneapolis: Fortress, 2003), 91.
2. Sharon Baker, *By Grace? (An)Economy of Salvation,* PhD dissertation, 142, 148.
3. Tony Bartlett in an e-mail to me December 26, 2006.
4. *House to House,* Vol. 11, No. 5.
5. Quoting George Allen Turner.

that the worst of all sinners would face…The truth of God needed the scape-goat to go into the wilderness… Jesus is the only man who ever lived who knew what it felt like to be that [the Levitical] scapegoat… Jesus took the place of sinners, so he experienced the separation that sinners faced (Isaiah 59:1-2). He was separated from God for three hours so that we might be with God for eternity."

There is a certain tragic serendipity in the juxtaposition of these two events, a shooting and a mailing. In both the shooting and the pastoral letter an innocent life is demanded as payment for sin. The juxtaposition of these two items highlights many of the concerns that will be addressed in the essays and discussions of this book. I suggest that the violence that was perpetuated in that Amish schoolhouse was a symptom of a larger disease, a disease nurtured by a 'Christian' theological worldview.[6] Yet the alternative to this cultural disease was evident in the forgiveness of the Amish. The atonement sought by the shooter, Mr. Roberts, is no different than that sought by the God of the mailing. For both, blood satisfies, and in both, innocent blood, truly innocent blood is shed. For the Amish, the blood of their little girls did not cry out for retaliation, for vengeance. Rather, the blood of the Amish girls cried out in the heart of the Amish community, "Forgiveness."

The identification by the Amish with the person of Jesus not only expressed his non-retaliatory ethic; it also embodied the character of Jesus in express-ing forgiveness as Jesus did (Luke 23:34). As Hebrews says, "Jesus' blood speaks a better word than that of Abel's (Hebrews 12:25). But what is this word? And what does it mean? How can we discern it? And what might this word mean for our understanding of Christian life and theology?

The literature on atonement theory has grown exponentially this past decade with a discernible shift occurring away from the Anselmic or satis-faction theory and its post-Reformation development, the penal satisfaction theory. Over the past century, particularly since the 1931 publication of Gus-tav Aulen's *Christus Victor*, the death of Jesus Christ has been reconsidered in ways not seen since the New Testament writers took quill to papyrus. And in this past decade, dominant theories of the atonement have come under intense scrutiny. Part of the impetus for this has been the various discussions around the doctrine of the Trinity and the death of Jesus in the twentieth cen-tury, discussions that rival those of the fourth and fifth centuries;[7] another

---

6. Charles Roberts' last words over the phone to the police were directed to the Amish girls, "I'm going to make you pay for my daughter." He refers to the death of his daughter (she lived twenty minutes) nine years before. It is the language of payment or exchange that is foundational to the shooting and the penal satisfaction theory of the mailing. On Charles Roberts' background see *The Lancaster New Era*, December 13 and 14, 2006.

key element has been the late twentieth century's interest in perspectives of the marginalized. Finally, René Girard's mimetic theory, as it relates particularly to the problem of sacrifice, has proved illuminating with regard to Christian understandings of atonement.

Now all credible authors on the atonement[8] observe that a sea change took place in understanding the death of Jesus with Anselm of Canterbury in his *Cur Deus Homo?* and again with Peter Abelard's critique a generation later.[9] Anselm argued the necessity of satisfaction to God's honor in order for the universe to remain just; Abelard said that the death of Jesus displayed the love of God, which moves us to repentance. These two competing understandings dominated the conversation on atonement from the twelfth through the nineteenth centuries. Post-Reformation Protestant dogmatics tended to come down in some version of Anselm, liberal Protestantism on

7. I especially note the influential role of Karl Barth, particularly regarding Jesus' death and Trinitarian relations (*The Judge Judged in our Place*), *Church Dogmatics* IV: 1 (London: T&T Clark, 1956) 211ff. Some might think we have to do here with judgment as wrath but such is not the case: "And it is to the point if we remember that the Judge is not simply or even primarily the One who pardons some and condemns the rest – whose judgment therefore we all have to fear. Basically and decisively – and this is something we must never forget when we speak of the divine Judge – He is the One whose concern is for order and peace, who must uphold the right and prevent the wrong, so that His existence and coming and work is not in itself and as such a matter for fear, but something which indicates a favor, the existence of One who brings salvation." See also Jurgen Moltmann's *The Crucified God* (New York: Harper and Row, 1974), esp. 235ff.

8. Authors on atonement referred to in this essay: J Denny Weaver, *The Nonviolent Atonement* (Grand Rapids: Eerdmans, 2001); Anthony Bartlett, *Cross Purposes* (Harrisburg: Trinity, 2001); S. Mark Heim, *Saved from Sacrifice* (Grand Rapids: Eerdmans, 2006); Peter Schmiechen, *Saving Power: Theories of Atonement and Forms of the Church* (Grand Rapids: Eerdmans, 2005); Marit Trelstad, ed., *Cross Examinations* (Minneapolis: Augsburg, 2006); Joel Green and Mark Baker, *Recovering the Scandal of the Cross* (Downers Grove: Intervarsity Press, 2000) and Mark Baker, ed. *Proclaiming the Scandal of the Cross* (Grand Rapids: Baker, 2006); Hans Boersma, *Violence, Hospitality and the Cross* (Grand Rapids: Baker, 2004); Darby Kathleen Ray, *Deceiving the Devil* (Cleveland: Pilgrim Press, 1998); Stephen Finlan, *Problems with Atonement*, (Collegeville: Liturgical Press, 2005); Scot McKnight, *Jesus and His Death: Historiography, the Historical Jesus and Atonement Theory* (Waco: Baylor University Press, 2005). Sharon Baker, *By Grace: (An) Economy of Salvation* (PhD dissertation Southern Methodist University, 2006); John Sanders, *ed., Atonement and Violence: A Theological Conversation* (Nashville: Abingdon, 2006); David Eagle, "Anthony Bartlett's Concept of Abyssal Compassion and the Possibility of a Truly Nonviolent Atonement" in *The Conrad Grebel Review* (Vol. 24, No. 1, Winter 2006). Leon Morris, *The Atonement: Its Meaning and Significance* (Downers Grove: Intervarsity Press, 1983); Timothy Gorringe, *God's Just Vengeance* (Cambridge: Cambridge University Press, 1996), Vincent Brummer, *Atonement, Christology and the Trinity* (Burlington: Ashgate Publishing, 2005); R. Larry Shelton, *Cross and Covenant*, (Paternoster Press, 2006); Robin Collins, "Girard and Atonement: An Incarnational Theory of Mimetic Participation" in Willard Swartley, ed., *Violence Renounced* (Telford: Pandora Press, 2000); John Milbank, *Being Reconciled: Ontology and Pardon* (Routledge: London, 2003); Thomas Schreiner, "Penal Substitution View" and Bruce R. Reichenbach, "Healing View" in James Beilby and Paul R. Eddy ed., *The Nature of the Atonement* (Downers Grove: Intervarsity, 2006). See also Vitor Westhelle, *The Scandalous God: The Use and Abuse of the Cross* (Minneapolis: Fortress, 2006); Miroslav Volf, *Exclusion and Embrace* (Nashville: Abingdon, 1996) and *Free of Charge* (Grand Rapids: Zondervan, 2005); John Carroll and Joel Green, *The Death of Jesus in Earliest Christianity* (Peabody: Hendrikson, 1995).

the side of Abelard. The debate was broken open when Aulen's *Christus Victor* demonstrated that Luther's theory of atonement was not to be framed within this dialectic but participated in a view that could also be attributed to the early church, notably seen in Irenaeus' recapitulation theory. We now conveniently classify atonement theories into three types: *Christus Victor*, Moral Influence, and Satisfaction, although these have each been modified into many different subtypes.

There are several ways contemporary authors enter the debate surrounding the atoning work of Jesus Christ. First there are authors that favor one type over others (Aulen, Weaver, Bartlett, Ray, Eagle, Morris, Finlan, Schreiner [in Beilby and Eddy], Daniels [in Sanders] and in some respects, Boersma). Second, are those authors that argue that the Bible has a plurality of metaphors for atonement and that none should be privileged (M. Baker, Green, Schmiechen, Sherman, Shelton and Finger). Third, there are authors who suggest that this plurality of metaphors is a biblical problem that can only be solved by ecclesiastical authority (Finlan). Fourth, there are those who engage mimetic theory in a substantial fashion (Bartlett, S. Baker, M. Baker, Heim, Alison, Weaver, Daniels and, in limited ways, Gorringe). With minor exceptions[10] though, almost all authors agree that the Anselmic theory and its popular distortions contain many a problem.[11]

In this essay, I want to suggest that we discern how atonement theories function, to what extent our atonement theories are influenced by pagan thought forms, and finally how Christian theology in the twenty-first century can learn how to do without the crutches of a violent deity. Marit Trelstad observes, "All categories in Christian theology collide in the discussion of the cross."[12] I will begin by looking at three areas that I think need exploration and clarification with regard to formulating an atonement theory: dualism, the use of Scripture, and God's honor. I do this admittedly as a mimetic theorist, as one who has been influenced by René Girard. The necessity of engaging mimetic theory is becoming more and more apparent as the implications for a mimetic theoretical hermeneutic become clearer across the disciplines of the human sciences. This can especially be seen in the spate of authors writing on Jesus' death that feel obliged to mention, use, or critique Girard.

---

9. S.N. Deane, *St. Anselm: Basic Writings* (LaSalle: Open Court, 1962); Eugene Fairweather, *A Scholastic Miscellany* (Philadelphia: Westminster, 1956).

10. Thomas Schreiner, "Penal Substitution View" in James Beilby and Paul R. Eddy, ed., *The Nature of the Atonement* (Downers Grove: IVP, 2006).

11. Schmiechen wonders if the problem with atonement lies "in the root images themselves, in the way they are developed or only in errant formulations? (16)." Part of my argument in this essay is that (sacrificial) images, development and errant formulations are all tied together.

12. Trelstad, *Cross Examinations*, 110.

Unexplored Questions in Atonement

Dualism

Part of our problem is that we read Scripture through the eyes of our western culture, which is grounded in Platonism.[13] In a recent lecture at Lancaster Theological Seminary, feminist theo-ethicist Mary Hunt pointed out that one of the pitfalls of contemporary theology is that it asks the wrong questions and suggested that current questions must be reframed. When a discipline runs out of fresh questions, it is on its last legs, preparing for its sojourn in the history department. This is especially true of the discipline of theology. It might be argued that one of the conditions of our postmodern situation is that the questions we are asking are revealed as the same old tired questions Christians have asked since the second century. These questions arise within a Hellenic worldview, a dualistic worldview.

If we recognize that the apostolic message did not arise primarily dependent upon a Hellenic worldview but rather a Jewish one,[14] we are given a fresh set of questions. We will see things differently. The ideal is not split off from the real; they are one and the same thing. God is one. This is the import of the Shema.

Dualism posits opposites. There is a good god (principle, force) and a bad god. These gods are locked in an eternal mimetic struggle, now one winning, now the other. Standard models of monotheism bring the two sides together and make the two one; there is only one God and this God is both good and evil or responsible for evil. For Jesus and the New Testament writers, God is good; it is humanity that 'is' satanic.[15] Evil is anthropologized; this does not diminish the power or tragedy of evil, it accentuates it, for it puts the burden of all the sins of humanity collectively on the whole human race, each and every one is completely culpable and complicit in evil, by thought, word and deed.[16] As Jesus has said, "God alone is good."[17]

How might this insight come about? Later I will suggest that mimetic theorists are asking a different set of questions than is typical of the Christian

13. Our contemporary 'Christian' dualism has been well documented by Philip Lee, *Against the Protestant Gnostics* (Oxford: Oxford, 1987).

14. I am aware that we are no longer to separate Judaism and Hellenism, especially since the groundbreaking work of Martin Hengel. And I tend to see an eastern dualism influencing Judaism at least from around the sixth century B.C.E. (Zoroastrianism). But it is western Platonic dualism that carries with it specific perceptions of epistemology, what can be known and how it can be known. While both eastern and western dualisms have much in common, it is the western that distinguishes between the real and the ideal or the noumenal and the phenomenal. In Zoroastrianism the dualism is cosmic and moral. See Yuri Stoyanov, *The Other God: Dualist Religions from Antiquity to the Cathars* (New Haven: Yale, 2000).

15. This is the suggestive anthropological meaning of Mark 8:33 over which commentators stumble.

tradition. For now, we can place our concern about dualism, and its effects on Christian theology, into a wider context. In fact, this context is historical and existential at one and the same time. Tony Bartlett argues convincingly that,

> The forcing issue is really violence itself. Old world cosmology generally, and then, very powerfully, Greek anthropology have set up a dualism of heaven/earth, spirit/ matter, soul/body, ideal/sensate, etc. So long as Christian thought remains embedded in this scheme then violence is secondary to essence, and the violence done to Jesus, in order to be redemptive, has to be some negotiation from the heavenly world above (hence sacrifice, penal substitution, etc). But contemporary thought from Durkheim, Frazer and Freud, through Girard, Derrida and Foucault see essence as secondary to violence. The only thing that Girard adds is to show how this shift is brought about precisely by the Bible. It's a matter of contemporary thought, which is in fact biblical thought. This shifts the whole ground of the debate in a most provocative way, and is, in fact, the authentic ground for it.[18]

How else do we / can we Think beyond platonism?

Scripture

Outside of those engaging mimetic theory, what is missing most in work on the atonement is an exploration of the presuppositions regarding the role of Scripture and the hermeneutic operative in the interpreter.[19] It becomes immediately apparent that some interpreters wish to be 'faithful to Scripture,' by which they mean the entirety of the Old and New Testaments. An implicit assumption here is some view of the inspiration or authority of Scripture; occasionally it is a (verbal) plenary inspiration (Morris, Schreiner, Boersma, perhaps Schmiechen). On the other hand, there are those who have a christologically-focused approach mixed with a hermeneutics of suspicion (Weaver, Ray, many authors in Trelstad). Finally, others see a progressive revelation that is self-critical (Bartlett, Heim, Alison, Gorringe, other authors in Trelstad).

16. See René Girard, *I See Satan Fall as Lightning* for a rich exposition of this theme. The 'anthropologizing' of evil does not take away its power; it is, as well, the acute awareness that humanity has become a 'duality.' The Adamic humanity is hell-bent on destruction, no matter how much the 'good' side of humanity might will otherwise. This, according to Ben Witherington, is how we might understand Romans 7, *The Problem with Evangelical Theology* (Waco: Baylor University Press, 2005), 3-92.

17. Schmiechen, op. cit., invokes dualism as a biblical construct when he says there is "a tension of holiness and love in God" and "this tension runs throughout the Bible and witnesses to God's holiness and love (41)." Again, "In one sense the entire Old Testament is the story of this tension, played out on two levels: the interaction between God and humankind and the tensions within God between justice and love (17)." A conflicted god is a sure sign that dualism is a hidden operational principle.

18. Bartlett, E-mail of Dec 26, 2006.

19. One who does (briefly) spell out a hermeneutic is Thomas Finger in *Atonement and Violence*, 90, 107n.9. One of the reasons this is not adequately addressed by mimetic theory is that Roman Catholic Girardians have not had to deal with the problems created by Protestant doctrines of the inspiration and authority of Scripture and the attendant sacrificial hermeneutics used to read the Bible (inerrancy, etc).

How one uses the Bible is a key as to how one will understand atonement. There are two groups of writers in current atonement theory that declare their hermeneutic up front, feminist, womanist and ethnic theologians and mimetic theorists. The approach of the former reads Scripture from the position of the ultimate Subject (the deconstructed postmodern 'self') questioning the "object," in this case, (a wrathful) God.[20]   The latter search for the origins of the 'mean' God and find this type of theology written in the process of ritual human victimage. Both essentially arrive at the same conclusions from different places, viz., that violence is not to be construed as a divine phenomenon but as human projection and that it is the violated that are asking the authentic questions.

It might be objected that this is to approach Scripture *tabula rasa* (as though one had no presuppositions) and we will discover in Scripture what we put there in the first place. To say that God is nonviolent (e.g., Weaver) or better yet, anti-violent (e.g., S. Baker) is not, however, eisegesis. This is absolutely not to make God in our image, as though God was really a liberal Democrat with Jesus Seminar leanings. I disagree with Hans Boersma when he indicts a deconstructive reading of the biblical text and the preference of such critics to criticize the 'perspective' (or 'intention') of the biblical authors. "We may desperately want to avoid blaming the God whom we worship for the violence in his story. But knowingly interpreting the biblical text against the intention of the author and the biblical tradition is an unsatisfying way of coping with the divine violence that we meet in the pages of the Bible."[21]

Jews and Christians don't need a perfect Bible; the perfect Bible will ultimately be distorted as myth.[22] The problem is with us, the interpreters! But a text that is self-critical allows us as humans to hear another voice besides the prevalent, prevailing and dominating voice of the gods of human culture. In Scripture we also find that still small voice, that one solitary life, the widow, the orphan, the helpless, the prisoner. And we have their voice; the voice of those who would not be silenced. The voice of a Joseph, a Job, a psalmist, Isaiah's Servant, the prophets, Jesus, the apostolic churches. Once you see the gospel this way, a hermeneutic shift takes place.[23] Bartlett, Heim, Alison,

---

20. This is the god behind what Elizabeth Schussler-Fiorenza terms 'kyriarchy.' Weaver, Ray and Trelstad do a good job of gathering contemporary 'voices from below' that critique the violent system of 'kyriarchy' and a sacrificial rendering of the atonement. Cf. also Green and Baker, op. cit., 171-183.

21. *Violence, Hospitality and the Cross,* 91. In spite of his appropriation of Derrida, Boersma lapses back into a metaphysics of presence in his biblical hermeneutic.

22. In mimetic theory, myth refers to stories that presume the guilt of victims and the right of the community to punish said victims.

S. Baker, M. Baker and Weaver have all demonstrated this shift in their writing on atonement in light of mimetic theory.

Judaism and Christianity, as well as their respective Scriptures, participate in varying degrees in myth and gospel; Christianity does not supersede Judaism, but joins her as a witness to one God, Maker of heaven and earth, revealed or exegeted (John 1:18) in Jesus of Nazareth. Yet, the history of the Christianity is identical to that of the Jews of the Older Testament; the Church has its fair share of myth and victims too. In Holy Scripture, however, the voice of the persecutor gives way to the voice of the persecuted.

Both Testaments tell the story of a loving, liberating, covenant making and keeping God, one who makes all things new, and leaves nothing untouched by divine Grace, Love, Mercy and Forgiveness. And it tells this story of a wandering God among the company of all the human gods. The God who is revealed in Scripture is no yin and yang God, no dualistic God, no Janus faced God. The God of the Bible is not to be found in the theology of the biblical writers, but in their anthropology as that 'voice' that haunts the edge of their violent structuring.

For Christians, Jesus is that voice. The life of Jesus, his character, his acts, his message, his hermeneutic, his call to discipleship, corporately suggest that God is love. This means that anything we can say about God's love for the beloved Son during his life and after his resurrection must also be said for Jesus' death. To speak otherwise is to mythologize the gospel, to once again revert to the human distortion of 'the Lie,' to hide the victim under the sick justice of ritual retribution.

I am asserting that biblical revelation posits violence and its correlates (substitution, satisfaction, reciprocity) as an anthropological datum, not a divine one. This is the revelatory aspect of Jesus' death and resurrection. It exposes the lie about 'divine' violence. "Violence is no attribute of God."[24]

Those who, by confession or training, must begin with a fully inspired

23. My essay "The Biblical Testaments as a Marriage of Convenience" (currently found at www.preachingpeace.org/biblicaltestaments.htm) explored the framing of this hermeneutic problem with Justin Martyr and Marcion while "Sacrificial Language in Hebrews" (Violence Renounced, op. cit.) sought to demonstrate this hermeneutic shift exegetically in the most allegedly sacrificial document of the NT. Some have associated the hermeneutic enterprise of mimetic theory with that of Marcion (see e.g., Boersma, *Violence, Hospitality and the Cross*, 56, 150-51). To be sure, there are parallels between the way mimetic theorists and Marcion approach Scripture in the distinction between God as revealed in the Gospel and God as revealed in the Older Testament. But unlike Marcion, mimetic theologians are thoroughgoing monotheists, reject dualism and affirm the creation. And unlike Marcion, blame for the death of Jesus is not grounded in the 'Creator god' but in human action, choice and will.

Bible are both blessed and cursed. They are blessed in that they have the domain correct; it is the conjunction of the Old and New Testaments that is important. These folks would not be caught dead being Marcionites! But because they have a 'flat' view of Scripture, they miss the richness and diversity of witness in the canonical tradition.[25] This 'flat' view of Scripture is their curse for it locks up a sacrificial rendering of the biblical text, inasmuch as it derives the meaning of non-sacrificial New Testament language from pagan sacrificial worldviews, rather than recognizing that the biblical tradition, the development of both the Jewish and the Christian Scriptures, is self-critical literature, it is constantly probing 'meaning.'[26] And this is a blessing. Tony Bartlett notes the interpretive problem right up front.

> ...the whole issue of Old Testament sacrifice is very murky. It never explains itself, it just 'works.' It's only when theologians come to the New Testament and they read Jesus' death as propitiatory sacrifice that they read back into the Old Testament the same thing. Thus, there is no evident scriptural meaning to sacrifice. What's more, there is a lot of critique. But there is a huge reflection on violence, as sin (Gen. 4:7 onward). Thus anyone who is a scriptural believer should sit up and take note of this.[27]

Those who assert that the logic of the New Testament is sacrificial fail to see that the early Christians understood sacrifice differently than those around them, both Jew and Gentile. Heim contends, "sacrifice was the natural point of friction between Christians and the world around them," and he further notes,

24. *The Epistle to Diognetus* 7:4. This is also very clearly affirmed by Sharon Baker, J. Denny Weaver, Tony Bartlett, Mark Heim, James Alison, Raymund Schwager and others, as well as René Girard (and Pope John Paul II). Schmiechen contends that "to deny divine holiness in favor of an all-accepting love inevitably lead to distortions in both the view of God and human life. It would also involve discounting major portions of both Testaments (17)." I do not see how our view of God is distorted if we speak of an all-accepting Love. The distortion is to keep together what Jesus and the New Testament writers sundered.

25. Paul Ricoeur, *Essays on Biblical Interpretation* (Philadelphia: Fortress, 1980), 73-118. John Howard Yoder, *To Hear the Word* (Eugene: Wipf and Stock, 2001), 94 rightly perceives that the Protestant Scholastic view of the authority of Scripture is grounded in a circular logic that has less to do with the Bible itself and more to do with later ecclesial politics, "it made more difference (than one first perceives) that what is recognized by the churches as a norming document is not a systematic text, not a catechism, and of course not a Summa, but a scattered series of documents emerging from the ongoing struggles of a community." On the political aspects of the canonization of the New Testament see David Dungan, *Constantine's Bible: Politics and the Making of the New Testament* (Minneapolis: Fortress, 2007); An alternative view of biblical authority can be found in my "Finding Our Way Home: A Brief Note on the Authority and Interpretation of Scripture" at www.preachingpeace.org/authority.htm.

26. John Howard Yoder, *Preface to Theology*, 299, (Grand Rapids: Brazos, 2002), "The Christian Gospel is different from paganism precisely in that paganism sees God as angry and requiring appeasement, whereas the gospel reveals God taking the initiative for redemption, and humanity as needing to be reconciled." Gorringe notes that this is true of sacrificial concepts as well, *God's Just Vengeance*, 223.

We could say that Christians rejected ritual blood sacrifice because even though it represented an advance on human sacrifice, it still embodied the logic of the sacred scapegoating that lay behind it (and continued to reproduce it, for instance in the persecution fed by the purity divisions that attended the practice of ritual sacrifice). The cultic altar still defined sacrifice in terms determined by the model of founding murders. Christians struggled to redefine 'sacrifice' as it figured in their own non-violent liturgical practice, not according to that fallen archetype but to the work of Christ to overcome it.[28]

In the light of mimetic theory, the question asked by those on the extremes of a naïve hermeneutic or a hermeneutic of suspicion, "how can God be both wrathful (violent) and loving?" is changed. Another way to put this is to say that the New Testament does not ask, "How is Jesus like God?" as though one 'knew' God but did not 'know' Jesus. The New Testament writers are asking "Is God like Jesus?" Can God really be this good, this loving, this kind, this self-giving, this forgiving, and this generous? What if God is really like Jesus?

What is needed today is a new understanding of biblical authority that is grounded first and foremost in the person, teaching and work of Jesus. The Anabaptists of the sixteenth century did just this. They related the Testaments differently than the magisterial Reformers. Calvin was prompted to make a profound shift in the way he structured the *Institutes* due to the challenge posed by the apparent 'Marcionism' of the Anabaptists.[29] This shift also occurred in the mid-twentieth century, when the Sermon on the Mount was 'rediscovered' and one could say that Mennonites were all but practical Marcionites![30] I would contend a major reason for significant theological polarization in the Mennonite church is the influence of the Sermon on the Mount, on the one hand, and the inerrancy driven view piped into Mennonite households by TV and radio. While we can reject Marcion's solution, it will always be important for Anabaptists to ask his question: How do the Testaments relate to one another? This question is a key energizing component of the radical and Jesus oriented character of Anabaptism.

I conclude this section with considerations drawn from an earlier essay:

27. Op cit., Bartlett, Dec 26, 2006 e-mail; see also *Cross Purposes*, 207ff, "scholarly caveats demonstrate a house that Jack built, in effect crystallizing an Old Testament theory of sacrifice by means of putative sacrificial patterns from the New, and then using the theory to corroborate the patterns!" On this 'backward reading' see also David A. Brondos, *Paul on the Cross*, (Minneapolis: Fortress, 2006), 19-26.

28. Heim, op. cit., 234-35.

29. Ford Lewis Battles, *Analysis of the Institutes of the Christian Religion* (Grand Rapids: Baker 1980).

was Jesus violent ?
- Temple cleaning
- demons to pigs .
- Ananias & Saphira

"[First], the church would do well to take its hermeneutic cue from Jesus and the apostles rather than inherited sacrificial theologies. I cannot emphasize this point enough. We will not recognize our sacrificial theology, hermeneutic and ethic, if we do not take the time to ask if our reading of Scripture is consistent with that of Jesus and the prophetic and apostolic witness. We can only do this when we see that the essential component is the question: what does God without violence look like? The answer of course is that God looks a lot like Jesus. But this means we must reconsider the sacrificial mythmaking of our theologies and correct them.

Therefore, second, we as Christians must own up to our sacrificial theologies and our tendency to mythologize and we must repent. If indeed we confess that humans are 'in sin' then we better accept the fact that our hermeneutics will tend also 'to sin.' As my professor Bernard Ramm used to say, "God forgives our theology… just like he forgives our sin." How do we recognize if we have a sacrificial theology? We look to see if the marks of victimage are present. Do we have a scapegoat? Do we justify ourselves? Do we lie? Do we create rivalries? Is our theology essentially dualistic? Do we sacralize the victim (and thus our violence)?

Third, the Protestant 'sola scriptura' principle without the controlling element of a theology of the cross will forever be a misplaced ideal. It will stand alone, defying interpreters to make sense out of its differentiation. It will be no more than a jigsaw puzzle without a box cover to give a clue as to what the end result looks like. Theology that does not begin and end as anthropology, with the humanity, death and resurrection of Jesus, will never be Christian theology. It will be more or less mythologized gospel. If we allow a theory of inspiration to control our hermeneutic, we will not be able to perceive the essential element that is the cornerstone of responsible Christian theology: the rejection of God in Christ on the cross by all humanity and the revelation of God's forgiving spirit.

Fourth, with Girard and others we may recognize the travail of revelation in the Hebrew Scriptures, just as we can recognize it, e.g., in certain early Greek playwrights. What is being birthed is the revelation of the forgiving God. This birth culminates in the life, death and resurrection of Jesus and the witnesses to his life that we call 'gospel.' As long as we insist on flattening out the biblical revelation with a theory of inspiration we will not be able to see the real character of God revealed in Jesus.

It is centrally important to readdress this issue of modern Christian hermeneutics from the perspective of mimetic theory. In so doing we also expose the underlying mythological (sacrificial) elements in our various doctrines, not the least of which is the doctrine of the authority, inspiration and interpretation of Scripture. I fear that the churches will not want to hear this. It will be far easier and more comfortable for them to remain in the la-la land of their 'first naïveté.' But I fear more for the world, for it is not hearing the good news of the gospel by those who claim to know Christ. I fear not that God will judge them, but that we will have missed so many opportunities

30. I recall reading this in an autobiographical essay by J.L. Burkholder. I found the omission of this discussion to be the most significant criticism I have of Thomas Finger's *A Contemporary Anabaptist Theology* (Downer's Grove: IVP, 2004). The hermeneutic consequences of privileging the Sermon on the Mount remain one of the most important aspects of the Anabaptist heritage.

to share the joyous message of liberation and peace that we have been given. Until and unless we re-examine this issue, we will remain in the vacuous sterility of our ignorance.[31]

God's Honor

This leads us to a final observation about our contemporary discussion. In the last decade the overwhelming majority of books published on the atonement, in one way or another, revise, critique, dismiss or outright reject the penal satisfaction theory of the atonement. While the problems associated with a penal theory of the atonement have been exposed time and again, still it dominates popular Christian culture. I would note that the mailing I received, which is mentioned earlier, and Schreiner's essay,[32] both have identical foci: the sinfulness of humanity, the holiness of God and the sacrifice of Christ. So the view of the mailing is not only 'popular' but also 'scholarly.' And this penal satisfaction view, in the words of Hans Boersma, is one that "juridicizes, individualizes and dehistoricizes the atonement."[33] Proponents of propitiation (the God-directed action of atonement) stress Jesus' divinity in his substitution, it is the 'eternal' character of his sacrifice that pays for our sins. Expiatory advocates (the human-directed action of atonement), more correctly in my judgment, emphasize Jesus' humanity in his death. Jesus' life and death are not discrete events; incarnation cannot be separated from atonement.

Now Boersma's 'modified Reformed' view of the atonement has much to commend it. It is developed within a hopeful recapitulation framework (that of Irenaeus) and it stresses incarnation as well as cross and resurrection. Finally, if one is going to do theology that is self-consciously Augustinian (western Christian), Boersma's understanding of the notion of divine punishment is the best one can hope for. But I find Boersma's apology to be unpersuasive in three major aspects.

In his essay, Boersma highlights divine intentionality. God had a role to

---

31. Hardin, "Finding Our Way Home: A Brief Note on the Authority and Interpretation of Scripture" at www.preachingpeace.org/authority.htm. John Howard Yoder pointedly observes that "the ability to perceive that what the Bible says is different from what we have always assumed it meant is very difficult to acquire and to act upon thereafter. This problem is the same for people who consider themselves 'liberal' and for those who consider themselves 'evangelical'" in *To Hear the Word* (Eugene: Wipf and Stock, 2001).

32. *The Nature of the Atonement*, 67-98; for this tripartite focus see Schmiechen, op. cit., 15-19.

33. Boersma, *Atonement and Violence*, 64. Even though I critique Boersma I want to affirm the giant leap he has made beyond the standard penal satisfaction theory. But it is still a penultimate step. The final step would be to engage the logic (logos) of nonviolence in the New Testament and the implications of that logic for theology proper.

play in the event of Jesus' death. I would agree. This is why, with Boersma and Weaver, I am sympathetic to a *Narrative Christus Victor*. Yet one might ask, what possible roles can be played in this 'divine drama?'

Boersma queries, "Is the cross an instance of human and divine violence, or is it an instance only of human violence?"[34] I presume his question is directed to two groups: the 'Girardians' whom he mentions in *Violence, Hospitality and the Cross*, and peace church scholars like Denny Weaver, Sharon Baker or Mark Baker. But how is this human violence understood? I suggest that for Boersma, human violence is minimalized with regard to Jesus' death. Prior to the question above Boersma asked, "Is the cross merely the result of the evil plot of human beings?" It is this "merely" that is troublesome to me. Critics of moral influence theory often assail the 'lack' of divine action in the atonement. But is it that, or is it, rather, that we have sublimated human responsibility for the death of Jesus and do not wish to acknowledge it? To say the cross is merely the result of the evil plot of human beings is like saying the genocide in Darfur or the Balkans or the Holocaust is merely the result of an evil plot. I respectfully disagree; there is nothing mere about human participation in the crucifixion event.[35] It is hubris of the highest order. The creature murders the Creator. It is the tragic ending that the play should never have had. There is no 'merely' to the ascription of the horror of Jesus' crucifixion to humanity.

Second, Boersma makes "a dual affirmation... (that the cross reflects both human and divine violence) along with the broad Christian tradition." He challenges Weaver, inter alia, "to face up to the fact that they are out of step with the broad Christian tradition" and that "[c]ontemporary advocates of nonviolent atonement theories posit an unfortunate disjunction with the broad tradition of Christian theology." Boersma deliberately contrasts "the broad Christian tradition" and Girard. He concludes, "[w]e do not need to abandon the broad consensus of the Christian tradition."[36]

Yes we do. Luther did. So did Calvin and Bullinger and Zwingli. And so did various Anabaptists. Today, we need to abandon conceiving and doing Christian theology within the Platonic tradition, with dualistic presuppositions. Today we can recognize that there is a difference, a significant difference, between the Greek (violent) Logos and the Gospel (nonviolent) Logos. The "broad Christian tradition" is a cipher for Augustinian influenced Christianity and it is this tradition we are saying is asking the wrong questions. "Broad Christian tradition" answers are only valid for its questions.[37] This is why it seems so difficult for Boersma to get handles on the Historic Peace

34. *Ibid*, 47.
35. On the horror of crucifixion see Martin Hengel, *The Crucifixion* (Philadelphia: Fortress, 1977).

Church perspective, as well as the Girardian one. The presuppositions are different and so the questions are different.

I have been suggesting that, in fact, it is necessary to contextualize the "broad Christian tradition" within the Platonism of Augustinian Christianity, exploring the great change that the Church underwent in the fourth century between Constantine and Augustine.[38] I would also argue that the deconstruction of western philosophy from Plato to Heidegger has taken with it the Christendom wedded to it. This especially means that the authority of Augustine must be deconstructed in the churches. The "broad Christian tradition" is but Plato's creek.

Finally, Boersma suggests that the negation of boundaries would be detrimental to the social fabric and that nonviolent atonement theory leads to such. Denny Weaver demurs from such a conclusion, but I believe Boersma is right. Unlike Boersma, I think boundaries are not the solution, but the problem. Boersma's anthropology suggests the western democratized Cartesian self, the bounded self of Greek philosophy.[39] This is the dualistic self (self/other).

I contend there is no such 'self.' This 'self' has been completely deconstructed. No one is an island. We are our relationships. I see the 'self' constituted differently than Boersma; for me, the self is structured triangularly, through the contagion of negatively mediated mimetic desire.[40] But Boersma is right in this: there is a problem with the negation of boundaries; it leads to chaos, or in more auspicious biblical language, to apocalypse, to the end of human civilization and culture, as we have known it.

Jesus' crucifixion is the apocalypse of human relationships. Structured on violence, he transforms them, in his resurrection, to relationships of love and forgiveness. Out of negative mimesis comes positive mimesis; cross and resurrection together is apocalypse.[41] How is this happening? Girard suggests

36. Boersma, *ibid*, 47, 53, 65, 155-56, 66.

37. Dietrich Ritschl, *Memory and Hope* (New York, Macmillan, 1967), 102-140.

38. I am in full agreement with John Howard Yoder, Denny Weaver and Stanley Hauerwas that there were extraordinary changes in ecclesial life and theology in the fourth and fifth centuries, not all of them for the better. Cf. my "Violence: René Girard and the Recovery of Early Christian Perspectives" in *Brethren Life and Thought*, Vol. 37, No 2.

39. Contrast this e.g., with the eschatological anthropology elucidated by John Zizioulas, *Being as Communion* (Crestwood: St Vladimir's Seminary Press, 1985), 62: "The truth and the ontology of the person belong to the future, are images of the future." For Zizioulas, this future is not locked into a 'historicized' temporal sequence, but is realized already in the person and work of Jesus and in the church by the Holy Spirit. This is precisely the critique that Bartlett uses against Anselmian atonement theory. Penal satisfaction theory "removes the historical-apocalyptic tone and content of the New Testament account of Jesus' death, and transfers it to some eternal presidium of judgment," *Cross Purposes*, 4. In the final analysis this is where I also part company with Volf and Boersma and the 'eschatological deferral of violence.' If we are all waiting for the other shoe to drop, of what benefit is the cross? Cf., Weaver, op. cit., 205-209.

that the Holy Spirit, as *paraclete*, has been active in both Church and culture and the historical influence of Christianity on western culture must be taken very seriously.[42] Indeed, Girard contends that as the gospel is preached, the systems that ground and interpret human culture become destabilized and cultures go into crisis. Mimetic theorists have noticed the systematic dynamic of these crises, and the predictable phases of victimage.[43] This victimizing of others is ours alone; the system of our creating is that which is coming undone. It is our 'devil' that has been exorcised. Evil is fully human. In the preaching of the gospel, the scandalous death of Jesus breaks into our cultural stupor and its macabre need for human blood. At the center of our quest for being, there stand... our victims. It is into this that "the Word was made flesh," God's (nonviolent) loving Word. James Alison puts it this way:

> The old default account, common to both Catholic and Protestant 'orthodoxy' was some variation on the 'substitutionary theory of the atonement.' That is, some version of a tale in which Jesus died for us, instead of us who really deserved it, so as to pay a bill for sin that we could not pay, but for whose settlement God himself immutably demanded payment. Not only does this not make sense, but it is scandalous in a variety of ways. It has been one of the principal merits of the thought of René Girard that at last it is enabling us to scramble towards a new account of how we are being saved which is free from the long shadow of pagan sacrificial attitudes and practice.[44]

Here is the rub: How do we begin to rid ourselves of the vestiges of pagan thought in our understanding of the atoning work of Jesus Christ? And if we do so, will we not be left with a very weak theory of atonement where God is some pie in the sky Santa Claus who just wants us to know how much God cares for us? Critics of the moral influence theory smell a rat when nonviolent atonement theorists want to anthropologize all violence. Need this be so?

40. A consequence of this is that sin is not primarily understood as something 'individual' but as social in character. Marit Trelstad (*Cross Examinations*, 14-15) observes that a new 'liberationist model' of atonement perceives sin as systemic, an insight congruent with Girard's triangular anthropology. This is not to say that individual concerns are ruled out of the picture for "a theology of covenant hold together individual and social salvation as two sides of the same coin" (123). Not for nothing, but the individualism rampant within Gnostic frameworks of modern Christianity is challenged by the fact that the New Testament consistently has the formula ὑπερ ὑμων not ὑπερ σου.

41. For example, note that the baptismal formula of Galatians 3:26ff eradicates the concept of boundaries; so does the doctrine of the divine *perichoresis*. There can be a positive way to perceive 'unbounded' life, which is 'life eternal.' Unboundedness is only anarchy to those enslaved to the 'arkh' of individualism. I would suggest that there is a correspondence here with the anthropology of both Jacques Ellul and Vernard Eller.

42. René Girard, *The Scapegoat* (Baltimore: Johns Hopkins, 1986), 198ff and *I See Satan Fall as Lightning* (Maryknoll: Orbis, 2001), 189ff. Cf. the theses of Radical Orthodoxy, esp. John Milbank, *Theology and Social Theory* (Oxford: Blackwell, 1990) and Thomas Torrance's arguments on the influence of Christian epistemology on modern scientific method in *Convergence and Transformation in the Frame of Knowledge* (Grand Rapids: Eerdmans, 1984).

43. E.g., Walter Wink, Robert Hamerton-Kelly, Eric Gans, James Alison, James Williams, Raymund Schwager and Michel Serres.

Boersma asserts that, "the problem with Girardian theory is that it keeps Christ at a distance. There is no participatory logic at work here, no identification between Christ and humanity. Moral influence theory, when viewed as the ultimate category of atonement theology, leads to a distancing between the Christ and those worshipping him."[45]

I would suggest that such is not necessarily the case. First, Girard's only neologism, interdividual, absolutely suggests a participatory anthropology; it is an imitative participation, even on the nonconscious level of desire. It is everywhere, pervasive throughout human culture (what theologians like to call original sin).

Second, Girardians need not reject substitution as a category. Whether propitiatory, expiatory, Anselmic, Abelardian, Girardian, Barthian or *Christus Victor*, every atonement theory can, in some sense, be called substitutionary. Substitution is the key concept of sacrifice. There is no sacrifice without substitution. Substitution is part of the economy of exchange and exchange is grounded in sacrificial violence. What might it mean to say Jesus was a substitute, in a qualified sense? For this we must turn to the concept of 'corporate personality.'

The biblical understanding of corporate personality, that is, that the one can stand for 'the many,' is a sacrificial sociology. The king, the priest and the prophet can all stand in for the people. So also do the Son of Man and the Suffering Servant. These corporate figures are representative and function substitutionarily. It is the particularity of this figure juxtaposed with its corporate character that opens up a strategy for interpreting Scripture anthropologically. As a substitute or representative (and I don't see much difference between these categories), corporate personality includes a dialectic, the one and the many. We are accustomed to seeing the one in relation to the all hierarchically, that is, the one stands over the many. But the perspective of the prophetic tradition is to see the many against the one.[46]

Mark Heim puts it this way:

> God enters into the position of the victim of sacrifice (a position already defined by human practice) and occupies it so as to be able to act from that place to reverse sacrifice and redeem us from it. God steps forward in Jesus to be one subject to the human practice of atonement in blood, not because that is God's preferred logic or because this itself it God's aim, but because this is the very site where human bondage and sin are enacted.[47]

---

44. James Alison, *On Being Liked* (New York: Herder and Herder, 2004). I owe this citation to Paul Nuechterlein at http://girardianlectionary.net/res/atonement_webpage.htm.
45. *Atonement and Violence*, 155.

Jesus as representative or substitute ought not to be an issue at stake in atone-ment theory, nor can it be, for without substitution there can be no break in the way sacrifice is understood.[48] At issue is our hermeneutic. It is how we perceive a sacrifice to be functioning that determines our understanding of sacrifice. Girardian biblical interpreters simply assert that rather than teach a theory of sacrifice, Scripture gives us a developing anti-sacrificial project. As Raymund Schwager has shown, as Israelite theology develops prior to and after the Prophets and through the Wisdom tradition, there is a decided shift away from a positive understanding of sacrifice, in many cases it took the form of the rejection of all sacrifice. The New Testament continues in this trajectory. It can be said that a sacrificial hermeneutic may quote the Bible but it is out of sync with the prophetic/wisdom approach to reading Scripture adopted by Jesus and the early church.

The inevitability ($\delta\epsilon\iota$) of the death of Jesus does not stem from God's need but from humanity's. There are only two roles to play in the tale of divine and human relationships, persecutor or persecuted. God can cause suffering or God can suffer. God in Christ chose the latter.[49] Many have said this well, from Barth to Moltmann and now Bartlett, but Douglas John Hall eloquently expresses it this way,

> If we posit a God who both wills the existence of free creatures and the preserva-tion and redemption of the world (and I take it that neither of these intentions can be dispensed with by Christians), then we must take with great seriousness the biblical narrative of a God whose providence is a mysterious internal and intentional involve-ment in history; a God, therefore, who is obliged by his own love to exercise power quietly, subtly, and, usually, responsively in relation to the always ambiguous and

46. On the prophetic reading cf. Heim, op. cit., 93-104; Raymund Schwager, *Must There Be Scapegoats?* (New York: Harper, 1987) passim; and Tony Bartlett's Bible Study series on Isaiah 40-66 at www.preachingpeace.org/biblestudies.htm.

47. *Saved from Sacrifice*, 143. Arland Hultgren, *Paul's Gospel and Mission* (Philadelphia: Fortress, 1985), 47-81, demonstrates that Romans 3:23-26 refers to this 'place' of atonement and not to an atoning sacrifice. His contends that Paul is using 'notes' from a synagogue homily he preached in the Diaspora on the Jewish Day of Atonement (in Ephesus). The ηλαστηριον of Romans 3:24 is, however, more than cultic, an insight missed by far too many interpreters. The cultic dimension is also political. Jesus becomes, in the words of John Milbank, *Being Reconciled*, 96, a *homo sacer*. Jesus "died as three times excluded: by the Jewish law of its tribal nation; by the Roman universal law of empire; by the democratic will of the mob. In the whole summed up history of human polity – the tribe, the universal absolute state, the democratic consensus – God found no place." The death of Jesus thus has extraordinary implications for social theory com-pletely missed by the penal satisfaction theory.

48. "Jesus evidently did not see his death in exclusively individualistic terms. From his pen-chant for the expression and imagery of The Son of Man to the last supper where he urged his followers to eat his body and drink his blood in order to share in his death, Jesus saw his death as not only his, it was a representative death,' Scot McKnight, op. cit., 337.

frequently evil deeds of the free creatures; a God who will not impose rectitude upon the world but labor to bring existing wrong into the service of good; a God, in short, who will suffer.[50]

In the language of both Derrida and Girard, Sharon Baker urges us to reconsider that the God of Scripture makes something out of nothing and out of the uttermost nothingness that is the Cross, God transforms the Cross into the climactic salvific event:

> [I]t is plausible to assert that the violence that befell Jesus Christ and that led to his death was not part of God's formal plan to liberate human beings from the power and consequence of sin. Instead, the death of Christ on the cross was a product of human free will that grieved the heart of God. At the same time, Christ's death revealed the salvific depth of God's love as well as the divine desire to deconstruct the violent religious sacrificial consciousness and its attendant ritual killing.[51]

In short, revelation takes place at precisely the same place as myth originates, the act of victimage. This is the scandal of the cross. It would be impossible to see apart from the resurrection. Resurrection is necessary for revelation.[52] Revelation as resurrection is the good news that God does not retaliate. I cannot find anywhere in the early church (30 C.E. to 110 C.E.), where an author brings together resurrection and wrath and this would be the logical place to do it. If God were retributive, then the resurrection would have been the terrible apocalypse of Jewish eschatology, the place of reciprocal retaliation for killing Jesus.[53] However, it is another reality that is testified to over and over again in the kerygma of the earliest churches. The resurrection of Jesus did not bring wrath but blessing, the blessing of the forgiving presence of God with humanity, not only in the time and space of incarnation, but also in the time and space of those who are the church, the Body of Christ, through the indwelling of the *paraclete*, the Holy Spirit. This is the kerygma of the earliest churches.

Mark Baker speaks of "proclaiming the scandal of the cross." I say "Amen to that." I especially appreciate that for Baker, mimetic theory opens

49. This is well explored by Arthur McGill in *Suffering: A Test of Theological Method* (Philadelphia: Westminster, 1982).

50. Douglas John Hall, *The Cross in Our Context: Jesus and the Suffering World* (Minneapolis: Fortress, 2003), 87.

51. *By Grace? (An)Economy of Salvation*, 140.

52. James Alison, *The Joy of Being Wrong*, 77-83, profoundly explores this. He suggests, "It is the forgiveness that the risen victim brought that enabled the fruitful separation of anthropology and theology into a distinct dependence rather than a violent confusion. It is the risen victim also who proved to be what enabled the apostolic group to glimpse the true nature of God's creation as being the same self-giving that lay behind the self-giving of Christ on the cross," 235. This is highlighted by Finger [in Sanders], 101f; also Heim, op. cit., 236, "...the New Testament sets out a decisive, initiating change made by Jesus' life, death, and resurrection."

kerygmatic windows on the biblical text.[54] But what is this scandal? The scandal of the cross is that where God says No, we say Yes; and where we say No, God says Yes. The scandal of the cross is forgiveness. At the place our theologies typically spy wrath, our eyes, like those of the disciples on the road to Emmaus, are opened, to see 'love divine, all loves excelling' and so embrace the scandal of divine forgiveness.

A theology of the cross will be scandalous, even and especially to "Constantinian Christianity." It will not be well received, particularly here in the United States, where the triple of evils of racism, militarism and poverty still reign in a Judeo-Christian (sic) culture. So-called "Christian" (sic) America is heavily invested in the victimage system. But the cross of Jesus cuts to the very core of our being and offers transformation to our whole person, our whole community. It can be said that Jesus' death kills, but it also makes alive and heals us.[55] But it will mean a costly understanding of discipleship. It will mean the active choice to live a life of non-retaliation, non-retribution or vengeance; a life grounded in forgiveness, reconciliation and peacemaking. Discipleship as 'cross-carrying' is life lived as Jesus died.[56] This is the witness of the Amish in Nickel Mines, PA.

John Stoner puts it this way:

> Any atonement theology, dealing with the cross as it does, must be able to make a credible interpretation of Jesus' words in Mark 8:34: 'He called the crowd with his disciples, and said to them, 'If any want to become my followers, let them deny themselves and take up their cross, and follow me.' In other words, a credible description of the meaning of the cross for the followers of Jesus is not adiaphora. Indeed, why should this not be equally important with our certainties about the meaning of Jesus' cross, since Jesus himself left no room for the disciple to avoid his or her own cross?[57]

What if, in the atonement, we are dealing not just with the only way we are reconciled to God, but also with the only way humans are reconciled to one another, i.e., through the nonviolent power of life grounded in forgiveness,

---

53. This appears to be the perspective of the crowds challenged by Peter's sermons in the early part of Acts.

54. See especially "A Beach Parable for Youth" in *Proclaiming the Scandal of the Cross*, 84-95.

55. I appreciate the contribution of Bruce Reichenbach on a 'Healing View' of the atonement in Beilby and Eddy, *The Nature of the Atonement*, in spite of its occasional sacrificial lapses. This is also one of Walter Winks theses in *The Powers* trilogy.

56. See my essay co-authored with Steven Berry, "Grasping God: Philippians 2:1-11 in Light of Mimetic Theory" at www.preachingpeace.org/documents/phil_2_covr_2005.pdf, esp. pages 10-19, for an explication of this self-giving dynamic of atonement. Denny Weaver (in Trelstad, 239) contends that the consequences of a nonviolent atonement ought to be "an intrinsic and integrating principle across the curriculum of Christian colleges and within each discipline by anybody anywhere who seeks to follow the way of peace with mind as well as body."

reconciliation and peacemaking? If that is the case, the atonement gives us not only a plan for "our salvation" but also a plan for the salvation of the world (which, after all, is really what John 3:16-17 are about). This would go a long way to giving meaningful content to the words in Jesus' prayer "forgive us our debts as we have forgiven our debtors."

New Horizons

As far as I am concerned, the deconstructive work of Gorringe, Ray, Heim, Weaver, S. Baker and Bartlett, as well as others, regarding exchange theories of atonement is complete. These theories muddy the waters of the good news and inevitably come under the spell of violence, reciprocity and vengeance. The world longs for the God of the Gospel of Jesus Christ, the One in "whom there is no shadow of turning," "who is light and in whom there is no darkness at all," who does not discriminate but gives bounteous blessing to all by "making the sun shine on both evil and good, and making rain to fall on both just and unjust."

So, is it possible that twenty-first century Christianity stands on the verge of trusting a God who is love alone and not a mixed god, a Christian version of divine schizophrenia? As we find our way forward, can we work with multiple models of atonement, or do we need to decide between them?

For example, David Eagle puts the question this way: Bartlett or Weaver?[58] It's a heavyweight match-up! The problem appears in that Weaver advocates a *Narrative Christus Victor* whereas Bartlett has thoroughly demolished the classic *Christus Victor* theory exposing its roots in Hellenic dualism. Bartlett is relentless in his marshalling of evidence against the 'ransom' theory, such as we find in Origen. Irenaeus and Marcion are both swept away with Bartlett's broom, and rightly so, as the ransom theory refers to a transaction between God and the devil (something both Anselm and Abelard reject as well).

However, Weaver eschews any Origenistic style ransom theory. Bartlett's critique of the *Christus Victor* eliminates the martial component but not the transformative one.[59] I do not see the *Narrative Christus Victor* as proposed by Weaver (and Finger) in antithesis to the modified Abelardianism of Bartlett (Heim, Sharon Baker); rather, for me, they complement one another.

---

57. E-mail of January 2, 2007. See also Brummer, op. cit., 91, "The Christian life is one in which we are to become Christ-like through the imitatio Christi. The primary focus of this imitatio is that we should relate to God as Jesus did." Cf. Collins, op cit., for an elaboration of the dynamics of incarnational mimesis.

58. "Anthony Bartlett's Concept of Abyssal Compassion and the Possibility of a Truly Nonviolent Atonement" in *The Conrad Grebel Review* (Vol. 24, No. 1, Winter 2006).

Weaver's *Christus Victor* names atonement in relation to negative mimesis (and the 'fallen' Powers), Bartlett's Abelard to positive mimesis (and the 'transformed' Powers). Both are necessary and complimentary.[60] Both are non-sacrificial in their hermeneutic. Both argue that God is not a violent actor in the atonement drama. Both contend against the propriety of the Anselmic sacrificial viewpoint. For both, the atonement produces an authentic model for Christian existence, a positive mimesis.

On the other hand, I would agree with David Eagle that something significant is being described by Bartlett's 'abyssal compassion.' The concept of abyssal compassion facilitates the bringing together of the cross and the Trinity. The cross of Jesus is the abyssal depth of the divine love expressed anthropologically. Yet we can see the divine love here as Jesus mirrors God in forgiving humanity. This is the conversive power of the cross. Bartlett's 'abyssal compassion' is comparable in insight for our time, as Luther's 'theology of the Cross' was in his time.

'Abyssal Compassion' is an atonement metaphor for the violence of the twenty-first century. It expresses the depth of the love of the one God Christians name as Father, Son and Holy Spirit. It answers all of the "How?" questions put by penal satisfaction adherents by describing in detail, the "infinite qualitative difference" between violent reciprocity and forgiveness and their consequent impact on theological systems. In particular, I would note that Bartlett's conclusions naturally lead to the ethics of the Historic Peace Churches and the renunciation of violence.

It all comes down to how we describe the Cross in relation to the Trinity. What is the relationship between the Father, the Son and the Holy Spirit in the cross event and does it change? Robert Sherman makes a solid and important case for conceiving of the work of Jesus in a Trinitarian framework woven in the theological matrix of the threefold office: king, priest and prophet (the three anointed offices in the Jewish Scriptures). More importantly, Sherman argues that each of these 'offices' is to be understood nonviolently and non-sacrificially.[61] If this is not done, one ends up with a split in 'God,' as many feminist and womanist critics have pointed out. All sacrificial theories of atonement ultimately crash on the rock of the '*homoousias*' (Nicene Creed).

If the Father and the Son are placed in a sacrificial relationship, Trinitarian relationships are being conceived within a pagan framework. There

59. For a nonviolent reading of both see Finger, *Atonement and Violence*, 95-97.

60. Shelton, *Cross and Covenant*, 212, suggests that a nonviolent atonement theory recognizes that both a modified moral influence and Christus Victor have a role to play in understanding the death of Jesus, but like so many other Evangelical authors fails to see the abyssal distance between these two and penal satisfaction. This is a significant blind spot in many writers on the atonement.

is a distinct difference between the reciprocity within Trinitarian relations and reciprocity among humans. Girard has demonstrated that reciprocity is an aspect of rivalrous mimesis and is embedded in the process of scapegoating. Reciprocity is the religious belief of *'Do ut des'* (I give to you so that you will give to me). Reciprocity is about exchange and balance. The mimetic theory illumines how humans facilitate social order through exchange, whether economically, mythically, religiously, psychologically or politically. Reciprocity, the need for opposites and cosmic balance, is the problem for those who begin from the premise that God is just and merciful, kind and vengeful, etc.

Within the dance of Love that is the divine *perichoresis*, is observed total and complete choice to exist 'for the other.' The other is completely and totally validated. Reciprocity is the generous giving back of one's 'self.' This 'self'-giving is writ large in the New Testament, from Paul and the early church (Phil 2:5-11), to Hebrews and the Gospel of John. This is the how of atonement, how one actively self-gives, how one acts in love, forgiving one's enemies, stopping the cycle of violence. Jesus' last words were that violent reciprocity might end with his death. His blood may have cried out from the ground but it spoke a better word than that of Abel, a Word that saves, redeems and liberates us all.

We are given perspective with this better word. We are not just shown two perspectives, that of persecutor and persecuted, we are given a third option. There are three kinds of victims. There is the victim of myth, who is guilty as charged. There is the retributive victim, revealed as innocent, yet still participating in the cycle of violence (as in the Older Testament). And there is the non-retaliatory, forgiving victim, such as we see on Calvary, and again under a pile of stones, with Saul consenting. You can be on top, persecuting victims, or you can be on bottom, being persecuted and demanding vengeance or justice. Either way you perpetuate the cycle of violence. The only way to stop violence, to put an end to violence, to rob it of its power, whether on top or bottom, is to forgive; it is to seek peace and pursue it, to announce the message that God forgives us and calls out from the world those who would do the same.[62] Forgiveness begins with the revelation of our own scapegoating and ends with our repentance.

This perspective is what Bonhoeffer referred to as "seeing from below." It is to read Scripture no longer through the eyes of the persecutor, the vic-

61. *King, Priest and Prophet*. Sherman (153) critiques the Reformed tradition for its triumphal rendering of the kingship of Christ wondering "might the Anabaptist tradition in fact be more faithful to the example and implications of Christ's redefinition of kingship than the Reformed tradition?"

tor or the successful, but to hear the voice of one crying in the wilderness, "Prepare Ye the Way of the Lord." It is the voice of the prophet crying out on behalf of the marginalized, the poor, and the defenseless that are victimized by society. It is the voice of Wisdom defending the righteous one who is victimized by enemies. It is the truly 'pathetic' voice of Jesus Christ dying.

Atonement is all about violence and how we perceive God's relation to violence. Mark Heim warns us that it is Pilate and Herod who have a sacrificial interpretation of Jesus' death and that, "the gospels make it clear that it is Jesus' antagonists who view his death as a redemptive sacrifice, one life given for many... Here is a caution for Christian theology. We must beware that in our reception and interpretation of the Gospel we do not end up entering the passion story on the side of Jesus' murderers."[63]

Atonement theories may come in various types but they will fall into one of two categories hermeneutically: sacrificial and non-sacrificial. The former is the message of myth, the latter, of gospel.[64] The latter speaks of the death of Jesus as truly good news, through the use of many metaphors, all of which reflect the forgiving victim. Some Christian atonement theories are structured as myth, justifying divine wrath; others from the perspective of the retributive victim. Those which do not perpetuate the cycle of violence, have, I think, participated in the Gospel. It seems to me that this is the horizon we are facing today. And it is this horizon that is truly evangelical, full of only good news.

---

62. So Paul in 2 Cor. 5:16-21.
63. Saved from Sacrifice, 125-26.
64. Finlan, op. cit.112, "To really understand Christ's life mission it is necessary to discard sacrificial thinking."

PART TWO

THE CROSS AND
THE HISTORICAL JESUS

Chapter Three

THE REASONS FOR JESUS' CRUCIFIXION

by N.T. Wright

1. Introduction

Of all the questions regularly asked about Jesus, the question, 'Why did Jesus die?' must be among the most frequent. It is certainly the most fascinating - and, as the researcher discovers soon enough, among the most frustrating. It has all the ingredients of a classic: dense and complex sources; the confluence of two great cultures (Jewish and Roman) in a single, swirling drama; characters who still leap off the page, despite the gap of two millennia; tragedies, and tragic ironies, both small and great; gathering storm-clouds of philosophy and theology; and, at the centre, a towering but enigmatic figure, who, if the sources are to be believed, had the capacity to evoke anger and admiration in full measure. Small wonder that not only historians and theologians, but also artists and musicians, have returned to the subject times without number.

'Why did Jesus die?', then - the third of the key questions we set ourselves at the start of this book - goes to the heart of our subject.[1] The question 'why', in such a case, involves us inescapably in the study of human intentionality. Why did the Roman authorities consider it appropriate or desirable to execute Jesus? Why did the Jewish authorities consider it right to hand him over to the Romans as deserving of death? And, in the middle of it all, what was Jesus' own intention in the matter? Nor is the question limited by these three aspects. It is also necessary to ask: why did certain first-century Jews, within an exceedingly short time, refer to the death of a messianic pretender - not in itself an uncommon or remarkable event in that time and place - in terms such as 'he loved me and gave himself for me'?[2]

As the historical questions focus at this point, so also do the problems of method. Consistent scepticism once more faces consistent eschatology. Either we know little or nothing about what actually happened, or we know that the ultimate explanation lies in the area of Jesus' beliefs about the imminent climactic moment in Israel's history.[3] The sources present particular problems;

---

1. See *JVG*, ch. 3.2.iii (106-9) for a preliminary discussion and setting of the scene.
2. Gal. 2.20; cf. too e.g. Phil. 2.6-8; Rom. 5.6-11, and plenty of other examples.

even if Q were admitted as a serious historical source elsewhere in the synoptic gospels, it necessarily falls away here, since Matthew, Mark and Luke overlap.[4] At one level, the texts are full of theological and exegetical reflection; at another, of just the sort of eye-witness detail that suggests that the reflection was caused by the events, not (despite the sceptics) vice versa. After all, if a first-century Jew believed that the events he or she had just witnessed, and indeed taken part in, really were the turning-point of history, they would be unlikely to describe them in the deliberately neutral language of someone writing up an experiment in inorganic chemistry. Changing the science, to distrust the sources because they show evidence of theology and exegesis is like distrusting an astronomer's report because the observations were not conducted during the hours of daylight.

In particular, it must be emphasized that here more than anywhere it is worse than futile to try to separate theology from politics.[5] The tired old split between the Jesus of history and the Christ of faith was never more misleading than at this point. Generations of gospel readers in search of atonement-theology, or at least atonement-homiletics, ignored the actual story the evangelists were telling, with all its rough political edges, in favour of the theological scheme the story was deemed to be inculcating, or at least illustrating. More recent generations of historians, not least those seeking to straighten out dangerous half-truths, have seen the accounts either as nothing but theology (and therefore historically irrelevant) or, worse, as politically motivated theology (and therefore historically damaging). As the eighteenth-century split between these different spheres is increasingly shown to be a mistake, it is time to attempt to put back together that which should not have been separated in the first place.[6]

One feature of the historical/political/theological mix needs special comment. It has become commonplace to claim that the gospel narratives of the

3. Scepticism: e.g. Crossan 1988a, 1991, 1994, and esp. 1995; Koester 1990, 216-40; 1992, following Bultmann and others, on which cf. Harvey 1982, 16; Hengel 1995b, 41-4. On scepticism in historiography, cf. Meyer 1979, 84f. Eschatology: Schweitzer 1954 [1906], 384-95; and e.g. Farmer 1956; Caird 1965; Wright 1985; de Jonge 1991a, ch. 3; and see below. On rationalizing views, the wry comment of Manson (1953, 76) remains potent forty years later: 'Jesus goes up to Jerusalem to give a course of lecture-sermons on the Fatherhood of God and the Brotherhood of man, and then becomes the victim of an unfortunate miscarriage of justice.' Alter 'lecture-sermons' to 'Cynic aphorisms', allow for a change in fashions as to Jesus' theme, and you have the Jesus Seminar in a nutshell.

4. This is not to say, of course, that if Q did exist it could not have had a passion narrative; only that, in the nature of the case, we could not know if it did. Seeley 1992 attempts to suggest that Q did take a view on Jesus' death, but that this corresponded, not to Jewish models, but to Stoic/Cynic ideals of the noble death.

5. See e.g. the protests of Borg 1984, ch. 1; Horsley 1994, esp. 395-8.

6. cf. ch. 4.2 *JVG*.

trials and death of Jesus are strongly coloured by anti-semitism.[7] This, I believe, has not been established. It is of course true that the narratives have been read and exploited in this direction, sometimes devastatingly; but that is a fact about subsequent readers, not necessarily about the stories themselves.[8] When the stories refer to 'the Jews', subsequent gentile Christianity could all too easily forget that Jesus, his family, his followers, the first Christians, and some or all of the writers of the gospels, were themselves Jewish. Paul, whose own Jewishness emerges, often explicitly, with every sentence he writes, can speak of 'the Jews' in general to mean 'non-Christian Jews'.[9] The phrase can be used simply to mean 'Judaeans' as opposed to 'Galileans' and so forth (the word in Greek is after all *Ioudaioi),* and some of the occurrences in John clearly belong here.[10] After all, even the Hebrew Bible can speak of 'the Jews' in this fashion.[11] For much of the narrative we must now examine, the phrase is used by the evangelists to denote the Jewish *leaders;* and it was not only the early Christians who had a quarrel with Caiaphas and his colleagues.

One must therefore guard against attempting to reconstruct history by studying the much later effects of stories and events. To suggest that a story is biased, or to suggest that continuing to tell the same story is likely to perpetuate a biased and perhaps violent point of view, is not to say anything one way or another about its historical value. The fact that lurid tales of British atrocities have goaded generations of Irish republicans to continue their campaign of violence against British rule in Northern Ireland does not (alas), in and of itself, indicate that the tales were false in the first place. The social responsibility of the historian to his or her own day must be balanced with the professional responsibility to follow the evidence wherever it leads. Society is not ultimately served by suppressing truth or inventing falsehood. The stories must speak for themselves. That, I hope, is what they will do in the present chapter.

One further task must be attempted, in line with some recent suggestions.[12] The reasons for Jesus' death must not be tacked on as a separate issue at the end of a discussion of his overall agenda; we must at least raise the question as to whether the two were in fact integrated. It is of course possible that Jesus' death was in that sense an accident, having nothing to do with the aims and agendas that he had been pursuing. But to take that line involves

7. e.g., recently, Crossan 1995.
8. So, rightly, Moule 1987, 177.
9. e.g. 1 Cor. 1.22; 10.32; 2 Cor. 11.24; 1 Th. 2.14. He can also use the phrase for Jewish Christians, e.g. Gal. 2.13.
10. e.g. Jn. 11. 7f.
11. e.g. Jer. 32.12.
12. cf. e.g. Meyer 1979, 218f.; Sanders 1985, 327-35; Wright 1985; Horsley 1994.

us in saying that *all* the sources are at this point *totally* wrong (as those who take this line readily admit), and that we must simply invent another narrative, however slight, to take their place.[13] But one should only resort to this desperate measure - the methodological equivalent of attempting to ski in bare feet - when all other solutions have failed. The plentiful literature on the topic suggests that we have by no means reached that point yet.

The method by which we may approach the threefold question - the combined intentions of the Romans, the Jewish leaders, and Jesus - must be the same as we have adopted throughout. We possess fixed points at either side of the question: in this case, Jesus' career as a prophet announcing the kingdom, and his death as a 'messianic pretender.' We have seen in the previous chapter that these two overlap: there is a 'prophetic' strand to the hearing before Caiaphas, and there are 'messianic' overtones throughout Jesus' public career. We are in a position to study not merely isolated or detached *sayings* - which always tilt the balance towards sceptical non- or pseudo- reconstruction[14] - but *actions* and *events* which, freighted with symbolic significance, create a context in which stories and sayings can settle down and make themselves at home. In and through it all, we are looking once more for appropriate continuity and discontinuity both with first-century Judaism and with emerging Christianity, though to define precisely what that might mean in this case, ahead of the actual discussion, would be, to say the least, unwise.

Since we have already examined the trial narratives to some degree in the previous chapter, we can be reasonably brief now in covering the same material from a slightly different angle, thus clearing the ground for our discussion of Jesus himself.

2. The Roman Charge

Crucifixion was a powerful symbol throughout the Roman world. It was not just a means of liquidating undesirables; it did so with the maximum degradation and humiliation. It said, loud and clear: we are in charge here; you are our property; we can do what we like with you. It insisted, coldly and brutally, on the absolute sovereignty of Rome, and of Caesar. It told an implicit story, of the uselessness of rebel recalcitrance and the ruthlessness of imperial power. It said, in particular: this is what happens to rebel leaders. Crucifixion was a symbolic act with a clear and frightening meaning.[15]

All this, though unpleasant, is not controversial. What follows, however,

13. e.g. Mack 1988, Part III; 1995, ch. 3.
14. As rightly pointed out by e.g. Meyer 1979, 84f.
15. On crucifixion see above all Hengel 1977.

is decidedly so: Jesus was executed as a rebel against Rome. At least, this conclusion is controversial in most orthodox circles. Whenever anyone suggests that Jesus was some kind of a political rebel, the protests are long and loud.[16] The impulse to rescue Jesus from politics, or at least from the wrong sort of politics, may also lie behind the futile attempts to rescue him from Messianism. But the evidence surveyed in the previous chapter leaves us little choice on the last point, and hence on its corollary: when Jesus was crucified, the general impression in Jerusalem that day must have been that he was one more in a long line of would-be, but failed, Messiahs.

However, matters are not as simple as the normal revolutionary theories would suggest, either. There is good reason to suppose that, although Jesus' accusers handed him over, and Pilate executed him, on this charge, *both parties knew he was not guilty of it,* or not in any straightforward sense.[17] It is true that Jesus' kingdom-preaching must have carried, to all his hearers, some sort of revolutionary sense: if YHWH was at last becoming king, all other rulers, from Caesar downwards, would find their power at least relativized. But Jesus' constant redefinition of the kingdom, in praxis as much as in words, meant that anyone who had observed him closely would have been aware that he did not fit the same category as Judas the Galilean had before him, or as Simon bar Giora would do a generation later. And, though the chief priests and Pilate had not, perhaps, done their homework on Jesus very thoroughly, I suggest that they were both aware of some serious differences.

Pilate was not, by any account, a particularly competent or distinguished official.[18] His rule in Judaea was often provocative and bullying. Philo's description of him, though undoubtedly exaggerated for rhetorical effect, is worth quoting. He describes the incident in which Pilate placed golden shields in the Herodian palace, causing offence which was, for Philo, a foretaste of what would have happened had Gaius' plan to erect a statue of himself gone ahead.[19] He tells how a delegation of princes confronted Pilate, threatening to tell Tiberius what was afoot,[20] Pilate's reaction is revealing:

He feared that if they actually sent an embassy they would also expose the rest of

---

16. cf. e.g. Hengel 1971; Bammel & Moule 1984, against Brandon 1967 in particular. Horsley 1987, 1994 and in other works attempts to rehabilitate a moderated and non-violent version of Brandon's thesis. So, in some ways, does Crossan 1991a. For the overtones of Jesus' crucifixion as a rebel, cf. e.g. Cullmann 1956, 6, 11 f., 22; Farmer 1956, 197.

17. cf. Sanders 1985, 294f.

18. On Pilate's rule cf. *NTPG* 174, with refs. to Josephus in particular; Schürer 1.383-7; Brown 1994, 693-705, with plentiful refs.

19. The description occurs in Philo's quotation *(Leg.* 276-329) of a letter ostensibly from Agrippa 1 to Caligula.

20. Philo *Leg.* 299-305; see the discussion in Brown 1994, 701f.

his conduct as governor by stating in full the briberies, the insults, the robberies, the outrages and wanton injustices, the executions without trial constantly repeated, the ceaseless and supremely grievous cruelty. So with all his vindictiveness and furious temper, he was in a difficult position. He had not the courage to take down what had been dedicated nor did he wish to do anything which would please his subjects. At the same time he knew full well the constant policy of Tiberius in these matters . . .[21]

Even on the correct assumption that Philo has over-egged the pudding, his picture is not so very different from that of Josephus. The scholarly spectrum of opinion on Pilate is not particularly wide, ranging from those who think he was an unmitigated disaster to those who, like Brown, say merely that he was 'not without very serious faults'.[22] The interesting thing to note for our present discussion is just how similar, underneath the rhetoric, Philo's account of the 'shields' incident is to John's account of Jesus' trial before Pilate. In both incidents, Pilate is caught between his desire not to do what his Jewish subjects want - he intends to snub them if he can - and his fear of what Tiberius will think if news leaks out. 'If you let this man go, you are not Caesar's friend.'[23]

This raises the point at issue in our present discussion. It has been fashionable for some time to say that the evangelists increasingly whitewashed Pilate's character in order to lay the blame for Jesus' death on his Jewish contemporaries.[24] But proponents of this view never quite come to terms with the fact that if John and the rest *were* trying to make Pilate out to be anything other than weak, vacillating, bullying, and caught between two pressing agendas neither of which had anything to do with truth or justice, they did a pretty poor job of it.[25] The later Christian adoption of Pilate as a hero, or even a saint, is many a mile from his characterization in the gospels: the famous scene of Pilate washing his hands must surely be read, both within history and within Matthaean redaction, as merely the high-point of his cynicism. He was the governor; he was responsible for Jesus' death; washing his hands was an empty and contemptuous symbol, pretending that he could evade responsibility for something that lay completely within his power.[26] What emerges from the

---

21. Philo *Leg.* 302f. (quoted from Loeb edn., tr. Colson).
22. Brown 1994, 704.
23. Jn. 19.12; cf. Robinson 1985, 265f.; Brown 1994, 843f., both with other refs.
24. cf. e.g. Winter 1974 [1961], ch. 6. Contrast Horbury 1972, 64f. Robinson 1985, 274 n.204 quotes a fascinating unpublished comment from C. H. Dodd, disputing the idea of an alleged increasing tendency to transfer responsibility from the Romans to the Jews: 'The only "steady growth" is between Mark and Matthew. Luke and John go no further than Mark, John perhaps not so far, and none of them goes any further than the most primitive form of the *kerygma* - or than Paul.
25. Lightfoot 1893, 187f. showed well how the 'cynicism, sarcasm and unbelief and the 'withering scorn' of Pilate is 'painted in deeper colours' by John than by the synoptists.

records is not that Pilate wanted to rescue Jesus because he thought he was good, noble, holy or just, but that Pilate wanted to do the opposite of what the chief priests wanted him to do because he always wanted to do the opposite of what the chief priests wanted him to do.[27] That was his regular and settled *modus operandi*.

In this case, however, he was thwarted. The comparatively brief accounts in the synoptic tradition make a lot more sense when placed against the larger screen of the Johannine narrative; taken together, they suggest four things.[28] First, Pilate recognized that Jesus was not the ordinary sort of revolutionary leader, a *testes* or brigand. If he was a would-be Messiah, he was a highly unusual one. Part of this recognition came, we may suppose, through the prisoner's own equivocation: 'the words are yours', as all four accounts have it.[29] Second, Pilate therefore realized that the Jewish leaders had their own reasons for wanting Jesus executed, and were using the charge of sedition as a convenient excuse. Third, this gave him the opening to do what he would normally expect to do, which was to refuse their request; he tried this, but failed.[30] He failed, fourth, because it was pointed out to him in no uncertain terms that if he did not execute a would-be rebel king he would stand

26. Mt. 27.24f. On the later Pilate-traditions cf. Brown 1994, 695f. The tragic and horrible later use of Mt. 27.25 ('his blood be on us, and on our children') as an excuse for *soidisant* 'Christian' anti-semitism is a gross distortion of its original meaning, where the reference is surely to the fall of Jerusalem (cp. Lk. 23.28-31). The legal situation is indicated by mSanh. 4.5: 'in capital cases the witness is answerable for the blood of him [that is wrongfully condemned] and the blood of his posterity [that should have been born to him]' (Danby 1933, 388).

27. As in the matter of the *titulus:* Jn. 19.21f.

28. Mt. 27.1-26/Mk. 15.1-15/Lk. 23.1-25/Jn. 18.28-19.16. Cf. Robinson 1985, 254-75; Sherwin-White 1969 (1963), ch. 2. Brown 1994, 721f. has a judicious summing-up which, though somewhat kinder to Pilate, follows a similar line to that adopted here.

29. Mt. 27.11/Mk. 15.2/Lk. 23.3/Jn. 18.37. The precise meaning of this phrase is of course much debated. Dodd's comment is perhaps pertinent (1968, 89f.): 'It would appear to be intentionally non-committal, meaning something like, "The words are yours", "Have it so if you choose",' He cites the C4 (Greek) *Apostolic Constitutions* 5.14.4, which, commenting on Mt. 26.25, distinguishes explicitly between *su eipas* ('you said [so]') and *nai* ('yes').

30. According to Mt. 27.15-23/Mk. 15.6-14/Lk. 23.17-23/Jn. 18.39-40, he tried to offer the crowds Jesus' release as part of a Passover custom, but was thwarted by their asking for Barabbas instead. This account has often been queried as part of the evangelists' attempt to shift the blame from Pilate to the Jews, but there is at least as strong a likelihood that it is historical: see, with full details, Brown 1994, 787-820. According to Lk. 23.6-12, Pilate sent Jesus to Herod, presumably so that he could say he acted on Herod's recommendation rather than that of the chief priests. (Parker 1987 proposed Herod as the real mover in the whole process; he is indeed more important in the gospel narratives than often acknowledged, but perhaps not to this extent.) Neither the Barabbas nor the Herod incident materially affects our present enquiry.

accused, himself, of disloyalty to Caesar.[31] Historically, emotionally, politically the sequence makes perfect sense. In terms of the Roman authorities, the answer to the question 'why did Jesus die?' is that Pilate not only put cynical power-games before justice (that was normal), but also, on this occasion, put naked self-interest before both. This, however, merely heightens the second and third aspects of our question. Why did the chief priests present Jesus to Pilate as a condemned criminal in the first place? And why did Jesus not defend himself against the charge of sedition?

3. The Jewish Charge

The historian's task in examining the Jewish hearing(s) would be a lot easier if we could begin at the end, as we can with the Roman trial. Just as there we are on safe ground with the *titulus* on the cross, from which we can work backwards, so it would be convenient to begin at the end of the Jewish hearing and reconstruct the process by which the court reached its verdict. Sadly, that is precisely what we cannot do, since, as we saw in the previous chapter, the verdict suggested by the synoptic gospels, especially Matthew and Mark, is normally regarded as historically puzzling. We are forced, instead, to work in towards the trial narrative from the two outer fixed points: Jesus' Temple-action on the one hand, and the charge before Pilate (which there is every reason to regard as historical) on the other.[32]

At the surface level, neither move is particularly difficult. Jesus' Temple-action led straightforwardly to the question about Messiahship; his unequivocal claim to Messiahship would translate without difficulty into the charge with which Pilate confronted him: 'Are you the king of the Jews?'[33] But, as with Pilate, we are faced with a curious phenomenon. The Jewish court, to be sure, wanted a charge that they could take to Pilate with some hope of having their conviction, and sentence, ratified and carried out. But they, like Pilate, knew very well that Jesus was not a would-be Messiah of the same sort as Judas the Galilean. If they had thought he was, they would most likely

---

31. One only has to read the account of Tiberius' 'reign of terror' in Tac. *Ann.* 5-6 to understand Pilate's nervousness.

32. cf. Harvey 1982, ch. 2.

33. Mt. 27.11/Mk. 15.2/Lk. 23.3/Jn. 18.33. This title reflects 'how a Roman would understand Jesus' in terms of 'an attempt to reestablish the kingship over Judea and Jerusalem exercised by the Hasmoneans . . . and Herod the Great' (Brown 1994, 731). One might add 'or in terms of a populist revolutionary movement, as mentioned by Josephus (e.g, *Ant.* 17.285)' (cf. Sherwin-White 1969 [1963], 24f.). Brown, however, makes unduly heavy weather of the transition from 'Messiah' to 'king of the Jews'.

have arrested his followers as well. In fact, however, *'no one* could think that [Jesus] posed an actual threat to the Jewish government . . . and certainly not to the Roman Empire.'[34] It was just not that sort of movement, and nobody seriously supposed it was. The very clarity of the historical sequence, focused on the idea of Messiahship, merely highlights the real problem: why, then, did the Jewish authorities determine to get rid of Jesus?

Later Jewish tradition, for what it is worth, highlights the motive that, as we saw in chapter 9, emerged as an undertone during the public ministry of Jesus. The Babylonian Talmud puts it like this:

> Jesus was hanged on the eve of Passover. The herald went before him for forty days, saying, 'He is going forth to be stoned because he practised sorcery and enticed and led Israel astray. Let everyone knowing anything in his defence come and plead for him.' But nothing was found in his defence, so he was hanged on the eve of Passover. [35]

In other words, the Jewish tradition, which certainly owes nothing to Christian interpretations of Jesus' death, is clear that Jesus was killed because of crimes punishable by death in Jewish law - specifically, Deuteronomy 13 and similar passages, and their later rabbinic interpretations.[36] This is, perhaps, as close as we come to a fixed point in the Jewish hearings, from which we can work inwards.

But in what ways did they think Jesus was 'leading the people astray'? It is not clear that leading a rebel movement would count in this category, though Josephus of course does his best to blacken the characters, and impugn the motives, of those 'prophetic' leaders he designates as 'brigands'. In any case, as we have seen, it is unlikely that either the chief priests or Pilate regarded Jesus as a serious revolutionary threat. No; as we argued earlier, they invoked Deuteronomy 13 and similar passages because Jesus was following, and advocating, an agenda which involved setting aside some of the most central and cherished symbols of the Judaism of his day, and replacing them with loyalty to himself. More specifically, his attitude to Torah (during his Galilean work) pointed towards his action in the Temple: one can imagine onlookers, aware of what Jesus had done and said in Galilee, saying 'There! I knew he was up to no good!' He appeared, so far as anyone could judge, to be speaking and acting in opposition to Torah and Temple, and leading

---

34. Sanders 1985, 329 (italics original); cf. 231, 295, 317f. and elsewhere. Sanders stresses that this contrasts Jesus with some other movements that the authorities might have been supposed to regard as parallel.

35. bSanh. 43a (cf. too 107b). Cf. *JVG* (Wright, *Jesus and the Victory of God*), 439-42. The apparent oddity of Jesus being stoned *and* hanged is explained by mSanh. 6.4: after stoning, the corpse must be hung on a gibbet, but taken down again before sunset in obedience to Dt. 21.23. The notion of a forty-day appeal for defence is normally discounted, e.g. by Klausner 1947 [1925], 28.

36. See *JVG*, 439-42.

others, by word, example and 'works of power', to do so the same. What could he be, in their eyes, if not a false prophet, performing signs and wonders to lead Israel astray?

The subtext of the hearing before Caiaphas is thus clarified. The surface text, as we saw in the previous chapter, was the framing of a charge which would stick before Pilate, who (as John's account makes clear) would not care a fig about someone 'leading Israel astray', but who would care, or ought to, about someone leading a rebel movement against Rome. The subtext, however, was the determination on the part of the court to find Jesus guilty of a crime in *Jewish* law. The general populus were *wanting* Jesus to be the sort of Messiah whom Pilate, if he caught him, would have to execute - the sort who, like Barabbas, would lead a violent revolution in the city.[37] If the Jewish leaders had found Jesus guilty of being a revolutionary Messiah, and had handed him over to Pilate on that charge, they might well have precipitated the riot they were anxious to avoid.[38] But if they were able to claim that he was guilty of a well-known capital crime in Jewish law, they might win the people over. Further demonstration that this was their aim can be found in the mocking by the Jewish court. Whereas Herod and the Romans taunt Jesus as a would-be Messiah, the Jewish leaders mock him as a would-be *prophet*.[39]

We should not, however, reduce the motivation of the Jewish court simply to the cynical and political. Serious Jewish observers were bound to conclude that Jesus was 'leading Israel astray' in terms of the agendas, and Torah-interpretations, current at the time.[40] Precisely because he would not endorse, but rather opposed, the movement of national resistance, the (Shammaite) majority of Pharisees would find him deeply unsatisfactory.[41] Precisely because he was 'stirring up the people', creating an excitement wherever he went in a highly volatile social and political setting, the chief priests and Sadducees were bound to see him as a serious trouble-maker. John's account of their anxiety bears all the hallmarks of historicity:

> The chief priests and the Pharisees called a meeting of the council, and said, 'What are we to do? This man is performing many signs. If we let him go on like this, everyone will believe in him, and the Romans will come and destroy both our holy

37. cf. Lk. 23.19, which reads like a sentence from Josephus: Barabbas had committed *phonos* [murder] during a *stasis* [uprising] in the *polis* [city].

38. As in Mt. 26.5/Mk. 14.2; cf. Lk. 22.2; Jn. 11.47-53. Riots, and Roman repression, at times of festival were nothing new: cf. *NTPG* 172-7, with refs.

39. Mt. 26.67f./Mk. 14.65/Lk. 22.63-5. Mt. has them call Jesus 'Messiah', but the point of the scene, for him as well, is that Jesus is being taunted as a false prophet.

40. cf. Klausner 1947 [1925], bk. 8, ch. 3.

41. On the Pharisees, their groupings, and agendas cf. *NTPG* 181-203, and *JVG*, ch. 9.

place and our nation.'[42]

He is performing signs; people will be led away after him; the Temple, and the national life itself, are at risk. These, I suggest, were the real issues underneath the night hearing at the chief priest's house. These issues, too, when coupled with the more obvious accusation that Jesus was a would-be Messiah, gave rise to the charge which, in Luke's account, the assembly put before Pilate:

> We found this man perverting our nation, forbidding us to pay taxes to the emperor, and saying that he himself is the Messiah, a King.[43]

Unless, then, we are to take the route of extreme scepticism and deny that we know anything at all about how and why Jesus was executed, we must say that the combination of charges we now have before us lay at the core of the hearing before the chief priests.

Did they, then, hold an official trial in haste, at night? Sherwin-White argued, not least from circumstantial evidence, that they probably did.[44] They wanted to be able to catch Pilate during working hours - i.e. first thing in the morning - and have the matter settled before the festival proper began.[45] Though certainty at this point is impossible - and is not necessary, either, for the argument of this chapter - I incline to the view that the meeting in John 11, held without Jesus present, was the real 'trial', at which it was agreed (a) that Jesus was a false prophet leading Israel astray, (b) that he was a serious political liability, and (c) that, since it seemed to be a choice between killing him and letting the Temple and nation be jeopardized, he should be killed.[46] All that remained was to extract some sort of confession of guilt in relation both to the Temple and to the charge of false prophecy. That was what the nocturnal hearing succeeded in doing.[47]

Succeeded, indeed, beyond their hopes. The prisoner, in agreeing to the charge of being a would-be Messiah, 'prophesied' his own vindication in such a way that a plausible charge of 'blasphemy' could be added to the list. He had now not only spoken false prophecy against the Temple, thereby placing himself clearly enough in the category condemned by Deuteronomy 13,

42. Jn. 11.47f.

43. Lk. 23.2. Mt. 27.11/Mk. 15.2 demand some such fuller account, since they have Pilate, without any prompting, asking Jesus 'Are you the King of the Jews?'

44. Sherwin-White 1969 [1963], 44-7.

45. This assumes that Jesus was executed during the day before Passover: see below.

46. Cp. Sanders 1985, 317f.

47. Harvey (1982, 30-2) suggests that the Jewish hearing was political, not judicial: what mattered was not that Jesus was formally convicted of a crime, but that the Jewish gathering heard enough to warrant handing Jesus over to the Romans with the suggestion that the Romans should try him as a would-be Messiah.

the category that might convince the crowds that the chief priests' verdict was correct. He had now not only confessed to messianic aspirations, placing himself clearly enough in the category necessary if Pilate was to carry out, despite his normal disregard for the chief priests, the sentence they had passed. He had done these two things in such a way as to prophesy that he, as Messiah, would sit on a throne beside the god of Israel. 'You will see "the son of man" "sitting at the right hand of Power", and "coming on the clouds of heaven".[48]

Since we have no evidence of anyone before or after Jesus ever saying such a thing of himself, it is not surprising that we have no evidence of anyone framing a blasphemy law to prevent them doing so. But, granted the charge of false prophecy already hanging over him, and the 'two powers' implication that the reference to Daniel 7 suggests, it seems to me likely that the reaction of Caiaphas, as in Matthew 26.65 and Mark 14.63-4, is substantially historical. Among other things, it explains John 19.7, where the chief priests say to Pilate, 'We have a law, and according to that law he ought to die because he has claimed to be the Son of God.'[49] Without the reference to Daniel 7, the phrase 'Messiah, Son of the Blessed' in Mark 14.61 would, as I insisted in the previous chapter, simply mean 'the true Davidic king'. With it, the option is at least open that the phrase is being given a new meaning: 'the one who will sit at the right hand of the god of Israel'. The only remaining objection to the historicity of the scene is, of course, that Jesus would never have said, or meant, any such thing. Discussion of this point must be deferred to the next chapter.

In terms of the Jewish authorities, then, the question 'Why did Jesus die?' evokes a fivefold answer. He was sent to the Roman governor on a capital charge

(i) because many (not least many Pharisees, but also, probably, the chief priests) saw him as 'a false prophet, leading Israel astray';

(ii) because, as one aspect of this, they saw his Temple-action as a blow against the central symbol not only of national life but also of YHWH's presence with his people;

(iii) because, though he was clearly not leading a real or organized military revolt, he saw himself as in some sense Messiah, and could thus become a focus of serious revolutionary activity;

(iv) because, as the pragmatic focus of these three points, they saw him as a dangerous political nuisance, whose actions might well call down the wrath of Rome upon Temple and nation alike;

---

48. Mt. 26.64/Mk. 14.62; cf. Lk. 22.69; see *JVG*, 360-5, 524-8.
49. cf. too Lk. 22.70.

(v)   because, at the crucial moment in the hearing, he not only (as far as they were concerned) pleaded guilty to the above charges, but also did so in such a way as to place himself, blasphemously, alongside the god of Israel.

The leaders of the Jewish people were thus able to present Jesus to Pilate as a seditious trouble-maker; to their Jewish contemporaries (and later generations of rabbinic Judaism) as a false prophet and a blasphemer, leading Israel astray; and to themselves as a dangerous political nuisance. On all counts, he had to die.

Their verdict was not, of course, a *sufficient* cause of Jesus' death. They needed Pilate to ratify and carry out the sentence. It was, however, a *necessary* cause of Jesus' crucifixion: Pilate himself would not have brought charges against Jesus, or, if he had, they would most likely have only resulted in a flogging.[50] Pilate's decision was both a necessary and a sufficient cause of Jesus' crucifixion. If he had refused to comply, Jesus would have been flogged and released; once he had agreed, the matter was concluded. This complex nest of causes explains the events; it does justice to the primary source materials – it does not reflect any bias as between Jewish and Roman authorities, since Pilate emerges at least as badly as Caiaphas; and it explains, not least by its complexity, the varied emphases found in pagan, Jewish and early Christian literature."[51] In both hearings, however, the prisoner had a role to play. He could have avoided arrest in the first place.[52] He could, perhaps, have chosen to mollify the Sanhedrin. He could have pointed out to Pilate that he posed no threat to public order, as his great-great-nephews were later to do before Domitian.[53] He could, in other words, have played all his cards differently, and might well have been either acquitted or let off with a lighter punishment. His own decisions, in other words, were themselves necessary, though insufficient, causes of his own death. Having examined Pilate and the chief priests, we must therefore turn our attention to Jesus himself, and ask once more, but now in relation to his own mindset: why did Jesus die?

---

50. On the analogy with Jesus ben Ananias (Jos. *War* 6.302-4); and cf. Lk. 23.16, 22.

51. Pagan: e.g. Tac. *Ann.* 15.44; Jewish: bSanh. 43a, etc. (see *JVG*). (The Roman text mentions only the Roman involvement, the Jewish text only the Jewish. Neither 'side' regarded responsibility for Jesus' death as something to be ashamed of.) Early Christian: e.g. Ac. 2.23; 3.14; 4.10, 27f.; 5.30; 7.52; 10.39; 13.28; 1 Th. 2.14f.

52. Even granted Judas' betrayal - a topic which, though of considerable interest, is not relevant to the present investigation.

53. Eus. *HE* 3.19f.: cf. *NTPG* 35lf.; Bauckham 1990, 94-106.

4. The Intention of Jesus (1): The Key Symbol

(i) Introduction

Did Jesus intend to die in something like the manner he did, and if so why? I argued earlier that it makes historical sense to ask this question, instancing three very different figures from roughly Jesus' own period: Seneca, Eleazar, and Ignatius of Antioch.[54] In each case, it not only makes sense to ask what the subject intended; it makes sense to explore the mindset which would sustain such an intention, and the worldview within which such a mindset might originate. It is a task like that which we now approach in relation to Jesus' understanding of his own death.

Albert Schweitzer suggested, nearly a century ago, that one might divide 'Lives of Jesus' into two main groups: those in which Jesus went to Jerusalem in order to 'work', and those in which he went there to die.[55] Schweitzer himself argued strongly for the latter route.[56] Most subsequent scholars have drawn back from it, regarding it (in the words of a recent writer who is otherwise much closer to Schweitzer than many) as implying that Jesus was 'weird'.[57] Since I propose to agree with Schweitzer, in outline though not in detail, it may be as well to say from the start that this counter-argument is flawed. It would of course be 'weird' for a comfortable modern western scholar to act deliberately in such a way as to occasion a capital charge, and then to incriminate him- or herself, partly by silence, and partly by cryptic but damning self-disclosures. But Jesus was not a comfortable modern western scholar.[58] Another worldview dominated his horizon, established his aims and beliefs, and generated his intentions. Four hundred years before him, Socrates had gone to his death rather than ingratiate himself with the Athenian regime; his followers mourned him greatly, but nobody thought him weird, or even inconsistent. Indeed, the point of Socrates' acceptance of the death penalty was that anything else would be radically inconsistent with his whole life and teaching.[59] It should be at least an open question whether

---

54. *JVG*, 106.

55. Schweitzer 1954 [1906], 389 n.1.

56. Recent followers of Schweitzer in this respect include e.g. O'Neill 1980, ch. 4; Bockmuehl 1994, 90; Hengel 1995b, 72.

57. Sanders 1985, 333 (though what he is criticizing is not strictly Schweitzer's view but what he describes as its 'logical implication').

58. Sanders (ibid.) claims that Jesus was 'a *reasonable* first-century visionary' (italics original). It all depends, of course, what you mean by 'reasonable'. Surely Sanders, who has done so much to expose the back-projection of certain later assumptions on to the New Testament, does not wish to fall into the same trap himself?

59. Plato, *Apology, Crito* and *Phaedo*. Cf. esp. *Apol.* 40-41: 'I [Socrates] suspect that this thing that has happened to me is a blessing, and we are quite mistaken in supposing death to

Jesus embraced a worldview (not of course the same as that of Socrates) within which his own death would make sense, and would indeed make more sense than anything else.[60]

As in our previous investigations, we must begin with praxis, story and symbol before investigating 'ideas', and the isolated sayings which may or may not disclose them. The idealist tradition, by starting with sayings, tends to lose sight of events and actions within the fog of hypothetical tradition-history. But it is events and actions, and the implicit narratives they disclose, that count within a world that knows the value of symbols. Modern western-ers, who live in a world that has rid itself of many of its ancient symbols, and mocks or marginalizes those that are left, have to make a huge effort of historical imagination to enter into a world where a single action can actually *say* something (it is ironic that philosophers within our words-and-ideas cul-ture have had to struggle to reclaim this notion, by means of such concepts as 'speech-acts'[61]). Unless we make the effort, however, we become the pris-oners of our own culture, and should give up even trying to be historians. Words focus, limit and sharpen symbolic actions, but do not replace them. And the central symbolic action which provides the key to Jesus' implicit story about his own death is, of course, the Last Supper.

(ii) The Last Supper: Symbol and Significance

(a) Introduction

Jesus' last meal with his followers was a deliberate double drama.[62] As a Passover meal (of sorts), it told the story of Jewish history in terms of divine deliverance from tyranny, looking back to the exodus from Egypt and on to the great exodus, the return from exile, that was still eagerly awaited. But Jesus' meal fused this great story together with another one: the story of Jesus' own life, and of his coming death. It somehow involved him in the god-given drama, not as a spectator, or as one participant among many, but as the central character.

---

be an evil . . . I am quite clear that the time had come when it was better for me to die and be released from my distractions.

60. For further discussion of Sanders' objection to Schweitzer, and his counter-proposals, see below.

61. See the discussion in Thiselton 1980, ch. 5.

62. For a recent survey of scholarly opinion, and bibliography, cf. O'Toole 1992.

(b) Last Supper and Passover

This presupposes, of course, that the Last Supper was in some sense or other a Passover meal.[63] The synoptic evangelists say as much: they date it; they have Jesus and the disciples speak of 'eating the Passover'; they have the disciples 'preparing the Passover-meal'.[64] John, however, indicates that the meal took place the day *before* the feast; he does not, however, describe the meal, or any symbolic actions concerned with the bread or the wine, but only the footwashing.[65] This fits with the Talmudic evidence, which as we saw had Jesus being executed 'on the eve of the Passover'.[66] Various attempts have been made to resolve this problem. Jesus may have been following a rival (perhaps Essene?) calendar; John has altered the chronology to make the theological point that Jesus is the true Passover lamb, slaughtered at the same time as the lambs were being killed in the Temple in preparation for the evening meal; the synoptists have turned the meal into a Passover meal in obedience to *their* theology or tradition; and so forth.[67] If we are to use the symbolic significance and implicit narrative of the meal as the starting-point for this part of our investigation, the question is of some importance.

It seems to me virtually certain that the meal in question was *some kind of* Passover meal. Several almost incidental details point this way. It was eaten at night, and in Jerusalem; Jesus and his followers normally returned to Bethany for the night, but Passover meals had to be eaten within the city limits, and after dark (days in the Jewish calendar began, of course, at sunset).[68] The meal ended with a hymn, presumably the *Hallel* psalms sung at the end of the Passover meal.[69] The best explanation for Jesus' crucial words is that the head of the household would normally explain certain parts of the Passover meal in relation to the exodus narrative. Likewise, the counter-arguments to the synoptic dating are not especially strong. Thus, for instance, Passover would normally be celebrated by families; but Josephus can speak of it being celebrated by what he calls 'a little fraternity', and in any case, as we have seen, Jesus regarded his followers as a fictive kinship

63. On this whole topic the work of Jeremias 1966a [1949] remains basic. It is impossible here to discuss in detail the many complex issues which his work has raised.

64. Date: Mt. 26.17 / Mk. 14.12 / Lk. 22.7. Jesus' words: Mt. 26.18 / Mk. 14.14f. / Lk.22. 11, 15. Disciples: Mt. 26.17 / Mk. 14.12. Preparation: Mt. 26.19 / Mk. 14.16 / Lk. 22.13.

65. Jn. 13.1; 18.28; 19.14, 31.

66. bSanh. 43a: *JVG*, 439. This evidence is of course much later, and as we saw contains other elements which label it as secondary,

67. Alternative calendar: Jaubert 1957. John's lamb-christology: Jn. 1.29, 36; 19.36 (cf. Ex. 12.46; Num. 9.12; 1 Cor. 5.7).

68. Night: 1 Cor. 11.23; Mt. 26.20/Mk. 14.17; cf. Lk. 22.14. Bethany: Mt. 21.17/Mk. 11.11; Mt. 26.6/Mk. 14.3.

69. i.e. Pss. 115-118; Mt. 26.30/Mk. 14.26.

group.[70] The only alternative to this conclusion is to adopt a quite radical scepticism about the whole event, which then leaves a major feature of very early Christianity completely inexplicable: Paul 'received' the detailed traditions about the Last Supper in (presumably) his earliest days as a Christian, i.e. in Damascus after his conversion in the early 30's.[71]

At the same time, we have no reason to suppose, granted all we have seen of Jesus' agenda and normal mode of operating, that he would have felt bound to celebrate the festival on the officially appointed day. Scriptural regulations permitted Passover to be kept, in case of necessity, at another time than that laid down, and if Jesus had been eager (as Luke has him imply) to force the issue that lay ahead of him, he might have considered that sufficient reason.[72] Though Jaubert's proposal about Jesus following the Essene (solar) calendar, as opposed to the official (lunar) one, has not received much subsequent support, there is no reason to suppose that Jesus might not have celebrated what we might call a *quasi-Passover* meal a day ahead of the real thing. This, of course, would have meant doing without a lamb (since the priests would not be killing them for Passover until the following day); that would be no bar to treating the meal as a proper Passover, since it was after all what happened in the Diaspora (and, of course, what was to happen throughout the Jewish world after AD 70).[73] Granted that Jesus had, throughout his work, reorganized the symbolic world of his contemporaries around his own life and mission (chapter 9 *JVG*), it certainly does not strain credulity to think that he might organize a special quasi-Passover meal a day early. All the lines of our investigation so far point this way, and suggest that Jesus saw the meal as the appropriate way of drawing the symbolism of Passover, and all that it meant in terms of hope as well as of history, on to himself and his approaching fate.[74]

What story did this deeply symbolic meal tell, before any words were spoken?[75] Granted a quasi-Passover setting, the meal itself said two very specific things.

---

70. cf. Jos. *War* 6.423f.; cf. *JVG*, 398-403, 430-2. For discussion of other problems, cf. e.g. O'Toole 1992, 236f.

71. 1 Cor. 11.23. For a recent discussion of early traditions about the Supper cf. Caird & Hurst 1994, 225-32.

72. cf. Num. 9.10f., specifying that those who are unclean or absent on Nisan 14 should keep the feast a month later instead; this, according to 2 Chr. 30.2-4, 13-15, was carried out by Hezekiah. For Jesus' eagerness, cf. Lk. 22.15.

73. cf. mPes. 10.3, reflecting awareness of the change from pre-70 to post-70 Passovers. Cf. Jaubert 1957.

74. For a similar proposal, cf. Bockmuehl 1994, 92-4.

75. Sanders 1985, 264 effectively asks the question in the same way, though his answer is somewhat different.

First, like all Jewish Passover meals, the event spoke of leaving Egypt. To a first-century Jew, it pointed to the return from exile, the new exodus, the great covenant renewal spoken of by the prophets. The meal symbolized 'forgiveness of sins', YHWH's return to redeem his people, his victory over Pharaohs both literal and metaphorical; it took place 'in accordance with the scriptures', locating itself within the ongoing story of YHWH's strange saving purposes for Israel as they reached its climax. This was the meal, in other words, which said that Israel's god was about to become king. This, indeed, is not especially controversial.

Second, however, the meal brought Jesus' own kingdom-movement to its climax. It indicated that the new exodus, and all that it meant, was happening *in and through Jesus himself.* This is extremely controversial, and needs to be spelled out in more detail.

The new meaning which Jesus gave to the old meal may be seen when we correlate it with his Temple-action. Both functioned as prophetic symbols, indicating an unexpected fulfilment of Israel's destiny, in which that destiny was being strangely redrawn around Jesus himself. Indeed, from this point of view we might almost suggest that it was *necessary* for Jesus *not* to celebrate the Passover on the regular night; he was precisely not keeping it as simply one more in the sequence, as part of the regular annual Jewish cult, dependent upon the Temple for the necessary sacrificial lamb.[76] If he believed that the kingdom was about to dawn, in other words that YHWH was about to inaugurate the new covenant, the end of exile, the forgiveness of sins, it becomes very likely that he would distinguish this meal from the ordinary Passover meal, while retaining enough of its form for the symbolism to be effective. If he believed that the kingdom was not merely a future event, waiting round some corner yet to be negotiated, but was actually bursting in upon the present moment, it would make sense to anticipate Passover night, celebrating a strange new Passover that would carry a kingdom-in-the-present meaning. And if he really believed that the Temple was due for destruction, that it had been solemnly judged by YHWH and found wanting, he might well regard it as appropriate that he should behave as though already in the Diaspora, already without the Temple, and celebrate his Passover meal without recourse to the system he had denounced, and whose imminent downfall he had predicted.

To calculate the symbolic and narratival significance of Jesus' action in the upper room, therefore, we must place it alongside the Temple-action. The two interpret one another.[77] Thus Jacob Neusner, for instance, has

76. Though cf. Sanders 1993, 250f. for the opposite view.
77. We should possibly understand the footwashing scene in Jn. 13.1-20 in this sense. According to the mBer. 9.5, one was supposed to wash the dust of the streets from one's feet

argued that the Temple-action and the Last Supper, taken together, indicated that Jesus was in effect intending to replace the Temple, as the symbolic focus of the Judaism, with his own newly instituted quasi-cultic meal.[78] Bruce Chilton, following a similar line of thought, has gone so far as to suggest that what Judas betrayed to the chief priests was that Jesus had performed a scandalous counter-Temple act in celebrating his own Supper as a new and radical alternative.[79] Neusner and Chilton have, I believe, put their finger on a vital point, but I do not think they have drawn from it quite the conclusion that it demands. The intended contrast is not so much between the Temple-system and the regular celebration of a meal instituted by Jesus, so much as between the Temple-system *and Jesus himself,* specifically, his own approaching death. This is not a peculiar idea imported into the picture from outside, but emerges clearly from the cumulative evidence amassed throughout the present book, and particularly in the previous chapter, that Jesus deliberately drew on to himself the whole tradition of Jewish expectation and hope. He saw himself as Messiah, the focal point of the great divine act of liberation. The symbols ordering Israel's life and hope were redrawn, focusing now upon Jesus himself. The final meal which he celebrated with his followers was not, in that sense, free-standing. It gained its significance from his own entire life and agenda, and from the events which, he knew, would shortly come to pass. It was Jesus' chosen way of investing those imminent events with the significance he believed they would carry.[80]

Within this wider context, Jesus' actions with the bread and the cup - which there is excellent warrant to regard as historical[81] - must be seen in the same way as the symbolic actions of certain prophets in the Hebrew scriptures. Jeremiah smashes a pot; Ezekiel makes a model of Jerusalem under siege.[82] The actions carry prophetic power, effecting the events (mostly acts of judgment) which are then to occur. They are at once explained in terms of those events, or rather of YHWH's operating through them. In the same

before approaching the sacred precincts. Jesus' action, in other words (in addition to all the other things that commentators normally say about it), could be seen as preparing his followers for something that would actually supersede the Temple. Whether or not we ascribe either the action, or this interpretation of it, to Jesus himself, this theme points us in the same direction as various recent historical studies which have placed the Temple-scene and the upper room in parallel.

78. Neusner 1989, esp. 290.

79. Chilton 1992b, 153f.; cf. too 1992a.

80. Cf. Jeremias 1966a [1949], 260f.

81. I find it simply incredible that so central and early a tradition as Paul recounts in 1 Cor. 11.23-6 would have been invented wholesale by the early church without a firm basis in Jesus' own actions.

82. Jer. 19.1-13 (cf, too e.g. 13.1-11; 27.1-28.17; 32.6-15; 35.1-19; etc.); Ezek. 4.1-17 (cf. too 5.1-12; 12.1-25; etc.). Cf. e.g. Beck 1970.

way, Jesus' central actions during the meal seem to have been designed to reinforce the point of the whole meal: the kingdom-agenda to which he had been obedient throughout his ministry was now at last reaching its ultimate destination. Passover looked back to the exodus, and on to the coming of the kingdom. Jesus intended this meal to symbolize the new exodus, the arrival of the kingdom through his own fate. The meal, focused on Jesus' actions with the bread and the cup, told the Passover story, and Jesus' own story, and wove these two into one.

(c) From Symbol to Word

If the symbolism and implicit story inherent in the action generated and sustained the meal's primary significance, the words spoken brought this into focus and articulation. What precisely was said at Passover meals at this period, and thus the extent to which Jesus mayor may not have adjusted the words for his new meaning, is impossible to ascertain. But there is every reason to suppose that the host at a Passover meal, then as now, would retell the story of the exodus, interpreting the actions and the elements of the meal in terms of that story, thereby linking the present company with the children of Israel as they left Egypt.[83] The words of Jesus at the supper would therefore have been seen, not only with later hindsight, but at the time, as performing a similar function. They would have been understood as reinterpreting the meal in relation to himself, claiming that the kingdom-events about to occur were the climax of the long history which looked back to the exodus from Egypt as its formative moment.

Debate will, no doubt, continue about what exactly Jesus said, and in what order, but since in any case we are dealing (a) with a Greek translation of dense Aramaic originals[84] and (b) with sayings which were reused (and perhaps retranslated) again and again in the life of the early church, we should not expect to be able to attain complete precision. What matters is that in the fourfold tradition, all the more impressive for its appearance in at least three independent forms (Mark and Matthew, as so often, seem to stand in closer relation than the others), it emerges that Jesus, in prophetic style, identified the bread with his own body, and the wine with his own blood, and that he spoke about these in language which echoed the context of Passover, sacrifice, and covenant which the meal, in any case, must already

83. cf. e.g. mPes., esp. 10.1-7.
84. The suggestion that Jesus spoke Hebrew on this occasion is rightly discounted by e.g. Fitzmyer 1985,1394.

have possessed.[85] The synoptic tradition also indicates that Jesus said something about the climactic events being so close that this would be the last such meal he would share with his followers before the kingdom arrived; this eschatological emphasis is appropriately modified in Paul's new situation.[86] All this may be spelled out in detail as follows.

1. Jesus' words about the bread identified it with his own body, as Ezekiel identified his brick with Jerusalem. Jesus' action thus indicated prophetically that he was to die, and that his death would be the source of life for his followers. According to the Mishnah, the unleavened bread of Passover was explained by Gamaliel (a contemporary of Jesus) as signifying the redemption from Egypt.[87] Unleavened bread was necessary, in the original story, because of the urgent haste of the exodus. In addition to identifying himself as the means of Israel's redemption, Jesus may have been alluding to the urgency with which his own mission was now at last to be accomplished.

2. Jesus' words about the cup (in Luke, the second cup) identify it, in similar prophetic fashion, with his blood. Behind the four versions there is a common meaning, with some of the accounts making more explicit what is implicit in the Passover setting anyway. The common meaning is that Jesus' coming death will effect the renewal of the covenant, that is, the great return from exile for which Israel had longed.[88] The phrase 'the blood of the covenant', which occurs in some form in all the accounts, echoes Exodus 24.8, in which Moses established the first covenant with the people at Mount Sinai.[89] It also evokes, perhaps equally significantly, Zechariah 9.9-11, which resonates closely with the themes we have studied already in this chapter and the previous one:

> Rejoice greatly, O daughter Zion!
>> Shout aloud, O daughter Jerusalem!
> Lo, your king comes to you;
>> triumphant and victorious is he,
> humble and riding on a donkey,
>> on a colt, the foal of a donkey.
> He will cut off the chariot from Ephraim,
>> and the war horse from Jerusalem;
> and the battle bow shall be cut off,
>> and he shall command peace to the nations;

---

85. Mt. 26.26-8/Mk. 14.22-4/Lk. 22.19-20/1 Cor. 11.23-6. Cp. Jn. 6.51-9. The longer reading of Lk. (including 22.19b-20, omitted by D) is now usually regarded as original: cf. Metzger 1971,173-7 and the commentaries (e.g, Fitzmyer 1985, 1387f.; still questioned by e.g. Evans 1990, 787f.).

86. Mt. 26.29/Mk. 14.25/Lk. 22.15-18; cf. 1 Cor. 11.26b.

87. mPes. 10.5.

88. On the meaning of 'drinking someone's blood', cf. 2 Sam. 23.13-17.

89. Ex. 24.6-8.

his dominion shall be from sea to sea,
    and from the River to the ends of the earth.
As for you also, *because of the blood of my covenant with you,*
    I will set your prisoners free from the waterless pit.
Return to your stronghold, O prisoners of hope;
    today I declare that I will restore to you double
    [or: I am declaring a second time that I will return to you].

The covenant is renewed in the context of the messianic victory, which will liberate Israel once and for all from her long exile.[90] As we have already stressed, Jesus' actions at the Last Supper are to be seen in close conjunction with his earlier actions in the Temple, including, as here, his quasi-royal entry. There is no reason to doubt that he intended, in speaking of the final cup of the meal in terms of his own death, to allude to this theme of covenant renewal.[91] It fits precisely with all that we have seen of his agenda so far.

All three synoptic accounts contain a further initial explanation: Jesus' blood will be shed 'on behalf of the many' (Luke has 'on behalf of you'). It has been common to link the Matthaean and Markan version of this to Isaiah 53; the meaning of the saying must then be more fully determined in the light of the larger picture of Jesus' explanatory words, for which see below.

To this, Matthew has added 'for the forgiveness of sins'.[92] Once again we must stress: in its first-century Jewish context, this denotes, not an abstract transaction between human beings and their god, but the very concrete expectation of Israel, namely that the nation would at last be rescued from the 'exile' which had come about because of her sins.[93] Matthew is not suggesting that Jesus' death will accomplish an abstract atonement, but that it will be the means of rescuing YHWH's people from their exilic plight. These words again make explicit the symbolic meaning of the meal.[94]

3. All three synoptists have a version of a saying in which Jesus insists that this will be his last meal with his disciples before the coming of the kingdom. Matthew and Mark refer to subsequent meals in the kingdom; Luke, simply to this being the last pre-kingdom meal.[95] These sayings, of course, make sense only if we postulate the eschatological and apocalyptic setting of Jesus' work for which we have argued throughout. But, within that, they fit extremely well. Jesus' Passover, like the original one, had a strong note of urgency.

90. The penultimate line clearly refers to the exile, still not undone (so Smith 1984, 259).
91. cf. Moule 1987, 194.
92. Mt. 26.28c; cf. Mt. 1.21.
93. On 'forgiveness' and 'return from exile' see *JVG*, 268-74; cp. Jer. 31.31-4, etc.
94. cf. Meyer 1979, 218f., with other refs.
95. Mt. 26.29/Mk. 14.25/Lk. 22.16 (eating the Passover); 22.18 (drinking wine). Cf. Hengel 1981a, 72f. Jeremias' suggestion that Jesus fasted at the meal, to pray for the coming of the kingdom (1966a [1949], 207-18), has not commended itself to later scholars.

4. Luke and Paul both include a command that the meal be repeated, and that this repetition be undertaken as a way of remembering Jesus himself.[96] As Jeremias has pointed out, this belongs closely with the words used at Passover meals from that day to this, in which prayer is made that God will remember, and send, the Messiah.[97] The command, though quite comprehensible in the setting we have described, again makes explicit what is in any case implicit in the symbolic action of the meal itself. If Jesus was about to perform the great messianic action, and if his last meal with his followers would function in relation to that action as Passover functioned in relation to the exodus from Egypt, then of course the meal would include the prayer that this messianic action would be successfully accomplished; and of course, as the meal was repeated by Jesus' followers, it would be done not with an eye to YHWH sending the Messiah at last - he had already done that - but with an eye to his remembering the messianic act which Jesus had already accomplished. All this, again, makes sense only once one allows that Jesus really did suppose that he was about to die, and that this was part of the eschatological plan for the fulfilment of YHWH's kingdom-purposes. Once that is supposed, however - and the present chapter argues for doing so on good historical grounds - it fits very well. Jesus' symbolic action deliberately evoked the whole exodus tradition and gave it a new direction.

(d) Conclusion

The great majority of scholars agree that Jesus did celebrate a final meal with his followers on the night before his death, and that this took place at least in the context of Passover week. Building on this strong consensus, I have argued that the meal, as an action, already contained such powerful symbolism, and such a strong retelling of one of Israel's most potent stories, that the endless debates about the words which Jesus mayor may not have used at the time ceases to be the central factor in determining the meaning he intended the meal to carry. When we then add the words, even in outline, to the action, there should be no doubt but that Jesus intended to say, with all the power of symbolic drama and narrative, that he was shortly to die, and that his death was to be seen within the context of the larger story of YHWH's redemption of Israel. More specifically, he intended to say that his death was to be seen as the central and climactic moment towards which that story had been moving, and for which the events of the exodus were the crucial and

---

96. Lk. 22.19b (part of the 'longer' text; see *JVG*); 1 Cor. 11.24 (the bread), 25 (the cup).
97. Jeremias 1966a [1949], 237-55, esp. 252, with refs.

determining backdrop; and that those who shared the meal, not only then but subsequently, were the people of the renewed covenant, the people who received 'the forgiveness of sins', that is, the end of exile. Grouped as they were around him, they constituted the true eschatological Israel.[98]

5. The Intention of Jesus (2): The Sayings and the Symbol

(i) Introduction

Jesus' symbolic action in the upper room, like his action in the Temple, must be set within two contexts: the larger picture of his work which we have built up in Part II, and the larger picture of the Jewish world within which that work made sense. And, just as in relation to the Temple we discovered that a good many of Jesus' sayings, clustered around the incident, functioned as riddles which explained the symbol, so we find in this case several sayings which, though cryptic in themselves, collectively point in one particular direction. Finally, as before, the symbolic action, and the riddles which explain it, create a historical context within which other material can settle down and, through coherence with the larger picture, make itself at home.

How does this work out?

In Part II of *JVG* I argued at length that Jesus was announcing the kingship of YHWH as something which was in the process of happening. It was not an idea, a new belief, a different way of regarding one's personal or social existence, only relating tangentially to the time and place of its announcement. It was something which would come to birth within actual history. Jesus' prophetic and symbolic praxis (chapters 5 and 9) constantly pointed in this direction; he told the story of the kingdom (chapters 6-8) as the movement through which Israel's history would reach its long-awaited goal. This all generates the question: what did Jesus think would happen next?

This question, in fact, presses upon any analysis of Jesus and his work.

Those who suppose that Jesus was essentially a teacher of timeless truths (whether political, religious or existential) are bound to ask, sooner or later, whether Jesus supposed his message was being widely accepted, and, if not (as seems to have been the case), what he should do next.[99] How much more must we ask it when we have rejected this model and embraced instead the

---

98. It is thus mistaken to suggest, as does Neusner 1989, 290 (and in several other places), that to see the Last Supper in relation to the Temple-incident suggests that Christianity was founded as a totally different religious tradition to Judaism. Cf. *NTPG* ch. 16.

99. cf. Barrett 1967, 38.

eschatological picture, with Jesus announcing that the great moment had come? What would the moment look like? How would the kingdom come?

Two strong clues emerge from our consideration of the answers Jesus implicitly gave to the worldview questions (chapter 10), and the story which he held out to his followers (chapter 7). From the former, it emerged that Jesus envisaged some sort of a battle; this was part of the messianic agenda, part of what had to be accomplished if the kingdom was to come. But the enemy against whom the battle would be fought would not be the pagan occupying forces. It would be the real enemy that stood behind them; the accuser, the satan, that had duped YHWH's people into themselves taking the pagan route, seeking to bring YHWH's kingdom by force of arms and military revolt. Jesus seems to have understood his own clashes with Israel's actual and self-appointed rulers and guardians of tradition as part of such a battle (chapter 9). If he were to meet these rulers head-on he would therefore be bound to regard such an encounter as the climactic confrontation between his agenda and theirs, his vocation to bring in the kingdom and their determination to keep Israel on the course which he had denounced. The stories which Jesus told, and the symbols he enacted, were not static or timeless indications of a religious or political system; they were events which were designed to lead to the great Event, the real battle with the real enemy.

But how would such a battle be fought? Here the kingdom-story of chapter 7 is enormously revealing. Jesus summoned his followers to a strange kind of revolution - a double revolution, in fact, through which Israel would become the light of the world, the heaven-sent answer to paganism, not through fighting a military battle like Judas Maccabaeus, but through turning the other cheek, going the second mile, loving her enemies and praying for her persecutors. This agenda was a revolutionary way of being revolutionary. It was not counter-revolutionary in the sense that it supported the *status quo;* it could hardly do that without abandoning the whole Isaianic kingdom-theology upon which it was based, in which YHWH revealed himself as the true king, the true God, in opposition to pagan gods and the regimes they support. Jesus held out the true, subversive wisdom, in opposition to the spurious conventional wisdom of his day. At the heart of that subversive wisdom was the call to his followers to take up the cross and follow him, to become his companions in the kingdom-story he was enacting.

My proposal is that Jesus took his own story seriously - so seriously that, having recommended to his followers a particular way of being Israel-for-the-sake-of-the-world, he made that way thematic for his own sense of vocation, his own belief about how the kingdom would come through his own work.[100] He would turn the other cheek; he would go the second mile; he would take up the cross. He would be the light of the world, the salt of the earth. He would be Israel for the sake of the world. He would be the means of the kingdom's coming, both in that he would embody in himself the renewed Israel and in that he would defeat evil once and for all. But the way in which he would defeat evil would be the way consistent with the deeply subversive nature of his own kingdom-announcement. He would defeat evil by letting it do its worst to him. Jesus' Jewish context supplied him, as we shall see presently, with several spheres of meaning in which such a line of thought, and of action, would make sense, albeit startling sense.

The particular sense it makes grows from every aspect of Jesus' kingdom-announcement. We saw at the end of chapter 9 that his action in the upper room functioned as the climax of his reconstruction of Israel's symbolic world. We can now see that this symbolic action gained its meaning from the entire thrust of his work, his retelling of the kingdom-story, and his prophetic praxis. Of course, if we remove Jesus from this context, it is easy to ridicule the suggestion that he believed himself called to defeat evil through his own suffering and death. But, as Schweitzer saw, once we put him back into his own world, the world of Jewish apocalyptic eschatology, such a suggestion makes very good sense in itself, and adds the not inconsiderable historical virtue that it draws together the different aspects of Jesus' work into a tight thematic unity. This reading, I suggest, possesses the very great strengths of getting in the data and doing so with an appropriate economy and elegance.

Once we grasp this, the various riddles which circle around Jesus' awareness of where his work was leading him begin to make sense as well. To these we must now turn.

(ii) The Riddles of the Cross

(a) The Rejected Son

We return once more to the key parable which gives theological depth to Jesus' Temple-action.[101] We have already seen that Jesus saw himself as the (messianic) son, coming as the last in the line of the prophets, coming to Israel on behalf of her god. But the truly disturbing thing about the story is of course that the tenants, in rejecting the son, and hence the message from

---

100. After writing this I came upon similar proposals in Manson 1953, 74-7; Farmer 1956, 201f.

101. Mt. 21.33-46/Mk. 12.1-12/Lk. 20.9-19; cf. *JVG*, esp. 497-501.

his father, kill him, and throw him out of the vineyard.[102] It is this that pre-cipitates the judgment of the vineyard-owner upon his wicked tenants.

As with so much of this material, it is open to anyone to object that the parable has been written up *ex post facto,* and that Jesus could not have told a story about himself, even cryptically, which ended this way. I reply (1) that this begs the question; (2) that the story fits so well with so many strands of Jesus' work and prophetic self-understanding that it is hardly straining historical credibility to ascribe it to him; (3) that the death of the son is not an addition, bolted on to the story from the outside, but belongs at its very climax; (4) that what may be the earliest version, that of Mark, does not have the son being first cast out of the vineyard and then killed (as Matthew does, reflecting perhaps later Christian awareness of Jesus being taken out of the city and then crucified[103]), but rather the reverse, which can hardly be regarded as a Christian retrojection; and (5) that the parable is remarkably free of any later Christian atonement-theology, focusing instead on the close connection between the death of the son and the destruction of the vineyard. I conclude that the prophetic narrative symbolism of this parable belongs to Jesus' awareness that his challenge to the Temple would result in his own death, as the guardians of Israel's traditions refused to respond to the mes-sage which he (of course) believed was from YHWH himself.

(b) The Great Commandment

A different viewpoint on the same symbols is provided by the little discus-sion as to which commandment is the greatest.[104] In its Markan context, this story is not about the relative value of different halakhic codes, though it is conceivable that that is how Matthew took it.[105] Mark continues the story with the scribe's reaction to Jesus' stress on the love of YHWH and of one's neighbour: yes, he says, these commands count for more than all burnt-offerings and sacrifices. Jesus, seeing that he answers shrewdly, replies in return: 'You are not far from the kingdom of god.'[106] This unusually warm commendation of a scribal interlocutor, not the sort of thing one expects to have been invented by the early church, points in the same direction as the other hints we have already examined. Jesus' kingdom-agenda, with the love of YHWH and of neighbour at its heart, suggested that the sacrificial system

---

102. Mt. 21.39/Mk. 12.8/Lk. 20.15.
103. cf. Heb. 13.12f.; Rev. 14.20; cpo Ac. 7.58.
104. Mt. 22.34-40/Mk. 12.28-34. Cf. the similar question and answer in Lk. 10.25-8.
105. cp, Mt. 22.40 (the end of the story in Mt.) with Mt. 5.17f.; 7.12.
106. Mk. 12.32-4.

was to be made redundant. This both confirms the meaning of the Temple-action and hints at the meaning of the supper-action. The one was an act of judgment; the other, a pointer towards the Temple's replacement.

(c) Anointing for Burial

All four canonical gospels record the action of a woman in anointing Jesus.[107] Matthew, Mark and John place the incident in the last few days of Jesus' life, Luke much earlier; Matthew and Mark have the woman anoint Jesus' head, Luke and John his feet. The action causes complaint, from the disciples (Matthew), the bystanders (Mark), the Pharisee whose guest Jesus was (Luke), and Judas Iscariot (John). In Matthew, Mark and John Jesus' response to the criticism (we must remember that a good many of his sayings respond to criticism either of himself or his followers; in other words, that the sayings belong with symbolic actions) includes the suggestion that what has been done has been a preparation for his burial.[108] Other overtones may also be present: a hint of a messianic anointing, perhaps,[109] or even the suggestion that the anointing is necessary at this stage because, since Jesus is to die a criminal's death, he may not receive proper anointing later.[110] The saying, though startling in its setting, does not provide the main thrust of the story by itself (which may also indicate its historicity); it is, however, a way of investing the woman's action with such great symbolic value that Jesus adds (in Matthew and Mark) the assurance that wherever the gospel is preached in all the world, what the woman has done will be told as a memorial to her. By itself, this incident, and the saying of Jesus embedded in it, hardly amounts to more than a strange hint. In the context of the symbolic actions in the Temple and the upper room, however, it functions as a further riddle, pointing towards Jesus' awareness of what lay ahead. His own death would somehow initiate a worldwide announcement of the 'good news'.

(d) The Green Tree and the Dry

One of the strangest, and yet ultimately most revealing, of these riddles is a passage peculiar to Luke:

---

107. Mt. 26.6-13/Mk. 14.3-9/Lk. 7.36-50/Jn. 12.1-8.

108. Mt. 26. 12/Mk. 14.8/Jn. 12.7. The text of the Jn. passage is awkward: lit. 'Let her alone, so that she may keep it for the day of my burial'; among other suggestions, NRSV supplies 'she bought it' before 'so that'. See the discussion in e.g. Barrett 1978 [1955], 413f.

109. So e.g. Manson 1953, 84f.

110. So Jeremias 1971, 284 (cf. his 1966b [1936],107-15).

A great crowd of the people followed him, including some women who were weeping and mourning for him. Jesus turned to them, and said, 'Daughters of Jerusalem, don't weep for me; weep for yourselves and for your children. For behold, the days will come in which people will say, "Blessed are the barren, the wombs that never bore, and the breasts that never gave suck." Then they will begin to say to the mountains, "Fall on us," and to the hills, "Cover us." For if they do this when the wood is green, what will they do when it is dry?'[111]

What could occasion a terrible beatitude such as this, overturning the normal first-century cultural assumption that barrenness was a woman's greatest curse? The answer, in the light of chapter 8 *JVG*, must be that Jesus was warning, one last time, of what would happen as a result of Jerusalem rejecting 'the things that make for peace'.[112] She had chosen the way of revolution, of confrontation with Rome; the youngsters playing in the streets in Jesus' day would become the firebrands of the next generation, and would suffer the terrible consequences. The mothers should save their tears for when they would really be needed.

How does the quotation from Hosea 10.8 ('they will say to the mountains, "Fall on us"', etc.) fit in to this?[113] The entire context of the original passage, though normally ignored, is most instructive:

> Israel is a luxuriant vine
>   that yields its fruit.
> The more his fruit increased
>   the more altars he built;
> as his country improved,
>   he improved his pillars.
> Their heart is false;
>   now they must bear their guilt.
> YHWH will break down their altars,
>   and destroy their pillars.
> For now they will say: 'We have no king,
>   for we do not fear YHWH,
> and a king - what could he do for us?'
> . . . The high places of Aven, the sin of Israel,
>   shall be destroyed.
> Thorn and thistle shall grow up
>   on their altars.
> They shall say to the mountains, Cover us,

---

111. Lk. 23.27-31. The version in *Thom.* 79 has subtly but decisively altered the emphasis, so that it suggests the voluntary renunciation of conception (so, rightly, e.g. Fitzmyer 1985, 1494; but cf. Soards 1987; Brown 1994, 924). For a full recent discussion of the passage cf. esp. Brown 1994, 920-7.

112. cf. Lk. 19.42.

113. The quotation has reversed the two verbs. The verse is also quoted in Rev. 6.16. For the idea cf. Isa. 2.19.

and to the hills, Fall on us.
. . . I will come against the wayward people to punish them;
  and nations shall be gathered against them
  when they are punished for their double iniquity
. . . You have plowed wickedness,
  you have reaped injustice,
  you have eaten the fruit of lies.
Because you have trusted in your power
  and in the multitude of your warriors,
therefore the tumult of war shall rise against your people
  and all your fortresses shall be destroyed,
as Shalman destroyed Beth-arbel on the day of battle
  when mothers were dashed in pieces with their children.
Thus it shall be done to you, O Bethel,
  because of your great wickedness.
At dawn the king of Israel
  shall be utterly cut off.[114]

It is all there: the vine that has become proud and gone to ruin, the judgment on the sanctuary, the rejection of YHWH and of the king, the terrible judgment which will result from trusting in military power, the dire warning to the mothers and their children - and, finally, the death of the king. The application to Jesus' contemporaries fits at every point with the picture we have drawn overall. The judgment of which Jesus was warning the women of Jerusalem was the devastation which would result from the city's rejection of him as the true king, and his message as the true way of peace. His own death at the hands of Rome was the clearest sign of the fate in store for the nation that had rejected him.

With this, we can understand the final cryptic saying. Jesus had announced the divine judgment on Jerusalem, for her failure to repent, for her persistence in militant nationalism. This was not simply a matter of the Jewish leaders judging him, and so pulling down upon their own heads a more severe judgment in turn.[115] It was a matter of the Romans condemning Jesus on a charge of which he was innocent and his compatriots guilty. He was the green tree, they the dry.[116]

114. Hos. 10.1-3, 8, 10, 13-15.
115. Brown 1994, 926f. (cf. too Fitzmyer 1985, 1498); this seems peculiar, since it makes the Jewish leaders first the subject, and then the object, of violence, spoiling the saying's parallelism. Johnson 1991, 373f. suggests that the Jewish leaders are the violent ones in both halves of the sentence; but Jesus is dying on a Roman charge and a Roman cross.
116. For the idea of wet and dry being destroyed together cf. Dt. 29.19; Ezek. 20.47 [MT 21.3]. Various rabbinic uses of the same imagery are collected in SB 2.263f. Leaney 1966 [1958], 283f. suggests that 'the times of the Gentiles' are compared to a tree, at present young and 'green', in the future mature and 'dry'; Evans 1990, 863f. proposes an allusion to the Tammuz-cult. The clearest statement of the view I regard as correct is in Caird 1963, 249f.; this is strongly supported by e.g. Lk. 11.49f.; 13.34f. (see below); 19.41-4; 21.20-4, where in each case the devastation of Jerusalem is to be at the hands of the Romans.

The saying does not carry any sort of atonement-theology such as characterized the church's understanding of Jesus' death from very early on. Indeed,
it holds out no hope of rescue, only the warning that what is happening to
Jesus is a foretaste of what will happen to many more young Jews in the not
too distant future. It belongs, not with even the earliest post-Easter reflection
on Jesus' crucifixion, but exactly where Luke places it. Its value in our current quest is therefore simple and powerful. It suggests, in its dark riddling
way, that Jesus understood his death as being organically linked with the fate
of the nation. He was dying as the rejected king, who had offered the way of
peace which the city had rejected; as the representative king, taking Israel's
suffering upon himself, though not here even with any hint that Israel would
thereby escape. The riddle belongs with the messianic riddles we studied
in the previous chapter, yet goes beyond them to point out the fate which
the true Messiah would suffer. Having announced the divine judgment upon
Temple and nation alike, a judgment which would take the form of awful
devastation at the hands of the pagan forces, Jesus was now going ahead of
the nation, to undergo the punishment which, above all, symbolized the judgment of Rome on her rebel subjects. If they did this to the one revolutionary
who was not advocating rebellion against Rome, what would they do to those
who were, and those who followed them?

(e) The Hen and the Chickens

A similar riddle, which again can only be fully understood when heard in
relation to Jesus' central symbolic actions, is found in two different contexts
in Matthew and Luke:

> Jerusalem, Jerusalem, that kills the prophets and stones those sent to her; how often
> would I have gathered your children, as a hen gathers her chickens under her wings,
> and you would not. Behold, your house has been abandoned. I tell you, you will not
> see me until you say, 'Blessed in the name of the Lord is the one who comes.'[117]

There are three elements to this saying. The first belongs closely with the
previous riddle; the second and third integrate this with the wider picture we
have been studying, not least with some aspects of the messianic riddles we
examined in chapter 11 of *JVG*.

First, the image of the hen and the chickens envisages a farmyard fire, in
which the hen gathers her brood under her wings for safety. When the fire is

---

117. Mt. 23.37-9/Lk. 13.34-5, with only minimal differences. Note that 'Blessed is the one
who comes' (Heb. *baruch ha-ba)* is the normal way of saying 'welcome', so that the final phrase
means 'welcome in the name of the Lord'; cf. Jeremias 1966a [1949], 260 n.62. Cp. LXX Ps. 128
[129].8; Sir. 45.15; Gen. 27.7.

over, she may have been scorched to death, but the chickens will be alive, protected under her wings. The picture is familiar in the Hebrew Bible, where it regularly suggests the children of Israel taking shelter under YHWH's wings.[118] This image indicates again that Jesus believed he would suffer the fate that was hanging over Jerusalem; indeed, that he desired to take it upon himself so that she might avoid it. To that extent, it goes beyond the picture of the green tree and dry, suggesting that there had at least been a chance that Jesus might, like Elijah in Ben-Sirach, turn away the divine wrath from Israel.[119] The riddle indicates clearly enough that the chance had come and gone; Jesus' fate and that of Jerusalem remain indissolubly locked together.

The second element brings together Jesus' despair at Israel's failure to seek and find the proffered shelter and the theme of judgment on the Temple in particular. The house has been abandoned. YHWH has left the Temple unprotected, open to enemy devastation. Again the image is familiar and biblical.[120]

The third element, quoting from Psalm 118.26, refers to the welcome offered to pilgrims on their way into Jerusalem. The psalm-verse occurs, of course, just after the passage about the stone which the builders rejected, and which has become the head of the corner[121]—which itself was used in the parable of the wicked tenants as part of the explanation of Jesus' action, coming at the end of the line of rejected prophets. The passages belong closely together and should be seen as mutually interpretative.

Putting the diverse elements together, we may suggest the following meaning. (1) Jesus envisaged himself as the true Temple-builder, coming on no ordinary pilgrimage to Jerusalem. (2) The present Temple, abandoned by YHWH, was under threat of destruction, having refused his message of peace, and his offer of a way of escape. (3) The only hope was to acknowledge him as the true pilgrim, and to welcome him, so that the stone rejected by the builders might indeed become the head of the corner.[122] The riddle

118. Dt. 32.11; Ru. 2.12; Pss. 17.8; 36.7; 57.1; 63.7; 91.4; Isa. 31.5.
119. Sir. 48.10.
120. cf. e.g. Jer. 12.7; 22.5; Isa. 64.10f.; Ps. 69.25; 1 Kgs. 9.7-8; Tob. 14.4; and of course Ezek. 8.6; 9.3; 10.1-22; 11.22-3. Fitzmyer 1985,1037; Johnson 1991,219 suggest that one might also understand 'house' as referring to the people; Nolland 1993, 742 suggests it should include the city as a whole. These may also be implied, but the Temple-theme in Jesus' riddles about his own messianic vocation (in addition to the regular implication of 'house') is so strong that the Temple itself is the much more natural referent. Sanders (1993, 259) points out that in Mt. 23.21 Jesus refers to YHWH as living in the Temple (not that Sanders thinks much of Mt. 23 is original to Jesus); if this is original, it may indicate Jesus' affirmation of the basic Jewish tradition, which is then followed in *v*. 38 by its prophetic subversion.
121. i.e. Ps. 118.22f.
122. According to Allison 1983, the saying is actually an oracle of hope: this is what Israel must do if she is to be saved. That element may be present, but is heavily modified by the

thus belongs closely with the messianic riddles we studied in the previous chapter, adding to them the powerful note that this Messiah understood his vocation to include rescuing Jerusalem from the coming devastation by taking it upon himself. She was bent upon refusing, but the offer remained open. Ironically, of course, the crowds in Jerusalem welcomed him (as one might have expected) with Psalm 118.26; but by then it was apparently too late.[123]

(f) The Baptism and the Cup

Working backwards through the synoptic tradition of riddles that explain Jesus' symbolic actions, we reach the strange saying about the fate that awaited Jesus, which he saw as a matter of vacation:

> I came to cast fire upon the earth, and how I wish it were already kindled! I have a baptism to be baptized with, and how I am constrained until it is accomplished![124]

> Can you drink the cup that I drink, or be baptized with the baptism with which I am to be baptized? . . . The cup that I drink you will drink, and you will be baptized with the baptism with which I am baptized, but to sit at my right or at my left is not mine to grant, but is for those for whom it has been prepared.[125]

By themselves, these are necessarily cryptic. In the context we have uncovered, they point unmistakably in one direction. Jesus was aware of a vocation, as part of his messianic work, to bring the battle for the kingdom to its head in an event which could be fully described only in metaphor. The first metaphor here, that of baptism, seems to envisage that Jesus' public career would end in the way it began: not now, though, with an initiation into the renewed people of Israel, but with something else for which that could stand as an appropriate sign and symbol. If John's baptism evoked the exodus; and if Jesus' central and final symbolic act, pointing to his own fate, was a further evocation of the exodus; then it is not unreasonable to see this cryptic reference to a 'baptism' still to be undergone as an allusion to the fate which he would have to suffer, and as investing that fate with exodus-significance.[126] Other uses of 'baptism' and its cognates in the metaphorical

---

preceding 'but you would not'.

123. Mt. 21.9/Mk. 11.10/Lk. 19.38/Jn. 12.13. On the crowds' reactions to Jesus cf. Farmer 1956, 198-201.

124. Lk. 12.49-50. Cf. Hengel 1981a, 71; 'What later community could have had any interest in subsequently constructing such an obscure, indeed questionable, saying as [this]?'

125. Mk. 10.38-40; the Mt. par. (20.22-3) omits the ref. to baptism.

126. cf. Dunn 1970, 42; cf. Zahl 1983, 328: 'by describing his own mission in terms of judgment, a baptism of catastrophe, Jesus proposed that the judgment fall on him'.

sense of undergoing suffering suggest that this allusion is on target.[127]

The same is true, *mutatis mutandis,* of the 'cup', which occurs again in the Gethsemane narrative.[128] This image is more frequent; and 'drinking the same cup' clearly means 'sharing the same fate'.[129] The cup can denote suffering, even martyrdom,[130] though the context can indicate that it can also be a cup of blessing.[131] Here the context indicates a warning for Jesus' followers, and a strange vocation for himself, to take upon himself the suffering predicted for the people.

As we cautiously allow the riddles to interpret one another, a picture grows up around the central action in the upper room. Jesus knew, somehow, that he was to suffer and die. He interpreted that event through a series of images by which he was saying, not only that this was his god-given lot, but that this was part of the vocation in which his work and Israel's fate were bound up together. We shall explore this further presently.

(g) Riddles and Authenticity

When we examined the messianic riddles which Jesus told in the aftermath of his Temple-action, I argued that their very form was a strong indication of their originality to Jesus himself. The early church was not reticent, or inclined to tell riddles, about his Messiahship; the only place such riddles belong is in Jesus' ministry itself. Something very similar can be said about the riddles that point towards the meaning of Jesus' death.

The early church was not reticent in speaking about Jesus' death, and in developing a rich and multifaceted interpretation of it. The first Christians had no need to speak of it in riddles. The cross was public knowledge, and, though it might be a scandal, it was a nettle that was grasped, not a strange fact that could be alluded to only with cryptic sayings. Putting this the other way around, the riddles are remarkably free of even the beginnings of that early atonement-theology which we see, for instance, so clearly in Paul. Indeed, some of them speak simply of approaching tragic death, without any sense of a redemption thereby achieved. They do not seem to be later history

127. The biblical use of flood-imagery for chaos or disaster is well known: e.g. Gen. 6–9; 2 Sam. 22.5; Ps, 69.1-2; 93.3; 124.4-5. For baptism-imagery in relation to suffering cf. e.g. Jos. *War* 4.137; cf. too Ps. 68.3; Job 9.31 in the Aquila version. For further refs. cf. e.g. Delling 1957. On the response to James and John cf. Muddiman 1987.

128. Mt. 26.39/Mk. 14.36/Lk. 22.42. Cf. Barrett 1967, 46-9.

129. See the passages cited in SB 1.836-8.

130. As in *Mt. Isa.* 5.13: 'for me alone the LORD has mixed the cup'. The biblical background for the cup of YHWH's wrath includes e.g. Isa. 51.17, 22, 23 (cf. Job 21.20; Ps. 60.3; Obad. 16); Jer. 25.15-17, 28; 49.12; 51.7; Lam. 4.21; Zech. 12.2.

131. e.g, Ps. 23.5; 116.13.

turned into prophecy: the prediction that James and John would suffer the same fate as Jesus was, so far as we know, only partially accurate.[132] If the story of the two brothers was made up to reflect positions held in the early church, it is very odd that Peter is not mentioned.[133] Nevertheless, though the sayings do not reflect anything that we know of early Christian atonement-theology, we can see how sayings such as these, surrounding Jesus' central symbolic actions, could have been part of the matrix from which that theology developed. They are thus both appropriately dissimilar, and appropriately similar, to the life of the early church.

The same is true (we shall explore this further presently) in relation to the Jewish context of Jesus' work. The riddles we have studied contain numerous links back, in particular, to the world of classical prophecy. But their particular form and direction is unique; we have no other examples of prophets applying to themselves anything like this combination of motifs. These riddles, once more, belong where we find them, namely, on Jesus' own lips. They functioned as cryptic but telling pointers to the event for which the main signpost was the Last Supper. Jesus' own death - the death of the strange non-messianic Messiah - was somehow bound up both with the fate of the whole nation and with the coming of the new exodus in which YHWH would at last establish his kingdom.

(iii) Predictions of the Passion

Working back further from the symbolic act of the Last Supper, and the short riddles which offer little flashes of interpretative insight into why Jesus did what he did on that occasion, we discover a context in which we can at last tackle the more substantial sayings on the subject which the synoptic tradition offers. By themselves, of course, these 'predictions of the passion' are regularly dismissed as *vaticinia ex eventu,* 'prophecies' after the event, reflecting early Christian apologetics and atonement-theology rather than anything characteristic of the mind of Jesus. Approaching them the way we have done offers a new route into Jesus' mindset, and to understanding how, from his point of view, his own death might actually function as part of the means of bringing in the kingdom.

The texts are well known:

---

132. James was killed by Herod Agrippa I (Ac. 12.2). John's fate is unknown (cf. Taylor 1952, 442, on the relevant Papias traditions) - even if, as Gundry 1993, 584 assumes without argument, he is the person referred to in Rev. 1.9.

133. So Sanders 1985, 147.

He began to teach them that the son of man must suffer many things, be rejected by the elders, the chief priests and the scribes, and be killed, and after three days be raised.[134]

How then is it written of the son of man, that he should suffer many things and be treated with contempt?[135]

He was teaching the disciples that the son of man will be given into the hands of men, and they will kill him, and that he will rise again three days after his death.[136]

Taking the twelve, he began to tell them what was to happen to him: 'Look, we are going up to Jerusalem; the son of man will be handed over to the chief priests and the scribes, who will condemn him to death, and hand him over to the Gentiles. They will scourge him, spit at him, flog him, and kill him; and after three days he will rise again.[137]

The son of man came not to be served but to serve, and to give his life as a ransom for many.[138]

You will all fall away because of me this night; for it is written, I will strike the shepherd, and the sheep will be scattered.[139]

For I tell you, this thing that is written must be fulfilled in me: 'And he was numbered among the lawless.' For that which concerns me has its fulfilment.[140]

The hour is at hand, and the son of man is betrayed into the hands of sinners.[141]

All this [Jesus' arrest] has taken place so that the scriptures might be fulfilled.[142]

There are other hints, too: the prophet cannot die except in Jerusalem (but presumably will when he gets there); the bridegroom will be taken away; there will be a time when the disciples will fend for themselves in Jesus' absence.[143] All in all, it is an impressive catalogue.

A great deal depends, of course, on what one deems to be possible, or thinkable, for Jesus himself. There is no problem about the language used here being available to him; no problem about showing that these sayings are very unlike both what we find in the Judaism of the time and what we find in

134. Mt. 16.21/Mk. 8.31/Lk. 9.22. Mt. adds 'must go to Jerusalem'.
135. Mk. 9.12.
136. Mt. 17.22f./Mk. 9.31/Lk. 9.44 (with variations).
137. Mt. 20.17-19/Mk. 10.32-4/Lk. 18.31-3.
138. Mt. 20.28/Mk. 10.45.
139. Mt. 26.31/Mk. 14.27, quoting Zech. 13.7.
140. Lk. 22.37.
141. Mt. 26.45/Mk. 14.41; cf. Lk. 22.22.
142. Mt. 26.56 (cf. 54)/Mk. 14.49. Goppelt 1981 [1975], 189 professes himself at a loss to know how Conzelmann 1969, 133 can dismiss these sayings so summarily as unhistorical.
143. Prophet: Lk. 13.33; bridegroom: Mt. 9.15/Mk. 2.20/Lk. 5.35; cf. *Thom.* 104; fending for themselves: Lk. 17.22; Mt. 24.9-14/Mk. 13.9-13/Lk. 21.12-19.

the atonement-theology of the early church. The real problem comes when we try to assess whether Jesus could or would have held such ideas in his head; in deciding, that is, the shape of his mindset.

I have already argued that Jesus saw himself as the focal point of Israel's long and tortuous story (and that this was not a particularly unusual thing for persons, under certain circumstances, to think at that time).

I have also argued that Jesus acted symbolically, and retold Israel's story, in such a way as to suggest strongly that he believed that this story would reach its climax in the great battle through which evil would be defeated and the people of YHWH rescued once and for all. The riddles we have just studied, in this light, point to a vocation of a particular shape, within which these predictions fit like a glove. The 'son of man' - the representative of the people of the saints of the most high - would find the beasts waging war upon him; but he would be vindicated. In order to study this further, and to get to the inside of the sayings, we must make a detour. We have got to the point where we must ask: what resources were available to Jesus for reflecting on how the kingdom might come through the suffering and death of Israel's representative?

6. The Intention of Jesus (3): Eschatological Redemption in Judaism

(i) Introduction

To answer this question, we return again to the variegated context of second-Temple Judaism. We proceed down two lines, namely story and symbol, aware of the praxis generated and sustained by these, and of the implicit answers offered as a result to key worldview questions, especially in this case: 'what's the solution?'

(ii) The Controlling Story: Exile and Restoration

We may begin on ground already well prepared. The overarching category within which first-century Jewish reflection could handle the whole question of present suffering and future vindication, of present woe and future redemption, and of the means by which YHWH might bring his people from the one to the other, was that of exile ('the present evil age') and restoration ('the age to come'). I use these terms, of course, as a shorthand; there are, no doubt, different ways of saying the same thing; but once again I must stress: for the bulk of first-century Judaism, the exile was simply not yet over. The promises of Isaiah and the rest had not been fulfilled. As long as Pilate and

Herod - and, for that matter, Caiaphas - were ruling, the kingdom had not yet come. Pagan oppression was the sign of the present evil age; the age to come would bring freedom and peace, when YHWH vindicated his people after their long period of suffering.

Once again, too, we must stress: return from exile, in this period, *meant* 'forgiveness of sins', and vice versa. 'The punishment of your iniquity, O daughter Zion, is accomplished; he will keep you in exile no longer.'[144] As long as Israel was still suffering under foreign rule, the 'sins' that had caused the exile had not been 'forgiven'. Forgiveness was concrete, as it would be for someone in prison: a 'pardon' that did not result in actual release would be no pardon at all. Psalms and prophets alike looked forward to the day when the promises would be fulfilled, when sins would be forgiven, and YHWH would have dealt once and for all with the evil that still oppressed his people.

In particular, the historical and theological theme that dominated the horizon of those longing for the real return from exile was of course the exodus. Celebrated every year at Passover, the exodus created the classic Jewish metanarrative, within which the hope for return from exile made sense, and in terms of which that return was described in some of the classic prophetic texts.[145] It is hard to overestimate the importance of the exodus-story within the historical, political and theological worldview of second-Temple Judaism; and, again and again, that story resonated in a world where most Jews were hoping and praying that it would come true once more, this time for good. That, as we have seen, was the world which Jesus deliberately set out to evoke in his last great prophetic and symbolic action. If we begin here, we are as likely as we shall ever be to track and trace the mindset of Jesus.

(iii) The First Sub-Plot: The Messianic Woes

As we saw in *NTPG,* some second-Temple Jews believed that the great deliverance would come through a period of intense suffering.[146] This functions as a story within the larger story: the time of suffering would be the means through which the apocalyptic drama would attain its goal. Though the theme is not ubiquitous in second-Temple Judaism, it occurs often enough (not least in Qumran, which offers a range of analogies with Jesus

---

144. Lam. 4.22, summarizing in effect the whole line of thought in Isa. 40-55 (cf. *JVG*, 268-74).

145. e.g. Isa. 51.9-11.

146. *NTPG* 277f., citing primary and secondary sources; in addition. cf. *Ass. Mos.* 9.1-10.10; 1 *En.* 47.1-4. Cf. too the (later) Sifre Dt. 333 on Dt. 32.43.

and his movement) for us to be able to postulate it with some confidence.

To grasp the significance of this sub-plot within the larger story of new exodus, of exile and restoration, we may return for a moment to Albert Schweitzer. Schweitzer saw the second-Temple expectation of the 'messianic woes' as the vital clue to Jesus' understanding, both of the moment in history at which he was living, and of his own vocation in relation to that moment. For him, the central idea was that of the *peirasmos,* the Testing:

> In order to understand Jesus' resolve to suffer, we must first recognize that the mystery of this suffering is involved in the mystery of the kingdom of god, since the kingdom cannot come until the *peirasmos* has taken place . . . The novelty lies in the form in which [the sufferings) are conceived. The tribulation, so far as Jesus is concerned, is now connected with an historic event: He will go to Jerusalem, there to suffer death at the hands of the authorities . . . In the secret of His passion which Jesus reveals to the disciples at Caesarea Philippi the pre-Messianic tribulation is for others set aside, abolished, concentrated upon Himself alone, and that in the form that they are fulfilled in His own passion and death at Jerusalem. That was the new conviction that had dawned upon Him. He must suffer for others . . . that the Kingdom might come.[147]

This idea, like a good deal that Schweitzer proposed, flew in the face of the theological sensibilities of the early twentieth century, and has for that reason not been much used, or even discussed, in subsequent research. Yet I am persuaded that, with certain important modifications (necessary not least because of our improved knowledge of Jewish apocalyptic), there is a core of historical insight here which should not be lost.

A comment on the likely reaction to such a proposal may be in order. It would of course be extraordinary to think of a cautious western scholar deliberately acting in obedience to a scheme of thought which provided, as it were, the script for a play to be enacted. (Actually, reflecting on the way in which some scholars plan their careers, it may not be so extraordinary as all that.) Western scholars, after all, not only believe in freedom to pursue their research in their own way. They also pride themselves on being detached flies-on-the-wall: observers, not participants. Here, once again, we face the danger of anachronism, imagining Jesus as a great teacher of truths-divorced-from-real-life. Only when we soak ourselves in the history of the time can we escape this imprisonment in our own culture. Schweitzer, I am persuaded, prised the prison door open a crack. I suggest that we push it open further, allowing both history and theology to escape from the clutches of those who have been dominated by anachronism disguised as (apparently sophisticated) scepticism. Only if we follow the first-century evidence where

---

147. Schweitzer 1954 [1906], 385-7 (the whole of 384-90 is significant). See too Schweitzer 1925 [1901], ch. 9, esp. 226-36.

it leads, after all, can we be justified in referring to 'Jesus' at all, whether in history or in theology.

My point at the moment is that, within the range of options available to a reflective Jew of the first century who believed himself to be a participant in the long-awaited drama of the kingdom of YHWH, it made a lot of sense to suppose that the kingdom would finally come through a time of intense suffering. We shall apply this to Jesus presently; for the moment we must fill in the picture with a second sub-plot, which likewise functions within the overarching metanarrative of the new exodus, the great return from exile, and which brings the concept of the messianic woes to a sharp point.

(iv) The Second Sub-Plot: Specific or Individual Suffering

The belief in the likelihood, or even the necessity, of suffering as part of the way in which the plan of YHWH would be brought to birth did not remain at a general level in the literature of this period. We can detect several categories of persons for whom specific suffering at the hands of the wicked, or the pagans, might be expected. Such suffering could be interpreted within the eschatological framework we have outlined. It was not arbitrary or random, but formed one sharp edge of the general sufferings of Israel. Within this, there are hints that such suffering *could* be seen, in some sense and in some cases, as part of the means whereby the coming liberation would be accomplished.

One of the most obvious categories of suffering individuals within Israel is that of prophets. The most obvious evidence for this is in the New Testament, where the idea has become proverbial,[148] but it has its roots in the biblical tradition,[149] and is reflected in books such as the *Martyrdom of Isaiah*. In Jesus' own day and experience, of course, the greatest of recent prophets was John the Baptist, and his fate must have weighed heavily upon the mind of the one who looked to him as forerunner.[150] The fearless prophet, opposed and perhaps killed by the Jewish authorities to whom he had spoken the word of YHWH, was a model which can never have been far from the self-understanding of the prophet from Nazareth.

---

148. cf. e.g. Mt. 5.11-12/Lk. 6.22-3; Mt. 23.29-36/Lk. 11.47-51; Mt. 23.37/Lk. 13.34 (cf. 13.33); Ac. 7.52; and, of course, the prophets in the parable of the wicked tenants. Cf. Jeremias 1971, 281; de Jonge 1991a, 34-7.

149. e.g, 2 Chr. 36.15f.; Neh. 9.26; Jer. 2.30; and, for the idea that the prophets (especially true prophets) were always rejected, cf. 1 Kgs. 19.10; 22.8; Ezra 9.10f.; Jer. 26.1-24; Zech. 1.4-6; 7.7-14. Cf. too Ezek. 4.4-6, on which see below.

150. cf, Schillebeeckx 1979 [1974], 299f. Lk. 13.33 ('no prophet can perish away from Jerusalem') is odd; Jesus regarded John as a prophet, yet he did not perish in Jerusalem.

Quite close to this is the important passage early on in the Wisdom of Solomon. Here, the wicked, out of a sense of the futility of their lives, plot to do evil. Specifically, they plan to kill the righteous man who has shown up their evil ways:

> Let us lie in wait for the righteous man,
> because he is inconvenient to us and opposes our actions;
> he reproaches us for sins against the law . . .
> He professes to have knowledge of God,
> and calls himself a child [or 'servant'] of the Lord . . .
> We are considered by him as something base,
> and he avoids our ways as unclean;
> he calls the last end of the righteous happy,
> and boasts that God is his father.
> Let us see if his words are true,
> and let us test what will happen at the end of his life;
> for if the righteous man is God's child, he will help him,
> and will deliver him from the hand of his adversaries.
> Let us test him with insult and torture,
> so that we may find out how gentle he is,
> and make trial of his forbearance.
> Let us condemn him to a shameful death,
> for, according to what he says, he will be protected.[151]

The writer comments, first, that when this happens Israel's god will hold the souls of the righteous in his hand, at peace though out of human sight; then, that at the appointed time he will raise them from the dead, setting them to rule over the world.[152] The ungodly, meanwhile, will be punished as they deserve.[153] This lesson is then applied more widely, with a further description of the fate which the righteous suffer at the hands of the wicked, and a further description of the bliss that awaits the righteous as a result, before being focused again as a warning to the kings of the earth that what they need more than anything else is Wisdom.[154] As has sometimes been pointed out, the language used to describe the fate of the righteous appears to be drawn from the 'suffering servant' passage in Isaiah 52 and 53, while the scene describing the judgment of the wicked is rooted in such passages as Isaiah 14 (the strange figure whose heaven-storming pride leads to downfall) and Psalm 2 (the Davidic king who routs his enemies).[155] There is good reason to suppose that this passage in the Wisdom of Solomon draws on an exegetical tradition which was used independently by 1 *Enoch* and other

151. Wis. 2.12-20.
152. 3.1-6; 3.7-9.
153. 3.10-19.
154. chs, 4-6; on the suffering and vindication of the righteous, 5.4-5; 5.15-16.
155. cf. Nickelsburg 1992,140 (e.g, echoes of Ps. 2.4, 9 in Wis. 4.18-19).

second-Temple writings.[156] The value of the passage for our present purpose is thus that it opens a window on a theme which we may cautiously presume to have been more widely known than just among the readers of a particular book.

This supposition is strongly confirmed by the evidence from Qumran. The sufferings of the Teacher of Righteousness are spoken of quite frequently, as for instance in the commentary on Habakkuk:

> Interpreted, [Habakkuk 1.13b] concerns the House of Absalom and the members of its council, who were silent at the time of the chastisement of the Teacher of Righteousness and gave him no help against the Liar . . .[157]

> The interpretation of [Habakkuk 2.15] concerns the Wicked Priest who pursued the Teacher of Righteousness to consume him with the ferocity of his anger in the place of his banishment, in festival time, during the rest of the day of Atonement . . .[158]

But the whole community will also suffer, and thus find their way towards the eventual salvation:

> Interpreted, [Habakkuk 2.4b] concerns all those who observe the Law in the House of Judah, whom God will deliver from the House of Judgment because of their suffering and because of their faith in the Teacher of Righteousness.[159]

> The sons of light and the lot of darkness shall battle together for God's might, between the roar of a huge multitude and the shout of gods and of men, on the day of calamity. It will be a time of suffering for all the people redeemed by God. Of all their sufferings, none will be like this, from its haste until eternal redemption is fulfilled.[160]

Thus, though it is very unlikely that anyone at Qumran thought in terms of a suffering Messiah, it is clear that there was a wider belief that the sufferings of the sect in general, and of one of its founders in particular, were pointers towards the coming liberation, and perhaps part of the means of its arrival.[161] This could sometimes even be expressed in terms of atonement:

> In the Council of the Community there shall be twelve men and three Priests . . . They shall preserve the faith in the Land with steadfastness and meekness and shall atone

---

156. Nickelsburg 1992, 138-42.

157. 1QpHab 5.10-11 (Vermes 1995 [1962], 342).

158. 1QpHab. 11.4-7 (GM 201).

159. 1QpHab. 8.1-3 (Vermes 1995 [1962], 344). GM 200 translates the key term, however, as 'deeds'.

160. 1QM 1.11-12 (GM 95). Cf. too e.g. 1QH 11 [=3].6-18 (GM 331f.) (quoted in *NTPG* 277 n.136). Of this psalm, Knibb (1987, 174) writes that 'the concern is entirely with the woes that would inaugurate the messianic age'.

161. Collins 1995, 123-6 rightly rejects the idea of a 'suffering Messiah' in 4Q451 fr. 9 & 24 (GM 270); Schiffman 1994, 346f. is right to dismiss the suggestion of a 'pierced Messiah' in 4Q285 fro 5 (GM 124).

for sin by the practice of justice and by suffering the sorrows of affliction . . .[162]

If Qumran offers further suggestions about the way in which innocent or righteous suffering could be understood within a second-Temple Jewish worldview, the same is true, perhaps more obviously, of the stories of the martyrs, particularly from the time of the Maccabees.[163] What matters here is not so much what actually happened as the way in which the stories of martyrdom were written up retrospectively. We must remember, too, that the Maccabees were celebrated in the big annual festival of Hanukkah, causing their story to be widely known; and that some of Jesus' symbolic actions and explanatory riddles seem deliberately to have evoked Maccabaean action.[164] The sufferings of the martyrs are described in 2 Maccabees as having the effect of dealing with the nation's sins in the present time, so that Israel might receive mercy in the future, unlike the other nations whose sins were mounting up until they were finally to be judged.[165] The martyrs therefore went gladly to their suffering and death, believing that they would be raised to new life in the future.[166] Their sufferings, they claimed, would make a way through the present time of wrath to the salvation which lay beyond, while their tormentors were storing up wrath for themselves:

> Our brothers after enduring a brief suffering have drunk of everflowing life, under God's covenant; but you [the Syrian king Antiochus], by the judgment of God, will receive just punishment for your arrogance. I, like my brothers, give up body and life for the laws of our ancestors, appealing to God to show mercy soon to our nation and by trials and plagues to make you confess that he alone is God, and through me and my brothers to bring to an end the wrath of the Almighty that has justly fallen on our whole nation.[167]

Or, again, in a work more or less contemporary with the time of Jesus:

> You know, O God, that though I might have saved myself, I am dying in burning torments for the sake of the law. Be merciful to your people, and let our punishment suffice for them. Make my blood their purification, and take my life in exchange for theirs.[168]

> Imitate me, brothers; do not leave your post in my struggle or renounce our courageous family ties. Fight the sacred and noble battle for religion. Thereby the just

162. 1QS 8.1-4 (Vermes 1995 [1962], 80). For this atoning activity cf. too 1QS 5.6; 9.4; and cp. jYom. 38b; tYom. 5.6ff.

163. On the Macc. passages cf. e.g. Hengel 1981a; de Jonge 1988, 174-84, 208-11; 1991a, 45-8. Droge & Tabor 1992 seems to me slanted to say the least; cf. *NTPG* 364f.

164. cf. Farmer 1956; and ch. II *JVG*.

165. 2 Macc. 6.12-17; cf. 7.18-19 .:

166. 2 Macc. 6.30; 7.9, 11, 14, 16-17, 22-3, 29, 30-8.

167. 2 Macc. 7.36-8.

168. 4 Macc. 6.27-9; cpo 1.11.

Providence of our ancestors may become merciful to our nation and take vengeance on the accursed tyrant.[169]

These, then, who have been consecrated for the sake of God, are honoured, not only with this honour, but also by the fact that because of them our enemies did not rule over our nation, the tyrant was punished, and the homeland purified - they having become, as it were, a ransom for the sin of our nation. And through the blood of those devout ones and their death as an atoning sacrifice, divine Providence preserved Israel that previously had been mistreated.[170]

Those who gave over their bodies in suffering for the sake of religion were not only admired by mortals, but also were deemed worthy to share in a divine inheritance. Because of them the nation gained peace . . .[171]

There are three strands of belief which run through these accounts. First, the fate of the martyrs is bound up with the fate of the nation as a whole. Second, as a result, their suffering forms as it were the focal point of the suffering of the nation, continuing the theme of exile-as-the-punishment-for-sin which we find in the great prophetic writings such as Jeremiah, Ezekiel, Isaiah 40-55 and Daniel, but now giving it more precise focus. Third, this representative exilic suffering functions *redemptively:* not only will the martyrs themselves enjoy subsequent heavenly blessing and/or resurrection life, but their sufferings will have the effect of drawing on to themselves the sufferings of the nation as a whole, *so that the nation may somehow escape.*[172] The fact that all these elements are found together in various different passages suggests that this complex theological (and political) train of thought was already well known by the time 4 Maccabees was written, i.e. most likely in the middle of the first century.[173]

This evidence from popular beliefs about prophets, from the Wisdom of Solomon, from Qumran, from the Maccabaean literature, and elsewhere indicates that we are here in touch with a tradition that was reasonably widespread and well known in the period of the second Temple. According to this tradition, the suffering and perhaps the death of certain Jews could function

---

169. 4 Macc. 9.23-4.

170. 4 Macc. 17.20-2.

171. 4 Macc. 18.3-4.

172. The atoning value of sufferings is a regular theme in various subsequent Jewish writings: e.g. Lev. R. 20.7; Sifre Dt. 333 (on Dt, 32.43); Midr. Pss. 118.18; ef. Moore 1927- 30, 1.546-52; Schechter 1961 [1909], 307-11; Barrett 1959, 11-15; Montefiore & Loewe 1974 [1938], 225-32; Hengel 1981a, 60-1.

173. cf. H. Anderson 1992, 453. Similar ideas occur fleetingly in later rabbinic literature, on which see below. Cf. too *TiBen.* 3.8, which, even in the shorter (Armenian) version, states unequivocally that 'in you will be fulfilled the heavenly prophecy which says that the spotless one will be defiled by lawless men and the sinless one will die for the sake of impious men'. This may, of course, be a Christian interpolation. Cf. Stuhlmacher 1986 [1981], 24, with other refs.; Hengel 1996, 81-3.

within YHWH's plan to redeem his people from pagan oppression: to win for them, in other words, rescue from wrath, forgiveness of sins, and covenant renewal. This by itself, I suggest, would be enough to give us some substantial clues as to the world of thought within which a prophet and would-be Messiah, in the first third of the first century, might find his own vocation being decisively shaped. But where did this tradition come from? The language, and frequent biblical allusions, suggest various sources; and, since what we find in the traditions about Jesus sometimes reflects similar passages, we must look at these in a little more detail.

(v) 'According to the Scriptures'

When is an allusion not an allusion? This question forms a powerful undercurrent in a good deal of New Testament study. The historical question (was Paul, or whoever, alluding to a particular text, and if so why) is often intertwined with literary questions about authorial intention and the like; about these things, as the writer to the Hebrews says, we cannot now speak in detail. It is highly probable that writers in second-Temple Judaism alluded to a good many biblical texts, deliberately conjuring up a world of discourse with a word or phrase. It is also highly probable that readers in the twentieth century, alert for such allusions, will hear at least some where none were intended. It is absolutely certain that modem readers who are alert to this danger, and hence unwilling to allow any allusions beyond more or less direct quotations, will radically misread important texts. There are times when the historian needs reminding that history is an art, not a science.[174]

With this uncomfortable introduction, we can proceed to enquire after the biblical roots of the tradition we have been examining. Working backwards, we come first to the book of Daniel. Whenever the Daniel-traditions reached their present form, it is clear both that they were of critical importance at the time of the Maccabaean crisis and that they were read eagerly during the first century as a charter for the revolutionaries who stood within the same Maccabaean tradition of holy revolt against the rule of paganism.[175] We have seen often enough the ways in which early chapters in Daniel were read in the first century, not least as part of the longing for the kingdom of YHWH to be established in place of the rule of the pagans. It is clear that such stories as the three young men in the fiery furnace, and Daniel himself in the lion's den, would have functioned in the Maccabaean period and thereafter as an

---

174. On the whole question of allusion cf. Hays 1989. Hooker 1959, 62-4, 101f. lays down extremely stringent criteria for what will count as a reference to 'the servant' in the NT. On the historical/literary questions cf. *NTPG* chs. 2-4.

175. cf. Farmer 1956, ch. 6.

encouragement to Jews under persecution to hold fast to their ancestral laws, even if it meant torture or death. In this context, we find again a close alignment between the fate of the nation, not least the Temple itself, and the fate of the martyrs:

> Forces sent by [the pagan king] shall occupy and profane the temple and fortress. They shall abolish the regular burnt offering and set up the abomination that makes desolate. He shall seduce with intrigue those who violate the covenant; but the people who are loyal to their god shall stand firm and take action. The wise among the people shall give understanding to many; for some days, however, they shall fall by sword and flame, and suffer captivity and plunder . . . Some of the wise shall fall, so that they may be refined, purified, and cleansed, until the time of the end . . .[176]

Much of this, clearly, suggests itself as a source for the themes just observed, not least in the Wisdom of Solomon and the Maccabaean stories. Shortly after this passage, the themes are repeated:

> There shall be a time of anguish, such as has never occurred since nations first came into existence. But at that time your people shall be delivered, everyone who is found written in the book. Many of those who sleep in the dust of the earth shall awake, some to everlasting life, and some to shame and everlasting contempt. Those who are wise shall shine like the brightness of the sky, and those who lead many to righteousness, like the stars forever and ever . . . When the shattering of the power of the holy people comes to an end, all these things would be accomplished . . . Many shall be purified, cleansed, and refined, but the wicked shall continue to act wickedly . . .[177]

Nation and martyr, wisdom and wickedness, 'apocalyptic' and covenant: the themes belong together within the same overall pattern. The fate of the Temple and its sacrificial system is closely bound up with the fate of the 'wise' who, as in Wisdom 2-6, are killed but will be vindicated. The 'time of great anguish' will give birth to the time of deliverance and purification.

Daniel, then, is an obvious source for first-century reflection on the way in which the fate of nation and martyr hang together. But where do these ideas in Daniel come from themselves? At one level, the idea of purification belongs with the Levitical code of sacrifices. In Daniel 12, as in 4 Maccabees 17, we are witnessing the transference to the sphere of human suffering of a theology which properly, or at least originally, belongs within the world of Temple and cult:

> Words like 'satisfaction,' 'blood,' 'purification,' 'ransom,' and 'propitiation' clearly recapitulate longstanding OT traditions, e.g. the levitical regulations for the Day of Atonement (Lev 16; 17:11; etc.). . .[178]

176. Dan. 11.31-5.
177. Dan. 12.1-10.
178. H. Anderson 1992, 453.

At another level, the traditions in question exhibit some connections with second-Temple reflection on the *Akedah,* the so-called 'binding' of Isaac (recounted in Genesis 22). It remains debatable whether this tradition was as clearly developed in our period as later. The issue is not urgent for our own question, since there is no suggestion that Jesus referred to this theme.[179]

There is no debate, however, on the place of the Psalter in forming the worldview and expectation of second-Temple Judaism. The Psalms continued throughout the period to be sung in the regular liturgical and praying life of Israel, not least in the Temple itself. Those going to Jerusalem would use the pilgrim psalms, and those worshipping at a festival the festive ones (the *Hallel* at Passover, for instance). In that the Psalter was collected into its present form long after the Davidic monarchy had ceased to function as such, the regular focus on the promise to David and his heirs was a major way in which the hope for a renewed kingdom was kept alive.[180] Within that, the psalms of lament, which form the bulk of Books I and II of the Psalter (i.e. Psalms 1-41, 42-72), speak again and again of the suffering of the people of YHWH, and of their trust in him to vindicate and deliver them. In one notable instance, an explicitly Davidic psalm becomes, half-way through, a psalm of lament (89.1-37, 38-52). Anyone whose spirituality and thinking had been even partially formed by regular use of the Psalms, and whose life was lived out under pagan oppression, would have no difficulty in making connections between the themes of the poems and their own situation.

A book which, as we have already seen, was arguably of great influence on Jesus, and which contained dark hints about the necessary suffering of the people of YHWH, is of course Zechariah, particularly its second part (chapters 9-14).[181] The writer promises the long-awaited arrival of the true king (9.9-10), the renewed covenant and the real return from exile (9.11-12), the violent defeat of Israel's enemies and the rescue of the true people of YHWH (9.13-17). At the moment, however, Israel are like sheep without a shepherd (10.2); they have shepherds, but they are not doing their job, and will be punished (10.3) as part of the divine plan for the return from exile (10.6-12). The prophet is himself instructed to act as a shepherd, but in doing so to symbolize the worthless shepherds who are currently ruling Israel (11.4-17). There will be a great battle between Israel and the nations, in which 'the house of David shall be like God, like the angel of YHWH, at the head' of the inhabitants of Jerusalem (12.1-9; quotation from verse 8). There will be

179. cf. *NTPG* 273f., and e.g. Hengel 1981a, 61-3 (suggesting that the tradition was already known in Jesus' day); Segal 1984.

180. e.g. Pss. 2; 18; 20; 21; 45; 72; 89; 101; 110; 132; 144. Ps. 45 is regarded as messianic, and applied to the Teacher of Righteousness, in 4Q171 4.24-7 (GM 206; Vermes 1995 [19621. 352).

181. On messianic hope in Zech. see recently Collins 1995, 31-4

great mourning for 'one whom they have pierced' (12.10); a 'fountain . . . for the house of David and the inhabitants of Jerusalem, to cleanse them from sin and impurity' (13.1); a judgment upon the prophets of Israel (13.2-6); and judgment, too, on the shepherd of Israel, who will be struck down, and the sheep scattered (13.7). In another reminiscence of Ezekiel, this will have the effect of destroying two-thirds of the people, while the remaining one-third will be purified, to be in truth the people of YHWH (13.8-9). The book concludes with the great drama in which all the nations will be gathered together to fight against Jerusalem, YHWH will win a great victory, becoming king indeed, judging the nations and sanctifying Jerusalem (14.1-21).

From this (to us) often confusing blur of images certain things stand out. The underlying theme of the passage, as of so much Jewish literature of the period, is the establishment of YHWH's kingship, the rescue of Israel from oppression and exile, and the judgment both of the nations and of wicked leaders within Israel herself. These events will focus on Jerusalem and the Temple; not surprisingly, the royal house of David will clearly have a hand in them, with the king riding into Jerusalem (chapter 9) and being like God at the head of the army (chapter 12). Whatever the actual relationship between the two parts of the book, this theme naturally dovetails with the picture of Zerubbabel in Zechariah 1-8.[182] One of the controlling images in the book is that of the sheep and the shepherd; building no doubt on Ezekiel 34, the prophet sees Israel as the flock, and the king as the shepherd, who eventually shares the fate of the people. The passage about the smitten shepherd is quoted, in a strongly messianic context, in one manuscript of the Qumran Damascus Document,[183] 'they shall look on the one whom they have pierced' (12.10) is taken messianically in a later Talmudic text, which may perhaps refer to Bar-Kochba.[184] These provide slender hints of how some Jews may have read the texts in our period.

A somewhat different biblical passage, which bears analogy both with the traditions described in the previous section and with the symbolic acts and riddling prophecies of Jesus, is found in Ezekiel, where the prophet symbolically undergoes the exile of the people:

> And you, O mortal, take a brick and set it before you. On it portray a city, Jerusalem; and put siegeworks against it, and build a siege-wall against it, and cast up a ramp against it; set camps also against it, and plant battering rams against it all around . . . This is a sign for the house of Israel.

---

182. cf. Collins 1995, 29-31. Zerubbabel is the likely referent of the 'Branch' prophecy of Zech. 3.8; 6.11f.
183. CD 19.7-11 (Vermes 1995 [1962], 102; GM 45); cf. Collins 1995, 78-82.
184. bSukk. 52a (cf. SB 2.583f.).

> Then lie on your left side, and place the punishment of the house of Israel upon it; you shall bear their punishment for the number of the days that you lie there. For I assign to you a number of days, three hundred and ninety days, equal to the number of the years of their punishment; and so you shall bear the punishment of the house of Israel. When you have completed these, you shall lie down a second time, but on your right side, and bear the punishment of the house of Judah; forty days I assign you, one day for each year . . .[185]

This, too, carries overtones of the Levitical sacrificial system, where the sacrificial animal is said to 'bear' the iniquities of the people.[186] Once again, there is nothing here that could be called a Christian 'atonement-theology'; only a sense that Ezekiel's vocation, first to portray the destruction of Jerusalem in symbolic fashion, and then to undergo in his own person the fate he had just symbolically enacted for the city, has some striking resemblances to the picture we built up earlier, in which Jesus' symbolic actions in the Temple and the upper room, and the riddles with which he explained those actions, pointed to a similar double effect, through which he would undergo the fate he had announced for the Temple.

More important even than Daniel or Ezekiel, as the biblical context for the stories of suffering and martyrdom in the second-Temple period, is the prophecy of Isaiah; particularly chapters 40-55, and particularly, within that, the figure of the servant. This has been a controversial topic, and we must approach the material with care. There are four main points to be made about pre- or non-Christian Jewish readings of this famous passage.[187]

First, the picture of the 'servant', whether in Isaiah 52.13-53.12 or in the other so-called 'servant songs', was only in very modern times abstracted from the message of Isaiah 40-55 as a whole.[188] If we are to stand any chance of understanding how a first-century Jew might have made sense of these passages, one of our first moves must be to read the surrounding contexts. And there we find, not a detached atonement-theology, but the prophecy which we have referred to a number of times in this volume: that YHWH would comfort and restore his people after their exile, would pour out his wrath upon the pagans who had held them captive, and would return in person to Zion to reign as king. Indeed, one of the passages in which these themes are stated most clearly (along with the opening oracle, 40.1-11), is the

185. Ezek. 4.1-6. Commenting on the two actions (laying siege to the brick, and lying prone), Eichrodt (1970 [1965], 85) remarks that 'if the prophet is a type of Yahweh in his first action, he evidently represents Israel in the second'.

186. cf. e.g. Lev. 10.17; 16.22. It also evokes one of Jesus' warning oracles over Jerusalem (Lk. 19.42-3); cf. Dodd 1968, 76.

187. On this whole topic see now above all Hengel 1996, in many ways superseding, and in some correcting, the very full treatment in Zimmerli & Jeremias 1967 [1957], 677-700.

188. cf. Hengel 1996 for the different ways in which the Qumran Isa. scrolls divide the book.

passage which leads in directly to the fourth servant song, namely 52.7-12 ('How lovely upon the mountains . . .'). Likewise, the chapters (54-55) which come after the fourth song celebrate in no uncertain terms Israel's restoration, the renewal of the covenant, and the forgiveness of the sins which led to exile; and chapter 55 throws open the invitation to all and sundry to come and join in the blessing. We would be quite wrong, in other words, to detach the picture of the 'servant' from this wider prophetic (and 'kingdom-of-god') context.

Second, it is fairly widely recognized that Isaiah 40-55, particularly the picture of the suffering righteous servant, was one of the main influences upon the second-Temple writings we examined a moment ago, and indeed on a good many other subsequent Jewish texts. Certainly the Maccabaean texts bear witness to this.[189] Daniel 11-12, in particular, should be regarded as one of the earliest extant interpreters of the servant-figure in Isaiah: it looks as though he saw the martyrs of his own day as at least a partial fulfilment of Isaiah 53.[190] This is hardly surprising. Whenever second-Temple Jews were struggling to make sense of their continued and harsh suffering, it makes sense to suppose that Isaiah offered a large-scale glorious hope, for return from exile and for the coming of the kingdom. Within that perspective, the present suffering of the righteous could be understood as falling somehow within the long-term purposes of YHWH.

Third, there is some evidence that some Jews at least interpreted the 'servant' figure messianically. The 'Branch' of Zechariah 3.8 is described as 'my servant'; a case can be made out for the messianic passages in Zechariah 12 and 13 making allusion to Isaiah.[191] and it can be argued that the subtleties within the two Isaiah scrolls found at Qumran, and within the LXX

189. cf. Hengel 1996; and e.g. H. Anderson 1992, 453 (for 4 Macc.); Nickelsburg 1992, 140 (for Wis.); etc. Despite (or perhaps because of) Christian use, Isa. 53 possessed some importance for the later rabbis: cf. e.g. bSot. 14a, joining Isa. 53.12 with Ex. 32.32 and applying it to Moses (possibly in response to Christian use, cf. Moore 1927-30, 1.550 with n.254); jShek. 48c, applying it to 'the men of the Great Assembly'; Sifre Num. 25.13, applying it to Phineas. Isa. 53.4 was used in bSanh. 98b (cf. too 98a), to suggest that the Messiah would be a leper (possibly in ironic deprecation of Messianism; so Collins 1995, 135 n.128, following Urbach). According to Origen *C. Cels.* 1.55, the Jews applied the chapter to the Jewish people as a whole. On the whole question cf. the older work of Neubauer & Driver 1876-77, and the standard studies such as e.g. Jeremias 1950; Zimmerli and Jeremias 1967 [1957]; Hooker 1959, chs. 2, 3; Schürer 2.547-9.

190. The allusion from Dan. 12.3 ('those who justify the many') to Isa. 53.11 ('he shall justify the many') - observed by e.g. Montgomery 1927,459, 472f.; Porteous 1965, 171; Lacocque 1979 [1976], 243, 245, 249; Fishbane 1985, 482-99 - is a sign that the whole passage about the suffering righteous ones, from 11.31 to 12.10, may be influenced by Isa. 52.13-53.12. Cf. von Rad's comment (1965 [1960], 315): 'the death of the wise in 11.33, 35, with its purifying effect, is reminiscent of the atoning function of the Isaianic servant.'

191. So Hengel 1996, 54-7: the sheep which go astray in Isa. 53.6 become the scattered flock of Zech. 13.7.

translations, suggest that those responsible in each case were aware of at least the possibility of messianic interpretations of some sort or another.[192] The strange 'son of man' figure in 1 *Enoch* looks as though it may well be a composite put together out of Daniel 7 and Isaiah 53.[193] It is well known that the Isaiah Targum, which some would date as early as the first century, identifies the 'servant' of 52.11 with the Messiah.[194] There is no reason to suppose that a messianic interpretation would have taken a first-century Jew by surprise.[195]

Fourth, although this messianic identification could be made (as a sharpening up and personalizing of the wider reference to the people as a whole), this does not mean that pre-Christian Judaism as a whole, or in any major part, embraced a doctrine of a *suffering* Messiah, still less a dying one. The Isaiah Targum demonstrates this strikingly: having identified the servant as the Messiah, the subsequent passages about suffering are referred to the sanctuary which was polluted because of Israel's sins (53.5), or to the suffering which the Messiah would inflict upon Israel's enemies (53.7, 9, 11), or to the tribulation through which the exiles would pass to salvation when pagan rule over Israel finally ceased (52.14; 53.3-4, 8), or (a variation on the same theme) to the suffering by means of which the true remnant would be refined and purified (53.10). Only at one point is there a different note: in the Targum's reading of 53.12 it seems to be the Messiah who 'delivered his soul unto death'.[196] Indeed, the use of Isaiah 40-55 as a whole, and in its parts, seldom if ever in pre-Christian Judaism includes *all* those elements which later Christian theology brought together (as, for instance, in 1 Peter 2.21-5): servant, Messiah, suffering, *and* vicarious sin-bearing.[197] It is conceivable that we find the idea of sin-bearing, with reference to Isaiah, in some Jewish texts, but this is far harder to prove than messianic meanings.[198] The main emphasis of the text in our period fell on the sufferings involved in Israel's still-continuing exile. Exile was, after all, the setting and referent of

192. cf. Hengel 1996, 63-6 (arguing that the A scroll indicates a *priestly* Messiah); 71-81. The question of whether Isa. 40-55 is used elsewhere in the Scrolls (e.g. 4Q491 =4QM8 fr. 11, 1.8-18 [GM 117f.], discussed by Hengel 1995b, 201-3; 1996, 83-6; 4Q540/541 [GM 269f.], discussed by Hengel 1996, 66-71) remains open for the time being.

193. Nickelsburg 1992, 139 (for 1 *En.* 62-3); Manson 1953, 173-4, and Black 1992 (for *1 En.* 37-71 in general).

194. On the Messiah in Tg. Isa. (and, indeed, the dating of the Tg. in question) cf. Chilton 1982, 86-96; 1984a, 197f.

195. So e.g. Hengel 1981a, 58f., 92f., against e.g, Rese.

196. Or perhaps 'exposed himself to the risk of death'; cf. North 1948, llf., with other refs.

197. Cf. Hooker 1959, 53f., 56-8.

198. Hengel 1996, conclusion: he cites 4Q540/541 as a possibility. This is not exactly a firm or wide base on which to build.

the original prophecy; later Jews, from Daniel's day onwards, would have thought themselves quite justified in reading the passage in relation to their own situation.

What follows from this in terms of the world within which Jesus read the Jewish scriptures, and came to an understanding of his own vocation? There was no such thing as a straightforward pre-Christian Jewish belief in an Isaianic 'servant of YHWH' who, perhaps as Messiah, would suffer and die to make atonement for Israel or for the world. But there was something else, which literally dozens of texts attest: a large-scale and widespread belief, to which Isaiah 40-55 made a substantial contribution, that Israel's present state of suffering was somehow held within the ongoing divine purpose; that in due time this period of woe would come to an end, with divine wrath falling instead on the pagan nations that had oppressed Israel (and perhaps on renegades within Israel herself); that the explanation for the present state of affairs had to do with Israel's own sin, for which either she, or in some cases her righteous representatives, was or were being punished; and that this suffering and punishment would therefore, somehow, hasten the moment when Israel's tribulation would be complete, when she would finally have been purified from her sin so that her exile could be undone at last.[199] There was, in other words, a belief, hammered out not in abstract debate but in and through poverty, exile, torture and martyrdom, that Israel's sufferings might be, not merely a state *from* which she would, in YHWH's good time, be redeemed, but paradoxically, under certain circumstances and in certain senses, part of the means *by* which that redemption would be effected.

(vi) Conclusion: Jesus' Jewish Context

Jesus' world, as we have seen, was structured around rich symbolism and vivid controlling stories. The texts we have just examined offer a set of symbols, and a composite story, within which Jesus' own symbolic act in the Last Supper, and the cryptic and coded riddles and stories with which he explained that act and indeed his whole final journey to Jerusalem, come to life in a fresh way. But I am not arguing that Jesus picked up a package of ideas that was current among Jews of his time and simply applied it to himself. He was challenging existing construals of the tradition, precisely at the point where his contemporaries were expecting a military victory over Israel's enemies;

---

199. cf. Isa. 40.2: 'Cry to her that she has served her term, that her penalty is paid, that she has received from YHWH'S hand double for all her sins'; 54.8: 'In overflowing wrath for a moment I hid my face from you, but with everlasting love I will have compassion on you, says YHWH, your redeemer.'

that was part of the whole point. We must not, however, allow ourselves to be forced on to the horns of the dilemma according to which Jesus is either made to conform to an existing Jewish view or made to 'oppose Judaism' by proposing something totally different. What we find in the gospels, I suggest, is a portrait of Jesus which both reaffirms the deep-rooted Jewish tradition that we have been studying and redefines it around his own vision and vocation of kingdom-bringing. That portrait seems to me, in those terms, very likely to be historically accurate.

There was, then, no such thing as a pre-Christian Jewish version of (what we now think of as) Pauline atonement-theology. There was a variegated and multifaceted story of how the present evil exilic age could be understood, and how indeed it could be brought to an end, through certain persons embodying in themselves the sufferings of Israel. Jesus, therefore, was not offering an abstract atonement theology; he was identifying himself with the sufferings of Israel. We are faced once more with appropriate similarity and dissimilarity. The symbolism and story-telling of Jesus make sense only within this Jewish world, but they play their own strange and unique variation on their dark theme. What Jesus did and said stands out a mile from what early Christianity said about him and his execution, but early Christian atonement-theology is only fully explicable as the post-Easter rethinking of Jesus' essentially pre-Easter understanding. We are back, methodologically, to a position we have been in more than once before. In order to move, as historians, from the Jewish world to the very similar, and yet very different, world of early Christianity, we have to postulate a middle term. The gospels offer us one.

7. The Intention of Jesus (4): The Strange Victory

(i) Introduction

But what precisely does that middle term consist of? How, in other words, can we clarify the mindset of Jesus as he came to terms with his strange vocation? How can we understand his predictions of his own sufferings, within his thoroughly Jewish pre-Easter context?

Let us quickly recapitulate the argument of this chapter so far. Jesus drew his work together in two great symbolic actions, of which the second, the Last Supper, clearly symbolized the new exodus, the renewal of the covenant, and 'the forgiveness of sins', the real return from exile. Around the time of these symbolic actions he told riddles which indicated that he saw his own fate and the fate of the nation as closely interwoven. The destruction hanging over her, and the death that awaited him, were somehow locked together. There are also repeated reports that he spoke quite explicitly (though puzzlingly to his hearers) about his awareness of a vocation to go to Jerusalem and die. Sometimes it seems that this awareness had a scriptural basis. When we place this picture - symbolic action, interpreted through a grid of riddles and stories - within the larger picture of second-Temple Judaism, we find, not an exact fit, but sufficient convergence to suggest the strong possibility of historicity, especially when we reflect on how unlike early Christian atonement-theology the resultant picture turns out to be. Why did Jesus die? Ultimately, because he believed it was his vocation.

I find, therefore, in favour of Schweitzer and against Wrede and his followers; against, too, those like Moule who have taken a cautious middle position.[200] Faced with the choice between consistent scepticism and consistent eschatology, I choose the latter: Jesus constructed his mindset, his variation on the Jewish worldview of his day, on the assumption that he was living in, and putting into operation, the controlling story which the scriptures offered him, which was now reaching its climax. This was not a matter of him plucking from thin air one or two proof-texts which might serve to generate or sustain a few abstract ideas or beliefs. Nor, for that matter, was it a case of him, as an individual, behaving in a manner which we have to designate as 'weird'.[201] It was a matter of his living within the story of YHWH and Israel as it drew towards its goal. Jesus lived in a world where it might well make sense to believe one was called to take upon oneself the fate, the exile, of Israel.

I propose, then, that we can credibly reconstruct a mindset in which a first-century Jew could come to believe that YHWH would act through the suffering of a particular individual in whom Israel's sufferings were focused; that this suffering would carry redemptive significance; *and that this individual would be himself.* And I propose that we can plausibly suggest that this was the mindset of Jesus himself.

This choice of consistent eschatology is far from being arbitrary. It is *not* a matter of choosing 'credulity' over scepticism'.[202] It is a matter of scientific, historical judgment. If you go the route of scepticism, you will neither

---

200. Moule 1977, 109 suggests that, though Jesus did not actually intend to die, he deliberately went to Jerusalem knowing that if he did there what his vocation demanded it might very well cost him his life. Following Schweitzer at this general level does not mean going with him all the way, into (e.g.) the trap spotted by Manson 1953, 78, or the position criticized by Sanders 1985, 327-9.

201. cf. Sanders 1985, 333; see *JVG*, 553. Sanders does in fact recognize a possibility not altogether remote from the one I shall propose.

202. On this spurious set of alternatives, and the importance in all spheres of knowledge of finding the way between them, cf. Polkinghorne 1994, ch. 2, esp. 31.

include the data, nor produce simplicity, nor shed light on other cognate areas of research. Choose eschatology, and you will achieve all three.

(ii) Proposal: Eschatology and the Cross

If, that is, you understand the eschatology. I have argued throughout that Jesus did not expect, or proclaim, the end of the space-time universe. Nor did he take the normal option of the military revolutionary. Nor, I have suggested, did he envisage the rebuilding of the Temple, whether by humans or by supernatural agency. Rather, he announced the end of the present evil age; the real, doubly subversive, revolution; and the reconstruction of the people of YHWH on a basis that would leave no future role for the Temple. The hypothesis I now wish to advance draws these three together into one, I propose that Jesus, consistent with the inner logic of his entire kingdom-praxis, -story and -symbolism, told the second-Temple story of the suffering and exile of the people of YHWH in a new form, and proceeded to act it out, finding himself called, like Ezekiel, symbolically to undergo the fate he had announced, in symbol and word, for Jerusalem as a whole.[203]

The picture can be put together step by step. Jesus believed that Israel's history had arrived at its focal point. More: he believed that Israel's *exile* had arrived at its climax. He believed, as we saw in the previous chapter, that he himself was the bearer of Israel's destiny. He was the Messiah, who would take that destiny on himself and draw it to its focal point. As a prophet, after the manner of Elijah, Jeremiah or Ezekiel, he had solemnly announced that Israel - Jerusalem - the Temple - were under judgment. The prophets had come and gone, and been ignored. He came as the last in the line, and they were planning to kill him.

The divine reaction to this, from Jesus' point of view, was not capricious or malevolent. Rather, the prophets, and the Messiah, had been trying to tell the people that there was a way of peace, a way to escape. They were

---

203. My proposal from this point onwards (cf. Wright 1985) is, I think, substantially new, and there is little point debating in detail with interpretations based on different foundations. I see myself standing on the shoulders of Schweitzer and Caird in particular, though disagreeing with both in certain (different) ways. Hints in the same direction are found in e.g. Farmer 1956, 200-2; Jeremias 1966a [1949], 261; Dahl 1974, 75; Zahl1983; Antwi 1991; de Jonge 1991a, 42-8. At the epistemological level, I again invoke Polkinghorne 1994 (cf. too Meyer 1979, 81-7): 'Why do I believe in quarks when no fractionally charged particle has ever unequivocally been observed in an experiment? Set your doubts aside for a while and see how belief in confined quarks enables us to understand a variety of phenomena (the hadronic spectrum of octets and decuplets; deep inelastic scatterings) which otherwise would have no underlying intelligibility' (32). Let the reader understand.

extending a lifeline. The prophets had warned Israel of the consequences of compromising with pagan cults; Jesus warned of the consequences of compromising with pagan politics. The Maccabees had denounced, as no better than pagans, those Jews who had compromised with Antiochus Epiphanes; Jesus denounced, as no better than pagans, not only those who compromised with Caesar by playing his power-games, *but also those who compromised with him by thinking to defeat him with his own weapons.* Those who take the sword will perish by the sword. Here is the doubly radical twist in Jesus' telling of the kingdom-story, which marks him out from his Jewish theological, eschatological and political context even while it insists that he is only comprehensible within it. His kingdom-announcement, like all truly Jewish kingdom-announcements, came as the message of the one true God, the God of Israel, in opposition to pagan power, pagan gods, and pagan politics. But, unlike the other kingdom-announcers of his time from Judas the Galilean to Simeon ben Kosiba, Jesus declared that the way to the kingdom was the way of peace, the way of love, the way of the cross. Fighting the battle of the kingdom with the enemy's weapons meant that one had already lost it in principle, and would soon lose it, and lose it terribly, in practice.

And Jesus determined that it was his task and role, his vocation as Israel's representative, to lose the battle on Israel's behalf. Like Jeremiah, he would warn the city of its impending doom even if he was regarded as a traitor for his pains. Like the Maccabaean martyrs, whom he may have had in mind, he would stand up to the tyrant and take the consequences. Like the Teacher of Righteousness, whom he almost certainly did not have in mind, he would confront the Wicked Priest, even if nobody took his part. Like the truly wise man, he would denounce the wicked and let them do their worst to him, believing that the dawning kingdom would see him vindicated. Like the young hotheads who pulled down the eagle from Herod's Temple, he would stand up against the corrupt central symbol of Judaism and face the wrath of its guardians.[204] He took upon himself the totally and comprehensibly Jewish vocation not only of *critique* from within; not only of *position* from within; but of *suffering the consequences* of critique and opposition from within. And, with that, he believed - of course! - that YHWH would vindicate him. That too was comprehensibly Jewish.

Yes, but radically new within that framework, and that in two ways. First, Jesus, unlike his predecessors in this paradigm, had announced and was enacting a programme aimed not at nationalistic victory over the pagans, but at making Israel what she was called to be, namely, the light of the world.

204. Jos. *Ant.* 17.149-66; *War* 1.648-55. Cf. *NTPG* 172, 327.

Indeed, the zeal which characterized both the Maccabees and their successors in the first century, making them intensify Torah-observance and draw their boundaries (actual and symbolic) ever tighter, was precisely what Jesus had opposed in his teaching and was now opposing in practice. Israel was called, he believed, to be the people of the creator god *for the world*. Whatever interpretation he put on his own death, therefore, it could not simply correspond to the interpretation the martyrs had put on theirs, namely that they were enabling the nation of Israel to escape from her exile while the rest of the world lurched towards its doom. His symbolic actions had pointed towards a renewal of Israel which broke the boundaries, the wineskins, the taboos, and which incorporated a new set of symbols. His last symbolic action, we may assume, was intended to continue and complete this process.

Second, Jesus therefore not only took upon himself the 'wrath' (which, as usual in Jewish thought, refers to hostile military action) which was coming upon Israel because she had compromised with paganism and was suffering exile. He also took upon himself the 'wrath' which was coming upon Israel *because she had refused his way of peace*. Like the Maccabaean martyrs, he suffered what he saw as the results of Israel's pagan corruption. Israel had flirted with paganism; suffering would come of it, as it always had; the martyrs took it upon themselves. Unlike them, he saw as pagan corruption *the very desire to fight paganism itself*. Israel had become a hotbed of nationalist revolution; suffering would come of it, specifically in the form of Roman swords, falling masonry, and above all crosses planted outside the capital city. He would go, as Israel's representative, and take it upon himself. As in so many of his own parables, he would tell Israel's well-known story one more time, with a radical and multiple subversive twist in its tail. Only he would tell it, not as a wordsmith, swapping aphorisms in the marketplace, but as the king, exiled outside the gate of his own beloved city.

My proposal, then, as the way of making sense of all the data before me, is that Jesus believed it was his god-given vocation to identify with the rebel cause, the kingdom-cause, when at last that identification could not be misunderstood as endorsement. Israel was in exile, suffering at the hands of the pagans; the Roman cross was the bitterest symbol of that ongoing exilic state. He would go ahead of his people, to take upon himself both the fate that they had suffered one way or another for half a millennium at the hands of pagan empires and the fate that his contemporaries were apparently hell-bent upon pulling down on their own heads once for all. The martyr-tradition suggested that this was the way in which Israel would at last be brought through suffering to vindication. Jesus' riddles, binding the fate of the nation to his own fate, suggested strongly that he intended to evoke and enact this tradition. The 'messianic woes' tradition indicated that this suffering and vindication would be climactic, unique, the one-off moment when Israel's history and world history would turn their great corner at last, when YHWH's kingdom would come and his will be done on earth as it was in heaven. The central symbolic act by which Jesus gave meaning to his approaching death suggests strongly that he believed this moment had come. This would be the new exodus, the renewal of the covenant, the forgiveness of sins, the end of exile. It would do for Israel what Israel could not do for herself. It would thereby fulfil Israel's vocation, that she should be the servant people, the light of the world.

(iii) The Cross and the Scriptures

It is within this model of understanding, I suggest, that Jesus' references to the scriptural paradigms standing behind the martyr and 'messianic woe' traditions make sense. For too long scholarship has asked, as though in a vacuum, whether Jesus thought of himself as 'the servant' or 'the son of man' - as though he lived in a world where only 'ideas' counted, where the symbols and stories of real life, politics, revolt, Torah-observance, Temple cult and the rest were secondary or irrelevant. Within this framework, small wonder that debate has been inconclusive, with those behind crying 'Forward!', and those in front shouting 'Back!'

Once we read the whole historical context, however, *as* history - that is, as the richly woven fabric of praxis, story, symbol and question which make up real life - then everything looks different. It should be beyond doubt that Jesus knew the scriptures intimately; if the Teacher of Righteousness at Qumran could give his followers a new interpretative grid whereby they were able to understand their own situation in the light of their Bible (and vice versa), there is no reason why Jesus should not have done something similar. Part of the evidence for this can be found, as C. H. Dodd observed, in the concentration of very early Christianity on certain particular books and passages, read in certain ways, but found in such diverse writings as to force us to postulate a great creative mind standing behind all the individual strands of early Christianity.[205] Even if this were not so, however, the argument of this book so far makes it virtually certain that Jesus must have thought, and taught, this way.

It then takes very little imagination to work out where some of the focal points of this creative exegesis can be found. The underlying narrative of the book of Daniel as a whole, with chapter 7 unarguably as one of its main

205. Dodd 1965 [1952], 109f.

focal points; of Zechariah, not least chapters 9-14; of the Psalms, with some in particular being of obvious importance; and of Isaiah 40-55 as a whole, with 52.13-53.12 unarguably as its main focal point: together these offer grand-scale, deeply poetic, and richly symbolic statements of exile and restoration, of suffering and vindication, and of the way in which, according to prophetic promise, YHWH would become king of all the world. Together they speak of YHWH's once-for-all defeat of evil, and his indication of his people, his servant, his Messiah, after their and his terrible, but redemptive, suffering. Whether or not it is true that Daniel 7 and Isaiah 52-3 had already been combined in the *Similitudes of Enoch,*[206] there is every reason to suppose that Jesus himself brought them together, stirring Zechariah 9-14 and certain psalms into the mixture as well, not as isolated or abstracted proof-texts but as what they manifestly were: climactic statements of the climactic moment in the long redemptive purposes of YHWH. Each of these passages was about the coming of the kingdom.[207] Each of them was about the radical defeat of the powers of evil.[208] Each of them, obviously, was about the vindication of Israel, and/or her representative. Each of them, despite popular impressions to the contrary, could be read in the first century as being about a messianic figure or figures.[209] Since we have already argued that these constituted the major elements of Jesus' kingdom-announcement, there is every reason to suppose that he would have felt free to draw on these texts, in his own way, as passages which in any case stood in the shadows behind the Maccabaean and other traditions that formed his more immediate context.

How, more specifically, does Jesus himself seem to have reread these four crucial parts of scripture, in relation to the vocation which led him to the upper room, the garden, and the cross?

I have already argued in some detail that Jesus made the book of Daniel thematic for his whole vocation. He understood it to be referring to the great climax in which YHWH would defeat the fourth world empire and vindicate his suffering people. He projected the notion of evil empire on to the present Jerusalem regime, and identified himself and his movement with the people who were to be vindicated. This provided him with a messianic self-

---

206. cf. *JVG*, 589f.

207. Isa. 52.7; Tg. Isa. 53.10 ('they shall look upon the kingdom of their Messiah'; does this in turn echo Zech. 12.10?); Dan. 7.14, 18, 22, 27; Zech. 14.9 ('YHWH will become king over all the earth'); Pss. 93; 97; etc.

208. Isa. 52.7-12 (where the whole point is that YHWH has revealed his power and kingship in defeating Babylon, so that Israel can at last return from exile); Dan. 7.11-12, 26 (as focal points of the whole book); Zech. 3.1-5; 9.1-8; 9.13-15; 12.3-9; 14.3, 12-15; Ps. 2; 110; etc.

209. cf. ch. 11 *JVG*.

understanding. Did it also, by itself, generate the expectation that he would have to suffer, and that that suffering would somehow be redemptive?

A case can be made out for this view.[210] The overall context of Daniel, in which the sufferings of YHWH's people at the hands of the pagans is such a major theme; and the historical context, from the Maccabees to Jesus, in which the suffering of the martyrs was made so much of; these should guarantee that the figure of the 'son of man' in chapter 7, who is exalted after the fourth beast has 'made war' upon him, should be understood as a suffering figure. We should be cautious, however. Nothing in chapter 7 itself indicates suffering; nothing in the book as a whole, except possibly 11.31-5 and 12.1-3, suggests that the suffering of the martyrs would be redemptive. Any attempt to show that Daniel 7 could by itself generate a picture of one who would suffer redemptively, and to marginalize other texts in which these themes stare us in the face, invites once more the comment of Schweitzer about watering the garden with a leaky bucket when a stream lies right alongside. However, there should be no doubt that the book of Daniel as a whole provided a framework of apocalyptic expectation, messianic hope, and the promise of vindication for faithful Israel the other side of present distress, which contributed substantially towards Jesus' sense of vocation.

Zechariah, too, was undoubtedly of great importance.[211] We saw in the previous chapter that Jesus used the shepherd-image of himself on a number of occasions;[212] Zechariah provided a setting and context within which the sufferings of the sheep were linked with those of the (royal) shepherd. Several of the riddles which we explored as belonging with Jesus' symbolic action at the Last Supper make exactly this connection between the sufferings of Israel and those of the Messiah. When, in this setting, we find Jesus quoting explicitly from Zechariah 13.7 ('smite the shepherd, and the sheep will be scattered'),[213] we should not suspect a cunning insertion by a later exegetically minded Christian theologian, but should see this as an indication of Jesus' own mindset. This is, of course, strikingly confirmed not by isolated sayings but by symbolic actions: Zechariah 9 focuses on the king riding into Jerusalem on a donkey, as the agent of the return from exile and the renewal of the covenant; Zechariah 14, which celebrates the coming of YHWH and his kingdom, ends with the Temple being cleansed of traders. There should be no doubt that Jesus knew this whole passage, and that he saw it as centrally constitutive of his own vocation, at the level not just of ideas but of

210. e.g. Barrett 1959, esp. 13-14.

211. Among the few writers to have explored this, cf. France 1971, 103-10; Lindars 1973 [1961], 110-34; Kim 1987a.

212. cf. *JVG*, 533-5.

213. Mt. 26.31/Mk.14.27; cf. Jn. 16.32.

agendas.[214] And this time we find the theme of suffering associated not just with Israel in general but with the shepherd, the Messiah, in particular.

The themes of suffering and kingdom emerge also, as we saw, in the Psalter. We have already observed Jesus' use of the pilgrim Psalm 118 ('the stone which the builders rejected') and of the royal Psalm 110 ('YHWH said to my Lord'). Without venturing down the road of psychology, we can claim as a strong historical probability that Jesus regarded the Psalms as providing a further set of bearings on his vocation, not least as it was focused on his strange royal and pilgrim journey to, and action in, Jerusalem. However, it was a psalm of lament that, according to Matthew and Mark, provided him with one of his last utterances: 'My God, my God, why did you abandon me?'[215] This has of course been the subject of endless discussion, at both the theological and the homiletical levels. For our purposes the critical thing to note is how well the psalm as a whole (never mind the Psalter as a whole) fits with what we have sketched as Jesus' mindset, aims and beliefs. It is, in a sense, the opposite of Psalm 89 (the royal psalm that turns into a lament), turning eventually from shame and despair to an affirmation not only of hope but of the coming kingdom of YHWH:

My God, my God, why hast thou forsaken me?
Why art thou so far from helping me, from the words of my groaning?
O my God, I cry by day, but you do not answer;
and by night, but find no rest . . .

I will declare your name to my brethren;
in the midst of the congregation I will praise you:
You who fear YHWH, praise him!
All you offspring of Jacob, glorify him;
stand in awe of him, all you offspring of Israel!
For he did not despise or abhor the affliction of the afflicted;
he did not hide his face from me,
but heard when I cried to him . . .
The poor shall eat and be satisfied;
those who seek YHWH shall praise him.
May your hearts live for ever!
All the ends of the earth shall remember and turn to YHWH;
and all the families of the nations shall worship before him.
For the kingdom is YHWH's,
And he rules over the nations.
To him, indeed, shall all who sleep in the earth bow down;
before him shall bow all who go down to the dust,
and I shall live for him.

214. cf. too e.g. Mt. 24.30, alluding to Zech. 12.10-12. Zech. 1-8 also furnishes themes for the ministry of Jesus; e.g. 8.19 with the fasting controversy (*JVG*, 433f.).
215. Mt. 27.46/Mk. 15.34; quoted from Ps. 22.1. Lindars (1973 [1961], 89) says that 'the genuineness of this saying, as actually spoken by Jesus, can hardly be disputed'.

My seed shall serve him;
future generations will be told about YHWH,
and proclaim his deliverance to a people yet unborn,
saying that he has done it.[216]

The combination of themes is remarkable, considering our whole reconstruction of Jesus' ministry and mindset. 'The kingdom is YHWH's'; that is the cry of the psalmist who has come through the terrible desolation of the first twenty-one verses to the vindication, the restitution, and indeed the resurrection of the final section. As with Daniel, the suffering is not explicitly said to be redemptive; but it is part of the strange process whereby the kingdom finally dawns. From the historical point of view there is no reason why Jesus should not have carried Psalm 22 (and a good many others) in his head, and why he should not have prayed its first verse as he underwent the agony of crucifixion.[217]

Daniel, Zechariah and the Psalms thus contribute to various elements of Jesus' mindset, his awareness of vocation. The kingdom would come through the suffering of the righteous; the true king would share the suffering of the people. But *redemptive* suffering is not stated explicitly; we only emerge with something that looks like that if we take into account the full context of these books, both literary and historical. That, of course, we must do, as the later use of such texts in martyr-literature, and the still later use in the rabbis, encourages us to do. But there is, as we have seen, one book which, not only in its literary and historical contexts but also in its clear and explicit statements, draws together all the themes we have been studying (the suffering of Israel at the hands of the pagans, and her subsequent vindication as YHWH becomes king of the world and redeems her from exile; the coming of a messianic figure; the *suffering* of a messianic figure), and adds to them a stone which the builders regularly reject but which has a strong claim to be the head of the corner, namely, the claim that the redemption of Israel from exile and the suffering of the messianic figure, are linked precisely as effect and cause. I refer, of course, to Isaiah 40-55.[218]

We begin on solid ground. Isaiah 52.7-12 was, as we have seen, thematic for the whole work of Jesus. The prophetic, heraldic announcement of the

---

216. Ps. 22.1-2, 22-31.

217. The psalm has obviously coloured the story of the passion in other ways: e.g. Mt. 27.43/Ps. 22.8; Jn. 19.23-5/Ps. 22.18. But these are best explained on the assumption that Jesus really did utter Ps. 22.1 on the cross.

218. The debate about Jesus' use, or non-use, of Isa. 53 is long-running and well known. As a small selection, cf. Barrett 1959; Hooker 1959; Jeremias 1967; France 1971; Lindars 1973 [1961], 75-88; Stuhlmacher 1986 [1981], 16-29; Caird & Hurst 1994,310-16. I am deeply indebted to fellow participants at a conference on this subject at Baylor University, Texas, in February 1996 - not least the central protagonists, Professors Morna Hooker and Otto Betz.

'gospel', telling Zion that her god was becoming king, that he had defeated Babylon and would bring her back from exile, could stand as a summary of all that Jesus was trying to say and accomplish. But if, then, we ask how the message of Isaiah 52.7-12 was to be put into effect, the prophecy as Jesus must have read it had a clear answer. The arm of YHWH, which would be unveiled to redeem Israel from exile and put evil to flight, was revealed, according to Isaiah 53.1, in and through the work of the servant of YHWH.

We have already seen that the 'servant', from chapters 42 to 53, could be seen in the second-Temple period as a reference to the Messiah. This is scarcely surprising, indeed, when we compare the picture of the servant in 42.1-9 with the messianic pictures in Isaiah 9.6-7 and 11.1-10. Indeed, the Isaianic 'herald' himself is seen as a messianic figure in one text from Qumran.[219] The whole passage, equally clearly, speaks of the suffering of YHWH's people at the hands of the pagans, and holds out the constant hope that, because of YHWH's love and loyalty, they will be forgiven their sins and released from exile. One of the main internal dynamics of the whole book is the fluidity of thought, often remarked upon, between Israel herself as the servant and servant-figure who clearly stands over against Israel.[220] All of this creates a context within which the themes of Jesus' ministry as we have studied them seem to fit like a glove. We thus emerge with the following argument:

(1)   Jesus announces and enacts the kingdom of YHWH, doing and saying things which dovetail very closely with the message of Isaiah 40-55 as a whole.

(2)   The kingdom-programme of Isaiah 40-55 as a whole is put into effect through the work of the servant, specifically his redemptive suffering.

(3)   Jesus acts symbolically as though he intends to put his kingdom-programme into effect through his sharing of Israel's suffering, and speaks as if that is indeed what he intends.

(4)   One of the relevant sayings quotes Isaiah 53 directly, and others can most easily be explained as an allusion to it.[221]

(5)   It is therefore highly probable that, in addition to several other passages which informed his vocation, Jesus regarded Isaiah 53, in its whole literary and historical context, as determinative.

---

219. 11Q13 2.15-20 (GM 140), referring also to Isa. 61; Dan. 9.

220. As Origen already saw: C. eels. 1.55.

221. Direct quotation: Lk. 22.37/Isa. 53.12. Allusion: Mk. 9.12/Isa. 53.3 (the only text which explains where 'it is written' that 'the son of man must be treated with contempt', showing also a fusion between Isa. 53 and Dan. 7, like 11Q13's fusion of Isa. 52 and Dan. 9); Mk. 10.45/Isa. 53.10, 12 (cf. Goppelt 1981 [1975], 193-5; Stuhlmacher 1986 [1981], ch. 2; Witherington 1990, 251-6; contrast Seeley 1993); Mk. 14.24/Isa. 53.12. Jeremias 1971, 286f. gives a longer list, including refs. to the Tg. and LXX. These have all of course been discussed *ad nauseam* in the literature; my overall argument is designed to set the debate in a wider context and so, I hope, to avoid getting bogged down.

(6) Jesus therefore intended not only to share Israel's sufferings, but to do so as the key action in the divinely appointed plan of redemption for Israel and the world.

This argument is strong, and it is specific. I am not suggesting that Jesus 'regarded himself as "the servant"', as though second-Temple Jews had anticipated modern criticism in separating out the 'servant songs' from the rest of Isaiah 40-55, or as though Jesus had created a 'role' for himself out of a few texts taken out of context. Nor am I saying that the Isaianic pattern was necessarily dominant in Jesus' sense of vocation; it provided one unique and specific element in a more complex whole. Jesus did not speak of Isaiah 53 when faced with Caiaphas; the trial setting called for the judgment scene of Daniel 7, and the question about the Temple called for a statement of messianic enthronement, neither of which were modified or softened by a statement of humble suffering. He did not speak of it directly when instructing his puzzled disciples; if they had understood it, they would not have followed him to Jerusalem. He spoke of it in his actions, particularly in the upper room, and in his readiness to go to the eye of the storm, the place where the messianic woes would reach their height, where the *peirasmos,* the time of testing, would become most acute, and to bear the weight of Israel's exile, dying as her Messiah outside the walls of Jerusalem. We catch echoes of this, rather than direct statements, as Jesus' words cluster round his actions. The son of man must, as it is written, suffer many things, and be treated with contempt; he came to give his life a ransom for many; this is my blood of the covenant, shed for you and for the many for the forgiveness of sins (in other words, for the end of exile); he was numbered with the transgressors. This is not a matter of assuming 'the influence of the Servant' on Jesus, and then finding 'passages which appear to support it'.[222] It is a matter of understanding Jesus' whole kingdom-announcement in the light of several major themes from the Jewish scriptures, and showing that it is absurd, granted the whole picture, to disallow reference, allusion and echo to Isaiah 40-55 in general, and to 52.13-53.12 in particular.

I suggest, then, that Isaiah 40-55 as a whole was thematic for Jesus' kingdom-announcement. His work is not to be understood in terms of the teaching of an abstract and timeless system of theology, not even of atonement-theology, but as the historical and concrete acting out of YHWH's promise to defeat evil and rescue his people from exile, that is, to forgive their sins at last. Within this, the allusions to Isaiah 53 should not be regarded as the *basis* of a theory about Jesus' self-understanding in relation

222. Hooker 1959, 20.

to his death; they may be, rather, the tell-tale signs of a vocation which he could hardly put into words, the vocation to be the 'herald' of Isaiah 40.9 and 52.7, and thence to be, himself, the servant, representing the Israel that was called to be the light of the world but had so signally failed to live up to her calling. The only way that such a vocation could be articulated without distortion was in story, symbol and praxis: all three came together in the Temple, in the upper room, and ultimately on the hill outside the city gate. Jesus' personal reading of Isaiah belongs not so much in the history of ideas, as in the history of vocation, agenda, action and ultimately passion. And he understood this vocation, agenda, action and passion as messianic.

(iv) The Messianic Task

I showed in the previous chapter that two tasks in particular awaited the would-be Messiah. He must cleanse, restore or rebuild the Temple; he must fight and win the battle against Israel's enemies. I now wish to propose, on the basis of my hypothesis so far, that Jesus intended his forthcoming death to accomplish these two tasks, albeit in a manner that was thoroughly, but not surprisingly, redefined.

Neusner has argued, as we saw, that Jesus' Temple-action and his Last Supper must be seen as deliberately mutually interpretative.[223] I agree, but question his conclusion. He suggests that the Supper itself was Jesus' replacement for the Temple cult. However, as we have seen, the symbolism of the Supper was not self-referential. Particularly when explained by Jesus' riddles and stories, never mind his explicit warnings and biblical allusions, it pointed not to itself but to the event which was about to take place; in other words, to Jesus' death.

What then does the parallelism between the Temple-action and the Supper say about Jesus' understanding of his death? It says, apparently, that Jesus intended his death to accomplish that which would normally be accomplished in and through the Temple itself. In other words, Jesus intended that his death should in some sense function sacrificially.[224] This should not surprise us unduly, or be regarded as necessarily meaning that the texts that suggest this viewpoint must be a later Christian retrojection. For a start, the things that point this way are not proof-texts, but actions and events which we have already seen good reason to regard as historically extremely plausible. For another thing, we argued earlier that, during Jesus' ministry, he regularly acted as if he were able to bypass the Temple system in offering forgiveness

223. Neusner 1989.
224. cf. e.g. Jeremias 1971, 290f.; Meyer 1979, 252.

to all and sundry right where they were.[225] Further, we have already seen that the Maccabaean martyrs were regarded as having, in some sense, offered themselves as a sacrifice through which Israel might be cleansed and purified.[226] We may also point out that near the heart of Isaiah 53 there is a strange phrase which, whatever it may have meant in its original setting, by the first century was certainly taken to refer to a sacrifice:

> When you make his life an offering for sin,
> he shall see his offspring and shall prolong his days;
> through him the will of the LORD shall prosper.[227]

It is not going beyond the evidence, then, to suggest that Jesus saw his own approaching death in terms of the sacrificial cult. But his would not be one sacrifice among many. The controlling metaphor that he chose for his crucial symbol was not the Day of Atonement, but Passover: the one-off moment of freedom in Israel's past, now to be translated into the one-off moment which would inaugurate Israel's future. In his last great symbolic action, Jesus was implying that he, as Messiah, would establish a reality which would supersede the Temple. He saw his approaching death, therefore, as one key part of his messianic task.

The other part was, of course, the battle. As we discovered in chapter 10, Jesus reconstrued the battle which had to be fought as the battle against the real enemy, the accuser, the satan. He renounced the battle that his contemporaries expected a Messiah to fight, and that several would-be Messiahs in that century were only too eager to fight. He faced, instead, what he seems to have conceived as the battle against the forces of darkness, standing behind the visible forces (both Roman and Jewish) ranged against him.

At one level, he was fighting this battle throughout his ministry, not least when battling with sickness and demon-possession ('this woman, whom the satan bound . . .'; 'If I by the finger of God cast out demons, then the kingdom of God has come upon you'). At another level, he was fighting this battle when he engaged in controversy with those opponents who were bent on driving forward their scheme for national security, national symbols, national hope, in the face of his challenge to a new way of being Israel, of being the light of the world. But at the fundamental level, there were two places where the battle had to be fought.

225. *JVG*, 268-74.

226. *JVG*, 582f.

227. Isa. 53.10. The word *asam*, translated in the LXX with *peri hamartias*, the regular phrase for 'sin-offering', may originally have had a wider range of meaning; by the first century we are safe in assuming that the Levitical, i.e. sacrificial, meaning would have been the first, and probably the only, meaning to be 'heard'.

First, Jesus must have believed that he was fighting the battle against the satan when he came face to face with Caiaphas as his accuser. ('This is your hour,' he said in the garden when the High Priest's servants came to get him, 'and the power of darkness.'[228]) Certainly the Teacher of Righteousness thought he was facing something like evil incarnate when he squared off against the Wicked Priest, and we have no reason to suppose that Jesus would have taken a substantially different view with the High Priest of his day. As we have seen, he seems to have regarded Jerusalem itself, tragically compromised as it was, as the new abode of the satan. His response to Caiaphas meant, among other things, that he was playing David to Caiaphas' Goliath; that he was playing the Danielic 'son of man' to Caiaphas' fourth beast. Small wonder that Caiaphas tore his robe.

Second, granted all we know about Jesus, he must have believed that he was also to fight the real battle, the messianic battle, when he faced the might of Rome, the enemy whom every Messiah for a hundred years either side of Jesus had to confront. The pagan hordes, with all their (to a Jew) blasphemous beliefs and vile practices, were widely regarded as the sons of darkness. Jesus, however, believed he had to fight the darkness itself, not simply its offspring. Hence, Gethsemane, the moment when the vocation was tested to the limit. He could have chosen, then and there, to slip away and establish a private counter-Temple movement, like the Essenes. He could have chosen to call for the twelve legions of angels, or more likely their earthly equivalent; there would have been plenty of people in Jerusalem ready to rally to him. The scene in Gethsemane, involving Jesus in weakness, fear, and (apparently) an agony of doubt, is hard to comprehend as a later Christian invention. It is entirely comprehensible as biography. It was, after all, failed Messiahs who ended up on crosses; the Jesus we have described throughout must have had to wrestle with the serious possibility that he might be totally deluded.

He had, however, already laid down the terms of the battle he had to fight.[229] 'He who saves his life shall lose it; he who loses his life shall save it.' This cryptic and subversive wisdom had always been the challenge he put before his followers; now it was to be revealed as the wisdom by which he was himself to live, and to die. Israel, he had urged, was to be the salt of the earth, the light of the world, through turning the other cheek, going the second mile; now he was to expose his whole body to the Roman lash, and to

228. Lk. 22.53.
229. Cf. Farmer 1956, 200-2, and the very suggestive passage in Meyer 1979, 218: 'The faith reflected in the esoteric teachings on repudiation, losing one's life, poverty, and the like followed no pattern of piety attested in contemporary Israel. A deft, assured, original foray into iniquity and redemption, it gave a new and matchless depth to the *anawim* thematic' [i.e. to the theme of 'the poor'].

set off on a forced march with the load the soldiers gave him to carry. And, despite all the overtones of the Maccabaean martyrs which clustered around the event, as he went to his death he seems not to have responded to his pagan torturers in the time-honoured manner. Instead of hurling insults and threats at them, he suffered either in silence or with words of forgiveness; a startling innovation into the martyr-tradition, which sent echoes across early Christianity in such a way as to be, I suggest, inexplicable unless they are substantially historical.[230]

They point, therefore; to the theme which was picked up in very earliest Christianity as the dominant note in Jesus' achievement. All through his public career he had acted on the basis of compassion for the multitudes, for the poor, for the sheep without a shepherd. When questioned as to the greatest commandment in the law, he highlighted the love of God and of one's neighbour. Not much is said in the scriptural text-base concerning the *love* which the Messiah might have for his people, but with Jesus this seemed to be uppermost, once more not simply as an idea but as a reality. We shall explore the roots of this theme in the next chapter, but it would be very odd not to draw attention to it at this point. The earliest Christians regarded Jesus' achievement on the cross as the decisive victory over evil. But they saw it, even more, as the climax of a career in which active, outgoing, healing love had become the trademark and hallmark. It is so easy to turn this point in a sentimental or pietistic direction that a historian may well be shy of raising the matter. But when we put the historical package together in the way that we have, this is the theme that emerges. Ben Meyer put it like this:

> What, in the end, made Jesus operate in this way, what energized his incorporating death into his mission, his facing it and going to meet it?
> The range of abstractly possible answers is enormous . . . But . . . it is above all in the tradition generated by Jesus that we discover what made him operate in the way he did, what made him epitomize his life in the single act of going to his death: He 'loved me and handed himself over for me' . . . ; 'having loved his own who were in the world, he loved them to the end' . . . If authenticity lies in the coherence between word (Mark 12.28-34 parr.) and deed (Gal. 2.20; Eph. 5.2; John 13.1; Rev. 1.5), our question has found an answer.[231]

Jesus, therefore, appears to have believed that victory in the real messianic battle would consist in dying at the hands of the Romans, dying the death of the rebel on behalf of the rebels. This was the climax of the way of being Israel which he had urged (without much effect) on his fellow countrymen. This, too, was the implication of his linking of his fate with that

---

230. e.g. 1 Pet. 2.19-25; 3.17f.
231. Meyer 1979, 252f. (the close of the book).

of the nation. He had announced judgment, the wrath of Rome no less, on nation and Temple for their failure to be the light of the world, to follow the way of peace. This judgment was not arbitrary; it was the necessary consequence of Israel's determination to follow the path of confrontation with Rome. But the way of the martyr was to take upon himself the suffering that hung over the nation as a whole. The way of the shepherd-king was to share the suffering of the sheep. The way of the servant was to take upon himself the exile of the nation as a whole. As a would-be Messiah, Jesus identified with Israel; he would therefore go ahead of her, and take upon himself precisely that fate, actual and symbolic, which he had announced for nation, city, and Temple. He would do, once and for all, what he had done in smaller, anticipatory actions throughout his public career, as he identified with the poor and sinners, as he came into contact with lepers, corpses and other sources of impurity. 'He has gone in to eat with a sinner' (Luke 19.7) would turn into 'he has gone out to die with the rebels'.

> At last, when there is no risk of misunderstanding, he can identify himself fully with the national aspirations of his people. He cannot preach Israel's national hope, but he can die for it.[232]

Thus

> [Jesus] goes to his death at the hands of a Roman judge on a charge of which he was innocent and his accusers, as the event proved, were guilty. And so, not only in theological truth but in historic fact, the one bore the sins of the many . . . [233]

This, then, was how Jesus envisaged the messianic victory over the real enemy. The satan had taken up residence in Jerusalem, not merely in Rome, and was seeking to pervert the chosen nation and the holy place into becoming a parody of themselves, a pseudo-chosen people intent on defeating the world with the world's methods, a pseudo-holy place seeking to defend itself against the world rather than to be the city set on a hill, shining its light on the world. One more time: this does not mean that Jesus rejected the concepts of chosen nation and holy place. The whole point is that he embraced them; that he discerned, and tried to communicate, what that chosenness, in its scriptural roots, actually meant; and that, discovering the nation as a whole deaf and blind to his plea, he determined to go, himself, to the holy place, and there to do what the chosen people ought to do. He would act on behalf of, and in the place of, the Israel that was failing to be what she was called to be. He would himself be the light of the world. He would be the salt of the earth.

232. Wright 1985, 87.
233. Caird 1965, 22 (= Caird & Hurst 1994, 419).

He would be set on a hill, unable to be hidden.

He would go, then, to the place where the satan had made his dwelling. He would defeat the cunning plan which would otherwise place the whole divine purpose in jeopardy. He would uphold the honour, the election, the true traditions, of Israel. He would stand, like Mattathias or Judas, against not only the pagans but also the compromisers within the chosen people, more particularly those who wielded power, those who ran the holy place, the shepherds who had been leading the people astray. Jesus, once more, was a first-century Jew, not a twentieth-century liberal.

As such, he must have known that he might have been deeply mistaken. The aims and goals which we must postulate if we are to make sense of his praxis, stories and symbols must have involved him in what we might call a great Pascalian wager, staking all on his vocation and vision. It was, after all, a huge gamble. Messiahs were supposed to defeat the pagans, not to die at their hands. Worse, dying thus actually demonstrated that one was not after all the Messiah; followers of a Messiah who was then crucified knew beyond question that they had backed the wrong horse. Ironically, if Jesus had been the sort of Messiah we may assume many Jews wanted him to be, the strong likelihood is that he would have ended up being crucified just the same. At every point, then, the messianic vocation to which he seems to have given allegiance led him into a dark tunnel, where the only thing left was sheer trust. But we can be confident of what he thought he was thereby going to achieve. He would bring Israel's history to its climax. Through his work, YHWH would defeat evil, bringing the kingdom to birth, and enable Israel to become, after all, the light of the world. Through his work, YHWH would reveal that he was not just a god, but God.

(v) The Victory of God

Jesus, then, went to Jerusalem not just to preach, but to die. Schweitzer was right: Jesus believed that the messianic woes were about to burst upon Israel, and that he had to take them upon himself, solo. I think that Jesus realized this considerably earlier than Schweitzer thought (for him, it was a secondary development, an adjustment of Jesus' earlier vision), but the point is not actually that important. What matters is that, in the Temple and the upper room, Jesus deliberately enacted two symbols, which encapsulated his whole work and agenda. The first symbol said: the present system is corrupt and recalcitrant. It is ripe for judgment. But Jesus is the Messiah, the one through whom YHWH, the God of all the world, will save Israel and thereby the world. And the second symbol said: this is how the true exodus will come about. This is how evil will be defeated. This is how sins will be forgiven.

Jesus knew - he must have known - that these actions, and the words which accompanied and explained them, were very likely to get him put on trial as a false prophet leading Israel astray, and as a would-be Messiah; and that such a trial, unless he convinced the court otherwise, would inevitably result in his being handed over to the Romans and executed as a (failed) revolutionary king. This did not, actually, take a great deal of 'supernatural' insight, any more than it took much more than ordinary common sense to predict that, if Israel continued to attempt rebellion against Rome, Rome would eventually do to her as a nation what she was now going to do to this strange would-be Messiah. But at the heart of Jesus' symbolic actions, and his retelling of Israel's story, there was a great deal more than political prag- matism, revolutionary daring, or the desire for a martyr's glory. There was a deeply theological analysis of Israel, the world, and his own role in relation to both. There was a deep sense of vocation and trust in Israel's god, whom he believed of course to be God. There was the unshakeable belief - Geth- semane seems nearly to have shaken it, but Jesus seems to have construed that, too, as part of the point, part of the battle - that if he went this route, if he fought this battle, the long night of Israel's exile would be over at last, and the new day for Israel and the world really would dawn once and for all. He himself would be vindicated (of course; all martyrs believed that); and Israel's destiny, to save the world, would thereby be accomplished. Not only would he create a breathing space for his followers and any who would join them, by drawing on to himself for a moment the wrath of Rome and letting them escape; if he was defeating the real enemy, he was doing so on behalf of the whole world. The servant-vocation, to be the light of the world, would come true in him, and thence in the followers who would regroup after his vindication. The death of the shepherd would result in YHWH becoming king of all the earth. The vindication of the 'son of man' would see the once- for-all defeat of evil and the establishment of a worldwide kingdom.

Jesus therefore took up his own cross. He had come to see it, too, in deeply symbolic terms: symbolic, now, not merely of Roman oppression, but of the way of love and peace which he had commended so vigorously, the way of defeat which he had announced as the way of victory. Unlike his actions in the Temple and the upper room, the cross was a symbol not of praxis but of passivity, not of action but of passion. It was to become the symbol of victory, but not of the victory of Caesar, nor of those who would oppose Caesar with Caesar's methods. It was to become the symbol, because it would be the means, of the victory of God.

(vi) Conclusion

The line of thought I have been exploring is complex from one point of view, but from another it is essentially very simple. Modern western minds do not, of course, habitually run in grooves like these. From a first-century Jewish point of view, however, it makes excellent if shocking sense. In offering a set of answers to our first three questions (Jesus' interaction with Judaism, his aims throughout his ministry, and the reasons for his death), the case has now been made that we are faced, not with a series of random or scattered events, but with a coherent historical whole. And within the history, as we shall see, there will be plenty of material for theology to go to work, though it may be surprised at what it finds. The silhouette of the cross against a darkened sky is more, not less, evocative for our having studied the portrait of the man who hung there. And the total historical picture, in all its complex simplicity, will challenge the most experienced iconographer.

Chapter Four

EXECUTED BY ROME, VINDICATED BY GOD

by Marcus Borg

Jesus's confrontation with the domination system during his last week in Jerusalem moves toward its climax. As we turn to the story of his final days, it is important to recall our characterization of the gospels in Chapter 3. Namely, they combine memory and metaphor, the story of Jesus remembered with the story of Jesus in metaphorical narrative. The metaphorical meaning of language is its more-than-literal, more-than-factual meaning. Metaphor refers to the surplus of meaning that language can carry.

The story of Jesus's death was remembered and told because of its more-than-historical meaning, even as it contains historical memory. In addition, as we will see, there are elements in it that are "purely" metaphorical. But even the parts that are probably historical were told because of their surplus of meaning. Combined with the stories of Easter, which will also be treated in this chapter, they were for his followers the most central stories they knew.

Mark, our earliest gospel, continues his day-by-day account of Jesus's last week. On Friday, it becomes hour by hour. With occasional and relatively minor variations, Matthew and Luke follow Mark's narrative. John's story is quite different, and some of the differences will occasionally be noted.[1]

THE LAST DAYS

Wednesday begins with the temple authorities continuing to seek a way to arrest Jesus. They want to do so in private, for they perceive the crowd to be sympathetic to Jesus and they fear a riot (Mark 14.2). Later that day, Judas, one of Jesus's disciples, provides the opportunity. He meets with the authorities and agrees to betray Jesus in a suitable place (Mark 14.10-11).

Mark provides no reason for the betrayal, though Judas's motive has been speculated about from ancient times. John's gospel implies that he did it for

---

1. Because I am writing this book during the same period of time that I wrote *The Last Week* (San Francisco: HarperSanFrancisco, 2006) with John Dominic Crossan, I occasionally use material from chapters 6 and 8 of that book in this chapter.

money; he speaks of Judas as a thief who stole from the money held in common by Jesus's followers (12.6). John also says that Satan made him do it (13.2, 27), as does Luke (22.3). In the recently discovered *Gospel of Judas*, written in the second century, Jesus orders Judas to make arrangements with the authorities for his death. Rather than Judas being a betrayer, he was the one disciple Jesus could trust to do this.[2] But scholars do not think this gospel tells us anything about the historical Jesus or the historical Judas. Other suggestions for his motivation have occasionally been made. Judas was perhaps afraid that they would all be arrested and punished, perhaps killed, and wanted to escape that fate by allying himself with the authorities. Judas was disappointed with the kind of kingdom he now realized Jesus was advocating and decided to turn Jesus over. Judas may have felt betrayed. But about all of this we must simply say that we do not (and cannot) know.

On Thursday, Jesus has a final meal with his followers. In the synoptic gospels, it is a Passover meal celebrating ancient Israel's liberation from Egypt. (In John's gospel, it is not; the Passover meal is the next evening, and the lambs to be eaten at that meal are killed at the same hour that Jesus dies in John).[3] In the course of the meal, Jesus speaks of the bread and wine as his body and blood. The words vary slightly in the various accounts, but the gist is clear. About the bread, Jesus said, "This is my body"; about the wine, he said, "This is my blood of the covenant."[4] A historical judgment about whether this language goes back to Jesus or is the product of the post-Easter community's ritualization of Jesus's meal practice is very difficult. Judas departs early.

The meal over, they leave the city and go to a garden called Gethsemane at the foot of the Mount of Olives just east of the walls of Jerusalem. There, in the dark, Judas arrives with a group of armed men. In the synoptics, they are sent by the temple authorities and are presumably temple police (Mark 14.32-50). In John, the arrest party includes a large number of imperial soldiers as well.[5] Jesus's disciples flee.

2. Discovered a few decades ago, the *Gospel of Judas* was made public early in 2006. Most likely written in the second half of the second century, the gospel expresses a form of early Christianity commonly (but perhaps unfairly) known as Gnosticism. It views the created world (and thus the body) as something to be escaped. As Jesus orders Judas to "betray" him, he says: "You will exceed all of them. For you will sacrifice the man that clothes me."

3. Moreover, in John, the meal does not include what Christians often call "the words of institution" of the Lord's Supper or Eucharist. These are found only in the synoptic gospels and Paul. Rather, in John "the last supper" is the occasion for Jesus to wash his disciples' feet and to deliver his "farewell discourse" (John 13-17).

4. Mark 14.22-25; Matt. 26.26-29; Luke 22.17-20; and in Paul, 1 Cor. 11.23-26.

5. John 18.3 reports a "cohort" (imprecisely translated "detachment" in the NRSV) of imperial soldiers—six hundred men! Oddly, after Jesus says to them, "I am he," they fall to the ground (18.6). In awe? In worship? Then they get up and arrest him. It is impossible to visualize this as a historical scene, though it works as symbolism. Jesus has just uttered the most sacred name of

Then Jesus is taken to a hearing before the temple authorities, presided over by Caiaphas, the high priest. Witnesses testify against Jesus, but they fail to agree. Their testimony includes garbled statements about Jesus threatening to destroy the temple. The high priest takes over. Having failed to find two or three witnesses whose testimonies agreed with each other, he asks Jesus directly: "Are you the Messiah, the Son of the Blessed One?"

Mark 14.62 reports Jesus's response. It begins with a terse, "I am." The Greek behind the English "I am" is ambiguous. It can be translated either as an affirmation ("I am") or as an interrogative ("Am I?"). Matthew and Luke both understand it as ambiguous. Matthew has, "You have said so" (26.64). Luke has, "You say that I am" (22.70).

Jesus's response continues: "And 'you will see the Son of Man seated at the right hand of the Power,' and 'coming with the clouds of heaven.'" This was enough for the high priest. He declares the statement to be blasphemy and asks his council, "What is your decision?" They condemn Jesus to death. Then the guards spit on him, blindfold him, and beat him.

For more than one reason, there is great historical uncertainty about this scene before the high priest and his council. First, it reports a meeting of the high priest's council at night on the day of the most important Jewish festival of the year. Trials were forbidden at night and on such days, but even if this meeting is understood as an "informal" hearing or kangaroo court, it is difficult to imagine.[6] Second, if it did happen, how did the followers of Jesus know *what* had happened at it? They had all fled. It is, of course, possible to imagine that someone who was there talked about what had happened, and the report reached Christian ears.

Yet a third reason is that the high priest's question and Jesus's response sound remarkably like a post-Easter Christian confession of faith. "Are you the Messiah, the Son of the Blessed One?" Are you the Christ, the Son of God? These are classic post-Easter affirmations about Jesus. Jesus's response sounds like a reference to his resurrection and second coming: "You will see the Son of Man seated at the right hand of the Power" echoes Psalm 110.1, one of the texts used by early Christians to express their conviction that God had raised Jesus to God's right hand. "Coming with the clouds of heaven" echoes Daniel 7.13-14, a text that also uses "Son of Man" language and that

God, "I am he," and so they prostrate themselves. Even the forces of empire recognize the sacred in Jesus—and then arrest and kill him anyway.

6. It is interesting to note that John does not report a trial or hearing before the council on the night or morning preceding Jesus's execution. John does mention that Jesus was brought before Annas and Caiaphas; the latter was the high priest, and the former his father-in-law (18.13, 24). But no councilor meeting is convened. Instead, John reports a meeting of the council some time before Passover Week at which they decided to put Jesus to death (11.45-53).

is associated in the New Testament with the expectation of Jesus's second coming (as in Mark 13.24-27). The symmetry is almost too good to be factual—Jesus was condemned for what amounts to an early Christian confession of faith. Jesus is the Messiah, the Son of God, who will come again on the clouds of heaven.

THE CRUCIFIXION

As dawn breaks on Friday, the temple authorities convey Jesus to Pilate. Jesus appears before him in the courtyard of the palace of the late Herod the Great, where the Roman governors stayed when they were in Jerusalem. Pilate looks at Jesus and asks, "Are you the King of the Jews?" We should probably hear mockery in his voice—you, a prisoner, bound, beaten, and bloodied, the king of the Jews? Jesus's response is nondeclarative: "You say so." Then Jesus remains silent (15.1-5). Refusing to respond to authority shows courage and suggests contempt. Indeed, Jesus does not speak again in Mark's gospel until the moment of his death.[7]

This is followed by a curious episode involving Barabbas, a prisoner awaiting execution as a Jewish insurrectionist. It is curious because it reports an implausible practice that at Passover Pilate customarily released whatever prisoner the crowd asked for. It seems an unlikely procedure for an imperial governor of a rebellious territory to follow. But as Mark tells the story, Pilate offers the "crowd" a choice between Jesus and Barabbas. They choose Barabbas and shout for Jesus's crucifixion (15.6-14).

This is a different crowd from the one that had listened to Jesus with delight during the week and whom the authorities feared. We have no reason to think that those in that crowd had changed their minds. Rather, this "crowd" (presumably a small group) had access to the courtyard of Pilate's residence (Herod's palace). The authorities didn't let just anybody in.

The Barabbas episode may be explained by the historical context in which Mark wrote, namely, near 70 CE and the Roman reconquest and destruction of Jerusalem and the temple. By then it was clear that the "crowd" had chosen the path of armed insurrection (Barabbas) that led to the catastrophic revolt of 66-70, rather than the path of nonviolence (Jesus).

So Pilate issues the order to have Jesus crucified. He is flogged. Soldiers

---

7. Only John reports an extended dialogue between Pilate and Jesus, and it is full of delicious irony (18.28-19.16). Pilate is like an errand boy, shuttling back and forth between Jesus and the temple authorities. Pilate asks "What is truth?" The irony is that within John's theology, Jesus is "the truth" (14.6). The truth is standing right in front of Pilate, and he doesn't recognize it. In the climactic scene, Pilate has Jesus sit on the judge's seat (19.13, variant reading); as Pilate passes judgment on Jesus, Pilate himself is being judged.

mock him as a would-be king; they dress him in a purple cloak and a crown of thorns and salute him: "Hail, King of the Jews!" Then they hit him, spit upon him, strip him, and take him out to be executed.

In a single sentence, Mark reports the crucifixion: "It was nine o'clock in the morning when they crucified him" (15.25). Mark doesn't narrate the details of what this kind of death entailed, which were well known to people in the Jewish homeland, who had often witnessed this form of imperial execution. Two others are crucified with him. Though called "bandits" in the English translation of Mark 15.27, the Greek word is the term commonly used for those engaged in armed resistance against Rome—"terrorists" or "freedom fighters," depending upon one's point of view. They join their voices to those mocking Jesus. Only in Luke (23.40-43) is one of them described as repentant.

At noon, darkness comes over the whole land and lasts until Jesus's death three hours later. It is idle to wonder if this was an eclipse of the sun; eclipses never last more than a few minutes. Moreover, if it were an eclipse, it would simply be a coincidental natural phenomenon. Nor does it help to suggest that this was a special darkness created by God. To see the darkness as something that happened risks missing the point.[8]

Rather, the darkness is metaphor. Ancient authors often associated highly significant events on earth with signs in the sky. Darkness is an archetypal symbol associated with suffering, mourning, and judgment. Such usage appears in the Jewish Bible. In Exodus 10.21-23, one of the plagues involved "darkness over the land." In the prophets, darkness is associated with mourning and God's judgment. In a reproach to Jerusalem from the sixth century BCE, Jeremiah refers to the sun setting at midday (15.9). Texts of judgment in Zephaniah 1.15 and Joel 2.2 refer to a day of "darkness and gloom." In a passage that threatens judgment upon Israel in the eighth century BCE, Amos says in the name of God, "I will make the sun go down at noon and darken the earth in broad daylight" (8.9).

Given this background, the darkness from noon to three o'clock is best understood as symbolism. How many resonances of meaning Mark intended is unclear, but it is reasonable to imagine a combination of grief and judgment. The cosmos itself joins in mourning, even as the darkness symbolizes judgment upon the rulers who crucified the "Lord of glory," to use a phrase from Paul.

---

8. Moreover, to imagine that darkness really covered the land for three hours leads to a very negative perception of the inhabitants of Jerusalem and the temple authorities. How could they be so obdurate as to miss the significance of what was happening? Why were they not terrified and led to rethink what was happening?

At three o'clock, Jesus dies. His last words are the opening line of Psalm 22: "My God, my God, why have you forsaken me?" (Mark 15.34). They are the only words spoken by Jesus from the cross in Mark and Matthew. Luke and John each add three more statements, thus producing what Christians know as "the seven last words."[9]

Then Mark narrates two events that provide interpretive comments about the death of Jesus. The first is the tearing of the temple curtain: "And the curtain of the temple was torn in two, from top to bottom" (15.38). Like the darkness, this event is to be understood symbolically and not as history remembered. The curtain separated the holiest part of the temple sanctuary—the "holy of holies"—from the rest of the temple building. It was the place where God was most particularly present and so sacred that only the high priest was permitted to enter it, and only on one day of the year. To say that the curtain was torn in two has a twofold meaning. On the other hand, it is a judgment upon the temple and the temple authorities. On the other hand, it is an affirmation: the tearing of the curtain, the veil of separation, means that God is accessible apart from the temple. So Jesus had taught, and so he knew from his experiences of God as a Jewish mystic.

In the second event contemporaneous with Jesus's death, the centurion in command of the soldiers who had crucified Jesus exclaims, "Truly this man was God's Son" (15.39). He is the first human in Mark's gospel to call Jesus "God's Son"; not even Jesus's followers do. That this exclamation comes from a centurion is very significant. Recall that, according to Roman imperial theology, the emperor was Son of God as well as Lord, Savior, and the one who had brought peace on earth. But now a representative of Rome affirms that this man, executed by the empire, is the Son of God. In the exclamation of the centurion, empire testifies against itself.

From a distance, some women watch. They had followed him and provided for him in Galilee. Mark tells us there were "many other women who had come up with Jesus to Jerusalem." They included: Mary Magdalene, and Mary the mother of James the younger and of Joses, and Salome (15.40-41). They will be at the tomb on Sunday morning.

WHY DID IT HAPPEN?

Why did it happen? Why did Jesus's life end this way? Those of us who grew up in the church do not come to this question without a preunderstanding. The most widespread one is that Jesus died for the sins of the world. In her

9. Luke 23.34, 43, 46; John 19.26-27, 28, 30.

reflections on growing up Christian, Roberta Bondi, a contemporary Christian scholar, speaks for many of us: "If you had asked me in fourth grade, 'Why was Jesus born?' I would have been glad to answer, 'It was because of sin. Jesus was born in order to pay the price for our sin by suffering and dying on the cross.'"[10] His death was central to God's plan of salvation: he had to die in order to atone for our sins. It was necessary.

Called "substitutionary atonement" or "substitutionary sacrifice," this understanding of Jesus's death continues to be bedrock for most conservative Christians, even as it is being set aside or relativized by many in mainline denominations. The cover of a recent issue of a well-known conservative-evangelical magazine proclaims "No Substitute for the Substitute," heralding an article titled "Nothing but the Blood." In it, the author criticizes some evangelical scholars for weakening the claim that Jesus's death was a substitutionary sacrifice and affirms that what is at stake is "nothing less than the essence of Christianity":

> If we have any assurance of salvation, it is because of Christ's Atonement; if any joy, it flows from Christ's work on the Cross. Apart from Christ's atoning work, we would be forever guilty, ashamed, and condemned before God.[11]

The author concludes the article with advice given by a father to his son Chad: "This is what I hold out to my young son as the hope of his life: that Jesus, God's perfect, righteous Son, died in his place for his sins. Jesus took all the punishment; Jesus received all the wrath as he hung on the Cross, so people like Chad and his sinful daddy could be completely forgiven."[12]

This understanding is part of a larger, familiar theological package in which all of us are sinners. In order for God to forgive sins, a substitutionary sacrifice must be offered. But an ordinary human being cannot be the sacrifice, for such a person would be a sinner and would be dying only for his or her own sins. Thus the sacrifice must be a perfect human being. Only Jesus, who was not only human but also the Son of God, was perfect, spotless, and without blemish. Only his substitutionary death makes our forgiveness possible.

Many people think this is the orthodox and thus "official" Christian understanding of Jesus's death, including many who have difficulty with it, whether within the church or outside of it. Hence it is important to realize that it is not the only Christian understanding. Indeed, it took over a thousand years for it to become dominant.

---

10. Roberta Bondi, *Memories of God*, (Nashville: Abingdon, 1993), p. 153-54.
11. Mark Dever, "Nothing but the Blood," *Christianity Today* (May 2006): 29.
12. Dever, "Nothing but the Blood," p. 33.

In fully developed form, it first appears in a book written in 1097 by Anselm, archbishop of Canterbury. It gradually became central in medieval Christianity and then in much of the theology of the Protestant Reformation. There it was foundational for the notion of radical grace: through Jesus's death, God has abolished the system of requirements by taking care of whatever you think separates you from God. Ironically and over time, it became for many Protestants the primary requirement in a new system of requirements: we are made right with God by believing that Jesus died as our substitute. Radical grace became conditional grace. And conditional grace is no longer grace.

But seeing Jesus's death primarily within the framework of substitutionary atonement goes far beyond what the New Testament says. Strikingly, Mark's story of Jesus's death says nothing about a substitutionary sacrifice. In the other gospels, it is only if one reads them within the framework of substitution that one finds the notion there.

Of course, some New Testament authors, including Paul, use sacrificial imagery. But it is one of several images they use to speak of the meaning of Jesus's death. The others include:[13]

- The cross as the domination system's "no" to Jesus (and Easter as God's "yes" to Jesus and "no" to the powers that killed him).

- The cross as revelation of the path of transformation: we are transformed by dying and rising with Christ.

- The cross as revelation of the depth of God's love for us. It is not the story of a human sacrifice required by a judging God, but a parable of God's radical grace.

In all of these, the notion of substitution is absent. Moreover, it is important to realize that the language of sacrifice does not intrinsically mean *substitution*. This is true in ordinary language as well as in the Bible. In our everyday use of the word, we speak of soldiers sacrificing their lives for their country, and of Martin Luther King Jr. and Gandhi and others sacrificing their lives for the causes—about which they were passionate. In *this* sense, was Jesus's death a sacrifice? Yes. But affirming this does not thereby imply that they and he died as a substitute for somebody else.

In the Bible, sacrifice is most commonly associated with a gift and a meal. The giving of a gift and the sharing of a meal are the classic means of bringing about reconciliation when rupture has occurred, whether with a person

---

13. For fuller but still concise expositions, see my *The Meaning of Jesus: Two Visions*, with N. T. Wright (San Francisco: HarperSanFrancisco, 1999), pp. 137-42; and *The Heart of Christianity* (San Francisco: HarperSanFrancisco, 2003), pp. 91-96.

or God. The giving of a gift to God makes it sacred, which is the root meaning of the word "sacrifice," "to make sacred." To say that Jesus's death was a sacrifice means that his death has become sacred for us. As the language of the Eucharist in liturgical churches puts it, "Christ our Passover has been sacrificed for us; therefore, let us keep the feast." Exactly. The Passover lamb was not a substitution, but food for the journey. Christ our Passover has been made sacred for us; therefore, let us share the meal of his body and blood.

To be candid at the risk of being offensive, I see the notion of substitutionary atonement as bad theology and bad history. I do not mean to mock people who think this way or to imply that thinking this way precludes being Christian. Millions of Christians have believed in substitutionary atonement and have been good Christians. Being Christian is not primarily about getting our beliefs right. Rather, I am inviting people who believe or think they are supposed to believe in substitutionary atonement to think again, to reconsider, to see again.

I think it's bad theology because it elevates one understanding of Jesus's death above all others and makes it normative. Moreover, it says something both limiting and negative about God. It limits God by saying God can forgive sins only if adequate payment is made. Is God limited in any way? Is God limited by the requirements of law? It is negative in that in it God demands a death—somebody must die. It implies that the death of Jesus, this immeasurably great and good man, was God's will, God's plan for our salvation.

In its emphatic form, the substitutionary atonement leads to what Dallas Willard, an evangelical author, vividly calls "vampire Christians"—Christians interested in Jesus for his blood but little else.[14] But, as he and I agree, the cross is about discipleship. Discipleship, following Jesus, is not about believing a correct atonement theology. It is about following the way of the cross—commitment to the path of personal transformation as symbolized by the cross, and commitment to the path of confrontation with domination systems, equally symbolized by the cross.

In his book *The Cost of Discipleship*, written in Germany in the late 1930s, Dietrich Bonhoeffer, one of the martyred saints of the twentieth century, said, "When Christ calls a man he bids him come and die."[15] He did not then know (though he may have intuited it) that the path of discipleship, the way of the

14. Dallas Willard, *The Divine Conspiracy* (San Francisco: HarperSanFrancisco, 1997), p.403, n. 8. The phrase "vampire Christians" was also included in his web site when I visited it in August 2006.

15. Dietrich Bonhoeffer, *The Cost of Discipleship* (New York: Macmillan, 1963), p. 7 (first published in Germany in 1937). Bonhoeffer was executed by the Third Reich in April 1945, a month before the war ended. He was only thirty-nine.

cross, would involve for him not only personal transformation but also a fatal confrontation with the powers that ruled his world. It would cost Bonhoeffer his life: he was executed by Nazi Germany. The way of the cross is about discipleship, not believing in the blood of Jesus as a substitute for our own.

I think it's bad history because it presumes that Jesus's death was part of the plan of God. But this is not a historical explanation, not an answer to the question, "Why was Jesus killed?"

EXECUTED BY ROME

That Jesus was crucified tells us that he was executed by Rome, the empire that ruled his world. It was an imperial form of execution, not a Jewish one. We do not know if the temple authorities had the power to impose capital punishment. According to John 18.31, they did not. But if they did have that power, the mode of execution would have been stoning. To say the obvious, Jesus was crucified, not stoned.

Crucifixion made a statement. There were other forms of Roman capital punishment, such as beheading. Rome reserved crucifixion for two categories of people: chronically defiant slaves and others who challenged Roman rule. What they shared in common was refusing to accept established authority.

Crucifixion was designed to be brutal and very public. Victims were nailed and sometimes also roped to a cross. Death was normally slow and excruciating (a word that comes from the Latin word for "cross"). The victim was naked and most often took several days to die. Death resulted from a combination of exposure to heat and cold, exhaustion, and respiratory failure. It was as public as possible. Victims were hung up near a city gate or other prominent place where many people would pass by. To imagine a different scenario, Jesus could have been killed in a back alley or a prison cell if the authorities had simply wanted to get rid of him. But he was crucified precisely because it made a public statement; it said this is what we do to people who oppose us. It was state-sponsored terrorism, imperial terrorism, torture and death as deterrent.

It has become a cliché among Jesus scholars to say that the most certain fact we know about him is that he was crucified. But it is an important cliché. Jesus was executed. He didn't simply die; the authorities killed him. For a sketch of the historical Jesus to be persuasive, it must account for this.

DID IT HAVE TO HAPPEN?

Was the death of Jesus foreordained? Did it have to happen, because of divine necessity, because of prophecies in the Jewish Bible, or both? In the decades after his death, his followers sometimes spoke of Jesus's death as foreordained by God and as God's providential purpose (see, for example, 1 Pet. 1.18-20 and Luke 24.26-27). These are, of course, retrospective and retrojective interpretations: they look back on the death of Jesus and see a purpose in it and they retroject this purpose back into the story.

This easily generates the inference that Jesus's death had to happen. But this is not a necessary inference. Consider the story from the Jewish Bible about Joseph and his brothers, the fathers of the twelve tribes of Israel. Envious of Joseph, they sell him into slavery and he ends up in Egypt. There, over a long period of time, rises to a position of authority second only to Pharaoh. Then, because of a famine in their land, his brothers come to Egypt seeking food. They do not know what has happened to Joseph or even if he is still alive.

Joseph meets with them and, when they learn who he is, they are afraid, understandably so. Their brother whom they sold into slavery is now in a position of power and can do to them whatever he wants. But rather than being vengeful, Joseph says:

> Do not be distressed, or angry with yourselves, because you sold me here; *for God sent me before you to preserve life* . . . *God sent me* before you to preserve for you a remnant on earth, and to keep alive for you many survivors. So it was not you who sent me here, *but God.* (Gen. 45.5-8)

The storyteller of Genesis affirms a providential purpose in Joseph's being sold into slavery: "*God sent me*—it was not you who sent me here, *but God.*"

Does this mean that it was God's will that his brothers sold him into slavery? No. It is never the will of God to sell a brother into slavery. Did it have to happen this way? No. It could have happened differently. His brothers were not foreordained to do this. Rather, the story affirms that God can use even the evil deed of selling a brother into slavery for a providential purpose.

Applying this story to how we might see Jesus's death, was it the will of God? No. It is never the will of God that a righteous man be crucified. Did it have to happen? It might have turned out differently. Judas might not have betrayed Jesus. The temple authorities might have decided on a course of action other than execution. Pilate might have let Jesus go or decided on a punishment other than death. But it did happen this way. And like the storyteller of Genesis, early Christians looking back on what did happen ascribed providential meanings to Jesus's death. But this does not mean that it had to happen.

Yet, though not required by divine necessity, the execution of Jesus was virtually a human inevitability. This is what domination systems do to people who challenge them, publicly and vigorously. It happened often in the ancient world. It had happened to Jesus's mentor John the Baptizer, executed by Herod Antipas not long before. Now it happened to Jesus. Within a few more decades, it would happen to Paul, Peter, and James. We should wonder what it was about Jesus and his movement that so provoked the authorities at the top of the domination systems of their time.

But Jesus was not simply an unfortunate victim of a domination system's brutality. He was also a protagonist filled with passion. His passion, his message, was about the kingdom of God. He spoke to peasants as a voice of religious protest against the central economic and political institutions of his day. He attracted a following, took his movement to Jerusalem at the season of Passover, and there challenged the authorities with public acts and public debates. All of this was his passion, what he was passionate about—God and the kingdom of God, God and God's passion for justice.

Jesus's passion got him killed. His passion for the kingdom of God led to what is called his passion in a narrower sense, namely, his suffering and death. But to restrict Jesus's passion to his suffering and death is to ignore the passion that brought him to Jerusalem. To think of Jesus's passion as simply what happened on Good Friday is to separate his death from the passion that animated his life. Did Good Friday have to happen? As divine necessity? No. As human inevitability? Virtually.

Good Friday is the collision between the passion of Jesus and the domination system of his time. What killed Jesus was nothing unusual. There is no reason to think that the temple authorities were particularly wicked people. We might have enjoyed their company. Moreover, as empires go, Rome was better than most. There was nothing exceptional or abnormal about it; this is simply the way domination systems behave. So common is this dynamic that, as suggested earlier, it can be called the normalcy of civilization.

This realization generates an additional reflection. According to the gospels, Jesus did not die for the sins of the world. The language of sacrificial substitution is absent from their stories. But in an important sense, he was killed because of the sins of the world. The injustice of the domination system killed him, injustice so routine that it is part of civilization's normalcy. Though sin means more than this, it includes this. Jesus was executed because of the sins of the world.

Jesus's passion was the kingdom of God. It led him to oppose the domination system of his time. The cross of Jesus, the central symbol of Christianity, was political. His death also has religious significance.

But any understanding that negates the political meaning of his death on the cross betrays the passion for which he was willing to give his life. His passion was God and the kingdom of God—and it led to his execution by the "powers that be." The domination system killed him.

EASTER: VINDICATED BY GOD

Of course, the story of Jesus does not end with his execution. His followers affirmed that God had raised him from the dead. Easter is so central to the story of Jesus that, without it, we wouldn't even know about him. If his story had ended with his crucifixion, he most likely would have been forgotten—another Jew crucified by the Roman Empire in a bloody century that witnessed thousands of such executions. Perhaps a trace or two about him would have shown up in Josephus or in Jewish rabbinic sources, but that would have been all.

But what is Easter about? On one level, the answer is obvious: God raised Jesus. Yes. And what does it mean to say this? Is it about a spectacular miracle—the most spectacular miracle there's ever been, and thus a testimony to the power of God? Is it about God demonstrating that Jesus was indeed his Son—that Jesus was who he said he was? Is it about the promise of an after-life-that death has been defeated? All of these? Or something else?

Those of us who grew up Christian have a preunderstanding of Easter, just as we do of Jesus's death. It commonly combines the stories of Easter from all the gospels into a composite whole and then sees them through the filter of Christian preaching and teaching, hymns and liturgy. In its most common form, this preunderstanding sees the stories as historically factual reports. Reading the stories carefully discloses differences in details, but these are seen as the product of multiple witnesses. As we all know, witnesses of an event can differ about the details (think of diverging testimonies about an auto accident), but still be reliable witnesses to the basic factuality of the event (the accident really happened).

This common preunderstanding includes at least three claims. First, the tomb of Jesus was empty. Second, this was because God had raised Jesus from the dead (and not because somebody stole the body or because his followers went to the wrong tomb). Third, Jesus appeared to his followers after his death in a form that could be seen, heard, and touched.[16]

This way of seeing the Easter stories affirms what might be called their *public factuality;* that is, anybody who was there would have experienced what is reported. You or I (or Pilate) would have seen the empty tomb and

---

16. For vigorous defenses of the historical factuality of the stories by conservative-evangelical scholars, see Lee Strobel, *The Case for Christ* (Grand Rapids, MI: Zondervan, 1988); *Jesus Under Fire*, ed. by Michael Wilkins and J. P. Moreland (Grand Rapids, MI: Zondervan, 1995); and Paul Copan, *Will the Real Jesus Please Stand Up?* (Grand Rapids, MI: Baker, 1998). For a more elaborate and sophisticated defense, see the massive volume by N. T. Wright, *The Resurrection of the Son of God* (Minneapolis: Fortress, 2003).

the risen Jesus talking to Mary Magdalene, appearing to his disciples, inviting Thomas to touch the wounds in his body, eating breakfast with them on the shore of the Sea of Galilee, and so forth. Public factuality means that the events could have been photographed or videotaped, had these technologies been available then. For many Christians, the historical factuality of the Easter stories is so central that, if it didn't happen this way, the foundation and truth of Christianity disappear.

But focusing on the public factuality of the Easter stories risks missing their meanings. They have a more-than-factual significance. When they are claimed to be factual reports, the question of faith most often becomes, "Do you believe they happened?" Debates occur about whether the tomb was really empty and whether the testimony of the witnesses can stand up to rigorous historical inquiry. Easter faith becomes believing that these utterly unique and spectacular events happened on a particular Sunday and for a few weeks afterward a long time ago. The factual question dominates, and the meaning question often remains unasked.

And so we turn to the question of meaning. What did Easter mean to the early followers of Jesus? To state my conclusion in advance, for them, including the authors of the New Testament, Easter had two primary meanings. First, the followers of Jesus continued to experience him after his death. They continued to know him as a figure of the present, and not simply as a figure from the past. Indeed, they experienced him as a divine reality, as one with God. Second, Easter meant that God had vindicated Jesus. As Acts 2.36 puts it, "This Jesus whom you crucified, God has made him both Lord and Messiah." Easter is God's "yes" to Jesus and God's "no" to the powers that killed him. Jesus was executed by Rome and vindicated by God. To put these two meanings as concisely as possible, Easter meant "Jesus lives" and "Jesus is Lord."

PART THREE

THE ATONEMENT
AND SACRIFICE

Chapter Five

GOD'S SELF-SUBSTITUTION
AND SACRIFICIAL INVERSION

by James Alison

I tried, over three chapters of *On Being Liked,*[1] to set out some bases for thinking through what it means to say that Jesus died to save us. That was, and is, very much an ongoing project. Since writing those chapters, I have been greatly helped by the work of Margaret Barker, especially *The Great High Priest*[2] and her study of the book of Revelation, *The Revelation of Jesus Christ,*[3] in taking this further. Barker's insights seem to me to combine extraordinarily well with the New Testament detective work of scholars like J. Duncan M. Derrett[4] and the anthropology of desire which René Girard has made luminous for us.[5] They offer the possibility of a richer and deeper understanding of the atonement, and one which will, I hope, not only help to overcome divisions within Christianity as to how Jesus' death is to be understood, but also give a far more positive account of the Jewishness of that saving death than we are used to.

So, I would like to give you a kind of progress report on where I think this understanding is going by trying to defend a thesis with you. My thesis is that Christianity is a priestly religion which understands that God overcomes our violence by substituting himself for the victim of our typical sacrifices. This opens us up to be able to enjoy the fullness of creation as if death were not.

The first thing that I ought to do, therefore, is to rehearse for you my brief account of what is traditionally called the substitutionary theory of atonement. This is what we are up against. It is a certain crystallization of texts threaded together in a way that has kept us captive, and my interest is in how

---

1. *On Being Liked* (London: DLT, 2003) chapters 2–4.
2. *The Great High Priest: The Temple Roots of Christian Liturgy* (London: Continuum, 2004).
3. *The Revelation of Jesus Christ* (Edinburgh: T&T Clark, 2000).
4. Derrett's *Law in the New Testament* (London: DLT, 1970) is classic, and his several volumes of *Studies in the New Testament* (Leiden: Brill) are jewels for those lucky enough to have access to them.
5. In more works than I can mention here. M. Kirwan's *Discovering Girard* (London: DLT, 2004) is, by Girard's own avowal, the best introduction to his thought.

we are going to move from this two-dimensional account to a three-dimensional account and see that, in reality, all the creative lines in the story flow in an entirely different direction. So, here's the standard story which, in one version or other, I'm sure you've all heard before:

God created the universe, including humanity, and it was good. Then somehow or another, humankind fell. This fall was a sin against God's infinite goodness and mercy and justice. So there was a problem. Humans could not, off our own bat, restore the order which had been disordered, let alone make up for having dishonoured God's infinite goodness. Nothing finite could make up for an offence with infinite ramifications. God would have been perfectly within his rights to have destroyed the whole of humanity. But God was merciful as well as being just, so he pondered what to do to sort out the mess. Could he have simply let the matter lie in his infinite mercy? Well, maybe he would have liked to, but he was beholden to his infinite justice as well. Only an infinite payment would do. Something that humans couldn't come up with; but God could. And yet the payment had to be from the human side, or else it wouldn't be a real payment for the outrage to be appeased. So God came up with the idea of sending his Son into the world as a human, so that his Son could pay the price as a human, which, since he was also God, would be infinite and thus would effect the necessary satisfaction. Thus the whole sorry saga could be brought to a convenient close. Those humans who agreed to cover over their sins by holding on to, or being covered by, the precious blood of the Saviour, whom the Father has sacrificed to himself, would be saved from their sins and given the Holy Spirit by which they would be able to behave according to the original order of creation. In this way, when they died, they would at least be able to inherit heaven, which had been the original plan all along, before the fall had mucked everything up.

Now, rather than making mockery of this story-line, I want to suggest that the trouble with it is that it is not nearly conservative enough. I want to put forward a much more conservative account. And the first way I want to be conservative is to suggest that the principal problem with this conventional account is that it is a *theory*, while atonement, in the first place, was a *liturgy*.

That doesn't sound like too much of a contrast in our world because we tend to have an impoverished notion of liturgy. And we do not realize how much our dwelling in theory complicates our lives. However, in fact, treating atonement as a theory means that it is an idea that can be *grasped* – and once it is grasped, you have "got it" – whereas a liturgy is something that *happens to and at you*. I want to go back and recover a little bit of what the liturgy of atonement was about; because once we understand that, we begin to get a sense of what this language of "atonement" and "salvation" is about.

Let's remember that we're talking about a very ancient Jewish liturgy about which we only know from fragmentary reconstructions of what might have gone on in the First Temple. For this liturgy, the high priest would go into the Holy of Holies. Before the high priest went into the Holy of Holies, he would sacrifice a bull or a calf in expiation for his own sins. He would then go into the Holy of Holies, having chosen by lot one of two lambs or goats – one goat which was the Lord, the other goat was to be Azazel (the "devil"). He would take the first goat with him into the Holy of Holies and sacrifice it; and with it, he would sprinkle the mercy seat (the throne above which were the Cherubim), the Ark and so on.

Only the high priest was allowed to enter the Holy Place. Now the interesting thing is that after expiating his own sins with the bull, he would then don a brilliant white robe, which was the robe of an angel. From that point he would cease to be a human being and would become the angel, one of whose names was "the Son of God." And he would be able to put on "the Name," meaning "the name which could not be pronounced," the Name of the Lord, represented by its four letters, YHWH. With the Name contained in the phylacteries, either on his forehead or wrapped around his arms, he would be able to go into the Holy of Holies. He was to be Yahweh-for-the-day, an angelic emanation of God most high. (Remember the phrase, "Blessed is he who comes in the name of the Lord"? This is a reference to the rite of atonement, the coming of the high priest – one of the many references to the rite of atonement we get in the New Testament – and of which we are largely ignorant!).

So, the high priest becomes an angelic emanation of YHWH; and one of the angel's titles is "the son of God." He sacrifices the goat that is "the Lord" and sprinkles his blood about the place. The purpose of this was to remove all the impurities that had accrued in what was meant to be a microcosm of creation, because the Holy of Holies, in the understanding of the Temple, was the place where the Creator dwelt, beyond and outside Creation. The idea was that Creation started from the Temple veil outwards, while the Holy Place was beyond time, matter and space. The rite of atonement was about the Lord himself, the Creator, emerging from the Holy of Holies so as to set the people free from their impurities and sins and transgression. In other words, the whole rite was exactly the reverse of what we typically imagine a priestly rite to be about. We tend to have an "Aztec imagination" with regard to the sacrificial system. The hallmark of the sacrificial system is that its priest sacrifices something so as to placate some deity.

The Jewish priestly rite was already an enormous advance beyond that world. They understood perfectly well that it was pagan rites that sacrificed victims in order to keep creation going. And one of the ways in which they had advanced beyond that, even before the fall of the Temple and the Exile to Babylon, was the understanding that it was actually *God* who was doing the work. It was *God* who was coming out, wanting to restore creation out of his love for his people. And so it is YHWH who emerges from the Holy of Holies, dressed in white, in order to forgive the people their sins and, more importantly, in order to *allow creation to flow.*

The notion is that humans are inclined to muck up creation; and it is God emerging from the place that symbolizes that which was before creation began: "the place of the Creator." The Holy of Holies was the place that symbolized "before the first day" – which meant, of course, before time, before creation was brought into being.

The priest emerged from there and came through the Temple veil. This was made of very rich material, representing the material world, that which was created. At this point, the high priest would don a robe made of the same material as the veil, to demonstrate that what he was acting out was God coming forth and entering into the world of creation so as to make atonement, to undo the way humans had snarled up that creation. And at that point, having emerged, he would then sprinkle the rest of the Temple with the blood that was the Lord's blood.

Now, here's the interesting point: for the Temple understanding, the high priest at this stage *was* acting "in the person of Yahweh," and it was *the Lord's* blood that was being sprinkled. This was a divine movement to set people free. It was not – as we often imagine – a priest satisfying a divinity. The reason why the priest had to engage in a prior expiation was that he was about to become a sign of something quite the opposite; he was acting outwards. The movement is not inwards towards the Holy of Holies; the movement is outwards from the Holy of Holies.

So the priest would then come through the veil – meaning the Lord entering into the world, the created world – and he would sprinkle all the rest of the Temple, thus setting it free. After that, as the person who was bearing the sins that had been accumulated, he places them on the head of what we call "the scapegoat," Azazel, which would then be driven outside the town to the edge of a cliff and cast down, where it would be killed so that the people's sins would be taken away.

That was, from what we can gather, the atonement rite. But here is the fascinating thing: the Jewish understanding was way ahead of the "Aztec" version we attribute to it. Even at that time, it was understood that it was not about humans trying desperately to satisfy God, but God taking the initiative of breaking through towards us. In other words, atonement was something of which we were the *beneficiaries.* That is the first point I want to make in emphasizing that we are talking about a liturgy rather than a theory. We are talking about something that we undergo over time as part of a benign divine initiative towards us.

This puts many things in a slightly different perspective from what we are used to. It means, for instance, that the picture of God in the theory that we have – that demands that God's anger be satisfied – is a pagan notion. In the Jewish understanding, it was, instead, something that God was offering to us. Now here's the crunch: the early Christians who wrote the New Testament understood very clearly that Jesus was *the* authentic high priest, who was restoring *the* eternal covenant that had been established long before. Jesus was coming out from the Holy Place to offer himself as an expiation for us, as a concrete living out and demonstration of God's love for us. And Jesus was acting this out quite deliberately.

There are a number of places where we get hints of this language. One of them is in Jesus acting out the role of Melchizedek. For example, the announcement of the Jubilee, which Jesus preaches in the synagogue in Nazareth,[6] was the way in which the high priest Melchizedek would come back and work for the liberation, the "atonement" or "redemption" of the people. In fact, what Jesus says and does in Luke is to fulfil the Melchizedek agenda, which includes going up to Jerusalem and being killed.

There are different ways in the other Gospels in which this is depicted. The classic example is in St. John's Gospel, chapter 17. Jesus' last speech to his disciples before the Passion is a speech based on the high priest's atonement prayer. Jesus then goes off to act out the role of the high priest who is making available the new Temple in his body (which, of course, John had given us a hint about in the beginning of his Gospel).

One of the ways in which this is told in St. John's Gospel is that Jesus is crucified on Thursday, not on Friday. On Thursday afternoon, he is going outside the city walls to be killed at exactly the same time – three in the afternoon – when the priests in the Temple were killing the lambs for the Passover feast. So, while they were killing the lambs, the real Lamb, the one who was identified as "the lamb of God," was going to the place of execution to be killed. But – bizarrely – he was going dressed in a "seamless robe," a *priest's robe*: hence the importance of his robe being "seamless," and lots having to be cast for it rather than it being torn.[7] So the high priest was going – *the Lord* was going – to "the Temple" where he would be "the Lamb," for, as we are told, when they look on him after he has died, they see that not a bone of his body was broken, alluding to the Passover lamb.

The identification is complete. And of course, Jesus' cry on the cross in

6. Lk 4:16ff.

7. That Christian tradition has never entirely lost sight of this can be seen by looking at Giotto's Scrovegni Chapel Crucifixion (1303-6), where the robe being handed over is very clearly priestly.

John's Gospel is "It is finished," "It is completed." The atonement, and therefore the inauguration of creation, is completed. In John's Gospel, the "I shall go to my Father" is always synonymous with "I shall go to my death, in which I shall be lifted up, and that is how I will glorify my Father." All of these things we know; but usually we do not see them in the context of Jesus being the authentic high priest doing the high priestly thing.

You can tell that this was how it was read because in John's Gospel, immediately after this, at the resurrection, we are transferred to the garden. We are back to the "first day" and we are in "the garden." Peter and John come to look, then Mary Magdalene comes in. What does she see? Two angels! And where are the angels sitting? One at the head and one at the foot of a space that is open because the stone has been rolled away. What is this space? This is the Holy of Holies. This is the mercy seat, with the Cherubim present.[8] The Holy of Holies is now open, because creation is able to flow completely freely. No more tangling up of creation. The Holy of Holies has been opened up. The high priest has gone in – one who did not need to sacrifice a bull for his own sins because he didn't have any. Then he was able to come out of the place of creation and into the whole world.

And remember that in the epistle to the Hebrews, as in much of the Pauline literature, and in John's Gospel, Jesus was the Word of God who was with creation from the beginning – "all things were created through him." This is the high priestly language of the One who is coming from God to offer atonement so as to open up creation. That is what is being fulfilled. And you get a sense of a realization in John's Gospel that this is what has been acted out: Jesus' fulfilling of the liturgy of the atonement. So far so good! This is an explanation that allows us to see Jesus' "subversion from within" of the ancient liturgy of atonement – which was also practiced in the Second Temple period.[9]

In the Second Temple there was no longer a mercy seat. There was no longer anything inside the Holy of Holies. The priestly mysteries had been lost. And this was one of the reasons that there was excitement: here was a priest who was going to fulfil the promises and restore the priestly mysteries. But of course "restored" in a skewed, "off stage" way – i.e. the real high priest was engaged in *being* the sacrifice, "the victim," the priest, the altar and the Temple on the city rubbish heap, at the same time as the corrupt city guys – which is how the ordinary Jews saw them at the time – were going through

8. For a particularly beautiful reading of this, see Rowan Williams' "Between the Cherubim: the empty tomb and the empty throne" in *On Christian Theology* (Oxford: Blackwell, 2000) pp. 183-196

9. Sirach 50 gives us a wonderful 2nd Temple account of the High Priest Simeon performing this liturgy with many of the ancient elements clearly recognizable.

the motions in the corrupt Second Temple, which was not of such great concern to the people. They didn't think it was the real thing. Many of Jesus' contemporaries would have regarded the Temple which they knew and the priesthood which ran it as, if you'll excuse the imagery, the diet-Pepsi version of a long lost real Coke.

From our point of view, these are all aspects of atonement. What Jesus was doing was fulfilling a set of prophecies concerning a liturgical happening, which is to us largely mysterious. The reason I wanted to tell you about it is that it is very important for us to understand that this is not simply an abolition of something that was bad, but the fulfilment of something that was considered good but not good enough. Do you see the difference? It means that our tendency to read the whole world of priesthood and sacrifice as an "unfortunate Semitic leftover" is really very wrong. The Jewish priestly thing – apart from being responsible for some of the most extraordinary texts that we have in what survives in the Hebrew scriptures – was also *the pattern* which enabled the relationship between creation and salvation to be held together. And that is the pattern of the Catholic faith, as I want to explore a little bit more. It is the notion of God making available for us the chance to participate in the fullness of creation by becoming a sacrifice for us in our midst.

We are all – quite rightly – allergic to liturgy by itself. We are absolutely right because that is one of the things that the New Testament is insistent on. The genius of Jesus lay, among other things, in bringing together the liturgical and the ethical, which is why atonement matters to us. Because what Jesus did was not really, as it were, to fulfil a series of prophecies regarding a somewhat bizarre ancient rite that involved lots of blood and a barbeque. What Jesus did – and this is the fascinating thing – was to make an extraordinary *anthropological* breakthrough. And this is where atonement is "substitutionary."

Here I want to offer a little aside: normally, in the *theory*-based approach to substitutionary atonement, we understand the substitution to work as follows: God was angry with humanity; Jesus says, "Here am I"; God needed to loose a lightning rod, so Jesus said, "You can loose it on me," thus substituting himself for us. Boom: lightning rod gets struck; sacrifice is carried out; God is happy. "I got my blood-lust out of the way!"

The interesting thing is that the New Testament points to an entirely different way of conceiving this: what Jesus was doing was *substituting himself for a series of substitutions*. The human sacrificial system typically works in the following way: the most primitive forms of sacrifice are *human* sacrifices. After people become aware of what they are doing, this gets transferred to *animal* sacrifices. After all, it's easier to sacrifice animals because they don't fight back so much, whereas if you have to run a sacrificial system, that requires you to keep getting victims. Usually you have to run a war machine in order to provide enough victims to keep the system going; or you have to keep pet "*pharmakons*" around the place[10] – convenient half-insider/half-outsiders, who live in splendour and have a thoroughly good time – until a time of crisis when you need people to sacrifice, and then you sacrifice them. But this is an ugly thing, and people are, after all, human; and so animals began to be sacrificed instead. And in some cultures, from animals you move on to more symbolic forms of sacrifice, like bread and wine. You can find the theme of sacrificial substitution in almost every cultural variation.

The interesting thing is that Jesus takes exactly the inverse route; and he explains to us that he is going in the inverse route. "The night before he was betrayed..." what did he do? He said, "Instead of the bread and the wine, this is the lamb, and the lamb is a human being." In other words he substituted a human being back into the *centre* of the sacrificial system *as the priest*, thus showing what the sacrificial system was really about, and so bringing it to an end. He was the Great High Priest giving portions of himself as Lamb to his fellow priests, just as the High Priest in office would distribute portions of the sacrificed lamb to the other priests.

So you do have a genuine substitution that is quite proper within the Christian living-out of atonement. All sacrificial systems are substitutionary; but what we have with Jesus is an exact inversion of the sacrificial system: he goes backwards and occupies the space so as to make it clear that this is simply *murder*. And it *needn't be*. That is what we begin to get in St. John's Gospel: a realization that what Jesus was doing was actually *revealing* the mendacious principle of the world. The way human structure is maintained is by people killing each other, convincing ourselves of our right and duty to do it, and therefore building ourselves up over and against our victims. What Jesus understands himself doing in St. John's Gospel is revealing the way in which the mechanism works. And by revealing it, he deprives it of all power by making it clear that it is a lie: "Your father was a liar and a murderer from the beginning." That is how the "prince" – or *principle* – of this world works.

So what we get in St. John's Gospel is a clear understanding that the undoing of victimage is not simply a liturgical matter; it is not simply a liturgical fulfilment. Jesus is substituting himself at the centre of what the liturgical tradition was both remembering and covering up, namely *human sacrifice*, therefore making it possible for us to begin to live without sacrifice. And

---

10. Some ancient Greek cities kept just such made-to-measure future victims in supply against the day when their sacrifice would be "necessary."

that includes not only liturgical sacrifice, but more importantly, the human mechanism of sacrificing other people so that we can keep ourselves going. In other words, what Jesus was beginning to make possible for us was to begin to live as if death were not, and therefore, to release us from having to protect ourselves over against death by treading on other people. Do you see how he is pulling together the ethical and the liturgical into the same space so that this is a space of dense anthropological revelation? When Jesus brings together the liturgical and the ethical understanding of victimhood, thus showing us what we typically do and how we need no longer do it, God is showing us something about *ourselves.*

Now, this was quite clearly seen at the time, as is clear from references in St. John's Gospel to Jesus' understanding of this mechanism as that of "the prince of this world." But there are also some give-aways in St. Paul that are very revealing.

Here is a story from 2 Samuel,[11] that takes us straight back into the world of expiation, propitiation and atonement – in the anthropological sphere, not the liturgical sphere. Remember, the two are linked, but they haven't yet been linked clearly:

> Now there was a famine in the days of David for three years, year after year; and David sought the face of the LORD. And the LORD said, "There is bloodguilt on Saul and on his house, because he put the Gibeonites to death." So the king called the Gibeonites. Now the Gibeonites were not of the people of Israel, but of the remnant of the Amorites; although the people of Israel had sworn to spare them, Saul had sought to slay them in his zeal for the people of Israel and Judah. And David said to the Gibeonites, "What shall I do for you? And how shall I make expiation, that you may bless the heritage of the LORD?" The Gibeonites said to him, "It is not a matter of silver or gold between us and Saul or his house; neither is it for us to put any man to death in Israel." And he said, "What do you say that I shall do for you?" They said to the king, "The man who consumed us and planned to destroy us, so that we should have no place in all the territory of Israel, let seven of his sons be given to us, so that we may hang them up before the LORD at Gibeon on the mountain of the LORD." And the king said, "I will give them." But the king spared Mephibosheth, the son of Saul's son Jonathan, because of the oath of the LORD which was between them, between David and Jonathan the son of Saul. The king took the two sons of Rizpah the daughter of Aiah, whom she bore to Saul, Armoni and Mephibosheth; and the five sons of Merab the daughter of Saul, whom she bore to Adriel the son of Barzillai the Meholathite; and he gave them into the hands of the Gibeonites, and they hanged them on the mountain before the LORD, and the seven of them perished together. They were put to death in the first days of harvest, at the beginning of barley harvest.

After a short time, the famine and the drought went way. A lovely story! The

---

11. 2 Sam 21:1-9.

interesting thing about it is that it makes clear something we often forget: how expiation worked. Here King David is expiating something, offering propitiation to the Gibeonites. In other words, the Gibeonites have a right to demand vengeance; they are owed something, and David is offering it to them. St. Paul seems to know about this story since he says in Romans,[12] "What then shall we say to this? If God is for us, who is against us? He who did not *spare his own Son* but gave him up for us all, will he not also give us all things with him?" Do you see what St. Paul is pointing to here? St. Paul is saying that God, unlike King David, did not seek someone else as a stand-in sacrifice to placate us, but gave his own Son (which, for a monotheist like St. Paul, means himself) to be the expiation, putting forth the propitiation.

In the Samuel text, who is propitiating whom? King David is propitiating the Gibeonites by means of Saul's sons. God is propitiating *us*. In other words, who is the angry divinity in the story? *We are.* That is the purpose of the atonement. *We* are the angry divinity. *We* are the ones inclined to dwell in wrath and think we need vengeance in order to survive. God was occupying the space of *our* victim so as to show us that we need never do this again. This turns on its head the Aztec understanding of the atonement. In fact, it turns on its head what has passed as our penal substitutionary theory of atonement, which always presupposes that it is *us* satisfying God, that *God* needs satisfying, that there is *vengeance* in God. It is quite clear from the New Testament that what really excited Paul was that from Jesus' self-giving, and the "outpouring of Jesus' blood," that this was the revelation of who God was: God was entirely without vengeance, entirely without substitutionary tricks. And that he was giving himself entirely without ambivalence and ambiguity for *us*, towards *us*, in order to set *us* "free from our sins" – "our sins" being our way of being bound up with each other in death, vengeance, violence and what is commonly called "wrath."

Now, what is particularly difficult for us, and why I want to remind us that this is a liturgy rather than a theory, is that the way we live this out as Christians is to remember that the one true sacrifice – that is to say, the place where God gave himself for us in our midst as our victim – has been done. It's over! The whole of the sacrificial system has been brought to an end. The Holy of Holies has been opened for good.

The way in which we depict this in our theological imagination is through the doctrine of the Ascension. Remember what happens at the beginning of the Acts of the Apostles. Jesus is with the apostles on a hillside outside Jerusalem, and then he is taken up into heaven. He blesses them on the way

---

12. Rom 8:31-32.

– i.e. we have the high priest. They stand looking up; and there are a couple of angels – who are, of course, our old friends the cherubim in the Holy of Holies, which has now become everywhere – saying, "Why are you standing there looking up to heaven? Go and wait to be empowered from on high." What we have here is Jesus going to "sit at the right hand of the Father": the place of the priest – the Word, the Creator – the sacrifice having been fulfilled. We live under *that*. And the way we live under it liturgically is by our participation in the Eucharist.

The purpose of the Eucharist is not for us to try to make Jesus come down here, but rather, our obedience to Jesus' instruction to invoke him, to do this in memory of him, so that we find ourselves transported into participation in the "heavenly banquet," the place where the Lamb is standing as one slaughtered, as in the vision described by the Book of Revelation. This is a Holy of Holies vision; this is a vision of the Holy of Holies now open and flowing everywhere. It is the one true sacrifice that has been done. That does not mean to say "over and done with." It means that the victorious Lamb is there; his blood is flowing out; the victim, the *forgiving* victim, is present. And we have access to participate in that atonement, which has been achieved and is made available to us in our Eucharist. The Eucharist is for us the high priest emerging out of the Holy of Holies, giving us his body and blood, as our way into being a living priesthood and a living Temple in the world.

Now, if that picture is true, then it seems that our Eucharistic life is supposed to be about us as a people, being turned into the new Temple by receiving the body and blood of the self-giving victim, who is already victorious. We are being turned into the new Temple that is able to participate in the life of God who is coming out to us here and now. That is what the doctrine of transubstantiation is about. It means that this is not merely our memorial supper; this is, in fact, the heavenly banquet where someone else is the protagonist and we are called out of ourselves into it. We are being called "through the veil" into participation. We are given the signs, which is why the body and blood are not something that hide the divinity but make it manifest. They are signs reaching out to us of what God is actually doing for us.

Now, all that is happening in heaven. That is the purpose of the doctrine of the Ascension: the Holy of Holies is fulfilled and we begin to receive all that flows from it.

This has ethical consequences. And these are tremendously important for our understanding, because, if you have a *theory* of atonement – something grasped – you have something that people can "get right," and then be on the inside with the good guys. "We're the people who are covered by the blood; we're the ones who are okay, the ones who are good; and then there are those others who aren't." In other words, rather than *undergoing* atonement, we're people who grasp onto the *idea* of the atonement. But the whole purpose of the Christian understanding is that we shouldn't identify too soon with the good guys. On the contrary, we are people who are constantly undergoing "I AM" – that is to say, God – coming towards us one who is offering forgiveness as our Victim. And we are learning how to look at each other as people who are saying, "Oh! So that's what I've been involved in." Which means that *we* are the "other" in this package; that *we* are the "other" who are being turned into a "we," in the degree to which we find our similarity with our brother and sister on either side of us. This, rather than: we are the people who, because we've grasped the theory, have become part of "I AM," and therefore the "other" is some "them." If you are *undergoing* atonement, it means that you are constantly in the process of being approached by someone who is forgiving you. That, it seems to me, is the challenge for us in terms of imagination when it comes to imagining and re-imagining atonement.

The difficult thing for us is to sit in the process of being approached by someone. Because we are used to theory, we want someone to say, "This is what it is. Get the theory right. Now put it into practice." This imagines that we are part of a stable universe that we can control. But if the real center of our universe is an "I AM" coming towards us as our victim who is forgiving us, then we are *not* in a stable place. We are in that place of being de-stabilized, because we are being approached by someone who is entirely outside our structures of vengeance and order.

Imagine what it is like to be approached by your forgiving victim. It is actually very difficult indeed to spend time thinking about our being approached by our forgiving victim! What is it like to actually undergo being forgiven? We tend to try to resolve this by saying, "Oh, it's not being forgiven that matters. It's *forgiving*: I must forgive!" So we work ourselves up into a moral stupor, straining ourselves to "forgive the bastard!" This then becomes very, very complicated. But in fact, the Christian understanding is quite the reverse: it's because we are undergoing being forgiven that we can forgive. And we need to forgive in order to *continue* undergoing *being* forgiven. But remember: it's because we are approached by our victim that we start to be undone. Or in Paul's language: "even though you were dead in your sins he has made you alive together in Christ." Someone was approaching you even when you didn't realize there was a problem, so that you begin to discover, "Oh! So that's what I've been involved in."

Now, this is vital for us: it means that in this picture "sin," rather than being a block that has to be dealt with, is discovered in its being forgiven. The definition of sin becomes: *that which can be forgiven*.

And the process of being forgiven looks like the breaking of heart, or "contrition" (from the Latin *cor triturare*). And the purpose of being forgiven

– the reason why the forgiving victim has emerged from the Holy of Holies offering himself as a substitute for all our ways of pushing away being forgiven, trying to keep order – the reason he has done that is because we are too small. We live in a snarled up version of creation, and we hold on to that snarled up version of creation because we are frightened of death. What Jesus was doing was opening up the Creator's vision, which knows not death, so that we can live as though death were not. In other words, we're being given a bigger heart. That is what being forgiven is all about. It's not, "I need to sort out this moral problem you have." It's, "Unless I come towards you, and enable you to undergo a breaking of heart, you're going to live in too small a universe; you're not going to enjoy yourselves and be free. How the hell do I get through to you? Well, the only way is by coming amongst you as your victim. That's the only place in which you can be undone. That's the place where you're so frightened of being that you'll do anything to get away from it. So if I can occupy that space, and return to you and say, 'Yes, you did this thing to me. But don't worry! I'm not here to accuse you. I'm here to play with you! To make a bigger space for you. And for you to take part in making that bigger space with me.'" And of course the way Jesus acted this out before his death was by setting up the last supper, in which he would give himself to us so that we would become him.

This is a risky project. That is the point! That is why I want to bring together the notion of creation and atonement, recovering the priestly dynamic. This is the risky project of God saying, "We don't know how this is going to end. But I want you to be co-participants with me on the inside of this creative project. And that means I'm running a risk of this going places I haven't thought of because I want to become one of you as you, so that you can become me as me." We get this in John's Gospel: "You will do even greater things."[13] And we think, "Oh Jesus is just being modest about his miracles." No, he is being perfectly straightforward anthropologically. To the degree in which, by receiving this sacrifice, we learn to step out of a world which sacrifices – tries to run things protectively over and against "them" – to that extent we will find ourselves – as we *have* found ourselves! – doing greater things than he could even begin to imagine. That's what the opening up of creation does.

The opening up of creation works in our midst through the Spirit who is the advocate, the defense counselor, who therefore rejects the accusatory tendency. While we accuse, while we live in a conspiracy theory, we never learn what *is*, so we never learn to take responsibility for it. We never learn to inhabit creation with fullness.

13. John 14:12.

Do you see that there is a huge movement in the atonement? The movement is from creation to us becoming participants in creation by our being enabled to live as if death were not. This is the *priestly* pattern of atonement; and it is the priestly pattern that Jesus had the genius to combine with the ethical, bringing together the ancient liturgical formula, the prophecies, the hopes of fulfillment of the anointed one, the true high priest who would come and create a new Temple, the true shepherd of the sheep who would come to create a new Temple. He came to fulfil those, and to reveal what it meant in anthropological and ethical terms: the overcoming of our tendency to sacrifice each other so as to survive. That is the world, which thanks to him, we now inhabit.

Now do you see why I said that I wanted to give you a much more conservative account than the atonement theory allows? What we are given is a sign of something that has happened and been given to us. What is *difficult* for us is *not* grasping the theory, but starting to try to *imagine* the love that is behind that. Why on earth should someone bother to do that for us? That's St. Paul's issue. "What then shall we say to this? If God is for us, who is against us? He who did not spare his own Son but gave him up for us all, will he not also give us all things with him?"[14] St. Paul is struggling to find language about the divine generosity. That is the really difficult thing for us to imagine. We can imagine retaliation, we can imagine protection; but we find it awfully difficult to imagine someone we despised, and were awfully glad not to be like – whom we would rather cast out so as to keep ourselves going – we find it awfully difficult to imagine that person generously irrupting into our midst so as to set us free to enable something quite new to open up for us. But being empowered to imagine all that generosity is what atonement is all about; and that is what we are asked to live liturgically as Christians.

---

14. Rom 8:31-32.

Chapter Six

GOD IS NOT TO BLAME: THE SERVANT'S ATONING
SUFFERING ACCORDING TO THE LXX OF ISAIAH 53

by E. Robert Ekblad

The tendency for communities and individuals to interpret calamities, fail-ures or any kind of suffering as God's judgment or punishment may well be (is potentially) the most destructive aspect of marginalization. The Hebrew oracles in Deutero-Isaiah were forged out of the crucible of Israel's exile in Babylon. The servant poems describe servant Israel's relationship to YHWH, its unique mission to the nations and its persecution and atoning suffering in ways that facilitate readings that attribute the servant's suffering to God. Modern doctrines of penal substitutionary atonement[1] base them-selves in part on Isaiah 53. The Greek translators of the LXX situated hun-dreds of years later than Deutero-Isaiah in the Diaspora of Alexandria Egypt appear to have deliberately interpreted these oracles in ways that exclude the attribution of suffering to *Kurios*. In the following, paper I will present four examples where the MT (Masoretic Text) has been interpreted as attributing the servant's suffering as God's judgment or sovereign will. Side-by-side, I will place the LXX translation, commenting on the translator's exegesis and theology of suffering.

In four places, the MT offers enough ambiguity that a way is opened for interpreters to attribute blame for suffering to YHWH.

1. In Isaiah 53:4. the MT can be read: "And we ourselves considered him stricken, beaten by God and afflicted" (חֲשַׁבְנֻהוּ נָגוּעַ מֻכֵּה אֱלֹהִים וּמְעֻנֶּה (וַאֲנַחְנוּ.

2. In Isaiah 53:5, the MT can be translated "the punishment for our peace was upon him and by his blow it has been healed for us" (נִרְפָּא־לָנוּ (מוּסַר שְׁלוֹמֵנוּ עָלָיו וּבַחֲבֻרָתוֹ.

---

1. This doctrine is often called "propitiatory atonement," which conveys the notion of payment for offences. The texts most often used to support this doctrine are Hebrews 10:11-12; Romans 5:6-11; Galatians 3:10-14; 1 Peter 2:24; 3:18 and 2 Cor 5:21. Expiation suggests the idea of covering. Assumption: there is something about God that requires God to punish. God is just, so forgiveness is not enough. Cf. J.I. Packer's essay *"What did the cross achieve?: The Logic of penal substitution,"* Leon Morris, *The Atonement,* p. 56, John Stott, *The Cross of Christ,* 145ff, all argue for penal satisfaction.

3. In Isaiah 53:6 the MT allows the following translation "but the Lord has caused to light upon him the iniquity of all of us" (גִּיעַ בּוֹ אֵת עֲוֹן כֻּלָּנוּ וַיהוָה הִפְ).

4. Finally the MT of Isaiah 53:10 reads "yet it pleased the Lord to crush him, making him sick, if his soul would make a guilt offering" (תָּשִׂים אָשָׁם־ וַיהוָה חָפֵץ דַּכְּאוֹ הֶחֱלִי אִם).

A careful reading of the MT of these passages shows that these texts are complex, defying reductionistic attempts to use them to support narrow doctrines. In Isaiah 53:4, "we ourselves considered him to be stricken, beaten by God..." reflects the speaker's misinterpretation of the servant's suffering. Covert identifications between the servant and YHWH abound,[2] suggesting God's own participation in suffering in contrast to the servant taking all the heat. Verbal forms show the servant to be both passive and active rather than a mere victim. This work, however, has already been done and is beyond the scope of this paper. The LXX translation itself however offers a careful interpretation of these verses which reflects a glimpse into the theology of at least one Jewish interpreter in the Diaspora of Egypt.

Broad literary context of Isaiah 52:13-53:12

The LXX's strong identification of the servant as Israel (though the servant is not completely reduced to collective Israel), may have led the translator to avoid attributing the servant's suffering directly to God. The LXX identifies the servant of Isaiah as Israel in ways that go beyond the MT.[3] The LXX's identification of the servant with Israel clearly includes Israel in his[4] sinfulness.[5] The people of Israel are described in the LXX of Isaiah 50:10 as

2. In most cases where הוּא appears in the MT of Deutero-Isaiah, it designates the Lord or the servant, inviting the reader to ponder a possible cryptic identification of the עֶבֶד as יְהוָה. הוּא designates the Lord in twelve out of twenty-one occurrences in Deutero-Isaiah (41:4; 42:8; 43:10; 43:13, 25; 45:18, 18; 46:4; 48:12; 46:4; 48:12; 51:12; 52:6, 6), the servant in five places (53:4, 5, 7, 11, 12) and other figures/things four times (41:7; 42:22; 45:13; 50:9).
3. Jacob ('Ιακώβ), Israel ('Ισραήλ), the people (λαός), the servant (παῖς), slave (δοῦλός), my chosen (ὁ ἐκλεκτός) are all linked in the LXX of Isaiah. In the LXX of 42:1, unlike the MT, Jacob/Israel is present directly in the text. In Isaiah 52:11, the people of Israel (addressed in the second person plural) are closely identified with the servant in 52:15. There is also a clear identification between the singular collective Israel as servant (52:13a) and the servant of (52:15). The LXX's use of (καλέω) also reflects this identification. When the Lord is subject of this verb, it always concerns Jacob/Israel or the servant.
4. The third masculine pronoun is used for Israel and the servant because in the LXX παῖς and 'Ισραήλ are masculine.
5. Intertextual links are present in the LXX between ἐκ κοιλίας in Isaiah 44:1-2, 24; 46:3 and 48:8, where Israel is labeled a "transgressor from the womb." Israel does not listen to the commandments (48:18). In addition, there are clear links between Isaiah 53:1ff and Isaiah 1:4ff's

"those who walk in darkness."[6] In the LXX of Isaiah, the phrase "the blind" consistently refers to Israel.[7] The LXX emphasizes more than the MT that all of Israel is considered blind and deaf; it does so when it places παῖς in the plural in the phrase "who is blind but my servants?" (42:19). Through numerous intertextual links to Isaiah 6:8-10 and other scriptures, the LXX emphasizes Israel's inability to see and hear apart from an act of divine revelation or liberation.[8]

Yet in spite of the LXX's willingness to depict servant Israel as radically broken, the servant people clearly have a universal mission. In Isaiah 42:1 the LXX clarifies the identity of the servant (παῖς) by adding the names Jacob and Israel, harmonizing with other texts in Isaiah 40ff where παῖς is clearly Jacob/Israel.[9] In Isaiah 42, the LXX identifies the whole people as those who have been chosen for a unique vocation.

The immediate literary context of Isaiah 52:13-53:12

The immediate literary context of the LXX of Isaiah 52:13-53:12 depicts Israel as having a missionary vocation among the nations, setting the stage for a unique interpretation of suffering in the fourth servant poem. In the LXX of Isaiah 52:1-7, the Lord speaks in the first person to Zion (Jerusalem the holy city, captive daughter of Zion). In Isaiah 52:8-10, a narrator—most likely the prophet—speaks about the Lord, Jerusalem and all the ends of the earth in the third person. Finally, in Isaiah 52:11-12, the same narrator addresses those who carry the vessels of the Lord (οἱ φέροντες σκεύν κυρί ου) with the command: "go out, go out from there." These appear to be the addressees before whom the Lord presents his servant in Isaiah 52:13.

The LXX differs significantly from the MT in Isaiah 52:11 with regard to the departure point of those who bear the vessels of the Lord. In the MT, the addressees appear to be called to depart from a place of exile to return to Jerusalem. The Lord is first described as returning to Zion in Isaiah 52:8. The LXX of Isaiah 52:8 matches the MT's בְּשׁוּב יְהוָה צִיּוֹן ("the return of the Lord to Zion") with ἡνίκα ἂν ἐλεήσῃ κύριος τὴν Σιων ("when the Lord will have mercy on Zion"). According to the LXX then, the Lord does not necessarily return to Jerusalem from anywhere (i.e. from Babylon). This

---

description of sinful Israel.

6. See the detailed presentation of intertextual exegetical links between Isaiah 50:10 and 9:2 in my commentary of Isaiah 50:10—E. Robert Ekblad Jr., *Isaiah's Servant Poems According to the Septuagint* (Peeters, 1999).

7. See Ekblad, *Isaiah's Servant Poems* on Isaiah 42:7.

8. Isaiah 42:7 is linked to Isaiah 6:8-10 and Isaiah 9:2.

9. Cf. 41:8, 9; 42:19; 43:10; 44:1, 2, 21, 21; 45:4.

textual difference prepares the way for the LXX's unique matching of the MT in Isaiah 52:9 and 52:11.

In Isaiah 52:9, the LXX first matches the MT's second person plural imperatives in "break forth into joy, sing together, you waste places of Jerusalem" with a third person plural imperative, "Let the waste places of Jerusalem break forth in joy together." The LXX follows this by matching the MT's "for the Lord has comforted his people" (עַמּוֹ) with "because the Lord has had mercy upon her" (αὐτήν). With Jerusalem and αὐτήν as antecedents, the LXX completes its transformation of the text in Isaiah 52:11's "go out from the midst of her" (αὐτῆς). According to the LXX, then, those who bear the vessels of the Lord are called to go out from Jerusalem.

It is likely that the LXX interpreted this call out of Jerusalem as part of the fulfillment of the Lord's revelation of his holy arm in Isaiah 52:10, when "all the ends of the earth shall see the salvation of our God." The LXX here reflects the Alexandrian Jewish community's self-understanding as a missionary vanguard sent out (ἀπόστητε) from Jerusalem (52:11) to all the ends of the earth (52:10), fronted and flanked by the Lord God of Israel (52:12).

Isaiah 52:13 marks the beginning of a new pericope with Ἰδού (like the MT). The Lord is clearly the speaker. The Lord presents his servant before those who have gone out from Jerusalem (the vessel bearers), assuring them of a future time when his servant will prevail.[10]

In the LXX of Isaiah 52:14. the Lord directly addresses those he has sent as a singular body.[11] This second person singular addressee, just addressed as vessel bearers, can at the same time be interpreted as the singular servant identified as Jacob or Israel in many places throughout Isaiah.[12] The future glorified servant then is introduced before the present servant, who

---

10. The vessel bearers were likely understood by the LXX translator as having a special vocation, and were probably associated with or identified as priests. Priests in the LXX of Isaiah 40:1-2 are called to comfort the people and to speak to the heart of Jerusalem (ἱερεῖς, λαλήσατε εἰς τὴν Ἰερουσαλημ). The association between vessel bearers and priests is common in the Greek Pentateuch (Num 3:5-9, 31-32; 4:15-16, 25-26; 7:8). The association here between the vessel bearers, priests and the servant of the Lord may suggest an understanding of the servant in 52:14 as being a select group of "righteous" who have a special vocation in the midst of Israel and the nations. This suggestion does not exclude other identifications of the servant, but reveals yet another layer of interpretation concerning the servant's mysterious identity.

11. Grelot is correct in noting how the LXX's primary difference with the MT in Isaiah 52:13-15 consists in the change of person which distinguishes each of these three verses as independent units. "... la principale différence réside dans le changement de personne qui fait adresser le discours de Dieu au Serviteur lui-même: c'est le signe d'une lecture qui découpe 52: 13-15 en trois morceaux indépendants, expliqués pour eux-mêmes." Les poemes du serviteur, 104. Unfortunately, neither Grelot nor Bastiaens note the distinction between the servant in 52:13 and the addressees (collective servant Israel) of 52:14. Cf. J. Ch. Bastiaens, Interpretaties van Jesaja 53, 184.

12. Isaiah 41:8, 9; 42:1, 19; 44:1, 2, 21; 45:4.

constitutes a collective that includes an undetermined number of people. This distinction between the collective servant and an unidentified, separate individual servant is visible throughout the poems.[13] The Lord warns this collective that people will be amazed by them and dishonor them—establishing a stark contrast to the servant's future glorification. In Isaiah 52:15, the Lord assures them[14] that nations and kings will also be astounded by the servant, whom they will finally see and understand.

In Isaiah 53:1, the speakers and addressees change. Those whom the Lord calls out from Jerusalem to the nations describe their report before the Lord. They now speak in the first person plural. The meaning of "we announced before him" most likely means that the speakers carried out their prophetic task with the suffering servant in mind before them. At the same time the announcers may have seen themselves as announcing against the servant.[15] This interpretation fits the context of the confession, wherein the speakers acknowledge their sin and the servant as their sin bearer (53:4-6). A remembrance of the rejected, persecuted servant and a constant reference to his paradoxical life serves as a reference for the announcing community, defining and orienting them in their vocation as the Lord's servant.

The LXX matches the MT's בַּיּוֹנֵק ("like a shoot") with ὡς παιδίον[16]

---

13. In Isaiah 49, the LXX, in contrast to the MT, clearly distinguishes a singular servant figure from servant Israel. While the servant is clearly identified as Israel (49:3), the servant cannot be Israel in 49:7, since the Lord speaks to the παῖς about one, apart from himself, whom the people are called to sanctify. In contrast to Israel, who does not trust (65:2), is the servant who trusts (50:5). The LXX establishes a contrast between the people who do not understand (Isa 6:9-10) and the servant who will understand (52:13). While the servant eventually will be exalted and glorified (52:13), the people react adversely to him (52:14). It is this servant alone who responds to the call in Isaiah 43:10 to be a witness and servant.

14. There is no evidence for J. Ch. Bastiaens' claim that there is a change of speakers from "others" in 52:13 to "the servant" in 52:14 to "all who would listen to the prophecy" in 52:15. The addressees in 52:15 are clearly the same collective servant consistently addressed in 52:13-15. The speakers' use of the past tense to describe the servant's suffering in 53:1-7 does not contradict the future tense in 52:14, as Bastiaens' maintains, but further supports a distinction between the collective servant who will face suffering and a separate servant who has suffered and died in the past and whose future glorification assures all future suffering servants that they will be glorified. Bastiaens' confusion regarding addressees in 52:13-15 leads him to the conclusion that the identity of the servant in 52:13-53:12 is vague. Furthermore, he claims that this very vagueness permits all who would count themselves among his seed to join in the servant's healing service and even his path of suffering. *Interpretaties van Jesaja 53,* 184-185. In contrast, it is the vagueness regarding the identity of those included among the collective servant addressees (52:13-15) and speakers (53:1-7), and their distinction from a servant who is differentiated and yet identified with them, which permits others to join the collective servant in the servant's mission at whatever moment in history they find themselves.

15. For these two meanings of ἐναντίον see J. Lust, E. Eynikel and K. Hauspie, *A Greek-English Lexicon of the Septuagint*. Part I, 149.

16. S*; 86*; 106; oII; 48ᶜ; 51 ᶜ; 90; 36; 87; 91 ᶜ; 309; 764 and Cyr. o have the variant πεδίον ("field, plain") in the place of παιδίον. This word does occur in Isaiah 16:8; 21:15; 40:4; 41:18

("like an infant/ little servant") only here in the entire LXX.[17] In the LXX of Isaiah, παιδίον often refers to a young child[18] or animal.[19] Παιδίον is also used to designate the prophet Isaiah's children who serve as signs[20] or the little child who is awaited as deliverer (9:6 (5)). The LXX's use of παιδίον may reflect an intertextual exegetical link that associates the speakers who announce their report in 53:1-2 with the awaited child of Isaiah 9:6(5), or more likely with Hezekiah's future children who will announce (ἀναγγελοῦσι) the Lord's righteousness (38: 19). The speakers can certainly also be identified with Jacob and all the remnant of Israel, who are described in 46:3 as the Lord's children, "taught [by him] from infancy (ἐκ παιδίου)."

Finally, παιδίον also reflects an understanding of the speakers as both identified with the παῖσ as Jacob/Israel, and at the same time distinct from the παῖς whom they describe in 53:2ff. Considering the semantic field of παιδίον in Isaiah and the larger literary context, παιδίον can well be translated "little servant."[21] The speakers in 53:2 see themselves as the "little servant" before the servant.

In Isaiah 53:1-7, they tell of a humble, suffering servant. They describe him as someone who lived before them, who suffered for their sins. Their confession may well represent their coming to understanding (52:13) and result in nations and kings being amazed and eventually understanding (52:15).[22] In the LXX the servant of Lord is embodied as suffering people, who learn this distinct presence by witnessing a truly righteous sufferer. The Lord addresses this "little servant/child" regarding the servant's past and future in 53:9-10 before the prophet (or apostles) speaks about the significance of the servant's life and death and of his future inheritance and deliverance (53:10-12).

---

and 63:14. While it appears to fit well with ἀνετέλλω, these words never occur together in Isaiah, nor do these authorities have ἀνετέλλω. In addition, while shoots spring up, never does παιδίον occur together with ἀνετέλλω in the LXX.

17. In the LXX of Isaiah, παιδίον occurs 16 times, most often matching the MT's נַעַר (Isa 3:5; 7:16; 8:4; 10:19; 11:6) or יֶלֶד (Isa 8: 18; 9:6(5); 11:7 or בֵּן (Isa 38: 19; 66:8). Grelot points out that παιδίον reflects a literal rather than metaphoric understanding of יוֹנֵק. "Le mot yoneq est entendu au sens pro pre et non au sens metaphorique ("bouture", hapax leg. en ce sens-la)." Grelot, Les poemes du serviteur, 104. The MT's יוֹנֵק does come from the verb יָנַק "suck" and can be translated "suckling" or "little child." Its feminine equivalent refers to a young shoot or twig (Hos 14:7; Ezek 17:22; Ps 80:12; Job 8:16; 14:7; 15:30).

18. Isaiah 3:5; 10:19; 11:6, 8; 49:15; 66:8, 12.

19. Isaiah 11:7; 34:15.

20. Isaiah 7:16; 8:4, 18.

21. This is the only place in Isaiah where the literary context invites the possible translation "little servant." "Child" is clearly the most common meaning. However it fails to alert the reader to the semantic association with servant present in the Greek.

22. J. Ch. Bastiaens, Interpretaties van Jesaja 53, 185. This notion is further developed in Paul's Epistle to the Romans 9.

The first LXX interpretation of the MT regarding God's perceived role in the servant's suffering is in Isaiah 53:4.

1. In Isaiah 53:4, the MT can be read: "And we ourselves considered him stricken, beaten by God and afflicted" (נָגוּעַ מֻכֵּה אֱלֹהִים וּמְעֻנֶּה וַאֲנַחְנוּ חֲשַׁבְנֻהוּ). The LXX here presents a distinct translation.

4 אָכֵן חֳלָיֵנוּ הוּא נָשָׂא	4 οὗτος τὰς ἁμαρτίας ἡμῶν φέρει
וּמַכְאֹבֵינוּ סְבָלָם	καὶ περὶ ἡμῶν ὀδυνᾶται
וַאֲנַחְנוּ חֲשַׁבְנֻהוּ נָגוּעַ	καὶ ἡμεῖς ἐλογισάμεθα αὐτὸν εἶναι ἐν πόνῳ
מֻכֵּה אֱלֹהִים וּמְעֻנֶּה:	καὶ ἐν πληγῇ καὶ ἐν κακώσει.

4 Surely he himself has carried our diseases,	4 **This one** our **sins he bears**
and our pains he has borne them,	and he **suffers for us,**
and we ourselves considered him stricken,	and we ourselves considered him **to be in pain**
beaten by God and afflicted.	**and in a plague** and in oppression.

The LXX of Isaiah 53:4 differs significantly from the MT. After presenting the servant as one who was unattractive, sick and completely marginalized, the LXX, through its variant οὗτος, emphasizes in a way similar to the MT that it is "this one" who bears our sins.

The LXX matches the MT's חֳלָיֵנוּ ("our diseases") with τὰς ἁμαρτίας ἡμῶν ("our sins") only here.[23] This matching is curious, since in Isaiah 53:3 the LXX matches the MT's חֳלִי with μαλακίαν following φέρειν. The repetition of φέρω alerts the reader of the LXX to an exegetical association between μαλακίαν and ἁμαρτίας. The servant's sickness is attributed to the people's sins. In the LXX, the servant's bearing of sickness is not a result of his own sins, but of the sins of the speakers: "this one bears our sins." With the exception of the servant's work in Isaiah 53:4-12, it is the Lord alone who responds to sin through pardon[24] or recompensation.[25] The LXX of Isaiah 53:4-12 quite

---

23. L'(22*)-62-96; 449'; Ath.II 988.1025 and Tht. have μαλακίας. In the LXX of Isaiah ἁμαρτία occurs 38 times, matching a number of different Hebrew words. In the LXX of Isaiah, ἁμαρτία matches the MT's עָוֹן (1:4; 5:18; 13:11; 14:21; 22:14; 30:13; 33:24; 40:2; 50:1; 53:5, 6, 11; 57:17; 59:3; 64:7(6), 9(8); 65:7); אָשָׁם (53:10); חֵטְא (1:18; 38:17; 53:12); חַטָּאת (3:9; 6:7; 27:9; 30:1,1; 43:24, 25; 44:22; 59:2, 12); מַחֲשָׁבָה (65:2); מְגוּרֹתָם (66:4) and פֶּשַׁע (53:5, 12). 'Αμαρτία occasionally appears in the singular to designate sin in general (Isaiah 3:9; 27:9; 33:24; 40:2) or a specific sin (Isa 22: 14; 30: 13). Most often it occurs in the plural to refer to wrong acts committed by a specific individual (Isa 6:7; 21:4; 38: 17), the people of Israel (Isa 1:4, 14, 18; 5:18; 14:21; 30:1, 1; 43:24, 25; 44:22; 50:1; 55:17; 59:2, 3,12; 64:7(6), 9(8); 65:2, 7; 66:4), and the whole world (Isa 13:11).

24. Isaiah 1:18; 6:7; 27:9; 33:24; 38:17; 40:2; 43:25; 44:22; 55:7.

25. Isaiah 13:11; 14:21; 59:2; 64:7(6); 65:7; 66:4.

possibly presents the servant as one through whom the Lord deals with human sin. This happens through the servant's voluntary suffering and dying for people's sins.[26]

The LXX's verb φέρει ("he bears") functions as a legitimate semantic equivalent for the MT's נָשָׂא ("he has carried").[27] The LXX associates the servant's bearing of sins with the language of atonement in a way that is far clearer than the MT. There are several places in Leviticus where φέρω and ἁμαρτία occur together,[28] providing the reader with a possible background for understanding the distinctiveness of Isaiah 53:4ff. The best example of the Greek Torah's use of this vocabulary is in Leviticus 5:6-8.

> And he shall bring (οἴσει) for his transgressions against the Lord, for [his] sin (περὶ τῆς ἁμαρτίας) which he has sinned, a ewe lamb from the flock (ἀπὸ τῶν προβάτων)...for a sin-offering (περὶ ἁμαρτίας); and the priest shall make an atonement for him for [his] sin (περὶ αὐτοῦ ὁ ἱερεὺς περὶ τῆς ἁμαρτίας) which he has sinned, and his sin shall be forgiven. And if he cannot afford a sheep, he shall bring for his sin (οἴσει περὶ τῆς ἁμαρτίας αὐτοῦ) which he has sinned, two turtle-doves or two young pigeons to the Lord; one for a sin-offering (περὶ ἁμαρτίας, and the other for a burnt-offering. And he shall bring (οἴσει) them to the priest, and the priest shall bring the sin-offering (περὶ τῆς ἁμαρτίας) first. (Lev 5:6-8a)

While Isaiah 53 and Leviticus 5 have similar vocabulary regarding the sin-offering, differences between the two must not be understated. In the first place Isaiah 53's construction φέρω + the accusative is quite different from Leviticus' φέρω + περί. While Leviticus uses the future of φέρω to describe a person or priest bringing or bearing an animal for sin, Isaiah 53:4 describes "this one," the servant, bearing "our sins" and suffering περὶ αὐτῶν ("for us"). Leviticus 5:6-7's mention of sheep is also repeated in Isaiah 53:6-7, where the speakers describe themselves as being ὡς πρόβατα going astray and the servant as like a sheep going to the slaughter. Yet in spite of these differences Isaiah invites the reader to examine a rapport and new interpretation.

Isaiah 53 is clearly the first place in the entire Old Testament where a human being is described as carrying/bearing sin on behalf of others.[29] In

---

26. The LXX's matching of different Hebrew words with ἁμαρτίας in Isaiah 53:4ff specifies the LXX's particular understanding of how the Lord responds to sin through the servant. In Isaiah 53:4-12, the LXX has ἁμαρτία six other times to match four different Hebrew words. In Isaiah 53:5, the LXX clearly states that the servant "became sick because of our sins" and 53:6b reads "the Lord has handed him over to our sins."

27. Φέρω is a common semantic equivalent for the MT's נָשָׂא both in Isaiah (Isa 17:13; 30:6; 52:11; 53:4; 60:6; 64:6(5)) and throughout the LXX.

28. Lev 4:28; 5:6, 7, 8, 11, 12; 14:19-20; 15:14-15, 29-30; 16:15; Num 6:10-11.

29. Numbers 18:1-23 describes the Levites' bearing the sins of the holy things and the iniquities of their priesthood. Leviticus 16:21-22's description of the scapegoat carrying the people's unrighteousness (Lev 16:22) is not linked to this passage through the vocabulary of the LXX.

the LXX of Isaiah, the servant displaces the sinner and priest by becoming himself the carrier or bearer for sin—just as the servant corresponds with the priest who brings/carries "our sins" corresponds with "ewe lamb" or the "two doves" which are carried for sacrifices.

The LXX differs from the MT in 53:4a by rendering perfect tense verbs with presents. This difference is best explained as editorial rather than *Vorlage* related. P. Grelot argues that the shift from the MT's past to the LXX's present: "suppose une permanence de la souffrance du Serviteur. La chose se comprend, s'il est la représentation figurée des justes souffrants qui existent au sein d'Israël."[30]

In contrast, the speakers in 53:1-8 are more likely the same collective servant Israel (possibly the very "représentation figurée des justes souffrants qui existent au sein d'Israël") whose eventual dishonor is foretold in 52:14. They emerge from out of this singular collective and speak of yet another servant figure distinct from themselves. They distinguish themselves as the child "little servant," distinct from another servant before whom they announce.[31]

Grelot is likely correct in arguing that the present tense reflects the LXX translator's tendency to actualize the servant poems for his audience. The present tense then opens the way for LXX readers of any time to identify the servant as their contemporary and themselves as disciples.

The LXX reinforces its interpretation of the servant's bearing sickness as "bearing our sins" with something stronger still: the servant "suffers pain for us." The LXX matches the MT's וּמַכְאֹבֵינוּ ("and our pains") quite freely with καὶ περὶ ἡμῶν ὀδυνᾶται ("and he suffers pain for us")[32] and has no semantic equivalent for סְבָלָם ("he has borne them").[33] Yet περὶ ἡμῶν may

---

30. Grelot, *Les poemes du serviteur*, 105.

31. Bastiaens argues that the servant in 53:1-7 is more closely identified with servant Israel in 49:1-9 and 42:1ff than is the we-figure, who he sees as being in the process of converting to join "obedient" Israel thanks to vision of the exaltation and glorification of the servant. While the servant whom the speakers describe in 53:2-6 is clearly identified through repeating vocabulary with collective Israel (cf. 49:3-4; 52:14), this servant is also unmistakably differentiated. Grelot and Bastiaens' hypotheses do not adequately take into account this somewhat cryptic identification and distinction between the community of announcers within Israel, collective Israel and the servant. The servant poems in the context of the whole of Isaiah better lend themselves to depicting Israel as simultaneously disobedient and obedient in her/his vocation as the Lord's servant rather than as two separate groups made up of the "obedient" and the "disobedient." At the same time, the speakers' confession is a liturgical statement that others are free to appropriate as they recognize the Lord's redemptive work through the servant. It is this saving work through suffering, rather than the Bastiaens' proposed vision of the exaltation and glorification of the servant, that inspires confession and conversion.

32. This contrasts to Matthew 8:17's literal match of the MT: καὶ τὰς νόσους ἡμῶν ἐβάστασεν.

33. Ottley rightly argues that the LXX simply omits סְבָלָם, *The Book of Isaiah*, vol. 2, 345. The LXX's ὀδυνω (which occurs three times in Isaiah to match three distinct MT words) – Isaiah

well have been facilitated both to harmonize with the first plural of 53:1ff and by the LXX's previous intertextual links to Leviticus' atonement texts, as seen above. Περὶ ἡμῶν also represents a collective rather than an individualist reading of the atonement traditions.

After a line of word-for-word renderings of the MT's וַאֲנַחְנוּ חֲשַׁבְנֻהוּ ("and we considered him") with καὶ ἡμεῖς ἐλογισάμεθα αὐτόν ("and we considered him"), the LXX matches the MT's נָגוּעַ ("stricken") with εἶναι ἐν πόνῳ ("to be in pain"). In addition, the following two participles מֻכֵּה ("beaten") and וּמְעֻנֶּה ("and afflicted") are matched with the nouns καὶ ἐν πληγῇ ("and in a plague") and καὶ ἐν κακώσει ("and in oppression"). Ottley is partially correct in arguing that these three participles "might have been read, with slight changes as nouns, but it seems to be a case of freedom in rendering."[34]

In the first case the LXX matches the MT's passive participle נָגוּעַ with εἶναι ἐν πόνῳ. While πόνος occurs eight times in the LXX of Isaiah,[35] this is the only place in the entire LXX where it matches נָגוּעַ. The translator may have misread נָגוּעַ as an infinitive absolute יָגוּעַ ("to be weary"). Εἶναι ἐν πόνῳ could conceivably function as a semantic equivalent for this infinitive, considering that יָגַע is often matched with πόνος in the LXX.[36]

God is not to blame

The LXX next matches the MT's מֻכֵּה אֱלֹהִים ("beaten by God") with καὶ ἐν πληγῇ ("and in a plague").[37] Πληγή is a common semantic equivalent for מֻכֵּה-- which was likely read here as a noun. Most significant here is the absence in the LXX of any semantic equivalent for אֱלֹהִים. This likely reflects the theological perspective of the translator.

The MT speakers confess their mistaken consideration that it was God who struck, beat and afflicted the servant, perhaps as some justifiable

21:10; 40:29; 53:4. This Greek verb occurs in only eight other places in the LXX (Tob 9:4; Prov 29:21: Wis 14:24; Hag 2:15(14); Zech 9:5; 12:10; Lam 1:13; 4 Mac 18:9), is an accurate semantic equivalent for a rare Hebrew word. מַכְאֹב occurs only here and in 53:3 in the MT of Isaiah. The *qal* of כָּאַב occurs four times (Gen 34:25; Ps 69:30; Job 14:22; Prov 14:22) and the *hiphil* four times (2 Kgs 3:19; Ezek 13:22; 29:24; Job 5:18) in the MT. It is likely that the LXX translator used καὶ... ὀδυνᾶται to match וּמַכְאֹב, read as a *hiphil* participle מַכְאִיב (e.g. Ezek 28:24). Περὶ ἡμῶν may have consequently been used to match וֹנוּ-- read as לֹ. It is curious that the LXX missed the MT's clear parallelism between וּמַכְאֹבֵינוּ and חֳלָיֵנוּ.

34. Ottley, *The Book of Isaiah*, vol 2, 346.

35. Isaiah 1:5; 49:4; 53:4, 11; 59:4; 65:14, 23(22); 66:7.

36. Deut 28:33; Pss 77(78):46; 108(109):11; 127(128):2; Hos 12:8(9); Jer 20:5; Ezek 23:29.

37. Several Greek miniscules have ἀπὸ θεοῦ following ἐν πληγῇ (106; V-88; 62; C; 403'; 407). The LXX's καὶ agrees with 1 QIsaᵃ, which has הֻמַּה, may reflect a Hebrew *Vorlage* distinct from that of the MT. It may also have been added for stylistic reasons.

punishment for his sin. This reading of the speakers' speculation concerning God's possible responsibility for the servant's suffering is absent from the LXX.[38]

1. Through the omission of God's name, the LXX makes it difficult to interpret God as the one who inflicts suffering on his servant.

2. The rendering of the MT's participles with nouns further facilitates the LXX's unique interpretation. The MT's "stricken, beaten ... and afflicted" invite the question: afflicted by whom? The LXX's nouns remove any direct exegetical basis for speculation about the subject of these participles.

In the LXX, the speakers confess that they simply considered the servant to be in pain, in a plague and in oppression, in ways that identify the servant clearly with the sin and pain of God's people. The LXX's vocabulary both here and in the following verses evokes the description of Israel in Isaiah 1:4ff.[39]

> Ah sinful nation, a people full of sins (ἁμαρτιῶν), an evil seed, lawless (ἄνομοι) children: ye have forsaken the Lord, and provoked the Holy One of Israel. Why should ye be smitten (πληγῆτε) any more, transgressing more and more? The whole head is pained (πόνον), and the whole heart sad. From the feet to the head, there is no soundness in them; neither wound (τραῦμα), nor bruise (μώλωψ) nor festering ulcer (πληγή) are healed (Isa 1:4-6).

This mysterious solidarity between the servant and the people is strengthened and broadened by the final LXX variant. The LXX matches the MT's וּמְעֻנֶּה ("and afflicted") with καὶ ἐν κακώσει ("and in affliction").[40] The LXX's use of κάκωσις together with ὀδυνάω (and πληγή) brings the servant's suffering into exegetical rapport with the Lord and the people in Exodus 3:7, where the Lord said to Moses:

> I have surely seen the affliction (κάκωσιν) of my people that is in Egypt, and I have heard their cry *caused* by their taskmasters; for I know their pain (ὀδύνη) and I have come down to deliver them from out of the hand of the Egyptians.

In Exodus 3:7, the people, like the servant of Isaiah 53:4, are oppressed

---

38. LXX removes any possible exegetical support of propitiatory atonement.

39. The Greek words in parenthesis in the following citation occur throughout Isaiah 53: πληγή (53:3, 4, 10), ἁμαρτία (53:4, 5, 5, 6, 10, 11, 12, 12), ἀνομία (53:5, 5, 8, 9, 12), πόνος (53:4, 11), τραυματίζω (53:5) and μώλωψ (53 :5). Grelot observes this intertextual link between Isaiah 1:4-6 and Isaiah 53:4ff. For Grelot, this shows a mysterious solidarity between the people and the servant (Grelot, *Les poemes du serviteur*, 105).

40. Though Isaiah 53:4 is the only place out of eighteen LXX occurrences (Exod 3:7,17; Num 11:15; Deut 16:3; Esth 1:1; 8:6; Pss 17(18):18; 43(44):19; Wis 3:2; Sir 11:27; 13:12; 29:12; Isa 53:4; Jer 2:28; 11:14; 28(51):2; Bar 5:1). Exod 3:7, 17; Deut 16:3) that מְעֻנֶּה is matched with κάκωσις, this Greek noun matches עֳנִי elsewhere in the LXX.

and suffering. As in Isaiah 53:4, the Lord in Exodus 3 is not described as inflicting suffering as a just punishment. Neither is the Lord a distant, disinterested God. Rather, the Lord sees the oppression of his people, hears their cry and even knows their pain. In Isaiah 53, it is the servant himself who manifests the Lord's solidarity with his people. In Isaiah 53:4, this solidarity represents total identification with the people's sin and suffering. In Isaiah 53:5 the LXX tailors its translation to respond to the deeper question concerning the purpose of the servant's suffering.

2. In Isaiah 53:5 the MT can be translated "the punishment for our peace was upon him and by his blow it has been healed for us" (נִרְפָּא־לָנוּ מוּסַר שְׁלוֹמֵנוּ עָלָיו וּבַחֲבֻרָתוֹ).

In contrast, the LXX presents a distinct understanding of punishment through its rendering of מוּסָר with παιδεία.

5 וְהוּא מְחֹלָל	5 αὐτὸς δὲ ἐτραυματίσθη
מִפְּשָׁעֵנוּ	διὰ τὰσ ἀνομιασ ἡμῶν
מְדֻכָּא מֵעֲוֹנֹתֵינוּ	καὶ ‛μεμαλάκισται διὰ τὰς ἁμαρτίας ἡμῶν
מוּסַר שְׁלוֹמֵנוּ עָלָיו	παιδεία εἰρήνης ἡμῶν ἐπ᾿ αὐτόν
וּבַחֲבֻרָתוֹ נִרְפָּא־לָנוּ׃	τῷ μώλωπι αὐτοῦ ἡμεῖς ἰάθημεν

5 But he himself was pierced because of our transgressions, he was crushed because of our iniquities, the punishment for our peace was upon him and by his blow it has been healed for us.	5 But he himself was **wounded** because of our lawless deeds **and he became sick because of our sins;** the **pedagogy** of our peace was upon him, with his **bruises** we **ourselves** were healed.

The speakers then go on to clarify the reason for the servant's suffering. The servant does not suffer at God's hands for his own sins. He suffers for "our" (the speakers') sins.[41] The LXX matches the MT's מִפְּשָׁעֵנוּ ("because of our transgressions") with διὰ τὰς ἀνομίας ἡμῶν ("because of our lawless deeds").[42]

---

41. This could mean that the servant suffers the consequences of the speakers' sins, as J. Ch. Bastiaens asserts in *Interpretaties van Jesaja 53,* 133. The dominant meaning here is that the servant suffers "in the place of" the speakers' sins. This meaning fits the context of 53:5b's "by his bruises we are healed." The use of τραυματίζω links Isaiah 53:5 to Isaiah 1:6 through the noun τραῦμα. This verse is also linked to texts that describe God's judgment of the people in both the MT and the LXX through the adjectival forms חָלָל and τραυματίας (Isa 22:2; 34:3 and 66:1).

42. Ἀνομία is a legitimate semantic equivalent for the MT's פֶּשַׁע, matching it nine (Isa 24:20; 43:25; 44:22; 50:1; 53:5, 8, 12; 59:12, 12) of its 25 occurrences in the LXX of Isaiah (1:5; 3:8; 5:7,18; 6:7; 9:18(17); 21:4; 24:20; 27:9; 33:15; 43:25, 26; 44:22; 50:1; 53:5, 8, 9,12; 58:1;

Ἀνομία, like its synonym ἁμαρτία,[43] matches a number of different Hebrew words in Isaiah[44] and establishes semantic links that do not exist in the MT. It appears to be used in Isaiah 53 to describe actions for which the servant is persecuted and led to death by his assailants.[45] The most significant contextual exegetical link is to Isaiah 53:9, where the servant is described as having not himself committed a lawless deed.[46] He was wounded because of the speakers' lawless acts.

The LXX matches the MT's מְדֻכָּא ("he was crushed") with καὶ μεμαλάκισται ("and he became sick") only here in the entire LXX. Μαλακίζομαι occurs in three other places in Isaiah, always to match the *qal* of חָלָה.[47] The three other occurrences of this Greek verb all concern Hezekiah's sickness (38:1, 9; 39:1). The LXX use of this verb may reflect an interpretive tradition that identified Hezekiah in some way with the Lord's servant. The perfect tense, in contrast to the present tense in 53:4, clearly places the servant's sickness in the past. The LXX's' choice of this Greek verb also clearly reflects contextual exegesis that links 53:5 to 53:3 through μαλακίαν. I have shown in my commentary on Isaiah 53:3-4 above how μαλακίαν and ἁμαρτία are linked through φέρω.

The LXX's matching of the MT's מֵעֲוֹנֹתֵינוּ ("because of our iniquities") with διὰ τὰς ἁμαρτίας ἡμῶν ("because of our sins")[48] further develops its unique interpretation of the servant's suffering. The LXX clarifies through its specific verb choice that people confess that the servant's bearing of sickness (53:3) and of sin (53:4) was not his own. Rather the servant bears the speakers' sickness which is a direct consequence of their sins.[49]

59:3, 4, 6, 12, 12; 64:6(5).).

43. Ἀνομία often occurs together with ἁμαρτία in Isaiah in a way that appears synonymous (Isa 1:4-5; 5: 18; 6:7; 27:9; 43:25; 44:22; 50:1; 53:5; 58:1; 59:2-3,12; 64:6(5)-7(6).

44. In the LXX of Isaiah ανομία matches the MT's עָוֹן (6:7; 27:9; 64:6(5)), סָרָה (1:5), שֶׁקֶר (53:9), חָמָס (53:9), בֶּצַע (33:15), רִשְׁעָה (9:18(17)), מַשְׁפֵּחַ (5:7), חַטָּאָה (5:18; 58:1), מַעֲלָל (3:8), אָוֶן (59:4, 6) and פְּלַצוּת (21:4).

45. These acts were against the νόμος, which in the context of the Diaspora may have been understood as referring to civil laws (as in crimes or acts considered by the state to be subversive). It is more likely that these lawless deeds represent transgressions of the *Torah,* since the translators were Jews and not pagans.

46. J. Ch. Bastiaens points out a significant intertextual link to Isaiah 59:1-15, which includes the people's confession of their lawlessness (59: 12-15), *Interpretaties van Jesaja 53,* 133.

47. Isaiah 38:1, 9; 39:1. Outside of Isaiah μαλακίζομαι, also matches some form of חָלָה (2 Kgs 13:5; 2 Chr 16:12; Dan Th 8:27) with the exception of (Gen 42:38; 2 Chr 16:12; Job 24:23).

48. עָוֹן occurs 25 times in the MT of Isaiah (1:4; 5:18; 6:7; 13:11; 14:21; 22:14; 26:21; 27:9; 30:13; 33:24; 40:2; 43:24; 50:1; 53:5, 6; 57:17; 59:3, 12; 64:5, 6, 8; 65:7). The LXX matches 17 of these occurrences with ἁμαρτία, as noted above in my treatment of 53:4a.

49. J. C. Bastiaens goes too far in asserting that the speakers' confession reflects a conversion that brings them to peace resulting in the servant offering them peace and healing. There is no hint from the text that the speakers' peace is a direct consequence of any action. *Interpretaties van*

In an otherwise word-for-word matching of the MT, the LXX matches the MT's מוּסָר[50] ("punishment") with παιδεία (instruction, learning, discipline, correction, chastisement)—its most common Greek semantic equivalent.[51]

By means of intertextual exegesis already discussed in my treatment of Isaiah 50:4-5, παιδείας links the servant's suffering in Isaiah 53:5 with the chastening of both Israel (26:16) and the servant (50:4-5).

> Lord, in affliction I remembered you, in slight affliction was your pedagogy/training (παιδεία) upon us (26:16).

The parallelism between slight affliction and "pedagogy/formation/training upon us" could suggest God's use of affliction for disciplinary purposes, παιδεία could also be translated "education" or "instruction." This meaning of the term is further supported by its use in Isaiah's third servant poem.

> The Lord gives me an educated/instructed (παιδείας) tongue in order to know at what time I must speak a word. He has presented to me in the morning, He has granted to me an ear to hear. And the chastening (παιδεία) of the Lord opens my ear and I do not disbelieve (ἀπειθω) nor do I contradict (50:4-5).

The intertextual links between Isaiah 53:5 and the above verses show the servant's solidarity with Israel and identification with the servant figure of 50:4-11. The servant's speaking the Lord's revelation clearly entails confrontation with oppressors and resistance from the violent. At the same time, the LXX invites the reader to interpret the servant's chastisement as coming from the Lord (cf. Isa 46:3). This is supported by the following verse's "and the Lord has handed him over to our sins" (53:6).

The LXX's use of παιδείας in 50:4 reflects an intentional, contextual exegetical tie to παιδίον ("child" or "little servant") in 53:2[52] and παῖς (52:13). This word choice may well show an understanding of the servant as embodying in his suffering the Lord's parenting and formation. In addition, as I have shown above in my treatment of Isaiah 50:4-5, there is a semantic tie with Isaiah's two occurrences of παιδεύω ("to discipline, bring up, instruct, train").

---

50. 1QIsaᵃ has a *waw* before this word (ומוסרי) that is not attested by either the MT or LXX.

51. As I have shown in my commentary on Isaiah 50:4, παιδείας frequently matches the MT's מוסר (discipline, chastening, correction), which corresponds to it 37 out of 55 occurrences in the LXX. Παιδεία appears four times in Isaiah 26:16; 50:4, 4(5); 53:5, matching מוּסָר here and in Isaiah 26:16. The most obvious meaning of this word in this context is chastisement or correction, as Grelot argues. "En 5b, on peut entendre la "leçon" (παιδεία) au sens péjorative de "châtiment" divin (cf. Prov 3:11-12LXX, cite par Heb 12:5-7): il s'agit d'une "correction" administree par Dieu à un people indocile (Grelot, *Les pemes du serviteur,* 105). J. Ch. Bastiaens rightly shows that "instruction" and "chastisement" are close together (Sir 22:6; 50:27), *Interpretaties van Jesaja 53,* 134.

52. See my above discussion of possible links between παιδία and παιδίον in 50:4, 5, 10.

So you will be educated/instructed (παιδευθήσῃ) by the judgment of your God, and will rejoice (28:26).

Hear me, o house of Jacob, and all the remnant of Israel, who are borne from the womb, and raised/instructed from infancy (παιδευόμενοι ἐκ παιδίου) to old age (46:3).

While in the texts above the Lord instructs Israel, here the servant experiences instruction, much like the individual servant figure in 50:4-5. The speakers confess their recognition that the suffering experienced by the servant is not to make peace between him and the Lord. The speakers recognize that the servant's suffering is instructional, achieves peace for them and showing them the narrow way.

The LXX matches the MT's וּבַחֲבֻרָתוֹ ("and by his blow") with τῷ μώλωπι αὐτοῦ ("and by his bruises"), its common semantic equivalent.[53] The LXX, like the MT, evokes Isaiah 1:6's description of broken Israel with whom the servant is identified. The speakers here confess their belief that the servant's bruises bring healing for their bruises.

The LXX matches the MT's נִרְפָּא־לָנוּ ("it has been healed for us") with ἡμεῖς ἰάθημεν ("we ourselves were healed").[54] The Lord is the subject of ἰάομαι in all but two of the ten occurrences in the LXX of Isaiah,[55] inviting the reader to see an identification between the Lord and the one who heals. In all but three of the ten occurrences of ἰάομαι in Isaiah, רָפָא is matched, bringing 53:5 into semantic rapport with verses in a way distinct from the MT.[56] An intertextual connection to Isaiah 61:1 identifies the Lord and his servant through the Lord's spirit. In Isaiah 61:1, the one upon whom the Lord has placed his spirit (like the servant of 42:1) heals the broken hearted. Here in Isaiah 53:5 healing is accomplished through the servant's suffering.

3. In Isaiah 53:6, the MT allows the following translation, "but the Lord has caused to light upon him the iniquity of all of us" in a way that has been interpreted as the servant being punished in the place of the guilty.

---

53. Μώλωψ always matches חַבּוּרָה or חֲבֻרָה (Gen 4:23; Exod 21:25; Judg 9:13; Ps 37(38):5; Sir 23:10; 28:17; Isa 1:6, 53:5.

54. The LXX's matching of the MT's third singular verb with a first plural likely reflects LXX translator's reading the MT's third singular *niphal* perfect with vowel pointings of a first plural *niphal* imperfect נֵרָפָא. The MT's נִרְפָּא could conceivably be read as either a third singular *niphal* perfect or a first plural *qal* imperfect. Since the latter, "we heal for ourselves" does not fit the literary context or the theology of this poem, I propose the above vowel markings.

55. Isaiah 6:10; 7:4; 19:22, 22; 30:26, 26; 57:18, 19.

56. Isaiah 7:4; 30:26; 61:1.

6 כֻּלָּ֫נוּ כַּצֹּאן תָּעִ֫ינוּ
אִישׁ לְדַרְכּוֹ פָּנִ֫ינוּ
וַיהוָה הִפְגִּ֫יעַ בּוֹ
אֵת עֲוֹן כֻּלָּֽנוּ׃

6 πάντεις ὡς πρόβατα ἐπλανήθημεν
ἄνθρωπος τῇ ὁδῷ αὐτοῦ ἐπλανήθη·
καὶ κύριος παρέδωκεν αὐτὸν
ταῖς ἁμαρτίαις ἡμῶν

6 All of us like sheep have wandered off,
we turned each one to his way,
but the Lord has caused to light upon him
the iniquity of all of us.

6 We have all gone astray like sheep,
each one has gone astray to his way,
and the Lord has delivered him over to our sins.

In the LXX, the speakers confess in 53:6b that the Lord has delivered the servant over to their sins in contrast to the MT, where the Lord causes everyone's iniquity to land on the servant. The LXX matches the expression הִפְגִּ֫יעַ בּוֹ ("has caused to light upon him") with παρέδωκεν αὐτὸν ("has delivered him over"). This Hebrew verb is matched with παραδιδόμαι only here and in Isaiah 47:3 and 53:12 in the entire LXX. In the LXX this verb most commonly matches the MT's *qal* of נָתַן. In Isaiah, it matches a broad range of Hebrew verbs, drawing together texts (intertextual exegesis) that are less clearly connected in the MT.[57]

The Lord is often described as directly (and indirectly) delivering over both Israel[58] and various nations.[59] People or nations are handed over (or not) to men (19:4; 25:5; 47:3), to the law (33:6), for plunder (33:23), to slaughter (34:2), to the King of Assyria (36:15; 37:10), to a lion (38:13), to death (53:12) and to the sword (65:12). The only other place in Isaiah where παραδιδόναι is concerned with ἁμαρτίας is in Isaiah 64:7(6), where people confess to the Lord: "you have delivered us up because of our sins" (καὶ παρέδωκας ἡμᾶς διὰ τὰς ἁμαρτίας ἡμῶν). The servant's solidarity with his people and the nations is so total that he experiences being delivered up by the Lord to their sins.[60]

The LXX matches the MT's אֵת עֲוֹן כֻּלָּ֫נוּ ("the iniquity of all of us") with ταῖς ἁμαρτίαις ἡμῶν ("to our sins"). Rather than being delivered over for his own sins (as the Lord delivers up people because of their sins in 64:7(6)), the Lord delivers over the servant for "our sins."[61] According to the

---

57. In the LXX of Isaiah, παραδιδόναι matches the *piel* of סָבַר (19:4), the *pual* of חָלַק (33:23), the *qal* (34:2) and *niphal* (36:15; 37:10) of נָתַן, שָׁלֵם (38: 13), the *qui* (47:3) and *hiphil* (53:6, 12) of פָּגַע, the *hiphil* of עָרָה (53:12), the *qal* of מָנָה (65:12) and a number of other words (23:7; 25:5, 7; 33:1, 6; 38:13; 64:7(6)).

58. Isaiah 25:5; 64:7(6); 65:12.

59. Isaiah 19:4; 23:7; 33:1, 23; 34:2.

60. The MT's "cause to light upon" appears stronger than the LXX's "hand him over to our sins." This verb choice may also reflect the LXX's apologetic for God visible in 53:4.

61. The LXX's dative ταῖς may indicate the translator's reading of אֵת as a preposition or as אֶל.

LXX, in response to each one [man's] wandering to his own way, the Lord delivers over the servant to "our" sins.

4. In Isaiah 53:10, the MT begins with a statement describing the Lord's delight in crushing the servant and making him sick if his life would make a guilt offering. In contrast, in the LXX a statement about the Lord's desire to purify the servant is followed by an invitation for the addressees to give a sin offering resulting in their seeing a long-lived posterity.

10 וַיהוָה חָפֵץ דַּכְּאוֹ הֶחֱלִי ֿ אִם־תָּשִׂים אָשָׁם נַפְשׁוֹ יִרְאֶה זֶרַע יַאֲרִיךְ יָמִים וְחֵפֶץ יְהוָה בְּיָדוֹ יִצְלָח׃	10 καὶ κύριος βούλεται καθαρίσαι αὐτὸν τῆς πληγῆς ἐὰν δῶτε περὶ ἁμαρτίας, ἡ ψυχὴ ὑμῶν ὄψεται σπέρμα μακρόβιον· καὶ βούλεται κύριος ἀφελεῖν
10 But the Lord delighted to crush him, making him sick, if his soul would make a guilt offering. He will see a descendant, he will survive days, and the delight of the Lord will prosper in his hand.	10 And the Lord desires to **purify** him of the plague; **If you would give a sin offering,** **your** soul **will see a long-lived posterity,** **and the Lord desires to take away.**

While the LXX matches the MT's חָפֵץ ("delight") with βούλεται ("desire") throughout Isaiah[62] and the LXX,[63] Isaiah 53:10 is the only place where καθαρίζω matches the MT's דָּכָא in the entire LXX.[64] Scholz and later Hengel explain this reading as due to the translator's hearing דַּכְּאוֹ as זָכָה ("be clear, clean, pure") with suffix.[65] However, καθαρίζω never appears as a semantic equivalent for זָכָה in the LXX.[66] Grelot is probably correct in

---

62. In the LXX of Isaiah βούλομαι matches the MT's חָפֵץ (Isa 1:11; 53:10, 10; 65:12; 66:4), חָמֵד (Isa 1:29), מָאַס (Isa 8:6), וּמְשׂוֹשׂ (Isa 8:6), אָבָה (Isa 30:9, 15; 42:24) and other Hebrew verbs (Isa 1:29; 8:6, 6; 30:9, 15; 36:16; 42:24).

63. Deut 25:7, 8; Judg 13:23; Ruth 3:13; 1 Kgs 2:25; 18:25; 2 Kgs 20:11; 24:3; 3 Kgs 18:33; 20(21):6; Job 9:3; 13:3; 21:14; Pss 39(40):8; 69(70):2; 113:11(115:3); Jonah 1:14; Jer 6:10; 49(42):22; Ezek 18:23; 33:11.

64. As I already showed above, the LXX matches the MT's מֻדְכָּא ("he was crushed") with καὶ μεμαλάκισται ("and he became sick") in Isaiah 53:5. The LXX's two distinct renderings of different forms of דָּכָא may reflect unfamiliarity with this verb. In fact the LXX matches the MT's other three occurrences of דָּכָא in Isaiah with ἀδικέω (3: 15), ὀδύνη (19: 1 0), πληγή (53: 10) and (συντρίβω).

65. Cited by Ottley, The Book of Isaiah, vol. 2, 348. Cf. M. Hengel, "Zur Wirkungsgeschichte von Jes 53 in vorchristlicher Zeit," 79.

66. The similar-sounding זָקַק, which underlies καθαρίζω once in Psalm 11(12):6, is a more likely possibility.

arguing that the LXX read יִדְכָּאוֹ as a *qal* infinitive construct יִדְכָּאוֹ of the Aramaic root דְּכָה which signifies "to purify."[67] While καθαρίζω occurs in only two other places in the LXX Isaiah,[68] it appears 55 times in the Greek Pentateuch, usually in texts concerning ceremonial purification.[69]

Once again the LXX permits a linking to traditions regarding ritual sacrifice through its distinct language. In the LXX, καθαρίζω often occurs together with ἀμνός in the Greek Pentateuch in scriptures that describe sacrifices of lambs for purification.[70] While the priests and people are usually the initiators of the rites of purification for their sins, here the LXX stresses that it is the Lord himself who desires to purify the servant of the plague. The people are still invited to offer a sin-offering, but this is separate from the Lord's desire to purify the servant. This represents a completely different emphasis from that of the MT.

Whatever the supposed underlying Hebrew word, literal Greek equivalents for the MT's דַּכְּאוֹ (read as "to crush") were certainly available.

Aquila has καὶ κύριος ἐβουλήθη ἐπιτίψαι αὐτοῦ τὸ ἀρρώστημα ("and the Lord wanted the sickness to crush him") and Symmachus has κύριος ἠθέλησεν ἀλοῆσαι αὐτὸν ἐν τῷ τραυματίσμῳ ("Lord desired to beat him in the beating"). The theological perspective of the translator(s) likely influenced their word choice. Rather than reinforcing an image of God as one who delights in crushing his servant and people, even if it were a means to some greater end, the LXX shows the same tendency visible in Isaiah 53:4, 6 to avoid implicating God in the oppression. According to the LXX, the Lord is disassociated from the persecutors. The Lord is not implicated as perpetrator of wrongdoing against the persecuted servant, whether that be an individual or the community. Rather, the Lord's desire is to restore his servant, purifying him of the plague.

The LXX variants here also clearly reflect contextual exegesis. Isaiah 53:10a forms a chiasm with 53:10b-11a that is hardly accidental. A brief look at the literary structure of this verse shows how carefully the LXX crafted its version.[71]

---

67. Grelot, *Les poemes du serviteur,* 107. Also see Marcus Jastrow, *Dictionary of the Targumim, the Talmud Babli and Yerushalmi, and the Midrashic Literature,* vol 1, (P. Shalom Publishing: Brooklyn, N.Y.), 307.

68. Καθαρίζω occurs in Isaiah 57:14 and 66:17, matching two distinct Hebrew verbs.

69. Gen 35:2; Exod 20:7; 29:36, 37; 30:10; 34:7; Lev 8:15; 9:15; 12:7, 8; 13:6, 7, 13, 17, 23, 35, 37, 59; 14:2, 4, 7, 8, 11, 11, 14, 17, 18, 19, 20, 23, 25, 28, 29, 31, 48, 57; 15:13, 28, 28, 16:19, 20, 30, 30, 22:4; Num 6:9; 8:15; 12:15; 14:18; 30:6, 9,13; 31:23, 24; Deut 5:11; 19:13.

70. Καθαρίζω appears in Exodus 29:36, 37; Lev 14:8, 11, 14, 20, 23; Num 6:9 in close proximity to αμνος (Exod 29:38, 39, 40, 41; Lev 14:10, 12, 13, 21, 24; Num 6:12) and twice in the same verses (Lev 12:8; 14:25).

71. The MT also connects A A' through 53:10a's יְהוָה חָפֵץ דַּכְּאוֹ וַיְהוָה and 53:10b's יַצְלִחַ

A   καὶ κύριος βούλεται καθαρίσαι [αὐτὸν τῆς πληγῆς·]
B   ἐὰν δῶτε περὶ ἁμαρτίας,
B'   ἡ ψυχὴ ὑμῶν ὄψεται σπέρμα μακρόβιον·
A'   καὶ βούλεται κύριος ἀφελεῖν [ἀπὸ τοῦ πόνου τῆς ψυχῆς αὐτοῦ]

While both καθαρίσαι and ἀφελεῖν differ significantly from their MT equivalents, each variant influenced the other. Together they are consistent in their expression of the LXX's distinct perspective. In both lines the Lord is clearly the servant's advocate. The Lord purifies him of the plague and takes away from the distress of his soul. In B B' the addressees are clearly distinct from the servant. They are invited to respond and assured of a long-lived posterity.

The LXX matches the MT's הֶחֱלִי ("making him sick")[72] with τῆς πληγῆς ("of the plague") only here in the entire LXX.[73] Hengel suggests that the translator perhaps read מֵחִיל ("from the pain/writhing") instead of הֶחֱלִי.[74] This hypothesis has neither external textual support nor an example in the LXX where πληγή matches any form of חוּל. A look at the immediate literary context offers a better explanation.[75] The use of πληγή here clearly reflects contextual exegetical linkage with other scriptures in Isaiah.[76] The LXX's "the Lord desires to purify him of the plague" invites the reader to see God as cleansing the servant of his vicarious immersion in the plague on behalf of his people (Isa 53:3 and 4). The Lord's purification of the servant of the plague may be read as [indirectly] including the people for and with whom he suffered. Both the servant's innocence (53:9) and the Lord's desire to purify the servant are the focus of this section. In contrast, those whom the Lord addresses are assumed transgressors who need to offer a sin-offering.

וְחֵפֶץ יְהוָה בְּיָדוֹ. This connection is even clearer in the LXX through the repetition of βούλεται and the infinitives καθαρίσαι and ἀφελεῖν in 53:10a's καὶ κύριος βούλεται καθαρίσαι and 53:10b's καὶ βούλεται κύριος ἀφελεῖν.

72. In the place of the MT's הֶחֱלִי attested also by 4QIsaᵈ's החלי, 1QIsaᵃ has ויחללהו (the imperfect, third masculine singular *piel* plus third masculine singular suffix of חלל "to bore, pierce" or "defile, pollute"). This reading is both longer and easier, since it clearly links the Lord's piercing of the servant in Isaiah 53:10 with his being pierced for our transgressions (מְחֹלָל) in 53:5. See Jan de Waard's thorough discussion in *A Handbook on Isaiah,* 196.

73. Aq has "the illness," Sym, "by wounding," and V *in infirmitate,* "in sickness," which Jan de Waard considers to each assume the noun הֳלִי. Ibid. 196. This hypothesis is possible, though there are no other occasions in the LXX where this matching occurs.

74. M. Hengel, "Zur Wirkungsgeschichte von Jes 53 in vorchristlicher Zeit," 79.

75. In Isaiah 53:3 the LXX matches the MT's חֹלִי with μαλακία and in 53:4 יְנוּ חָלָ is matched with τὰς ἁμαρτίας ἡμῶν. In both Isaiah 53:3 and 53:4 πληγή is closely associated with these two matchings for חֳלִי.

76. Πληγή occurs eleven times in Isaiah, as noted above (Isa 1:6; 10:24, 26; 14:6, 6; 19:22; 30:26, 31; 53:3, 4, 10).

* * * * *

The LXX's ἐὰν and following second person plurals mark the beginning of a new phrase rather than a condition for the Lord's purification of the servant. "If you give (δῶτε) a sin offering, then your soul will see (ὄψεται) a long-lived descendent," departs markedly from the MT, where the Lord's delight in crushing and making the servant sick is related to the latter serving as a guilt offering. In contrast, ἐὰν begins a phrase that states the condition, interpreting the MT's new line beginning with יִרְאֶה as the result.

The LXX's distinct interpretation is achieved through its matching of the MT's אִם־תָּשִׂים אָשָׁם ("if [his life] would make a guilt offering") with ἐὰν δῶτε περὶ ἁμαρτίας ("if you would give a sin offering"). The LXX variant may reflect a Hebrew *Vorlage* with תָּשִׂימוֹ. It is more likely that the translator read תָּשִׂים as a second masculine singular[77] but matched it with the second plural δῶτε to reflect the distinct interpretation that the Lord is here addressing the plural speakers of 53:1-7.[78] The Lord addresses the plural speakers of 53:1ff, inviting them to give a sin-offering so as to see a long-lived posterity. Hengel's assertion that the congregation must make a sin-offering in order to share in the salvation promised to the servant is unwarranted."[79] While the promise to see a long-lived posterity is certainly a desirable benefit for those who offer sin-offerings, the servant's bearing of their sins is not dependent upon their religious efforts. Bastiaens is probably right in interpreting the call to offer sin-offerings as reflecting the importance that the addressees take responsibility for their sins and take steps themselves in response to the servant's work for them. He also rightly cautions that the emphasis here is less on the sin-offering and more on the promise that those who do so will see a long-lived descendant.[80] The LXX's shift to the second person reflects the translator's didactic concern to actualize the text for his hearers and readers, as Grelot argues.[81] Regardless of the original motivation for this

---

77. The majority of commentators correct this text, reading תָּשׂוּם as תָּשִׂים though נַפְשׁוֹ is clearly the subject. P. Grelot, *Les poemes du serviteur*, 62. Dhorme reads this as a second masculine singular, See E. Dhorme, *La Bible I 'Ancien Testament, II, Bibliothèque de la Pléade*, Paris: Gallimard, 1959, 190 «si tu fais de ta vie un sacrifice d'expiation.»

78. J. Koenig argues that the LXX agrees with the MT here: "De même a été négligé ou minimisé le fait que G (ἐὰν δῶτε) implique, avec passage au plurielen grec, par déduction (tu places = chacun place = vous donnez) un text H(G) identique à TM. Les deux témoins les plus antiques et, de loin, les plus importants, étayent done la leçon TM." *Oracles et Liturgies de l'Exil Babylonien*. Paris: Presses Universitaires de France, 1988, 108.

79. M. Hengel, *"Zur Wirkungsgeschicht von Jes 53 in vorchristlicher Zeit"* 79.

80. J. Ch. Bastiaens, Interpretaties van Jesaja 53, 140.

81. According to Grelot, "C'est donc le prophète qui donne une instruction à ses auditeurs, ou plutôt son interprète grec qui assume son rôle en s'adressant directement aux auditeurs de la lecture biblique. En conséquence, le texte est recomposé ... Mais la recomposition complète du texte montre que, pour l'interprète, l'édification des auditeurs et lecteurs prime la fidélité matérielle a sa

interpretation, the LXX readers may well experience themselves as addressed.

The Greek expression δῶτε περὶ ἁμαρτίας (literally "give for sins") occurs only here in the entire LXX. Δίδωμι does occasionally signify "give up" or "sacrifice."[82] Here it may well function as a synonym for one of the many verbs that are used together with περὶ ἁμαρτίας in the Pentateuch.[83] In contrast to the detailed ritual prescriptions concerning sin-offerings in the Pentateuch, the LXX of Isaiah 53:10 does not specify what the addressees are to give as a sin offering. They are simply told that giving for sin will result in their seeing a long-lived posterity.

The LXX matches the MT's אָשָׁם ("guilt offering") with περὶ ἁμαρτίας ("sin offering") only here in Isaiah. However, ἁμαρτια does occasionally match אָשָׁם in the Pentateuch[84] as well as in the Prophets and Writings.[85] Leviticus 5:7 is once again brought into relationship with our passage, this time through the LXX's matching of the MT's אֶת־אֲשָׁמוֹ with περὶ τῆς ἁμαρτίας αυτου. Most importantly περὶ ἁμαρτίας serves as the semantic equivalent for הַחַטָּאת ("sin offering") in the Pentateuch.[87] This language harmonizes with the LXX's language elsewhere in this poem that evokes ritual sacrifice. It also reflects intertextual exegesis, evoking the prescriptions concerning sin-offerings in Leviticus and Numbers. Hengel may be right in suggesting that the congregation's recognition that God is acting through the servant and confession of their guilt might function as "spiritual sin offering."[88] The speaker (prophet or Lord) invites the addressees to give a sin offering so they will see a long-lived posterity.

The MT's accent and third feminine singular invite the reader to identity נַפְשׁוֹ as the subject.[89] In the light of the LXX's above variant, δῶτε, ἡ ψυχὴ

---

littéralité." Grelot, *Les poemes du serviteur,* 108-109.

82. 1 Macc 6:44; 2:50; 2 Cor 8:5; Matt 10:45; 20:28; Luke 22:19.

83. In the Greek Pentateuch a number of verbs are used with περὶ ἁμαρτίας in the context of ritual sacrifice of animals for sin offerings. Διδωμι may be understood in Isaiah as synony-mous with φέρω "bring" (Isa 5:6, 7, 11; 12:6), ποιέω "offer" (Lev 14:31; 15:15, 30; 23:19; Num 6:11; 8:12; 15:24; 28:15), προσάγω "bring forward" (Lev 16:9; Num 15:27) and even λαμβάνω "take" (Lev 9:2, 3; 12:8; 16:5; Num 8:8).

84. Gen 42:21; Lev 5:7; Num 18:9.

85. 4 Kgs 12:16(17); Isa 53:10; 1 Chr 21:3; 2 Chr 28:13.

86. The Greek expressions περὶ τῆς ἁμαρτίας (Lev 4:14, 35; 5:6, 8, 9; 6:25(18), 30(23), 37(7:7); 8:2, 14; 9:8, 10, 22; 10:16, 17, 19; 14:19; 16:11, 15, 27; 19:22; 29:11) or περὶ τῆς ἁμαρτίας plus pronoun (Exod 32:30; Lev 4:3, 3; 5:6, 7; 5:10, 13; 9:7; 10:19; 16:6; Num 6:16: 15:25) also match the MT's term הַחַטָּאת.

87. Lev 5:6, 11; 7:27(37); 9:2,3; 12:6, 8; 14:13, 13; 14:22, 31; 15:15, 30; 16:3, 5, 9; 23:19; Num 6:11, 16; 7:16, 22, 28, 34, 40, 46, 52, 58, 64,70, 76, 82, 87; 8:8, 12; 15:24, 24, 27; 28:15, 22, 29; 29:5, 11, 16, 19, 22, 25, 28, 31, 34, 38.

88. Hengel, *"Zur Wirkungsgeschichte von Jes 53 in vorchristlicher Zeit,"* 79.

89. While many scholars correct נַפְשׁוֹ making it a third person masculine singular, יָשִׂים is

ὑμῶν could not have been read as the subject.[90] In contrast, the LXX clearly read נַפְשׁוֹ as the subject of the following verb יִרְאֶה. It is unlikely that the LXX's matching of the MT's third masculine singular suffix of נַפְשׁוֹ with a second plural suffix ἡ ψυχὴ ὑμῶν reflects a *Vorlage* with וְנַפְשְׁכֶם. There is no textual evidence outside of the LXX to support this variant. Rather, this difference with the MT clearly shows contextual exegesis consistent with the LXX's move to the second person plural.

According to the LXX, the addressees' soul will see a long-lived descendent if they give a sin-offering. This reading departs significantly from the MT, which describes the servant as seeing a descendent and surviving days. Here the singular ψυχή appears to designate the soul of a collective group. In the LXX of Isaiah ψυχή appears as both a plural[91] and as a singular noun with plural pronouns.[92] The LXX appears to be suggesting that the singular ψυχή represents the whole people or a collective group of addressees. This group will see a long-lived posterity.

* * * * *

The LXX clearly presents Israel as broken and alienated from God. The LXX appears to emphasize a greater distance between servant Israel and the Lord than is present in the MT.[93] While Israel describes himself as weary, discouraged and exhausted in his role as the Lord's servant in both the LXX and the MT (49:4), the LXX appears to place even greater emphasis on the servant's brokenness.[94] In both the LXX and the MT, the slave (MT servant) Israel is clearly in need of being gathered by someone outside of herself. Here we see a differentiation between the servant and another figure that is also present.

I have demonstrated in my book, *Isaiah's Servant Poems According to the Septuagint,* that the intensification of persecution against the servant appears

---

clearly the subject of חַיִּים, Grelot, *Les poemes du serviteur,* 62.

90. The LXX reading may here reflect concern for style. Koenig argues that "une lecture du verb a la 3ᵉ pers. fem., avec *napso* 'son ame' pour sujet serait un style improbable." *Oracles et liturgies de l'exil babylonien, 108.*

91. Isaiah 1:16; 19:10; 32:6, 6; 58:3.

92. Isaiah 3:9 ψυχῇ αὐτῶν (Isa 3:9; 66:3); ἡ ψυχῇ τοῦ λαοῦ αὐτοῦ (Isa 7:2), ἡ ψυχὴ αὐτῆς— as in the region of Moab (Isa 15:4); τὴν ψυχὴν αὐτῶν (Isa 47:14); ἡ ψυχὴ ἡμῶν (Isa 26:8); ἡ ψυχὴ ὑμῶν (Isa 33:18; 53:10; 55:2, 3); ψυχῇ αὐτοῦ (Isa 44:20; 49:7) and τῇ ψυχῇ σου (Isa 51:23).

93. The clearest example of this is in Isaiah 49:3 and 49:5, where in the LXX the speaker refers to himself as the Lord's slave, using δοῦλος instead of the usual παῖς. This likely reflects an editorial change emphasizing the speaker's self-abasement before God, as discussed in my commentary of 49:3.

94. The LXX of Isaiah 49:4's use δοῦλος and πόνος suggests a greater emphasis on Israel's abasement and suffering than is present in the MT.

to correspond with his differentiation from Israel. Even as this differentiation becomes increasingly evident, the LXX reader is continually reminded or the servant's identification with Israel. The servant does not turn from shame (50:6), evoking scriptures throughout Isaiah associating Israel's shame with sin, political alliances, and idolatry.[95]

There are numerous texts that describe the appalling appearance of the servant. While these texts generally occur in sections of the servant poems where the servant is differentiated from Israel, this separate servant's condition must also be read as encompassing Israel. The servant is associated with Israel's past and present suffering (i.e. Exodus) as can be seen in the use of the term πληγη. The servant (as distinct from Israel) is clearly associated with the pain of the people.[96]

The marginalized state of the servant results in his being despised and disregarded.[97] The servant's appearance and glory will be dishonored from among humankind (52:14; 53:3) and will provoke amazement (52:15). The servant is described as having no appearance, glory nor beauty (53:2). Rather, he is oppressed by the plague, sickness, ignominy. Everyone (παρὰ πάντας ἀνθρώπους) perceives the servant as lacking. The LXX appears to include Israel with the nations among those who abhor the servant (49:7).[98]

While the speakers in the LXX of 53:1ff are not overtly identified as Israel, there are clear links and they appear to speak for all when they describe the servant's suffering for their sin. The speakers in the LXX describe themselves as being led astray, presumably by others (53:6a).[99] Yet at the same time the speakers take full responsibility for their disorientation. "Each one has gone astray in his way" (53:6). They recognize that the servant suffers because of their sin. Their confession that the servant became sick because of their sins shows an exegetical link particular here to the LXX between sickness and sin (53:3-5). The servant bears sin, suffers pain and oppression (53:4), and is wounded and punished because of and on behalf of the people (53:5).

Even as servant Israel is described as broken by sin, oppression, and the differentiated servant as the people's sin-bearer and healer, servant Israel is linked both to scriptures describing the awaited Messiah[100] and to prominent characters in Israel's past. The LXX associates the servant with

95. The LXX associates the shame of the servant in 50:6 with that of Israel (Isa 3:9; 30:3, 5; 42:17; 45:16) and the nations (19:9; 20:4; 46:3, 10). See above commentary on Isaiah 50:6.

96. See intertextual connection between Isaiah 53:4 and 1:4ff.

97. This condition may well reflect the experience of certain elements of the Jewish community in the Diaspora.

98. "Slaves of rulers" likely refers to Israel (cf. Isa 49:7).

99. πλάναω.

100. Note the above-mentioned ties between Isaiah 42:1 and 9:6-7 in the LXX.

Hezekiah through numerous intertextual links.[101] The Lord describes his servant as finally understanding, being lifted up, and exceedingly glorified (52:13). Even though the servant here is differentiated from Israel, their close identification permits the reader to interpret these words about the servant as including Israel. The servant's judgment will be taken away (53:8). He will be purified (53:10) and justified (53:11). Finally, the servant will inherit many and divide the spoils of the strong (53:12).

At the same time the LXX clearly differentiates the servant from the whole people throughout the preceding three servant poems.

The servant as distinct in Isaiah 53

The collective Jacob/Israel as servant (52:14) is identified with, yet distinct from, the servant of 53:2ff. Both the identification with and distinction between the Israel and the servant are clearest in 53:1ff, where the plural speakers describe themselves as a "little servant" (παιδίον) who announce before the servant (παῖς) (53:2). The people's vocation is clearly to announce what they have heard and seen (53:1)—though no one has believed the report (hearing).

The people confess that a separate servant's bearing of sickness results from their sins (53:3).[102] The servant is innocent (53:9-10a) in contrast to sinful Israel. He is righteous, yet persecuted. The servant is a righteous sufferer: the servant's bearing of sickness is not a result of his own sins, but of those of the speakers. "This one bears our sins" (53:4). The servant embodies in his suffering the Lord's training of the people. The servant's education through suffering achieves the peace for the people. The LXX presents the servant as the one through whom the Lord deals with human sin, voluntarily suffering and dying on people's behalf.

The Lord's purification of the servant from the plague invites the reader to see God as cleansing the servant of his vicarious immersion in the plague on behalf of the people (53:10). The servant's suffering and death are depicted as linked to Israel's traditions regarding animal sacrifice (53:7).[103]

The LXX exhibits a tendency to de-emphasize the enemies or persecutors in favor of placing everything under the sovereignty of God. The people's dishonoring of the servant results from the Lord's handing him over to their sins. Rather than focusing on those who punish in 50:6, the LXX emphasizes the means of persecution (i.e. whippings, blows) or the punishment itself (50:6).

---

101. Μαλακία (53:5 = 38: 1,9; 39:1), turn away face (53:3= 38:2). Ἀναφαίρω (53:l0b).
102. See notes on φέρειν.
103. Slaughter is an intertextual verb as is "like a lamb."

The LXX presents suffering as the deserved punishment for collective sin (1:4-6). Though the servant is righteous, he demonstrates total solidarity with the people by suffering pain for them (53:4).[104] The LXX emphasizes more clearly than the MT that the servant's persecution results in his death (53:8). The servant's total solidarity with sinful Israel and suffering for their sins gives meaning to persecution and suffering experienced by the innocent (53:9).

There is an eschatological tension in the LXX between the present "you are my slave" and the future: "and in you I will be glorified" (49:3). The servant's eventual purification (53:10), justification (53:11) and deliverance (53:12) give hope to both the righteous who suffer and to the whole people who benefit from the servant's expiatory work.

Conclusion

In this paper, I have argued that the LXX translators' many differences with the MT of Isaiah 53:3-7 can be interpreted as theologically motivated. They seek to disassociate God from the servant's (Israel's) suffering in verses where the MT could be (wrongly, I believe), and often has been, interpreted to support a notion of atonement through penal substitution.

---

104. See the intertextual rapport between Isaiah 53:4 and Exodus 3:7.

Chapter Seven

THE FRANCISCAN OPINION

by Richard Rohr

"I will pour out on them a spirit of kindness and prayer, when they look upon the one they have pierced" (Zechariah 12:10).

Most people, Catholic, Orthodox, or Protestant, do not realize that what is commonly accepted as the mainline opinion—on Jesus' death as an atonement or heroic "sacrifice" of some type—was not the only Christian opinion in the 13th century. It was a subject open to debate. The Franciscan spokesman and scholar was a Scotsman named "Blessed" John Duns Scotus (1266-1308), who held the early theology chairs at Oxford and Cologne, after studying at the University of Paris.

He is known as the "Subtle Doctor" of the Church, and such subtlety is surely exemplified in his teaching on *Cur Deus Homo?* (Why did God become a human being?). Duns Scotus did not question God's redemptive work in Jesus, but only the precise "how?" and "what?" of it. "*How* did God transfer transformative love to humanity?" Not if, but *what* is the precise nature of Jesus' redemption?"[1]

Our Franciscan interpretation was never condemned or denied by the orthodox Catholic tradition, and was considered a legitimate "minority position." When the Reformation occurred, the Protestant reformers largely accepted and even furthered the "majority position" (necessary blood sacrifice) rather uncritically. This opinion was, of course, developed by early church fathers, Anselm, St. Thomas Aquinas and the mainline Catholic tradition. This very issue is an example of two telling patterns: First, Catholicism was once more broad-minded and allowed for alternative interpretations of doctrine more often before the Reformation than it does today. And second, the Protestant Reformation often either *reacted to—or continued with*—popular Catholicism much more than it realized.

In short and simple form, John Duns Scotus was not swayed or limited by the numerous metaphors of ransom, debt, redemption as "buying," blood sacrifice, payment of price (the Hebrew *goel*), "purchased in blood"

---

1. Duns Scotus' thought was so subtle that his very name was used as an insult by his detractors, and his followers were called "dunces"!

vocabulary that we frequently find in the Bible. Recognizing that he was primarily a philosopher, I would assume that Scotus saw them for the metaphors that they were—images that would have spoken powerfully to a people formed by temple sacrifice, animal offerings, a *quid pro quo* kind of mind, a biblical text that did use frequent sacrificial imagery and even images of Divine vengeance from Genesis to Hebrews. Duns Scotus saw these metaphors as limited because they made God's redemptive action a rather anthropomorphic "reaction" to human sin *instead of God's perfect and utterly free initiative.* This he could not tolerate.

These sacrificial and atonement metaphors would have appealed, or even seemed necessary, to a judicial mind uncomfortable with the concept of forgiveness, or any dualistic mind that prefers tit for tat explanations for things. Jesus came to change all of that, of course, and it became our central concept of grace. Duns Scotus' systematic philosophy and theology was utterly committed to *protecting the perfect freedom of God, and also the necessary inner freedom of each creature.*[2] The freedom of the will (to love!) was a higher attribute than knowledge for him, and this differentiated the Franciscan from the Dominican schools. We were almost the official "debating society" at that time.[3]

John Duns Scotus, however, was more in harmony with Colossians and Ephesians, which would have appealed to his philosophical-aesthetic sense of the whole and of history, more than any of the literal symbols of sacrificial payment found elsewhere in the Bible. These letters saw Jesus as the "first image in the mind of God" (Ephesians 1:3-6, 10-11), which is even further described in the hymn in Colossians 1:15-20. Jesus, Scotus said, was not "necessary" to solve any problem whatsoever—no mopping up exercise after the fact—but a pure and gracious declaration of the primordial truth from the very beginning! The incarnation of God in Jesus gives us the living "icon of the invisible God" (Colossians 1:15), who is the template for all else (1:16), who reconciles all things in himself (1:17), the headmaster in a cosmic body which follows after him (1:18) and, if I may use a contemporary image, Jesus is the "hologram" for all that is happening in a holographic, constant, and

---

2. Dr. Mary Beth Ingham, *Scotus for Dunces* (Franciscan Institute, St. Bonaventure University, 2003). This is the best source which makes John Duns Scotus' rarefied and largely untranslated Latin text available for contemporary readers.

3. Together the Franciscan and the Dominican schools formed a genuine wholeness in the 13th century Church, but the Franciscan school saw freedom of the will as the necessary prerequisite for love, more than intellectual understanding or "knowledge." In that sense, Scotus was almost a premonition of modern psychology, which learned to account for human unfreedom and defences, and our inability to know and see the truth. For us, free will (*voluntas*) precedes knowledge (*scientia*).

repetitive universe (1:19). He does what we also must do, which is why he says "follow me."

The human Jesus, in other words, is God's pre-emptive statement to humanity about history and the soul—all distilled and focused in one visible life—which is "secretly" Divine but overtly human. We called this Scotus' doctrine of "The Primacy of Christ." *Whatever happens to Jesus is what must and will happen to the soul:* incarnation, an embodied life of ordinariness and hiddenness, initiation, trial, faith, death, surrender, resurrection and return to God. Such is the Christ-pattern that we all share in, either joyfully and trustfully (heaven), or unwillingly and resentfully (hell). Christ's primacy and pattern is ironically undone and even made unnecessary when all that really matters is the last week of his life.[4]

Jesus, of course, communicates the Godself most graphically and dramatically on the cross itself, *where we see and learn to trust* the free offer of God's love in a brutal and utterly compelling image, one that assaults the defended psyche, mind and heart. Self-giving love calls forth love in return, Father Francis would say. But the trouble is that we emphasized paying a cosmic debt more than communicating a credible love—which is the utterly central issue. It became more an image of a Divine *transaction* than an image of God's *free action* in human transformation. The primary problem with the crucifix/cross as image is that it has now become commonplace, or in most "left brain churches" largely rejected. *Many substituted a theological explanation for a transformative story and image.* Nevertheless, the cross is still our official icon of transformation, and not surprisingly became the very corporate logo of Christianity itself.

The motive for the Incarnation, says John Duns Scotus, was simply God's desire to effectively and freely communicate Divine and Perfect Love. That was more than enough of a task for God, and more than we could handle, as history has largely shown. *If Jesus had any debt to pay, he was paying the "debt" to the human soul and human seeing, so it could gaze upon God properly, truthfully and without fear.* The Franciscan sense is that the "substitutionary atonement" theory, as it was later called, has achieved the exact opposite. In order to turn Jesus into a Hero we ended up making the Father into a "Nero." This is not good and radically subverts the whole Christian economy of grace.

---

4. The problem is that we can then ignore most of his teaching as long as we allow Jesus to be the "blood sacrifice for our sins." We end up "worshiping Jesus" as a quasi-substitute for following him, which is of course what he actually proposed. It also bases the whole Christian life in sin and guilt atonement instead of a journey of transformation into conscious sons and daughters of God.

For "Scotists," as the Franciscan School was called, Jesus was not needed or required to change the mind of God about humanity. The Father did not need to be talked into loving his own creation. The loving mind of God was directed toward us totally from the very beginning of time, as both the doctrine of the Primacy of Christ, and any Trinitarian understanding, make clear and absolute. God never changed. *We do consistently,* however, in our perennial inability to believe such incomprehensible grace and steadfast love, and by our various attempts to save ourselves, clearly symbolized by Adam and Eve leaving the garden.

The doctrine of the eternally outpouring and receiving Trinitarian God is absolutely central to John Duns Scotus' theological worldview. For Scotus, Jesus cannot and must not be understood apart from his life as the "Second Person of the Blessed Trinity, and within the eternal "procession" of persons that we call the Mystery of a Trinitarian God.[5] We ended up with a Father God who appears—*at least unconsciously*—to be vindictive, violent, and petty, not at all free, subject to supposed laws of offended justice—and a Son who is mainly sent to solve a problem instead of revealing the heart of God. Sin becomes the very motive for redemption instead of love.

The Son of God is presented as reacting, whereas a free and loving God would always act from God's own primordial and eternal truth. *Divine love is not determined by the worthiness of the object but by the goodness of the subject.* Such problem-based and sin-based Christianity is a very uninviting and even unsafe universe to the Franciscan mind. No wonder mainline Christianity has produced so few mystics and so many detractors. True Christianity beguiles, seduces, invites, cajoles, creates spiritual yearning and draws humanity into ever more desirable mystery, healing and grace. When Christianity is not rightly mystical (read "experiential"), it always settles for mere moralisms, belief systems, and explanations (which can remain extrinsic, behavioural and even egocentric). God instead wants us to become "an altogether new creation" (Galatians 6:16), "with the mind of Christ" (1 Corinthians 2:16), "friends not servants" (John 15:15).

In Franciscan parlance, *Jesus did not come to change the mind of God about humanity, Jesus came to change the mind of humanity about God.* This grounds Christianity in love and freedom from the very beginning. It creates a very coherent and utterly attractive religion, which draws people toward lives of inner depth, prayer, reconciliation, healing and even universal "at-one-ment," instead of mere sacrificial atonement. Soon we have an ener-

---

5. Christianity has poorly interpreted much of the Gospel by trying to convert people to Jesus before it "converted" them to Trinity! (Bible quotes without a life of prayer, doctrines without inner experience, church growth without living in the Spirit.)

getic basis for a joy-filled and mystical Christianity, as Franciscanism always preferred. A non-violent atonement theory says that God is not someone we need to fear or mistrust (versus "What will God ask of me if he demands violent blood sacrifice from his only Son?"). Our only desire is "to fall into the hands of [such a] Living God" (Hebrews 10:31). But like any trust fall, first we have to trust him.

Jesus, for us, is the mediator of a Christianity that is much more about Divine Union than a "moralistic" payoff or a solution to a cosmic problem. Such "ungracious" religion has only led to a kind of false idealization of egotistic self-sacrifice, a *quid pro quo* universe that Jesus himself never taught and even rejected: "Go, learn the meaning of the words, what I want is mercy not sacrifice. I did not come for the virtuous, but for the sick." (Matthew 9:13). As much of the brilliant work of René Girard has taught in our time,[6] Jesus was precisely the "once and for all" sacrifice given to reveal the lie and the absurdity of the very notion and necessity of sacrificial religion itself (much of the point of Hebrews 10).

But we perpetuated such regressive and sacrificial patterns by making God the Father into the Chief Sacrificer, and basing the very notion of divine redemption on a kind of "necessary violence."[7]   Can God do no better than that? Or were we attracted to such a theory to legitimate our own conscious or unconscious desire to be violent? Is dominative power not *our humanly* preferred way of dealing with our problems? (We *must* ask that question!) A violent theory of redemption legitimated punitive and violent problem solving all the way down—from Papacy to parenting! There eventually emerged a huge disconnect between the founding story and the message of Jesus itself! "If even God uses and needs violence, maybe Jesus did not really mean what he said in the Sermon the Mount." Remember, *how* you get there determines where you finally arrive!

Our bellicose Christian history has made this core problem rather clear. If

---

6. Girard, Rene, e.g. *The Scapegoat, Things Hidden Since the Foundation of the World, Violence and the Sacred, The Girard Reader,* and many more.

7. The universal history of religion moved from human sacrifice (Isaac story), to animal sacrifice (which Jesus exposes and liberates, e.g. John 2:13-17), to a two thousand year history of dualistic Manichaeism, Catharism, Jansenism, Puritanism, and the ping pong game of body hatred and body worship that we face today. *Some body, some body part, or some one—always needs to be sacrificed*—at least for anyone who has not experienced grace and mercy. A scapegoat *will* be found. So Jesus instead became the Scapegoat—to expose the lie of scapegoating—not to perpetuate it. But the idealized history of—"something must be sacrificed"—has largely continued unabated—even though Jesus came to reveal and end this violent mechanism in the paradoxical revelation of the cross—by showing us how wrong scapegoating could be, how easily we misperceive evil, and how this can be done at the highest levels of power (high priest and imperial authority).

God solves problems by domination, coercion and violent demand, then we can too. Grace, mercy and eternal generosity are no longer the very shape of God, as the Trinitarian nature of God seemed to say. Free will, grace and love became less admirable than some theoretical cosmic justice, law and blind obedience. We ended up making God very small, and drew the Godhead into our own egoic need for retribution, judicial resolution and punishment. Exactly what Jesus came to undo! If God can forgive, then God can forgive! We do not need one major exception where we need atonement and payment of price. But theoretical religion has always been more comfortable with cosmic problem-solving than with personal surrender to the healing and transformative mystery of Divine Love. Healing and forgiveness have not been in the forefront of Christian history, even though it is almost the only thing Jesus does.

But sacrificial thinking is in the human hard-wiring, and has been so glorified in myth, ego and war, that most people are unable to live without some form of blood expiation and vengeance toward problems. Now if the Godself even needs appeasement and atonement and necessary victims—we are in an utterly closed system of supposed *redemptive violence.* Exactly the "useless" offerings that most of the prophets, and many of the Psalms (40, 51, 69) railed against. Such a worthiness-based mind cannot "imagine" or allow grace and forgiveness—even in God. Remember that mercy and compassion is first experienced as weakness (witness our governments), whereas sacrificial thinking strengthens our sense of egoic structure and what we call "self." The creating of a necessary ego structure is a first half of life task; whereas surrendering to a perfect Love from elsewhere takes away our power and always feel like a defeat to the ego. If we get there, it is more often in the second half of life,[8] unless of course we suffered young and were loved young. Some manner of "buying and selling" is the only way the dualistic or mercenary mind can understand things, it seems. Yet this is the very notion that drove Jesus to rebellion against the temple, the very action that got him killed (John 2:14-17) and that began Luther's necessary revolt against formulaic religion, the buying and selling of indulgences. The mind and heart untouched by the utter illogic of grace always needs a formula, an explanation, a buy off, a sacrificial payment to restore the human scales of justice. Whereas "Through *his goodness revealed* (emphasis mine) to us in Christ Jesus, he showed us how infinitely rich God is in grace, saving us by pure gift ... so that we are God's work of art, created in Christ Jesus to live the good life as

---

8. Rohr, Richard, "The Spirituality of the Two Halves of Life" (Center for Action and Contemplation, Albuquerque, NM, 2003), Recorded Conferences with Ron Rolheiser, and another with Paula D'Arcy.

from the beginning he had meant us to live it" (Ephesians 2:7-10). *Jesus is not the afterthought here, but the forethought, the first thought, the distilled icon of all that God is doing in creation.* And what it says is that what God is doing "is good, very good!"

Jesus Christ is, therefore, both the medium and the message ("way, truth, and life")—all combined in one compelling and convincing human body (Jesus) and cosmic body (Christ)! Jesus is not a necessity for us Franciscans. Jesus is pure gift and grace and glory! And why would a gift be less good than a necessity? "From his fullness (*pleroma*) we have all received, grace in return for grace. . . No one has ever seen God, it is the only Son, who is nearest to the Father's heart, who has made him known" (John 16,18).

Practically, however, the only way out of our historical fear of God (which seems to be in the human hard-wiring) is quite simply to "gaze upon the one we have pierced" (John 19:37) so that the crucified Jesus can "draw [us] unto himself" (John 12:32). This is a contemplative and prayerful knowing, not a logical or judicious knowing. It cannot be proven by marshalling texts for or against. It is known by those who stand before the crucified, and those who pray from inside their own littleness and unworthiness, as our Father Francis did. It is a knowing preserved for those who "become like little children" before the mystery of a Perfect Love. In our Franciscan spirituality, "the wise and learned" can never understand this; it is the offered "foolishness" of a crucified God—who only makes sense to other fools, as Paul teaches (1 Corinthians 1:18-31).

In closing, it has always surprised me that many Catholics, and those who know through story, inner image, prayer and art, are not so invested in any sacrificial atonement theory as those who begin and end with books and texts. In fact, Catholics often say, "What is the atonement theory?" They do not even get upset if you deny it! How shocking. I have a strong opinion why this is true.

Although the Dominicans might have formally won the debate back in the 13th century, and the Protestants largely followed them, God actually won— through the many who learned how to pray, look and listen. They just gazed upon the crucifix long enough—and they knew. They knew it was all OK. They knew "Jesus died for our sins," but not through any needed heavenly transaction or convincing Bible quotes. *They knew it by gazing upon the one that we have pierced,* praying from a place of needed mercy, and allowing Love to change them from the bottom up. They needed no top-down theory. God gazed at them through the suffering and sad eyes of Jesus, and they looked back—and up. And redemption happened again.

To stand under is still the best way to understand.

PART FOUR

ATONEMENT AND
FORGIVENESS

Chapter Eight

THE FORGIVENESS OF SINS
HOSEA 11:1-9; MATTHEW 18:23-35

by Rowan Williams
with comments after by Mark D. Baker

Belief in forgiveness is just as much a matter of *faith* as anything else in the creed. It is no more obvious and demonstrable than the existence of God or the divinity of Jesus Christ. This is perfectly clear if we think a little about the meaning of forgiveness and the realities of human existence and relationship. I am what I am because of what I have been and done, good and bad. My self is woven out of a great web of complicated motivation reflections, intentions, and actions, some of which have turned out to be creative, while others have been destructive for myself and for other people. And mature persons need to be able to see and accept all this, to take responsibility for some things and to accept the inevitability of others—to *own* the whole of ourselves, to acknowledge realities both past and present, to destroy all the crippling illusions about ourselves that lock us up in selfish fantasies about our power or independence. I depend on the past, and it is part of me; to deny it is to deny myself. I am my history.

People will often talk about forgiveness in a way that suggests this is not true. "Forgive and forget," we say; we'll say no more about it. We look at forgiveness as if it were the same as acquittal—leaving the court without a stain on our character as if it simply obliterated the past. If that is how we think of forgiveness, it really does become incredible—an arbitrary fiat which unties all the knots we are bound in by simply pretending certain things haven't happened. It is rather like the attitude of those who seem to think that the resurrection cancels out the crucifixion. But we know this is not true: if we have been badly hurt by someone, then whatever happens the scars and memories will still be there, even if we "forgive" them. And if we have hurt someone, the same is true: we may be "forgiven," but we can see the effects of what we have done, perhaps for years after. If forgiveness is forgetting, then it isn't only incredible: it is a mockery of the depth and seriousness of the suffering that human beings inflict on each other. The monument at Auschwitz to the Jews killed there has the inscription, "O earth, cover not their blood." There are things that should never, never be forgotten—Auschwitz is one of them—and if forgiveness means forgetting, then forgiveness is a trivial and profoundly offensive idea, as that monument indeed suggests.

Well, though, isn't forgiveness still a possible idea even if we agree that the past can't be changed? Can't we say that forgiveness is an agreement not to forget, but at least to suspend judgment on the past? In other words, I deserve your anger, I deserve punishment, but you kindly excuse me what I owe you. This approach has a good deal of support in the New Testament; it is the basis of a lot of Christian thinking on the subject. I am a sinner, but God graciously treats me as if I weren't. This is important, and it is an advance on the "forgive and forget" idea. But is it enough on its own? Surely not. This is a forgiveness that changes nothing—something that sounds almost cynical if we're not careful. A forgiveness that says only, "I know exactly what you are and what you have done, but I'll say no more about it," can be, in fact, a terrible, negative judgment. I don't take you seriously enough to do anything: do what you like, I won't make any difficulties.

That's a travesty, of course, but it is something to beware of. No, we need something more positive to say about forgiveness. We need to recognize both the reality of the past and the hope of a future forgiveness. Because real forgiveness is something that changes things and so gives hope. The occasions when we feel genuinely forgiven are the moments when we feel, not that someone doesn't care what we do, but that someone does care what we do because he or she loves us and that love is strong enough to cope with and survive the hurt we have done. Forgiveness of that sort is creative because it reveals new dimensions to a relationship, new depths, new possibilities. We can find a love richer and more challenging than before. If someone says to me, "Yes, you have hurt me, but that doesn't mean it's all over. I forgive you. I still love you," then that is a moment of enormous liberation. It recognizes the reality of the past, the irreversibility of things, the seriousness of damage done, but then it is all the more joyful and hopeful because of that. Because this kind of love doesn't have illusions, it is also all the more mature and serious. It can look at and fully feel my weaknesses, and still say, "I love you."

But what does this say about the unhealed human injuries, about the death and catastrophe that can find no human resolution? Who is to forgive the camp commandant at Auschwitz, the murderer of a child, the tyrant waging genocidal wars? Only the victim has the "right" to forgive: I can't forgive on someone else's behalf. I can't intrude into that dreadful intimate relation between the one who hurts and the one who is hurt. So it seems as if there can be no forgiveness if the victim doesn't forgive—and the dead, you might say, don't forgive. We might find a reason for pardoning the murderer, but that is not the same thing. Are there, then, wounds never to be healed, personally as well as globally?

After all, our love is not very strong. It is hardly surprising if we come to a point where we say, "I can't take that. That is the end of love." Is forgiveness to depend on this, on our hopeless, inept struggles to love?

The reply of the gospel is "no." Christian faith here pushes right against the limits of the credible once again in saying that *God* forgives and has the *right* to forgive. God is the ultimate victim of all human cruelty, says the gospel: God bleeds for every human wound. Inasmuch as we do good or ill to any human person, it is done to God. Forgiveness is not only a matter to be settled among ourselves—or left unsettled because of our inadequacies. It is God's affair too. And the good news of Christianity is that, since God suffers human pain, since God is the victim of human injury, then there is beyond all our sin a love that is inexhaustible. God's love for this creation never comes to a point where it can take no more. In the old Prayer Book epistle for today, we hear Paul reminding us that *agape*, God's love, never comes to an end. So God can always survive the hurt we do him; whenever we turn to him in sorrow and longing, after we have done some injury, this love is still there, waiting for us, a home whose door is always open. Whatever we do can never shut that door to his merciful acceptance. The only thing that can keep us out is the refusal to ask for and trust in that mercy.

And the gospel proclaims all this in virtue of the cross of Jesus. Without that, we cannot begin to understand the forgiveness of sins. Jesus crucified is God crucified, so we believe. Jesus is the total and final embodiment in history of God's loving mercy; and so this cross is a unique, terrible, extreme act of violence—a summary of all sin. It represents the human rejection of love. And not even *that* can destroy God: with the wounds of the cross still disfiguring his body, he returns out of hell to his disciples and wishes them peace. Because Jesus as preacher and teacher had proclaimed and enacted God's identification with the world of human beings, Jesus the condemned criminal speaks of God's presence in the extremity of suffering, in abandonment and death—God as victim. And thus he proclaims God as the one who, above all others, has the right to forgive. "In all their affliction he was afflicted." The prophet in the Old Testament saw a little of that, but here in Jesus it is spelled out in the detail of a human life and death. There is our hope—the infinite *resource* of God's love, the relationship with his creatures that no sin can finally unmake. He cares what we do because he suffers what we do. He is forever wounded, but forever loving. The possibilities of our relationship with him are indeed "new every morning."

So our sins become not stopping points, but starting points. They can be the occasions of constantly fresh, constantly wider visions of the grace of God. It's often been said, boldly, that the saints in heaven rejoice over their sins, because through them they have been brought to greater and greater understanding of the endless endurance of God's love, to the knowledge that beyond every failure God's creative mercy still waits. We have a future because of this grace.

A matter of *faith*: yes, indeed, not of clear knowledge or vision. To see God in Christ crucified is a matter of faith; to believe in the r unyielding and inexhaustible love of God is a matter of faith; and to believe there is a future for us despite the reality of our sins is a matter of faith. Still more difficult to imagine is how God can forgive in the name of those most desperately and terribly hurt. How can God forgive the tyrant and the murderer? We can't talk too glibly about reconciliation and resolution here. It is hard to see how some people might ever let themselves be forgiven, even if forgiveness is offered. But it's not our business to work that out. All we can be sure of is that whatever the deficiency and the drying-up of human capacity to love, the killing of love by pain, there is still, at the heart of everything, a love that cannot be killed by pain. That is a warning against regarding or treating any human being as unforgivable; that is the positive side of this problem, this brick wall for the imagination. We don't know how some situations can issue in forgiveness, and we have to bear their dreadfulness without pious evasion, but it would be worse to deny the possibility of grace, however unthinkable. That possibility is our only hope, and it is the only clue to what "grace" can mean in our relations with each other—the refusal to set the limits to our love.

As Jesus' parable forcibly reminds us, the man who forgets how much and in what way he has been loved and forgiven, how much hurt he has inflicted on the eternal heart of God, and who clings to his "rights" and nurses his unforgiven injuries—that man is in mortal danger. He has understood nothing and sees forgiveness as a thing canceling the past. And of course he duly finds out that the past is not canceled. But we who profess belief in the forgiveness of sins must see forgiveness as something creative of the future, the future of our own love. It is never a possession; it is not something finished; it is a gift and a hope, and also a call.

The gift is itself a task. We can pray in gratitude to God for being forgiven, but we must pray too for help to live with forgiveness, and to live it in our own future.

Comments by Mark D. Baker

Rowan Williams models for us an approach to contextualizing the message of atonement through leading his audience to reflect on their experiences of forgiving and being forgiven. Instead of starting with a concept or theory that may feel abstract or unintelligible and then working to connect it to life, he does the opposite. He leads the listeners to develop a concept of forgiveness from their experiences in life.

Although I would not endorse a theological approach that lets human experiences and reasoning serve as the foundation and guide for theological thinking, at times (as here) human experience can function well as a means of communicating a theology rooted in God's self-revelation. For instance, Williams uses experience not to end up with a watered down concept of forgiveness. Instead, through logic and reflection on real-life experience he leads the listener to sense the cost of forgiveness and also the impossibility of forgiveness being offered in some cases. In the process he helps the listener recognize that some of the things commonly said about forgiveness, in everyday life and sometimes in theological statements, do not match reality. We cannot forgive and forget. Simply suspending judgment can be a way of not taking seriously the hurt caused and communicating a sense of, "Do what you like; I will not hold it against you."

In contrast, he helps us feel the richness of a forgiveness that acknowledges the hurt, that does not deny its pain and consequences, but states: "I forgive you. I still love you." He also, however, points out the impossibility of many receiving this forgiveness. There is no human way. It is a beautiful point of transition in the sermon. Is there then no way? The reply of the gospel is "no." At this point Williams turns our attention to the cross—the extreme act of violence and summary of all sin—to help the listeners comprehend both that the forgiveness God offers is true, deep, and rich, and that God can offer it to all.

Williams's proclamation on forgiveness has a different feel than many other presentations on the cross and forgiveness, not simply because of how he explores the theme of forgiveness in "real life," but also because of where he situates God. Rather than placing God in a legal system and saying that God is unable to forgive without first demanding punishment, Williams portrays God as the one most able to forgive, and entitled to do so, because of the pain and hurt God suffered at the cross. As in penal satisfaction, here the cross allows God to offer forgiveness to all, but for quite different reasons- reasons much more consonant with the theological guidelines derived from the New Testament writers (see chap. 1).

In an additional way Williams's sermon matches those theological guidelines for proclaiming the atonement: he not only communicates in a way that connects with his audience; he also challenges them. By referring back to the Gospel text they have heard, he not only proclaims forgiveness through the cross, but also calls them to be forgiving people.

Chapter Nine

THE REPETITION OF RECONCILIATION:
SATISFYING JUSTICE, MERCY, AND FORGIVENESS

by Sharon Baker

Religion Gone Bad

Postmodern artist Anselm Kiefer works extensively with the ambiguity between heaven and earth. He paints provocative and haunting images of human depravity and the unvoiced heavenly response. Wrestling with the problem of justifying God in a world fraught with evil, he says: "Religion can pretend to be pure, history cannot."[1] Horrendous acts of terror find asylum in the refuge of religion, rationalizing that if God condones or even commands violence it must be right. Historically, much of the large scale human violence appears to be motivated by religious convictions.[2] Without the lens of religion through which to peer, however, we are presented with a bleak history of human violence that stains the historical landscape with spilled blood, putting the human race to shame. In fact, a violent history is in the making as we speak with the war in Iraq, the genocide in Darfur, and the terrorism of political fundamentalists. As a result, religion and those who practice it can no longer pretend to be pure. History reveals our impurity; we are guilty of merciless violence against humanity in God's name. The time for indictment is long overdue.

Christians alone have generated violence and abuse beyond measure. Because these "holy" warriors marched to the drum beat of a violent God, the ones whom Christ longed to liberate were instead tied up and tortured; those whom Christ sought to love were instead slaughtered in hate. Why do these atrocities occur? What motivates such dutiful killing and imperturbable oppression?

"From the time we are children, we create ourselves by imagining a heaven. We each have a different one. It's like color. No one sees the same blue. Some may see black."[3] I would substitute "heaven" for "God." We

---

1. Anselm Kiefer, *Heaven and Earth*, organized by Michael Auping (Fort Worth: Modern Art Museum of Fort Worth: Prestel, 2006), 32.
2. The crusades, the Spanish Inquisition, the many holocausts throughout history, the war in Iraq are a few examples of violence executed under the guise of religion.
3. Keifer, *Heaven and Earth,* 32.

create ourselves a God. We each have a different one . . .

Changing the Lens

In his book, *Jesus Against Christianity*, Jack Nelson-Pallmeyer makes the case that the "overwhelming image of God in the Bible is that of a brutal, violent, and vengeful judge."[4] God's violent vengeance occurs in the Old Testament over one thousand times, speaking of "Yahweh's blazing anger, of his punishments by death and destruction, and how like a consuming fire he passes judgment, takes revenge, and threatens annihilation."[5] In actuality, Nelson-Pallmeyer says, the magnitude of avenging divine violence in the Old Testament far exceeds human violence. God directly and indirectly instigates monumental amounts of violence that according to contemporary ethical standards would be considered incredibly unjust. Traditional readings of the Old Testament seem to reveal a violent deity bent on getting his own way regardless of the cost. Questioning the actions of God revealed in scripture appears heretical to some, which only works to preserve the traditional perception of God as violent. Is this perception important? Why should it matter to us if the image of God is one of violence and retributive justice?[6]

For theologian A. W. Tozer, our perception of God is the most important thing about us. We do not merely believe in God, we believe in a certain kind of God. He states that "[t]he images used to speak about God not only decisively determine the way one thinks about God, they have a powerful impact on the shape of the life of the believer."[7] Comedian and actor Steve Allen agrees, saying: "that mankind is still capable of the murderous evils that have been committed in the 20th century may be due in part to the fact that Jews and Christians have totally incorporated, into their unconscious perhaps, extremely vengeful and 'righteous' behavior as characteristic of

---

4. Jack Nelson-Pallmeyer, *Jesus Against Christianity: Reclaiming the Missing Jesus* (Harrisburg, PA: Trinity Press International, 2001), 21. See also Jack Nelson-Pallmeyer, *Is Religion Killing Us?* (Harrisburg, PA: Trinity Press International, 2003), 10, 16. Deut. 7:1-2; 1 Sam. 24:1. See also Eric Seibert, *Disturbing Divine Behavior: Dealing with Problematic Portrayals of God in Old Testament Narratives* (publication pending).

5. Raymund Schwager, *Must There Be Scapegoats? Violence and Redemption in the Bible*, trans. by Maria L. Assad (New York: Crossroad, 2000), 55.

6. Seibert, *Disturbing Divine Behavior*. In his book, Eric Seibert makes a valid and insightful case for critical historical, literary, and cultural studies in order to get to the bottom of the portrayal of God as violent in human history. He provides us with an alternative way to read the Old Testament that places the blame for violence where it belongs—at the hands of human beings, writing their history for their faith community.

7. A.W. Tozer, *The Knowledge of the Holy: The Attributes of God: Their Meaning in the Christian Life* (New York: Harper and Row, 1961), 7.

the God they worship."[8] Our view of God has a profound effect on the way we behave and on the decisions we make, especially when those decisions include whether or not to go to war. For example, on the one hand, those Christians who view God as a warrior, commanding armies of people to fight and kill, may also believe that God commissions nations and people to go to war, killing others in order to protect the innocent. Consequently, taking up arms to fight and kill is a valid response. On the other hand, Christians who focus on God as loving, forgiving, and reconciling, see God as nonviolent, as a God who rejects violence and killing. As a result, killing others for any reason, even in war, is inappropriate.

The Old Testament is not the only text culpable for portraying God as violent and vengeful. Notions of a violent God also lie in the traditional interpretations of the atonement. The very act of God fashioned to bring lasting peace in the face of inordinate violence and evil was somehow turned into a basis for violence. Traditionally, Christian atonement theology and its varying motifs have focused on the cross and the efficacy of Christ's violent death. The passion of Christ has been described in metaphors analogous to the historical or political context, including images from the temple, the battlefield, the courts of law, the slave market, feudalism, courtly love, account-keeping, and family life. Most of the traditional theories have been those that reduce the passion to an equation, "formulated by a divine mathematician" so that a special death is necessary in order to balance the cosmic accounts. That death was afforded by Jesus Christ.[9]

Although each of these atonement theories entertains various nuances more complex than I have indicated, one thing remains clear and common to all: God would not simply wipe the slate clean. God would not or could not write off the loss of offended honor or debt owed in order to forgive sin. Instead, God required payment either through satisfaction, punishment, or a victory forged through violence. Accordingly, we can receive forgiveness only through some sort of economy, of *quid pro quo,* of a balancing of the divine account books.[10] Lurking behind these theories is the ghost of a punitive father, haunting the image of forgiving grace by finding the death of his own son an agreeable way to negotiate forgiving the world.[11]

Many contemporary biblical scholars and theologians argue that doctrines

8. Steve Allen, *More Steve Allen on the Bible, Religion, and Morality* (Prometheus, 1993), 313. See also Seibert, 2.8-9.

9. Paul S. Fiddes, *Past Event and Present Salvation* (Louisville, KY: Westminster/John Knox Press, 1989), 4-5, 83.

10. P.T. Forsyth, *The Cruciality of the Cross* (London: Independent Press, 1948), 98.

11.William Placher, *Jesus the Savior: The Meaning of Jesus Christ for Christian Faith* (Louisville: Westminster, 2001), 139.

of atonement endorsing penal substitution or satisfaction theories are not true to the biblical text. The heart of the New Testament witness seems to indicate reconciliation rather than retribution. In other words, they see reconciliation as justice and mercy, rather than as punishment or as satisfying an offended deity. Instead, we should interpret the life, death, and resurrection of Jesus as a revelatory event, expressing a theology of divine protest against violence and a divine movement toward restoration and reconciliation. Because "God was in Christ reconciling the world to himself," would not an atonement metaphor that focuses on reconciliation and the restoration of a broken relationship, rather than on forms of retribution, harmonize more effectively with divine love?[12] Take, for example, the protest against racial segregation seen in the American South during the 1960's. Violent act upon violent act was inflicted on black American communities nationwide. One response was to retaliate with retributive violence in the name of justice, matching hatred for hatred and violence for violence. These actions fed the escalating cycle of repetitive violence. Some black American leaders, however, responded differently to the violence. In the hopes of reconciliation and the restoration of black/white relationships, they sat peaceably at lunch counters while others shouted insults and inflicted bodily harm. They moved silently and peacefully to the front of buses, responding to hatred with love. They loved their enemies and prayed for them and they interrupted the cycle of violence with the way of peace and of love. As a result, the repetition of violence decreased as the repetition of reconciliation increased.

In an analogous way, God in Christ interrupted the cycle of violence with divine love. God in Christ worked to tear down structures of violence and to redeem the world with love and forgiveness. The life, death, and resurrection of Christ reveal to us that God does not prefer violence.[13] Christ reveals to us that God's justice is mercy in the form of restoration, reconciliation, and redemption, from the strong powers of the world. Where reconciliation is the focus, violence is cut short. Where restoration of relationship is foremost in theories of atonement, violence is precluded from the divine character. Where violence is seen as a human act free from any connection with God's way of acting or redeeming humanity, "legitimate" use of coercive power no longer holds sway over society or state.

I realize that connections between atonement theory and social violence cannot be established with certainty, for causes and their effects are often difficult to prove. Yet, if traditional atonement theory lends legitimacy to social and personal violence in any way whatsoever, it must be rethought. We need

---

12. 2 Cor. 5:19; Eph. 2:16.
13. Placher, *Jesus the Savior,* 148.

new metaphors for a new community of God that speak to our contemporary issues in language that expresses the Good News as good news.

Traditional language describing Christ's work of redemption served specific communities of faith. The New Testament's conflated use of sacrificial, ransom, and expulsion language to explain the work of Christ were ones that the people of that culture could understand. If read and understood as correspondent truth, in a literal manner, these images stand in tension with one another.[14] For instance, mixed within the atonement language of scripture we see a God that is both just and merciful, producing a tension between justice and mercy. God forgives freely yet at the same time demands a substitute to take away the debt, compromising the nature of forgiveness as complete pardon. A just God finds satisfaction in Christ's unjust death, therefore begging the question, "Is injustice ever just?" Conceptions of the Father demanding the death of the innocent Son pit the persons of the Trinity against one another, portraying an image of God against God.[15] Such contradictions and views of God, taken literally, cannot be helpful for Christian ethics or for a healthy image of God (who appears to have split personalities—loving and compassionate one moment, angry and vengeful the next). The New Testament explains Christ's life, death, and resurrection as economic, substitutional, militaristic, sacrificial, and priestly.[16] Can all of these motifs be literal, concrete cosmic transactions that take place between God the Father and God the Son with God the Holy Spirit looking on in appreciation? Or might these motifs be metaphors, language employed for the sole purpose of helping God's community to understand the extent of divine love and the extravagance of divine forgiveness?

Throughout the Old and New Testaments metaphorical language is used in order to teach a truth that is otherwise difficult to comprehend. Metaphors abound, depicting God as a rock, as an eagle, as a compassionate mother, as a strong tower, a shepherd, a king, a servant, and many others. The stories of creation, Jonah in the belly of the big fish, the flood, Job, all reveal

---

14. Vincent Taylor, *The Atonement in New Testament Teaching* (London: The Epworth Press, 1958), 184-215. In this section Taylor argues that the New Testament atonement metaphors work in tension with one another.

15. See Jürgen Moltmann, *The Crucified God: The Cross of Christ as the Foundation and Criticism of Christian Theology*, trans. by R.A. Wilson and John Bowden (Minneapolis, MN: Fortress Press, 1993).

16. 1 Cor. 7:23; 2 Cor. 5:19-21; Col. 2:14-15; Heb. 9:26; Heb. 9:24-25; Mtt. 20:28. See also Stephen Finlan, *The Problem with Atonement* (Collegeville, MN: Liturgical Press, 2005), 5-9; Mark Heim, *Saved From Sacrifice: A Theology of the Cross* (Grand Rapids, MI: William B. Eerdmans Publishing Company, 2006), 213. Heim believes that some images of God may be harmful to our health—so true. The same cross carried on banners in the Crusades is the same cross hanging in hospitals, places known for healing, love, and compassion.

important truths through metaphor and through story. Jesus taught profound truth through parables—storytelling using metaphorical language that helps the community of readers comprehend the mind, heart, and actions of an incomprehensible God. The language used to explain the redemption of the human race through Jesus Christ is also metaphorical language. Paul and the other writers of the New Testament books interpret the saving life, death, and resurrection of Christ in ways that their own communities could understand and apprehend through the use of figurative or metaphorical language, borrowing well-known images from the social structure.[17] The contemporary Christian community has the responsibility to continue the tradition through reinterpreting these divine truths, to make them relevant for the world in which we all live.

We see throughout Christian history faithful theologians reinterpreting the passion of Christ according to their contemporary situation. For example, Irenaeus, one of the earliest advocates of the *Christus Victor* theory, lived in conflict with the social structure of his day. Christianity was illegal and Caesar was lord. He related the earthly conflicts between Caesar and Christianity to a cosmic battle between celestial powers.[18] Anselm's satisfaction theory interprets the atonement according to the feudal system prevalent in his age. Abelard interprets the atonement according to the notions of "courtly love" and the new humanist culture just becoming popular in his society. With the assimilation of Aristotle, Aquinas interprets the atonement according to and in harmony with the philosophical categories and ethical principles of his day. With the growth of the nation state in the thirteenth and fourteenth centuries, judicial power was transferred from the community to the state, which brought about a focus on punitive measures and the popularity of penitentiaries. In a culture obsessed with sin and guilt along with the institution of newer civil laws, the reformers interpreted the atonement through the lens of punishment and justification.[19] The liberal social theologians reinterpreted atonement according to the Enlightenment's positive humanistic attitudes and the new scientific discoveries that appeared to undermine faith in an invisible, non-verifiable God. After the devastation of two world wars, theo-

---

17. For a good treatment of metaphor and story telling in scripture see Seibert, *Disturbing Divine Behavior.*

18. Joel B. Green and Mark D. Baker, *Recovering the Scandal of the Cross: Atonement in New Testament and Contemporary Contexts* (Downers Grove, IL: Intervarsity Press, 2000), 116ff.

19. See Timothy Gorringe, *God's Just Vengeance* (New York: Cambridge University Press, 1996), 85-219; Anthony Bartlett, *Cross Purposes: The Violent Grammar of the Cross,* (Harrisburg, PA: Trinity Press International, 2001), 56-78; Peter Schmiechen, *Saving Power: Theories of Atonement and forms of the Church* (Grand Rapids, MI: William B. Eerdmans Publishing Company, 2005), 315.

logians like Karl Barth reinterpreted atonement for a world reeling from profound suffering and disenchantment with humankind. The liberation theologians, concerned with making the Gospel of Christ relevant for the scores of
thousands of innocent people oppressed, abused, and murdered by empires,
wars, and crooked governments, reinterpreted the atonement for their suffering communities.[20] The layers of reinterpretation in both the biblical texts and
in the history of Christian doctrine lead to the realization that the tradition *is*
to reinterpret the tradition. We reinterpret continually, repeatedly, with a repetition of reinterpretation that preserves the relevance of the living and active
Word of God. The responsibility to reinterpret the character and heart of God,
from that of violent to anti-violent, looms before us as we work toward a theology of peace, reconciliation, and restoration through Christ.

Unlike some contemporary theologians, I do not want to discard the tradition. Our Christian tradition richly expresses the community's efforts to
understand the divine mind and hands down to us valuable insights that we
can continue to treasure and remember. At the same time, we need to re-
evaluate, continually putting tradition to the test of time, preserving what
enriches and serves the community and reinterpreting those portions of the
tradition that no longer speak relevantly to the contemporary situation.

Unfortunately, tradition does not always come to us in the form of a rich
heritage. The New Testament word commonly translated "tradition" (*para-
dosis*), which means "to hand down" or "to hand over," is also translated as
"to betray" in the story of Judas who betrayed Jesus to the authorities, *handing him over* to be crucified. According to this double-meaning, therefore,
tradition either enriches or betrays us with the wisdom of the past. Tradition, then, needs to be wisely rethought so that we can identify the points of
betrayal. Yet at the same time, attempting to sift through the tradition handed
down to us with the intent to reinterpret gives the impression of arrogance on
our part. T.S. Eliot hauntingly expresses both the potential folly of clinging to
the wisdom of old traditions and need for the wisdom of humility:

Do not let me hear
Of the wisdom of old men, but rather of their folly,
Their fear of fear and frenzy, their fear of possession,
Of belonging to another, or to others, or to God.
**The only wisdom we can hope to acquire
Is the wisdom of humility: humility is endless.**[21]

---

20. I realize the simplistic nature this short summary of social cause and theological effect in
Christian history. Of course, it is more complicated and many other factors are involved. I use this
section of the essay for illustrative purposes only.

21. T.S. Eliot, *The Four Quartets—East Coker*. Many thanks to Professor B. Keith Putt who

With the wisdom of humility, we can realize that there are instances in which our tradition is folly, has betrayed and deceived us. When we discover these betrayals we can reinterpret the scriptural and theological events in ways that redeem and preserve the tradition so that it can remain relevant for our own communities. We reinterpret, however, with a mind and attitude of wise humility, knowing that the tradition we set in motion through our reinterpretations may require further reinterpretation in the future. My goal, therefore, is to reinterpret the tradition by reading scripture through the lens of a peace-loving, anti-violent God, preserving the language of sacrifice and satisfaction, justice and mercy, forgiveness and love, with a mind and an attitude of what I hope is wise humility.

Referring to God as *anti*-violent rather than as *non*-violent needs clarification. The death of Jesus on the cross was violent. Whether seen as stemming from God or from sinful humanity, the Bible reveals that the violence was real nonetheless. Consequently, the term "anti-violent" seems more faithful to the biblical text and expresses my own perception of God. "Anti" in the Greek means "face to face" or "in front of" which later came to mean "to take the place of." Perceiving God this way, therefore, expresses a *face to face* encounter with God in the biblical text and in redemptive history in a manner that enables us to perceive an anti-violent God *in the place of* a violent God.[22]

Because we still wrestle with the tensions between divine justice and divine forgiveness, as if God's justice is somehow compromised by God's forgiving sin, I will discuss both justice and forgiveness before moving on to atonement. But as you read, keep this question in mind: have we traditionally misinterpreted divine justice? As a thought experiment, suppose that we have, and consider another interpretation of divine justice in the former's place.

Reconciling Justice

In Shakespeare's *Merchant of Venice*, Antonio, who owes Shylock a substantial amount of money, is financially ruined. Shylock demands justice before the royal court. He wants his pound of flesh in payment for Antonio's debt. Appeals to him to show mercy, to forgive at least a portion of the debt owed by Antonio, fall on deaf ears. No amount of pleading for mercy, persuasive argument, or appeal to prayer moves Shylock from his resolve for justice; he will not forgive the debt. In response to these appeals, he shouts vehemently,

---

first brought this passage to my attention in a philosophy class.

22. Thanks to a conversation with Willard Swartley on 1/9/07. See also "Ἀντι," *Theological Dictionary of the New Testament,* vol. 1, ed. by Gerhard Kittel (Grand Rapids, MI: Wm. B. Eerdmans Publishing Company, 1964), 372-373.

"I crave the law!"[23] Shylock must have justice, the debt must be requited—in full—through cutting off a slab of Antonio's flesh equal to the amount owed. As Shylock prepares to raise the knife to cut off a pound of Antonio's flesh, Portia, posing as a lawyer, reminds him that justice must be served, the law upheld. He can take his pound of flesh, as the law dictates, but he must take his pound of flesh *only*, nothing more; he must do so without shedding one drop of blood. Otherwise, justice will be demanded from him as well. He will lose all he owns and be thrown in prison. Shylock is reminded here of Portia's earlier words comparing mercy and justice: "Therefore, Jew, though justice be thy plea, consider this, that, in the course of justice, none of us should see salvation."[24]

Outraged, horrified, and scared, Shylock rescinds his demands for a pound of flesh. Since he has demanded justice, however, the court remains firm and only pauses to enquire of Antonio, who has now been granted half of Shylock's wealth, "What mercy can you render him?"[25] Shylock, the one who minutes before demanded justice instead of mercy in his dealings with Antonio, stands trembling in humility before the same Antonio, hoping against hope for mercy instead of justice.

Do we not all stand in Shylock's place? Do we not all hope against hope for divine mercy rather than divine justice? In doing so, we place justice and mercy in polarity as opposites. Yet does the polarity define divine "justice" and "mercy"? Shakespeare sheds some light on this question. Earlier, in the midst of the courtroom scene, Portia insists that Shylock show mercy, to which he responds, "On what compulsion must I?" In true Shakespearian form, Portia expresses the nature of justice from the heavenly perspective:

> The quality of mercy is not strain'd,
> It droppeth as the gentle rain from heaven
> Upon the place beneath: it is twice blest;
> It blesseth him that gives and him that takes:
> 'Tis the mightiest in the mightiest: it becomes
> The throned monarch better than his crown;
> His sceptre shows the force of temporal power,
> The attribute to awe and majesty,
> Wherein doth sit the dread and fear of kings;
> But mercy is above this sceptred sway;

23. William Shakespeare, *The Merchant of Venice*, IV. I. 106.
24. Shakespeare, IV. I. 199.
25. Shakespeare, IV. I. 377.

It is enthroned in the heart of kings;
It is an attribute to God himself.
And earthly power doth then show likest God's
When mercy seasons justice.[26]

According to Shakespeare, in order for justice to be most like God's, it must be infected with mercy and not stand as mercy's opposite. As a result, mercy and justice do not live in tension, butting heads in a contest over how to render to us our just deserts. Antagonism between the two actions results from a human construction of justice. Where human justice is retributive, quantitative, and destructive of relationships, God's justice is restorative, qualitative, and builds relationships. Although Shakespeare is not a theologian or a biblical scholar, his conception of justice resonates with the biblical witness.

A search for justice through scripture leads me to the conclusion that we have misconstrued its meaning due to our Western lens. First, in the biblical texts, justice is often set in opposition to violence. In Isaiah 5:7, God "expected justice [from Israel] but saw bloodshed" instead. Isaiah 59:3-4 begins with the violent, wicked actions of the people, stating that "your hands are defiled with blood, and your fingers with iniquity; your lips have spoken lies, your tongue utters wickedness. No one brings suit justly, no one goes to law honestly." Because of these unjust, violent actions "justice is far from [them]" (Is. 59:9). Comparably, Isaiah 16:4-5 indicates that once oppression and violence are gone, justice is established. From these verses we can conclude that justice and violence have nothing in common. In other words, when violence takes place, justice is absent. We may even be able to say that justice and violence stand in polarity as opposing actions in which one cancels out the other. The absence of justice in acts of violence begs this question: If justice is not present in violence, how then can we conceive of a God who executes justice through violence, especially through the violent murder of an innocent man on the cross?[27]

Second, justice almost always has a parallel relationship to righteousness, both expressed in the form of action. Proverbs 8:20 clarifies this relationship: "I walk in the way of righteousness, along the paths of justice."[28] Justice, like righteousness, is a way or a path. The word "way" or "path" in the middle-Eastern perspective speaks of a collection of right actions, an active doing,

---

26. William Shakespeare, *The Merchant of Venice*, IV. I. 184ff.
27. See also Isa. 1:15-17 in which God tells the people to stop shedding blood and do justice and Job 19:7 in which Job seeks justice and only finds violence. Again, justice is absent in the presence of violence. C.f., Isa. 32:16-18; Jer. 22:15-17; Mic. 3:1-3; 7:2-3; Hab. 1:3-4.
28. Prov. 2:8-9 also speak of justice as a "good path." In Isa. 59:8-9 justice is absent from the people's path.

a certain way of negotiating through life.[29] The word "righteous" in Hebrew actually means "a collection of right actions," again implying *doing* rather than an abstract condition of the heart and mind. Often the words "righteousness" and "justice" are paired with the Hebrew word *'āśâ*, meaning "to do," indicating that both justice and righteousness are action words—we *do* justice and we *do* righteousness.[30] Isaiah 56:1 gives divine expression to this parallelism, stating: "Thus says the Lord: Maintain justice, and do what is right, for soon my salvation will come and my deliverance be revealed." Additionally, maintaining justice and doing what is right also inaugurates the advent of divine salvation and deliverance, a significant connection to God's redemptive action.

Justice and righteousness in the biblical witness are not abstract, ontological conceptions that remain hidden in the heavenly places, hoped for and prayed for but never quite arriving. For example, justice and righteousness acted out, according to scripture, include loving compassion for others, taking care of the oppressed, the poor, the outcast, and even the enemy.[31] God's righteousness, God's carrying out right actions, is an extension of God's justice, which does not include violence, but instead, indicates a loving compassion even for the enemy.

Third, the nature of justice is expressed through acts of mercy. Justice and mercy appear in parallel in the well known verse, Micah 6:8: " . . . what does the LORD require of you but to do justice, and to love kindness [mercy], and to walk humbly with your God?" Justice and mercy are also often paired with the word *'āśâ*, "to do." In another passage, the words of God come to Zechariah, again coupling the actions of justice and mercy, by exhorting Zechariah to "render true judgments (*mišpat 'e meṭ*), show kindness and mercy to one another" (7:9). The text explains in the next verse how true judgment or justice is to be accomplished through merciful actions: "do not oppress the widow, the orphan, the alien, or the poor; and do not devise evil in your hearts against one another" (v. 10).[32] We see then that mercy describes

---

29. Gordon Brubacher, "Just War and the New Community: The Witness of the Old Testament for Christians Today, *Princeton Theological Review*, (Fall, 2006): 24.

30. *Anchor Bible Dictionary*, "Righteousness," 731. The Hebrew word *'āśâ* in the phrase "righteousness and justice" indicates the *doing* of the pair.

31. For example: Ps. 10:17-18; 33:5; 82:1-8; 99:4; Isa. 1:15-17; 30:18-19; 32:1-2; 42:1-4; 61:1-8; Jer. 9:24; 22:3; Ez. 34:11-16; Hos. 2:19. When the word *mishpat* is translated in the English Old Testament, it is done so in a manner that indicates the justice served in a courtroom. Not so in the Hebrew. The word instead implies continuous, repeated actions, *doing* justice rather than exacting justice.

32. Greifswald J. Zobel, "*hesed*," *Theological Dictionary of the Old Testament*, ed. by G. Johannes Botterweck and Helmer Ringgren, trans. by David E. Green, vol. 5 (Grand Rapids, MI: William B. Eerdmans Publishing Company, 1986), 49.

the nature of justice. As such, it includes maintaining the cause of the needy (Ps. 140:12; Ez. 34:16), giving food to the hungry (Ps. 146:7), rescuing the oppressed (Isa. 1:17; Jer. 22:3), and peace-making (Isa. 42:1-4; Jer. 22:3). In these verses and in others, mercy and justice complement each other so that in doing mercy, we also do justice. In other words, justice is the catalyst for mercy and mercy executes and establishes justice.

Fourth, doing justice is redemptive. Isaiah 1:27, asserts that, "Zion shall be redeemed by justice." [33] In another text, the Psalmist begs for deliverance and redemption according to God's justice (Ps. 119:153-156). God also promises Jeremiah that the day will come when God will do (*'āśâ*) justice and redeem the people (Jer. 23:5-6; 33:15). Isaiah makes the connection between justice and redemption through the negative expression of no justice, no redemption: "We wait for justice, but there is none; for salvation, but it is far from us (59:11). Consequently, it appears that redemption is the result of doing justice. To redeem, therefore, is to *do* justice.

In addition, the biblical text uses the imagery of flowing streams of fresh water to describe justice (Amos 5:24). Water is a rare and precious commodity in the communities of the middle-East. Particularly rare, almost non-existent, are streams that continually flow through the arid land. Water provides and ensures that life in will continue—no water, no life. Justice, like water, is pro-life. Water, especially that in the imagery of Amos as a perennial, ever-flowing stream, restores the dry ground and parched throats to life, satisfying the longing of the land and of the thirsty inhabitants. In other words, the imagery of justice as a continual flowing stream over the land imposes upon us a beautiful picture of something redemptive, restorative, and life-giving that satisfies the longing of those in need. God's justice, therefore, acts like a stream that flows continually, repeating over and over again redemptive life-giving activity, a repetition of justice flowing along like water over the land.[34]

Fifth, justice is seen as a great light that drives away the blindness imposed by darkness. Isaiah incisively expresses this metaphor:

> Therefore justice is far from us, and righteousness does not reach us; we wait for light, and lo! there is darkness; and for brightness, but we walk in gloom. We grope like the blind along a wall, groping like those who have no eyes; we stumble at noon as in the twilight, among the vigorous as though we were dead. . . We wait for justice, but there is none; for salvation, but it is far from us (Isa. 59:9-11).

Without justice, darkness prevails and we grope around as blind people,

---

33. See also Isa. 33:5-6; 51:4-5;
34. See also Ps. 65:9-14; Ps. 1:3.

separated from the light of divine justice.

Interestingly, scripture provides us with the image of blindness rather than sight when injustice rules the land. Consequently, from a divine point of view, injustice is blind to the path of justice. In contrast, the image of justice expressed in the imperial structures of government and civil judiciary systems is portrayed by an unseeing, blindfolded woman. In this case, the human concept of justice is blind, not sighted; it is represented by darkness, not light. If the *biblical* notion of justice coincides with righteousness and with seeing a divine light, implying that injustice is blind, could it be that the human notion of justice as blind is actually injustice in God's eyes? Do the empires of the world have their eyes blindfolded to justice so that injustice, under the guise of justice, reigns? As retributive and punitive, human justice exacted by the world's governments does not appear to offer redemption or restoration. Divine justice, on the other hand, does.

Sixth, divine justice satisfies God. Proverbs 21:3 actually gives expression to this statement: "To do righteousness and justice is more *acceptable* to the LORD than sacrifice." The passage then proceeds to explain what justice and righteousness look like in practice. Doing righteousness and justice are acceptable—dare we say—satisfying, to God, more satisfying than the cult's bloody sacrifices offered on the altar. The words of God spoken in Jeremiah 9:24 shed more light on justice that satisfies God, saying, "I act with steadfast love, justice, and righteousness in the earth, for in these things I *delight*." In other words, God is delighted, or can we say, satisfied, by love, justice, and righteousness worked out practically on earth. Matthew, quoting Isaiah, provides us with further insight into the anti-violent, restorative nature of the justice that satisfies God. Talking about Jesus he says:

> Here is my servant, whom I have chosen, my beloved, with whom my soul is well *pleased.* I will put my spirit upon him, and he will proclaim justice to the Gentiles. He will not wrangle or cry aloud, nor will anyone hear his voice in the streets. He will not break a bruised reed or quench a smoldering wick until he brings justice to victory. (Isa. 42:1-3; Mt. 12:18-20)[35]

In this passage, the spirit of God empowers Jesus to proclaim divine justice, not through offensive hollering and yelling in the streets or through coercive force, but through non-violent means. As a result, God is pleased, or could we say, satisfied, with Jesus and his actions that bring justice to victory by

---

35. Italicized emphasis is mine. See also Isa. 42:1-4, which includes justice in a list of what pleases or satisfies God, things in which God's soul delights. Verse 4 is particularly interesting and indicates that Jesus will not be crushed until he has established justice. Can we conclude from this that justice was established or revealed through his ushering in the Kingdom of God while he was still alive? Isa. 59:15.

peaceably restoring us to God. Isaiah reveals God's displeasure in the lack of justice, writing: " . . . The LORD saw it, and it *displeased* him that there was no justice" (Is. 59:15b).[36] God was displeased, unsatisfied, therefore, that justice could not be found in the land. We can conclude from these passages that restorative justice forged through Christ's actions during his life, death, and resurrection satisfied God.

The justice as expressed in the biblical texts resonates with the justice Jesus preached and modeled for us. Jesus and the redemption and restoration brought to us through his acts of justice and righteousness appear as a light shining in the darkness.[37] Forgiving enemies, breaking down boundaries between Jew and Greek, slave and free, male and female, all reveal divine justice at work in Jesus Christ.[38] Seeing it as anti-violent, right in action, merciful, redemptive, and restorative, reveals justice in a new light—a redemptive light that breaks through the darkness of violence and oppression, retribution and vengeance.

In contrast, retributive justice sticks to the letter of the law, requiring its pound of flesh, demanding re-payment, compensation, an eye for an eye, in order to forgive sin. Conversely, divine restorative justice requires neither payment nor retribution. Instead, it seeks restoration, peace, and the fore-giving[39] of pardon so that restoration and qualitatively new relations can take place between offended parties. In other words, divine justice is infected with mercy. It lights the way to forgiveness and restores without violence. Richard Rohr, in his commentary on the book of Job writes that "[t]he general belief in the scriptures . . . is that God's justice is not achieved by punishment, but by the divine initiative we call grace. . ."[40]

A painting in the courtroom of the Pennsylvania state capitol building illustrates for us an image of justice that will help us to understand and to reinterpret it in a manner that brings us more closely in touch with the reality

---

36. The Hebrew words I am equating with divine satisfaction are bāhar, in Pr. 21:3, which means to chose based upon the best, most desired or desirable choice; rāsâ, in Is. 42:1, which means to delight it, to take pleasure in, which expresses satisfaction; and hāpēs, in Jer. 9:24, which means that God (in this case) finds great pleasure in doing something. God is pleased or satisfied with doing something. It is not an arbitrary pleasure, but one based upon the best, most serviceable act. All these words can lead to the interpretation that God is satisfied with God's choice of servant, that God is satisfied by the servant's work, and that God is satisfied with the results. See G. Kittel and G. Friedrich, *Theological Dictionary of the Old Testament.*(Grand Rapids, MI: Eerdmans, 1985).

37. Jn. 1:4-9.

38. Lk. 23:34, 43; Gal. 3:28; 2 Cor. 5:18-19.

39. Fore-giving expresses the notion of "giving *before*hand" or giving something *before* a person repents or pays back a debt.

40. Richard Rohr, *Job and the Mystery of Suffering: Spiritual Reflections* (New York: The Crossroad Publishing Company, 2005), 57.

of divine justice. The painting, entitled "Divine Law," by Violet Oakley does not depict a scale of balances held by a blindfolded woman that typically epitomizes justice, but instead, presents us with a musical scale played by a celestial harpist. An "L" adorns the left edge of the painting with the letters "LOVE" running down the vertical leg of the "L." The middle of the painting portrays an "A" above a "W," spelling out the word "LAW." This symbolizes the artists representation of the divine harmony between LOVE and LAW, both working together for the good and peace of all people. Consequently, in a room where justice is served hangs a painting suggesting a form of justice that expresses the purpose of the law—to mediate justice in love and thus to fulfill the law. Violet Oakley's portrayal of justice as a musical scale plays not a dirge but a doxology of justice tempered with love, and served through mercy. Rather than a blindfolded justice, one that does not see, Ms. Oakley presents us with a concept of justice that has its eyes wide open, that sees the offenses through the eyes of love and mercy. The justice of love, revealed by the law of love, seeks to overcome condemnation with mercy; after all, mercy triumphs over judgment.[41]

Charles Moule, who works in the field of criminal and civil justice, also argues that divine justice—the deepest level of justice—is restorative rather than retributive. Whereas retributive justice seeks to fit the punishment to the crime, attempting to control wrongdoing through punishment, restorative justice forgives the crime and seeks to redeem wrongdoing through a repairing of the relationship. He states that "the first great step towards justice at the deepest level is, paradoxically, when the victim [in this case, God] abandons quantitative justice [such as penal and satisfaction requirements], waives the demand for 'just' retribution, and begins to become ready to forgive—that is, to meet the damage by repair."[42] The Gospel accounts of Jesus reveal to us a God who meets the damage by repair through forgiveness.

Conceptions of divine justice as restorative and qualitative rather than as retributive and quantitative carry significant implications for theories of atonement. We see in the New Testament evidence of a movement away from the pursuit of retribution, vengeance, and retaliation. Instead we see a movement towards a pursuit of forgiveness, restoration of relationship, and new life together in the community of God in the words of Paul: "God in Christ was reconciling the world to himself, *not counting their transgressions against them*" (2 Cor. 5:19, emphasis mine). A comparison of the Old Testament portrait of divine justice with the actions of Jesus reveals God's justice

---

41. Jam. 2:13. See also Gorringe, *God's Just Vengeance,* 234ff.
42. C.F.D. Moule, *Forgiveness and Reconciliation* (London: SPCK, 1998), 41-42 [bracketed additions are mine].

at work to forgive and to redeem, to repair and to restore. Through the actions of Jesus during his lifetime and in his passion, we gain an understanding of the divine response to retributive violence and conceptions of human justice. Rather than shouting threats of retaliation in the name of God, Christ set in motion the ultimate expression of divine justice and its restorative character by asking God to forgive us in a moment that may have instead provoked vengeance and retribution.[43] As revealed in the Christ event, the process of forgiveness, reconciliation, and restoration without retaliation demonstrates the deepest, most profound level of justice.[44]

Human beings tend to have difficulty accepting the possibility that God forgives sin unconditionally since, from a human viewpoint, forgiveness of such magnitude is impossible. For some reason we have trouble accepting an infinitely loving God, who forgives without the use of violent power or punitive measures. We prefer a God who exacts justice through violence, through sending the wicked to eternal punishment without a hope for redemption and reconciliation with the God who created and loves them.[45] We prefer to cling to what I believe are human notions of justice and forgiveness. Philosopher and theologian John D. Caputo points out that 'unaccountable' forgiveness "disturbs our sense of law and order, disrupts our sense of economic equilibrium, undermines our desire to 'settle the score' or 'get even', blocks our instinct to see to it that the offenders are made to 'pay for' what they did."[46] Divine justice as restorative and redemptive, however, does not keep accounts with records of retributive actions or satisfaction. It is un-accountable. God applies just such justice through forgiveness.

Theologians in touch with intense suffering, however, rightly protest theories of atonement that advocate divine forgiveness without satisfaction or punishment. Some of these protests are valid and must be addressed. Those who live under the abuse and violence of unjust governments, who have suffered much at the whims and agendas of political oppressors, need to believe that, when all is said and done, God will vindicate them; their oppressors will be brought to justice.[47] The hope of vindication understandably enables

---

43. Lk. 23:34.

44. Moule, *Forgiveness and Reconciliation,* 44-46. Moule states the notion of divine justice well: "The life of Jesus and his death—the inevitable consequence of total dedication to the way of God—and his total aliveness through and beyond (not in spite of) death, all point in this direction, and exhibit the justice of God at its deepest level: "God in Christ was reconciling the world to himself" (2 Cor. 5:19). No hangover of retributive systems still showing itself in the New Testament can negate this . . ." See also e.g.: Rom. 3:24; 1 Cor. 1:30; Eph. 1:17; Eph. 2:4-6; Col. 1:14.

45. Nelson-Pallmeyer, *Jesus Against Christianity,* 295.

46. John D. Caputo, *Weakness of God,* 208.

47. Based upon a conversation with Scott Holland of *Cross Currents,* Nov. 19, 2006 in Washington, DC.

victims to retain their faith in a good God even in the midst of profound suffering. Yet, the exhortation to love our enemy includes loving those who cause extreme suffering. Divine justice in the form of restoration, however, still vindicates the oppressed and calls the guilty to account.

I believe that restorative rather than retributive justice is more effective and complete. Take for instance, by way of illustration, an event in the life of Peter the Great. In an attempt to squelch the Streltsy revolt, many men and women who betrayed the Tsar were imprisoned and tortured in order to exact a confession of guilt and bring forth repentance. After suffering horrendous pain through the infliction of various tortures, one such prisoner still remained silent. No amount of punishment or pain drew a confession from him. In fact, the torture seemed to harden his resolve to keep silent. Having heard of the prisoner's cold determination, Peter released him from torture, embraced the man, kissed him, and promised that he would not only pardon him, but would also make him a colonel in the Tsar's army. Peter's biographer writes that "[t]his unorthodox approach so unnerved and moved the prisoner that he took the Tsar in his arms and said, 'For me, this is the greatest torture of all. There is no other way you could have made me speak.'"[48] The prisoner confessed all and repented. As promised beforehand, he was pardoned and admitted into Peter's army as a colonel, serving Peter faithfully for the remainder of his days. Brought face to face with unexpected love and grace, the man realized the full extent of his betrayal, repented, and was restored to the Tsar. Remorse for his betrayal took the place of his hardened heart. I admit that God does not torture people as Peter advocated. Consequently, the analogy does not accurately describe divine actions in procuring repentance, but the point I wish to make still holds. The man still suffered great pain for his sin; not from the pain of punishment, but from the realization of magnitude of his sin. Justice in the form of mercy accomplished redemption and restoration where punishment could not. Was justice served?[49]

Peter's act of mercy that resulted in the restoration of relationship may have something in common with God's form of justice. Unselfish love seeks to redeem and restore; punishment (typically conceived as justice) seeks revenge and retribution.[50] In order for divine justice to work in harmony with divine love, mercy, and forgiveness, shouldn't it be redemptive and restorative at the same time? How does eternal damnation, burning forever in unquenchable fire, redeem and restore? Is it possible that divine justice *is* the

---

48. Robert K. Massie, *Peter the Great: His Life and Work* (New York: Ballantine Books, 1980), 262.
49. Of course, all analogies break down at some point and this one is no exception.
50. Gorringe, 245, 248ff.

path of mercy and forgiveness?

Let me offer a hypothetical illustration that instead of taking place in a Russian prison in the presence of the Tsar, occurs in the "throne room" of heaven in the presence of God. Hitler (typical stand in for someone very evil) stands before God to give an account of his life. Trembling in terror, expecting the equivalent or more in punishment, he explains his motives and deeds done while alive. He knows without doubt that the sentence will be harsh and eternal, and he hates God and God's justice. Much to his astonishment, instead of receiving the expected eternal death sentence, he is confronted with extravagant, unexpected love and forgiveness, and promised a place in God's kingdom as if he were God's own son. Unnerved by such an unorthodox approach, Hitler realizes completely the depth and depravity of his own sin. Filled with remorse and repentance he falls on his face before God, completely undone, horribly and inconsolably grief-stricken over the suffering and injustice he has caused. Yet, forgiven by a just God, Hitler finds redemption and restoration. He is transformed by divine justice.

Justice that effects non-retaliatory forgiveness may have profound consequences for the one forgiven with such sacrificial abandon. In fact, the expenditure of forgiveness often results in a response of repentance that proves just as costly. St. Thomas Aquinas comments that "an equal gift of grace means more to the penitent who deserves punishment than to the innocent who has never incurred it."[51] As articulated by Gil Bailie, "Jesus seems to have understood that the only real and lasting contrition occurs, not when one is confronted with one's sin, but when one experiences the gust of grace that makes a loving and forgiving God plausible."[52] Reconciling justice and non-retaliatory forgiveness form two sides of the same coin that both call the guilty to account and yet redeem peacefully with love.

Justice, therefore, does not mean "getting let off the hook," or "getting away with murder" (or worse). It means coming face to face with the shameful depravity of personal sin by coming face to face with the one who has the right and the power to punish but who instead loves and forgives. Love and forgiveness instead of anger and punishment bring repentance and redemption and in this manner, justice is served.[53] The biblical witness testifies to

---

51. *ST* IIaIIae, q. 106, a. 2, ad 3; Ia, q. 20, a. 4, ad 4.

52. Bailie, *Violence Unveiled,* 208-209.

53. "By the blood of Christ" may possibly be synonymous with cleansing away sin. The word "kippur" often translated as "to atone," literally means "to cleanse." When the blood of Christ is mentioned in the New Testament, it is also connected with "kippur," indicating that the blood of Christ cleanses us from sin. In both testaments there is no connection between "kippur" or "cleansing" to penal or satisfaction theories of atonement. There is a connection, however, between cleansing and forgiveness so that we may be able to say that to cleanse means to forgive. We can see this

this picture of divine justice that casts out fear of judgment and punishment through forgiving love:

> So we have known and believe the love God has for us. God is love, and those who abide in love abide in God, and God abides in them. Love has been perfected among us in this: that we may have boldness on the day of judgment, because as he is, so are we in this world. There is no fear in love, but perfect love casts out fear; for fear has to do with punishment, and whoever fears has not reached perfection in love. We love because he first loved us (1 Jn. 4:16-19). [compare with Rom. 5:8-10]

Justice embraced by divine love, mercy, forgiveness, and restoration removes the fear of punishment with the extravagant outpouring of love, which in turn kindles repentance and love in us. This is a love that seeks to restore a relationship in spite of an offense.

Raymund Schwager beautifully expresses this process of divine restoration, that in the face of human hatred and hardness of heart still manages to redeem. He says that on the cross "the law of revenge became the law of redeeming love. The curse was repaid with blessing. The conspiracy of hatred was answered with an outpouring of love."[54] Seen in this light, love redeems us, not by winning a victory over us, but by winning us over, filling us from the source with love for God. God's love and the resulting redemption are not given on the basis of merit earned, but are God's gratuitous gifts to humankind. No one is excluded; no one is turned away.[55]

Although the forgiveness given as a result of Jesus' work of atonement does not entail an economic transaction of any sort between Father and Son, the gift of forgiveness is nonetheless costly.[56] The New Testament story of

---

connection in Heb. 9:22: "all things are cleansed with blood, and without shedding of blood there is no forgiveness." This topic is an entire chapter of a book project in which shedding blood may be symbolic for sacrificial obedience as in Rom. 12:1 and in Jn. 15:13. Hopefully, more to come. For a more complete treatment of "kippur" and the concept of cleansing see Finlan, *Problems with Atonement,* 11-20; Anchor Bible Dictionary, "Atonement." J. Denny Weaver also describes sacrifice as self-giving obedience. See J. Denny Weaver, "Narrative Christus Victor: The Answer to Anselmian Atonement Violence," *Atonement and Violence: A Theological Conversation* (Nashville, TN: Abingdon Press, 2006), 24.

54. Schwager, *Must There Be Scapegoats?*, 214. Heim says that "Jesus didn't volunteer to get into God's justice machine. God volunteered to get into ours." See Heim, 218.

55. The Thomistic notion of redemption based upon merit earned by Christ and applied to our account is one of the areas that I depart from Aquinas. Aquinas notes that the love of Christ compels us and in Christ we have our example of perfect love. See *ST* III, q. 48, a. 1, r; Miller, "Inclusivist and Exclusivist Issues," in *Perspectives in Religious Studies,* 129; Moule, *Forgiveness and Reconciliation,* 38; Quinn, "Abelard on Atonement," 298: Quinn argues that God has made his transformative love available to all humanity, churched or un-churched, Christian and non-Christian, good and evil.

56. Moule, *Forgiveness and Reconciliation,* 23-24. Moule suggests that forgiveness includes a type of death to self in that the self gives up or sacrifices the selfish desire for revenge or retribution; Fiddes, *Past Event and Present Salvation,* 16; Jacques Derrida, *The Gift of Death,* trans. by

the forgiving father in Luke 15 hints at the costly nature of forgiveness. The father is willing to suffer the pain from the wrong done to him by his son and still offer forgiveness. He neither demands that his son return his inheritance, nor that the son beg the family's pardon. Instead he prepares a banquet for his son. Forgiveness, as this father knows, is not merely a matter of words spoken, "I forgive you," or of an embrace given. "It is a creative act, costly and achieved only by the output of energy. It means thinking nothing about one's rights or about abstract justice, but surrendering one's self concern altogether. It means absorbing the wrong instead of retaliating; giving, and not demanding any *quid pro quo*."[57] In other words, the father's gift of forgiveness has cost him a great deal. As a gift, forgiveness costs something; it involves costly sacrifice—the sacrifice of giving up on receiving something in return. In forgiving sin, God in Christ sacrificed receiving the debt we owed God for sin.[58]

God's sacrificial and redemptive justice enacted through forgiveness reveals the nature of atonement as "at-one-ment." No atoning bloody sacrifice that appeases an angry God, no punishment of an innocent man that absolves us from guilt. In fact, according to Rita Nakashima Brock, violence never saves, never restores, but only creates something worse, something violent in return.[59] Rather the restoration of relationship through the power of forgiveness, describes our at-one-ment with God. I argue that Jesus did not "make" atonement for our sins; he "did" at-one-ment through restorative, forgiving justice.

In fact, the costly sacrifice of Jesus continues "doing" at-one-ment through unending forgiveness, the repetition of forgiveness that we too are called

David Wills (Chicago: University of Chicago Press, 1995); B. Keith Putt, "Prayers of Confession and Tears of Contrition: John Caputo and a Radically 'Baptist' Hermeneutic of Repentance" in *Religion With/Out Religion: The Prayers and Tears of John D. Caputo*, ed. by James H. Olthuis (New York: Routledge, 2002), 62-79; B. Keith Putt, "Faith, Hope, and Love: Radical Hermeneutics as a Pauline Philosophy of Religion" in *A Passion for the Impossible: John D. Caputo in Focus,* ed. by Mark Dooley (New York: SUNY Press, 2003), 237-250; John D. Caputo, "Holding by Our Teeth: A Response to Putt" in *A Passion for the Impossible: John D. Caputo in Focus,* ed. by Mark Dooley (New York: SUNY Press, 2003), 251-254.

57. Moule, *Forgiveness and Reconciliation,* 22. Cf. P.T. Forsyth, *The Cruciality of the Cross*, 2nd edition (London: Independent Press, 1948), 29. Forsyth proclaims that a feeble gospel preaches that God is ready to forgive. A strong and impelling gospel announces the good news that God has already forgiven.

58. See Gorringe, *God's Just Vengeance,* 60, 78-81. Gorringe addresses the concept of sacrifice as internal, wrought through obedience to God, rather than external through the literal shedding of blood.

59. Rita Nakashima Brock, "The Cross of Resurrection and Communal Redemption," *Cross Examinations: Readings on the Meaning of the Cross Today* (Minneapolis, MN: Fortress Press, 2006), 242.

to "do." Peter asked, "how many times should I forgive?"[60] The answer amounted to saying—repeatedly. Always. Continually. Don't stop. Keep on doing it. Only through loving forgiveness does reconciliation occur. Only through loving forgiveness does at-one-ment with God and others transform a violent world. In so doing, we follow in the footsteps of Jesus' dis-arming love with continual sacrifices of forgiveness, repetitions of reconciliation that dis-arm others. Through the Spirit of God we respond with loving living, not out of an economy of violence for violence, but out of love. God's imagined violence upon Christ begets human violence upon one another. Rather than a repetition of violence that only begets violence, we embrace the repetition of love that begets love. I dare to dream of a world dis-armed by the reconciling repetition of God's forgiving justice re-enacted in the lives of Christ followers throughout the world. Such extravagant forgiveness, reconciliation, and love serve justice and truly satisfy God. In other words, to serve justice through forgiveness satisfies God—God is satisfied through forgiveness by which justice and mercy redeem creation and fulfill God's promise of restoration for all.[61]

---

60. Mt. 18:21-22. Thomas Finger also expresses atonement as at-one-ment. See Thomas Finger, "Christus Victor as Non-Violent Atonement," *Atonement and Violence*, 88.
   61. Isa. 61:1-7, 11; 66:17-25; Acts 2:17-21; Rev. 22:1-5.

Chapter Ten

DIE WITH ME: JESUS, PICKTON AND ME[1]

by Brita Miko

Sometimes I get scared by what the life of Christ might mean.
Now is one of those times.
The life of Christ happens in every moment—the moment we scream,
the moment we laugh, the moment we die, the moment we hesitate. It is not
only in the mind (like a disembodied Word), rather it is forever incarnated,
born anew into every circumstance. The lived reality is where we must know
the life of Christ and receive it and be in it. It cannot be magical words for
another world. It must be the way through in this world—a world where DNA
is found in freezers and we swallow fury and our inability to understand.

My fear began in a run-of-the-mill moment. I was reading theological
ideas on a newsgroup and Brad Jersak was writing about redemption. Nothing alarming, simply:

1. Redemption is accomplished and applied to all humanity on the Cross.

*"And he is the propitiation for our sins: and not for ours only, but also for the
sins of the whole world" (1Jo 2:2 KJVA).*

2. Redemption is enjoyed / experienced by those who believe and follow.

*First, guilt is already removed from all at the Cross. Experiencing this hap-
pens upon belief... but even as enemies we're already forgiven, which allows
me to make such strong statements to unbelievers as "You are forgiven. Your
guilt has been taken care of. Believe that and you'll be free of existential
condemnation that makes you sick and keeps you alienated from God... Your
shortcomings, your guilt-trips, your self-condemnation became irrelevant the
moment the Father answered his Son's prayer, 'Father, forgive them'...*

It's the message of forgiveness, grace, and the cross. It is what we believe.
My mind pushes, though; my mind needs to put flesh on words. Into my mind
comes Robert Pickton.

1. This piece began in a newsgroup. Brad Jersak's words are italicized, enfolded in mine.

Pickton has received some press over the last five years. The poorest postal code in Canada is in Vancouver—the Downtown Eastside. When I worked there, women were going missing. The conventional wisdom said the women were somewhere—absent—and would return, like they always did. The women I talked with did not believe this, though. In organizations, there are layers of policy, there are protocols and boundaries for the safety of the employees—all get warned about Carpal Tunnel Syndrome. When you are sick and poverty-stricken and desperate, however, safety becomes unaffordable. Poverty (having no shelter, no income, no resources) creates vulnerability. Prostitution exacerbates the risks. In industrial areas, the women stood alone in the dark, they climbed into strange SUVs and trucks, they were driven away in the darkness. Sometimes in the night I would wake up because a woman was screaming below on the street after a trick gone bad. Through the window, I would hear the rage and the pain. The edges of my heart would curl. I felt powerless.

Economically, there is no harder place to survive in our nation. Everyday, however, I saw a community surviving. They lived on. And there was so much beauty there—raw beauty. People sharing nickels and smokes and kindness. People accepting their neighbours—even if their neighbour was labelled dual-diagnosis or a rice wine drinker or violent. There was no hierarchy. There was no higher status. But not everyone survived. Not the ones who jumped off roofs or out sixth floor windows. Not the ones overdosing because of unpredictable changes in drug purity. Not the ones who got knifed in the park or on the street. And not the ones whose DNA was found on the Pickton farm.

There were over sixty women who disappeared. There were over sixty women who were in the community and then were gone. One by one, over years they vanished. Now, DNA from 27 different women has been uncovered in the ground—26 of whom have been identified as women the Downtown Eastside lost. They were the most vulnerable. They were the poor, desperate and afflicted. They were God's.

To me, Robert Pickton[2] seems like an example of not-saved-and-going-to-hell. He is accused of killing the forsaken and the abandoned. He fills me with pain and anger.

Into my theology he goes.

I can say that Christ died for Robert Pickton. I can say that Christ's death atoned for Robert Pickton's sins. I can even agree with Brad that *redemption is accomplished and applied to* Robert Pickton *on the cross*. Even while

---

2. Or the one responsible for the remains. Other people may have been involved or may be completely responsible for the deaths. As I am writing this, however, Pickton is on trial.

saying that, I am not saying he is going to heaven. He has not received the forgiveness he is offered.

But what do I see?

He is stabbing the woman. He is stabbing Jesus. Jesus is the woman. Jesus, incarnate in the least; Jesus present in every moment. They are both dying—Christ and her. Into this moment, Jesus speaks, "God forgive him, he doesn't know what he's doing." Continuing with Brad's words, *"...the Father answered his son's prayer, 'Father, forgive them' with a big, 'For you, Son? Of course!' and opened wide the doors of heaven to everyone. He declares, "All is forgiven! Ho, all who are thirsty! Come! Come to the table freely prepared for you! [And here's where repentance comes in:] You've looked for life at so many other tables and I see you are still hungry and emaciated. Come to my table and taste to see that I'm good."*

It is hard to hear this word offered to him.

The "God forgive him."

The "Of course."

The "Come to my table."

In fact, I cannot believe I am hearing this word.

But Pickton has yet to eat.

Pickton has not tasted.

I am looking down the table saying,

"Don't you dare eat.

Don't you dare touch that food.

It isn't for you.

Damn.

God damn you."

God is saying "Ho, all is forgiven! Come to my table and taste to see that I'm good."

However, I am filled with rage, and I am not saying that. This is Pickton. On earth, all is not forgiven.

I do see that Christ was forgiving him, even as it was happening. I can hold together that Christ was forgiving him, but he is not in heaven (although there may come a day). I can hold together that all (the whole world) have been reconciled; all (the whole world) have been forgiven. But all will not be in heaven.

The invitation is given to all to taste God, though.

If Pickton does taste, if Pickton does eat, if Pickton does see God is good then...

Then...

Then...

Another part of me will die.

Then I might not survive.

But as I am carrying my cross, what was I to expect?

Really.

What was I to expect?

Did I think the good news would not hurt?

Did I think the good news would not kill me?

Did I think that being crucified with Christ would be anything but the worst thing I could imagine?

Loving and forgiving will kill us.

 Carrying my cross equals loving.

 Carrying my cross equals forgiving.

Or perhaps

 loving equals dying,

 forgiving equals dying.

We have known this for years, but as I write these words I begin to comprehend them—their magnitude, their infinite scope. We know love is THE WAY. We know forgiveness is THE WAY. But to walk through what it means in this world—Pickton, me, and worst of all, the Father "opened wide the doors of heaven to Pickton"—is something else entirely.

I know it in the abstract, but to see it in the concrete kills me.

I feel damned both ways. If it is true, what are the implications for the families of the women? Am I not in solidarity with their grief? How can I let the Father open wide the doors of heaven to Pickton without betraying them? without betraying truth? without betraying love? without betraying their lives? without betraying justice? without betraying..... If I embrace it, part of me dies. The part of me that can respect myself dies. The part of me that can justify myself dies. The part of me that loved them dies. The part of me that loved the Father dies. People will hate me justifiably if I embrace it.

This is not what I wanted being a Christian to mean.

If it isn't true, though, then the knowledge I had before in the abstract (love is THE WAY, forgiveness is THE WAY) was just a nice idea.

This is why Christ's teachings and Christ's death on the Cross are not two separate issues. Christ's WAY, the narrow path, is the road of loving and forgiving even unto death. And He didn't say, "Let me do that for you." He said, "Come die with me."

Forgiving is the very thing I am most unwilling to do. That's the very thing I want to say, "Do that for me." Or in fact, "Don't."

 Don't do that, God. If you do, my anger will be upon you. If you do, the fury I feel toward Pickton will fall on you. If he goes free, you will die. It's the position of my gut—not my mind. If you forgive him, then you become culpable in the destruction of the vulnerable. Don't you see that if you do that, you become like him? You will make us do this. You are only giving us a reason to kill you. What we would release upon him, we will instead release upon you.

I need you to be like me. We cannot be gracious to one who annihilates the vulnerable. We cannot be gracious to these destroyers. Do you understand me, God? Do you know what you do? Do you see that I might kill you? Do you see… but then I see it. What is inside Pickton, is inside me. I could kill. I could kill even God, because of my beliefs.

I do not want to have only these two choices.

Your forgiveness would mean I either satiate my need for justice by killing you, or I forgive him with you and die myself. Your forgiveness leaves me only two options. I become like him or I become like you. This is not what I want. I want a third option to be that we damn him. You and I survive and he is dead.

That's why we can say all are forgiven and invited, but few choose to follow.

Pickton is a good example of those who are invited freely to the table because all the prerequisites for his invitation have been satisfied by Jesus' love and forgiveness.

I am a good example of those who have trouble following him from the table because of the expectation that I will have to love and forgive.

Let me try that again:

> *a. the call to believe = all are loved and forgiven*
> *b. the call to follow = I must love and forgive*

Both are bad news to the Pharisee in me.
I want a. for me and not for Pickton.
I don't want b. if by that he means Pickton.
A wide open door to a lavish banqueting table.
A hard narrow road that doesn't just lead to the cross: it is one.

This road is harder than I thought. The way of love is much, much harder. It's so hard in fact, I don't know if I'm ready to do it. It's easier to follow the rules than to love. It's easier to believe the right things than to love.

This is what we mean by the righteousness that exceeds that of the Pharisees.

We sometimes assume a call to love is wishy-washy. But a call to love is terrible and terrifying and relentless and in every moment unattainable. A call to love is the worst thing ever.

Yes. A seventy-times seven love. A Gethsemane love. A Golgotha love.

I can go through an entire day believing the standard evangelical statement of faith—"bodily resurrection of the dead" and all. I can get up the next day and do it, again. Easy. And the whole program of evangelical morality—I passed it today. I didn't get drunk on absinthe. I didn't create, pass or smoke a hookah pipe. I did not become a meth cook. The things we measure ourselves by, are the things we succeed at daily. However, I truly lack the ability to love, again and again. Today I failed at love. But there is redemption. Even my small daughter forgives me. Even my baby forgives me. So I do keep trying. I am just a failure at it. By looking at the doctrines and rules, instead of love, I feel better about myself. If I MAKE it about the doctrines and the rules, instead of love, I feel fine.

Correct behavior to the religious leaders (and to us): whitewashing

    versus

Correct behavior to Jesus: love.

Suddenly I am face-to-face with the tenuousness of my faith. The slightest shift in Christianity's requirements could exclude me. If it's about love and forgiveness, I have been failing, even while keeping "the letter of the law." Have I been blind to the way of Christ? And if this is the way, can I follow Him in it? Even the thought of naming the name Pickton in a context of forgiveness makes me scared—and nauseated.

...My flesh somehow still wants to divorce the Picktons from the "It is finished" work of love and forgiveness. Not that Pickton has grafted himself to Christ. Not that he has believed and followed. But this is true (I think, with knees trembling): On Good Friday, Christ grafted himself to Pickton. He voluntarily submitted to being nailed to Pickton and all his sin. Flesh to flesh. Love and murder, skin on skin. Christ's blood washing Pickton. Cleansing Pickton. Drawing out the guilt and poison. Finishing it... way back then. And then, face to face, nailed there together, Christ whispers to Pickton and to Brita and to me... "Die with me." Not, "You don't need to die because I died" but, "If you die with me, you will rise with me." And then we say yes or no, probably over and over.

I am immersed in blood. I am under blood. Drowning. Blood is all over Jesus, too—the blood of each of those beautiful, desperate women that were loved. He is covered in their blood. The blood is deep because it is the blood from all their wounds. It is on him. Dear Jesus. It is on you.

And He holds it out to me,

"This cup is my blood, my new covenant with you" (1 Cor. 11:25, *The Message*).

The new covenant is blood. Did I know it was blood—real blood?

This cup he drank from.

He too pleaded, "Take this cup from me." It was too hard for him to walk down this road, but he did it. It is too hard for me, too. I do not want this cup. I do not want blood. I like Christianity-lite. I want rules and doctrine, the old-school way. I want safety. I want a nice cup of coffee, double cream, double sugar, please, Jesus.

I want air.

He tells me,

> This is my blood of the covenant, which is poured out for many for the forgiveness of sins. I tell you, I will not drink of this fruit of the vine from now on until that day when I drink it anew with you in my Father's kingdom (Matt. 26:28-29, NIV).

I realize it is not their blood anymore. Maybe it never was. It is His blood that is all over me. Making me wet and sticky and scared. Why do I feel so much shame?

> *Shame is based in a lie. That is why Christ scorned the shame of the cross. The lie was that love, forgiveness, nonviolence, even silence were marks of impotence and failure. Shame shame. But He knew something. "Look mother, I make all things new."*

Loving and forgiving does feel shameful to me. Not in an everyday context, but in a Robert Pickton world, loving and forgiving is shameful. Forgiving the terrorist is shameful. I feel like I will deserve the world's anger if I forgive him. You will want to kill me. You will be right.

The cup, the blood, and the fruit are all connected, though. They are all manifestations of the same thing. In Matthew 26 (above), Christ spoke of drinking of the fruit of the vine, which is blood. If we remain in Him, if we remain in the vine, we bear fruit. In the fruit is blood. Bearing fruit involves blood. The drink is this fruit of the vine. The drink is His blood. Bearing fruit, loving and forgiving, the way of the cross, the blood—it's all one red pool. It's all spilling.

> Remain in me, and I will remain in you. No branch can bear fruit by itself; it must remain in the vine. Neither can you bear fruit unless you remain in me (John 15:4 NIV).

It's red and wet and sticky.

It's all over us.

It covers us and makes all things new.

For my flesh is real food and my blood is real drink. Whoever eats my flesh and drinks my blood remains in me, and I in him... the one who feeds on me will live because of me (John 6:55-57, NIV).

It's red and wet and sticky.
It's all over me.
It covers me and makes me new.

And the only way through is to drink it.

Take this cup from me, please—if there is any other way; if there is any other road.

Maybe we can't do it AND we can't avoid it. So we cast ourselves on Christ, pleading with him to do it in us. Surrender, not despair.

Surrender. Die with me. Drink my blood.
Jesus didn't drink it for me. He drank it, and I need to drink it with him. Union.
God, help me not choke.

Jesus said, "Yes, in fact you will drink this cup... and be saved. And because it is a cup of salvation, you enter into the work of redemption. Grace is released... real grace that can transform a Pickton or rescue a prostitute. I want to rescue you. But more than that, I want to let this kernel of wheat in you fall into the ground and die, then sprout up to bear much good fruit."

For every Pickton that knows the love and forgiveness of God, we save how many prostitutes? for every pedophile that hears the good news that they are forgiven and their guilt IS atoned for, how many children grow up whole? for the joy set before us, we endure the cross of love and forgiveness, despising its shame, and anticipate the fruit that Christ bears.

The life of Christ must be the way through in this world. Can we walk in it at all? It is the way of union. It is the way of the cross. It is the way of blood. The new covenant is blood.

Our justice crushes mercy.

His kisses it.

PART FIVE

THE ATONEMENT
AND JUSTICE

Chapter Eleven

PUNISHMENT AND RETRIBUTION: DELIMITING THEIR SCOPE IN N.T. THOUGHT[1]

by C.F.D. Moule

Introduction by Pierre Allard

The honour of writing an introductory paragraph to the re-publishing of Dr. Charles Moule's article, *"Punishment and Retribution: An attempt to delimit their scope in New Testament Thought"* (first published in 1965), came to me a few days after my return from Rwanda where the consequences of a vindictive spirit among a Christianized population led to unspeakable atrocities.

Considering how sound and solidly biblical Moule's thesis is, it is sad indeed that such an eminent scholar needs in his opening words to warn "that many readers—perhaps most— will find themselves in disagreement with the radical thesis I am about to present." It shows, once more, how through the centuries, the restorative dynamic of biblical justice has been lost and replaced by a punitive and vengeful spirit in much of Christendom. We are so far from Augustine who, fearing the sentence of death for the murderer of some of his friends, writes in 412 CE to Judge Marcellinus: "We do not wish the suffering of the servants of God avenged by the infliction of precisely similar injuries in the way of retaliation... be not provoked by the atrocity of their sinful deeds to gratify the passion of revenge, but rather be moved by the wounds which these deeds have inflicted on their own souls to exercise a desire to heal them."[2] We are closer to Aquinas who affirms that "heresy is a sin which merits not only excommunication but also death, for it is worse to corrupt the faith which is the life of the soul than to issue counterfeit coins which minister to the secular life. Since counterfeiters are *justly* [my emphasis] killed by princes as enemies to the common good, so heretics deserve the same punishment."[3] When one combines the Gregorian Reform/Revolution

---

1. Among relevant publications since this paper, note especially W. Moberly, *The Ethics of Punishment*, London, 1968, and E. Moberly, *Suffering, Innocent and Guilty*, London, 1978.

2. *Nicene and Post-Nicene Fathers,* ed. by Philip Schaff and Henry Wace, (Buffalo, New York: The Christian Literature Co., 1896), vol. 1, "The Confessions and Letters of St. Augustine," Letter CXXXI11, to Marcellinus (412 A.D., p. 470-471).

3. Thomas Aquinas, *Summa Theologica,* 11-11, art. 3.

with the emergence of the theology of satisfaction under the influence of the *Cur Deus Homo* (in the closing years of the 11th century) by Anselm of Canterbury, one has great difficulty recognizing the good news of the gospel. And "for those who hope to find in the witness of the church some signs of the work of the Holy Spirit an examination of the role of the church in the penal debates of the nineteenth century is depressing indeed. From start to finish the bishops proved staunch supporters of flogging and hanging..."[4]

Having been involved in the criminal justice system for 35 years, I cannot but wonder what would happen if Moule's article were to be taken seriously by Christians. I dare to say that it would lead to the following:

- Evangelical churches would no longer be the strongest proponents of capital punishment.

- Christian communities around the world would become forgiving and welcoming and would find in their midst a place for healing for returning offenders.

- Many more theologians and biblical scholars would seek to publish works challenging, from a biblical perspective, current punitive theories of satisfaction and atonement.

- Our governments would think twice, in countries where a majority of their constituents declare themselves to be Christians, before introducing restrictive punitive measures in the area of criminal justice, knowing they would be met with opposition instead of with silent connivance or outright support.

So, I say, read and re-read Moule's article until it challenges and transforms your way of thinking about punishment from a biblical perspective. You will find his article life-giving because "the gospel announces a new relationship to God based on grace, forgiveness, and love, and this emphasis virtually eclipses the concept of retributive punishment."[5]

Rev. Dr. Pierre Allard
Just Equipping, President
And former Assistant Commissioner
with the Correctional Service of Canada

---

4. Timothy Gorridge, *God's Just Vengeance,* Cambridge University Press 1996, p. 211.
5. Christopher D. Marshall, *Beyond Retribution: A New Testament Vision for Justice, Crime, and Punishment*, p. 146.

Punishment and Retribution
Delimiting their Scope in N.T. Thought

It is likely, I know, that many readers - perhaps most - will find themselves in disagreement with the radical thesis I am about to present. But my hope is that time will not have been wasted - whatever the conclusions reached - because the thesis leads us in any case to ponder, once more, the very heart of the Gospel.

What I offer for your consideration is the thesis that the word "punishment" and other words related to it (especially "retribution") have, if used in their strictly correct sense, no legitimate place in the Christian vocabulary. The word "punishment" is often loosely applied, it is true, in modern parlance, to suffering inflicted for other purposes - disciplinary or deterrent. But for such inflictions I believe that it is an incorrect and misleading term. Similarly, in many places where the notion of punishment (even if not the actual word) appears in the New Testament, careful pondering shows that what is meant is, again, not strictly speaking, punishment. There is no denying, however, that there are further passages in the New Testament where the idea of retribution is most deliberately intended. But here, I would dare to say, the essentially personal character of the Christian gospel is temporarily obscured. In other words, what I want to ask is whether suffering inflicted for disciplinary and deterrent purposes (which are entirely relevant to the gospel) is not too lightly confused with suffering inflicted for the purposes of punishment and retribution, so that the latter have been dragged into a Christian context where they do not properly belong.

Let me start from what, in England at any rate, is a widely held view, among Christians as well as others, and from a formulation of it by a distinguished British theologian, Dr. Leonard Hodgson, formerly Regius Professor of Divinity at Oxford. In his book, *The Doctrine of the Atonement* (London, 1951), embodying the Hale Lectures, Dr. Hodgson devotes a considerable section of a chapter (Ch. III) to the subject of punishment and forgiveness. In the course of this he describes punishment as, essentially, the disowning by the community of evil done by its members (p. 57, etc.). By this I think we have to understand that, quite apart from anything that is done to rescue and reform the offender, and quite apart from any action that may be deemed likely to serve was a deterrent to prevent a repetition of the offence - over and above these, and distinguishable from them - Dr. Hodgson maintains that a purely *punitive* duty is laid upon the community. Quite apart from their duty to try to reform the offender and their need to protect themselves from again becoming victims of his offence, the members of a society have to maintain the moral standards of that society by expressing their disapproval of the offence: they have formally to repudiate it as something they refuse to accept in their system, by judicially assessing it and awarding an appropriate penalty. Over against the offender's "Yes" to the offence, the community has a duty to utter its equivalent "No".

In an entirely different context, here is a concrete example of the same attitude, though expressed very much more diffidently and without any confessedly Christian presuppositions. It is in a short book-review by Philip Toynbee, which appeared in *The Observer* for the 11th June, 1961. The book under review was *The Case of Adolf Eichmann* by Victor Gollancz - a moving plea against Eichmann's trial and, most of all, against his execution. The reviewer went a long way with Gollancz, but, at the end, came to precisely the point which I am raising. 'Mr. Gollancz', he wrote, 'points out that it would be absurd to defend the trial of Eichmann on deterrent grounds: it would, I think, be almost equally difficult to defend it on reformatory grounds. But are there other legitimate grounds for the infliction of punishment by human beings on one of their kind? Retribution is an ugly and an arrogant word, but are we quite sure that punishment is morally improper simply *qua* punishment? Are we quite sure that our motives are *only* bad when we feel indignant that some evil-doer has 'got away with it'? Does Eichmann deserve at least his arrest and trial simply because it is, in however helpless a way, *fitting* that he should be exposed to the world for what he is or was? I can only say that I am *not* sure about these points . . .'

Now, all of us, I know, can understand that reviewer's instinctive query and Hodgson's reasoned affirmation. But, nevertheless, I venture to think that this sense of the fittingness of retribution and the idea that punishment is proper, simply *qua* punishment, do need to be challenged in the name of personal values and, especially, in the name of the Christian gospel. I want to ask whether there is any room at all for this principle inside the good news of the death and resurrection of Jesus Christ, or, indeed, inside any relationship between persons as persons. May it not be one of those alien bits of secularism and sub personal standards that still adhere to thinking that has got beyond their stage, and subtly cloud the issue?

The facts may, I hope, become clearer if, for a start, we look briefly at two famous New Testament themes - namely, the wrath of God, and sacrifice.

About wrath, {*orge*}, it seems to me that three things may be said by anyone who presupposes the long and familiar debate around the word.

The first is that it is probably a mistake to imagine that Paul - let alone any other New Testament writer - thought of 'wrath' {*orge*} impersonally. As D.E.H. Whiteley, one of the most recent writers to discuss the word, says: "When he (Paul) says 'wrath', he means 'wrath of God', though he seldom includes the words 'of God'. In referring to what *we* should call 'impersonal, automatic' processes, he employs 'personal language'.[6] In this, Whitely follows C.K. Barrett[7] and others against C.H. Dodd.[8]

The second thing that may be said (again, with Whiteley)[9] is that - for Paul, at any rate, {*orge*} relates not to a *feeling* (*affectus*) in God, but to his *action* (*effectus*). In this, Whiteley is in agreement with Dodd.

Thus, thirdly, even if {*orge*} is not merely some impersonal phenomenon but is *God's* {*orge*}, we are still not compelled to assume that it must be retributive and punitive - least of all, if it denotes less a *feeling* than an *action*.

If God has willed the dire consequences that ensue on sin, it does not necessarily follow that he has willed them retributively, punitively. It may be that he has willed them as the only way of doing justice to the freedom and responsibility of the human personality, as he has created it. There are, it is true, passages, as we shall shortly remind ourselves, where the sense seems, in fact, to be retributive, but they are strikingly few, and I shall argue that they are not really integrated with the logic of the gospel. Indeed, I suspect that, once we have eliminated *affectus* in favour of *effectus*, we have logically eliminated any need to associate punishment in its strict sense with *orge*.

About sacrifice, I have written at some length elsewhere.[10] Very briefly, I would submit that, although it is *possible* to interpret the ritual and cultic offering to God of material objects - animal or other - as a gesture of pure adoration, it is, in the main, extremely difficult to dissociate from the word sacrifice, and from the action we so denote, the notion of bribery and barter and propitiation. If the word sacrifice has, in fact, been rescued from these associations, that is due to the astounding discovery that God himself initiates, provides, and, indeed, offers the sacrifice - the discovery adumbrated by Hebrew prophecy and implemented in Jesus Christ. But in so far as God's initiative does become evident - in so far as he is thus revealed as the subject rather than the object of the action - the notion of sacrifice, in any cultic sense, is correspondingly weakened. And precisely because the initiative is God's, it becomes impossible any longer at all to think of him as requiring to be propitiated or capable of being bribed. The language of sacrifice is, indeed, used metaphorically in the New Testament of the death of Christ, but comparatively seldom, and, in terms of Christ offering sacrifice to God, only

6. *The Theology of St Paul*, Oxford, 1964, p. 67
7. *The Epistle to the Romans*, London, 1957, p.33
8. *The Epistle to the Romans*, London, 1932, pp. 21 f.
9. *Theology*, 69.
10. *The Parish Communion Today*, ed. D.M. Paton, London, 1962, pp. 78 ff.

in Eph. v.2 and in Hebrews.[11] And the root *hilask* - is notoriously stood on its head by the New Testament, so that it can no longer logically be rendered by words of propitiation. Sacrificial language is used metaphorically also of the self-dedication of Christians to the service of God. But, for both these actions - Christ's and ours - the word "sacrifice" tends to be misleading, because it is so heavily charged with notions of propitiation and satisfaction - terms which consort badly with an action initiated by God himself and effected at his own infinite cost.

It may be that the cultic language of sacrifice is still the only language which sufficiently preserves the idea of adoration and worship and dedication on man's side, but I have my doubts. Costly self-surrender must surely be capable of being described in other ways. Meanwhile, the matter is at any rate germane to our inquiry, because the more cleanly and clearly the notion of compensation and satisfaction is eradicated from the Christian doctrine of atonement, the less clouded will be the issue about the place of retribution inside the gospel. If words like "compensation" and "satisfaction" could be successfully specialized, so as to relate exclusively to what has to be done in order to restore the wrong-doer to his proper personhood, to his full stature and dignity as a responsible person, then they would be tolerable - perhaps even desirable. But it seems to me extremely difficult to detach them from the suggestion of compensation and satisfaction to a feudal lord for injuries done to him; and this is something which is alien to the gospel. *eye m eye* ?

With this preliminary, we come specifically to the question of rewards and punishments. It seems, at first sight, that, in the Gospels, at any rate - most obviously in the parables, but also in many other contexts - we are moving in the realm of quantitative justice, and that the language of retribution, of penalty and punitive measures, as also of reward and merit, is here, at any rate, perfectly clear - indeed, inescapable.

Even here, however, in the Gospels, I question whether, on closer scrutiny, one is not driven to recognize that what is described (though less often than we sometimes think) in popular terms of reward and punishment is (usually, at least) something much more organically related to the actions and attitudes in question than these words suggest. It may be that the language of reward and punishment may only be used in these passages because it is the plain man's way of talking - perhaps the plain man's only way of understanding. But, if so, it is so rough and ready that it needs much qualification and amplification the moment one attempts to be more precise.

11. ix. 14, x. 10, 14.

For instance, in Lk. xiv. 12-14 Jesus is represented as saying that one should give generous meals not to the rich who might offer hospitality in return but to the poor, because then one will be rewarded {*antapodothesetai*} at the resurrection of the just. But this is not necessarily different from saying that virtue is its own reward. "Reward" in its normal sense is a mercenary word, and the mercenary-minded would be intolerably bored by the resurrection of the just - by heaven. The very notion of heaven compels us to transvalue the word "reward" by some such paradox as this. Similarly, the so-called "rewards" named in the beatitudes, and the so-called "penalties" in the corresponding woes in the Lucan version, are not mercenarily or arbitrarily fixed. They are organically related to the attitudes for which they are so-called "rewards" and "penalties". The avaricious, because they are avaricious, do not know how to enjoy anything other than material riches: they already have {*apechete*, Lk. vi. 24 f..) the only "reward" they are capable of receiving. Conversely, it is because the poor and the distressed may become thereby aware of their dependence on God that they, as a class, are capable of the permanent and inexhaustible riches of fellowship with him.

There are exceptions, and Luke, in particular, is prone to quantitative ideas, but there are instances of the same paradoxical use of mercenary terms in Tannaitic literature. Morton Smith[12] quotes the saying: "The pay for a commandment is a commandment, and the pay for a transgression is a transgression". It is difficult, as a matter of fact, to find more than a few parallels from the New Testament to the use of "pay" in a sinister sense (*in malam partem*), to denote the results of sin. Acts i. 18 (Judas {*ektesato chorion ek misthou tes adikias*}) is not an instance, for there the *misthos ('pay')* evidently means the literal silver he was paid by the Jewish authorities for betraying Jesus; and II Pet. ii. 13 {*adikoumenoi misthon adikias*} is too obscure for us to be confident. I can think of no more than three clear examples - though two of them are very striking. The first is in Rom i. 27, where homosexuals are described as {*ten antimisthian hen edei tes planes auto en heautois apolambanontes*}, ". . .paid in their own persons the fitting wage . . ." (New English Bible). The second is in Rom. vi. 23, where the contrast between the two halves of the verse is instructive: {*ta gar opsonia tes hamantias thanatos to de charisma tou theou zon aionios en ChristoIesou to(i) kuri(i)) hemon*}. This is perhaps a deliberate attempt to express the ruthlessly mercenary nature of sin as an employer and to contrast this with God's huge generosity which makes terms

---

of merit or reward on God's side wholly ridiculous. The New English Bible translation sharpens the contrast: "For sin pays a wage, and the wage is death, but God gives freely, and his gift is eternal life . . ." Thirdly, there is Heb. ii. 2, which says that, even under the Mosaic Law, every disobedience received its appropriate requital - {*endkon misthapodosian*}. Of course, there are other passages where the same idea is expressed without precisely the "pay" metaphor (e.g. II Thess. i. 6, {*antapodounai*}). But these are not relevant to the present point.

Thus, the New Testament uses the "reward" metaphor seldom for the consequences of evil; and whatever use it makes of it for good, is offset by such passages as the one just quoted from Rom. vi, where the utterly paradoxical, unmerited graciousness of God is stressed; and, in any case, the New Testament uses the metaphor in such a way as to show that it is really inadequate for its theme.

Even in the parables, where one might expect the vividly pictorial presentation to employ this sort of language extensively, it is comparatively restrained. To say, for instance, as in Lk. xvi. 19 ff., that a person who is blind to the needs of the beggar on his doorstep is bound to suffer irreparable remorse - indeed, that regard would not otherwise have been paid to his responsibility as a person, and that there is no way of forcibly making a man do good without violating that personal responsibility - is not the same thing as saying that he *deserves* this pain *as a punishment*, or that it has been determined *as a punishment* for such conduct. Again, the parables of Matt. xiii merely describe consequences: the wheat is garnered and weeds are burned; and "that is where the weeping and the gnashing of teeth will be". There are other parables in which the "rewards" and "punishments", so-called, are as thinly disguised as in the beatitudes. The parable of the money in trust, for instance, is - at least on its "rewarding" side - notoriously like that Tannaitic saying I quoted just now. The "pay" for the "commandment" to use the money well, turned out to be another "commandment" to exercise the same acumen and diligence in a still wider sphere. Virtue has, in that sense, become its own reward. Even in the allegory of the sheep and the goats, the two classes are merely invited into the kingdom or ordered off to misery. It is true that that misery is described as "prepared" for them (*to pur to aionion to hetoimasmenon to(i) diabolo(i) kai tois aggelois autou*}, Matt. xxv. 41, cf. 46);[13] and it is perfectly true that, in such a hint as this, and occasionally elsewhere, the dire consequences of wrong are described as penalties judicially

13. Cf. the similar use of *hetoimazein in bonam partem* in Matt. Xx. 23, Mk. X. 40.

imposed. For instance, two undeniable examples are Matt. xviii. 35, *houtos kai ho pater mou ho ouranios poiesei humin*, i.e. something comparable to the enraged king who ordered the unforgiving servant off to the torturers; and the savage finale to Luke's version of the money in trust, Lk. xix, 27: *plen tous echthrous mou tous me thelesantas me basileusai ep' autous agagete hode kai katasphaxate autous emprosthen mou.* Here, too, it must be added that Luke manifests (whether by selecting traditions or by his own shaping of them I will not here discuss) a clearer tendency towards a quantitative scheme of justice and responsibility than the others. Lk. xii. 47 ff definitely assumes degrees of responsibility and of deserts: to know one's duty and to neglect it deserves a severer flogging than unwitting failure. To have more gifts is to be more responsible. The same principle is implied in Acts iii. 17, where Peter says that he knows it was in ignorance that the Jews killed Jesus.[14] Again it is in Luke (if it is an original reading - though this is doubtful) that we find (xxiii. 34), "Father, forgive them, for they know not what they do" - a prayer which in this respect contrasts, as a matter of fact, with the unconditional prayer of Stephen (Acts vii. 60), "Lay not this sin to their charge". There is also, in Lk. xxiii. 41, the dying robber's statement that, while Jesus suffers innocently, he and his companion deserve all that they get {*kai hemeis men dikaios, axia gar hon epraxamen apolambanomen*}. But I believe it is fair to say that this kind of thing is the exception rather than the rule, even in the realm of parable, where, in any case, we have learnt to accept the picture as a whole, and not press details in an allegorical spirit.

Thus far, our discussion of the language of reward and punishment in the New Testament has chiefly concentrated on the traditions of the words of Jesus. Apart from my excursion into the meaning of *orge* and of sacrificial terms, I have stayed inside the evidence of the rest of the New Testament. The answer is "Now"; and my conclusion will be that there are passages, indeed, which are quite clearly retributive and even vindictive; but, once again, that they are fewer and more limited than is sometimes imagined; and, as I believe, peripheral and alien to a strict exposition of the Gospel.

Before we look at the passages in question, I beg you to remember that I am at no point denying - who in his senses could? - that, throughout the New Testament, dire consequences are attached to sin; neither am I saying that these are not "willed" by God. That sins leads to suffering, and that, without suffering, there is no reconciliation, nobody could hope to deny. Precisely

---

14. D. Daube has observations on this principle in Judaism, e.g., "'For they know not what they do': Luke 23, 34" in *Studia Patristica* IV = *T.U.* 79, 1961, 58 ff. But all this, I think, is exception rather than rule in the Gospels as a whole.

because God's grace is, by definition, respectful towards personality and recognizes the dignity and responsibility of a free person, it cannot "pauperize" the recipient. Grace is stern, it is challenge and demand, precisely by reason of its generous concern for the whole, undiminished entirely of personhood. But to say that is not the same thing as saying that punishment, penalty, retribution belong within the compass of grace, any more than reward does, except in the extremely paradoxical senses already indicated.

With that reminder, we face the chief passages outside the Gospels in which punitive words are used with precision and cannot but imply a definite notion of retribution.

(1) In Rom. ii. 5-11 Paul is in what anyone belonging to a Reformed tradition might be tempted to call a distinctly unpauline mood. He speaks quite specifically in terms of retributive justice: v. 6, God will give everyone his due (*apodosei*), each in proportion to his deeds (*kata ta erga autou*).[15] To those who, by patiently doing good, seek glory and honour and immortality he will give eternal life; to those whose concern is nothing but self-interest (*tois ex eritheias*) and who reject truth and accept falsehood he will give *orge* (wrath) and *thumos* (anger) (v. 8) . . . For God is impartial in his verdicts (*ou gar estin prosopolempsia para to theo*}, v. 11). In short, the theme of the whole paragraph is God's exact justice – (*dikaiokrisia*) (v. 6).

Well: justification by works! But it has always been recognized that, in these opening sections of his mightiest epistle, the Apostle is building up a massive indictment against mankind, Jew and Gentile alike, and is arguing from the premises accepted by anyone who recognizes a moral code.[16] It is not until we are shown to be all alike legally without defense that the good news of grace is introduced. In a sense, therefore, this section is deliberately taking up a pre-evangelic, pre-Christian standpoint.

I am not pretending by this that Paul at any point consciously repudiates the system of justice it implies; but it is worth observing that the point at which he develops to its extreme a system which, as I am arguing, has no real place within a fully personal relationship, is precisely the point at which he is consciously taking a pre-Christian stance - as it were, deliberately leaving the Gospel out of account for a while.

(2) Not so, however, the next passage, Rom. xii. 19-21. Whatever this means in detail, nobody can deny that it is firmly within a confessedly Christian standpoint. And it is here that the same note of retribution occurs, with

---

15. Cf. II Tim. Iv. 14.
16. In the same section of Romans, another clear example of the retributive idea of *deserving* is Rom. I. 32, *oi ta toiauta prassontes axioi thanatou eisin*.

a quotation again, as in Rom. ii, from the Old Testament; *emoi ekdikesis, ego antapodoso* is quoted (v. 19) with approval from the Pentateuch. It is perfectly clear that, while Christians are here forbidden to vindicate themselves by retaliation (*me heautous ekdikountes. v. 19*), this is not because vindication, as such, is deemed undesirable, but because the proper person to achieve it is God himself. The phrase *dote topon te(i) orge(i)* is extremely difficult to interpret in any sense except "give *God's* wrath room" - stand aside and let God wreak vengeance.[17]

K. Stendahl, in a very forceful article,[18] maintains that we must face the fact that, as in much of the Old Testament and Qumran, so in Paul, there is no feeling that the Lord's enemies ought to be spared, but rather a confident expectation of the vindication of the Lord's own against them. The New English Bible hints that the Pentateuchal affirmations are intended to be transcended and replaced by a better way at the point at which Paul goes on to quote Prov. xxv. 21 f., "If your enemy hungers, feed him", etc. In the Greek, this quotation is introduced merely by *alla ('but' or 'in another way')*. The New English Bible expands the *alla* to "But there is another text". Stendahl objects[19] that there is no instance to support such a translation, and that the *alla* must be either a straight adversative, giving the correct alternative to self-vindication, or else a heightening particle (meaning, I suppose, something like "No: rather, if your enemy hungers, you must feed him"). I think that Stendahl is probably right grammatically. I only wonder whether the New English Bible may not be right *as a paraphrase*, and whether Paul, by his very introduction of the Proverbs passage and by his application of it, is not giving a new meaning to retaliation. Are we bound to accept Stendahl's paraphrase of the idea in *soreuseis*:[20] "If you act in non-retaliation, your good deeds are stored up as a further accusation against your enemy for the Day of Wrath to which you should defer all judgment"? May it not be even if we abandon the New English Bible's rendering of *alla* that Paul is *reinterpreting* vengeance in terms of remorse? And, if so, remorse being capable of leading to penitence, it would no longer be necessary to regard this sort of "retaliation" as retributive or vindictive. Paul's climatic summary (v. 21), {*me niko hupo tou kakou, alla nika en to(i) agatho(i) to kakon*} is suggestive - particularly when the object of conquest is carefully placed in the neuter - *to kakon.*

---

17. Cf. 1 Sam. xxvi: 18, Sir. xix: 17.
18. "Hate, Non-Retaliation, and Love," *H.T.R.* 1, 4, Oct., 1962, 343 ff.
19. *H.T.R.* 1, 4, 1962, 346, n. 9.
20. *H.T.R.* 1, 4, 1962, 348.

I am bound to say that what looks like a dreadfully vindictive passage seems, after all, to be not far from that paradoxical transvaluation which we have already watched in the Gospel sayings: and I am not persuaded by Stendahl's closing remark,[21] that perhaps even in the Sermon on the Mount the injunction to non-resistance ought similarly to be interpreted as meant to point to the quickest way to vengeance.

(3) But now, thirdly, within the Pauline corpus, we come to II Thess. i. 5-11. The authenticity of this epistle is sometimes questioned, but I have never been able to find persuasive grounds for believing that it is not Pauline. If it is Pauline, it strikes a distinct discord in the Pauline symphony. Within the space of these few verses we have a number of phrases specifically welcoming revenge.

The theme is that the Christians are to face their sufferings with a good heart, because these are evidence, not that God is unjust but, on the contrary, that he is just: they are (v.5) *endeigma tes dikaias kriseos tou theou*, and they are going to result in the Christian's being deemed worthy of God's Kingdom (*eis to kataxiothenai humas tes basileias tou theou*); for (v. 6) it is only fair {*dikaion*} if God compensates {*antapodounai*} with anguish *(thlipsis)* those who are anguishing them *(tois thlibousin humas)*, and compensates with relief *(anesis)* those who are now experiencing anguish. For the Lord Jesus will be revealed (or, accompanied by?) a flame of fire, dealing vengeance *(didontos ekdikesin)* to those who do not know God or obey the gospel. These (v. 9) shall pay the penalty of eternal destruction, excluded from his presence (or destruction which proceeds from before him?), {*diken tisousin olethron aionion apo prosopou tou kurion*}. Short of certain parts of the Apocalypse, this comes as near as anything in the New Testament to the vindictive gloating of a Tertullian. The interesting thing is that in this respect it is unique in the Pauline corpus.

(4) Going outside Paul, we meet, first, in Heb. x. 29, the only New Testament occurrence of (*timoria*), "penalty", and it is used with a word of deserving: if law was ruthless in the Mosaic dispensation, {*poso dokeite cheironos axiothesetai timorias. . .,*} how much worse a penalty will be deserved, do you think, by the apostate from Christianity? There is no vindictiveness here, only dread of apostasy, but the language of deserving and of retribution is plain enough. Three times in the same epistle - and, in the New Testament, only here - occurs the word *misthapodosia*. It occurs at ii. 2, where it is in the rare sense of penalty. The other two are *in bonam partem* - x. 35, do not cast

21. *H.T.R.* 1, 4, 1962, 355.

away your confidence (*parresia*), for it carries a high remuneration; and xi. 26. Moses counting the stigma of the Christ *(ton oneidismon tou Christou)* greater riches than all the treasures of Egypt, because his eyes were on the recompense (*apeblepen gar eis ten misthapodosian*). These last two uses fall easily inside the category of metaphor which we found in the Gospels, and there is no need to interpret them in a mercenary way. The remuneration of *parresia* (boldness and unashamed Christian confession) and of accepting the stigma of being a follower of the Messiah is a fuller realization of the same - it is fellowship with the Christ, not some arbitrary prize.

So far as our concern goes, then, Hebrews yields us one definite phrase of deserving punishment: not a very large result.

(5) II Peter and Jude furnish notorious examples of a retributory justice. Note that in II Pet. ii. 4-9 God is spoken of, as clearly as one might expect, as bringing retributory punishment on evil. He is said to have brought disaster on the rebellious angels and the antediluvian world and Sodom and Gomorrah, and this to have judged them (*v. 6, katekrinen*) and made an example of them (*v. 6, hupodeigma . . .tetheikos*). It is not till v. 9 that we meet the phrase about keeping the wicked under chastisement until the Day of Judgment *(adikous . . . eis hemeran kriseos kolazomenous terein)*. But the tone of the passage is vindictive, as in that of -

(6) - the more condensed phrase in the corresponding passage in Jude 7: *prokeintai deigma puros aioniou diken hupechousai.*

(7)   Finally, the Apocalypse contains a number of not only retributive but positively vindictive passages. There is no lack of emphasis on the necessity for Christians to *suffer*, like their Lord and Master; and there is no suggestion in the Apocalypse (a point sometimes forgotten) that Christians ought ever to resist the secular power. They are to suffer passively; and the blood of the martyrs, like the blood of the Lamb has indeed redeemed the Christian community, it is now viewed as powerful, not to redeem the enemies of Christ, but to smash them with a rod of iron; and there is never any sign of doubt that that is what they deserve.

This is too familiar a fact to need illustrating at length. Let me remind you simply of xvi. 5 f., *dikaios ei, ho hon kai ho en, ho hosios, hoti tauta ekrinas, hoti . . . haima autous dedokas pein; axioi eisin*; and xix. 1 f., where there is an exultant shout of "Alleluia!" in Heaven, because God, in his justice, *exedikesen to haima ton doulon autou ek cheiros autes}* (that is, the Great Whore). In the light of such passages, I find it almost impossible to believe (must as I should like to) that the blood that flows like a great river out of the winepress of the wrath of God, in xiv. 20 is - by a splendid paradox - meant by the Apocalyptist to be the redemptive blood of the suffering Christ. This has been suggested - but can it be so?

This, I believe, completes my review of the main passages of the sort we are considering. There are undoubtedly scattered phrases here and there which could be added to the list, but I do not believe that they would amount to anything considerable. What conclusions, then, is it legitimate to draw?

One thing, I think, is undeniable, namely, that the New Testament writers as a whole (not least St Paul himself) do their thinking in a framework of ideas in which quantitative justice and retribution are axiomatic. Indeed, for the most part, their framework is that of the Old Testament Law; and if there is any reason to think of St. Luke as a Gentile (though this is being questioned by some), it is remarkable that his writing, even more than those of known Jews, shows particularly clearly, as we have seen, the consciousness of a quantitative system.

But, this being so, is it not the more significant that - apparently without realizing it themselves - these writers have so remarkably confined and reduced their expressions of this attitude? The passages we have considered where retribution *in its strict sense* is favoured are comparatively few, and mostly evoked by the stress of persecution and set in a context of apocalyptic. The language of punishment and retribution, also, is strikingly confined. *Poine* (punishment) does not so much as occur in the New Testament; *timoria* (punishment) occurs only in Heb. x. 29 (the verb, {*timorein*}, being applied only to Paul's persecution of Christians before his conversion - Acts xxii. 5, xxvi. 11); *kolasis* (punishment) - except in I Jo. iv. 18, where it is specifically criticized, comes only once again, in Matt. xxv. 46; *(kolazesthai)* (apart from Acts iv. 21, where it describes what the opponents of Christianity wanted to do) comes only in II Pet. ii. 9; and, in any case, it is a neutral word for infliction of pain, without necessarily carrying retributive notions. It can easily be reformatory. The same applies to (*zemia*) and (*zemiousthai*), which denote deprivation, for whatever reason - it could be deterrent (as in a fine) or educative.

Am I, then, asking you to believe that the deliberate infliction of suffering has no place in a Christian society? Am I an eccentric, advocating the removal of sanctions from community life? Indeed not! What am I trying to say can, I hope, be gathered up in a few sentences as follows.

(1) First, I am pleading for a clear recognition of distinctions between the various purposes for which suffering may be deliberately inflicted - by God on man, or by man on man.

Ignoring mere cruelty, suffering may be deliberately inflicted with the hope of reforming and educating the offender, or in order to deter from a repetition of the offence. Both these motives, I would say, are perfectly compatible with the Gospel - indeed, required by it. But there is a third motive

- that of seeing justice done or causing it to be seen that justice has been done. This motive - distinguishable from the other two - concerns abstract justice; it is essentially retributive and retaliatory; and it is the appropriateness of this motive within a Christian system that I am questioning. The best that can be said for it, I fancy, is (what I quoted L. Hodgson as saying) that it may be the only way of maintaining standards, the only way in which a community can say "We disapprove of this action". But I fail to see that that declaration is not already implied by the other two motives. If a community tries to reclaim and reform the offender and to prevent a repetition of the offence, surely that is a clear enough expression of its disapproval.

You may say, the one amounts to the other - so why quibble? I reply, because the satisfaction of abstract justice (although in many cases it may *look* (and, indeed, feel!) exactly the same and take exactly the same forms as the others) is a sub-personal motive; and to allow it into one's scheme of thought does, in the end, distort one's judgment and one's idea both of God and man.

(2) For, secondly, the moment one comes to the level of personal relations - and, most of all (so far as one can conceive them) to the absolute heights of the love of God - mere justice ceases to be relevant. The father of the prodigal son does not say, "Here comes my son: before I receive him back, I must secure that the family sees justice done".

(3) Instead - and this is my third point - whereas the suffering involved in a reconciliation is almost infinitely intensified, it is never, when we stand inside the Gospel, *retributive* suffering. Suffering there is in plenty. If a reconciliation could be effected without suffering, it would not be a reconciliation between persons. (The only painless reconciliation I can think of is a mathematical one - as between two columns of figures in an account-book.) A person is, by definition, responsible. If he has committed an offence, he cannot be restored to fellowship until he has accepted the pain of responsibility for his offence and (so far as possible) made reparation. Anything less would be a diminution of his personality. To demand of him less would not be "grace"; it would be insult. But his responsibility is not to some abstract system of justice: it is to God and to his fellow-men. That, and nothing abstract or sub-personal, is the measure of his responsibility. On the side of the injured party - who, ultimately, is God himself - the suffering of forgiveness is boundless. This too, is the cost involved in the structure of personal relationship, as God has created it.

But, on both sides, the suffering is creative and restorative and healing, and in obedience not to abstract laws of justice but to the demands of the living organism of persons which is most characteristically represented by the Body of Christ. That is why I also query the ultimate appropriateness of a word like "sacrifice" in its strict sense.

Therefore - to conclude - while I say, with deep conviction, "I do not deserve God's love", that is not because I have fallen short of some divine code of laws, but because love, by definition, cannot be *deserved* (least of all infinite, divine love). And, accordingly, I am not sure that it is a Christian attitude to say "I deserve damnation" either. Certainly I may be on my way to damnation as long as I reject God's love, as long as I remain ungrateful and unresponsive; for to be my true self is to respond to God's love, and to fail to respond is to forfeit selfhood. But I doubt if *deserve* or *merit* is the right word on the debit side of the account, any more than it is on the credit side. (*Axios*) is doubtfully at home in the Christian vocabulary except in the cry of pure *adoration* - "Worthy is the Lamb . . .!" In a word, I am asking whether there is any *ultimate* obligation or moral imperative (however necessary intermediate sanctions may be for the time being) except the obligation to gratitude, which is a personal, not a legal, response. Many other, and secondary, levels of obligation may in fact be needed as scaffolding (so to speak), to build the ultimate structure; a legal code may help, as a temporary crutch, to attain to the level of personal relationship. But the moment we use the secondary as primary and normative and confuse ends with means, we are on the less than Christian track; and this applies as much to the principle and motives behind a so-called penal code as to a preaching of the Gospel in terms of penal substitution.

Chapter Twelve

FORGIVENESS, RECONCILIATION, AND JUSTICE[1]

by Miroslav Volf

Introduction

It is not what the mainstream sociologists who followed in the footsteps of Karl Marx, Max Weber, and Emil Durkheim were predicting over the past century or so, but it happened. Instead of slowly withering away or lodging itself quietly into the privacy of worshipers' hearts, religion has emerged as an important player on the national and international scenes. It is too early to tell how permanent this resurgence of religion will be. The processes of secularization may well continue, though not so much in the older sense of the increasing loss of religious observance, but in the newer sense of the diminishing influence of religion in contemporary societies. Be the fate of secularization in the contemporary societies as it may, presently religion is well and alive on the public scene, so much so that a collection of essays with the title *Religion, the Missing Dimension of Statecraft* can become obligatory reading for diplomats in many countries, Western and non-Western, and that despite the fact that it bears all the marks of an initial effort to push at the boundaries of a discipline.[2]

In the public perception, the reassertion of religion as a political factor has not been for the good. It seems that gods have mainly terror on their mind, as the title of Mark Jurgensmeyer's book on the global rise of religious violence suggests.[3] In the Western cultural milieu the contemporary coupling of religion and violence feeds most decisively on the memories of the wars that plagued Europe from the 1560s to the 1650s and in which religion was "the burning motivation, the one that inspired fanatical devotion and the most

---

1. This paper was originally given at J. F. Kennedy School of Government, Harvard University, and at London School of Economics. I want to thank audiences at both places for their helpful comments. Special thanks to my research assistant, Ivica Novakovic.

2. Douglas Johnston and Cynthia Sampson, *Religion, the Missing Dimension of Statecraft* (New York: Oxford University Press, 1994).

3. *Terror in the Mind of God. The Global Rise of Religious Violence* (Berkeley: University of California Press, 2000).

vicious hatred."[4] It was these wars that contributed a great deal to the emergence of secularizing modernity. As Stephen Toulmin has argued in *Cosmopolis*, modernity did not emerge, as often claimed, simply as a result of its protagonists' endeavor to dispel the darkness of tradition and superstition with the light of philosophical and scientific reason. It is not accidental that Descartes "discovered" the one correct method to acquire knowledge in a time when "over much of the continent ..., people had a fair chance of having their throats cut and their houses burned down by strangers who merely disliked their religion."[5] A new way of establishing truth "that was independent of, and neutral between, particular religious loyalties" seemed an attractive alternative to war fueled by dogmatic claims.[6]

As was the case with their Enlightenment forebears, many of our contemporaries see in religion a pernicious social ill that needs to be treated rather than a medicine from which cure is expected. The resurgence of religion seems to go hand in hand with the resurgence of religiously legitimized violence. Hence it is necessary to weaken, neutralize, or eliminate religion as a factor in public life.

In this essay I want to contest the claim that the Christian faith, as one of the major world religions, predominantly fosters violence, and to argue, instead, that it should be seen as a contributor to more peaceful social environments. I will not argue that the Christian faith was not and is not often employed to foster violence. Obviously, such an argument cannot be plausibly made; not only have Christians committed atrocities and other lesser forms of violence but they have also drawn on religious beliefs to justify them.[7] Neither will I argue that the Christian faith has been historically less associated with violence than other major religions; I am not at all sure that this is the case. Rather, I will argue that at least when it comes to Christianity, *the cure against religiously induced or legitimized violence is not less religion, but, in a carefully qualified sense, more religion*. Put differently, the

---

4. Scott R. Appleby, *The Ambivalence of the Sacred. Religion, Violence, and Reconciliation* (Lanham, MD: Rowman and Littlefield Publishers, 1999), 2. See Ronald Asch, *The Thirty Years War. The Holy Roman Empire and Europe, 1618-48* (New York: St. Martin's Press, 1997).

5. Steven Toulmin, *Cosmopolis. The Hidden Agenda of Modernity* (New York: Free Press, 1990), 17.

6. Toulmin, 70.

7. For a survey see Gottfried Maron, "Frieden und Krieg. Ein Blick in die Theologie- und Kirchengeschichte," in: *Glaubenskriege in Vergangenheit und Gegenwart*, Ed. Peter Herrmann (Goettingen: Vandenhoeck und Ruprecht, 1996), 17-35. See also Karlheinz Deschner, *Kriminalgeschichte des Christentums*, 6 Vol. (Reinbeck bei Hamburg: Rohwolt, 1986ff) and a response to his work, H. R. Seeliger (ed.), *Kriminalizierung des Christentums? Karlheinz Deschners Kirchengeschichte auf dem Pruefstand* (Freiburg im Breisgau: Herder, 1993).

more we reduce Christian faith to vague religiosity or conceive of it as exclusively a private affair of individuals, the worse off we will be; and inversely, the more we nurture it as an ongoing tradition that by its intrinsic content shapes behavior and by the domain of its regulative reach touches public sphere, the better off we will be. "Thick" practice of the Christian faith will help reduce violence and shape a culture of peace.

I will first offer some general remarks on the relation between Christian faith and violence, and then, in the main body of the paper, attempt to show that at Christianity's heart, and not just at its margins, lie important resources for creating a culture of peace. Before I proceed, one comment about the focus of my exploration and two disclaimers are in place. First, the focus. I cannot offer here a perspective on the entire complex of issues that relate to the reassertion of religion as political factor on national and international scenes. For instance, I leave such crucial issues aside, like the question whether in international relations a shift has taken place toward religiously driven conflicts and, if so, what are the dynamics characteristic of security action on behalf of religion.[8] Instead of looking at religion as an object of securitization, I am exploring dimensions of the impact a particular religion—the Christian faith—should have upon the security action taken in defense of *any object* and upon the way in which relations between the parties after such action are negotiated. And now the disclaimers. First, by concentrating on religious resources I am neither excluding other resources nor suggesting that they are less important. "Shared democracy," "interdependence," and "dense international organization network," for instance, are crucial, as Bruce Russett has argued,[9] echoing major themes of Kant's essay "Eternal Peace."[10] Second, by concentrating on the resources of the Christian faith I am not claiming that other religions are by nature violent or even that Christianity owns the comparative advantage. I merely want to argue, by exploring the religion I know best, that, contrary to the opinion of many academics, politicians, and of the general public, religion can be associated with the very opposite of the violence-inducing passions.

---

8. See "In Defense of Religion: Sacred Referent objects for securitization."

9. Bruce Russett, "A neo-Kantian perspective: democracy, interdependence, and international organizations in building security communities," in: *Security Communities*. Eds. Emanuel Adler and Michael Barnett (Cambridge: Cambridge University Press, 1998), 368-394; see also Bruce Russett, *Grasping the Democratic Peace. Principles for a Post-Cold War World* (Princeton: Princeton University Press, 1993).

10. Immanuel Kant, *Perpetual Peace*. Transl. Lewis White Beck (New York: Bobbs-Merrill, 1957).

1. Christian Faith and Violence

In the past, scholars have argued in a variety of ways that the Christian faith fosters violence. I will concentrate here only on two types of arguments that, in my opinion, go to the heart of the matter. Other arguments, such as the one based on the combination of divine omnipotence, omniscience, and implacable justice—the omnipotent God, who sees everything, wills the punishment of every transgression—will take care of themselves, if adequate response is given to the two kinds of arguments I address here.

The first type of argument claims that religions are by nature violent, and that the Christian faith, being a religion, is also by nature violent.[11] In his book *Prey into Hunter* Maurice Bloch has, for instance, argued that the "irreducible core of the ritual process" involves "a marked element of violence or . . . of [a] conquest . . . of the here and now by the transcendental."[12] He explains,

> In the first part of the ritual the here and now is simply left behind by the move towards the transcendental. This initial movement represents the transcendental as supremely desirable and the here and now as of no value. The return is different. In the return the transcendental is not left behind but continues to be attached to those who made the initial move in its direction; its value is not negated. Secondly, the return to the here and now is really a conquest of the here and now by the transcendental.[13]

It is this violent return from the transcendental sphere, Bloch continues, that explains "the often-noted fact that religion so easily furnishes an idiom of expansionist violence to people in a whole range of societies, an idiom which, under certain circumstances, becomes a legitimation for actual violence."[14]

Let us assume that Bloch has analyzed the core of the ritual process correctly. The question still remains whether one should look at the core of the ritual process, stripped of the texture as well as of the larger context that a concrete religion gives it, in order to understand the relation of religions to violence. Here is a thought experiment: Imagine that the first part of the

11. Juergensmeyer's *Terror in the Mind of God* rests on such a belief. One central reason why violence has accompanied religion's renewed political presence, he argues, has to do with "the nature of religious imagination, which always has had the propensity to absolutize and to project images of cosmic war" (242). Of course, cosmic war is waged for the sake of peace, so that precisely as a phenomenon at whose core lies cosmic war "religion has been order-restoring and life-affirming" (159). But if it is not to be violent, religion cannot be left to itself; it "needs the temper of rationality and fair play that Enlightenment values give to civil society" (243).

12. Maurice Bloch, *Prey into Hunter. The Politics of Religious Experience* (Cambridge: Cambridge University Press 1992), 4-5.

13. Bloch, 5.

14. Bloch, 6.

ritual—the leaving of the here and now by the move toward the transcendental—were understood by a religion as the death of the self to her own self-centered desires and as her entry into a transcendental space of harmonious peace. And suppose that the second part of the ritual consisted in the conquest of the here and now by the transcendental precisely as understood in this peaceful way. If this were how the formal structure of ritual were filled in materially, would such a religion serve as "a legitimation of actual violence"? Would not the "conquest," if successful, be precisely the victory of "transcendental" peace over the violence of the here and now?

As you are most certainly aware, such a religion need not be imagined as hypothetically existing. For what I have asked you to imagine is precisely how the Christian faith understands itself.[15] It will foster violence in a way Bloch suggests only when its notion of the "transcendental" is stripped of its proper content and then infused with the values of the "here and now" around which the conflict rages. One could object that *any* conquest of the here and now by the transcendental involves violence. But if non-coercive victory of peace over violence is itself seen as implicated in violence, then one may well wonder whether the notion of violence has been hopelessly muddled.

Other scholars, like Regina Schwartz in her book *The Curse of Cain*, try to explain the Christian faith's complicity in violence by pointing not to the general features of the Christian faith as religion, but to one of its characteristic components. Along with Judaism and Islam, Christianity is a *monotheistic* religion, and therefore, Schwartz argues, an *exclusive* religion that divides people into "us," who know the one true God, and "them," who do not. Such monotheistic exclusivity, which imports the category of universal "truth" into the religious sphere, is bound to have a violent legacy, the argument goes.[16] "We," the faithful, have on our side the true God who is against "them," the infidels and renegades.[17]

15. Bloch engages the Christian faith directly, and envisages a possibility of it not underwriting violence. But in his account such a possibility is predicated on a "refusal of the second phase of rebounding violence, that is, a refusal of the conquest of external vitality which is therefore ultimately a refusal to continue with earthly life" (pp. 90-91). St. Paul's Christianity, he believes, is an example of such a refusal—or rather, an example of a half-hearted refusal since Paul also undertook "prudent organization of a well-organized church firmly embedded in the continuing practical and political world" (94). On my reading, St. Paul's Christianity is not an example of refusal of conquest of the here and now, but of the kind of conquest for which non-violence is constitutive; communities of faith were meant to instantiate precisely such conquest.

16. Jakov Jukic sees the heart of monotheism's exclusivity precisely in the insertion of the question of truth into the religious domain which the belief in the one God inescapably makes. To believe in one God means to believe in one *true* God. The claim to truth in religious domain has immediate consequence in the public realm (*Lica i Maske Svetoga. Ogledi iz drustvene religiologije* [Zagreb: Krscanska sadasnjost, 1997, 242f).

17. Regina Schwartz, *The Curse of Cain: The Violent Legacy of Monotheism* (Chicago: The University of Chicago Press, 1997).

But is the divine oneness necessarily violent? Is *any* notion of divine oneness violent? Does not, for instance, universalism, which is implied by divine oneness, work also *against* the tendency to divide people into "us" and "them"? More significantly, would not a pressure be exerted against self-enclosed and exclusive identities if the monotheism in question were of a Trinitarian kind?[18] Let me explicate this last rhetorical question.[19] One of the socially most important aspects of the doctrine of the Trinity concerns the conceptualization of identities. To believe that the one God is the Father, the Son, and the Spirit, is to believe that the identity of the "Father" cannot be understood apart from the "Son" and the "Spirit." To be the divine "Father" is from the start to have one's identity defined by another and therefore not to be undifferentiated and self-enclosed. Moreover, the divine persons as non-self-enclosed identities are understood by Christians to form a perfect communion of love; the persons give themselves to each other and receive themselves from each other in love. It would be difficult, so it seems to me, to argue that *such* monotheism fosters violence. Instead, in Bloch's terminology, it grounds peace here and now in the transcendental peacefulness of the divine being. The argument for inherent violence of monotheism works only if one reduces the thick religious description of God to naked oneness and then postulates such abstract oneness to be of decisive social significance.

Again, my point is not that the Christian faith has not been used to legitimize violence, or that there are no elements in the Christian faith on which such misuses build. It is rather that at the heart the Christian faith is peace-creating and peace-sustaining so that such misuse is less likely to happen when people have deep and informed commitments to the faith, commitments with robust cognitive and moral content—at least when these commitments stem from historic Christian beliefs rather than being recast arbitrarily by leaders of short-lived and oppressive communities. Strip religious commitments of all cognitive and moral content and reduce faith to a cultural resource endowed with a diffuse aura of the sacred, and you are likely to get religiously inspired or legitimized violence. Nurture people in the tradition and educate them about it, and if you get militants, they will be militants for peace. As R. Scott Appelby argued recently in his book *The Ambivalence of the Sacred*, contrary to the misconception popular in some academic and political circles, religious people play a positive role in the world of human conflicts and contribute to peace not when they "moderate their religion or

---

18 . For a critique of Schwartz along these lines see Miroslav Volf, "Jehovah on Trial," *Christianity Today* (April 27, 1998), 32-35.

19. For the following see Miroslav Volf, "Trinity is Our Social Program."

marginalize their deeply held, vividly symbolized, and often highly particular beliefs," but rather "when they remain *religious* actors."[20]

There are two main ways in which religions contribute to the violence between the conflicting parties: (1) by assuring the combatants of the (absolute) rightness of their cause and the correlative (absolute) evil of their enemies[21] and (2) by sacralizing communal identity of one party and correlative demonizing of others.[22] In hope of showing that the Christian faith puts pressure on its mature and informed practitioners not to act out of persuasion in the absolute rightness of their cause, I will explore the nexus of issues around the questions of forgiveness, reconciliation, and justice which lie at the heart of what this faith is about. As the example of South Africa with its "Truth and Reconciliation Commission" paradigmatically attests, these issues are particularly relevant to the post-conflict situations. An argument similar to the one I make here about religion and absolute rightness of one party in conflict could be made in relation to sacralization of communal identities, though I will not pursue that argument here.[23]

In the following I will first discard two wrongheaded ways to relate forgiveness, reconciliation, and justice, and then argue for an alternative.

2. Cheap Reconciliation

The first wrongheaded way to relate justice to forgiveness and reconciliation goes under the name of "cheap reconciliation." It attained prominence in theological circles through the *Kairos Document*, written by theologians critical of the South African regime before the dismantling of apartheid. They coined the term in analogy to the notion of "cheap grace"—which designates the readiness to receive love from God with no sense of obligation toward one's neighbors. Significantly, the term "cheap grace" was coined by Dietrich Bonhoeffer, a theologian who for religious reasons participated in the resistance against the Nazi regime.[24] The drafters of the *Kairos Document* set up the context for understanding what they mean by "cheap reconciliation" as follows:

> In our situation in South Africa today it would be totally unchristian to plead for reconciliation and peace before the present injustices have been removed. Any such

20. Appleby, 16.
21. So, for instance, Juergensmeyer, 242.
22. So, for example, Sells, *Bridge Betrayed*.
23. See Miroslav Volf, *Exclusion and Embrace. A Theological Exploration of Identity, Otherness, and Reconciliation* (Nashville: Abingdon Press, 1996).
24. Dietrich Bonhoeffer, *The Cost of Discipleship* (New York: MacMillan, 1963 [1937]), 45-47, 59.

plea plays into the hands of the oppressor by trying to persuade those of us who are oppressed to accept our oppression and to become reconciled to the intolerable crimes that are committed against us. That is not Christian reconciliation, it is sin. It is asking us to become accomplices in our own oppression, to become servants of the devil. No reconciliation is possible in South Africa without justice.[25]

As I will argue shortly, I am not persuaded that reconciliation should be pursued only *after* the injustices have been removed but rather believe that struggle against injustices is part of the more fundamental pursuit of reconciliation. But if we put this temporal sequencing of justice and reconciliation aside for a moment, the critique of cheap reconciliation that emerges from the text is clear. Cheap reconciliation sets "justice" and "peace" against each other as alternatives. To pursue cheap reconciliation means to give up on the struggle for freedom, to renounce the pursuit of justice, to put up with oppression.

If I am not mistaken, some such usage of the term "reconciliation" predominates in public discourse today. One speaks of "national reconciliation" and expects from it "collective healing" and greater "political unity" or fears that behind it lurk organic notions of the social "body" and the centralization of power. Stripped of its moral content, reconciliation is contrasted so starkly with "justice" that one has to weigh the relative values of "justice" and "unity" in order to assess to what extent the sacrifice of justice can be morally acceptable and politically desirable in order to achieve political unity.

To advocate cheap reconciliation clearly means to betray those who suffer injustice, deception, and violence. Though the Christian faith has been all too often employed to advocate such reconciliation—indeed, the *Kairos Document* as a critique of "cheap reconciliation" was directed against theology of the pro-apartheid churches—such a concept of reconciliation really amounts to a betrayal of the Christian faith. It is almost universally recognized by theologians and church leaders today that the prophetic denunciation of injustice has a prominent place in the Christian faith. This prophetic strand cannot be removed without gravely distorting Christianity. The struggle against injustice is inscribed in the very character of the Christian faith. Hence an adequate notion of reconciliation must include justice as its constitutive element. And yet it is precisely here that watchfulness is needed. For the imperative of justice, severed from the overarching framework of grace within which it is properly situated and from the obligation to non-violence, underlies much of the Christian faith's misuse for religiously legitimizing violence.

---

25. *The Kairos Document. Challenge to the Church. A theological comment on the political crisis in South Africa.* (Braamfontein: Skotaville Publishers/Grand Rapids, MI: W.B. Eerdmans Pub. Co., 1986), Art 3.1.

In the context of cheap reconciliation, forgiveness is best described as acting toward the perpetrator "as if their sin were not there."[26] The offense has happened—or one party thinks that it has happened—but the injured party treats the offender as if it had not. At the popular level, one is told simply to shrug one's shoulders and say, "Oh, never mind." This "never mind" exculpates the offender even from "moral reproach."

In *The Genealogy of Morals* Friedrich Nietzsche advocated a version of "as-if-not" attitude toward transgression. He suggested it in the context of the opposition between "slave morality" and "noble morality." The first, which operates along the axis of "good-evil," is reactive in the sense that it is shaped by the situation with respect to which it defines human conduct; the second is purely positive, existing in sovereign disregard of the situation. In the process of this distinction, Nietzsche advocates an attitude toward transgression untouched by concerns for justice as desert. He writes,

> To be unable to take his enemies, his misfortunes and even his *misdeeds* seriously for long - that is the sign of strong, rounded natures with superabundance of a power which is flexible, formative, healing and can make one forget (a good example from the modern world is Mirabeou, who had no recall for the insult and slights directed at him and who would not forgive, simply because he - forgot.) A man like this shakes from him, with one shrug, many worms which would have burrowed into another man; here and here alone is it possible, assuming that this is possible at all on earth - truly to 'love your neighbour.'[27]

Such sovereign disregard for injuries from others demands extraordinary strength, almost that of an *Uebermensch* and a person with sensibilities nurtured by the culture of late modernity may be tempted to reject Nietzsche's proposal simply on that count. This, however, may be less an argument against Nietzsche than against the weakness of the victims of offenses. At least for those who, unlike Nietzsche, think that moral concerns are legitimate, the crucial question is whether the "as-if-not" attitude toward transgression is morally acceptable. The answer is arguably "No." It is morally wrong to treat a murderer "as if" he had not committed the murder—or at least it is wrong to do so until some important things have happened, for example, until the murder has been named as murder and the murderer has distanced himself from the deed. One may also suggest that disregard for justice as desert entails the abdication of responsibility for the transformation of the perpetrator and the world at large. For it is hard to imagine how one could induce offenders to change without at least implicitly morally reproaching their deeds.

26. John Milbank, *Theology and Social Theory. Beyond Secular Reason* (Oxford: Blackwell, 1990), 411.
27. Friedrich Nietzsche, *On Genealogy of Morals*. Transl. Carol Diethe (Cambridge: Cambridge University Press, 1994), 23-24; Part 1, Section 10.

Significantly, Nietzsche himself never described the "as-if-not" attitude as forgiveness. Mirabeau, his example of the "virtuous," *could not forgive* because he had forgotten! Because forgiveness is conceptually tied to justice as desert, Nietzsche had little positive to say about it and tended to replace it with "forgetting."[28] Nietsche rejected forgiveness precisely because he saw rightly its positive relation to justice. Forgiveness is more than just "the overcoming of anger and resentment."[29] It always entails foregoing a rightful claim against someone who has in some way harmed or offended us. Such a foregoing of a rightful claim makes forgiveness unjust and precisely thereby prevents forgiveness to fall outside of concern for justice.

The concern for justice is integral to forgiveness and reconciliation. But what is the precise relation between justice on the one hand and forgiveness and reconciliation on the other?

3. First Justice, Then Reconciliation

One way of relating positively justice to reconciliation is to suggest that the process of reconciliation can begin only *after* injustice has been removed. This, as I noted earlier, seems to be the position of the *Kairos Document*, which so rightly denounced "cheap reconciliation." But is this "first justice, then reconciliation" stance plausible? There are major problems with it.

First and most fundamentally, the "first justice, then reconciliation" stance is impossible to carry out. All accounts of what is "just" are to some extent relative to a particular person or group and are invariably contested by that person's or group's rivals. In any conflict with prolonged history, each party sees itself as the victim and perceives its rival as the perpetrator, and has *good reasons for reading the situation that way.*

Even more significantly, as Nietzsche rightly noted in *Human, All Too Human*, given the nature of human interaction, every pursuit of justice not

---

28. See Nietzsche, *Beyond Good and Evil. Prelude to a Philosophy of the Future.* Transl. Marion Faber (Oxford/New York: Oxford University Press, 1998), 110, Aphorism 217. In *Human, All Too Human* Nietzsche argued for the impossibility of forgiveness by tying it to (1) the knowledge of the evil-doer about what he or she is doing and (2) to the right of the offended or of the third party "to accuse and to punish." Since the evil-doer can never fully know what he or she is doing and since we do not have the right to accuse and to punish, Nietzsche argued, forgiveness is impossible. So clearly, for Nietzsche forgiveness presupposes the framework of justice.

29. So Jeffrie G. Murphy, "Forgiveness and Resentment," *Forgiveness and Mercy*, ed. Jeffrie G. Murphy and Jean Hampton (Cambridge: Cambridge University Press, 1988), 14-34, 24. Pamela Hieronymi's response to a prevalent claim that forgiveness is primarily a matter of manipulating oneself out of resentment is to the point: "Ridding one's self of resentment by taking a specially-designed pill, for example, would not count as forgiveness" ("Articulating an Uncompromising Forgiveness," *Philosophy and Phenomenological Research* [forthcoming], 2).

only rests on partial injustice but also creates new injustices.[30] In an ongoing relationship, as the temporal and spatial contexts of an offense are broadened to give an adequate account of it, it becomes clear that any action we undertake now is inescapably ambiguous, at best partially just and therefore partially unjust. No peace is possible within the overarching framework of strict justice for the simple reason that no strict justice is possible. Hence the demand at communal or political levels is often is often not for "justice" but for "as much justice as possible." But the trouble is that, within the overarching framework of strict justice, enough of justice never gets done because more justice is always possible than in fact gets done.

Second, even if strict justice were possible, it is questionable whether it would be desirable. Most of us today feel that the legal provisions of the Hebrew Bible which insist that the punishment be commensurate with the crime are excessive. "An eye for an eye, a tooth for a tooth" strikes us as too severe. Originally, of course, the provision was meant to restrict the excesses of vengeance. And yet it is precisely the demand for more than equal retribution that is strictly just. If a person's tooth is broken in retribution for her breaking of mine, we are *not* even for the simple reason that the situation of offense is manifestly not one of exchange. In a situation of exchange, both of us would have disposal over our teeth, and I would give you mine under condition that you give me yours. But in a situation of offense, the consent to the exchange is lacking. By breaking my tooth you have violated me, and therefore you deserve greater punishment than just the equal breaking of your tooth. Most of us, however, don't think that a world in which corrective justice was pursued even with strictness as the principle "tooth for a tooth" demands would be a desirable one; and so, even when we demand "justice," we are in fact after something much less than strict justice, which is to say that we are ready tacitly to "forgive" part of the offense. We are at least implicitly aware that the normal functioning of human life is impossible without grace.

Third, even if justice could be satisfied, the conflicting parties would continue to be at odds with one another. The enforcement of justice would rectify past wrongs but it would not create communion between victims and perpetrators. Yet some form of communion—some form of positive relationship—needs to be established if the victim and perpetrator are to be fully healed.

30. Friedrich Nietzsche, *Human, All Too Human. A Book for Free Spirits* (transl. Marion Faber; Lincoln: University of Nebraska Press, 1996), 216. For a related but different critique of justice see Jacques Derrida, "Force of Law: The 'Mystical Foundation of Authority'," in *Deconstruction and the Possibility of Justice*, eds. Drucilla Cornell, Michel Rosenfeld and David Gray Carlson (New York and London: Routledge, 1992), 24-26.

Consider the fact that personal and group identities are not defined simply from within an individual or a group, apart from relationships with their near and distant neighbors. We are who we are not simply as autonomous and self-constituting entities but essentially also as related and other-determined. I, Miroslav Volf, am who I am not simply because I am distinct from all other individuals but in part also because over past two years, for instance, I have been shaped by interaction with my son, Nathanael. Similarly, to be a Serb today *is* in part to have Albanians as one's neighbors and Kosovars as a minority within one's borders, to be a citizen of a country that waged wars against Bosnia and Croatia and was bombed by NATO. If we are in part who we are because we are embedded in a nexus of relations which make others to be part of ourselves, then we cannot be properly healed without our relationships being healed too.

The pursuit of justice, even if *per impossibile* fully successful, would satisfy our sense of what is right, but would not heal us. It would bring us peace only as the absence of war, but not as harmonious ordering of differences.

The "first justice, then reconciliation" stance implies that forgiveness should be offered only after the demands of justice have been satisfied. Forgiveness here means no more than the refusal to allow an adequately redressed wrongdoing to continue to qualify negatively one's relationship with the wrongdoer.

Strange as it may seem, forgiveness *after* justice is not much different from forgiveness *outside* justice. Forgiveness outside justice means, you will recall, treating the offender as if he had not committed the offense. Forgiveness after justice means doing the same—only that the demand that justice be satisfied before forgiveness can be given is meant to redress the situation so that one can *rightly* treat the wrongdoer as if he had not committed the deed. Whereas in the first case forgiveness is the stance of a heroic individual who is "strong" and "noble" enough to be unconcerned with the offense, in the second case forgiveness is the stance of a strictly moral individual who shows enough integrity that after the injustice has been redressed he or she refuses to feel and act vindictively. To forgive outside justice is to make no moral demands; to forgive after justice is not to be vindictive. In both cases it is to treat the offender as if he had not committed the offense or as if it were not his.

The first and decisive argument that I brought against the "first justice, then reconciliation" stance applies to this notion of forgiveness too. If justice is impossible, as I have argued, then forgiveness could never take place. There is another important argument against this notion of forgiveness. If forgiveness were properly given only after strict justice has been established, then one would *not* be going beyond one's duty in offering forgiveness; one would indeed *wrong* the original wrongdoer if one did not offer forgiveness. "The wrong has been fully redressed," an offender could complain if forgiveness were not forthcoming, "and hence you owe me forgiveness." But this is not how we understand forgiveness. It is a *gift* that the wronged gives to the wrongdoer. If we forgive we are considered magnanimous; if we refuse to forgive, we may be insufficiently virtuous—for, as Robert Adams argues, "we ought in general be treated better than we deserve"[31]—but do not wrong the other.

We need to look for an alternative both to forgiveness and reconciliation outside of justice and to forgiveness and reconciliation after justice. I want to suggest that such notions of forgiveness and reconciliation are to be found at the heart of the Christian faith—in the narrative of the cross of Christ, which reveals the very character of the God. On the cross, God is manifest as the God who, though in no way indifferent toward the distinction between good and evil, nonetheless lets the sun shine on both the good and the evil (cf. Matthew 5:45); as the God of indiscriminate love who died for the ungodly to bring them into the divine communion (cf. Romans 5:8), the God who offers grace—not cheap grace, but grace nonetheless—to the vilest evildoer.

4. Will to Embrace, Actual Embrace

So what is the relationship between reconciliation and justice that is inscribed in the very heart of the Christian faith? Partly to keep things rhetorically simpler, I will substitute the more poetic "embrace" for "peace" as the terminal point of the reconciliation process as I explore this issue in the reminder of my text. The Christian tradition can be plausibly construed to make four central claims about the relation between justice and embrace.

4.1. The Primacy of the Will to Embrace

The starting point is the primacy of the will to embrace the other, even the offender. Since the God Christians worship is the God of unconditional and indiscriminate love the will to embrace the other is the most fundamental obligation of Christians. The claim is radical, and precisely in its radicality, so socially significant. The will to give ourselves to others and to welcome them, to readjust our identities to make space for them, is prior to any judgment about others, except that of identifying them in their humanity. The will

---

31. Robert M. Adams, "Involuntary Sins," *The Philosophical Review*, 104 (1985), 24.

to embrace precedes any "truth" about others and any reading of their action with respect to justice. This will is absolutely indiscriminate and strictly immutable; it transcends the moral mapping of the social world into "good" and "evil."

The primacy of the will to embrace is sustained negatively by some important insights into the nature of the human predicament. Since the Christian tradition sees all people as marred by evil and since it conceives of evil not just as act but as a power that transcends individual actors, it rejects the construction of the world around exclusive moral polarities—here, on our side, "the just, the pure, the innocent," and there, on the other side, "the unjust, the defiled, the guilty." Such a world does not exist. If our search for peace is predicated on its existence, in its factual absence we will be prone to make the mistake of refusing to read conflicts in moral terms and thus lazily fall back on either establishing symmetries in guilt or proclaiming all actors as irrational. Instead of conceiving of our search for peace as a struggle on behalf of "the just, the pure, the innocent," we should understand it as an endeavor to transform the world in which justice and injustice, innocence and guilt, crisscross and intersect, and we should do so guided by the recognition that the economy of undeserved grace has primacy over the economy of moral desert.

4.2. Attending to Justice as A Precondition of Actual Embrace

Notice that I have described the will to embrace as unconditional and indiscriminate, but not the embrace itself. A genuine embrace, an embrace that neither play-acts acceptance nor crushes the other, cannot take place until justice is attended to.

Hence the will to embrace includes in itself the will to determine what is just and to name wrong as wrong. The will to embrace includes the will to rectify the wrongs that have been done, and it includes the will to reshape the relationships to correspond to justice. And yet, though an actual embrace requires attending to justice, it does not require establishment of strict justice. Indeed, the pursuit of embrace is precisely an alternative to constructing social relations around strict justice. It is a way of creating a genuine and deeply human community of harmonious peace in an imperfect world of inescapable injustice.[32] Without the grace of embrace, humane life in our

---

32. Robert Burt, "Reconciliation with Injustice," *Transgression, Punishment, Responsibility, Forgiveness. Studies in Culture, Law and the Sacred* (Madison: University of Wisconsin Law School, 1998), 106-122 (=*Graven Images* 4 [1998]).

world in which evil is inescapably committed but our deeds are irreversible would be impossible.[33]

4.3. Will to Embrace as Framework for the Search for Justice

To emphasize the will to embrace means more than to advocate learning how to live with inescapable injustice while not giving up on the pursuit of justice. For the will to embrace is also a precondition of (even tenuous) convergences and agreements on what is just in a world of strife. Without the will to embrace, each party will insist on the justness of their own cause, and strife will continue. For, given the nature of human beings and their interaction, there is too much injustice in an uncompromising struggle for justice.

The will to embrace—love—sheds the light of knowledge by the fire it carries with it. Our eyes need the light of this fire to perceive any justice in the causes and actions of our enemies. Granted, our enemies may prove to be as unjust as they seem, and what they insist is just may in fact be a perversion of justice. But if there is any justice in their causes and actions, only the will to embrace will make us capable of perceiving it, because it will let us see both them and ourselves with their eyes. Similarly, the will to exclude—hatred—blinds by the fire it carries with it. The fire of exclusion directs its light only on the injustice of others; any justness they may have is enveloped in darkness or branded as covert injustice—a merely contrived goodness that makes their evil all the more deadly. Both the "clenched fist" and the "open arms" are epistemic stances; they are moral conditions of adequate moral perception. The clenched fist hinders the perception of the possible justness of our opponents and thereby reinforces injustice; the open arms help detect any justness that may hide behind what seems to be the manifest injustness of our opponents and thereby reinforces justice. To agree on justice in situations of conflict you must want more than justice; you must want embrace.

4.4. Embrace as the Horizon of the Struggle for Justice

As in many of our activities, in the struggle for justice much depends on the *telos* of the struggle. Toward what is the struggle oriented? Is it oriented simply toward ensuring that everyone gets what they deserve? Or is it oriented toward the larger goal of healing relationships? I think the later is the case. Hence the embrace should be the *telos* of the struggle for justice. If not,

---

33. On the need for forgiveness against the backdrop of the irreversibility of deeds see Hanah Arendt, *The Human Condition. A Study of the Central Dilemmas Facing Modern Man* (Garden City: Doubleday, 1959), 212f.

reconciliation will not even be attempted until the "right" side has won. And unless reconciliation is the horizon of the struggle for justice from the outset, it is not clear why reconciliation should even be attempted after the victory of the "right" side has been achieved.

Pulling all four features of the relation between reconciliation and justice together we can say that reconciliation describes primarily a process whose goal is the creation of a community in which each recognizes and is recognized by all and in which all mutually give themselves to each other in love. As such, the concept of reconciliation stands in opposition to any notion of self-enclosed totality predicated on various forms of exclusion. And far from standing in contrast to justice, for such a notion of reconciliation justice is an integral element. Though reconciliation may be seen from one angle to issues *ultimately* in a state "beyond justice," it does so precisely by attending to justice rather than by circumventing it.

5. Forgiveness and the Primacy of Embrace

Forgiveness can be properly understood and practiced only in the context of the stance which gives primacy to reconciliation but does not give up the pursuit of justice. So what is the relation between forgiveness and justice?

First, forgiveness does not stand outside of justice. To the contrary, forgiveness is possible only against the backdrop of a tacit affirmation of justice. Forgiveness always entails blame. Anyone who has been forgiven for what she has *not* done will attest to that. Forgiveness should therefore not be confused with acceptance of the other. Acceptance is a purely positive concept; any notion of negation is foreign to it, except, obviously, that it implies negation of non-acceptance. But negation is constitutive of forgiveness. To offer forgiveness is at the same time to condemn the deed and accuse the doer; to receive forgiveness is at the same time to admit to the deed and accept the blame.[34]

34. It is important to note that human forgiveness cannot remove guilt. As Nicolai Hartmann rightly pointed out in his *Ethics*, human forgiveness is "a moral act on the part of him who forgives and solely concerns his conduct toward the guilty... Forgiveness may very well take from the guilt that special *sting of guilt* which inheres in the deserved contempt and hostility of the man who has been wronged; and it may give back to the guilty the outward peace which he had spurned; but it can never remove the moral guilt itself" (Nicolai Hartmann, *Ethics III. Moral Freedom*, transl. Stanton Coit [London: George Allen & Unwin, 1932], 271-272—italics added). Only divine forgiveness actually removes guilt. When human beings forgive they (1) forego resentment, (2) refuse to press the claims of justice against the other and therefore also (3) bear the cost of the wrongdoing . As a result of human forgiveness, the guilty *is treated* as if he or she were not guilty (to be distinguished from *defining* forgiveness itself as treating the other as if he or she had not committed the offense). But unless forgiven by God, he or she remains guilty, human forgiveness notwithstanding.

Second, forgiveness presupposes that justice—full justice in the strict sense of the term—has not been done. If justice were fully done, forgiveness would not be necessary, except in the limited and inadequate sense of not being vindictive; justice itself would have fully repaid for the wrongdoing. Forgiveness is necessary because strict justice is not done and strictly speaking cannot be done.

Third, forgiveness entails not only the affirmation of the claims of justice but also their transcendence. More precisely, by forgiving we affirm the claims of justice in the very act of not letting them count against the one whom we forgive. By stating that the claims of justice need not be (fully) satisfied, the person who forgives indirectly underscores the fact that what the sense of justice claims to be a wrongdoing is indeed a wrongdoing.

Fourth, since it consists in forgoing the affirmed claims of justice, forgiveness, like any instantiation of grace, involves self-denial and risk. One has let go of something one had a right to, and one is not fully certain whether one's magnanimity will bear fruit either in one's inner peace or in a restored relationship. Yet forgiveness is also laden with promise. Forgiveness is the context in which wrongdoers can come to the recognition of their own injustice. To accuse wrongdoers by simply insisting on strict justice is to drive them down the path of self-justification and denial before others and before themselves. To accuse wrongdoers by offering forgiveness is to invite them to self-knowledge and release. Such an invitation has a potential of leading the wrongdoer to admit guilt and to repent, and thereby healing not only wrongdoers but also those who have been wronged by them.

Fifth, the *first step* in the process of forgiveness is unconditional. It is not predicated on repentance on the part of the wrongdoer or on her willingness to redress the wrong committed. Yet, full-fledged and completed forgiveness, is not unconditional. It is true that repentance—the recognition that the deed committed was evil coupled with the willingness to mend one's ways—is not so much a prerequisite of forgiveness as, more profoundly, its possible result. Yet repentance is the kind of result of forgiveness whose absence would amount to a refusal to see oneself as guilty and therefore a refusal to receive forgiveness as forgiveness. Hence an unrepentant wrongdoer must in the end remain an unforgiven wrongdoer—the unconditionality of the first step in the process of forgiveness notwithstanding.

Finally, forgiveness is best received if in addition to repentance there takes place some form of restitution. Indeed, one may ask whether the repentance is genuine if the wrongdoer refuses to restore something of what she has taken away by the wrongdoing—provided that she is capable of doing so. In sum, forgiveness is an element in the process of reconciliation, a process in which the search for justice is an integral and yet subordinate element.

Conclusion

In the later part of this essay I sought to explicate the social significance of the foundational act of the Christian faith—the death of Christ. This step from the narrative of what God has done for humanity on the cross of Christ to the account of what human beings ought to do in relation to one another was often left unmade in the history of Christianity. The logic of God's action, it was sometimes argued, was applicable to the inner world of human souls plagued by guilt and shame; they outer relationships in family, economy, and state ought to be governed by another logic, more worldly logic. At least in Protestantism, this disjunction between the inner and outer was one important reason why the Christian faith could be misused to legitimize violence.[35] Emptied of their social import, religious symbols nonetheless floated loosely in the social world and could be harnessed to purposes that are at adds with their proper content. Significantly, this disjunction is never to be found in the New Testament; instead, the central religious narratives and rituals are intended to shape all domains of early Christian's lives. Arguably, the central Christian rituals, Baptism and Eucharist, enact the narrative of divine action precisely as the pattern for lives of believers.

It may well be the case, someone may respond, that the Christian faith at its heart fosters peace rather than violence. But in what ways can it do so in concrete social and political settings? First, the narrative of divine action can motivate and shape behavior of individual actors in conflict situations. Depending on their position, such individual actors can be significant and even decisive for the future of conflicts. Second, this narrative can shape broader cultural habits and expectations that make peaceful solutions possible. It takes a particular cultural soil for the seed of peace to bear fruit. Of course, the narratival portrayal of the divine redemptive action cannot be simply mirrored in human interaction, be that on individual, communal, or political planes. Instead, one has to aim at culturally and situationally appropriate practical analogies as near or distant echoes of the divine redemptive action that lies at the heart of the Christian faith.

Finally, the narrative of divine action as it applies to human interaction can help shape social institutions. One way to think about how this may be the case is to recall the concluding words of Anthony Giddens' book

---

35. See, for instance, Paul Tillich, *Against the Third Reich. Paul Tillich's wartime addresses to Nazi Germany* (Louisville: Westminster John Knox Press, 1998).

Stricken by God ?

Modernity and Self-Identity. After noting the emergence in the high modernity of what he calls "life politics" (as distinct from "emancipatory politics") which demands a remoralization of social life, he writes,

> How can we remoralize social life without falling prey to prejudices? The more we return to existential issues, the more we find moral disagreements; how can these be reconciled? If there are no transhistorical moral principles, how can humanity cope with clashes of 'true believers' without violence? Responding to such problems will surely require a major reconstruction of emancipatory politics as well as the pursuit of the life-political endeavors.[36]

The narrative of the God of unconditional love who reconciles humanity without condoning injustice along with its intended patterning in the lives of human beings and communities, contains, I suggest, at least some resources for such a reconstruction of politics.

---

36. Anthony Giddens, *Modernity and Self-Identity. Self and Society in the Late Modern Age* (Stanford: Stanford University Press, 1991), 231.

Chapter Thirteen

FREED TO BE HUMAN AND RESTORED TO FAMILY: THE SAVING SIGNIFICANCE OF THE CROSS IN A HONDURAN BARRIO

Mark D. Baker

In our book, *Recovering the Scandal of the Cross,* Joel Green and I encourage readers to view afresh the variety of contextual understandings of the death of Christ in the New Testament and to reconsider how we can faithfully communicate with fresh models the atoning significance of the cross and resurrection for specific contexts today.[1] I have taken up the challenge myself, and developed a number of contextual images of the atonement. In this article, after a general description of one neighborhood in Tegucigalpa, I retell two people's stories to provide a concrete basis for the theological reflection in the rest of the article in which I offer an answer to the question of how the cross and resurrection provide salvation in the context of a Honduran barrio.[2] This article presupposes and builds on the biblical and theological work of *Recovering the Scandal of the Cross.* As you read this article you might picture it as a conversation between the Bible, the insights of our book *Recovering the Scandal of the Cross* and the context of a Honduran *barrio.*

The Context: Life in the Barrio

Flor del Campo, with a population of over 15,000, is one of the numerous poor neighborhoods that have sprung up on the hills surrounding Tegucigalpa in the past 25 years. The inhabitants live in a climate of violence and most are trapped in poverty. They dream of living in a simple house instead of a shack; they worry about having enough food to eat; and as they encounter others with higher status they experience continual shame and humiliation that crush their sense of dignity and self-worth. Politicians promise solutions, but structures and corrupt practices continue to allow a small number of Hondurans to get richer and richer while most languish in poverty. Inefficient governmental institutions function best at providing jobs for the small

---

1. Joel B. Green & Mark D. Baker, *Recovering the Scandal of the Cross: Atonement in New Testament & Contemporary Contexts* (Downers Grove, IL: InterVarsity, 2000).
2. An atonement image I have developed for another context is part of a book of atonement images I have edited titled: *Proclaiming the Scandal of the Cross* (Grand Rapids, MI: Baker Academic, 2006).

number with political connections.

Some in Flor del Campo turn to crime as a way to escape poverty–whether selling drugs, stealing at work, or assaulting people on the street. In Flor del Campo people never leave their houses unattended. If they did, someone might break in or even steal the clothes off the line. Many seek momentary escape through drugs or alcohol. Teens seeking status and security join surrogate families, gangs, only to be forced to prove themselves to other gang members who humiliate them. At night gangs roam the dirt streets of Flor del Campo creating a climate of terror.

What they see and hear in the media and everyday life constantly reminds the people of Flor del Campo how they fail to measure up to society's concept of a successful human: a person of note. Although some accept with fatalistic resignation the subservient role they play out in relation to people of higher status, others in Flor del Campo grasp for symbols of status in order to give the appearance of having achieved higher social standing than they actually have. Some men go hungry so they can save money to buy a pair of Nikes; some mothers buy cosmetics and clothes rather than the school supplies their children need. To avoid admitting they are from Flor del Campo, a number of residents tell people at work or school that they live in La Pradera, a nearby middle-class neighborhood. One woman, who is actually a cleaning lady, lies to neighbors about the nature of her work, and leaves her house each day dressed as if she had an important office job. Others have been so beaten down and stepped upon that their concern is not to appear to belong to a higher strata, but to survive.

Yet in a twisted way many of those who do not attempt to mask the reality of their social status still do not live as authentic humans. Unlike the above examples where people try to appear as something superior to what they really are, cultural norms press the poor to live as less than authentically human. Those of lower status are called *humilde* which literally means humble, and is used to refer to people with little education or economic resources who are commonly peasant farmers or manual laborers. The *humilde* are expected to act with deference and humility when they encounter those of higher status. To live up to the cultural norm of appropriate behavior for a *humilde*, that is to be good in the eyes of society, these people must come close to acting like they are animals—deserving of very little and at the service of those above them.

At the same time, cultural norms of *machismo* and *marianismo* provide all those living in Flor del Campo, even the *humilde*, with ways to rise above others of their economic status and be considered a "real man" or a "good woman." *Machismo* is an exaggerated awareness and assertion of masculinity. *Machismo* includes an emphasis on masculine virility and male superiority and domination over women. Even a very poor man can prove he is a "real man" and demonstrate his superiority over other poor men by drinking more, "conquering" more women, engendering more children, demonstrating control of his household, and responding aggressively to insults against his honor.

Marianismo looks to the Virgin Mary as the ideal of a "good woman." Marianismo venerates a woman who comes to marriage as a virgin. In contrast to men, married women are to remain "cloistered" at home in the sexual sense. Elvia Alvarado, a Honduran *campesina* (peasant), explains the double standard. "If a woman lives with one man and sleeps with another, it's a terrible scandal. Men kill their wives for sleeping with another man. But *campesino* men are free to sleep with other women."[3] Purity is central to *marianismo's* portrait of a good woman; being long suffering is also a key trait; being industrious and hard working is praised as well as necessary for survival. A good woman provides her family good meals and keeps her house in order, and in contrast to the macho men, submits and meekly endures her husband's unfaithfulness and often drunken abuse.

A Honduran man's effort to prove he is macho, a real man, is an example of what I earlier described as human efforts to grasp to be more and thus mask one's finiteness or true humanity. In a sense, women striving to live up to the ideal of a good woman, do the same. But grasping the status of a good woman actually requires women to pull back and live as less than the authentic human they are. They suppress their physical and emotional well-being and personal development as they live out the ideals of *marianismo*.

Church is another avenue for the *humilde* to grasp status and mask their sense of inferiority by being "true Christians." If they obey the list of rules and faithfully attend the nightly church services they can rise above others and amount to something in the church. The price of this form of legalism is high. A spirit of judgmental condemnation fills many churches. Church is viewed as family, members call each other brother and sister, but membership in the family is conditional on following the rules, on being "good." There is little room for sharing one's struggles or other forms of transparency. Rather than facing the shaming, accusing looks of others in the church, many who stumble and break a rule simply never return.[4]

People live in fear, not just of their "brothers" and "sisters" in the church, but of God: the supreme father of this family. One man described God as an

3. Elvia Alvarado, *Don't Be Afraid Gringo: A Honduran Woman Speaks From the Heart*, trans. and ed. Medea Benjamin (San Francisco: Food First, 1987) 46.
4. For a more complete discussion of legalism in the evangelical churches of Flor del Campo see Mark D. Baker, *Religious No More: Building Communities of Grace and Freedom* (Downers Grove, Illinois: InterVarsity, 1999) 17–33.

old man with a stern face, a large beard, and a thick leather strap for whipping people. Although descriptions would vary, most people view God as a distant accusing figure eager to punish any misstep. He loves, but conditionally. Theirs is a God who keeps track of their deeds, handing out blessings to the good, and meting out punishments like sickness to those who fall short of his standards. Many Hondurans, especially evangelicals, interpreted hurricane Mitch, which devastated the country in 1998, as a punishment sent by God.[5]

Clearly, Flor del Campo is a difficult place to be authentically human and experience family. At the physical level many have inadequate nutrition, housing, and health care, and this lack prevents them from living to their full human potential. Poverty hinders many from educational development, and a climate of violence creates fear and stymies the full flowering of human relationships. Like Adam and Eve, some in Flor del Campo grasp to be more and give the appearance of being something superior to the vulnerable humans they are. Others attempt to protect their humanity from being discovered by pulling back. Most of the *humilde* in Flor del Campo live out a mix of grasping and pulling back through *machismo, marianismo,* religious rules, and other cultural definitions of what it means to be good. But rather than giving them a sense of acceptance and belonging, of being part of a true family, these actions serve to disconnect and alienate them further from God, themselves, and others.

As we state in the last chapter of *Recovering the Scandal of the Cross,* the nature of the human situation to which the cross addresses itself is one coordinate for answering the question of its saving significance.[6] We will take a brief interlude in our description of the context and begin to think of this human situation in theological terms.

Defining "Human" and "Family"

Everyone living in Flor del Campo is, in a biological sense, *homo sapiens*–a human being. For the sake of this exploration, however, we need to move past this most basic definition of the word. For instance, those who have adequate nutrition, housing, and health care have the potential to live a fuller human experience than those who do not. A ten-year-old girl who was malnourished as an infant, who suffers chronic sickness due to contaminated drinking water, and who sits listlessly in an overcrowded class because she

---

5. For a more in-depth discussion of their concept of God see Baker, *Religious No More,* 40-46; Stanley Slade, "Popular Spirituality as an Oppressive Reality," in *New Face of the Church in Latin America,* ed. Guillermo Cook (Maryknoll, New York: Orbis, 1994) 135-49.

6. Green and Baker, 201.

had so little breakfast will have a significantly diminished educational experience in comparison to someone not suffering those limitations. Even so, broadening our definition of being human to the basic components a United Nations study might list does not fully capture what I have described above.

We can be helped by thinking biblically and theologically about the term "authentic humanity." Adam and Eve lived as authentic human beings when their lives were characterized by peaceful interdependence with creation and each other, when they lived in trust of God, each other, and themselves. In the security of God's love they accepted their finiteness with its limitations without self-accusation, doubt, and shame. Exactly because they did not try to be God and accepted their vulnerable state as dependent beings they were free to be fully and authentically human.

A day came, however, when they refused to trust God and to accept that their finite state was good. They overreached, grasping for the forbidden fruit in order to be like God, more than human. They rejected what they truly were. This led them to feel shame for what they had rejected: their true humanity. Without prodding, Adam and Eve began covering up and hid themselves from a kind and loving God. Alienated from God, others, and ourselves we have been hiding ever since. In the words of psychologist and theologian Margaret Alter,

> Adam and Eve's story illustrates ubiquitous human fear of exposure and humiliation. . . In our minds we have failed to achieve an inner desire to transcend our finite nature; we have overreached and appeared foolish. We have invented an unnecessary obligation to be as God. As a result, we feel the stinging humiliation of not being good enough, of being inferior and out of control.[7]

As we have seen in Flor del Campo, some respond to the ubiquitous fear that Alter describes by grasping to be more and thus mask their finiteness. Others attempt to protect themselves from being discovered by pulling back. In a sense they live as less than human. Many live out a mix of grasping and pulling back. Either way, they cut themselves off from the possibility of living as authentic humans in loving relationship with others.

Just as all the people who live in Flor del Campo are humans, all of them, to varying degrees, are part of a family. In this essay I want to use the word family in an expanded sense, so as to think of "family" as a group of persons relating to each other as authentic humans who embrace their vulnerability and live out honest relations of trust and interdependence. So, when I say "family" I am not necessarily referring to people connected by blood ties, but people who are relating to each other as fully human.

---

7. Margaret G. Alter, *Resurrection Psychology: An Understanding of Human Personality Based on the Life and Teachings of Jesus* (Chicago: Loyola University Press, 1994) 16-17.

"Authentic Christian community" would be another label we could put on what I am calling family in this essay. I use the term "family" because it is a biblical image, one used by Paul in a discussion of salvation (Galatians 4:1-7), but more importantly because it is a term more readily understood and embraced by the people of Flor del Campo. They are more likely to respond to an invitation to join a group of people who relate to each other as true family than to an invitation to join a group people who live as a true community.

In this barrio, many people's experience of family, both in the traditional sense of the word and in this expanded, qualitative sense of a place where they can belong, be loved, and feel supported, leaves much to be desired. It is characterized by alienation more than by trust and love. Many long to experience authentic family.

To further clarify our understanding of alienation in Flor del Campo, and to be able to more concretely discuss the saving significance of the cross and resurrection I will introduce you to two people. Alba is a real person and her story is true. Ramon and his story are fictional, but reflect events that have happened in Flor del Campo.

Ramon

Ramon grew up in a small village in the southern part of Honduras. He went to school for two years, but did not pass first grade or learn to read. As an adult he farmed the tiny piece of hillside land that he inherited from his parents, but deforestation and his slash-and-burn agricultural methods left his soil depleted and more arid. He had trouble growing enough corn and beans to feed his wife and three children. He began to escape through increased drinking. Feeling impotent to provide for his family and to acquire symbols of status like a watch, a revolver, a horse, or a few head of cattle, he tried to prove he was a "real man" by acting more aggressive towards others in the village: insulting and fighting other men, and pursuing other women. He had three more children, one with his wife, one with a teenage neighbor, and another with a woman his age who already had children.[8] He decided to sell

---

8. Male *machismo* is a significant cause for disintegrated families in Flor del Campo where more than 25 percent of the homes are headed by single mothers. In some cases the father has been killed by someone defending his honor. In others the father has fled because he killed someone or has gone to the United States to find a job or better wages. Most often, however, men leave one woman and set of children behind and have more children with another woman. It is not uncommon in Flor del Campo for a household to consist of a mother and her children fathered by two or three different men, none of whom now live with her. Many times when a father does live with the family they might prefer that he did not because of his drunkenness and demanding or abusive ways of relating to them.

his land and leave after a drought had led to an especially poor harvest and a number of people had told him that the husband of his most recent lover was planning to kill him.

Ramon took his wife and their four children and moved to Tegucigalpa with hopes of getting a job and having a better life. He built a small shack beside his sister-in-law's house in Flor del Campo. He could not find steady work, and he felt even more of a failure than he had in his village. He had trouble adapting to the ways of the city. When he saw people looking at him, or heard his name mentioned at the bar, he imagined they were ridiculing him as an ignorant peasant. He felt especially belittled by his neighbor Jorge who had a good job, and who Ramon thought was too friendly with Ramon's wife. Ramon soon was spending his nights drinking, insulting, fighting, and chasing women, much as he had done in his village.

During the day, however, he roamed Tegucigalpa knocking on rich people's gates meekly asking for work. One time someone offered him a regular job. He said he would take it, but fearful that the person assumed he could read Ramon never returned. After a hard day's work using a machete to cut the lawn of an electrical engineer in a wealthy neighborhood, the engineer asked Ramon how much he should be paid. Ramon responded as *humilde* people usually do. He bowed his head slightly, made no eye contact and softly said, *"Usted sabe"* (literally "you know"—in essence, "who am I to tell you?").

Later that day Ramon was about to enter the bar when he heard Jorge talking about him. Ramon went home and took his brother-in-law's revolver. When Ramon walked into the bar Jorge immediately felt a mix of both shame and anger. People had told him that Ramon had been belittling him in numerous ways. Jorge stood up, emboldened by alcohol, and insulted Ramon who insulted him back and shoved Jorge against the wall. Jorge grabbed a bottle to attack Ramon, but Ramon pulled out the gun, shot him, said a few more words to emphasize who was the real man of the two of them, and left Jorge dying on the floor.

Alba

Alba grew up in a town near Tegucigalpa. She was the second of fourteen children. Her father inherited a large farm from his parents, but he spent more time drinking than working. He sold the property little by little to support his family and his drinking habit. Eventually the family ended up in the street. A neighbor took pity on them and let them stay rent-free in a house she owned. Alba's mother started working as a maid, and brought home food her employers gave her for the family. If her father, who did not work, caught her mother bringing the food home he would throw it out, accusing her of getting the food by sleeping with other men. Other times he would hit her and take the money she earned so he could go drink. Alba lived in fear of her father. He beat all of them, including her mother, with electrical wires. When he came home in a drunken rage Alba and her bothers and sisters jumped out of bed and ran outside. Alba rushed home from school each day, not because she was eager to be with her family, but to avoid possible punishment. She never asked if she could go to a friend's house to play, but quietly did her chores, and then went to work for food and money at a neighbor's house. Instead of risking saying something wrong and being ridiculed or beaten, Alba learned to say as little as possible. She carried this practice with her to school where she talked much less than the other students, and usually only participated in class if the teacher forced her to.

When she was in third grade a cousin told Alba's mother that she would like to help Alba by letting her live at her house, giving Alba food, clothing, and covering her school expenses. The cousin lied. The cousin "rescued" Alba only to make her a slave. She never paid Alba, did not let her go to school, made her work all day, never let Alba eat with the family, and gave her the leftovers if there were any. Alba used to get up at four in the morning and surreptitiously eat because her cousin punished her whenever she caught her taking food.

Boys began showing interest in Alba when she turned 14, but the way her father treated her mother made it hard for her to believe the boys' talk of love. She ignored or rejected them.

Alba learned how to survive. Her silence and low profile protected her from the beatings and rejection she feared, but over the years she gradually rejected herself. She did not love herself, and could not imagine that anyone else could either. She once tried to kill herself by drinking pesticide, but she did not even get sick.

She eventually did trust a young man enough to want to start a family with him. Her cousin ridiculed her, saying he was poor trash. But Alba ran away from her cousin's home and eventually moved to Tegucigalpa with her husband. As an adult and mother in Flor del Campo Alba joined a church and strove to be a "true Christian" and live up to the expectations of this new family. She went to church every night, followed the rules, and worked hard in various projects to raise money to construct a church building. She did not, however, feel loved or cared for. She sensed she did not measure up because she did not speak in tongues. Someone looked displeased with what she said the first time she shared in a church meeting, so she returned to her childhood practice of remaining quiet.

The Saving Significance of the Cross and Resurrection, Part One

What is the saving significance of the cross in the context of Flor del Campo? How can it free people to live as authentic humans and allow them to be part of a group of people who are truly family for them? I lived in Honduras for ten years. I spent a lot of time in Flor del Campo, walking the dirt streets, teaching and preaching in some of the churches, and sitting in people's tiny homes talking about life and the gospel. One question I discussed with people in Flor del Campo was, "What is the saving significance of the cross and resurrection for Flor del Campo today?" What follows grew out of those conversations.

Paul wrote the Corinthians that he proclaimed Christ crucified (1 Corinthians 1:23). In a similar way, in Flor del Campo I have observed the importance, not only of talking about what was accomplished on the cross, but also on who was crucified. I have divided my answer to the question of the saving significance of the cross into two sections. The first focuses on the revelatory nature of the cross. What does the Crucified One reveal to us about the character of God and what it means to be truly human? And how that can help people like Ramon and Alba? The second section will explore how God acted through the cross to provide freedom from the powers of alienation and estrangement that have distorted their relationship with God, others, themselves, and creation.

The first section is also divided into two sub-sections. In the first we reflect on how the cross can connect with each person's experience of having their authentic humanity crushed, what I will call being a crucified one. In the second we will reflect on how the cross reveals that each crucified person also engages in hurting themselves and others, what I will call being a crucifier.

Crucified Humans

As a *humilde* person, Ramon stooped at times and buried his true humanity in acts of deference to those of higher class, but generally he lived a life of macho maneuvering in an effort to present himself as a "real man," superior to others, and thus masking his true humanity. He feared how others might respond if they discovered the real Ramon, the one beneath the macho mask, a human that, in contrast to his mask, often felt powerless, felt inept and out of place in the city, and worried about what he and his family would eat. When Alba was a child, life felt dangerous, and drawing attention to herself seemed to make it even more dangerous. Alba protected herself by pulling back and hiding. Her suicide attempt was the ultimate attempt to hide. She carried to the extreme what life had taught her: the less she expressed herself, the more she stayed curled up in her protective turtle shell, the safer she was. In church she "hid" at times, and in other situations stepped out to try to perform as a "true Christian." Neither Ramon nor Alba were experiencing true family. They did not live in loving connection with the people around them. Alba and Ramon did not trust others enough to live openly as the humans. There was no space for Alba or Ramon to live truly as human beings. Their authentic humanity, the persons they had been fashioned by a gracious God to be, had been squashed and strangled—crucified.

Although in a biological sense Ramon and Alba are alive, in the face of worries, fears and threatening life situations their fragile true humanity has been hidden and masked to the point of being smothered or crucified. Through the incarnation, cross, and resurrection God invites and enables the crucified human buried within each of us to come to life. In the incarnation God embraces the very human finitude and vulnerability that the people in Flor del Campo try to mask or hide through their attempts to live as "real men," "good women," "true Christians," and to be appropriately "humble." It is hard to imagine a situation of greater vulnerability than that of a newborn baby or a naked man nailed to a cross. Certainly the manger and the cross are the moments that Jesus' finite humanness, his vulnerability, are most evident, but his life as a whole reveals to us what it means to live as an authentic human.

It is probable that in Alba's church experience she did reflect on the human life of Jesus, but mostly to extract certain actions that could be translated into rules one must obey in order to earn the honor of being considered a true Christian. Instead of using Jesus' life as a means to help construct religious masks that hide one's true humanity, those in Flor del Campo could more appropriately see in Jesus a man who did not succumb to the pressure to bury his humanity and act as a "real man," and a "true Christian,"or behave in the ways expected of a *humilde* person. Of course, Hondurans cannot actually do what the previous sentence implies because Jesus lived in a different time and place and did not experience Honduran *machismo* or the religious distortions of Christianity present in Flor del Campo. We can be sure, however, that people in Jesus' culture had similar ways of grasping for superiority and similar pressures to behave according to one's status. If we mentally flip through the pages of the gospels we can think of a number of examples of some grasping for superiority, such as the rich through publicly giving huge offerings, the Pharisees through religiosity, members of the Sanhedrin, the kings, and Pilate through political power. Equally we can observe others stooping to the roles ordained by society: outcast lepers, children, and women, and some, like toll collectors, that mixed grasping and hiding.

Jesus lived as a man free from alienation, and thus in a trusting relationship with God, with others, and with himself—an authentic human. Jesus did not live according to a program. We might say he was unpredictable, but perhaps we could more appropriately say that since he did not enter into games to cover up his humanity and worry about what others thought of him, he was free to respond in honesty and love to those around him. Jesus ate with outcasts—people with whom a pious person should not have associated. He allowed strong feelings to flow—feelings of sadness, compassion and anger. Sometimes he spoke, other times he was silent; sometimes he was harsh, other times gentle. Attuned to human suffering, he healed and saved people, yet he was not driven to heal all; he did not move frantically from town to town with a strategy to reach all of Palestine by year's end. He seemed relaxed; he took time alone. At times he spoke directly, but more often he told parables and asked questions. We are told he spoke with authority, but it was not an authority based on status or position, rather it arose from his complete trust in God the Father and thus his freedom to be who he truly was. We cannot be sure but we can imagine that people respected his authority because of the way he looked them in the eye, his tone of voice, and the way he carried himself as a person who was content to be fully himself. In Jesus, God affirms our humanity by entering into it so completely, as if to say to those in Flor del Campo, "I have experienced true humanity, with all of its limitations and vulnerability, but also in all of its potential. You can too."

Of course, when people are fully human and do not hide, on the one hand, and do not attempt to be more than human and wear masks, on the other, they make others around them uncomfortable. They are inconvenient to the rest of us, for they threaten the security of the accepted norms of our lives and the worlds around us. Jesus did this. I will explore this in more detail in the next section. In a general way, however, we can say that as an authentic human Jesus did and said things that so upset others they killed him. Jesus was willing to demonstrate total solidarity with us despite the costly consequence of that commitment, his death by crucifixion.

The scandal of God-incarnate hanging on the cross in weakness, nakedness, and humiliation is a moment of salvation for us. It invites us to be a human being, to recognize, embrace, and truthfully represent ourselves in all our fleshly physicality, our emotional complexity, and our frightened vulnerability.[9]

What is more, the resurrection validates the life Jesus led. In a sense,

9. Doug Frank, "Approaches to an Ethic of the *Real*," unpublished manuscript, 11.

through the resurrection God says to us, "This is the life to imitate." It is an invitation to live in freedom from the voices and powers that tell us we must mask our true humanity. God does not promise, through the resurrection, that if we will live as the true human we were created to be we will not suffer; quite the contrary, Christian existence as authentic loving humans in the midst of evil invites reviling and suffering. But the resurrection is a promise that in an ultimate sense Jesus has died for us, in our place, so that we are no longer enslaved to masking and hiding our humanity as a way to protect ourselves. We can freely live as authentic humans without fear. Life, not death, has the final word.

I have stated that at root there is a relational problem of alienation from God, others, and one's own self. Restored relationships of trust are the solution. As long as Ramon and Alba think of God as a stern demanding figure, however, they will feel alienation not trust, and the Christian family will not feel much different than the homes they grew up in. The cross liberates here as well.

Up to this I point have emphasized the humanity of Jesus. In Jesus, God has revealed to us what it means to be truly human, but as God incarnate, Jesus is also the ultimate revelation of God. So, when we point Alba and Ramon to the cross we are not just pointing to the salvation found in God's taking on the crucified experience they live; we are also pointing to the salvation experienced as the cross exposes the lie of our misconstrued images of God. Instead of a distant accusing figure all too willing to use his awesome power to punish human error, in Jesus God reveals himself to be accepting and forgiving, a God whose ultimate solution is not to destroy through awesome power, but to heal and restore by shouldering suffering that is not rightly his. When Ramon and Alba comprehend that the God they meet in Jesus and God the Father are the same God, we can imagine a fearful part of them relaxing and trusting.

The People of Flor del Campo as Crucifiers

We first reflected on Alba and Ramon identifying with Jesus as ones being oppressed, suffering, facing death. This is because I believe that if Jesus were walking the streets of Flor del Campo this is how he would relate to most people. He would not accuse them of failing to live as authentic humans, but he would invite and empower them to do so. Understanding more profoundly how their humanity is being crucified will naturally awaken Ramon's and Alba's awareness of people, forces, and systems that are crucifying them. To experience salvation fully, however, Alba and Ramon will also have to recognize that they themselves are crucifiers: that they crucify others, as well as themselves.

Jesus' Life and Death

Jesus' life and death were integrally connected. In the context of Jerusalem and the Roman Empire, Jesus' death on the cross was not an incomprehensible legal mistake that God had to orchestrate to satisfy the divine need for a death of a sinless person to balance legal ledgers in heaven. Jesus did not die through chance or misfortune. Jesus' life provoked hostility that led to his death. Jesus took the initiative to help others live as the humans God had created them to be. He lifted up many by countering self-crippling, alienating shame with loving acceptance. Out of love he also attempted to pull down those who tried to rise above others, to make others less so that they might be more. Jesus did more than just reach out to individuals. He confronted systems, practices, and beliefs at the heart of the society that stood as barriers to people living fully as humans in true family. For instance, as in Flor del Campo today, in Jesus' time many people drew strict religious boundary lines of separation and exclusion. Jesus challenged this line-drawing through word and deed. He clashed not only with religious leaders, but also with ideas the general population had about God. In contrast to seeing God as a righteous avenger who would bring glory to Israel and punish Israel's oppressors, Jesus revealed a God of incomprehensible graciousness who would include many in the kingdom of God whom others would deem as unworthy.

Certainly religious leaders had reason to see Jesus as a threat, but Jesus' subversive action reached far beyond the religious. As in Honduras today, the society of Jesus' Palestine provided clear status markers[10] that Jesus continually upended by treating with honor and respect those who lacked status. He did this not to raise them to positions of power and privilege, but to subvert the very structure of society that supported and perpetuated such distinctions. In first-century Palestine people gave and accepted gifts within families without concern for reciprocation. Outside of families, however, the norm was balanced reciprocity: the direct exchange of goods of approximately equal value within a relatively narrow period of time. Similarly, in Honduras today people keep track of favors given and received and seek to reciprocate, both to do what is proper and to avoid being beholden to someone else. In Jesus' Palestine another barrier to living as authentic humans in loving connection

---

10. This is not to imply that the two societies measure status in the same way. Also we must remember that status in Jesus' world (and to a lesser extent in Honduras also) was not simply a function of one's relative income or standard of living, but a complex of phenomena—religious purity, family heritage, land ownership, vocation, ethnicity, gender, education, and age. See Joel B. Green, "Good News to Whom? Jesus and the 'Poor' in the Gospel of Luke," in *Jesus of Nazareth: Lord and Christ. Essays on the Historical Jesus and New Testament Christology*, ed. Joel B. Green and Max Turner (Grand Rapids, Michigan: Wm.B. Eerdmans, 1994) 59-74.

with others was the patronage system: a system of relationships grounded in inequality between the two principals. Patrons had social, economic, and political resources needed by clients; in exchange, clients gave expressions of loyalty and honor useful to the patron. The patronage system is not as strong in Flor del Campo as it is in rural Honduras. It does, however, thrive in the political realm where the more powerful hand out benefits in exchange for the support of those under them, and in a general way people in Flor del Campo are still involved in relationships where those in need are controlled by "patrons" to whom they are indebted. The result, in Palestine as in Flor del Campo, is a never-ending circle of obligation, where the giving of "gifts" is part of a cycle of repayment and debt.

Jesus subverted the patronage system and practice of the balanced reciprocity by teaching his followers to give without expectation of return, and stating that among them the greatest would be servants of the least. In general, Jesus overturned distinctions based on social status as defined in the larger world and challenged people to accept the previously unacceptable as though they were family. This attack on the status quo, however, met resistance.

Residents of Flor del Campo feel trapped by a political and economic system that they experience as having helped the rich get richer even as the poor find it harder and harder just to buy food for their family. They talk disdainfully of government officials grown wealthy through corruption, but people in Flor del Campo feel powerless to change this situation that hinders their ability to live fully as human beings. The common people of Jesus' day had similar complaints, and some saw armed revolt as the solution. Although Jesus differed in significant ways from these revolutionaries, his proclamation of the coming of the kingdom of God and his critique of the rulers of the day provided sufficient political similarities with a revolutionary position that Jesus could be credibly presented as a threat to the Roman social and political order. His encounters with the devil and demons demonstrate that it was not just human rulers that perceived Jesus as a threat.

We may find it easy to praise Jesus' approach to life. Yet we must take very seriously the fact that his approach to life led the powers and people of his day to kill him. In Jesus, humans encountered God incarnate, and they rejected and killed him. Apparently the God Jesus proclaimed, whose kingdom Jesus introduced into human history, did not match the kind of God people wanted. The people of his day joined together and killed the human Jesus just as groups have found unity throughout the ages through violence against a common enemy. They rejected Jesus just as throughout history people have been willing to ridicule, ostracize or kill those who challenge the norms of a community's existence. Israel's prophets, we may recall, exercised a destabilizing force among the people, and the lot of the prophets was consistently rejection by the people to whom they were sent. Prophets are not the only ones who have suffered. Many people have hurt, stolen from, stepped on, and even killed neighbors because they saw it as a way to improve their own lot in life. In Jesus, however, people encountered not just another human, but God's own Son who lived in obedience to his Father and who faithfully represented God's purpose in word and deed. Here people encountered one who lived as a true human as God created us to live. And their response was to kill him. Enraged, they did to Jesus' humanity what they had done each day to their own: they killed it. As Margaret Alter writes: "Righteous rage insisted that . . . Jesus had to die, and he did die. The rage was not God's. It was human: our own. It was fear of losing control over . . . our own worthiness before God, our terrible fear of finitude."[11] In killing Jesus they killed God, their neighbor, and their true selves, and thus graphically displayed their alienation from God, others, and themselves.[12]

This three-faceted crucifixion–of God, others, and self–is repeated daily in Flor del Campo as people chose to think of God as a powerful, distant, and accusing figure instead of a merciful God who bears our pain. Crucifixion is repeated whenever people hurt and step on others, whenever people reject their true selves by grasping to be more than the finite human they are, or whenever they have been worn down to the point of living as less than the human God created them to be. As Gayle Gerber Koontz observes, "We humans sin when we contribute to corruption, distortion or breaches in what are intended to be Christ-like relationships to God, neighbors and the earth–when we foster foundational postures of 'being alone, being against, being above or being below,'...rather than "being with, being for, being together."[13]

The Cross as Mirror

We need to look at the cross not just in the sense of what *they* did in the first century, but as a mirror enabling our own honest look at how we express the same three-faceted alienation. When Ramon and Alba, together with other Christians, engage in this form of self-examination, they will see the sad truth that they were participating in their own deaths. Alba's attempt to end her own life was in this sense nothing less than a severe expression of the full

---

11. Margaret Alter, "Theological Insights as Therapeutic Interventions," *Radix* 26 (1) 26.
12. See Karl Barth, *The Church Dogmatics*, IV:1 (Edinburgh: T. & T. Clark, 1956) 399.
13. Gayle Gerber Koontz, "The Liberation of Atonement," *The Mennonite Quarterly Review* 63 (1989) 172.

extent of her self-destructive attitudes. The crucified are also crucifiers.

Evangelists in Flor del Campo often try to arouse people's feelings of guilt and fear, accusingly telling them that they killed Jesus, that they nailed him to the cross. I have sat with people like Alba and Ramon and together looked at the cross as a mirror of our lives and reality, not to scare them or to stir up feelings of guilt, but so that they might experience freedom from their crucifying ways. Of course in actual conversation I might use other words besides "crucifier" to help them recognize their self-alienation! Also, and very importantly, unlike the evangelists who talk about killing Jesus as a point of contact, a beginning, I would be sitting with Alba and Ramon to look at this mirror only after they have already begun to experience God's compassionate love for them as those who are crucified. Only then are they able and ready to experience the message of the cross as a word of judgment as well as of love.

Notwithstanding these qualifications, for Alba and Ramon to look at the cross as a mirror of themselves as crucifiers, and not just as the crucified, will hurt. It will be painful to see how cruelly alienated they have been from themselves, others, and God; and how ensnared they have been by powers and forces, like *machismo, marianismo*, religion, and society's imposed roles and status markers, that hinder authentic human life and stand as barriers to living as true family. It will be painful to see that through their own commitments and behaviors they have participated in the human dispositions and actions that nailed Jesus to the cross.

Looking at the cross in this way can bring to light how Alba's withdrawn quietness, self-rejection, and religious striving, and Ramon's macho strutting as well as his stooped acquiescence serve to fuel a cycle of mutual falseness between them and people with whom they relate. Grasping higher or hiding lower have only made the cycle of alienation spin with greater power.

When I sat with groups of people in Flor del Campo and looked at the cross as a way to illuminate our crucifying ways and our enslavement to the powers of death, we observed much more than is evident in Ramon and Alba's stories. We reflected not so much on people like drug dealers and corrupt politicians who are commonly labeled as "bad," but on people, much like those who actually killed Jesus, who would not look on their actions as evil. We talked together of the newly wealthy Honduran who sets up or takes advantage of structures that exploit others; or the faithful church member who self-righteously condemns her neighbor for her sporadic church attendance and tells her she is no longer saved since she cut her hair. We thought about a public health worker who sees the importance of the slow hard work of education, yet who continues, almost in spite of herself, to focus her work on projects that produce quick measurable results that demonstrate the effectiveness of her institution to the donors who support it. We mentioned the man who plots revenge to protect the honor of his family. And we spoke painfully of the woman who listens silently, staring at the dirt floor, as her common-law husband once again accuses her of not really going to the food cooperative meeting, but of seeing other men (even though in reality he is the one sleeping with other women). She is relieved he did not hit her this time. When he leaves to go to the bar she neatly irons his shirt and pants so that he will look sharp the next day, and so she will not feel the shame of people making derogatory comments about a wife who would send a man off with a wrinkled shirt.

These people would not likely interpret their actions as a consequence of alienation from God, themselves, and others, nor would they likely see themselves as formed by and enslaved to principalities and powers. More likely they would see their actions as necessary, normal, and appropriate, perhaps even good. Yet each act leaves them spiraling helplessly downward, trapped in a never-ending cycle of alienation. The combined effect of these "necessary," "normal," and "good" actions is the suffering and violence seen in Flor del Campo today.

We can draw together the two strands of the revelatory significance of the cross by returning to the account of Adam and Eve I used to define authentic humanity. The New Adam Jesus Christ reveals to us a human living without shame or fear as the pre-Fall Adam and Eve had lived. Jesus validates our finite humanness and invites us to live without masks. As God incarnate, on the cross, Jesus Christ reveals to us a God markedly different from the God that people in Flor del Campo live in fear of. In that the cross addresses a key element of our estrangement from God. Yet, as we have seen, Jesus as the New Adam and Jesus as God incarnate were rejected and killed. In this way the cross reveals to us and the people of Flor del Campo how we are children of the post-Fall Adam and Eve and deeply mired in sin. We are alienated from God, ourselves, and others.

At the cross, however, the New Adam does more than reveal and illuminate; he liberates. As Paul states forcefully, through this one man's righteous act all have the possibility of a new life of right relationship with God and others (Romans 5:18-21).

The Saving Significance of the Cross and Resurrection, Part Two

When actually proclaiming an atonement message on the streets of Flor del Campo there is little reason to separate and distinguish between ways the cross's saving action is revelatory and in what ways God acted objectively through the cross and resurrection to heal the breach between us and God. I have made the distinction to help us better understand both the scandal of the cross, and the depth and breadth of the saving significance of the cross and resurrection in a setting like Flor del Campo. I caution, however, against thinking too strictly in these terms. There are subjective elements in what follows, just as one could argue that there were objective aspects in the previous section.

How did God act to save us? Perhaps the simplest answer is the biblical statement that Jesus died for us; he died for our sins.[14] One way of understanding the meaning of these phrases is to recognize that those who killed Jesus acted out a tragedy we all are involved in. As we observed in the previous section Jesus proclaimed a message of radical graciousness and acceptance, and then lived out that message. Many, however, resisted and rejected the Kingdom of God as lived and proclaimed by Jesus. In response Jesus spoke words and parables of judgment. In doing so, however, he did not retract his message of unconditional love, of invitation to all to join him in table fellowship. He did not say, "You have not done what is necessary to achieve God's love and acceptance." Rather out of loving concern he warned them of the consequences to themselves, and others, of their rejecting God's graciousness and rooting themselves every more firmly in a society of tit-for-tat reciprocity, in a religiosity of status seeking and drawing lines of exclusion and, fundamentally, in a paradigm that mistakenly imagined a God of conditional love. They would suffer, as well as cause others to suffer, the very real punishments of that society and religiosity and live in fear of the "God" they believed in.[15] In his unrelenting gracious effort of love and inclusion, however, Jesus took on himself the fate that he had warned others about. Jesus had not sinned, but he bore the ultimate consequences of our sin, of our lack of trust in God. We can say Jesus died for us both in the sense that his death was directly caused by human sinful action, and because he entered into our situation and shouldered the ultimate consequences of an alienation that was not his but ours. He suffered in our place to save us from suffering the ultimate consequence of our sin.

How does Jesus dying as a result of human sin provide Alba and Ramon freedom from the alienation and enslavement that leads them to crucify God, themselves, and others? That question could be answered in a number of ways. I will explore three images that communicate the answer to this question in a way that matches up well with the Flor del Campo context. God in

14. For example: Rom. 5:6; 1 Cor. 15:3; 1 Thes. 5:10.
15. Raymund Schwager offers an insightful interpretation of Jesus' parables of judgment that contributed to my understanding of the rejection/judgment dynamic I describe in these two sentences. *Jesus in the Drama of Salvation: Toward a Biblical Doctrine of Redemption* [New York, NY: Crossroad, 1999] 53-69, 195-96.

Jesus Christ provides salvation through the cross by acting as a whirlpool-stopping-rock, by providing forgiveness, and by exposing the fallacy of the supposed dominance of the powers.

Stopping the Cycle

The people of Flor del Campo are trapped in cycles of anti-human and anti-family attitudes and actions. It is like they are in a huge whirlpool in a raging river, like the ones they have seen when storms transform the small river that twists through the ravine on the edge of their neighborhood into a raging torrent. Since their actions are rooted in alienation they end up kicking and thrashing in a way that makes the whirlpool spin faster and pull them down even deeper. For instance, both Alba's hiding for protection through quiet withdrawal and her religious striving left her less connected with herself, others, and God. To withdraw further or to adopt even stricter and more demanding religious practices only increased her alienation. Ramon's overly humble refusal to say how much he deserves for a day's work does not stop the whirlpool that traps him in oppressive poverty of body and spirit. His fear to stand up with dignity as the true human he is causes the whirlpool to spin faster. The bar room scene with Ramon attempting to hide his fear and insecurity with assertive violence provides the clearest example of this whirlpool dynamic.

One might think that Ramon's killing Jorge ended this macho maneuvering, but one of Jorge's relatives will likely act to defend the family's honor. As long as the men involved continue to live according to the macho definition of honor and true manhood the cycle will continue like a whirlpool in a raging river. The actions of trying to upstage another definitively, or to kill another, do not stop the whirlpool. They always and inescapably make it spin faster because they are part of the same current of alienation and insecurity that started the whirlpool in the first place.

Jesus' life reveals a freedom from this dynamic and his death on the cross breaks the cycle in a way that makes this freedom available to others. As we observed, Jesus confronted patterns, systems, and powers that hindered people from living together as a family of authentic humans. He did not simply promote a new religious option or political faction, nor did he just rearrange definitions of status and privilege. All those actions, although giving an appearance of radical change, would have merely redirected whirlpools, but not stopped them. As Vernard Eller observes, the only effective way to stop a whirlpool is to introduce a fixed point. A whirlpool dissipates quickly

16. Vernard Eller, *War and Peace from Genesis to Revelation* (Scottdale, Pennsylvania: Herald, 1981) 161-63. Eller borrows this image from Søren Kierkegaard and develops it in relation to the cross.

when it hits a rock that refuses to whirl.[16]

Ramon's shoving Jorge and Jorge's attacking Ramon with a bottle both caused the whirlpool to spin faster. Either one of them could have acted as a rock and dissipated the whirlpool by ignoring the shove or insult and leaving quietly, just as Jesus did in Gethsemane when he told Peter to put his sword away. That incident happens to line up well with this particular bar room example, but in reality most of Jesus' actions, which promoted life and resisted forces of division and death, can be understood as whirlpool smashing, whether healing a leper, responding to the woman caught in the act of adultery, teaching of the dangers of wealth and money, challenging the patronage system, or eating with those despised by society.

As we observed, Jesus' refusal to spin along in the same direction as others created tension and hostility. This came to a head at the cross when alienated people caught up by the principalities and powers attempted to put a stop to Jesus once and for all through bribery, falsehood, humiliation, and a shameful death. Jesus did not violently oppose those forces, but instead acted as a rock against which those forces might batter, absorbing the energy of the whirlpool and stopping it. In a definitive way the cross broke the cycle of increasing alienation and violence because it absorbed the worst act of violence in the world—the killing of God incarnate. God did not respond to this lashing out with a vengeful counterblow, but with forgiving love. The ultimate act of hatred was answered with the ultimate act of forgiving love.

Cycles of alienation continue to spin in our world. It seems that they are on display at every turn in Flor del Campo. But because of the cross's decisive whirlpool smashing affect Alba and Ramon, together with their Christian families know that whirlpools of sin are not ultimately the most powerful force and that, enabled by the Spirit of Jesus, they can resist their drag, and stand together as a rock that stops whirlpools.

Forgiveness

The saving significance of the cross reaches even deeper into life in Flor del Campo. Alba's and Ramon's alienation is not abstract. As crucifers they have concretely hurt others, God, and themselves. They are estranged from God, and this broken relationship with God leads them to live out alienating relationships with others and creation itself. Recognizing their crucifying ways through the illumination of the cross is helpful, but does not in and of itself restore the damaged relationships. Through the cross, however, God also takes the initiative and provides forgiveness, a key to restoring relationships.

At the cross humans acted out our unbelief and alienation. God experienced the worst that humans could do. Jesus suffered a humiliating and painful death, and God the Father suffered the loss of his son through that shameful means of execution. Yet on that cross Jesus said, "Father forgive them; for they do not know what they are doing" (Luke 23:34). When Jesus forgave those who crucified him, he forgave them not just for the specific act of crucifixion, but more profoundly for the attitudes and behaviors that had led to the cross. He forgave them for their rejection of the gracious God revealed by Jesus and the rejection of the true humanity modeled by Jesus. God, however, provides more than a decree of forgiveness. Through the resurrection Jesus returned to the disciples as a concrete forgiving presence intent, not on scolding, shaming or seeking revenge for their betrayal and desertion, but on reaching out in love and restoring relationships.

Of course, God had forgiven before, and Jesus had previously demonstrated a forgiving stance to his disciples and others; But the depth of the offense at the cross means that God's forgiveness of that offense also reaches down to the very depth of human sin–God has and will forgive the worst we can do. The powerful waves of that forgiveness extend to Flor del Campo today forgiving people for the acts of crucifixion repeated daily in Flor del Campo when people reject God, hurt and step on others, and reject their true humanity.

Forgiveness removes a barrier that stands between us and God. It is a step toward renewed relationship that starts with the graciousness of God acted out on the cross and through the resurrected Jesus. When God forgives Ramon, however, this is not an isolated event, an exchange between Ramon and God only. God's forgiveness marks the inclusion of Ramon in the family of God's people, and also calls forth from Ramon acts of forgiveness toward others.

Disarming the Powers

Paul writes of Jesus, "He disarmed the rulers and authorities and made a public example of them, triumphing over them in it" (Colossians 2:15). This affirmation has immediate relevance in Flor del Campo. The earthly leaders, as well as the principalities and powers that used them, certainly thought they had won the day when Jesus breathed his last breath. Paul is clear, however, that the crucifixion of Jesus has exposed the powers, revealing the delusion of their supposed dominance. It must have seemed ironic in Paul's day, just as it does in Flor del Campo today, but the witness of the New Testament is clear that, in the weakness of the cross the power of God is revealed. [17] Other

17. Note how in 1 Corinthians Paul writes of both the cross's perceived foolishness and weakness of the cross (1:18-25), and of its power to save and his specifically noting that had the powers ("rulers of this age") understood this they would not have crucified the Lord (2:8).

powers can only be labeled as pseudo-powers. Today in Flor del Campo the powers continue to act as if humans have no choice but to follow and obey, but their claim is a false one. Jesus has triumphed over the powers. The lie of the powers has been exposed by the cross. Therefore, humans can be freed from their influence when they come to recognize and to treat the powers as the mere "things" they are. People in Flor del Campo can resist powers such as: *marianismo, machismo,* materialism, the patronage system, and religious and social status markers that divide and separate.[18] Together with other Christians, Ramon and Alba can say "no" to the forces that shaped their lives in ways that hindered them from living authentically as family.

As is implied in the previous paragraph the image of the cross disarming the powers could be developed in relation to a number of enslaving powers in the context of Flor del Campo. The text of the second chapter of Colossians lends itself to talking about this theme in relation to the power of religion since Paul's statement of Christ's triumph over the powers comes within a discussion of religion as an enslaving power. The section leads off with principality and powers language in (2:8) and is followed up by a "therefore" (2:16) which then goes on to talk about the sort of thing I have categorized as enslaving religion and to which people in Flor del Campo could easily illustrate with examples from their lives. Religion accuses people in Flor del Campo of not measuring up, just as forces of religion defined Jesus as an outsider worthy of death. Through the cross, however, Jesus exposed the falsity of religion and in essence "erases the record" of misbehavior that religion accuses us of (2:14). Therefore we can understand God as forgiving us of our trespass of misconstruing our relationship to God and allowing religion to define how we establish that relationship (2:13), as well as erasing the legal demands that religion tells us we must comply with to be part of the people of God. God forgives us of even the ultimate trespass of crucifying the Son of God thus undermining the power of religion. How can religion place a legal bond against us for something God has forgiven? The bond imposed by the powers imprisons us in our trespasses making them bigger than they are even to God. God forgives our trespasses and exposes the lie of the power of religion. That is good news for Alba and others like her in Flor del Campo.

---

18. I have argued elsewhere on why it is appropriate to include forces like those listed in this sentence within the Pauline concept of principalities and powers (Mark D. Baker, "Responding to the Powers: Learning From Paul and Jesus" [M. A. Thesis, New College for Advanced Christian Studies, Berkeley, 1990]).

I began this section by saying that Jesus Christ died in our place and suffered the ultimate consequences of our sin. We have seen that in doing so on the cross Jesus entered into our unending cycle of violence and alienation and stopped it, not through overcoming it with power, but through absorbing its force. We also observed that Jesus bore the full brunt of our sin, yet responded with forgiveness, removing a barrier to our relationship with God. Finally I noted that through the cross and resurrection Jesus exposed the lie of the enslaving powers and removed them from their position of domination. These actions combined with the previously discussed subjective aspects of the cross and resurrection provide the possibility of new life in Flor del Campo: the possibility of living as an authentic human in a true family with others who have experienced the saving power of the cross and resurrection. In reality, today Alba is part of a Christian community, or what I have called family in this essay. I will end our discussion by briefly observing how she and a few others in this family have experienced the saving significance of the cross and resurrection.

Family Members Under the Cross

Although in certain situations Alba still struggles with her tendency to hide, the cross and the love she has experienced in a family produced by the cross and resurrection have helped her to blossom. Alba loves and has now opened herself to receive love. She shares her ideas in Bible studies, visits others who are hurting and in need. She has had the courage to go against the norms of marianismo and work alongside her husband in a shoemaking shop–an all male profession in Honduras.

For Mario, Alba's husband, through an encounter with the resurrected crucified Jesus he experienced forgiveness for past sins and restoration to the family of God. Mario has seen the lie of machismo and been freed to leave alcoholism and macho ways. He has become a caring father, a man not ashamed to cry, a man willing to ignore those who taunted him for not being able to supply his family's needs (that is, for not "keeping his wife in her place" when Alba started making shoes). He now participates in church, not out of fear of hell, but as a response to the love he has experienced from God including God's love expressed through others in the church family. Mario and Alba have also deepened their loving connection with each other and have invited neighboring couples to weekly get-togethers in their home where they all talk about their struggles in their families. Mario and Alba share from their experience of seeking to have a marriage characterized by honest vulnerability and mutual support.

Mario and Alba are not alone. Juan, another member of their church family, has spent years working to counter injustices and alleviate poverty through participation in various political movements and organizations, both Christian and secular. For Juan the salvific work of the cross and resurrection has helped expose the lies of both the forces that maintain his people trapped in poverty and the lies of quick-fix solutions administered by people sitting in plush offices. The cross and restoration to the family of God has provided Juan the hope and support necessary to stand against the current and work tirelessly at long term grassroots solutions.

And Arely has experienced the saving significance of the cross through its exposure of the lies of legalistic religion and the exposure of the false god she feared. Arely was quite active in a legalistic church, but as an older teenager she truly became restored to the family of God. She longed to feel like she belonged and was accepted by the other church members and God–the Father of the family. She lived under the burden of keeping all the church's rules, striving to become part of the select group that had leadership positions–the only ones she thought would get to heaven. The judgmental climate of that church was not the family she had hoped for. Through the cross she came to understand that God had taken the initiative to save her. Through the cross and resurrection she experienced God's forgiveness and restoration of the fractured relationship. The cross revealed to her that God was far more interested in loving her than in scaring her into compliance with a strict dress code. Through the love of God and the acceptance of others in God's family, Arely experienced a new freedom in a different church. Freed from fear and shame she emerged as a capable leader guiding others to experience God's love.

As these make evident, the salvific significance of the cross and resurrection is not grounded in a divine adjustment of peoples' legal status in record books in heaven. Jesus through the cross and resurrection provides us the possibility of living differently today, and God's presence with us through the Holy Spirit enables us to live out this possibility. This is not, however, something that can be done individually. It is not something that Alba, Mario, Juan, or Arely have done alone. To be brought into restored relationship with God is to be brought into a community, a family, the people of God.

This is not only a theological truth. It is a practical necessity. As the women and men in Flor del Campo who have experienced salvation begin to raise their heads and speak eye to eye with those supposedly superior to them instead of accepting the self-deprecating role assigned them by society, they will spark conflict and will need the support of a Christian family. The men or women who seek to live without putting on masks that provide the appearance of being more than human will experience insecurity and will need the support of others. Any attempt to live as the humans God intends us to be requires the context of a group of people who are doing the same thing, rather than a single person attempting to do it in a home, church, or work setting where others will respond according to the norms and standards of the day.

The cross and resurrection may have disarmed the principalities and powers, but most people continue to live in submission and slavery to them. It will take the strength and support of a Christian community to live in freedom from the powers; to reject the lies of the media and commercials that tell people that possessing things will bring them status and happiness; to resist the pressure of religion to draw lines of division and to view one's acceptance by God and others as based on following a list of clearly defined rules; to resist being so controlled by the spirit of an institution that one does not do what is best for the neighborhood or city, but what is best for the institution; and to resist the culture's definition of a "true man" or "true woman."

The cross and resurrection of Jesus Christ offer the possibility of restored relationship with God, with oneself, and others. They bring people in Flor del Campo into a family of loving support and loving confrontation that enables them to escape the burden of attempting to live up to the destructive ideals of machismo, marianismo, legalistic religion, and free them from the bondage of playing out the expected role of humilde people.

Conclusion

I invite you to respond to what you have read in two ways. First I invite you to reflect and meditate on how the facets of the saving work of the cross explored in this essay can help you to experience the gospel in a more profound way. Allow God's Spirit to work in areas of your life that have similarities with characteristics we observed in Ramon and Alba's life. How is it that through Jesus' life, the cross and the resurrection God can enable you to live a more authentically human way?

Second, I invite you to use not just one explanation of how the cross saves, but to use various images that together more adequately communicate the depth and breadth of the saving significance of the cross. In this article we saw how God worked through Jesus to provide salvation through the means of the cross that acted as a whirlpool-stopping rock, that provides forgiveness and that displayed as false the supposed dominance of the principalities and powers. You may use and adapt these images and develop others that relate to your context and experiences. I also invite you to ask God to reveal to you people around you who, like Ramon and Alba, are enslaved by powers of alienation and who need to experience the freedom provided through the cross.

I hope and pray that through reading this and sharing the message of the cross with others, you can experience in a more significant way genuine Christian community–what in this article I have called authentic family.

Appendix: Reflections on Contextualization

Why did Jesus have to die? Discussion of the atonement typically starts with that question. This essay, however, reflects a different approach. It begins by looking at the reality of a poor Honduran neighborhood and observing how hard it is for people to live authentically human lives and to relate to others in open and loving relationships: as true family. I then asked, what is the saving significance of the cross and resurrection in this situation? The approach is contextual not because it takes a single, predetermined, model of the atonement and translates and adjusts it so that it will be understandable in a different setting. Rather it is contextual because the context itself helps to determine which models and images are used.

To say that we begin with questions that arise from the social environment and allow those questions to influence how we talk about the atonement does not mean that the context has the final and ultimate word about the meaning of the cross. If that were the case the cross could too easily lose its scandalous character; it would lack any capacity to confront its culture. Rather, we must seek to talk about the atonement in a way that is profoundly shaped by the biblical materials and the history of theological reflection, and at the same time in a way that is shaped in a new context by the symbols and values that characterize this context. To proclaim the saving significance of the cross and resurrection is not, on one extreme, simply to repeat the narrative of the cross as this might be found in the Gospel of Mark or in the theology of Anselm. Nor, on the other extreme, can we proclaim the atonement simply by recounting life-episodes from a particular setting. Proclaiming the saving significance of the cross and resurrection requires that these two narratives be woven together, so that the relevance of the cross and resurrection for human salvation is brought to bear in circumstances where it can be heard and embraced as good news.

Of course, discussion that distinguishes too sharply between "text" and "context" is somewhat artificial. It is true that this essay begins with a particular social environment in a Honduran barrio, then inquires into the saving significance of the cross for the problems encountered there. Even so, I know that even the way I have framed the description of the problems is deeply influenced by our interactions with biblical texts and theological resources. My point then is not to privilege context or to pretend that in some "neutral" way we need to analyze the context. Rather, I hope that this article communicates the great value in taking a contextual, missional approach to our articulation of the atonement.

I believe that atonement theology must find its ground in the kind of depth and breadth of connection with people's lives to which this article points. I would argue, in fact, that we are much better off to think of communicating the atonement in a way that is enmeshed in narratives of Jesus' life and our lives, enmeshed in relationships, enmeshed in experience of Christian community, and talked about in a variety of ways consistent, then, with this form of embodied ministry. The totality of the saving significance of the cross cannot be communicated in one church service; rather, it can be and must be approached from various angles at different times.

PART SIX

ATONEMENT AND
NONVIOLENT VICTORY

Chapter Fourteen

THE NONVIOLENT ATONEMENT: HUMAN VIOLENCE, DISCIPLESHIP AND GOD

by J. Denny Weaver

Introduction

Questions of violence are a key element in turning atonement into one of the hotly perking theological topics of our day. A traditional understanding of atonement doctrine is that it responds to the question, "Why did Jesus have to die?" As my discussion unfolds, it becomes clear that I consider that question quite inadequate as an indicator of what should be the real concerns of atonement theology. The violence in the atonement discussion comes in several forms, from observations about violence embedded in the standard atonement images themselves to concerns raised by feminists and womanists about what the dangerous model of an innocently suffering Jesus implies for persons in abusive and oppressive contexts. Thus both theological and pastoral dimensions keep the question of atonement theology fermenting vigorously.

I believe that nonviolence is intrinsic to the story of Jesus. Thus nonviolence should be a constitutive, shaping element of Christian theology, rather than emerging as an issue to deal with after one has established the theological foundation or the framework on some other basis. A quick caveat: this statement does not reduce Jesus or the gospel to nonviolence. It does mean that any defining statement about Jesus or the gospel that does not have rejection of violence as a constitutive element is an incomplete statement about Jesus or the gospel.

My approach to atonement begins with the assumption that Jesus is normative for Christian ethics and Christian discipleship, which makes it imperative to deal with the violence contained in the standard atonement theories.[1] Given the intrinsic violence of the standard theories of atonement, which I will demonstrate briefly below, I am in the camp of those several individuals who advocate abandoning much of the standard tradition of atonement and

---

1. In fact, I believe it is arguable that the incorporation and rationalization of violence in Christian thought and Christian practice that entered the church in the fourth and fifth centuries is the most fundamental error in the entire history of Christian thought.

making a new beginning in discussing the saving work of Jesus. I recognize that one can never begin entirely new, without recourse to anything that has gone before. However, even as I am in conversation with the long history of the discussion of the work of Christ, and even as it is possible to locate my approach within one of the traditional categories, I have proposed a new image of atonement, one that is not built on any of the received theories. In so doing, I use the Bible—most particularly the book of Revelation but also the Gospels—in ways that do not appear in any other approach I am aware of, either ancient or modern. This new atonement image avoids the various forms of violence embedded in the standard theories, and it is an atonement image that undergirds discipleship to Jesus. It is a theology for living; it shapes Christian living. And beyond this pastoral dimension, this atonement theology impacts our understanding of God. It becomes clear, I believe, that the beyond the life, death and resurrection of Jesus, the discussion of atonement is actually a conversation about our view of God.

The paper develops the argument in three main sections. The first presents some presuppositions and preliminary considerations of content and methodology, which are inextricably intertwined. The following section sketches my new paradigm for nonviolent atonement, under the name narrative Christus Victor.[2] The final section then provides a few comparisons between narrative Christus Victor and the standard atonement images as well as engaging in supportive conversation with other recent efforts either to defend the standard views or to articulate a new approach to atonement.

Preliminary Considerations

My initial point may sound like a truism. It is that theology begins with the narrative of Jesus. In a general sense, all Christian theology refers to or explains the meaning of Jesus Christ, but I intend more than that basic affirmation. First, it means that the discussion of the saving work of Jesus—atonement theology—focuses not on the meaning of the death of Jesus but encompasses his life and resurrection as well as his death. This statement is not to deny the significance of Jesus' death. But rather than showing how Jesus' life and/or resurrection are compatible with the meaning of his death, I want to say that his life and resurrection are integral to his work. In other words, without the

---

2. To date, the most complete statement of this new paradigm is the book J. Denny Weaver, *The Nonviolent Atonement* (Grand Rapids: Wm. B. Eerdmans Publishing Co., 2001). There may be differences of nuance between this book and the essay in hand. Such differences, if any, reflect the ongoing development of the paradigm. The essay proceeds without a specific attempt to ensure complete consistency between the two, but the present essay is most certainly a continuation of the direction first charted by the book.

life and resurrection of Jesus, discussion of his saving work—atonement theology—is incomplete.

John Howard Yoder's well-known *Politics of Jesus*[3] developed the argument for taking Jesus as the norm for ethics. Identifying Jesus as the norm for theology is a further application of Yoder's argument. That theology begins with the narrative of Jesus means to take the humanity of Jesus seriously for theology. The corollary is that Christians should take the humanity of Jesus seriously because of the belief that the presence of God is found in Jesus.[4] Discussion of the salvific dimensions of the totality of Jesus' life, death and resurrection happens because it is the particular story in which God and the reign of God are present in human history. Extending the import of Yoder's *Politics of Jesus*,[5] I work from the assumption that theology and in particular atonement theology should reflect the narrative of Jesus just as Christian ethics is determined by the story of Jesus.

Further, identifying the narrative of Jesus as theological norm applies to theology what Yoder said about the priority of Christian commitment for ethics.

> The church precedes the world epistomologically. We know more fully from Jesus Christ and in the context of the confessed faith than we know in other ways. . . . The church precedes the world as well axiologically, in that the lordship of Christ is the center which must guide critical value choices, so that we may be called to subordinate or even to reject those values which contradict Jesus.[6]

This priority of a confessional claim does not negate other ways of knowing. It is rather an assertion that we understand these ways of knowing within the framework Jesus.

Insights which are not contradictory to the truth of the Word incarnate are not denied but affirmed and subsumed within the confession of Christ. Values which are not counter to his suffering servanthood are not rejected but are affirmed and subsumed in his lordship, becoming complementary and

---

3. John Howard Yoder, *The Politics of Jesus: Vicit Agnus Noster*, 2d ed. (Grand Rapids, MI: William B. Eerdmans, 1993).

4. This language is my paraphrase and adaptation of the language of Yoder, who was writing of the normativeness of Jesus for discipleship in several paragraphs that referred to his earlier *Politics of Jesus*. John Howard Yoder, *The Priestly Kingdom: Social Ethics as Gospel* (Notre Dame, Ind.: University of Notre Dame Press, 1984), 8–9. Yoder's discussion concerned ethics while my application in this instance is to theology, although as following paragraphs indicate, ethics and theology are integrally related.

5. Yoder, *Politics of Jesus*.

6. Yoder, *The Priestly Kingdom*, 11.

instrumental in the exercise of ministry to which he calls his disciples.[7]

To give one example, René Girard's theory of mimetic violence and scapegoating provides one important analysis of the function of violence in human society. At the same time, as Girard himself recognizes, developing an understanding of the salvific meaning of Jesus' life, death and resurrection does not necessarily depend on his theory.

Integral to this narrative of Jesus is his rejection of violence. Most evidently, the narrative concerns more than the rejection of violence, and the story cannot be reduced to the rejection of violence. But it is also true that omitting the rejection of violence results in an incomplete story. The question is then how to account theologically for this rejection of violence. If it is intrinsic to the story, as I believe it is, then it belongs at the beginning of theologizing as a shaping element rather than a secondary issue that finds a place—if at all—in a subcategory of standard theology. In my development of an understanding of atonement, this rejection of violence that is intrinsic to the story of Jesus is a criterion that exposes the intrinsic violence of received or standard atonement theology.

If theology has the same norm as ethics, namely the narrative of Jesus, then theology and ethics are integrally related. A simple image illustrates. Every person is oriented by and giving expression to a variety of commitments. These commitments may comprise any combination of a host of things—one's family, one's career, the nation, the nation's war effort, the Republican or Democrat party, a desire to be famous or wealthy, the Green Bay Packers who are omnipresent where I live, and much more. Actually, we live from a host of commitments simultaneously, with some having more importance than others. If we are Christian, then Jesus Christ should be the most important of those commitments, the supreme commitment that shapes all other commitments. Then the question becomes, How do we give expression to those commitments? Or, How does someone else know what our commitments are? These commitments are communicated in two basic ways—living them and talking about them. Ethics is the lived version of the commitments. Ethics consists of the practices by which we live out our commitments, ethics consists of commitments made visible by living them. Theology is then the words and images we use to describe those commitments. If one's ultimate commitment is to Jesus Christ, then the practices of one's life should reflect the story of Jesus while theology expresses the meaning of that story in words and images. In other words, ethics and theology comprise two versions or two forms of the same commitment. One might

7. Yoder, *The Priestly Kingdom*, 11.

ethics vs theology

Some work needed on action / other's words

both are needed

what of Jesus' threats?

see this image as akin to the common aphorism, "Actions speak louder than words." It would be incongruous to have a theology that purported to give the meaning of Jesus as Lord but to have ethics that were shaped not by the narrative of Jesus but by exigencies of the social order. Stated most specifically, since rejection of violence belongs to the narrative of Jesus, it would be incongruous to have theology that claimed the centrality of Jesus Christ but ethics that accommodated or defended the violence or the sword that Jesus rejected, or to claim a foundation in Jesus but to develop theology that rationalizes the sword he rejected.

Identifying the narrative of Jesus as the norm for theology has implications for the use of the entire biblical text in theology. The Bible was written by multiple authors over an extended period of time. This complex text reveals a conversation—which means disagreements—about issues related to sacrifice and atonement as well as about the nature of God. Identifying the narrative of Jesus as norm in no way implies the discarding biblical texts. It does mean that the entire biblical text is read through and interpreted through the narrative of Jesus. Given the conversation that the Bible contains, it is not required to turn every conceivable image into a theory of atonement; nor is it a goal of atonement theology to incorporate every conceivable utterance into an atonement theory any more than the Bible's stories of multiple wives obligates the incorporation of polygamy into our theology of marriage. While the entire canon is important and relevant and may be made use of in developing the context of atonement theology, the canon or the entire biblical text is not a norm for atonement theology on the same level as the narrative of Jesus through which the entire canon is read and interpreted.

Taken together, these preliminary considerations concerning the narrative of Jesus point to an attitude toward the received history of doctrine. This story constitutes a norm for evaluating the development of doctrines in history. The implication is that the history of doctrine in and of itself is not a norm for theology. Stated more particularly, the existence of a particular formula, or the fact that an atonement doctrine has been passed down to the present by tradition does not in and of itself obligate us to conserve and make use of that formula. Stated from the other side, the norm of the narrative of Jesus can and does call for the abandonment of some formulas.

With these considerations in mind, I move to sketch an understanding of atonement. More particularly, I will provide a reading of the narrative of Jesus that draws out its salvific meaning, which I call an atonement theory. This reading explains why the narrative of Jesus is important, and why we, that is Christians, want to commit our lives to living within it. At first glance, this reading may not sound particularly novel. However, when fully explicated it is quite challenging. To begin I simply recite a version of the narrative of Jesus, which I project as an image of atonement.

Constructing Atonement Theology

The Gospels as narrative Christus Victor

Jesus launched his public ministry in Nazareth when he read from Isaiah 61.1-2. His words signaled that his ministry had a strong social component, bringing "good news to the poor," "release to the captives and recovery of sight to the blind," and freeing of oppressed people (Luke 4.18-19). Throughout his ministry Jesus went out of his way to minister to outcasts like lepers and prostitutes. He paid attention to widows, orphans, and strangers—those without representation in the patriarchal society of first-century Palestine.

As the Gospels tell the story, Jesus carried on an activist mission whose purpose was to make the rule of God visible. This ministry had confrontational components. He plucked grain on the sabbath (Luke 6.1-5), healed on the Sabbath (Luke 6.6-11; 13.10-17), travelled through Samaria and interacted with a Samaritan woman (John 4.1-38), freed rather than stoning the woman caught in adultery (John 8.1-11), disputed with the Pharisees, cleansed the temple (Luke 19.45-47), and more. With such actions, Jesus confronted the purity code taught by the religious leadership. In contrast to the structures defined by the code and the religious leadership, these confrontations showed what the rule of God looked like. The reign of God valued women equally with men, valued the despised Samaritans as much as the majority ethnic group, sought restoration of relationships rather than punishment, and more.

Jesus healed people and he cast out demons—actions which show that the reign of God encompasses the created order. Jesus sent out the twelve (Luke 9.1-7) and then seventy (Luke 10.1-17) to "proclaim the kingdom of God" (9.2) and to say that "the kingdom of God has come near you" (10.9). The reign of God was near because in his person Jesus made the reign of God present. His acts, such as confronting the purity code, his healings, and his teaching, such as the Sermon on the Mount (Matthew 5-7), showed the comprehensive character of the reign of God for those who would live within it.

To complete the story, Jesus' actions to make present the reign of God in human history provoked opposition. That opposition increased to the point of wanting him eliminated. He was tried, condemned, and with the connivance of the religious leadership he was executed by the Romans, the highest political authority of the day. But according to the foundational doctrine of Christian faith, three days later God raised him. Jesus' story culminates with his resurrection from the dead. The resurrection is God's affirmation that the life and teaching of Jesus were the reign of God present in human history.

The acts and the teaching of Jesus show that the reign of God cares about the powerless—those without advocates in a given society. But equally as important as who Jesus identified with is *how* he identified with them. Those who would be Jesus' disciples will adopt his way of being on the side of the victims. Equally important as that Jesus confronted injustices is *how* he confronted them. Jesus' way of confronting injustice and uplifting the poor rejected violence as a way to alleviate suffering. As reported in Matthew 5.38-42, Jesus suggested turning the other cheek, giving the cloak with the coat when sued, and going the second mile. I accept Walter Wink's analysis, which interprets these injunctions as strategies of nonviolent resistance, which enable the victim of oppression to turn the tables nonviolently on an oppressor.[8] The following injunction about love of enemies is extremely important—it shows that the resistance strategies dare not become mere means to belittle an enemy, but are strategies for turning the situation in ways that preserve the humanity of those involved and keep open the possibility of restored relationships.

When Jesus was arrested, he forbade his companions to defend him with swords, rebuked Peter for using his sword, and healed the damage Peter had caused (Luke 22.49-51; John 18.10-11). Apparently Jesus chided those who arrested him for thinking that they needed swords and clubs. He had been teaching every day in the temple, where it was obvious that he could be taken without weapons (Luke 22.52-53). These observations indicate that rejection of violence belongs intrinsically to Jesus' witness to and making present the reign of God, which means that nonviolence is an intrinsic dimension of *how* Jesus' identified with and pursued justice for the suffering and oppressed.

Jesus' life and his teaching are visible and particular manifestations of the reign of God. In Jesus, the reign of God is present in human history. That is the meaning of incarnation: that in Jesus God and God's reign are present in human history. To be *Christ*ian, to be identified by and with Christ, means to join with and follow Jesus in his mission of witnessing to the peaceable reign of God. And to be *Christ*ian means to witness to the reign of God in the same

---

8. The sayings in Matt. 5.38-42 about not resisting evil, turning the other cheek, giving the cloak with the coat, and going the second mile have usually been interpreted as statements of passivity, of not responding to unjust actions, of commands for "nonresistance." As such, these commands would stand in tension with the activist confrontation of injustice in the interpretation of Jesus' life just sketched. However, Walter Wink has shown that the sayings of Jesus in Matt. 5.38-42 are actually tactics of nonviolent resistance by means of which seemingly powerless individuals living in economic exploitation or under Roman military occupation can nonviolently turn the tables on their oppressors. See Walter Wink, *Engaging the Powers: Discernment and Resistance in a World of Domination*, The Powers, vol. 3 (Minneapolis: Fortress Press, 1992), 175–84.

manner that Jesus did. The reign of God becomes visible in the world when Christians—people identified with and by Christ—live in ways that make the reign of God visible. The Christian calling—the mission of the church—is to carry on Jesus' mission of witnessing to and making present the reign of God in human history. I have just identified Jesus by means of a story. You could call it a narrative Christology. This story identified Jesus as one who makes the presence of God visible. This story used the Gospel account to identify Jesus by his actions—actions that make present and depict the character of the rule of God.

But alongside this narrative Christology, I also interpret this story as an atonement motif. My first point is to observe that there is no indication of any kind that the death of Jesus in this story satisfies anything.[9] The death in this story is produced by the forces that opposed Jesus. This death, produced by the powers that opposed Jesus, is clear evidence that their means differ from God's means that are made visible in Jesus, if God is truly present in the life of Jesus. Stated another way, nothing about the narrative just rehearsed turns it into a death needed by God to satisfy a divine need, whether that need is punishment demanded by divine law, or restoration of honor to an offended God, or restoration of distorted order of creation in God's universe, or restoration of worship that was wrongfully withdrawn from God. Those elements, lifted from some of the several satisfaction atonement theories, are simply not there when we rehearse the narrative of Jesus as given in the Gospels. These requirements of satisfaction are composed in some other paradigm and brought from somewhere else and placed on—imposed on—this story from outside.

The second point concerns the kind of atonement image the narrative presents. Recall the three-fold taxonomy of atonement doctrines given currency by Gustav Aulén's *Christus Victor*,[10] namely Christus Victor, satisfaction and moral influence. It is easily observed that the narrative just recited fits under the umbrella of Christus Victor, but with significant elements that clearly distinguish it from the classic version given credence by Aulén. One difference concerns the arena of the confrontation. In the several versions of classic Christus Victor, which is identified with Irenaeus and other early church Fathers, the struggle is cosmic and the victory of Christ is cosmic. Aulén does attempt to find the motif throughout the New Testament, but he has only one page on the Gospels, and his comments there focus primarily on the language

---

9. This point in agreement with Anthony Bartlett's analysis from a Girardian perspective. Anthony W. Bartlett, *Cross Purposes: The Violent Grammar of Christian Atonement* (Harrisburg, Pa, Trinity Press International, 2001), 189.

10. Gustaf Aulén, *Christus Victor: A Historical Study of the Three Main Types of the Idea of Atonement*, trans. A. G. Herbert (New York: Macmillan Publishing, 1969).

of Jesus' words about confronting Satan.[11] In contrast, in my version the first level of struggle between reign of God and rule of evil occurs not in the cosmos but on earth, where the life and teaching of Jesus as a whole engage the struggle. I am not denying the cosmic or universal dimension. Rather, I am arguing that the struggle begins in our history, in the life and teaching of Jesus. To emphasize its beginning in this narrative, and to provide a name for ease of reference, I have called my paradigm narrative Christus Victor, in order to distinguish it from the classic versions.

The beginning point in the narrative of Jesus, and the location of the confrontation in the life of Jesus in our history, brings to the fore a decisive contrast to classic Christus Victor. Its beginning point in the Gospel narratives makes eminently clear that narrative Christus Victor is not building on nor derived from classic Christus Victor, nor is it simply a variant of it. Narrative Christus Victor precedes the classic version. If a relationship exists between them, it is classic Christus Victor that is derived from narrative Christus Victor, having stripped away the narrative of Jesus and retaining only the image of cosmic triumph. Calling this narrative designation of Jesus an atonement image is not strictly necessary for understanding the story. However, the name narrative Christus Victor does serve a purpose—it shows the particular theological category in which we are thinking about the meaning of the story, and it provides a short-hand designation for ease of reference.

This sketch of the narrative of Jesus is one dimension of the biblical foundation for narrative Christus Victor. The book of Revelation is a multi-faceted statement of narrative Christus Victor that makes clear the cosmic dimension. As a by product of the discussion of Revelation for atonement purposes is the rehabilitation of the book for the cause of nonviolence and away from interpreters of several stripes who enlist it on the side of a violent God.

Revelation as narrative Christus Victor

The book of Revelation constitutes one of the most important components of understanding narrative Christus Victor as an atonement paradigm. Given the way the interpretation of Revelation suffers in common perception, I begin with a brief introduction on how to read Revelation.

It is more than obvious that Revelation uses a lot of symbols. The big question, to be decided fundamentally before one ever cracks the book, is where one will look to find the antecedents of those symbols. If Revelation is making predictions that are coming true in our time, as dispensationalists

---

11. Aulén, *Christus Victor: A Historical Study of the Three Main Types of the Idea of Atonement*, 75–76.

believe, then one is assuming that the symbols refer to things in our present age, things that we have read about in *Time* or *Newsweek* during the last
few months or years. However, Revelation was written almost 2000 years
ago, and in the first chapter the author clearly address it to churches in seven
cities in Asia Minor, located in what today is Turkey. If we take seriously
its address to those first readers, and if those first readers to whom it was
addressed were to understand it, then the antecedents of the symbols must
be located in the first century or earlier, where they could be understood
by the readers to whom the book was originally addressed. If its symbols
refer to entities in our time—such the European Economic Union, the UN
located in a building on a continent that was unknown in the first century, the
international banking and credit card system linked together by computers
invented in the last fifty years, the internet which appeared in the last two
decades, commercial air travel which is not a century old, political alliances
formed in the last 10 or 15 years, political entities in the Middle East that are
derived from late nineteenth- and early twentieth-century colonial practices,
and more—then Revelation is referring to a host of products and materials
entirely outside of and beyond the comprehension and frame of reference of
first century readers. And in this case, then, the book would be meaningless
to first century readers. In this light, it seems obvious that we should read
Revelation with the assumption that it was directed to readers in the first century, and that we should understand it in terms of a message directed to those
readers. And when we do understand its message to first century readers, as I
will make clear, it also becomes exceedingly meaningful and relevant for us
as well. And in the process, it emerges as an atonement motif.[12]

From among the classic images of atonement, recall the cosmic battle
version of Christus Victor. The twelfth chapter of Revelation features the
specific image of a heavenly battle between the forces of Satan, represented
by the dragon, and the forces of God led by the angel Michael. This is the
cosmic battle version of Christus Victor. This cosmic battle in chapter 12
follows the birth of a baby who was snatched up to heaven after the dragon
tried unsuccessfully to kill him. The image of the baby snatched up to heaven
clearly refers to the death and resurrection of Jesus, which means that the
woman with a crown of 12 stars is Israel that produced Jesus and then the
church that is identified with Jesus. The dragon is called "the Devil and Satan"
(Revelation 12:9). However, the seven heads and ten horns and seven crowns

---

12. For a somewhat longer discussion of these methodological considerations, see J. Denny
Weaver, "Reading the Past, Present, and Future in Revelation," in *Apocalypticism and Millen-
nialism: Shaping a Believers Church Eschatology for the Twenty-First Century*, ed. Loren Johns
(Kitchener: Pandora Press; co-published with Herald Press, 2000), 98–101.

identify it as a symbol of Rome. The seven heads recall the seven hills on which legend says Rome was built, while the horns and crowns represent emperors, which I will identify in a moment. This cosmic battle between the forces of God and Satan depicted in chapter 12 is then really an image of the reign of God in the *person of Jesus* confronting the evil of the world, symbolized by *Rome*. This confrontation is continued by the life of the church. The so-called cosmic battle of Revelation 12 is really imagery that testifies to the cosmic significance of the *real* confrontation *in history* between the Roman empire and Jesus and his church. Note that I have brought Revelation down to earth and located it in the first century. When we understand it this way, it is a book about Jesus, another Gospel. Identifying the historical antecedents of Revelation's symbols brings us back to the narrative of Jesus and the first-century church—except now that narrative is told in a way that portrays its cosmic significance. Revelation 12 is not a description of a cosmic battle nor a prediction of any kind of future events. It is an image of narrative Christus Victor, with real world, historical dimensions, which make clear that it both precedes and is distinguished from classic Christus Victor that features only an extraterrestrial, cosmic battle.

A similar interpretation applies to the seven seals in Revelation 6-7, which also casts additional light on the images of Revelation 12. I suggest that the seven seals correspond to the seven imperial regimes between the crucifixion of Jesus under emperor Tiberius (14-37 CE) and the reign of Domitian (81-96 CE), during whose rule the book likely was written. Each seal contains a symbolic reference to an event during the reign of the corresponding emperor.[13]

The "conquering and to conquer" of seal one is a subtle reference to the crucifixion and resurrection of Jesus, and the emperor rider's failed attempt to conquer Jesus. In seal two, the blood red horse and threat to take peace from the earth recall the threat to Jerusalem in 40 CE, when emperor Caligula (37-40 CE) commissioned a statue of himself in the form of the god Zeus, and ordered an army commanded by Petronius to occupy Jerusalem and to install the statue on the high altar of the temple. Caligula died before that order was carried out, and the city was spared.

Seal three has symbols of famine, which was widespread under emperor Claudius (41-50 CE), and cross-referenced in Acts 11.28. The double ugly riders and the multiple means of spreading death and destruction in seal four certainly represent emperor Nero (54-68 CE), whose reputation for cruelty is

---

13. For a detailed discussion of the seven seals and their historical antecedents, see Weaver, *The Nonviolent Atonement*, 20–28.

still remembered after nearly two millennia. Seal five shifts viewpoint from earth to heaven. The vision of the heavenly altar in the fifth seal parallels an eighteen-month break in the succession of emperors in 68-69 CE when three rivals—Galbo, Otho, and Vitellius—each claimed the imperial crown but did not survive long enough to consolidate power.

The imagery of astronomical collapse and earthly chaos and devastation in seal six has been frequently interpreted as a description of the end of the world. It is not. This imagery depicts an event in the historical arena of this world, but one which seemed like the end of the world to those who experienced it. In 70 CE, an army commanded by Titus, son of the reigning emperor Vespasian (69-79 CE), invaded Jerusalem and sacked the city. Images of celestial chaos and terrestrial pandemonium together symbolize the breakdown of order and the feelings of loss and devastation for the inhabitants—both rulers and commoners—when the army of the occupiers utterly destroyed Jerusalem and the temple.

Opening the seventh seal does not occur until chapter eight. The opening was followed by "silence in heaven for about a half hour." After Vespasian, his son Titus (79-81 CE) had a short reign as emperor. Domitian followed, ruling from 81 to 96 CE. Since the sequence of emperors ends here, it indicates that Revelation was most likely written during the reign of Domitian, with little of note to symbolize during the brief rule of Titus. The seven emperors from Tiberius through Titus and the total of ten emperors and pretenders constitute the seven crowns and ten horns of the dragon of chapter 12 that we examined just above.

The important point in interpreting the seals is that the worst events in the first century—culminating with destruction of Jerusalem in 70 CE—are not the end of the story. The entirety of chapter 7 also belongs to the sixth seal. Here one encounters the renowned image of the 144,000, which consists of 12,000 from each of the twelve tribes of Israel. 144,000 is obviously a symbolic number, obtained by squaring the number 12, which symbolizes Israel, and then multiplying by the large number of one thousand, a biblical figure used to mean "very large number." One thousand would have seemed much larger to a first century reader than to us in the computer age who routinely encounter extremely large numbers. One hundred forty-four thousand ought not be read as a number of mathematical precision any more than it is mathematically precise today when a busy person proclaims that she has "a million things to do." With the number 144,000, the author John has provided a symbolic way to display God's people, who descend from Israel, as a very large multitude.[14]

The vignette of the exceedingly large number of God's people descended from Israel is followed immediately by another "great multitude that no one could count" (v. 9), composed of people from every conceivable nation and tribe and language of the earth. When one understands the symbolic character of 144,000, it should be apparent that the two multitudes are comparable in size—each a symbolic depiction of the people of God, one emphasizing continuity with Israel, the other making the point that no ethnic or national group is excluded from the people of God. They proclaim that "salvation belongs to our God who is seated on the throne, and to the Lamb" (v. 10). In verse 14 the reader learns that this white-robed throng has "come out of the great ordeal" and their robes have been washed "white in the blood of the Lamb," and they are pictured as worshipping God "day and night" while the "Lamb at the center of the throne" protects them. The "great ordeal" could refer to martyrs generally but it may well be a specific reference to the devastation of Jerusalem by Titus' army. What does it mean that this worshipping throng is juxtaposed with the devastation so graphically depicted in the first scene of seal six?

That chapter 7 is four times longer than the scene of devastation indicates relative importance. More substantively, the juxtaposition of scenes of devastation and celebration displays the rule of God, revealed triumphant in the death and resurrection of Jesus, victorious over the worst imaginable devastation meted out by the forces of evil—symbolized by Rome. With eyes on the resurrected Jesus as the living and embodied representative of God, those who have come through the "great ordeal" of Rome, including the mayhem and destruction of Jerusalem, can celebrate life in the reign of God where salvation is found. This set of images is another depiction of what I have called narrative Christus Victor, with the symbols giving the cosmic significance of events involving Jesus and the first century church.

Revelation was written during a period of relative calm in the empire, without widespread persecution of Christians, and the churches in Asia Minor were perhaps becoming comfortable with a seemingly benevolent empire. In addition to and alongside the point about the victory of the reign of God over evil meted out by Rome as depicted by the sequence of seven seals, Revelation delivers a warning. It cautions readers in the seven churches not to be complacent and seduced by a tolerant-appearing empire. Remember the true

---

14. M. Eugene Boring, *Revelation*, Interpretation: A Bible Commentary for Teaching and Preaching (Louisville, Kentucky: John Knox Press, 1989), 130–31.

character of empire and what it is capable of doing, the message says.

It bears pointing out specifically that the images of Jesus in Revelation represent the resurrected Jesus. Begin with the vision of Christ in Revelation 1.12-20, a living, post-resurrection Jesus. When John heard the voice, and saw the magnificently arrayed figure who was "like the Son of Man," he fell at the figure's feet "as though dead." But the figure of Christ said, "Do not be afraid; I am the first and the last, and the living one. I was dead, and see, I am alive forever and ever; and I have the keys of Death and of Hades" (vv. 17-18). Of the many things to say about this vision of Christ, for present purposes the point is that this is a vision of the resurrected Christ. It is this Christ who lives forever and has the power of the keys.

Consider the vision of the heavenly thrown room in chapters 4 and 5. Following the fourth chapter's vision of worship around the heavenly throne, chapter 5 opens with the sight of the scroll in the "right hand of the one seated on the throne." After John's despair at thinking that no one could open the scroll, he is informed that the Lion of the tribe of Judah has "conquered" and earned the right to open the seals on the scroll. But then, to John's surprise, he sees the Lamb who takes the scroll and begins to open the seals. This Lamb is among the heavenly court around the throne, "standing as if it had been slaughtered." This Lamb obviously was slaughtered, as the heavenly host sings, but just as surely, the Lamb is now alive. It is the living, resurrected Lamb who proceeds to open the scrolls. The slaughtered Lamb, the slain Jesus, is the one lauded, but the Lamb designated in this manner is praised as a living, resurrected Lamb, who reveals the purposes of God as symbolized by the scroll in the hand of the image of God. It is to the living God and the living Lamb that the heavenly chorus directs its worship:

> "To the one seated on the throne and to the Lamb
> be blessing and honor and glory and might
> forever and ever!" (Rev. 5.13)

The refrain of blessing to the one seated on the throne and to the Lamb returns again in chapter 7, as the object of worship of the two throngs of the 144,000 and the countless multitude (5.10,12). It is the resurrected Jesus, and the God with whom he is identified, who are the recipients of the heavenly worship.[15]

---

15. This identification of the resurrected lamb—Jesus—and the one seated on the throne—God—in this depiction of narrative Christus Victor is one place to show the error of David Eagle, who claimed that narrative Christus Victor "enshrines violent conflict within God's own nature." David Eagle, "Anthony Bartlett's Concept of Abyssal Compassion and the Possibility of a Truly Nonviolent Atonement," *The Conrad Grebel Review* 24, no. 1 (Winter 2006): 67.

The vision of woman in labor, baby, and dragon in chapter 12 also features a resurrected Jesus. The snatching of the baby to heaven (12.5) in the vision of woman, dragon and baby is most certainly an image of resurrection. In terms of chapter 12, the heavenly battle follows the resurrection. The heavenly announcer proclaimed that the comrades have conquered the accuser "by the blood of the Lamb and by the word of their testimony, for they did not cling to life even in the face of death" (12.11). Such testimony does not make sense unless there is resurrection, and in fact the conquering—the victory—occurred with the resurrection, the snatching of the baby away from the jaws of the dragon. Revelation uses images with cosmic significance to depict the earthly confrontation of forces of reign of God with forces of reign of evil. Evil forces kill Jesus, but reign of God triumphs in resurrection. Revelation is a multi-faceted statement of what I have called narrative Christus Victor.

The victory of the reign of God over the forces of evil, symbolized by Rome that killed Jesus, occurs through resurrection. Of particular importance for the moment is to point out that this victory through resurrection is a *nonviolent* victory, that is, a victory without divine violence. Disciples of Jesus, the church, those who commitment themselves to live within the story of Jesus, participate in this victory as they continue his confrontation of evil in the face of adversity and even death. It is the resurrection of Jesus, signaling a future culmination of the reign of God, which validates the truthfulness of this confrontational witness.

That the victory through resurrection is a nonviolent victory is clear from observations of the narrative in the Gospels and in the symbols of Revelation, which portray the cosmic significance of that narrative. However, nonviolence is more than an observation extracted from the narrative. It is an intrinsically necessary characteristic of the victory of the reign of God. Dealing death to Jesus exposes the fundamental, mutually exclusive means between the forces of evil, symbolized by Rome, and the reign of God made present in the life of Jesus. The ultimate weapon of the forces of evil is death, which is an act that annihilates existence. Destruction of existence—denial of the capacity to exist— is the worst that the powers of evil can do to a human being. It is this denial of existence that the reign of God overcomes through resurrection. In order for the victory of the reign of God to be complete, the forces of evil must have free rein to do their worst. No subsequent complaint about limitations on their freedom can diminish the victory of the reign of God. That complete freedom for the powers of evil to act thus requires the reign of God to act nonviolently, that is, to act without responding in kind— with violence—to the action of the powers. Thus one sees the nonviolence of Jesus when observing the story of his life, but one can also note the intrinsic necessity of nonviolence in the manner in which the reign of God confronted evil. The powers of evil are afforded the freedom to deny Jesus his existence. It is this denial of existence that resurrection vanquishes, a victory complete precisely because evil was allowed to do its worst. The triumph of the reign of God depends not on God's capacity to exercise either retributive violence or the greatest violence, but on the power of the reign of God to overcome in spite of and in the face of the violence of evil.

Although the nonviolent victory through the resurrection appears clearly in the vignettes of the seals in Revelation 6-7 and the heavenly battle of chapter 12, the image of the rider on the white horse in Revelation 19 seems at first glance to present a different image. It is cited in a variety of contexts to display God's supposed violence and the ultimately violent character of God's judgment of evil.[16] Thus it bears pointing out the nonviolent character of that image. First, simply note that the rider's robe is dipped in blood *before* the supposed battle, and that his name is "the Word of God" (19.13)—two attributes that clearly identify the rider as the resurrected Jesus. Then note that no actual battle is depicted; rather the armies of the kings of the earth are defeated by the sword that extends from his mouth (Rev. 19.21), which makes it the word of God and not violence that defeats evil. This sword is the same one depicted for the resurrected, triumphant and reigning Christ in 1.16. Ephesians 6.17 and Hebrews 4.12 also used a two-edge sword as an image for the word of God. The vivid image of the rider on a white horse actually conveys a message about the nonviolence of the reign of God. It is another statement that in the resurrection of Jesus, the victory of the reign of God over evil occurs without violence. This image as well contributes to Revelation as a statement of narrative *Christus Victor*.

Mention of the rider of chapter 19 calls for a brief analysis of the culminating vignette of Revelation, namely the vision of the New Jerusalem in 21.10-27. As the New Jerusalem descends from heaven, the heavenly announcer proclaims, "The home of God is among mortals, he will dwell with them as their God; they will be his peoples, and God himself will be with them" (21.3). Thus the New Jerusalem is where God is, and one would expect it to be run as the reign of God is governed.

---

16. Three diverse examples are Albert Curry Winn, *Ain't Gonna Study War no More: Biblical Ambiguity and the Abolition of War* (Louisville, Ky.: Westminster/John Knox Press, 1993), 183–85; Karen Baker-Fletcher and Garth KASIMU Baker-Fletcher, *My Sister, My Brother: Womanist and XODUS God-Talk*, Bishop Henry McNeal Turner/Sojourner Truth Series in Black Religion, vol. 12 (Maryknoll, New York: Orbis Books, 1997), 106–8; Miroslav Volf, *Exclusion and Embrace: A Theological Exploration of Identity, Otherness, and Reconciliation* (Nashville: Abingdon Press, 1996), 276, 295–301.

Highly symbolic language depicts the city. It abounds with twelves, a number that symbolizes God's people. The city has twelve gates—three for each side of the city—with twelve angels at the gates, and the names of the twelve tribes inscribed on the gates. The wall of the city has twelve foundations, inscribed with the twelve names of the twelve apostles.

The dimensions of the city also abound in twelves.[17] It is a cube of 12,000 stadia per side. With one stadium being 600-660 modern feet, the cube that is the city would be about 1500 miles per side. But recall that one thousand means "very big number" so that 12,000 is a big symbolic number involving the divine twelve—and it seems obvious that the number is not meant to define a real dimension. The walls are built of jasper, the foundations adorned with precious gems, the city gates made of enormous pearls, and the streets paved in gold. Construction using these precious objects points to the value of the city, but may also show that the worth of these mundane objects pales before the real content of the city. This city is where God resides—the glory of God replaces the light of sun and moon and the Lamb is the lamp of the city.

This city, the New Jerusalem, provides the culmination of the book of Revelation. The important point concerning the city of the New Jerusalem is to know what it signifies. The seemingly obvious answer, given that it follows a judgment scene in chapter 20, is that the New Jerusalem is a vision of heaven. But I accept a different answer.[18] The New Jerusalem is a symbolic representation of the church living in the midst of the world. The cheering throngs in chapter 7 portray the supremacy of the reign of God over the worst that the powers of evil can generate. Now as the culmination of the book, the reader encounters a vision of the gloriousness of living as an inhabitant of the church that gives witness to the victory of the reign of God over against the evil that still abounds in the world. The vision of the New Jerusalem is a vision of the church as it continues the mission of Jesus to witness to the presence of the reign of God in the world. This vision completes Revelation as an image of the reign of God in Jesus confronting the injustice of the world—the atonement image I have called narrative Christus Victor.

For note, the powers and expressions of evil continue to exist right along with the New Jerusalem, whether one sees those evils in terms of direct

---

17. A reader has to recover those twelves from the footnotes when using the New Revised Standard Version, which renders the distance in miles rather than stadia. Other recent translations retain 12,000 furlongs or stadia.

18. The following discussion of the New Jerusalem draws on Wes Howard-Brook and Anthony Gwyther, *Unveiling Empire: Reading Revelation Then and Now* (Maryknoll, N.Y.: Orbis Books, 1999), 184–95.

threats to the church, or more likely as reminders of the character of even a benevolent-appearing empire. In words attributed to the one seated on the throne,

> It is done! I am the Alpha and the Omega, the beginning and the end. To the thirsty I will give water as a gift from the spring of the water of life. Those who conquer will inherit these things, and I will be their God and they will be my children. But as for the cowardly, the faithless, the polluted, the murderers, the fornicators, the sorcerers, the idolaters, and all liars, their place will be in the lake that burns with fire and sulfur, which is the second death (Rev. 21.6-8).

The point here is that evil doers are still present and surround the New Jerusalem. This point should jump out since the wicked were supposedly already judged and vanquished in the previous chapter. Since the wicked are still around with the New Jerusalem, it appears that the New Jerusalem is not a post-judgment vision of heaven, but a vision of the gloriousness of living in the church that participates in the life of the resurrected Jesus even in the face of the threat from Rome.

That the New Jerusalem is a vision of the church living in the world and not post-judgment heaven is reinforced by other comments. Following the statement that the glory of God provides the light of the city, one reads about who does and does not enter the perpetually open gates of the city.

> Its gates will never be shut by day—and there will be no night there. People will bring into it the glory and the honor of the nations. But nothing unclean will enter it, nor anyone who practices abomination or falsehood, but only those who are written in the Lamb's book of life (Rev. 21.25-27).

In other words, those who follow God and those who do not exist side by side, but only the children of God enter, that is, belong to the New Jerusalem. This statement does not concern physical boundaries. It depicts belonging, belonging understood in terms of loyalty and adherence to the rule of God. It is a statement about living in the resurrected Jesus versus being defined by loyalty to Rome. Do not be seduced, the image warns, by the seeming benevolent power of an empire not currently harassing Christians. Those who live within the rule of God are in the city and those who do not are not within the city. A similar observation applies to a sentence in the book's epilogue.

> Blessed are those who wash their robes, so that they will have the right to the tree of life and may enter the city by the gates. Outside are the dogs and sorcerers and fornicators and murderers and idolaters, and everyone who loves and practices falsehood (Rev. 22.14-15).

The idea is here clearly expressed that the faithful and faithless exist together in time, and those who wash their robes—apparently in the blood of Jesus—

may enter the city. This is given an even clearer expression by the reading of some ancient manuscripts which replace "wash their robes" with "do his commandments." The import of the text, and of the vision of the New Jerusalem, is to portray the joy and the glory of living in the reign of God in face of either the seduction or the threat of Rome.

This interpretation of the New Jerusalem demands an explanation of the binding of Satan for one thousand years and the seeming last judgment of Revelation 20. Briefly stated, this chapter uses images of time to portray the victory of the reign of God through the resurrection of Jesus.

The binding of Satan is not a new event, encountered only for the first time in Revelation 20. The "binding" for a thousand years is another symbolic reference—this time in terms of time—to the triumph of the reign of God over the evil perpetrated by the Roman empire. Since the "one thousand" really means a very large number—perhaps like a "zillion" in twenty-first century slang—this is one more image to portray the victory of the reign of God over the rule of evil. The resurrection of Jesus "binds" Rome for the unfathomably large expanse of God's time (a symbolic thousand years) in comparison to the limited time of Rome's power in human history (a very finite three and a half years). The binding of Satan parallels the defeat of the dragon in 12.9-10, resulting in a celebration of salvation that belongs to God and the Lamb in 7.10. Thus the supposed "millennium" of Rev. 20, which actually occupies only a small space in the book and appears only here in the Bible, does not refer to a specific period of history yet to be inaugurated. It affirms symbolically that regardless of the apparent power of evil abroad in the world, those who live in the resurrection of Jesus know that that evil has been overcome and that its power is already limited. When one considers the power of Satan from the perspective of the reign of God, Satan's power is indeed limited within the vast scope—a "thousand years"—of God's time.

Three-and-a-half as a symbolic reference to the limitation of evil's time appears more clearly when note is made that seven is one of the sacred numbers frequently used of things related to God. We read of seven flaming torches, which are the seven spirits of God (3.5), and of the Lamb, "with seven horns and seven eyes, which are the seven spirits of God sent out into all the earth" (5.6). Half of the sacred seven designates the earthly time that Satan harasses the church in Revelation 12.6. When compared with God's limitless time of a "thousand" years, Satan's time is short and finite: just three-and-a-half years or 1260 days.

The contrast in times—one vastly expansive, the other quite limited—emphasizes the limited and defeated power of the earthly representatives of Satan when seen in light of the resurrection of Jesus. During the symbolic three-and-a-half years, God limits Satan's power by preparing a place in the wilderness where the woman can be nourished, by providing the wings of the eagle with which she can fly into the wilderness, and by making the earth swallow the river that flows from the mouth of the dragon. Since the dragon represents Rome, the "millennium" text of chapter 20 proclaims yet another version of the message from the seven seals motif in chapters 5-7 and the woman and dragon of chapter 12. It is a message of encouragement to Christians confronting the power of the Roman empire. Revelation displays how transcendent reality differs from perceived reality. Christians therefore need not ultimately fear the suffering and destruction meted out by Rome, the earthly manifestation of Satan.

The text of judgment at the "great white throne" (20.11-15) shows that the choice between living in the reign of God and under the rule of Satan has consequences. It does make a difference where ones loyalties lie and who one serves. It is a choice about one's ultimate destiny. Surely after seeing the many images through Revelation of the victory of the reign of God in the resurrection of Jesus, any aware reader of Revelation will choose the side of the reign of God. To encourage that choice, the vision of the New Jerusalem in chapter 21 brings Revelation to a climax with a vision of the gloriousness of that choice for God.

Locating the message of Revelation in the first-century confrontation between church and imperial Rome does not undercut the idea of Jesus' return or a future culmination of the reign of God. The future still belongs to God. The culmination of the "thousand years" in 20.7-8 and the judgment at the "great white throne" (20.11-15) reveal what those who believe in the resurrection of Jesus Christ already know, that Jesus is Lord and that the reign of God encompasses all of reality. That future begins already in the New Jerusalem of chapter 21—an invitation to live within the reign of God that is already established on the resurrection of Jesus.

Narrative Christus Victor is an atonement motif that draws on the narrative of Jesus from the Gospels and the imagery of the book of Revelation, showing that they present two different perspectives on the same story. It is a story that portrays God's working in the world in Jesus. It is a story that invites our participation in it. It is a story of salvation. As sinners, in one way or another, we are accomplices with those sinful forces that killed Jesus.[19]

---

19. Two reasons make it important to underscore our participation in the forces of evil that killed Jesus. Theologically, it asserts universal sinfulness as well as stating the link that enables us to share in the victory of Jesus' resurrection over those powers of evil. Historically, it is important to lay responsibility for resistance to the reign of God and the death of Jesus on all of humanity, beginning with the Roman political establishment which had the final human responsibility. This

Jesus died making the reign of God present for us while we were still sinners. To acknowledge our human sinfulness means to confess our participation in the forces of evil that killed Jesus, including their present manifestations in such powers as militarism, nationalism, racism, sexism, heterosexism and poverty that still bind and oppress.

Because God is a loving God, God invites us to join the rule of God in spite of the fact that we participated with and are captive to the powers that killed Jesus. We cannot compensate for or undo our participation with the powers that killed Jesus. But God invites us to participate in the reign of God anyway. That invitation to participate in spite of our guilt for opposing the reign of God and collusion with the powers that killed Jesus is grace. It is grace because under our own power, we cannot resist and overcome the powers of evil. Only God can do that, and if we are resisting and overcoming, it is because God has enabled it and transformed us and in spite of ourselves brought us to the side of the reign of God. Some folks, particularly in the Reformed tradition, will want to call that invitation in spite of ourselves election or predestination. At the same time, we are free moral agents who are responsible for our actions. We have to make a choice whether to remain in league with the forces that oppose God or to accept God's invitation to join with the reign of God. Everyone indebted to the Arminian tradition will want to call that choice free will. Together these two impulses of divine call and human free will express Paul's paradox of grace: "But by the grace of God I am what I am, and his grace toward me has not been in vain. On the contrary, I worked harder than any of them—though it was not I, but the grace of God that is with me" (1 Cor. 15.10).

This invitation to join the reign of God envisions both those who are oppressed and their oppressors. When the oppressed accept God's invitation, they cease collaborating with the powers that oppressed and join the forces who represent the reign of God in making a visible witness against oppression. Although they may still suffer as a result of the struggle, they have ceased being victims who submit willingly to unjust suffering. And when the oppressors accept God's invitation, they cease their collaboration with the powers of oppression, and join the forces who represent the reign of God in witnessing against oppression. Thus under the reign of God as depicted in narrative Christus Victor, former oppressed and former oppressors join together in the saved life of witnessing to the reign of God.

universal participation in the death of Jesus specifically counters the claim that "the Jews" killed Jesus, which became the basis of anti-semitism through the centuries since Constantine. See James Carroll, *Constantine's Sword: The Church and the Jews: A History* (New York: Houghton Mifflin Company, 2001), 71–88, 175–76.

Narrative Christus Victor is an atonement motif that accounts for the life of Jesus, and in particular the nonviolence of Jesus that is intrinsic to his life. Discipleship belongs intrinsically to this motif—one experiences the salvation it offers by living within the narrative of Jesus that it presents. It is also the case that narrative Christus Victor avoids the problems of violence that have been raised in recent decades against the standard, received images of atonement.

The following section demonstrates how narrative Christus Victor deals with the problems of violence by putting it in conversation with other atonement images.

Atonement Image Comparisons

The significance of narrative Christus Victor as an atonement motif, in particular its character as a nonviolent motif, becomes apparent through some comparisons with the standard or traditional atonement images. Narrative Christus Victor does contain violence, but it is not God's violence nor violence sanctioned or needed or used by God. The violence in narrative Christus Victor comes from the side of the forces of evil that killed Jesus. In fact, it is the resort to violence that makes clear the differing modus operandi of reign of God and the rule of evil represented by Rome.

Gustav Aulén's *Christus Victor* gave currency to a three-fold taxonomy of atonement doctrines—Christus Victor, satisfaction, and moral influence theory. My use of three categories is derived from but not wholly dependent on Aulén's categories. Aulén distinguished objective and subjective views. I distinguish among the standard theories on the basis of the object or direction or target of the death of Jesus—aimed toward the devil, aimed God-ward or toward God, and aimed toward sinful humankind. Of course, there are multiple ways of envisioning the death aimed at each of the objects. The fact that narrative Christus Victor has no object for the death of Jesus distinguishes it from any of the standard views.

With one possible exception, all the standard atonement themes contain elements of divinely sanctioned violence. Contrast the appearance of violence in narrative Christus Victor with the violence in the classic version of Christus Victor. For the ransom theory, Jesus constituted the payment God owed to the devil in exchange for the devil's release of captive souls. In this case, the devil is the object of the death of Jesus. In this image, God sanctioned the devil's violence against Jesus as the price of freeing the rest of God's children from the clutches of the devil.

The exception to divinely sanctioned violence in standard atonement theories is the cosmic battle version of Christus Victor. In this cosmic confrontation, Jesus is not offered as a ransom and there is not an apparent "target" for his death. Rather, he suffers as a casualty of the devil's violence in the cosmic battle between forces of God and of the devil. This motif reflects the image of cosmic battle in Revelation 12. It can be said that the cosmic battle version of classic Christus Victor is the trimmed-down version of the reading of Revelation that forms part of the basis of narrative Christus Victor. In any case, cosmic battle Christus Victor is the one motif of the classic atonement images that does not feature some form of divinely sanctioned violence.

Contrast the appearance of violence in narrative Christus Victor with the violence of satisfaction atonement, the predominant atonement motif for much of the last seven or eight centuries. In the first section of *Cur Deus Homo?*, Anselm specifically rejected the ransom version of Christus Victor. He removed the devil from the atonement equation and made human beings responsible directly to God. For Anselm's satisfaction version, the death of Jesus is aimed God-ward in order to satisfy the offended honor of God. Thus Jesus does what sinful humans cannot, namely offer an innocent death to God in order to restore the honor of God. And since the devil is eliminated as an actor in this scenario, God remains for Anselm as the only actor with agency in the equation. Unavoidably, therefore, the satisfaction theory implicates God in the sanction of violence. Stated crassly, in satisfaction atonement, God orchestrates the scenario in which Jesus is sent to earth for the purpose of dying to satisfy the offended honor of God. God arranges the death of Jesus in order to satisfy, that is restore, the offended honor of God. When analyzed from a nonviolent perspective, it is apparent that satisfaction atonement depends on violent imagery—death is needed to satisfy God—with the attendant implication that the sanction on this violence is intrinsic to the character of God. God is the one who arranges for that death to satisfy God. This is intrinsically an image of a violent God or a God who sanctions violence. This image stands in contrast to narrative Christus Victor in which violence opposes God rather than being sanctioned or needed by God.

For satisfaction atonement, the object of Jesus' death has shifted from the devil to God.[20] This providing of Jesus' death in order to satisfy or restore the offended honor of God brings to the forefront a conundrum for the story of Jesus' death. On the one hand, the various figures who conspire to kill Jesus—the mob, some religious authorities, Pilate and the Roman occupation force—obviously oppose the rule of God. After all, they kill the one in whom God is present on earth. But on the other hand, in satisfaction atonement

---

20. Anthony Bartlett, using Girardian analysis, says that the shift from ransom theory to Anselm's satisfaction theory is a shift in the agent of exchange from the devil to God. Bartlett, *Cross Purposes: The Violent Grammar of Christian Atonement*, 76–86, esp. 83.

Jesus' death is needed as that which satisfies the offended honor of God. As a result, those who kill Jesus are actually acting according to the will of God, or assisting God in providing the death needed to satisfy God's honor.

Abelard agreed with Anselm in rejecting the idea that Jesus' death was owed to the devil. However, Abelard also had difficulty with the view of God in satisfaction atonement, namely God the judge, who judges whether sinners had made sufficient use of the merits of Christ's satisfying death. As Abelard's proposal has been understood, Jesus was given to die in order to display the great love of God for sinful humankind—divine love great enough to give God's most precious possession, the Son, to die as a sign of divine love. As it has become identified, the moral influence theory thus features the death of Jesus as a loving act of God aimed toward us. Sinful human beings are established as the object of the death of Jesus. Because of sin, humankind is alienated from God and fearful of God perceived as a judge. In order to show these sinners—us—that God is really loving and accepting, God the Father performs an act of great, infinite love, giving us his most precious possession, his Son, to die for us. When sinners perceive that love, according to this image, they will want to cease rebelling and return to the loving embrace of the Father.

In comparison with narrative Christus Victor, it also becomes apparent that the moral influence image does not escape divinely sanctioned violence. The display of God's love in moral influence depends on Jesus' death. It is the fact that God gives up Jesus to die—a death of one to show love for the many—that shows the intrinsic, divinely needed violence of this motif. It also contains the conundrum present in satisfaction atonement, namely that the people who kill Jesus both oppose and assist the will of God.

Protestantism shifted the emphasis in satisfaction atonement to produce penal substitutionary atonement. Jesus took the place of sinners and submitted to the punishment that divine law decreed for sinful humankind. In this motif it is not God's honor but God's law that becomes the object of the death of Jesus. Jesus submitted to the punishment required by God's law. But again with the devil removed from the equation, God is the agent who orchestrates the scenario in which Jesus is punished in order to satisfy God's law. Penal substitution thus emerges as a variant of the atonement imagery in which Jesus' death is aimed God-ward. Again one notes the contrast with narrative Christus Victor, in which God neither needs nor sanctions violence, as well as the problem of those who kill Jesus both opposing the rule of God and also exacting the punishment that God's law demanded. In contrast, rather than being what God needs, as in satisfaction and penal substitution, the violence in narrative Christus Victor is what characterizes the rule of evil that opposes the reign of God.

Violence that fulfills a divine agenda is not a factor for narrative Christus Victor. The saving element of narrative Christus Victor is resurrection and God's call that reconciles the sinner to the reign of God. Narrative Christus Victor has no need for a divinely orchestrated death in order to satisfy some demand—any demand—of a God who needs to be placated.

Another way to characterize the absence of divinely necessitated violence in narrative Christus Victor is to say that God is nonviolent or that the reign of God is characterized by nonviolence. Ultimately atonement theology is actually a discussion of our image of God—one who defeats violence with superior violence and reconciles sin on the basis of a violent death, or a God who triumphs over evil and reconciles sinners nonviolently through resurrection.

Other contrasts between narrative Christus Victor and satisfaction atonement are also enlightening. The high point, the necessary element from the story of Jesus for satisfaction atonement is death. It is Jesus' death that satisfies whatever element is lacking in the divine economy. In contrast, narrative Christus Victor needs the life and teaching of Jesus, since these are what identifies the reign of God for the would-be disciple of Jesus. Further, for narrative Christus Victor the culmination is not the death but the resurrection of Jesus, since that is the event which fully manifests God's presence in Jesus, and which fully validates the life of Jesus as the will of God. Stated another way, in any of the versions of satisfaction atonement, the ultimate purpose of Jesus' mission is to die. It is his death that satisfies the divine demand, however defined. Death also satisfies the divine agenda for moral influence. In contrast, for narrative Christus Victor, the mission of Jesus is to live. It is his life that witnesses to the presence of the reign of God in him and in the world, and that calls the would-be disciple of Jesus to immerse himself or herself in that life.

The contrasting places of ethics in narrative Christus Victor and in satisfaction atonement is significant. As implied above, ethical living—discipleship—belongs intrinsically to narrative Christus Victor. To be saved is to participate in, to be shaped by, the story of Jesus. It portrays an activist Jesus, who cares for poor people and people without clout in the political system. To be saved means to follow Jesus—to be his disciple—in caring about those same concerns. To be saved means to carry on the mission of Jesus to witness to and make present the reign of God in the world. This is the mission to which Christians are called. To describe narrative Christus Victor is to portray the story in which Christians find themselves, and which guides the life of discipleship. Compare this activist Jesus with the image of Jesus portrayed in any version of satisfaction atonement, in which Jesus' mission is to die in order to satisfy a divine requirement. This Jesus is an innocent sufferer who submits to unjust suffering because a higher order, namely God the Father, needs it. This aspect of satisfaction is the image that has proved so offensive for feminist and womanist writers. For womanists and feminists, to portray this Jesus as the model of discipleship for an abused woman is to advise her to submit to the abuse from her husband in the hope that such submission may change the spouse's violent behavior. I am in full sympathy with these writers who find this ethical implication of satisfaction atonement distasteful and who call for abandonment of satisfaction atonement.

A number of suggestions exist for defending satisfaction atonement and salvaging it from the charges of harboring or condoning violence. One method acknowledges the violence of these motifs but then develops proposals that proclaim either the usefulness of limited violence, which renders moot the presence of violence, or declare that the violence of the satisfaction motifs is limited to a divine mission and is therefore not to be imitated. Well-known authors who use these techniques are Richard Mouw and Hans Boersma.[21] Space permits only two brief comments. First, this sanction of violence stands in sharp contrast with Jesus' rejection of violence.[22] Further, if God is fully revealed in Jesus, then the God revealed in the nonviolent story of Jesus could not be a violent God or a God who sanctioned violence. The implication of these defenses of violence within satisfaction atonement is that neither theology nor ethics reflect the particular narrative of Jesus.[23]

Another commonly used strategy for defending satisfaction atonement is to accept one version as problematic and then to discover another, supposedly inoffensive satisfying motif. Penal substitution often emerges as the offending version. One suggested solution is to abandon penal substitution and to recover Anselm's original version, in which the concern is not punishment but some more acceptable concern such as the honor of God or

---

21. Richard J. Mouw, "Violence and the Atonement," in *Must Christianity be Violent? Reflections on History, Practice, and Theology*, ed. Kenneth R. Chase and Alan Jacobs (Grand Rapids, MI: Brazos Press, 2003), 159–71, and Hans Boersma, *Violence, Hospitality and the Cross: Reappropriating the Atonement Tradition* (Grand Rapids, MI: Baker Academic, 2004).

22. Boersma attempts to avoid this problem by arguing that every action beyond passive nonresistance involves violence. But defining every action as violence renders virtually pointless the discussion of violence. For a longer response to Boersma, see J. Denny Weaver, "Response to Hans Boersma," in *Atonement and Violence: A Theological Conversation*, ed. John Sanders (Nashville: Abingdon Press, 2006), 73–79.

23. These issues obviously merit more discussion and analysis that this essay allows. For a beginning of this discussion, see John Sanders, ed., *Atonement and Violence: A Theological Conversation* (Nashville: Abingdon Press, 2006). This book has essays from both Boersma and myself, along with responses from each author to the other, focusing primarily on the issues of violence.

restoration of creation.[24] A parallel suggestion argues that Anselmian atonement was not about a transaction, and therefore rejects any satisfaction atonement that features an economy of exchange whether of punishment or honor. Rather, the solution proposed is a satisfaction atonement in which the death of Jesus restores true worship to God on our behalf.[25] Yet another, related defense attempts to overcome the problem of the Son satisfying the Father or the Father abusing the Son by arguing that God was identified with Jesus so that Jesus was not satisfying the Father or the Father requiring something of Jesus, but rather on the cross Godself was bearing the burden of sin.[26]

Such adjustment of motifs does not solve the problem, however. There are more such defenses than can be addressed here individually, but once one has such defenses in mind, it is not necessary to address each one individually in order to address them as a whole. As long as the death of Jesus is aimed God-ward, one cannot avoid the implication that death is the means through which God enables reconciliation, and thus God uses or sanctions a violent death, nor the implication that the powers which killed Jesus perform a service for God and are thus functioning within God's will. Whether Jesus' death is a matter of restoring God's honor or holiness or the order of creation, or offering obedience or worship to God, the death is still directed God-ward. And that is true for any future efforts to find other emphases and nuances and redefinitions not yet contemplated. Changing the emphasis or definition within the framework of the satisfaction image does not deal with the implication of Anselm's deletion of the devil, which leaves God as the sole actor with agency in the salvation equation. One can distinguish Anselm's language from penal substitution, and one can claim that the death restores obedience and worship rather than restoring honor or paying a debt, *but* it is still death that accomplishes the saving work. Note that having God so identified with Jesus that Godself is on the cross bearing the burden of sin does not solve the problem—the burden God is bearing is still a burden that comes from God or God's justice and that is satisfied only by a suffering death. And

24. Two examples of this argument are Catherine Pickstock, *After Writing on the Liturgical Consummation of Philosophy* (Oxford: Blackwell Publishers, 1998), 156–57, and Peter Schmiechen, *Saving Power: Theories of Atonement and Forms of Church* (Grand Rapids, MI: William B. Eerdmans, 2005), 194–221.

25. Daniel M. Bell, Jr., *Liberation Theology After the End of History: The Refusal to Cease Suffering* (London: Routledge, 2001), 146–53; Daniel M. Bell, Jr., "Sacrifice and Suffering: Beyond Justice, Human Rights, and Capitalism," *Modern Theology* 18, no. 3 (July 2002): 344–54.

26. A recent example of this approach to atonement is Miroslav Volf, *Free of Charge: Giving and Forgiving in a Culture Stripped of Grace* (Grand Rapids, MI: Zondervan, 2005), esp ch. 4. The idea that Godself suffers and bears the burden of sin resembles the view that was called patripassianism in the early church.

also that people still have to kill Jesus in order for honor or worship to be offered to God on behalf of sinners or for Godself to bear the burden of sin. No amount of nuancing and redefining and reemphasizing this or that element will rescue satisfaction atonement from its intrinsically violent orientation, and from the image of God as the agent ultimately behind the death that satisfies God—because satisfaction in any form retains only God as the actor of agency to engineer the saving death of Jesus.[27]

Another common defense of satisfaction atonement appeals to the writings of Paul. Paul uses language that works within satisfaction atonement imagery, and it has been generally assumed that satisfaction atonement builds on Paul. I dispute, however, that Paul must necessarily be interpreted as the basis of satisfaction atonement, or that Paul's letters should be read over against the narrative of Jesus from the Gospels.

Narrative Christus Victor is developed from a reading of the Gospels and from the book of Revelation. For a variety of reasons I believe that one should interpret Paul within rather than against those New Testament bookends. In *The Nonviolent Atonement*, I based the discussion of Paul on J. Christiaan Beker and Raymund Schwager, neither of whom interpret Paul in terms of satisfaction atonement.[28] The earliest statements about Jesus in the New Testament appear in the sermons in the book of Acts, which tell how the apostles identified and spoke of Jesus in the first weeks and months after he was no longer with them bodily. These sermons, found in Acts 2.14-41, 3.17-26, 4.8-12, 5.30-32, 10.34-43, 13.17-48, use the same outline. It includes some version of statements that Jesus was killed, that God raised him, that this is the promised age or a fulfillment of scripture, that the apostles were witnesses to these events, and that the story calls for repentance and forgiveness of sins.[29] This outline identifies Jesus in terms of a narrative. The gospels expand this narrative. Paul called this narrative "the good news" that he had received and passed on, using it as the basis for his defense of a general resurrection in

---

27. Peter Schmiechen, *Saving Power: Theories of Atonement and Forms of Church* (Grand Rapids, MI: William B. Eerdmans, 2005), 2, 314 objects to the three-fold taxonomy of atonement theories given currency by Gustav Aulén. Schmiechen argues that not all theories fit under Aulén's three categories and suggests that there are at least ten theories. However the analysis here, which identifies the varying God-ward directed objects for the death of Jesus, shows that several of those he describes as individual theories belong to the conglomerate of satisfaction views, each of which features a God-directed death of Jesus.

28. J. Christiaan Beker, *Paul the Apostle: The Triumph of God in Life and Thought* (Philadelphia: Fortress, 1980), ch. 8; Raymund Schwager, *Jesus in the Drama of Salvation* (New York: The Crossroad Publishing Company, 1999), 160–69.

29. John Howard Yoder, *Preface to Theology: Christology and Theological Method* (Grand Rapids: Brazos Press, 2002), 54–56.

1 Corinthians 15. Further, I follow the analysis of John Howard Yoder, in his *Jewish-Christian Schism Revisited*, where Yoder interprets Paul as an interpreter of Jesus.[30] These pieces indicate that one should interpret Paul in line with the narrative of Jesus in the Gospels and Revelation.

Finally, in line with narrative Christus Victor I provide a brief exegesis of Romans 3.24-26, a text frequently cited as proof of Paul's congruency with satisfaction atonement. The verses:

> they are now justified by his grace as a gift, through the redemption that is in Christ Jesus, whom God put forward as a sacrifice of atonement by his blood, effective through faith. He did this to show his righteousness, because in his divine forbearance he had passed over the sins previously committed; it was to prove at the present time that he himself is righteous and that he justifies the one who has faith in Jesus.

Recall that the sacrifices of Leviticus happen in times of joy as well as failure. Therefore they cannot be interpreted as rituals that required blood as the necessary payment for sin. Thus even if "sacrifice of atonement" is modeled on Old Testament sacrifices, it need not be read in an Anselmian manner. One can understand sacrifice as a self-giving or re-dedication of self to God without it being any kind of payment or restoration of honor or worship to God. Moreover, Jesus' faithfulness even unto death did reveal his righteousness in the face of the evil powers—his righteousness became obvious in light of the treatment he received. The result of his self-giving death is reconciliation between God and sinners, when sinners come to accept God's invitation to join freely—that is, through grace—the reign of God. And as noted above, when God accepts that sinner into the reign of God, sins are certainly passed over, by grace, and the sinner's faith in Jesus reconciles that sinner to God.

This section has compared narrative Christus Victor as an atonement image with versions of standard atonement images, and engaged in conversation with a few of the efforts to defend the traditional images. These comparisons and conversations emphasized the nonviolent dimensions of narrative Christus Victor. The following section engages a different kind of conversation, a conversation with writers who share many of the concerns about violence in theology.

A Girardian Conversation

In contrast to efforts to salvage or refurbish the standard atonement images, I have identified a particular perspective—the rejection of violence in the narrative of Jesus—from which to evaluate these several theories. This

---

30. John Howard Yoder, *The Jewish-Christian Schism Revisited*, ed. Michael G. Cartwright and Ochs Peter (Grand Rapids, MI: William B. Eerdman's Publishing Company, 2003), ch. 3.

perspective allows for acknowledgment of the incompatibility of theories with each other, as well as providing the basis to challenge and abandon the received, traditional theories. On the basis of the rejection of violence in the narrative of Jesus, I also suggested a specific, new atonement image, namely narrative Christus Victor, which avoids the problems with violence.

However, narrative Christus Victor is not the only approach to atonement, which critiques the standard images out of concerns about violence and suggests a new beginning. My suggestion for a new beginning shares a number of points in common with the recent work of Anthony Bartlett and S. Mark Heim. Both Bartlett and Heim bring analysis shaped by René Girard's theory of mimetic violence and scapegoating to their discussion of atonement. I am in substantial agreement with them that the received atonement images are intrinsically violent, and we are in particular agreement in discovering the intrinsic violence of all versions of Anselmian and satisfaction atonement in that they make God the ultimate source of the violence exercised on Jesus. If recent suggestions on atonement are divided into two camps—those who want to refurbish a received version of atonement, whether Irenaeus or Anselm or Abelard—and those who seek a new beginning or to bring a new element to the table, with due allowances for the awareness that one can never fully begin tabula rasa, both Bartlett and Heim fall to the side of new beginnings, along with the effort to construct narrative Christus Victor. Beyond these important agreements, there are differing emphases and perhaps some disagreements between my view and that of the Girardians. The following offers a beginning of this conversation.

For Bartlett and Heim, the innocent, nonviolent death of Jesus exposes the violence of scapegoating. If Jesus had responded with violence, that violence would have been merely one more disruptive act that appeared to justify the violence of those who sought to kill him, and his death would have been one more scapegoat death in the repetitive cycle of scapegoat violence whose purported purpose is preservation of order in society. But the nonviolent, innocence of his death exposed the practice of scapegoating for what it is—the killing of an innocent person. Although using a different basis of analysis, the Girardians and myself have each articulated an understanding of Jesus' death in which nonviolence is a logical necessity.

I do not disagree with the conclusion of Bartlett and Heim, as far as they go. However, in my view, Jesus' mission was more than dying in order to expose the violence of scapegoating.[31] Jesus' mission was to witness to the

---

31. Heim certainly acknowledges as much, but nonetheless his book on the saving work of Jesus focuses on the salvific element of Jesus' death. S. Mark Heim, *Saved from Sacrifice: A Theology of the Cross* (Grand Rapids, MI: William B. Eerdmans, 2006), 134. This discussion brings to the fore

reign of God in history on earth, to make the reign of God and the very presence of God present on earth. This mission is short-circuited, along with the function of incarnation, if the focus of Jesus' saving work is a death in the abyss to escape scapegoating. It is Jesus' life that witnesses to and displays the character of the reign of God in human history. It is that witness, that way of living, that produced opposition which subsequently led to Jesus' death. However, the purpose of his life goes beyond dying to expose scapegoating. The purpose of his life was the living witness to the reign of God. The activity of his life demonstrated what the reign of God looked like—defending poor people, raising the status of women, raising the status of Samaritans, performing healings and exorcisms, preaching the reign of God, and more. Jesus' mission was not to die. He carried out an activist mission, to live and to bring life, to make the reign of God present in the world in his person and in his teaching, and to invite people to experience the liberation it presented.

Girardians refer to this making present of the reign of God by Jesus as positive mimesis or imitation of God. The difference between my view and that of Bartlett and Heim at this point is one of emphasis. Where I have emphasized the life of Jesus, with its liberationist elements, as revelatory of the reign of God, Bartlett and Heim see the death of Christ as the pinnacle of the revelation of victimage. However, both also recognize that Jesus' life cannot be divorced from his death. The resurrection as vindication thus points back to the life of Jesus as the model for discipleship, which would include the liberationist elements emphasized in my version. Even if it is differently emphasized, I agree with Bartlett and Heim that the resurrection is the vindication of the life and death of Jesus, that it is the eschatological event that vindicates the fully human Jesus which the Christian community is to follow.[32]

Although Bartlett gets to the point by a different route than I followed, I am in accord with him in asserting the nonviolence of Jesus, that Jesus confronted evil nonviolently, that this nonviolent challenge to evil renders prevailing atonement images untenable. I am in agreement that this story of

the question of divine intent in the death of Jesus. I discuss that issue in a following section.

32. See Anthony W. Bartlett, *Cross Purposes: The Violent Grammar of Christian Atonement* (Harrisburg, Pa.: Trinity Press International, 2001), 186–89; S. Mark Heim, *Saved from Sacrifice: A Theology of the Cross* (Grand Rapids, MI: William B. Eerdmans, 2006), 220. See also James Alison, "Resurrection Hope and the Intelligence of the Victim," in *Consuming Passion: Why the Killing of Jesus Really Matters*, ed. Simon Barrow and Jonathan Bartley (London: Darton, Longman and Todd, Ltd., 2005), 129, and René Girard, *I See Satan Fall Like Lightning*, trans. and foreword by James G. Williams (Maryknoll, N.Y.: Orbis Books, 2001), 187-91. In addition, it is the intent of the exegetical work on the Girard-shaped website, PreachingPeace at http://www.preachingpeace.org/ to explore discipleship to the risen Christ.

Jesus, whose death halted the cycle of mimetic violence, reshapes the meaning of God and sets out a new direction of transformation for those who identify with Jesus in this messianic event.[33] However, my different approach to the question of violence in atonement gives my theological construction some different emphases from Bartlett's.

Bartlett focuses on Jesus' death, while I have emphasized resurrection as the saving event, the sine qua non of this narrative. In my estimation, the focus on death provides a passive cast to the saving work of Jesus. Jesus' work was to face death nonviolently. Jesus did not retaliate. That act of nonretaliation, however, has a more active appearance when put in the context of Jesus' life as portrayed in the Gospels. Jesus ministered to women when that was unexpected, he travelled through Samaria when that violated strictures against mixing with the unclean Samaritans, he healed on the sabbath in violation of the purity code, he used sarcastic language, and more that could be named. I accept Walter Wink's analysis that interprets the sayings about turning the other cheek, giving the cloak with the coat, and going the second mile as strategies for nonviolent resistance.[34] This activist Jesus continues an already centuries-long practice of living as the people of God as a witness to the surrounding society, with Daniel and his three friends, Esther and Ruth serving as examples.[35] Thus the historical line in which Jesus stands extends far back into the Old Testament. The act that precipitated his death, the cleansing of the temple, was thus not a surprising event but one more action that challenged unjust practices and settings that violated the reign of God. Jesus' mission was to witness to, to make present in his person, the reign of God and the presence of God in the face of these injustices. It is in these actions that one sees the character of the reign of God on earth, in human conditions.

Killing Jesus was the ultimate assault by the forces of evil that opposed the reign of God. I agree with the Girardian analysis makes sense that his nonviolent death exposed and halted the cycle of mimetic violence and is a statement of abyssal compassion. But it was his life that was the revelation of the reign of God, with nonviolence an intrinsic characteristic of that life. And most of all, it was resurrection that revealed and validated that life as the very life of God. If the focus of being Christian is a life transformed by

---

33. Anthony W. Bartlett, *Cross Purposes: The Violent Grammar of Christian Atonement* (Harrisburg, Pa.: Trinity Press International, 2001), 224.

34. Wink, *Engaging the Powers*, 175–84.

35. John Howard Yoder, "Jesus the Jewish Pacifist," in *The Jewish-Christian Schism Revisited*, ed. Michael G. Cartwright and Ochs Peter (Grand Rapids, MI: William B. Eerdman's Publishing Company, 2003), 69–92.

the narrative of Jesus, which I believe it is, then that narrative validated by resurrection is the foundation of restructured atonement theology. But as just noted, the difference between my construction and that of Bartlett or Heim is that I place more emphasis on the exposition of the narrative of Jesus. Furthermore, as displayed in the account of the disciples on the road to Emmaus, encountering the resurrected Jesus does have the capacity to transform lives and empowers witness.

With Bartlett I can say that this witness of nonretaliation displays abyssal compassion, which is an invitation to uncoerced transformation. It is important to say that this transformation is uncoerced—only a nonviolent witness, which allows and accepts refusal as an answer, makes transformation genuine. Nonetheless, I believe that resurrection adds an additional element. Even when the cross displays the unconditional love of God in the abyss, when transformation is uncoerced it is still the case that nothing changes in the historical realm until a person makes that transformation. Resurrection changes that dynamic. One can still interpret the death in terms of a witness of nonretaliation that stops the cycle of mimetic violence, but resurrection means that something has indeed changed in the cosmos. Even if sinful humans choose to continue to participate in mimetic violence, the resurrection means that the reign of God has been vouchsafed as the ultimate power of all reality. This is not the objective transaction of Anselmian atonement, but it is a statement that the victory of the reign of God does not depend on the voluntary transformation of individual sinners.

In an article supporting Bartlett's proposal of a modified moral influence theory developed as abyssal compassion, David Eagle poses two challenges to my proposal of narrative Christus Victor. First of all, Eagle rejected the claim that narrative Christus Victor reflects a pre-Constantinian ecclesiology while Anselm reflects a medieval ecclesiology that has separated ethics from the narrative of Jesus. Eagle's evidence is a claim by Hans Boersma that finds the "roots" of the Anselmian tradition in pre-Nicean tradition, plus a rather dated statement by A. James Reimer that Nicea stands in continuity with the New Testament. Space permits only the briefest of responses. The most basic point to make is that it is widely recognized, I presume, that the early church did not espouse the sword and that later, by the late fourth or fifth century, the church came to accommodate the sword via justifiable war arguments, and by the end of the eleventh century it was advocating redemptive violence in the form of crusades. The arguments about Anselm (as well as about Nicene and Chalcedonian Christology) concern the various, overlapping stages in these developments to the eleventh century, points at which new stages became solidified, and so on.

Those who attempt to separate fourth century creedal theology from these developments, however the theological trajectory is traced, or to separate Anselm's satisfaction atonement doctrine from his medieval context, are attempting to separate theological development from the historical context of the writers of theology. Extremely interesting in this regard is Bartlett's description of Anselm accepting an invitation from a Norman knight, and eventually also in the company of Pope Urban II, to spend several days at ease, observing the siege of Capua "and assisting at a cruel act of war almost as entertainment."[36] I would argue that it is no more possible to separate theology from this historical context of the evolving accommodation of violence than it is to separate liberation theology from the context of Latin and South America where it developed or to separate Karl Marx's or Adam Smith's economic theory from their socio-economic contexts or to separate black theology from the context of enslavement of African Americans and ongoing racism in North America.

Another component of the argument such as Eagle's is the attempt to say that violence is not intrinsically a theological issue related to the story of Jesus. To that I simply say that we would not be discussing ideas of violence and theology if violence was not a problem of Christian theology generally and of the narrative of Jesus in particular.[37]

Eagle's second complaint is that narrative Christus Victor displays traces of a "divided, and hence violent, God." As I hope the above sketch of narrative Christus Victor has made clear, that charge is simply not true. I presume Eagle's error results from the fact that he assumes incorrectly that Bartlett's critique of Gustav Aulén's work also applies to narrative Christus Victor,[38] which I have taken pains to distinguish from the classic Christus Victor described by Aulén.

S. Mark Heim uses a thorough-going Girardian analysis in his book *Saved*

---

36. Bartlett, *Cross Purposes: The Violent Grammar of Christian Atonement*, 95.

37. In addition to the discussion of context in Bartlett, *Cross Purposes*, for other recent discussion of these issues see J. Denny Weaver, "Nicaea, Womanist Theology, and Anabaptist Particularity," in *Anabaptists and Postmodernity*, The C. Henry Smith Series, vol. 1 (Telford, Pennsylvania: Pandora Press U.S.; co-published with Herald Press, 2000), 251–79; J. Denny Weaver, "Renewing Theology: The Way of John Howard Yoder (Musings from Nicea to September 11)," *Fides et Historia* 35, no. 2 (Summer/Fall 2003): 85–103. For a very important discussion of the shift from a resurrection-oriented theology of the early church to a focus on dead Jesus and redemptive violence in the eleventh century, see Rita Nakashima Brock, "The Cross of Resurrection and Communal Redemption," in *Cross Examinations: Readings on the Meaning of the Cross Today*, ed. Marit Trelstad (Minneapolis: Augsburg Fortress, 2006), 241–51.

38. See the progression of Eagle's argument in the first three paragraphs of Eagle, "Anthony Bartlett's Concept," 67. Michael Hardin also recognizes Eagle's error in his essay in this volume, "Out of the Fog: New Horizons for Atonement theology."

from Sacrifice.[39] As was the case for Bartlett's analysis, much of Heim's analysis takes a different but parallel path to my own analysis of atonement violence. To name only a few points of confluence: I agree that maintaining silence in the face of violence makes its rule absolute;[40] that the Bible's story shows God siding with the outcasts and victims of violence;[41] that the error in Anselm's theology is that the death of Jesus is offered to God, which makes God the one who requires sacrifice and death, which in turn establishes God as the ultimate practitioner of scapegoating;[42] that we should decisively reject some theological formulations, such as violent atonement images;[43] and that it is possible to transform our perspective and understanding of the language of sacrifice by providing a nonviolent, nonscapegoat reading of it.[44] Where we differ is that Heim's solution is most concerned to transform our understanding of the standard language of sacrifice, whereas I take the route of advocating a new image.

I read the book of Revelation in a significantly different way than does Heim. For Heim apocalyptic literature pictures future violence, visualized on one of two paths—either as a result of increased frustration as the exposing of the scapegoat mechanism lessens that outlet for violence, or as divine vindication of victims that calls forth new forms of human solidarity. The apocalyptic passages in the Synoptic Gospels tend to picture the future apocalyptic according to the first path, with God rescuing the faithful from the chaos of self-destructing human communities caught up in cycles of destruction and violence. When divine judgment appears, it is in a form that focuses on "the practice of mercy and the avoidance of sacrifice." Apocalyptic violence takes the second form in Revelation. The image of the fifth seal has the martyred souls calling for vengeance, and Revelation 12 pictures a full battle on behalf of victims against the powers of evil. Violence from the human sides builds up as the exposure of scapegoating lessens its practice. The violence of "divine rectification" then looks like the "mirror image of the sacrificial forces whose destruction it describes." This future violence in apocalyptic literature is not a prediction, however. Beside these two violent apocalypses

---

39. S. Mark Heim, *Saved from Sacrifice: A Theology of the Cross* (Grand Rapids, MI: William B. Eerdmans, 2006). See also S. Mark Heim, "Saved by What Shouldn't Happen: The Anti-Sacrificial Meaning of the Cross," in *Cross Examinations: Readings on the Meaning of the Cross Today*, ed. Marit Trelstad (Minneapolis: Augsburg Fortress, 2006), 211–24.

40. S. Mark Heim, *Saved from Sacrifice*, p. 102.: *A Theology of the Cross* (Grand Rapids, MI: William B. Eerdmans, 2006), 102.

41. *Ibid,* Heim, 103.

42. *Ibid,* Heim, 299–302.

43. *Ibid,* Heim, 325.

44. *Ibid,* Heim, 326.

of self-destruction and climatic battle, Heim gives the final word to the New Jerusalem, a "new creation into which people are adopted," "a new contagion of reconciliation and peace to substitute for the unanimity of sacrifice." This new Jerusalem is not a future prediction, but that to which we are called now, but it comes with the sober realization that exposing of the violence of scapegoating "is compatible with the unleashing of new depths of violence.[45] In contrast to Heim, my reading of Revelation emphasized the historical antecedents and first century context of Revelation. As a result, rather than being an apocalyptic image that includes the divine violence of rectification and vengeance and picturing Revelation as primarily symbols, my reading location of Revelation in first century history uses apocalyptic imagery to give a message much closer to Heim's reading of Jesus from the Gospels.

I also pose an additional question for both Heim and Bartlett. The question concerns divine intentionality. According to my analysis, a flaw in all the standard atonement theories is the image of a God who intends that Jesus die or the image of a purposeful sending of Jesus in order to die. This divine intentionality is there whether it concerns the transaction with the devil in which Jesus' life is traded for the souls of sinners, the action of God to send Jesus to provide the death that satisfies the divine need (whether understood as restoring divine honor or the order of creation or obedience or worship), and the demonstration of divine love by the act of giving the precious Son to die in order to show love to the rest of God's children. Girardian analysis, which pictures Jesus dying in abyssal compassion or stepping into the scapegoat mechanism in order to stop it, successfully invalidates all of these exchangist or transactionist images of atonement. However, the Girardian perspectives walk right up to the line of divine intent (to suggest an image) without quite passing over it. When the intent is to show compassion and halt the scapegoat mechanism, that comes painfully close to the divine intention that Jesus should die, which allows the idea of a God who uses or sanctions violence in through the back door. This is a bothersome element of the Girardian analysis even when resurrection asserts that God overcomes this death and validates Jesus' life as the model of Christian discipleship.

Narrative Christus Victor also encounters the same question of divine intentionality, but I believe that it responds more satisfactorily than does the Girardian approach. If Jesus' mission was the life-bringing, life-affirming mission of witnessing to the reign of God as I proposed, then I cannot say that

---

45. *Ibid,* Heim, 263–70, quotes 266, 267, 268, 269.

his death was intrinsically necessary to the divine will. If God is fully present in the nonviolent life of Jesus, then one cannot posit a nonviolent Jesus and a God who sanctions violence or intentionally works through violence.[46] A God whose specific intent was that Jesus die, such as in sending Jesus on a mission of dying to expose the scapegoat mechanism is, in my view, uncomfortably close to a God who had a purpose in divinely intended violence.

However, from another perspective, using different images, it is possible to say that God willed for Jesus to die or that the death of Jesus fulfilled the will of God. Given the ultimate nature of the confrontation of reign of evil and reign of God that took place in the life of Jesus, the death of Jesus was inevitable. It was the ultimate character of the confrontation that made it inevitable. In order to avoid death, Jesus would have had to abandon—that is, fail—his mission. Rather than abandoning and failing, Jesus choose to die. Because God did not want Jesus to abandon and fail his mission, God willed that Jesus should die. But it was the circumstances of his mission, rather than a specific divine need for a death, that necessitated Jesus' death. In this formulation, Jesus' mission concerned his lived witness to the reign of God. His mission was to live in ways that made the reign of God visible and present. When this is his mission, it is possible to say that his death—even though inevitable—is the byproduct of carrying out his mission. And in that formulation, God is not willfully sending Jesus for the specific purpose of dying, but God nonetheless willed that Jesus die. If we truly believe that the nonviolence of Jesus is an intrinsic element of the reign of God, it is important to talk about the God revealed in Jesus in ways that do not visualize God in the position of intending or needing violence to achieve purposes of the reign of God, even as we believe that the death of Jesus fulfilled God's will that he remain faithful to his mission even unto death.[47]

A similar question of intentionality concerns Jesus' attitude to death. If Jesus' mission was to give living witness to the reign of God breaking into the world, then his mission was not to die. Jesus did not conduct his mission in such a way as to court death as the necessary end result; he was not on a mission to provoke his death. However, as I already noted, the ultimate

46. This is an application of standard trinitarian doctrine, pointed out in Yoder, *Politics of Jesus*, 17–18, and John Howard Yoder, "How H. Richard Niebuhr Reasoned: A Critique of *Christ and Culture*," in *Authentic Transformation: A New Vision of Christ and Culture*, ed. Glen H. Stassen, D. M. Yeager, and John Howard Yoder (Nashville: Abingdon Press, 1996), 61–65.

47. This discussion of divine intentionality responds to the analysis of Christopher Marshall, who sympathizes with narrative Christus Victor but argues for a specific divine intentionality in the death of Jesus. Christopher D. Marshall, "Atonement, Violence and the Will of God: A Sympathetic Response to J. Denny Weaver's *The Nonviolent Atonement*," *The Mennonite Quarterly Review* 77, no. 1 (2003 January 2003): 69–92.

character of his mission produced an ultimate response, namely killing him. From one perspective, as his comments in Gethsemane make clear ("My Father, if it is possible, let this cup pass from me" (Matt. 26:39), Jesus did not relish dying, and he did not want to die. Apparently he could have saved his life (Matt. 26.53), but that would have meant failing his mission. He chose to die rather than to fail his mission. Thus he could say, "No one takes [my life] from me, but I lay it down of my own accord" (John 10.19), and Philippians 2.8 speaks of his obedience to the point of death on a cross.[48]

Heim raised an interesting and important question concerning the extent or the kinds of violence that are exposed and opposed in the cross. He rightly argues that there are kinds of violence that can but do not necessarily turn into sacrificial violence—tax codes, economic structures and legal systems that favor some people over others, abortion, a police force, even war. Christians can oppose participation in these structures without making reference to the cross. (I would even add that there are rational reasons for opposing these structures that do not depend on theology.) Thus the question concerns the extent to which participation in all violence is opposed in the theology of the cross, a matter on which there is significant disagreement among theologians.[49] Heim suggests that at a minimum, this analysis of the cross offers "an understanding of sacrifice and an invitation to live without scapegoating. Therefore at the very least Christians must challenge any of these systems or practices, or others, when and insofar as they become instruments for that sacrificial violence."[50] I agree with that assessment as far as it goes. However, the greater use I make of the narrative of Jesus and in particular its liberating elements leads and allows me to say that the life, death and resurrection of Jesus call us to lead lives shaped by a commitment to nonviolence.

This conversation with Bartlett and Heim displays a number of parallel concerns about violence in theology between my approach that produced narrative Christus Victor and the analysis of these Girardian-influenced

---

48. This difference between pursuing death as a specific end versus accepting death as the result of Jesus' mission is perhaps illustrated by the story of Tom Fox, the member of a Christian Peacemaker Team delegation who was kidnapped and eventually killed in Baghdad. All members of the delegation knew the risks, but none of them went to Baghdad for the purposing of being killed. They were willing to accept the risk of death in order to carry out a living mission of peace. In the case of Fox, death was the result of his peace mission, but he did not journey to Baghdad for the purpose of getting killed, and the directors of Christian Peacemaker Teams did not send Tom Fox to Iraq for the purpose of dying.

49. For two views that represent perhaps the extreme positions on this question, see the essays and responses of Hans Boersma and myself in John Sanders, ed., *Atonement and Violence: A Theological Conversation* (Nashville: Abingdon Press, 2006).

50. S. Mark Heim, *Saved from Sacrifice: A Theology of the Cross* (Grand Rapids, MI: William B. Eerdmans, 2006), 254.

scholars. Our different approaches have produced parallel and complementary results. This result makes the obvious point that there is more than one way to deal with the violence in the standard images of atonement, and also that theology is always an ongoing conversation, whose results are always under discussion. But more importantly, the independence of these results, particularly for Bartlett and myself whose books appear nearly simultaneously and without awareness of the other, which arrived at complementary conclusions is a clear testimony to the importance of recognizing and dealing with the violence that is contained in the standard, received approaches to atonement theology.

In Place of Summary

This conclusion uses a brief commentary on the Parable of the Prodigal Son to summarize issues outlined in this paper.

In the familiar story, the prodigal son took his share of the family inheritance and squandered it. His life spiraled out of control until he hit bottom. The jolt of hitting bottom moved him to return home and proclaim his unworthiness. He threw himself on his father's mercy—and the father welcomed him back and proclaimed the grand celebration while the older brother sulked. Given the last 900 years of the history of atonement theology, what is not said about the attitude and actions of the father in the parable is as important as what is said in understanding what this story implies about atonement imagery.

Think about what did *not* happen. Satisfaction atonement in any of its forms assumes that some satisfaction is required for forgiveness, that forgiveness cannot happen until the debt to God is paid—whether what needs satisfying is understood in terms of divine honor or the order of creation or worship of God or the divine law. Modern legal systems model this assumption of the need for satisfaction before forgiveness can happen. But the father did not demand such a restitution or satisfaction. The father did not demand repayment of the money wasted before he could pronounce forgiveness. There was nothing of the father as a stern judge, who as a matter of justice demanded reparations or an act to restore family honor or an undertaking to restore the order of the family before the prodigal could return to the bosom of the father. The father did not demand that the son first undergo some form of punishment or "pay his debt to the family" before he could rejoin them. We do not see a father, whose attitude changed from stern judgment to merciful acceptance *after* reparations were paid. However, judging from the response of the older brother, we might infer that such actions are the kind of move that he thinks should occur. Thus the responses of the father and the older brother really do reveal two very different attitudes toward forgiveness, with the father of the story imaging God's forgiveness.

The story foreshadows our contemporary conversations about atonement theology. Picture the father in the role of God. The range of non-acts imagined above for the father, as well as any others we might come up with, are earthly, human acts and attitudes that mirror the numerous ways of envisioning divine satisfaction in the several versions of satisfaction atonement, whose roots can be traced to Anselm of Canterbury. The father forgiving without anything being restored or returned or without punishment being exacted but in response to an act of contrition by the prodigal, anticipates the atonement image I have come to call narrative Christus Victor.

When the son declared his unworthiness, the father proclaimed the beginning of the celebration that would mark the prodigal's return to the family. The father always loved the prodigal, even when he was a lost son. The father was continually waiting and eager to accept the prodigal, if and when he returned. And when the prodigal did appear in the distance, the father expressed what he had been feeling all along, namely that this was his child who belonged in the family. And he proclaimed a celebration to mark that return. The attitude of the father is shaped by presuppositions from what I have called narrative Christus Victor, while the desire for punishment and satisfaction reflects some version of satisfaction atonement.

A point to emphasize is that the father's forgiveness was not a declaration that the prodigal's behavior had no consequences, nor was it a declaration of accepting the prodigal "just the way he was." To experience the mercy of the father, the prodigal had to accept responsibility for his deviant behavior and make a change in his life. He left the path of estrangement and switched to the path of the family. And that is all that he could do—he could not reclaim the money that he had wasted, and nor could he undo the immoral things he had done with prostitutes. But he could change his life, and start to live morally from that point on, again in the bosom of the family. This change in the prodigal's life reflects the emphasis on discipleship in narrative Christus Victor. Accepting the prodigal home—forgiveness—did not mean pretending nothing had happened nor acting as though the prodigal had done nothing wrong, nor was it predicated on some form of restitution. In fact, when the father said, "The son that was dead is alive again; he was lost and is found," that is a very frank recognition of the son's sin. But when the prodigal confessed his sins, he was already forgiven—the father did not hold the son's past, which could not be undone, against him in welcoming the prodigal back into the family. This parable embodies much of the image I have called narrative Christus Victor.

Chapter Fifteen

THE CROSS: GOD'S PEACE WORK–
TOWARDS A RESTORATIVE PEACEMAKING
UNDERSTANDING OF THE ATONEMENT

by Wayne Northey

Introduction

"Atonement" refers to a theory (theology) about the effects of the death of Christ on humanity.

The New Testament employs several images to interpret the impact of Christ's death on the cross. Some are:[1]

- A conflict-victory-liberation motif called "Christus Victor." This was the title of a famous study by Gustaf Aulén (1969). Christ is victor over the "powers." A key Scripture is Phil. 2:9–11.

- One of vicarious suffering, mostly found in the Gospels. This arises from Jesus' self-understanding based upon the "Suffering Servant" songs of Isaiah, in particular chapter 53. Key Gospel Scriptures are Matt. 3:17, Luke 4:18–22, Matt. 8:16–17, Mark 10:45, 14:24.

- Certain archetypal images. Jesus, in his death is referred to as: representative man (Rom. 5:12–21; 1 Cor. 15:20–22, 45–49; Eph. 2:11–22), pioneer (Acts 3:15; 5:30–31; Heb. 2:9–19; 12:2), forerunner (Heb. 6:20), firstborn (Rom. 8:29; Col. 1:15, 18; Heb. 1:6; Rev. 1:5).

- There is also a martyr motif. Seven times the martyr-witness of Jesus is mentioned in the book of Revelation, such as Rev. 1:5.

- There is also a sacrifice motif that draws heavily on Old Testament sacrificial background. Key Scriptures are 2 Cor. 5:21 and much of Hebrews. This is a motif for understanding the nature of life in Christian community: praising God, doing good to others, living in communion with others, etc.

- There is an expiation theme with reference to the wrath of God. It is a dynamic related to living a life of forgiveness towards others. Some key Scriptures are Rom. 3:25; 1 John 1:7–2:2; 4:10–11.

- A redemption-purchase image picks up on the Old Testament redemption of Israel that is now a "new Israel" redeemed by Christ. A key Scripture is Rom. 3:21–26.

- Reconciliation, the restoration of broken relationships, what widely in criminal justice is known as "Restorative Justice," is another image. Key Scriptures are

---

1. From John Driver, *Understanding the Atonement for the Mission of the Church* (Scottdale/ Kitchener: Herald Press, 1986), pp. 15–36. Some of the following is also drawn from Driver.

Rom. 5:6–11; Eph. 2:14–16; 2 Cor. 5:17–20; Col. 1:20; 3:10–11, with reference to the new humanity of reconciled relationships and to the reconciliation of humanity with God.

- Justification as justice, righteousness, setting right, or making righteous are essential metaphors of biblical justice as in Micah 6:1–8, the high water mark of the Hebrew Scriptures' spirituality. Key Christian Scriptures are Rom. 1:16–17; Rom. 3:21–26.

- An adoption-family image is also part of New Testament revelation. Key Scriptures are Rom. 8:23; Gal. 4:4–5; Eph. 1:5–7; Gal. 4:4. They underscore the depth of intimacy in Christ's work, permitting God to be called "Abba," a deeply tender term of endearment. The entire prodigal son/father story of Luke 15:11ff is a powerful instance.

Beginning before the era of Emperor Constantine (early fourth century), but intensified during and since, the early church's emphasis on becoming "Christlike" shifted to becoming merely "Christian." This abstraction or legal fiction is based upon physical sacraments performed (baptism and Eucharist in the Catholic tradition) or an intellectual change of beliefs (justification by faith in the Protestant tradition). It allowed people to become "Christian" without really having to change anything about their lives, lifestyles or political commitments/actions/realities, not least without having to become "Christlike."[2]

Several factors emerged in the Church since the fourth century to buttress a movement away from understanding the work of Christ as, above all, a call to an ethical/political/lifestyle "imitation of Christ," a change of behaviour so drastic Jesus called it denial/death of self (Matt. 16:24 and *passim*), and Paul dubbed it "clothing oneself" with the Lord Jesus Christ (Rom. 13:14 and *passim*).

First, the onset of **rationalism** in the history of the church demanded that the various atonement images be wrestled into a coherent "dogma" that often put at arms' length the necessary change needed in one's personal *behaviour* in favour of changes only in one's personal/religious *rituals* or *belief.*

Second, there was change in **conceptions of law** away from an emphasis upon right relationships, maintained and restored, to one of retributive/punitive justice. Just desserts and punishments became the primary thrust of law in the course of Christian thinking rather than an understanding of a call to forgiveness and repentance. The dominant image of God became and

---

2. "The literal ethical components of Christ's saving work have gradually atrophied, and the transcendent aspects, especially of sacrifice and expiation which lent themselves more easily to sacramental expression, became almost exclusively the lens through which the saving work of Christ was viewed. The practical results of this Constantinian shift in the way of perceiving the atoning work of Christ soon appeared. Admittedly un-Christlike people could be assured of the benefits of the saving death of Christ, bereft of its power to transform" (Ibid, Driver, 1986, p. 31).

remains, in Western Christianity, the sentencing Judge.[3]

Third, the central preoccupation of law gradually came to be **guilt needing expiation** through punishment, rather than grace as undeserved gift. The setting for the jewel called law was grace, not guilt, biblically. Guilt is hardly a New Testament category.[4] But in Constantinian and post-Constantinian Christianity, guilt became the dominant setting for law, necessitating expiation or satisfaction for the wrong or sin committed.

Four Dominant Theories of the Atonement

In the history of the church, three theories of the work of Christ, the atonement, have been developed, according to John Driver, to which Charles Bellinger adds a fourth. They are:

1. Conflict-Victory (Christus Victor);
2. Satisfaction (Saint Anselm – 1033–1109);
3. Moral Influence (Peter Abelard – 1079–1142);
4. Penal substitution (John Calvin – 1509–1564, *et al.*).

The first was never systematized like the second; the third was systematized, but was eclipsed by the second, though Abelard was a younger contemporary of Saint Anselm; the fourth was developed during the 16th century Reformation.

The Conflict-Victory or Classic Dramatic or Ransom theory flourished between the second and sixth centuries, and was revived this century in particular through Gustaf Aulén's book, *Christus Victor* (1969). In this view, Christ the Victor fights against and overcomes the evil powers of the world. Sin as submission and enslavement to evil powers is overcome through Christ's death and resurrection. This view has known widespread revival in the West this past century, and "has always been foundational for the Eastern Orthodox tradition built upon the Fathers such as Irenaeus and Gregory of Nyssa."[5]

---

3. I have often asked in teaching on this: How many times did Jesus call God "Judge" in the Gospels? The answer is *never*. How many times did Jesus call God (nurturing, caring, and forgiving) "Father" in the Gospels? The answer is a staggering *170 times*!

4. Krister Standahl argued brilliantly that it is hard to find "any evidence that *Paul the Christian* had suffered under the burden of conscience regarding personal shortcomings which he would label 'sins'." Krister Standahl, "The Apostle Paul and the Introspective Conscience of the West," *Paul Among Jews and Gentiles* (Philadelphia, PA: Fortress Press, 1976), p. 82, italics in original. His entire essay,first published in English in *Harvard Theological Review*, 56 (1963), pp. 199-215, is a watershed in modern Pauline studies in reinterpreting Paul in the opposite direction of St. Augustine, as one with a very robust conscience and rarely plagued by guilt.

5. Charles K. Bellinger, *The Genealogy of Violence: Reflections on Creation, Freedom, and*

The Moral Influence understanding demonstrates God's matchless love. There is a strong ethical thrust based on Christ's life and death.

The Satisfaction theory has been seen as basic to Western orthodoxy and a non-negotiable pillar of evangelicalism in terms of its appropriation. Its essential logic is:

- Sin is transgression of God's law.

- God's honour is paramount, and sin takes away honour due God.

- Satisfaction must be at least equal to the sin committed (tit for tat):

> The main justification [for 'new concepts of sin and punishment based on the doctrine of the atonement'] given by Anselm and by his successors in Western theology was the concept of justice itself. Justice required that every sin (crime) be paid for by temporal suffering; that the suffering, the penalty, be appropriate to the sinful act; and that it vindicate ('avenge') the particular law that was violated. As St. Thomas Aquinas said almost two centuries after Anselm's time, both criminal and civil offenses require payment of compensation to the victim; but since crime, in contrast to tort, is a defiance of the law itself, punishment, and not merely reparation, must be imposed as the price for the violation of the law.[6]

The only satisfaction equal to the guilt of humanity is death, but it can only be offered if the person paying it is without guilt himself, argued Saint Anselm. Only Jesus fits this need, and he is furthermore God, and thus his expiation pays for all humanity. The logic is straightforward:

> Only God can complete this work of restoring his honor, but the work must be done by man: 'otherwise man does not make satisfaction'... Thus Christ makes the payment needed to restore God's honor and cancel the debt of the human race. His death satisfies God's justice and opens up the way of salvation once again, reestablishing the right and fitting order of the universe.[7]

This theory is set out mainly in forensic and commercial terms. In Anselm's day, the sacraments received made one the beneficiary of this expiation. For Protestants, faith leading to justification made one the beneficiary.

The satisfaction theory of Anselm, closely followed by the Reformers in the penal substitution theory, shows a central preoccupation with rationalistic scholastic theology in Western Christianity. It elicits two fundamental questions: Is the Bible primarily a book of timeless propositional truths and law codes, necessitating only categorization of its pronouncements to know exactly how to live or be damned? Or, is the Bible primarily God's Story

---

Evil (New York, NY: Oxford University Press, 2001), p. 134.

6. Harold J. Berman, *Law and Revolution: The Formation of the Western Legal Tradition* (Cambridge: Harvard University Press, 1983/1997), p. 183.

7. *Ibid*, p. 135.

inviting us to join our story to God's, so that on the way, we can learn how to live as God intended through imitation of Christ?

In the history of the Western Church since the era of Constantine, God as stern-moral-sentencing Judge eclipsed God as loving Story-teller, who weaves a transformative tapestry of faith, hope and love through the ages. All humanity and the entire creation are invited into God's grand gesture of ceaseless, elicitive and everlasting *love (hesed* in the Old Testament, *agape* in the New Testament)—God's ultimate words for the cosmos become flesh (incarnated) in Jesus.

Charles Bellinger presents a fourth view, "penal substitution," close to the hearts of the 16th century Reformers, easily confused with the satisfaction theory since they are strictly aligned:

> The substitution theory stresses the idea that Christ, the innocent one, took upon himself the penalty for sin that human beings deserve... The wrath of God the Father is turned away from us by being turned toward the Son on the Cross.

> The power of this vision has exerted great force down through history to the present day. It is seen particularly in the preaching of Protestant Christianity from the Reformation to Jonathan Edwards to Billy Graham.[8]

Commentary

On the surface of it, perhaps the most remarkable fact about Christian understandings of the atonement is the dominance of the satisfaction theory in Western Christendom.[9]

A character, Hans, in my novel, *Chrysalis Crucible*, agonizes:

> My conclusion from simple observation is that Evangelicals routinely practice an under-your-breath ideologized footnote theology that reads repeatedly, 'Except our enemies,' when quoting John 3:16 and all similar New Testament ethical teachings. How could Billy Graham tell the North Vietnamese that God loves them when he fully blessed his own country in displaying the exact opposite feeling—hatred unto death? How could he do this when he was still praying with the President for victory in the War, when he apparently willed the utter inversion of the Gospel regarding treatment of neighbor, enemy, and Creation?[10]

---

8. *Ibid*, Bellinger, pp. 136-137.

9. St. Anselm of Canterbury developed his satisfaction theory of the atonement against the dominant political background of feudalism in a book entitled *Cur Deus Homo–Why God Became Man*. God was the Feudal Lord of Creation, who could exact Ultimate Punishment/Satisfaction for humankind's sins only through sacrificing the perfect God/Man Jesus Christ. The 16th century Reformers developed this further into the idea of a "penal substitution" that saved humans from God because God took the punishment from God that humans deserved. This was against the backdrop of well-developed penal law preoccupied with what criminologist Nils Christie called "pain delivery." Cf. Nils Christie, *Limits to Pain* (Oxford: Martin Robertson, 1981).

10. Wayne Northey, *Chrysalis Crucible* (Abbotsford, BC: Fresh Wind Press, 2007), p. 397.

The short answer to Hans' questions is: because of the penal satisfaction view of the atonement. There is an enormous punitive dynamic in this doctrine that permits Christians, of course through "legally constituted authorities" (i.e. the state) to destroy its enemies. Judeo-Christian revelation says the opposite. One theologian writes, after concluding that the univocal New Testament ethic for both church and state is nonviolence,

> One reason that the world finds the New Testament's message of peacemaking and love of enemies incredible is that the church is so massively faithless. On the question of violence, the church is deeply compromised and committed to nationalism, violence, and idolatry.[11]

Columnist Matt Miller wrote ironically of Evangelicals' take on John 3:16, their all-time most quoted Bible verse, "For God so loved the world that he temporarily died to save it from himself. But none of that really matters because most people will be tortured for eternity anyways."

This was not the understanding in Eastern Orthodoxy, to which Matt Miller unwittingly points. Alexandre Kalomiros wrote in *The River of Fire*:

> Some Protestants consider death, not as a punishment, but as something natural. But, is not God the creator of all natural things? So in both cases, God—for them—is the real cause of death.

> And this is true not only for the death of the body. It is equally true for the death of the soul. Do not Western theologians consider hell, the eternal spiritual death of man, as a punishment from God?

> The "God" of the West is an offended and angry God, full of wrath for the disobedience of men, who desires in His destructive passion to torment all humanity unto eternity for their sins, unless He receives an infinite satisfaction for His offended pride.

> What is the Western dogma of salvation? Did not God kill God in order to satisfy His pride, which the Westerners euphemistically call justice? And is it not by this infinite satisfaction that He deigns to accept the salvation of some of us?

> What is salvation for Western theology? Is it not salvation from the wrath of God?

> Do you see, then, that Western theology teaches that our real danger and our real enemy is our Creator and God? Salvation, for Westerners, is to be saved from the hands of God![12]

---

11. Richard Hays, *The Moral Vision of the New Testament: Community, Cross, New Creation; A Contemporary Introduction to New Testament Ethics* (San Francisco, CA: Harpers, 1996), p. 343. This is likewise the conclusion of Willard Swartley in *Covenant of Peace: The Missing Peace in New Testament Theology and Ethics* (Grand Rapids, MI: Eerdmans, 2006), the most extensive theology to date on *peace* as central Gospel ethic in the New Testament.

12. Alexandre Kalomiros, *The River of Fire* (Seattle, WA: St. Nectarios Press, 1980), pp. 4–5.

In *Chrysalis Crucible*, the protagonist, Andy, muses about

> ... what it would mean to be the son of a feudal lord in some ancient time who fell madly in love with the beautiful daughter of a serf. The lord of the manor would finally approach the daughter's father at the repeated bidding of his son. "My son would have your daughter's hand in marriage," he would declare, and proceed with an announcement of all the arrangements to be made.
>
> He imagined if, when the father presented this to his daughter, she refused the son's intentions.
>
> "But you must understand," the lord of the manor would declare to the father, with his son present, "my son does love her greatly, and has a marvellous plan for her life that he cannot wait to unfold for her. *But*," his tone would turn menacing, "if she refuses my son's hand, then hear this: After a fixed time, which I forthwith decree as two months, if your daughter will not have my son's hand in marriage, then we have together agreed that she shall be subject to the most abject tortures and mutilations for three days, after which she shall be fully dismembered and thrown to the wild dogs."
>
> Then the lord and the son would withdraw to await the daughter's decision.
>
> Could it be truly said that the son ever loved the daughter if he could contemplate such retributive vengeance for not taking his hand in marriage? Could it ever be said that God truly loves us if He was perfectly prepared to exact everlasting conscious punishment upon us for failure to make a decision for Christ? "Once to die, and after this judgment." Could such love and hatred abide together in the same bosom? Did God love the whole world—except those, of course, He consigned to hell, whom he "loved" with a pure hatred?[13]

A few pages later we read:

> Andy pondered this for a time. "Janys," he began, "what would be one time of total contentment for you in your life? Think about that. I'm guessing one such is beyond memory, when you were a newborn child totally surrounded by your mother's warmth, love, and nurture. Think about the image of a newborn baby, Janys, of a mother's total care of and love for her. Then imagine God in that role. That fits what we know and say about God. Remember, Jesus wanted to gather the people of Jerusalem to himself like a mother hen gathers her chicks. Remember all those biblical images of God nurturing His people like a mother?
>
> "Then switch your imagination to a torture room in Central America, where that same little baby, now grown to mature adult, is stretched out on a cold mattress, is viciously raped and undergoes routine indignities beyond imagination. She cries out for the release of death, but that does not come. And the pain and torture are endless.
>
> "Now, can you honestly imagine the same mother in both roles, arranging for and superintending the second reality, no matter what the rationalization? Yet that is precisely what teaching you and I have been led to believe, that the same "god" who created us out of an enormous free act of love—who loved us so desperately that

---

13. *Ibid*, Northey, p. 552.

He gave 'His only begotten Son' to birth us a second time—somehow just as determinedly plans the most malicious eternal outcome imaginable if we do not *believe* in Him. In that case, Jesus dies *above all to save us from God!* That's crazy! It boggles my mind, Janys, that this has been taught for two thousand years! If this is the only way we can think about God according to the Bible, I'm checking out. It is sick beyond all human imagining! But the reason I say this now, Janys, *is precisely because I read my Bible!*

"Meanwhile, I have to hand out an evangelistic tract, as do you, about God's love for us that forewarns, at the same time, that any who reject Christ's offer *werden Schmerzen, Kummer und Pein erleiden in der ewigen Dunkelheit der Hölle.* That's what it says, Janys, in just about those exact words. That if we reject Christ we will experience everything that woman tortured in Central America experienced *in the eternal darkness of Hell.* And Dr. Harlow's book says the same thing: that if we reject Christ we will experience *Furcht, Trauer und Zorn.* Fear, sadness, and wrath, Janys. He quotes several passages from Matthew to prove it. That's what we're saying God is planning for each person who rejects Him! Do you really believe that? I don't. I can't. I won't!"[14]

A final scene from the novel finds Andy riveted by an epiphany while touring Dachau Concentration Camp:

Then a realization blasted into his consciousness like the imagined sudden blistering heat of those ovens at full burn: *Dachau is Christendom's most perfect human picture of hell!*

The parallels overwhelmed. *God is Hitler. The ovens are God's specially built chambers of eternal conscious torment,* to which human victims by the billions are fed because they refused to take the hand of the feudal lord's son in marriage. Jesus the Jilted Lover, whose cry of wrath echoed throughout the Corrupted Cosmos. Only unlike Daniel and his companions in Nebuchadnezzar's fiery furnace, these victims would experience the full suffering of the oven for ever and ever, God be praised, amen! For there even the worm "dieth not." This was Christendom's "god." This was Evangelicals' hell. This was what Billy Graham warned his listeners about... This was the deep dark open secret about... Bill Bright's, Evangelicals' "God who loves you and has a wonderful plan for your life."

"Nein!" Christendom, Evangelicals, Christians and Billy declared. But their eyes betrayed them. Deep down, they all said, "Yes!" This was the fundamental, fundamentalist, Evangelical footnote theology of John 3:16. This was the truth about their god: God is the Ultimate Sadist of the Universe...[15]

Herald Berman, in a magisterial work on the formation of Western penal law, writes:

However broadly Anselm conceived justice, reason required that he stop at the boundary of grace. God is bound by his own justice. If it is divinely just for a man to pay the

---

14. *Ibid,* Northey, p. 561.
15. *Ibid,* Northey, p. 577.

price for his sins, it would be unjust, and therefore impossible, for God to remit the price. In *Cur Deus Homo* Anselm's theology is a theology of law.

Before the time of Anselm (and in the Eastern Church still) it would have been considered wrong to analyze God's justice in this way. It would have been said, first, that these ultimate mysteries cannot be fitted into the concepts and constructs of the human intellect; that reason is inseparable from faith—one is not the servant of the other, but rather the two are indivisible; and the whole exercise of a theology of law is a contradiction in terms. And second, it would have been said that it is not only, and not primarily, divine justice that establishes our relationship with God but also, and primarily, his grace and his mercy; that is his grace and mercy, and not only his justice, which explains the crucifixion, since by it mankind was ransomed from the power of the devil and the demons of death—the very power which had procured the slaying of Jesus in the first place but which then itself was finally conquered through the resurrection.[16]

The satisfaction theory of the atonement led to brutal political realities in Western culture down to the present:

For the Church Fathers, it is the devil who—illegitimately—insists on the payment of the debt incurred by humankind. Anselm inverts this. Now it is God who, legitimately, exacts the payment of debt... In both Old and New Testaments an indebted person could be 'redeemed' by the payment of his or her debt. Jesus, following Deuteronomy, insists on the cancelling of debt as a fundamental aspect of Christian practice. Anselm, however, makes God the one who *insists* on debt. The debt humanity has incurred must be paid with human blood. The God who rejected sacrifice now demands it... From the start sacrifice and satisfaction run together... The God who liberates from law is now, in Anselm, understood as hypostasised, personified law... What remains... is a mysticism of pain which promises redemption to those who pay in blood. In this move a most fundamental inversion of the gospel is achieved, which prepares the way for the validation of criminal law as the instrument of God's justice instead of what it is in the gospel, an alienating construction which is at best a tragic necessity.

The penal consequences of this doctrine were grim indeed. As it entered the cultural bloodstream, was imaged in crucifixions, painted over church chancels, recited at each celebration of the Eucharist, or hymned, so it created its own structure of affect, one in which earthly punishment was demanded because God himself had demanded the death of his Son.[17]

In the belief that God would give God's enemies "Ultimate Hell" according to the satisfaction theory of the atonement, it was only a small step for Christians to authorize and to participate in the state's giving its enemies penultimate hell in the death penalty (with many forms of exquisite punishment and torture), and in war.

16. *Ibid,* Berman, p. 180.
17. Timothy Gorringe, *God's Just Vengeance: Crime, Violence and the Rhetoric of Salvation* (Cambridge: Cambridge University Press, 1996), pp. 102–103.

The exegetical problems of the satisfaction/penal substitution view of the atonement may be addressed under four considerations:

1. Penal theorists set God as object, not agent, of reconciliation. But God did not break with humanity; humanity broke with God (cf. 2 Cor. 5:18–20). God is not an angry deity like a feudal lord needing appeasement by expiation. Humanity, not God, needs reconciliation. The central text is the picture of God the Father in the Prodigal Son story (Luke 15:11ff), endlessly yearning for reconciliation with his son—a picture of us all, "like sheep [who] have gone astray" (Isa. 53:6).

2. There is hardly mention in the New Testament of humanity's guilt. The texts speak rather of humanity's separation from God. Likewise, in the Old Testament, "atonement" had to do with restoration of a broken relationship with God, not with guilt requiring punishment. "The central concern of the Anselmian theory for guilt and its removal would appear to find inspiration more in Western concepts of justice and punishment than it does in the Bible and its world of thought."[18]

3. Redemption is not, as in Anselm, freedom from indebtedness and punishment. Rather, it is liberation from the former master, sin, to freedom under the new Master, Jesus (Gal. 5:1). It is a change of lordship, not decree of punishment, that is in view.

4. Atonement is an historical cleansing, righting and healing of community and the earth:

> I often wonder why, when the Old Testament and the Gospels see atonement through the perspective of becoming clean from ritual uncleanness; when it is filled with so much about both becoming unclean and being an unclean person contaminating the community and the land, and with an elaborate system of atoning and cleansing administered by the priesthood; that now that the lamb of God who takes away the sin of the world comes, it is suddenly understood in a narrow forensic sense. That does not make sense to me. Anselm in a newly Norman world of power and control creates a contractual system of atonement, moving away from the relationship-oriented feudal one. The concept becomes more abstract and contractual from the 15th to the 18th centuries by the rapidly increasing influence of the emerging burgher class with its economic and utilitarian interests. The classical school of criminology emerges with a forensic rational choice theory (choice by the individual and reason to deter) and Kant's a-historical concept that punishment rights a metaphysical imbalance. It is about time that atonement theory is looked at in its historical context, and that we return to a biblical understanding of atonement, atonement as an historical cleansing, righting and healing of community and the earth. And what does it mean to say that 'It is finished'? It means: No more executions are needed for satisfaction to be satisfied.[19]

---

18. *Ibid*, Driver, p. 58.
19. Prison Chaplain Henk Smidstra, British Columbia, personal e-mail, Feb. 23, 2007.

Toward A Restorative Peacemaking *Understanding of the Atonement (Part 1)*

Hans Boersma has written a brilliant book entitled *Violence, Hospitality, and the Cross: Reappropriating the Atonement Tradition.*[20] There is so much to commend this book on the atonement, especially his appreciation of atonement as *recapitulation*, following Church Father Irenaeus.[21] Sadly, Boersma introduces a concept of "violence at the boundaries" into a reading of the atonement that simply is not in the founding texts.[22] I choose to discuss this book since it is perhaps the most sophisticated contemporary statement of violence in the atonement.

No one reads the Bible without ideological glasses. In Boersma's case, those glasses are explicitly the Reformed tradition, that I submit is *deformed* on the issue of violence. Timothy Gorringe uses the term "deformation of biblical faith."[23] This *deformation* tarnishes Boersma's superb work. It is helpful to explain why, since this has been endemic in Western theological studies on the atonement since Anselm.

Immediately in the preface, Boersma declares:

> This [Reformed tradition] comes to the fore in my re-evaluation of violence as something that is not inherently negative; in my insistence that boundaries can function in wholesome ways and need at times to be defended; as well as in my argument that restorative justice can only function if we are willing to include the notion of punishment.[24]

As one discovers in reading the entire manuscript, Boersma never becomes specific on these issues. Just how much or exactly what kind of state violence is "not inherently negative" is never indicated.[25]

---

20. Hans Boersma, *Violence, Hospitality, and the Cross: Reappropriating the Atonement Tradition* (Grand Rapids, MI: Baker Academic, 2003).

21. Boersma argues that "recapitulation" incorporates elements of all three of the traditional models (collapsing satisfaction theory and penal substitution into one). "Christ [takes] the place of Adam and of all humanity and as such [gives] shape to the genesis of a new humanity (*Ibid*, Boersma, p. 112)." But how? "This is where the three atonement models come in. As the representative of Israel and Adam, Christ instructs us and models for us the love of God (moral influence). As the representative of Israel and Adam, Christ suffers God's judgment on evil and bears the suffering of the curse of the Law (penal representation). As the representative of Israel and Adam, Christ fights the powers of evil, expels demons, withstands satanic temptation to the point of death, and rises victorious from the grave (Christus Victor) (*Ibid*, Boersma, p. 113)."

22. See also the essays in this volume by Hardin, Bartlett and Klager.

23. *Ibid*, Gorringe, pp. 81-82. Cf. a fuller quote below.

24. *Ibid*, Boersma, p. 10.

25. I have found in debates and presentations on violence in warfare, that my dialogue partners fall silent or become angry the moment it is suggested that they insert even one of their loved ones into the inevitable "collateral damage" of the civilian deaths picture, and still say that "accidental" killing of their loved one is a (mere) regrettable part of warfare. The stakes suddenly become

Boersma writes that "The exclusionary practices of the Christian Church, the violent suppression of internal dissenters throughout its history, and the collusion of the Church with the sword of the state all seem to illustrate the fact that violence, not hospitality, lies at the heart of the Church."[26] He says later: "Put provocatively, God's hospitality in Christ needs an edge of violence to ensure the welcome of humanity and all creation."[27] And again: "A tragic view of reality can hardly uphold non-violence as an absolute or non-negotiable standard but would have to recognize that violence lies at the heart of things and cannot possibly be avoided."[28] *With this line, he introduces perhaps the most ethically objectionable piece of ideology of the entire Reformed tradition*—and of most Western church traditions—one that stretches back theologically to Augustine in his formulation of the Christian "just war" tradition: *Realpolitik.* Notice that he did not claim that "violence lies at the heart of biblical Kingdom witness," for such is simply false. Over against biblical revelation, *Realpolitik,* to which rival revelation Boersma points as moral lodestar, claims that human institutions from state governments to Microsoft to Church, are indeed "fallen," "sinful," and "under God's judgment." But they're all we have, and they will not change this side of Kingdom Come, especially the violence endemic to them, to all human culture. "So if we can't beat 'em, join 'em!"[29]

I suggest that the fundamental political error of Reformed and most Western church traditions is that they choose to serve both God and *Realpolitik.* As with mammon (money), God brooks no rival (Matt. 6:24; Luke 16:13).

---

personal. Are we, in defence of "just war," so anesthetized to believe no one's loved ones are ever sacrificed in "collateral damage" from warfare? I suggest that in company with others, Boersma is okay with violence at the boundaries so long as he and his loved ones are not impacted—so far an almost exclusive luxury of North American existence. Raising this consideration is strategically a conversation stopper, the Ultimate Trump Card.

Since the introduction of aerial warfare in World War I, the civilian death rate in warfare has not surprisingly soared. Tami Biddle wrote that when aerial warfare was still only imagined in the 19th century, it meant "English-speaking peoples raining incendiary bombs over the enemy to impose the customs of civilization." Tami Biddle, *Rhetoric and Reality in Air Warfare: the Evolution of British and American Ideas about Strategic Bombing, 1914-1945* (Princeton: Princeton University Press, 2002). In Luke 9:55, Jesus' disciples wanted to rain fire down upon a Samaritan village, and Jesus "rebuked them." So ever is the Way of Jesus. Willard Swartley comments, "Rather than eradicating the enemy, as was the goal of Joshua's conquest narrative in the earlier story–in a similar location [Samaria]—the new strategy eradicates the enmity... Instead of killing people to get rid of idolatry, the attack through the gospel is upon Satan directly (Luke 10). Instead of razing high places, Satan is toppled from his throne!" [Note 48 reads: 'Hence the root of idolatry is plucked from its source...'] *Ibid,* Swartley, 2006, p. 144.

26. *Ibid,* Boersma, p. 16.

27. *Ibid,* Boersma, p. 93.

28. *Ibid,* Boersma, p. 199.

29. This fatalism is only present amongst Christians *politically.* The alcoholic, drug addict, sex addict, *sinner!*, are never so admonished.

Jean Bethke Elshtain, author of *Just War Against Terror*,[30] on a website defending her book says: "Just war restraint and indiscriminate slaughter belong to different moral and political universes."[31] She is correct of course. However, as John Howard Yoder argued, there has never been "just war restraint" in the history of Western warfare, let alone a just war according to its advocates' own developed criteria.[32] *There never can be* is the counter-*Realpolitik* challenge.

Father George Zabelka was the Catholic U.S. military chaplain who blessed the men who dropped the bombs on Hiroshima and Nagasaki in 1945. He said in an interview:

> The mainline Christian churches still teach something that Christ never taught or even hinted at, namely the just war theory, a theory that to me has been completely discredited theologically, historically, and psychologically.

> So as I see it, until the various churches within Christianity repent and begin to proclaim by word and deed what Jesus proclaimed in relation to violence and enemies, there is no hope for anything other than ever-escalating violence and destruction.

---

30. Jean Bethke Elshtain, *Just War Against Terror: The Burden of American Power in a Violent World* (New York, NY: Basic Books, 2003. See my online review at: http://clarionjournal. typepade.com/clarion_journal_of_spirit/wayne_northey/index.html.

31. Stanley Hauerwas and Paul J. Griffiths, "War, Peace and Jean Bethke Elshtain," *First Things*, 136 (October 2003), pp. 41–47. (http://firstthings.com/ftissues/ft0310/articles/hauerwas. html).

32. John Howard Yoder, *The Politics of Jesus: Vicit Agnus Noster* (Grand Rapids, MI: Eerdmans, 1984).

World War II has often been called a "just war." James Berardinelli in a review of Errol Morris' 2004 film, *The Fog of War*, writes: "Long before [Robert] McNamara became president of Ford motor company or entered the public spotlight, he served in World War II under the unrelenting command of General Curtis LeMay, the commander of the 20th Air Force. In 1945, LeMay was in charge of a massive firebombing offensive in Japan that resulted in the deaths of nearly 1 million Japanese citizens, including 100,000 in Tokyo during a single night. LeMay's B-29 bombers raked 67 Japanese cities, sometimes killing more than 50% of the population. McNamara points out that, had the United States lost the war, he and LeMay would have been tried as war criminals. But, of course, it's the victors who write the rules and determine what is justified." James Berardinelli, *The Fog of War:* Film Review (http://movie-reviews.colossus.net/movies/f/fog_war.html).

The Chief of staff for Presidents Roosevelt and Truman wrote of the atomic bombs dropped:

"It is my opinion that the use of this barbarous weapon at Hiroshima and Nagasaki was of no material assistance in our war against Japan. The Japanese were already defeated and ready to surrender because of the effective sea blockade and the successful bombing with conventional weapons. The lethal possibilities of atomic warfare in the future are frightening. My own feeling was that in being the first to use it, we had adopted an ethical standard common to the barbarians of the Dark Ages. I was not taught to make war in that fashion, and wars cannot be won by destroying women and children." William D. Leahy, *I Was There: the Personal Story of the Chief of Staff to Presidents Roosevelt and Truman* (New York, NY: Whittlesey House, 1950), p. 441.

Leahy begs the question: when has war been other than "in that fashion," one that invariably is "barbarous," all just war theory notwithstanding? "War is hell," observed Civil War General William Tecumseh Sherman. Just war theory claims in Orwellian doublespeak: "War is peace."

To fail to speak to the utter moral corruption of the mass destruction of civilians was to fail as a Christian and as a priest as I see it... I was there, and I'll tell you that the operational moral atmosphere in the church in relation to mass bombing of enemy civilians was totally indifferent, silent, and corrupt at best—at worst it was religiously supportive of these activities by blessing those who did them... I, like the Catholic pilot of the Nagasaki plane, "The Great Artiste," was heir to a Christianity that had for seventeen hundred years engaged in revenge, murder, torture, the pursuit of power, and prerogative violence, all in the name of our Lord.

I walked through the ruins of Nagasaki right after the war and visited the place where once stood the Urakami Cathedral. I picked up a piece of censer from the rubble. When I look at it today I pray God forgives us for how we have distorted Christ's teaching and destroyed his world by the distortion of that teaching. I was the Catholic chaplain who was there when this grotesque process that began with Constantine reached its lowest point—so far.[33]

Boersma asserts: "The limitation of Eucharistic hospitality to those who are baptised indicates again that the Church has boundaries that the Church's hospitality cannot be absolute if the Church wants to remain the Church."[34] True, as far as it goes. One must rejoin: Nor can its violence in warfare or criminal justice be absolute/terminal, which it is in warfare and capital punishment by definition. While the Church practises discerning discipline, it must be ever restorative in intent on this side of the "age to come." This can be seen in Jesus' parable of the wheat and the weeds in Matthew 13; his teaching about conflict resolution in Matthew 18; Paul's call for restoration in Galatians 6, etc. Boersma himself writes correctly: "Confession and penance... constitute one of the ways in which the Church safeguards and protects its character as a hospitable community."[35] Vengeance is God's purview, which in itself is God's wrath in an agony of restorative covenant love (Rom. 12:19 and context; cf. Hosea, especially 11:8).[36] The Church is tasked to offer endless invitation to the sinner, to carry out incessant peace evangelism.

Dr. Boersma mentions theologian James Alison's book *Raising Abel* with reference to René Girard, discussed below. But he never discusses the book. Alison posits a Christian call to embrace *now* an "eschatological" (non-violent) imagination/praxis *vis-a-vis* dominant "apocalyptic" (violent) practices

---

33. George Zabelka, "I Was Told it Was Necessary," [interview] *Sojourners* 1980, 9/8, pp. 12–15.

34. *Op. cit,* footnote 37, p. 220.

35. *Ibid,* Boersma, p. 228.

36. John Driver argues thus: "God's response to the unfaithfulness of humanity... is wrath. However, in the biblical perspective the wrath of God is not an abstract law of cause and effect in a moral universe to which somehow even God must subject himself. Biblical wrath is an intensely personal response of God to the unfaithfulness of his people with a view to protecting the salvific covenant relationship which he has established in the Old Testament and the New... "Inasmuch as God's wrath is his wounded covenant love, it is in reality more salvific than punitive in its intention" (Driver, *op. cit.*, 1986, p. 183).

in the Church and world. "This whole book," Alison writes, "is structured around this principle of analogy: God's revelation is known thanks to a subversion from within of human violence."[37] He says later:

> The phrase 'God is love' is not one more slogan which we can tack on to the end of other things we know about God and which we can brandish when we feel like it. It is the end result of a process of human discovery which constitutes a slow and complete subversion from within of any other perception of God... The perception that God is love has a specific content which is absolutely incompatible with any perception of God as involved in violence, separation, anger, or exclusion.[38]

Finally, with reference to the ultimate violence of the traditional doctrine of hell, Alison writes:

> The commonly held understanding of hell remains strictly within the apocalyptic imagination, that is, it is the result of a violent separation between the good and the evil worked by a vengeful god. It seems to me that if hell is understood thus, we have quite simply not understood the Christian faith; and the Christian story, instead of being the creative rupture in the system of this world, has come to be nothing less than its sacralization. That is, the good news which Jesus brought has been quite simply lost.[39]

Boersma moves us towards a restorative peacemaking theory of the atonement, but ultimately posits Christ's work as ahistorical, its imitation beyond human attainment or attempt.

If violence is the ultimate addiction of the human race, Boersma with most of his Reformed and Western theological colleagues would not join Violence Anonymous–or the church!–to learn the ways and practices of abstention from it.

Toward A Restorative Peacemaking *Understanding of the Atonement (Part 2)*

René Girard is an historian, literary scholar, and anthropologist who is compared in intellectual impact in the 20th and 21st centuries to figures such as Freud, Hegel, and Nietzsche in the 19th century. He is also a Christian (Roman Catholic) who taught in U.S. universities from 1950 until his retirement in 1995. A meeting of scholars and others takes place annually to discuss application of Girard's thought to a vast array of academic disciplines.[40]

---

37. James Alison, *Raising Abel: The Recovery of the Eschatalogical Imagination* (New York, NY: Crossroad, 1996), p. 33.
38. *Ibid,* Alison, p. 48.
39. *Ibid,* Alison, pp. 174-175.
40. See: http://theol.uibk.ac.at/cover/.

Girard takes pains to state he is not a theologian. He says he reads the Bible "anthropologically"[41] and considers it the most revolutionary text of all human history.[42]

A discovery made by him in his observation of human culture in terms of the question of the origins of violence is a universal "scapegoat mechanism." He discerns that such scapegoating constantly operates to create social cohesion (peace) out of disintegrating violence that would threaten social cohesion (human culture). This is the ongoing saga of all cultures, no less Western "civilization."

In other words, all cultures in all history, according to Girard, are based upon violence to guard it against violence leading to dissolution. He claims that all cultures, and all cultural institutions, are based upon a "founding murder" that places violence at the very core of human culture, time and world over.

After Girard's presentation of this universal phenomenon throughout recorded history in *Violence and the Sacred,*[43] he wrote, with two others, another book entitled *Things Hidden Since the Foundation of the World.*[44] In the interval between publication of these, Girard made (for him) the astounding discovery that the Bible alone stood out in world literature as that place that began to question the legitimacy of a "scapegoat mechanism" in response to violence, and ultimately subverted its legitimization.

This subversion was to be seen supremely in the story of Jesus, and supremely again in his death on the cross.[45] It is the story of a small group of dissenters who begged to differ with the scapegoating violence of the mob that cried "Crucify him!" and justified his death as a way of bringing law and order to Israel in the face of resistance to Roman occupation.

The words of Caiaphas, the High Priest are illustrative of the scapegoating dynamic/mechanism universal in all cultures:

> Then the chief priests and the Pharisees called a meeting of the Sanhedrin. "What

---

41. "His method is to begin, not with theology or the revelation of God, but with an understanding of human beings and human relations that the Bible and the early Christian tradition disclose." René Girard, *I See Satan Fall Like Lightning* (New York, NY: Orbis, 2001), p. ix, foreword.

42. He writes: "In the Hebrew Bible, there is clearly a dynamic that moves in the direction of the rehabilitation of the victims, but it is not a cut-and-dried thing. Rather, it is a process under way, a text in travail... a struggle that advances and retreats. I see the Gospels as the climactic achievement of that trend, and therefore as the essential text in the cultural upheaval of the modern world." René Girard, *Things Hidden since the Foundation of the World: Research Undertaken in Collaboration with Jean-Michel Oughourlian and Guy Lefort,* edited by Hamerton-Kelly (Stanford, CA: Stanford University Press, 1987), p 141.

43. René Girard, *Violence and the Sacred* (Baltimore: Johns Hopkins University, 1977).

44. *Ibid,* Girard, *Things Hidden.*

45. "...Paul's exalted idea of the Cross as the source of all knowledge is anthropologically sound (Girard, 2001, p. 3)."

are we accomplishing?" they asked. "Here is this man performing many miraculous signs. If we let him go on like this, everyone will believe in him, and then the Romans will come and take away both our place and our nation."

Then one of them, named Caiaphas, who was high priest that year, spoke up, "You know nothing at all! You do not realize that it is better for you that one man die for the people than that the whole nation perish." He did not say this on his own, but as high priest that year he prophesied that Jesus would die for the Jewish nation, and not only for that nation but also for the scattered children of God, to bring them together and make them one. So from that day on they plotted to take his life (John 11:47-53).

This for Girard is a classic illustration of the "scapegoat mechanism" at work: to make one person die for all. The author of John's Gospel ironically says this happened indeed, but not because of God's will. Rather, Christ was crucified because of the scapegoating violence endemic to the human condition in all cultures.

Girard contradicts all readings of the Gospel that would understand Christ's death primarily in terms of a bloodletting sacrifice, willed by God, which otherwise would be required of every one of us, and will in fact be required by all who reject Jesus' substitutionary death. He states:

... it is important to insist that Christ's death was not a sacrificial one. To say that Jesus dies, not as a sacrifice, but in order that there may be no more sacrifices, is to recognize in him the Word of God: 'I wish for mercy and not sacrifices.'[46]

Girard is saying that the revelation that comes through Jesus is of a God completely without violence. Therefore, it is a total misreading of the Gospels to believe that God required "satisfaction" for humanity's sins through the (violent) sacrificial death of his Son. Rather, living out a consistent life ethic of nonviolence will always elicit violence, which in Jesus' case meant violent death on the cross. The early church understood that this very submission to humanity's violence (not God's demand for sacrifice!) became, paradoxically, its ultimate overthrow.

There is consequently a new light put on 1 John 2:2: "[Christ] is the atoning sacrifice for our sins, and not only for ours but also for the sins of the whole world." Why is this so?

We know that we have come to know him if we obey his commands. The man who says, "I know him," but does not do what he commands is a liar, and the truth is not in him. But if anyone obeys his word, God's love is truly made complete in him. This is how we know we are in him: Whoever claims to live in him must walk as Jesus did. Dear friends, I am not writing you a new command but an old one, which you have had since the beginning. This old command is the message you have heard. Yet I am

---

46. *Ibid*, Girard, *Things Hidden*, p. 210.

writing you a new command; its truth is seen in him and you, because the darkness is passing and the true light is already shining. Anyone who claims to be in the light but hates his brother is still in the darkness. Whoever loves his brother lives in the light, and there is nothing in him to make him stumble. But whoever hates his brother is in the darkness and walks around in the darkness; he does not know where he is going, because the darkness has blinded him (1 John 2:3-11).

Christ's death is effective in all humanity, like leaven in flour, to enable us to fulfill our ultimate human calling: *love*—what James calls "the royal law." "If you really keep the royal law found in Scripture, 'Love your neighbor as yourself,' you are doing right" (James 2:8). Paul says, "Love does no harm to its neighbor. Therefore love is the fulfillment of the law" (Rom. 13:10).[47]

1 John puts it bluntly: "If anyone says, 'I love God,' yet hates his brother, he is a liar. For anyone who does not love his brother, whom he has seen, cannot love God, whom he has not seen. And he has given us this command: Whoever loves God must also love his brother" (1 John 4:20–21). *The biblical test case for love of God is love of neighbour; the biblical test case for love of neighbour is love of enemy. Failure to love the enemy is failure to love God.*

It is hard to reconcile a message that says, "God loves you, and has a wonderful plan for your life (heaven) based upon Christ's blood sacrifice for you," with "But if you ignore this sacrifice, God hates you, and has a terrible plan for your after-life (hell), based upon your rejection of God's blood sacrifice."

Does this not make God into a god of unparalleled violence? For who has that kind of power to effect "eternal conscious punishment" upon one's enemies except God? Does this not paint a picture of God that is worse than the worst the world has seen of violent tyrants? Does this not paint a picture of a schizophrenic god, at once overwhelmingly loving, but likewise eternally violent?

Timothy Gorringe argues no to such a god, based upon the founding texts, referencing Girard. I shall quote him at some length:[48]

> If the New Testament were quite unambiguous, there would be no argument. Most commentators wish to hold both that Jesus preached a gospel of non-retaliation, of love for the enemy, *and* that he died a vicarious death. The problem is that, to the extent the notions of vicarious suffering presuppose scapegoating, then they presuppose violence. The New Testament can certainly be read as supporting satisfaction

---

47. Love is, above all, external (nonviolent) action towards the other, as is God's action towards us in Christ. Not mere internal (loving) disposition–pace Augustine–on which misreading of the biblical text and atonement (tragically for Western culture!) Augustine's just war doctrine turned.

48. *Ibid,* Gorringe, p. 81–82. I have indicated insertions of Gorringe's footnotes in square brackets.

theory. What I have tried to argue is that it does not *have* to be read in this way, and that there is much which points in other directions. Suspicions about the conventional reading are raised both by the fact that it did not form a part of the understanding of the early Church Fathers, and also by the way it functions.

'According to this argument, the Father of Jesus is still a God of violence, despite what Jesus explicitly says. Indeed he comes to be the God of unequalled violence, since he not only requires the blood of the victim who is closest to him, most precious and dear to him, but he also envisages taking revenge upon the whole of mankind for a death that he both required and anticipated.

In effect, mankind is responsible for all this. Men killed Jesus because they were not capable of becoming reconciled without killing' [Girard, *Things Hidden*, p. 213].

[Girard]... has put his finger on a profound truth about the way in which this interpretation of the crucifixion has functioned. Not only were the scapegoat and sacrificial themes amalgamated, but these were read *politically* in conjunction with a series of texts (Romans 13, 1 Peter 2, Titus 3) which taught that 'the powers that be are ordained of God'. The judicial arm of the state, exercised above all in capital punishment, was understood, quite explicitly by Luther[49], as the exercise of God's rule. Thus a story which was a unique *protest* against judicial cruelty came to be a *validation* of it. The community which was supposed to be not conformed to the world now underwrote its repressive practice. That this could happen, and not be perceived, was due not just to the ambiguity of the New Testament texts, but to the fact that profound and necessary truths about vicarious love are concealed within the conventional interpretation. The justification of retributivism by Christianity does not represent the intrusion of an 'alien element' but, like the justification of crusading, is a deformation of biblical faith. The church has contributed both to the mentality in which people make war, and to vengeful attitudes towards offenders. It is this which makes the work of exegesis on the founding texts so important [I am alluding to Yoder, *The Politics of Jesus*, p. 247].

Gorringe states near the outset of his book:

I shall argue that whilst a powerful tradition in Christian atonement theology reinforced retributive attitudes, an alternative tradition, as I hope to show more squarely rooted in the founding texts, always existed to critique these. In understanding the roots of retributivism I hope at the same time to contribute to its deconstruction.[50]

He follows two writers, Norbert Elias and David Garland, in his positing of the "structures of affect"[51] which for several centuries predisposed an entire Western culture towards the practice of retributive/punitive justice in response to crime. Given that "satisfaction theory emerged, in the eleventh

---

49. Luther wrote: "Let no one imagine that the world can be governed without the shedding of blood. The temporal sword should and must be red and bloodstained, for the world is wicked and is bound to be so. Therefore the sword is God's rod and vengeance for it." James J. Megivern, *The Death Penalty: An Historical and Theological Survey* (New York, NY/Mahwah, N.J: Paulist Press, 1997), p. 142.

50. *Ibid*, Gorringe, p. 7.

51. *Ibid*, Gorringe, p. 8.

century, at exactly the same time as the criminal law took shape,"[52] there was a fateful interplay between law and religion for the next millennium— to the despite of the gospel and criminal alike! Domestic and international state enemies equally could be brutalized and eliminated, in direct political consequence of the satisfaction/penal substitution theories of the atonement. To quote again Gorringe's commentary:

> The penal consequences of this doctrine were grim indeed. As it entered the cultural bloodstream, was imaged in crucifixions, painted over church chancels, recited at each celebration of the Eucharist, or hymned, so it created its own structure of affect, one in which earthly punishment was demanded because God himself had demanded the death of his Son.[53]

James Megivern has written the most comprehensive English text to date on the history of the death penalty in the West. In it he interweaves significant theological reflection. At one point he writes,

> Once Christianity had become the state religion, the imperial values articulated in Roman law tended to overwhelm gospel values… As a result, the legacy of Con-stantinian-Theodosian Christianity to subsequent ages was highly ambiguous on the ethics of killing, whether in the case of war or capital punishment. Less and less attention was paid to that most troublesome of the teachings of Christ: the prohibition of the taking of revenge.[54]   *what other values were "overwhelmed"?*

In the introduction he states:

> As is evident, the problem being addressed extends far beyond the issue of capital punishment as such, since this practice is symptomatic and only one piece of the much larger puzzle, the puzzle of accounting for the oxymoronic phenomenon of 'Christian violence' in its many forms.[55]

The *locus classicus* text on the atonement is Romans 5:6–11. It is a text not only completely devoid of violence modelled for humanity to execute, rather to endure; it is, on the contrary, peacemaking to the core. It reads:

---

52. *Ibid,* Gorringe, p. 22.
53. *Ibid,* Gorringe, pp. 102–103.
54. *Ibid,* Megivern, p. 50. Alistair Kee wrote, "But there is one conquest made by Constantine, the effect of which still continues to the present day, his most surprising yet least acknowledged... He conquered the Christian church. The conquest was complete, extending over doctrine, liturgy, art and architecture, comity, ethos and ethics... But this achievement, unheralded then, unrecog-nized now, represents Constantine's greatest conquest, the one which has persisted largely unchal-lenged through the centuries in Europe and wherever European Christianity has spread...
"To be declared heretical by the norms of orthodox Constantinian Christianity may be a source of relief and encouragement to those who seek to follow Christ." Alistair Kee, *Constantine versus Christ: The Triumph of Ideology* (London: SCM Press Ltd, 1982), pp. 154, 169.
55. *Ibid,* Megivern, p. 4.

[handwritten margin note: what wrath?]

You see, at just the right time, when we were still powerless, Christ died for the ungodly. Very rarely will anyone die for a righteous man, though for a good man someone might possibly dare to die. But God demonstrates his own love for us in this: While we were still sinners, Christ died for us. Since we have now been justified by his blood, how much more shall we be saved from God's wrath through him! For if, when we were God's enemies, we were reconciled to him through the death of his Son, how much more, having been reconciled, shall we be saved through his life! Not only is this so, but we also rejoice in God through our Lord Jesus Christ, through whom we have now received reconciliation.

Another classic text on the atonement reads, "Be imitators of God, therefore, as dearly loved children and live a life of love, just as Christ loved us and gave himself up for us as a fragrant offering and sacrifice to God" (Eph. 5:1-2).

This is, I submit, the direction that Girard's ground-breaking work on sacrifice and the scapegoat mechanism takes us *politically*.

A third classic text on the atonement reads:

Therefore, if anyone is in Christ, he is a new creation; the old has gone, the new has come! All this is from God, who reconciled us to himself through Christ and gave us the ministry of reconciliation: that God was reconciling the world to himself in Christ, not counting men's sins against them. And he has committed to us the message of reconciliation. We are therefore Christ's ambassadors, as though God were making his appeal through us. We implore you on Christ's behalf: Be reconciled to God. God made him who had no sin to be sin for us, so that in him we might become the righteousness of God (2 Cor. 5:17-21).

The first line in this passage (verse 17) does not read "he is a new creation"! There is no (male) pronoun in the original (nor verb). It reads rather: "[*there is a*] *new creation*"–and should be trumpeted across the cosmos[56]! For that short packed phrase explodes with the magnificent peacemaking thrust of the atonement, hence the title I chose for this essay: *The Cross: God's Peace Work*. The Cross reverses all brokenness throughout the cosmos through reconciliation: between God and humanity (*theologically*); within ourselves (*psychologically*); amongst ourselves (*sociologically*); and within all creation (*ecologically, cosmologically*). It is all seamless, all equally part of God's work, all to be lived out *now* in light of Kingdom Come *then*.

Conclusion: The cross—God's peace work[57]

New Testament theologian Walter Wink, author of a significant three-volume study on the Powers, writes:

---

56. Note also the use of ιδου in verse 17.

57. A recent conference explored the "peace work" of the atonement. An article about it is found at this site: http://peace.mennolink.org/articles/atonementconf.html. Two related sites are: http://ecapc.org/; http://www.preachingpeace.org.

I submit that the ultimate religious question today should no longer be the Reformation's 'How can I find a gracious God?' It should be instead, 'How can I find God in my enemy?' What guilt was for Luther, the enemy has become for us: the goad that can drive us to God.[58]

He continues a little later: "It is our very inability to love our enemies that throws us into the arms of grace. What law was for Luther, the enemy has become for us."[59]

The New Testament witness is consistent: there is no love of God without love of enemy. How we treat the enemy is the ultimate indicator of how we respond to God. Avowed love of God is a religious farce if it is not shown in concrete love of the enemy. We read: "But someone will say, 'You have faith; I have deeds.' Show me your faith without deeds, and I will show you my faith by what I do" (James 2:18).

Justification by faith is legal fiction if not demonstrated in the identical attitude towards neighbour and enemy that God takes towards us in the offer of justification in the first place. This is the biblical "plan of salvation" so central to the Gospels.

> The strength of this plan of salvation [lies] in the tight bond it [creates] between divine grace and a total human response. Christian conduct [does] not follow (by some kind of inference or induction) as a consequence of salvation: it [is] itself salvation. The salvific gift of God and its human answer in following Jesus [are] two sides of one reality.[60]

This "reality" I submit is biblically Ultimate *Realpolitik*, that is *restorative peacemaking* to the core.

To a persecuted 16th century Anabaptist leader belongs the final word: "Mere faith alone is not sufficient for salvation... Yea, I confess... that mere faith does not deserve to be called faith, for a true faith can never exist without deeds of love."[61]

58. Walter Wink, *Violence and Nonviolence in South Africa: Jesus' Third Way* (Philadelphia, PA: New Society Publishers, 1987), p. 49.

59. *Ibid,* Wink, p. 50.

60. James Wm. McClendon, Jr., *Doctrine,* Systematic Theology, Volume II (Nashville, TE: Abingdon Press, 1994), p. 118.

61. Balthasar Hubmaier, quoted in *Ibid,* McClendon, p. 117.

Chapter Sixteen

GOOD NEWS FOR POSTMODERN MAN: CHRISTUS VICTOR IN THE LUCAN KERYGMA

by Nathan Rieger

I began seminary in the year that Modernity died. No bells tolled at the funeral; instead, there was the mighty crashing of the Berlin Wall, resounding across the landscape of the latter twentieth century like some colossal sonic boom, breaking the windows of entire cultures and marking a dividing line through history like a vapor trail in the sky.

Modernity had been the mother of many ideologies and not a few civilizations, and through her long terminal illness, her children grew weak, and many of them shall shortly follow her. Those numbered among her children include such diverse notables as Marxism and Darwinism, Robespierre and Picasso, Captain Kirk and Sigmund Freud; but not least among them were many bearing the name of *Christian.* These all seemed to be children born not of the Spirit, but of the 'will of men'—that venerated mother, and being Enlightened, had no place in her life for Spirit, nor for anything transcendent at all. (She felt that she was on a level with anyone; she went to lengths to make plain that she abhorred the very idea of anything or anyone above her in any way. Her conversations always began and ended with herself—a bad habit to be sure, but she could not break it as hard as she tried.)

But as to her children called Christian—to those who watch, a startling thing is apparent. Some of the children *named Christian* loved mother *modernity* enough to follow her to the grave, not able to conceive of life without her. Others, however, have discovered that they indeed are not her children, nor ever were. These are ones born not of the 'will of men,' but of God; now they have begun to trace their lineage back, back before the Enlightenment, back to a cataclysmic struggle that they had been told was nothing more than a myth; back to *Christus Victor.*

What follows is part of the great adventure of discovery that has befallen these step-children of the Enlightenment. What is the truth of their birth? And how can they explain that genesis to others who are motherless since the death of Modernity?

This experiment-in-thought is occupied with the question of how Christians understand and portray the atonement today as the church struggles to re-contextualize its mission in the postmodern world. To exegete accurately or speak relevantly today, however, we must first overcome the historical amnesia that locked modernity into the existential present, and remember what has gone before. To do this we will cut small cross-sections into three particularly formative times in the Christian understanding of the atonement: the patristic, the High Medieval and the Enlightenment periods. After glancing backwards, we can look further and more intently backwards to the kerygma in Luke-Acts itself, and ask again if what we find there has not actually been bastardized by the enlightenment. And what then?

Then, it may appear to you as it does to this writer that a New Testament metaphor-complex for the atonement, so-called *Christus Victor¹*, was adopted and ardently articulated by the church fathers, but rejected by the scholastics in the high medieval period, and its coffin tightly sealed by modernity. In Christianity, however, tightly-sealed tombs have been known to fail…

The Christus Victor motif, dominating the Lucan Kerygma, should be repopularized in the church's evangelism of the postmodern world.

I. Three Slices of History *(of atonement theory)*

A. The Fathers

Risus Paschalis–the Easter laugh. From the days of Gregory of Nyssa until today in some Christian circles, the time after Easter has been time for jokes. After mass, the priest descends from the altar into the congregation and plays stand-up comic. It is not just comic relief to loosen up after the sadness of Good Friday; the jokes are told to commemorate the divine joke, played on the devil, of the resurrection of Jesus.

This view of Christ's atonement as a victory over dark powers dominated the patristic period. Though at some points diverging, the early theologians of Christianity came to general agreement on certain ideas, and together they may be seen to present a paradigm, which, if not without paradoxes, nonetheless still has theological coherence. Presented more systematically² than was

---

1. This term was first applied to a specific view of the atonement by the Swedish theologian Gustav Aulen in 1931, *in Christus Victor* (New York: Macmillan, 1976). Since then, although it has become something of a technical term in theology, it still evades precise definition because of intrinsic paradoxes. Our working definition will be given below.

2. The following is my own collation and synthesis of the Fathers from primary sources, Aulen, Culpepper, Driver, Finger, Heick, and Mackintosh. Regarding the systematizing of Christus Victor, a view often criticized for its lack of coherence, a careful reading of *primary* sources would suggest that this criticism sometimes stems from presuppositional differences with the highly supernaturalistic worldview of the Fathers; in other the words, an extrinsic rationale is portrayed as intrinsic. patristic scholars like Thomas Oden have found more internal consistency in patristic writings than has generally been given them credit.

done in the first millennium of Christianity, the Fathers generally held:

1. The idea that through sin humankind was made subject to the devil. Humankind had placed itself under his oppressive domination, which was manifest through the powers of death,[3] political authorities,[4] pagan deities,[5] sickness,[6] and demon-possession.[7]

2. The quasi-legitimacy of the Devil's claim to authority. Though the devil was himself an unjust robber,[8] authority had been voluntarily given to him by people through their own sin; as well, it had been permitted by God, who judges sin indirectly through the oppression of the devil.

3. A ransom had to be paid to redeem those under Satan's power.[9] Christ, in no bondage to Satan, was made that ransom.[10]

4. The Devil and the human authorities acting with him were deceived (or self-deceived) into the murder of Christ.[11]

5. In Jesus' life and death, two "recapitulations" had occurred; firstly, Jesus was righteous through all stages of his life in every area that Adam was not, thereby recapitulating (lit., *re-heading)* the human race;[12] secondly, all sins committed by the human race were recapitulated in the killing of Jesus. His murder epitomized and representatively enacted all Sin, and in this very real way Christ bore the Sin of all.[13]

6. In the murder of Christ, the Devil overstepped all bounds, overreaching any authority he may have had by killing someone not legitimately subject to

3. Cf. Finger, 320.
4. Origen, *Contra Celsum, I.I.*
5. Justyn, *First Apology* V.14.
6. Garrett, 40, 57.
7. Cf. Garrett, 39.
8. Gregory of Nazianzus de-emphasized, but probably did not deny this point. See Aulen; 50; Finger, 337.
9. Advocated esp. by Gregory of Nyssa, who spoke graphically and crudely of the ransom being given directly to the devil, *Great Catechism*, XXIV. Also, John of Damascus, De Fid. Iii. 27. It should be noted, however, that there was both diversity and caution in other Fathers, who spoke of a ransom, but one which only "perhaps" was given to the devil. Cf. Origen in Heick, 121.
10. Origen, taking his cues from the N.T. use of λυτρον (Mk 10.45, 1 Tim 2.6, Heb 9.15) developed this metaphor in numerous places , e.g., Joann ii.21, Matt 16.8, Rom ii.13.
11. Aulen, Loc. cit. Here too note the common affirmation that the devil was deceived, but whereas in Origen the sphere of deception is the power of Christ, in Gregory of Nyssa it regards his deity. Augustine referred three times in his writings to the devil's mousetrap, *muscipula diaboli,* reiterating the metaphor of deception apparently without systematizing a theology around it.
12. Irenaeus understood recapitulation to mean that Christ obeyed all that Adam should have, and thus became the new Adam, this time refusing to give to the devil the authority that the first Adam did. "But when He became incarnate and was made man, He summoned up in Himself the long line of human beings, and furnished us, in a brief, comprehensive manner, with salvation; so that what we had lost in Adam ... that we may recover in Jesus Christ." *Irenaeus, Against Heresies, III, 18.1.*
13. "... the recapitulation that should take place in his own person of the spilling of blood from the beginning... and that by means of Himself there should be a requisition of their blood." Ibid, V.14.1.

death.[14] By doing so, he forfeited his rule.

7. The resurrection/exaltation of Jesus was God's great reversal of the judgment on Christ; the devil was now judged instead, all authority taken from him and given to Jesus.[15] Those calling on the name of Jesus would receive deliverance from evil.

In observation one may note that this view of the atonement is both highly supernaturalistic while at the same time maintaining that the drama of the atonement was played out on a historical plane. In this cosmology, there is inter-penetration between the levels of the cosmos.[16]

Note as well the dramatic form this view takes; it is a story as much as a set of propositions. This was even more true when the Fathers set it forth. The Christus Victor idea dominated the first millennium of Christian thought on the atonement, until Anselm (1033-1109). With him, the scholastics began the first serious reformulation of the doctrine of atonement.

B. The Scholastics

Anselm, one of the great archbishops of Canterbury, is known for his approach of "faith seeking understanding." However, it is clear that in *Cur Deus Homo?* ("Why did God become human?") he was intending to show "by plain reasoning and fact that ... all things were to take place which we hold in regard to Christ."[17] He wanted to prove the necessity of the atonement through reason alone, without relying on Scripture. In doing so, he set a pattern that influenced thought about the atonement for the next millennium.

Anselm's motivation was largely apologetic; he addressed "Christians, Jews and Gentiles."[18] His presentation of the atonement was in part, I suggest, so seminal because it was not merely intended for "in house" use; Anselm provided a model by which those outside the *corpus christianum* could be addressed. He concerned himself not only with repeating dogma, but with the question of contextualization, how in the high middle ages the gospel could

---

14. Aulen, Loc. cit. See also Origen in Heick, Loc. cit.

15. Finger, I, 333.

16. Bultmann correctly says that the cosmology assumed here is three-tiered: "The world is viewed as a three-storeyed structure, with the earth in the centre, the heaven above, and the underworld beneath. Heaven is the abode of God and of celestial beings... The underworld is hell... The earth is the scene of the supernatural activity of God and his angels on the one hand, and of Satan and his demons on the other. These supernatural forces intervene in the course of nature and in all that men think and will and do." 'New Testament and Mythology', in *Kerygma and Myth: A Theological Debate,* ed. H.W. Bartsch (ET London, 1972), 1.

17. Anselm, qtd. in T. Finger, *Christian Theology ,* vol.1 (Scottdale: Herald, 1985), 305.

18. Heick, 267.

be understood in terms familiar to that era, and thus his reference to feudal social structure.

Anselm's method in *Cur Deus Homo?* was to argue his discussion partner, Boso, into a corner (Book I), and then out of it (Book II). In the process, Boso learns:[19]

1. Sin is "not to render God his due."[20]

2. What is due to God is "honor," in the medieval sense. This is not honor as the vague sort of respect that we would speak about today, but something "objective, social in its nature, the guarantee of social stability."[21] Failure to pay it meant the possible loss of property or position. Feudal society demanded that honor be shown according to social class, at the top of which, of course, was God.

3. God, as the ultimate feudal lord, would have been irresponsible to let the violation of his honor go without either repayment of the debt to God's honor, or punishment. But the only thing we humans could use to pay back the debt, we owe anyway—perfect obedience. And this we are unable to pay, let alone repay. The situation is desperate, and like a good Hitchcock mystery, Book I ends there, "to be continued..."

4. With this double-fault on the part of humankind, the first part of Anselm's syllogism is complete, and Book II launches its completion: "none but God can make satisfaction."

5. Because, however, humankind had been given the task of perfect obedience and overcoming Satan, "none but a man ought to do this."[22]

6. Jesus, the God-man, fulfills both responsibilities that humankind had reneged on: perfect obedience, and the enduring of the punishment that would give "satisfaction to God's honor."

7. Jesus had no need of the merits that his punishment earned him; graciously, he paid them to God in our name, transferring the reward, eternal life, to us as well.

This is familiar theological turf to anyone who has done time handing out tracts on a street-corner. Our concern here is not to critique it, but to observe several differences with Christus Victor:

First, note that the main conflict is not between God and the powers of darkness, but a dual conflict between the divine lord and his recalcitrant yet helpless tenants; also, there is conflict between God and the God-man, who

---

19. The following is garnered from Finger, Heick, Mackintosh. All page numbers are from *Cur Deus Homo?* as quoted in these three authors.

20. p. 200.

21. R. Southern in Finger, 306.

22. p. 245.

acts as a substitute for the peasants in taking the punishment from the lord.

Secondly, whereas in Christus Victor, the direction of salvation is human-ward, God coming "down" to break the bondage of humankind to evil pow-ers, Anselm sees the direction of salvation as primarily "up" from the God-man to God, fulfilling the upward obligation of obedience and suffering of punishment.

Thirdly, the main purpose of Jesus" struggle with the powers of darkness in Christus Victor is to break their hold on creation, which is seen as the main problem; in Anselm, Christ still struggles with the devil, but it is only to fulfill humankind's obligation to do that, and *thereby* earning merit for them. The lack of that merit is the main deficit, and deficit, not bondage, is the main problem.

Fourthly, though Anselm retains supernatural elements other than God, they stand at the periphery of his schema, with the main dynamic being a struggle to maintain the divine-human "class" relationship in its proper balance. The transcendent order breaks in briefly in history, with Christ's struggle with the devil seen as only part of his vicarious task of obedience, which in turn is only part of his task of earning merit. Besides the incarnation itself, the drama of the inter-penetrating layers of the cosmos is minor.

Anselm's chief theological opponent in real life was not Boso, but Abelard, a younger contemporary. Whereas Anselm began at least in theory with faith, and then proceeded towards understanding, Abelard was a de *facto* rationalist in both philosophy and methodology.[23] Though his formulation of the atone-ment differed radically from Anselm, he also rejected vehemently the Chris-tus Victor idea on the grounds that it did not have enough internal cohesion. Thomas Aquinas, in his *Summa Theologica,* the greatest work of the scholas-tics, did likewise soon after, and on the same grounds of rationality.

C. The Moderns

Thomas Oden has characterized Modernity, as an era, with four motifs: autonomous individualism, narcissistic hedonism, reductive naturalism, and absolute moral relativism.[24] Of these, naturalism that has had the most pro-found effect on atonement theology.

Bultmann could be said to epitomize this reductionism in his "demytholo-gizing" of the New Testament. Though he comes late in the modern period, he

---

23. Heick cautions on too close an association with the Enlightenment rationalists, in that Abelard never questioned the authority of the Bible. Cf. 278.

24. Thomas Oden, *Two Worlds: Notes on the Death of Modernity In America and Russia* (Downers Grove: Intervarsity, 1992), 33.

illustrates well the extreme of what modernity has done to the atonement.
Firstly, Bultmann ruled out *a priori* the existence of the three-tiered realm
he accurately described as that of the New Testament worldview.[25] Science
makes it impossible to believe in anything acting in history from a transcendent order.[26]

Secondly, Bultmann took the hermeneutic of suspicion to its ultimate.
There is almost nothing that can be learned about the *historisch* of the death
and resurrection of Jesus from the New Testament.[27] "The salvation event is
viewed more as a memory in the minds of struggling, despairing rememberers than an actual historical event."[28]

What is left after the demythologization is done? Neither Anselm nor Origen, to be sure. Perhaps only influence; the influence of the a-historical story
of a good man. This is indeed the trend of atonement theologizing in the last
two hundred years: the story of the cross acts as *a moral influence.*[29]

This theory became the chief rival of those derived from Anselm,[30] with
Christus Victor out on two counts: not only did it maintain that atonement
was made in history, but it saw the transcendent breaking into the natural.

Anselm kept his following; he was only down on one count, the insistence
on the historical sphere of the atonement. The in-breaking of a transcendent
realm remained a motif, but relatively minor, and kept neatly to a smallish
role in the first century and before, and expected again in a major way at the
parousia.

Of course, none of this is to say that naturalism prevailed completely in
the church. I am arguing only that it became a miasma that could be smelled
to some degree almost everywhere. The whole of modern culture, not just
the liberal stream of the church, acquired a strong distaste for relating immediately to any kind of transcendent order; for instance, even the conservative dispensationalism that has fought tooth and nail with "Modernism" has

---

25. See quote on p. 6 above.

26. *"Man's knowledge and mastery of the world* have advanced to such an extent through
science that it is no longer possible for anyone seriously to hold the New Testament view of the
world... we can no longer believe in spirits, whether good or evil... no longer any heaven... the
same applies to hell... Sickness and the cure of disease are likewise attributable to natural causation, not the result of daimonic activity ... we can no longer look for the return of the Son of Man
on the clouds of heaven or hope that the faithful will meet him in the air." R. Bultmann, New
Testament and Mythology' in *Kerygma and Myth: A Theological Debate.* Bartsch, H.W., ed. (ET
London, 1972), 4.

27. Ibid, 1-8.

28. Oden, p. 37.

29. This focus did not limit itself to the liberal stream of thought. Both evangelicals such
as Finney, or liberals such as Harnack used 'influence' as a primary metaphor in describing the
atonement. Cf. Bultmannn, 13ff.

30. Finger, I, 318.

been extremely militant against the idea of an in-breaking of the transcendent order at any time and place other than in the Bible; to many in that camp, the cosmos is a "uniformity of cause and effect in a closed system."[31]

Though they would never admit to a philosophical affinity with naturalism, as Fundamentalism has developed in the twentieth century it has tended *in practice* to be anti-supernaturalistic.[32] Evangelicals should mark well: being theologically conservative never made anyone immune from the *praxis* of Modernity.

Thus the naturalistic paradigm has not been contained to the upper echelons of academia; one of the characteristic marks of the period of Modernism was that people rejected or minimalized transcendent reality at a popular level. The universe was looked on as a mechanistic, closed order.

> We may summarily reject all miracles, prophecies, narratives of angels and demons, and the like, as simply impossible and irreconcilable with the known and universal laws which govern the course of events.[33]

How positive and hopeful did this look in the early days of the Enlightenment! It really seemed to many as if humankind could come to knowledge of absolutes beginning from themselves, using reason alone, and in this process find the kernel within the husk of the atonement. But today, the modern hope is weary indeed. Reason has not proven sufficient to lead us to universal absolutes; even transcending the absurdity of existentialism is despaired of. Thomas Oden has made a case for defining modernity, as an era, to be the two hundred years between the French Revolution and the fall of the Berlin Wall, where the political system based on naturalism collapsed.[34] Whatever historians will ultimately say, at least some of the Enlightenment's most basic presuppositions have been widely questioned at a popular level.

As this dying continues, Christians are beginning to wake up to the fact that the Enlightenment was maybe not so enlightening for our understanding of the scriptures, set as they were in a vastly different worldview. Many of the former rationalistic objections to Christus Victor are now dying with modernity. Aulen and others following him have broken ground for us; now, with the advent of mercurial changes in the worldview of the West, does Christus

---

31. Sire, 63.
32. One might note the works of John F. MacArthur, or Charles Ryrie.
33. David Straus in Allen, *Christian Belief*, 166.
34. This is beyond the scope of this paper to argue his thesis; I am positing only his general accuracy. Whether or not historians in years to come will agree on the fall of the Berlin wall as the dividing line between epochs remains to be seen, and is irrelevant to my argument, but there are many who would agree with him that the West is in what A. Wallace has called the "mazeway," a period of transition between world-views. See Wallace, Anthony. "Revitalization Movements," AA 58 (1956), 264-81.

Victor offer us help through the 'mazeway'? As we die to one cosmology and give birth to another, let us see if Christus Victor still speaks from the pages of the New Testament.

I believe that perhaps the most crucial step in exegesis is our self-understanding, the accuracy with which we can understand our own worldview and its intrinsic bias. Having stirred our corporate memory first, remembering something of how our times have biased us, now, let us bring that light to the text.

II. Exegesis of Acts 3

Assuming, with C.H. Dodd, that the kerygmatic speeches in Acts 2-5, 10, and 13 represent the kerygma of the church in Jerusalem at an early period,[35] let's look at one of the first presentations of the gospel with form-critical and narratological tools. Found in Acts 3, it suits our purpose of examining a representative Lucan text.

A. Background

Of the many purposes which have been conjectured for the writing of Acts, there is some degree of consensus on two that have immediate relevance for us. The first one can be seen in the "thesis statement" of Acts in 1:8, where the progress of the gospel is outlined from Jerusalem to the farthest corners of the gentile world. Acts begins in Jerusalem and ends in Rome, and as a book it functions to explain how a Jewish movement became so gentile.

These questions would have been further intensified after the destruction of the temple in 70 CE.[36] Why was Simon bar Giora defeated? Were the promises of Scripture to Israel not to be fulfilled? Was Israel being judged for a particular sin?

Secondly, there was a serious question that arose because of the political scandal that Jesus' death on a Roman cross had created.[37] Luke wrote partly to show that Jesus and his movement were innocent of the charges of political insurrection. In Acts, the Romans are often portrayed positively, vindicating Paul's activities.[38]

---

35. C. H. Dodd, *Apostolic Preaching and its Developments* (New York: Harper and Row, 1964.) p. 37.
36. Craig Evans, *Luke* (Peabody: Hendrickson, 1990), 6.
37. See Bruce's "Introduction" in *Acts,* NICNT (Grand Rapids: Eerdmans, 1988).
38. See 13:7ff; 16:35ff; 18:14ff; 19:35ff; 21:37ff; 22:29.

Luke's editing shows a major concern to set the events of the apostles in their secular, often political setting. I count no less than seventeen pericopes in Acts where there is direct interaction with governing authorities: Pilate, Gallio, Felix, Festus, Agrippa, etc. I agree with the consensus that Luke wanted to deny that Christianity was a political rebellion, and this prompted the concern for the relationship of the gospel to these political events. However, much of the political interaction occurs while the apostles, Paul and Peter especially, are proclaiming the kerygma. Our passage is one of these. Is there then a connection between the proclamation of the way of salvation and the varied dealings with civil leaders? Is there soteriological significance there?

Redaction-critical scholarship often assumes that Luke is simply putting his own apologetic agenda into the apostles' mouths; there is no soteriological significance to those passages which address the political question, we are told.[39] Yet there are three things that cause me to question whether there is a connection here.

First, the themes are so frequently and deeply intertwined, and at important places in the narrative. One notices that right from the first moments of Paul's conversion there is a political agenda connected with the preaching of the gospel: "This man is my chosen instrument to carry my name before the Gentiles *and their kings..."* (Acts 9:15). One can hardly read modern missiology into this and derive a strategy of focusing on reaching influential people! No—kerygma and kings must intertwine for other reasons.

Second, Luke claims to want to present to us "an orderly report" from "eyewitnesses" (Lk 1:2-3). There is good reason to believe that Luke was historically accurate in his reporting of events, more reason than just an a *priori* doctrinaire assumption.[40] It follows that even if Luke edited for the apologetic purpose of defending Christianity from various accusations made against it, the apostles could not have had the same agenda when the events he described first happened, for the accusations had not yet been made. There had to have been a more soteriological function to the kerygma in its infancy.

Third, there is the internal structure of pericopes such as we have before us, where statements of a political nature can be seen through form and literary analysis to have a central place in the narration of the kerygma.

As we have noted, one of the hallmarks of Christus Victor as elucidated by the Fathers is that it sees the ministry of Christ as a struggle with the

---

39. See H. Conzelmann, *The Theology of St. Luke* (Philadelphia: Fortress, 1961), 201.
40. So argues Richard Cassidy in *Jesus, Politics, and Society* (Maryknoll: Orbis, 1978). Cassidy is by no means just reciting a conservative creed.

powers of darkness. In Origen and Justyn especially, political rulers were seen as agents through which the demonic worked. This is true in Lucan thought as well; Satan, the authorities, and Judas were in collusion to kill Jesus. Because Christus Victor has often been dismissed as a serious soteriology, these conflict motifs with the authorities were able to be dismissed also as having "no soteriological significance."

I submit that the consensus of scholarship is right: Luke's purpose is partly apologia against accusations of insurrectionism, and as well to deal with the problem of Jewish rejection of the gospel, the divine reasons for the destruction of the temple, and the hellenization of Christianity. But I cannot accept that Luke re-drew the lines of the kerygma—which was first and foremost a message of salvation—in order to accomplish these two points of agenda. He would not have betrayed the heart of the Christian message for the sake of secondary issues.

Thus we are forced to find other ways to explain the deep intertwining of soteriological and political motifs.

A third major purpose to Luke-Acts is described by Susan Garrett in her work in Lucan studies, *The Demise of the Devil*. She sees Hellenistic magic in the background, and argues cogently that Luke wrote partly to defend the early Christians against accusations of magic. She maintains that Luke saw Jesus' and the early church's miracles as quite distinct from, even opposed to magic, falling much more in line with intertestamental rabbinic thought on the two ages.[41] As our passage deals directly with a "miracle" and its explanation, this background has a bearing on our exegesis as well.

B. Text Unit

For our purposes the text unit includes the whole of Acts 3. This has two major components that function as a unity; the sign of the healed cripple, and the proclamation of the *kerygma* immediately afterwards. The latter functions as an explanation as the former and the former functions as a witness to the thrust of the latter (see II.B.3.b in the structural outline below). It is clear that the larger unit, united by the theme of the healing of the crippled man and its consequences, extends to 4:31,[42] so we will carefully examine this as well when we consider the immediate context.

---

41. pp. 4, 130.
42. As in F.F. Bruce, *Acts,* NICNT (Grand Rapids: Eerdmans, 1988), 76.

C. Textual Criticism

Metzger deals with no less than twenty-four variants in this passage, most of which, however, are either theologically insignificant or poorly attested to. I will deal with three that are theologically relevant to our study.

Verse 6: εγειρε και ("get up and") is missing from several ancient manuscripts (v.6). The combination of B and D is "particularly impressive" and thus the {D} rating. However, it is still likely that they were originally present.[43] This reading simply provides emphasis of commanding authority over the infirmity.

Verse 12: εξουσια ("authority") as substituted for ευσεβια to ("piety") in Chrysostom and several versions, but ευσεβια is undoubtedly correct. εξουσια would have seemed to the scribe to be a better word to pair with δυναμει to describe a miracle.[44] This reading broadens Peter's disclaimer, emphasizing the authority of Christ.

Verse 13: εβαρυνατε (oppressed), a western reading, replaces ἠρνησασθε ("denied") in B, probably to avoid repeating ἠρνησασθε in the previous clause. It is also used in Acts 28:27, but nowhere else in Luke-Acts. It is "manifestly inappropriate."

In verse 16 there is no textual variant, but an extremely awkward construction that literally reads, "his name, by faith in his name, has healed this man." C. Torrey suggests that a change occurred in an Aramaic stage of the transmission that altered the original "he has made whole" to "his name has strengthened," very similarly constructed phrases. This would justify the NIV, "By faith in Jesus, this man . . . was made strong."[45]

D. Structural Outline of Acts 3

    I. Sign
        A. Setting & Characters 1-2
        B. Event 3-10
            1. Request of the Crippled Man 3
            2. Action of the Two Disciples 4-6
                a. Attention commanded 4-5
                b. Healing commanded 6
            3. Healing Described 7-8

---

43. B. Metzger, *A Textual Commentary on the Greek New Testament* (Stuttgart: United Bible Societies, 1971), 307.
44. Ibid, 309.
45. Bruce, *Acts, 80.*

E. Key Words

*1. **Wonder and amazement*** (vs. 10). Twenty-seven times in Luke-Acts there are words denoting the response of the people as one of awe, amazement or wonder. Used here are the nouns θαμβος, "amazement" and εκστασεως, "to be beside oneself." Luke often uses these and others like θαυμαζω, εξιστημι, and φοβος in pairs, multiplying word upon word to emphasize the utter amazement of the people to the works of God. Only three of twenty-seven times do they have an object other than the work of Jesus or God himself. Terms like these are fitting in the narration of a drama that has just seen the irrupting of the Kingdom of God.

2. *Glorified* (vs.13). Glory (δοξα) and its derivatives are used twenty-seven times in Luke-Acts. In only two spots, Luke 9:31 and Acts 7:2, is it related to something other than Jesus, his coming, death or resurrection. It means primarily "brightness, splendour, radiance."[46] Lucan metaphors of light/darkness are present twenty-nine times besides the references to glory, and are very interconnected with it.[47]

3. *Servant* (vss.13, 26). Though "servant" is common enough in our English Bibles, παδια is an unusual Greek word to be translated as such, and it is even more unusual to see it used as a title for Jesus. In that capacity it appears only here, where it is repeated, showing emphasis, and in 4:30. Its repetition here is especially significant in that it indicates strong intertextuality with Deutero-Isaiah's Servant Songs. Jesus is portrayed as that Servant.

4. *Deliver up* (vs.13a). Bauer says that in this passage the meaning of παραδιδωμι is "to hand over, turn over, give up a person, hand over into custody."[48] Though it has been argued that this verb is strictly juridical and devoid of theological content,[49] one might ask whether juridical and theological meanings are exclusive to each other. Mark had already used this verb in a theological sense (9:31, 10:33).[50] This verb helps to confer the sense of judicial murder, which the resurrection reversed, emphasizing the patristic theme of the recapitulation of evil.

Luke uses παραδιδωμι in predictions of the Passion (9:44; 18:32; 20:20; 22:21-22; 24:7), in the passion narrative itself (22:4ff), and in retrospective allusions (24:20 and our passage). There are only three instances in Luke and three in Acts where the verb is used for a "giving over" that is other than that of Jesus'; the verb is profoundly tied to the passion. O.T. background for the use of this verb can be found in the Servant Song of Is 52:13-53:12, as we will see below.

5. *Suffer* (vs.18). πασχω has as its root meaning to "suffer, endure something."[51] The whole phrase παθειν τον Χριστον αυτου is a common Lucanism (Luke 24:26; 24:46; Acts 3:18; 17:3; 26:23). Although it is often

---

46. W. Bauer, A *Greek Lexicon of the New Testament and other Early Christian Literature* (Chicago: University of Chicago, 1958), 205.

47. For example, Acts 22:6 "... About noon as I came near Damascus, suddenly a bright light from heaven flashed around me..."

48. Bauer, 614.

49. Norman Perrin, qtd. in Joel Green, *The Death of* Jesus (Tubingen: Mohr, 1988), 289.

50. Green, 289

51. Bauer, 63.

assumed that this suffering must be substitutionary, that is nowhere implied by any Lucan context in which it used. If there is a substitutionary implication, it would have to be derived from elsewhere, perhaps in an allusion to the suffering servant of Deutero-Isaiah, who endures judgement 'for' others. If this meaning is present it is not at all explicit; what we do see explicitly is that all five pericopae refer to suffering as the fulfillment of Old Testament prophecy; three connect it to the exaltation that was to come immediately after, and the other two emphasize his Messiahship in a missiological function.

6. *Refreshing* (vs.19). αναφυξις has as its root meaning—"to give breathing space, revive, refresh."[52] This is used once in the LXX, in Exodus 15:11, where Pharaoh sees that there is relief from judgement. Philo uses it with the same meaning.[53] Some have suggested that the phrase "times of refreshing" means the Messianic Age of salvation.[54]

7. *Restore* (vs.21). Though literally ἀποκαταστσις means "restoration,"[55] Bruce contends for the meaning of "establishment" or "fulfilment" and suggests that here it is the Messianic Age.[56]

These last two words suggest a cosmic drama unfolding. While personal forgiveness is mentioned, it gives way quickly to the bigger picture that a shift in the ages has taken place. This is of course relates better to the patristic picture of Christus Victor's overthrow of the powers than it does to an Anselmian schema.

F. Analysis and Intertextuality

First, let us look at the major divisions: sign and kerygma. Dividing the chapter in two clear units is not an irrelevant point; one is clearly narrative and one is proclamation (kerygma comes from a root meaning to preach or proclaim). The use of "sign" to describe the first section of narrative, however, must be justified, as in the Lucan corpus, σημειον is used the majority of times in a negative sense.[57] Here I am using it as an etic category to bring across the intimate connection between the healing and the proclamation.

---

52. Ibid, 63.
53. Loc. cit.
54. Bruce, 84.
55. Bauer, 92.
56. "... it makes good sense in the present context, in reference to the fulfilment of all Old Testament prophecy, culminating in the establishment of God's order on earth. If Jesus must remain in heaven until this consummation, this is in line with Paul's exposition of Ps. 110:1: Christ must reign until all hostile powers are overthrown." Bruce, 85.
57. See Luke 11:16; Luke 11:29; Luke 21:7.

Before we examine the conceptual links, note the literary: in 15b and 16, we see in the outline that the disciples are paralleled in function with the healing. That function is explicit: to witness (μαρτυρεω) to the resurrection of Jesus. The disciples are giving verbal witness; the healing has given a tangible witness. The Greek brings this out in the phrase απεναντι παντων ὑμων (before all of you); this is reminiscent, though not verbatim of the phrase in 9:15, "bear my name before nations, before kings, and before the sons of Israel." It connotes open declaration of truth.

Just what this truth is is not defined in the narrative section. To know more accurately what the healing witnesses to, we shall have to let the second section help us. Before that, however, note several more literary devices used by Luke in the narrative section:

The characterization is typically Lucan. The man is going about business as usual, which for him is the lowly task of begging; he was one of the poorest of the poor, which highly qualifies him for the ministry of Jesus. Jesus singled out cripples in Luke for ministry (Luke 13:11; 14:13); now the continuity between him and his disciples is being stressed.

The local and temporal settings bring us to the very core of the Jewish cultus. One must note that the temple does not have the same completely negative connotation as it does in Mark's gospel. Yet the thrust is still negative; the fact that the man had been there at the center of Judaism "from birth," "where he was put every day," emphasizes Judaism's inability to do what Jesus did all the time, what the disciples were about to do, and what Jesus declared was a key sign of the dawning of the Messianic age (Luke 7:22).

Luke piles word on word to emphasize the extraordinary nature of the miracle: instantly, walking, jumping, running, astonished, wonder, amazement, praising God. As we noted above, the people's reaction is described in terms that almost without exception apply to the scene of a mighty work of God. Thus ends the narrative.

The second section begins with Peter humbly disclaiming his own authority, and ascribing the power of the healing to Jesus. This provides a segue into the main section of the kerygma, which I would like to suggest is set in a trial-form. This formal structure has as its background several Danielic and Isaianic passages, to which I would now turn.

In Daniel 7 we have an example of apocalyptic in which the narrative embraces the following themes: authority to rule is given to a creature. However, that authority is used to judge, oppress and destroy the saints of God. The creature becomes very arrogant, but is allowed to do its worst. When pride has overcome it, a throne is set up for the Ancient of Days, and in a court setting the creature is stripped of its authority, its judgements on the righteous reversed, and its sovereignty given to the saints who had endured. "...this horn was waging war against the saints and defeating them, until the Ancient of Days came and pronounced judgment in favor of the saints of the Most High, and the time came when they possessed the kingdom" (Dan 7:21-22).

In Daniel, this motif is repeated a number of times, in different forms, some highly apocalyptic, others in historical narrative with Nebuchadnezzar as the central figure. But the same basic structure remains: authority is given but wielded unjustly over the righteous. When pride has taken its course, then its authority is nullified and given to another, usually one that has endured the unjust authority.

A similar theme is found in Isaiah 14, a taunt song for the King of Babylon. His oppressive rule over nations was brought to an end when his desire for divinity filled him with arrogance and desire for worship. Then God brought him to judgment and removed him from authority.

This common thread found its way into apocalyptic literature of the intertestamental period. In *Life of Adam and Eve,* written around the first century, this passage from Isaiah is reinterpreted it to refer to Satan.[58] The Qumran War Scroll, 11QMelch, and the Sibylline Oracles all contain this same theme.[59] 11Q Melchizedek is the most important of these for our understanding; there, a cosmic event takes place in the year of the Lord's favor, when release is proclaimed to the captives. Melchizedek is exalted to a throne in the heavens, above the assembly of the heavenly beings, displacing and judging Belial in the process.[60] This is remarkably similar to Luke's portrait of Jesus both in Jesus' apocalyptic saying in Luke 10, as well as the kerygma throughout Acts.

This theme is also strongly present in Isaiah's Servant Songs, in particular, Isaiah 52:13-53:12. God says of the Servant: "Therefore I will give him a portion among the great, and he will divide the spoils with the strong, because he poured out his life unto death."[61]

Note that none of these four points are directly related to any substitution motif. Vicarious substitution is so often read back into this Servant Song that it is almost strange to think that when the early church quoted this passage, it may have been used in other ways besides support for a substitutionary view of the atonement.

58. Susan Garrett, *The Demise of the Devil* (Minneapolis: Fortress, 1989), 50.

59. U.B. Muller in Garrett, 52.

60. Ibid.

61. "The influence of Is 52:13 on Acts 3:13a is widely acknowledged... Of course, the correspondence is not precise..., but we are not arguing for any literal or 'midrashic' citation of the Fourth Servant Song in Acts 3 ... all four points of correspondence ... are likewise very much at home in the trial scene: Jesus' (anticipation of his) glorification, his innocence, his suffering, and, naturally, his 'being delivered up.'" Green, 290.

Luke does not use the substitutionary concept. Nowhere in Luke or Acts does it appear,[62] with only one possible exception in Acts 20:28, where there is a highly problematic textual reading. The question arises then, is the Lucan kerygma finding intertextuality with this trial motif? If it does, then we would expect to see it in other places in the Lucan corpus, especially in regards to Jesus' death and resurrection.

Our expectation is fulfilled in a number of places. Firstly, in the wilderness temptations in Luke 4:6-7, Satan, claiming to have authority over "all the kingdoms of the earth"—and Jesus does not dispute this—craves Jesus' worship, bargaining for it. After Jesus' refusal, we are told that Satan withdrew from Jesus for a while, in temporary defeat. Garrett suggests that should be linked with Luke 10:18, where Jesus speaks of Satan's fall from heaven:

> Luke regarded the desire for worship by any being but God or Jesus as cause for the most severe punishment. "Because he did not give God the glory," Herod was "immediately smitten by an angel of the Lord, and was eaten by worms and died. Given Luke's horror at the prospect of misdirected worship, Satan's arrogation of divine glory—culminating in his brazen effort to persuade even Jesus to worship him—must have drastic consequences.[63]

Turning to 10:18, one is struck by several similarities with the passage we have just explored in Daniel. First, there is the obvious similarity of content, but then one notes the introductory phrase, "I was watching Satan fall from heaven." Here εθεωρουν (I was watching, imperfect tense) is the same word used in the LXX to introduce Daniel's apocalyptic visions. If Jesus is describing an apocalyptic vision, and both content and grammar suggest this, like Daniel it could be proleptic—yet to happen. Jesus is looking forward to the day when Satan will be judged and dethroned.

What we have seen so far is that there was a common motif both in the Old Testament and Rabbinic writings that bears a great deal of similarity to the way that Luke presents the career of Jesus in relation to the devil. However, there is one obvious divergence that can be seen. Peter, in his proclamation, is not addressing some cosmic being as in Daniel or Isaiah or the War Scroll. He is speaking to Jews, probably many ordinary citizens. How can one be dethroned in some cosmic fashion if one is a bricklayer in southeast Jerusalem, and has never seen a throne, let alone sat in one?

Let us make several observations about Luke's use of repetition. First, of the numerous times in Acts where the kerygma is proclaimed with this judgment theme—you killed God's Christ!—the subjects vary

---

62. Joel Green, in a personal conversation.
63. Garrett, 40.

significantly. In Acts 2, a similar pronouncement is made against Jews and proselytes who had come to the city from all parts of the Empire for the feast:

"...fellow Jews *and* all who live in Jerusalem..." In 4:10, he speaks the same pronouncement against the rulers of Jerusalem. Stephen pronounces it on the high priest and those with him; even further, he extends it even to their fathers, who stood in solidarity with their murder of Jesus by murdering the prophets who came in ages past (7:52). Even when Paul is in Athens in ch. 17, the judgement motif remains; in fact, it is perhaps the most salient commonality between the kerygma proclaimed to the pagan philosophers and that proclaimed in Jerusalem.

The variety of subjects that the judgment motif was applied to in early preaching argues for some larger theme here that would account for its consistent application in such diverse situations. Irenaeus found such a theme.[64] As we noted on p. 5, he spoke of all the sins of all time being "recapitulated" in the murder of Christ. Thus, Stephen can argue that the ancestors of those he addressed partook of the murder of Christ, because they in their own time resisted the Holy Spirit—the Spirit of Jesus. Jesus himself taught this principle of solidarity in sin:

> So you testify that you approve of what your forefathers did; they killed the prophets, and you build their tombs. Because of this, God in his wisdom said, 'I will send them prophets and apostles, some of whom they will kill and others they will persecute.' Therefore this generation will be held responsible for the blood of all the prophets that has been shed since the beginning of the world (Luke 11:48-50).

Luke thus teaches that sin in all generations and places found its culmination (recapitulation, as Irenaeus said) in the murder of Christ. To the degree that a person is found in solidarity with the forces that killed Jesus, the apostles are able to say, you killed him!

In Luke, this solidarity is wider even than the human race. Satan lies behind all the institutional and individual plotting, and all forces in the narrative that conspired against Jesus are seen in solidarity with Satan:

> Then Satan entered Judas, called Iscariot, one of the Twelve. And Judas went to the chief priests and the officers of the temple guard and discussed with them how he might betray Jesus. They were delighted... He consented (Luke 22:3, 4).

This solidarity was not an either/or condition; it was a dynamic; there were differing degrees of solidarity with evil. For instance, both the Romans

---

64. For a more in-depth treatment, see John Driver, *Understanding the Atonement for the Mission of the Church* (Scottdale: Herald, 1986), 284.

and the Jews co-conspired against Jesus, yet Luke sees the Romans as somewhat more willing to repent than are the Jewish authorities, painting them more positively throughout Acts. Yet the Jewish authorities are not ruled out by anything but themselves. They are allowed to disqualify themselves, with Jesus in Luke and the apostles in Acts continually holding out the offer of repentance.[65]

As narrative time elapses, the portrayal of the authorities follows the same thematic line that we saw previously in the trial-form:

> In point of fact, far from triumphing over Jesus, the authorities set the stage for their own demise: Under the lordship of the exalted Jesus, the apostles, not they, will be the leaders of God's reconstituted people, and they make themselves responsible for the destruction of Jerusalem.[66]

In summary of what we have said about solidarity of evil in Luke, first, it is not limited to geographical or temporal proximity to the death of Jesus. Second, it is not limited to individuals or even institutions, but is cosmic in dimension, uniting both human and spiritual powers. Lastly, it is dynamic, and can change, as illustrated by the continual call to repentance.

All this, both the trial-form and what we have said to be the Lucan view of the solidarity of evil, all this provides rationale for seeing the murder pronouncements ('accusation of judicial murder' in my outline) as an intrinsic and not an occasional part of the kerygma in Acts.

Now that some of the meaning of the proclamation has been clarified, we can return briefly to the meaning of the healing as "demonstration." We have already established the linkage between proclamation and demonstration; now we can see that the healing reveals, or is a manifestation of the judgement on the coalition of darkness. The healing is not just a "miracle" or attention-getter, a platform from which to proclaim the "real" message; it is itself an integral part of the proclamation.

This is borne out by the way that Luke structures the narrations of apostolic preaching in Acts. Excepting the two testimonials required of Paul by magistrates, which can not be included as kerygma per se, out of nine instances where the preaching is narrated, seven are intimately connected with a similar "sign." Proclamation and demonstration both declare one reality: Jesus is the Lord.

In the healing of the man in Jesus' name, Jesus is seen to have authority,

---

65. "In Luke, there are three phases to Jesus' ministry, with the religious authorities featured as the main antagonists from 3:1-21:38. During this period, their conflict with Jesus assumes the form of a lengthy but intermittent conversation: Jesus remains open to the authorities because he would summon them to repentance." Kingsbury, 106.

66. Ibid.

or lordship, specifically over sickness. Lucan thought holds that the healing of a person is tantamount to a victory over Satan, though not implying that all sickness is caused by him. Whenever Jesus healed someone he claimed to be "plundering" Satan's dominion, preempting spoil from its master (Lk 11:22).[67] Luke describes Jesus healing a woman "whom Satan had bound" (Lk 13:16); in proclaiming the gospel Peter declared that Jesus had gone around "healing all oppressed under the power of the devil" (Acts 10:38). In this Luke was in full agreement with a plethora of rabbinic writers of the intertestamental period that saw healing as a sign of the dawn of the messianic age.[68]

Next in our outline we have the "offer of clemency" as I have titled it. In its three subpoints, we observe that a) deception is acknowledged to have been at work in the minds of those who killed Jesus; b) God's sovereignty is asserted, and c) repentance is given as the condition of pardon. All three are important themes in Christus Victor.

Regarding the deception theme (αγνοιαν, "ignorance," here) we have already established that the Fathers, especially the two Gregory's, disagreed on the nature of it. When attempting to systematize the deception theme, their language and thought became very graphic at times, describing how Christ used his flesh as bait for the devil to swallow, with the hook being his divinity. Our pericope is much simpler, and only asserts that there was ignorance involved in the murder of Christ. We needn't go beyond that ourselves.

Regarding the repentance theme, it should be noted that it is not a repentance from purely personal sin, but from the solidarity of evil concept that we have argued for. Any reduction of this to purely personal sins is not true to the context. Repent in this context would be to "turn around" from solidarity with that which murdered the Christ.

Finally, we see the statements from vss. 19b-26 united around the theme of the inauguration of the New Age. This was a beloved theme in rabbinic thought. History was divided into the "present evil age" and the blessed "age to come." What Peter is claiming in his proclamation is nothing less than the inbreaking of the age to come. G. Ladd has argued extensively that the whole New Testament embraces this dualistic view, *not of the cosmos*, but of history, with several important differences from the rabbinic teaching:[69] first, the age to come was not a nationalistic dream, but a wholistic kingdom; second,

---

67. Ibid.

68. For one example - and it could easily be multiplied - consider jubilees 23:29: in the messianic age "there will be no Satan and no evil one who will destroy, because all of their days will be days of blessing and *healing."*

69. *See Presence of the Future* (Eerdmans: Grand Rapids, 1974) and Dale Allison, *The End of The Ages Has Come* (Philadelphia: Fortress, 1985).

with the first coming of Christ, the Kingdom was inaugurated, but would not be completely fulfilled until the *parousia*. We live in the "presence of the future" but not wholly in it yet. The nature of this "in-between age" can be seen especially in 20-21a, where the tension is put forth as neatly as anywhere in the New Testament; times of refreshing come as we repent—this can be realized now but the time has not yet come for Christ to restore everything.

The reference to the prophets ties the theology of this passage in with the Old Testament—especially Isaianic—expectation of a transcendent, eschatological kingdom established on earth "as the waters fill the sea", as well as the prophetic drive for a very earthy righteousness manifested in society.[70]

We have now seen in the Lucan kerygma, by implication or explicitly, six of the seven motifs that we listed at the beginning as belonging to Christus Victor.

1. Humanity under the bondage of evil powers.
2. The devil's claim to authority.
3. The recapitulation of sin at the cross.
4. The deception of the coalition of darkness into their murder of Jesus.
5. The disqualifying from authority of the powers of darkness.
6. The exaltation of Jesus to authority.

The remaining motif, the notion of ransom, could very easily be added by implication. Finger suggests that the root idea is that sin has consequences; we are locked into a network of evil that we could not escape unless Jesus gave himself to suffer himself within this network of evil. An equivalent price had to be paid, not to satisfy God, but by the intrinsic necessity of what redemption entailed for Jesus, living under the powers.[71] In Acts 3 we certainly see that for Jesus, sin had terrible consequences.

III. Contemporary Implications: Proclaiming the Good News in the Twenty-first Century

There is no small division today between the average world of the Christian scholar and the Christian evangelist. They often think and work as far apart as the east is from the west. I have worked in an organization that sends out fifty thousand young evangelists every year; yet there must be very few of them that explain the gospel using any other metaphor but those derived from Anselm or moral influence theories. Fewer still would suspect that the formulation of the atonement they know as "gospel truth" was not known in

---

70. For example, Isaiah 65 and Micah 2.
71. Finger, 331.

such a form for the first thousand years of Christianity.

As we have suggested, the collapse of the modern paradigm in our society begs for new ways of formulating the gospel that have not so heavily imbibed rationalistic reductionism. Christus Victor is that, as we have seen.

The church at large could benefit immensely, I believe, from a popularization of its essential concepts. Its implications are broad, much broader than the scope of this paper; our self-understanding is rooted so deeply in the atonement, and we function according as we believe we are—axiology naturally derives from ontology.

Though I began to write only with the notion of using Christus Victor as metaphor for explaining the gospel, to me it becomes apparent that we have here an agenda for action, and not just explanation. Indeed, this very well could be a prime distinction between it and the traditional evangelical gospel, to which may or may not be tacked on any social or transcendent dimension. With Christus Victor, the model contains within itself an inherent wholistic agenda, that encompasses all of life, and is not just occupied with the question of one's soul, narrowly conceived.

What, then, does Christus Victor have to say to our praxis of evangelism? We can hardly do more than identify some starting points.

A. Solidarity

Christus Victor recognizes the interconnectedness of personal, structural, and demonic forces for evil. There is no dichotomy which prioritizes according to a platonic dualism. The interpreters of Anselm have not been kind to our humanness, nor to the place of all of creation in the schema of redemption. Rather, the preoccupation with the formal honour of the feudal lord would intrinsically tend to be satisfied with the redemption of his status as honourable and ours as forgivable. But in Luke-Acts, the atonement brings "the restoration of all things". There is a solidarity to creation: it has conspired in its wholeness against the Christ, and in its wholeness it can be redeemed.

The widespread recognition of this itself is one of the most significant results that could follow a popularization of the Christus Victor schema. From there, however, it must be taken in all directions possible. In other words, the solidarity of all evil means that the body of Christ need not polarize around one or another agenda in being salt and light in our society. The activists confronting our Herods may be in solidarity with charismatics casting out our Satans. And, the cancelling of third-world debt is part of the celebration of the resurrection just as much as the redemption of one prostitute or wealthy businessperson.

B. Theodicy

Christus Victor has something valuable to contribute to our evangelistic apologetic for theodicy. Any Christian who has spent time talking to non-Christians about our faith knows how often this issue comes up. Why does God let the innocent suffer? Why is there evil if God is good?

It was in light of the unspeakable evil of the second world war that a theology of the powers was given new impetus. It is not hard to see why: can this degree of evil be simply attributed to human choice? Or are there also cosmic forces intertwined with what we can see? In the modern era, few would listen to a cosmology like this. Now, there is a growing awareness in the west of a spiritual malaise abroad in this world that cannot be easily overthrown by four spiritual laws on the evangelical front or by more brotherhood of man on the liberal.

Theodicy questions the justness of God, seeking to understand how God can be in any way seen as righteous in light of the disastrous state of the planet, if it really is *his* planet. Christus Victor would say that it is ultimately his, but both sin and redemption go deeper than human choice: creation has for a time been to some extent *given over* to powers under which the Christ suffered. here is no claim to helpless victimhood for humans here. Christus Victor sees us in a solidarity of sin with the soldiers pounding the nails, with murderers of Christ. When he suffered under Pontius Pilate, he suffered under *us*.

While this is certainly not even close to a simple and comprehensive explanation of the way things are, it does beg us to see God not as the feudal lord who preoccupies himself with questions of legalities of his status among us, but as the one who has struck the decisive blow against them only by suffering under them, under us. And it creates space for wrestling with the issues of cosmology that were reduced to simplisms under modernity.

The resurrection, seen as the beginning of the end of the reign of evil, also asserts the ultimate justice of God. It is God's ultimate statement that he is against them, and will eventually but surely consummate his anger against sin.

C. Structures and Repentance

In doing evangelism using the metaphors of the satisfaction theories, repentance is often neglected, turning the gospel into a message of the cheap grace that Bonhoeffer decried. When it is emphasized, it is often the sins violating one's personal conscience that we declare must be turned away from.

The kerygma in Acts called for a repentance that meant turning away from the whole old order; loosing one's loyalty from this present evil age. This meant a turning away from participation in institutions of any kind that held solidarity with the purposes of darkness. This repentance very well might be a process as well as a crisis; the different stances towards Rome between Mark and Luke illustrate that disentanglement from these all-pervasive entities is not simple, or uniform for all disciples, for all time.

In a time where there has never been more freedom to act, it is ironic that such a sense of helplessness to change the big picture pervades us in the west. A view of the atonement that views solidarity with evil as something to be repented of is a shock to our lethargy. But to be born into Kingdom of God is such a shock! It is only our modern pietism, reducing sin down to issues of personal, and never public morality, that props up the illusion that we can be cozy to the corporate evils of our time while confessing Christ. This modern pietism could have only existed under a view of the atonement that emphasized an individualistic and purely personal salvation.

"In the end it was not demons that killed Jesus, it was humans and their institutions—the Sanhedrin and the Roman Government—that did so. Today, opposition to God on earth is still centered in humans."[72] It is from the evil of those human institutions that we must also turn away from, and call others to as well.

D. Structures and Judgement

Part of preaching the gospel in Acts was the pronouncement of God's judgement on whatever forces had aligned themselves against the Messiah. Part of preaching the gospel for us is to confront contemporary institutions that are manifestations of the demonic.

In Christus Victor, as well as rabbinic thought of the first century, judgment on the old order was a sign that the new had come. Our evangelism loses definition if we are announcing less than a complete overthrow of the old order within society, the individual, and even the cosmos. Conversely, by confrontation with the "present evil age" we express in negative terms what the kingdom is about—but showing what it is not.

Luke has engaged behind the scenes in some evaluation of solidarity of various parties in his society, and seemed to say that in some respects, the Roman institution of government, at that time, on certain points was less in solidarity with cosmic darkness than were the authorities of Israel. This resulted in a more positive portrayal of Rome than Jerusalem in Acts. His discerning example is one worthy of following, still remembering our Lord's

---

72. Paul Hiebert, "Spiritual Warfare: Biblical Perspectives" in *Mission Focus* (Vol. 20, no. 3: Sept. 1992), 41-46.

words to be slow to judge, and remembering that we killed the Christ. If we are to confront institutional evil, however, we must discern where it exists.

E. Proclamation and Cosmic Demonstration

In several areas we have seen the unity of proclamation and demonstration in Luke-Acts. The casting out of demons and the healing of the sick was tangible evidence of the presence of the future. They signified, in a way that no social or personal-ethical act could have, that the authority of Satan had been stripped from him. We must continue to learn how to unite our verbal proclamation with the signs that Christ's victory is cosmic, and not merely ethical or societal. Modernity must no longer limit our view of Christ's victory to the reductively materialistic.

F. Metaphor and Worldview

It must be made clear that Christus Victor is not here portrayed as being the exclusive way that Christians should see the atonement. It is one metaphor among several, though admittedly a major one, perhaps one that is large enough to contain the others.

Christus Victor is appropriate for our times in two ways; it is a model that our culture will be increasingly open to as more people weary of naturalism and the mechanistic world view. It could be received for partly the same reason that the New Age movement is being received: transcendence to a rationalist is water in the desert. We can learn to be flexible with metaphors for reasons of contextualization to our culture.

However, there is a point where changing metaphors can be unfaithful to the Biblical world view, and this is what I have argued has happened in Modernity. In our evangelism, we should be encouraged to make use of flexible metaphors to increase the relevancy or clarity of the gospel, but not to supplant the Biblical world view.

A very old metaphor is commending itself to our times for its biblicity and its contemporary relevance. As our society moves away from the Enlightenment in both time and thought, Luke would speak to us new encouragement to declare by proclamation and demonstration the judgment of the Old Order and the presence of the New.

PART SEVEN

ATONEMENT, REBIRTH
AND DEIFICATION

Chapter Seventeen

ATONEMENT: BIRTH OF A NEW HUMANITY

by Anthony Bartlett

The world and the church in it are at a moment of unparalleled crisis. And yet in the midst of crisis it seems to be the character of human beings to wall ourselves off from its depth, until perhaps the truth is absolutely impossible to avoid. Look at the paralysis of the world's nations confronting the problem of global warming: even as the ice caps melt, species disappear and our weather turns more and more freakish, the nations still concern themselves with issues of sovereignty, power, war and wealth. There is a profound mismatch between politics and human reality.

These physical phenomena are also not unrelated to the question of Atonement to be addressed here. How we see the world is causal of the kind of world we get. A violent theory of atonement—a theory that employs violence as generative of its meaning—such a theory will serve to redouble the violent way in which we respond to the world and, then, the way the world/the earth responds to us.

However, the crisis I am referring to goes deeper than the environment, and even of the violence with which we treat it. It is a crisis brought about by the Gospel itself when God introduces God's truth to the world and does so in the most intimate depths of our humanity. It is a kind of radiation therapy, pinpointing the most secret cancer of our being. The cancer is the deep spring of violence within human history and the pinpointing of God is not to destroy by reciprocal violence, but to bring to light and at once to offer the healing of love.

But we are loathe to change, loathe to be other than violent-human. It's as if our core humanity lives in a deep dark cave within us and is convinced by its own spelunker existence that hardness, revenge and violence is the only way to be. When Jesus enters that cave and shows the possibility, right there in the cave, of gentleness, forgiveness, nonviolence and love, the bitter old spelunker can either see his familiar darkness completely made over so that it is almost unrecognizable, or he can storm and rage ever more absolutely in an attempt to put out the light.

In other words, the core crisis of humanity is not of the environment, or even of violence, but of identity and at the most originary level. The violence experienced in the cross, therefore, is not a matter of changing God or of paying off the devil, but of entering the murderous cancer tissue of humanity to make possible a re-programming for the sake of life. The image tells us at once that this version of the work of Christ is nothing like a gnosticism, for it is neither to do with the heavens or with knowledge, but with the depths of human life and with human relationship. Furthermore, it is not simply waiting around for individual souls to be enlightened but, because it works at the generative level of our collective humanity, of itself it provokes a rolling crisis of history and culture. Because the light has shone in the darkness the darkness can no longer behave with impunity. So, as I say, it must find further and further reactive and extreme formations to survive.

Here then is the heart of the matter for this paper and for the way in which I will attempt to respond to the other scholars and writers. The whole human situation has *already* changed because of the cross and it is this change that sets the scene for our contemporary meaning of atonement. In fact, all the theological work and writing represented here and the papers being presented, they all in one way or another recognize this sea-change brought by the cross. And it is from this perspective I wish to approach them.

But there is need to back up here for a moment. As many will already understand, the argument made here is dependent on the work of René Girard, on his development of mimetic anthropology. In a nutshell, Girard has shown that human culture emerged from pre-historic crises of imitative or mimetic desire, rivalry and violence between our hominid ancestors. (For a quick reinforcing image we may think of the work of Jane Goodall with chimpanzees in the Gombe Stream National Park and her descriptions of the strange, periodic and dietetically aberrant hunting of red colobus monkeys, accompanied by frenzied intra-specific behavior. *My Friends The Wild Chimpanzees* National Geographic (1967) It seems the chimps do not enter fully the mimetic abyss and kill one of their own.) The surrogate or collective victim of such crises, by virtue of its ability to bring peace out of chaos, became the foundation of culture, the birth of the sacred, the first god, the principle of human semiotics, the beginning of human language.

Clearly this is not the place to rehearse the evidence for Girard's hypothesis. Suffice to say that this scenario is played out structurally in a million ways in a million places in what we commonly call making someone else a scapegoat. And then, most importantly, Girard views this as a disclosure brought above all by the biblical text. It is the biblical record, beginning with Cain and culminating in the crucifixion of Jesus, that demonstrates the foundational violence of human culture and allows us to trace it back, generatively, to the dawn of humanity. In consequence, mimetic anthropology is also aptly named biblical anthropology.

My own work in *Cross Purposes* was intended to draw out the reverse side of Girard's hypothesis, which was in fact the traditional notion of the compassion of Jesus on the cross, but now understood not in any simply emotive way but as the strict anthropological agency and counterpart to the disclosure of violence. I named it "abyssal compassion," arguing that unless Jesus humanly refused and forgave every violent provocation, then true disclosure of the victim would never have taken place. Rather the cross would have been swallowed up immediately in the cyclical logic of offense and revenge. (Compare the seven brothers in 2 Maccabbees.) But in fact Jesus endlessly, abyssally, suffers with and forgives our violence while even so revealing it, and thus, at the all important personal level (saving grace), evokes in us an answering sorrow, love and conversion, a compassion reciprocal to his.

Here then is a version of atonement, an explanation the meaning and effect of the cross, equal parts disclosure and forgiveness, forgiveness and disclosure. It is evocative of Abelard's account but has the added advantage of basing itself on a fundamental anthropology and, furthermore, being able to explain the content of violence in the other two major doctrines. Cosmic mythological victory over the devil and satisfaction of God's honor/justice are simply reformulations of the actual violence of the cross in terms of mimetic rivalry: worked out in both cases as a mimetic exchange; in the case of the devil, the antagonist didn't know it until it was too late; in the case of God, he intended it all along. Such is the power of generative violence in culture it was almost inevitable that the further the church journeyed from its original eruptive experience of forgiveness such reformulations would take place. Nevertheless, at another, more hidden but dynamic level, the steady effect of the gospels on spiritual, artistic, reflective, ethical and political culture progressively produced the awareness of the victim, and then, finally, late in the day, but still, I believe, before too late, it gave birth to the Girardian understanding of desire, violence, the bible, and the revolutionary meaning of forgiveness.

Having laid this out these aspects of *Cross Purposes*, I now want to show how the logic takes a further step, and here I rejoin my initial remarks. Just as in *Cross Purposes* I drew out the reverse side of Girard's revelation of the victim, viz. the abyssal compassion of Christ, so now I want to draw out, in parallel, the reverse side to the rolling crisis of culture provoked by the cross. Girard certainly remarks on this crisis, but he does not accent it as his main argument. It is present as the generative function of the cross, but he does not develop its meaning, and I think this is the case because he does not clearly foresee an historical solution to this crisis. In contrast, I wish strongly to affirm the biblical hope for a new creation; and by that I mean a transformation of the historical human space into a world of peace, justice, mercy and life. Moreover, I believe this hope is furthered by some of the best elements of postmodern thought. (See Sharon Baker)

Because of the disclosure of the victim it is more and more difficult in global human relationships to make the old ordering effect of "good violence" (i.e. state violence, political oppression, war, capital punishment etc.) actually work. Then, on the intellectual level, the objective rational order of the universe has collapsed into constructed forms, manufactured choice, disposable discourse, semi-existent particles. Philosophy, social theory, physics, all these disciplines participate in the loss of the metaphysical heavens, and developmentally they result from and then go on further to produce the perspective of generative violence by which we compose the human cosmos. The old constitutive order of culture is dissolving through our fingers, like castles made of sand. This is the postmodern world but I believe in concert with Girard it is the gospel revelation of the victim that is the core destabilizing and deconstructive agent.[1]

However, it would be contradictory in theological terms for the biblical creator God to destabilize or disable the old order without at the same time offering, with a parallel insistence and progressively greater clarity, the alternative of a new creation. God's life-giving intent is to lead creation to its completion and this is witnessed in both Old and New Testaments. The seventh day of creation is characterized by blessing, in the same way that human beings who are made in God's likeness receive a blessing (Genesis 1.28-2.3); this would strongly suggest an eventual time-produced earth (the seventh day) where humanity and its authentic blessing converge. Paul in first Corinthians (7.31) tells us "the form of the world is passing away" (i.e. not the world as such), using the word *schēma* for form. This word, *schēma*, then produces the compound, transform/*metaschēmatizein*, as in when he comes "Christ will transform our humble bodies" (Phil.3.21). The Corinthians verse together with the Philippians verse implies that the present form of this world gives way to another.

Here then is the key point of the essay and itself a substantive progression from Girard (even if it still by virtue of mimetic anthropology): not only does the gospel de-constitute the old generative anthropology; necessarily hand-in-hand with this de-constitution it is brings about a human re-constitution. Even if it is not at first apparent—no more apparent, for example, than the de-constitutive revelation of violent cultural origins was initially apparent—it must be supposed that the revelation of generative violence is accompanied by an equal and alternative revelation of generative love and peace. (Note the

---

1. See presentation by author at Theologia Pacis, Akron, PA, Jan. 07, and *The Jonah Zone,* especially chapter three.

importance of "generative;" it is not a matter of ethical or political ideals, but a life-giving, culture-forming power in the world.) This also obviously means that eschatology, the final revelation of Christ to humankind, is neither placed in another sphere, alien to the world, nor is it something characterized by a single, abrupt, violent break. As Jesus said, and on more than one occasion, the kingdom of God is to be compared to something organic and growing, like a seed; and yet, at the same time, not excluding the marked experience of stress and difficulty which a woman has in childbirth (John 16.20-22)

It would be possible then to say that I am presenting a thought of atonement as a kind of cultural atonement, but it goes well beyond that. When the writers of the New Testament grasped the enormous transforming power of Christ they concluded that he was in fact the constituting source of creation itself. In first Corinthians Paul, talking about the multitude of cultural gods and lords, suddenly, and in contrast, concludes, "yet for us there is one God . . . and one Lord, Jesus Christ, through whom are all things and through whom we exist" (1 Cor. 8.6). Similarly the author of the prologue of John announces "All things came into being through him, and without him not one thing came into being" (John 1.3). It's as if the human regenerative experience of Jesus was so enormous, so profound and so endless in its implications, that the whole cosmos was felt to begin all over again through him. And what was true epistemologically, in terms of meaning, then became true ontologically—everything did in fact come into being through him.

The process itself is instructive, for it suggests that the New Testament already sees ontology as subsequent to relationship, and this then would be determinative for eschatology: the world in fact becomes how we relate to it. I will return to these thoughts below, but for the present moment I want simply to hold to view the simple sketched dimensions of the concept. The atonement I am suggesting is a radical re-creation of the human space and to such an extent that it amounts to creation itself, for the first time. Christ is what God for ever purposed in creation and he is the true beginning of all. Jesus' life, cross and resurrection are not an afterthought, nor are they a desperate remedy in a world gone wrong, even less are they the grim fulfillment of a penal judgment. They are the very stuff of life itself, the miracle of the creation of the other out of the infinitely self-giving womb of God, of the other who has the opportunity to return in absolute freedom a reciprocal, infinite self-giving to God. And here of course is the rub: it is a matter of absolute freedom. There are no guarantees. It is always possible the world will refuse the invitation of hospitality, and all we will be left with is ever more desperate crisis. But—and here is the dynamic point of the essay—even as that progressive crisis unfolds the true, singular, redemptive dimensions of the gospel become ever clearer. It is a theme akin to a "vanishing point":

two parallel lines, one of violence, the other of forgiveness, may go on and on into infinity. And yet to our eyes, to the crisis-ridden vision of humanity they can only get closer and closer together. The more the one insists on itself, the more the other does too. And so the gospel choice for forgiveness, for the other who is the enemy, can only continue to grow in thematic and spiritual power in our contemporary world.

I want now to develop these themes in conversation with other writers and thinkers on atonement, many of whom are represented here in this symposium. This will have the merit of further mutual development of themes and ideas. I begin with J. Denny Weaver and his important book, *The Nonviolent Atonement.*[2] Weaver's work represents the best known rejection of traditional atonement formulae, and it has the added advantage of speaking out of the Radical Reform tradition, articulating the Anabaptist existential and historical grasp of nonviolence as a cardinal Christian theme. Weaver rejects the three standard models, ransom from the devil, satisfaction of God, moral influence, because of what he sees as their inherent violence. In all three cases, God is the ultimate agent of Jesus' death and therefore responsible for the violence of his murder. And in the first two instances, at least, Jesus is completely passive, making him a paradigm of the submissive victim. It is at this point that Weaver finds the most compelling contemporary weight for his argument, citing feminist authors like Joanne Carlson Brown, Rebecca Parker, Rita Nakashima Brock, Delores Williams. These authors have written persuasively, including their own experience, that substitutionary atonement has served to condone and reinforce the abuse of women, children and others. There is an appalling truth in the grain of their testimony, and it provides the ethical urgency of Weaver's argument. In these critiques God is convicted of "divine child abuse," or "divine suicide," or modeling the "ultimate surrogate."

In contrast, Weaver presents a version of atonement which is a rediscovery of a pre-Constantinian *narrative Christus Victor*, the story of Jesus' triumph over the forces of evil in his life, death and resurrection. Here the agent of Jesus' death is never God but the historical forces of oppression at loose in the world, in particular the power and violence of the Roman empire. The focus here on the historical context is also a feature of Weaver's treatment of the other models of atonement: he is aware that nothing arrives out of clear blue sky; for example, the satisfaction model substantively repeats themes from medieval society and culture. Rather than think ahistorically, the awareness of context is vital for our understanding of Jesus' death on the cross, as

2. J. Denny Weaver, *Nonviolent Atonement* (Grand Rapids, MI: Wm. B. Eerdmans Pub. Co, 2001).

also our understanding of past understandings of that death. (He also treats violence as a differentiated phenomenon, distinguishing between harmful or lethal coercion, and nonviolent or beneficial coercion.)

In sum Weaver's book represents a decisive break with violence as a thematic in God's action or in God's good pleasure and, behind that, it provides a significant weathervane in the contemporary awareness of religion as giving comfort to abuse and violence. However, Weaver's argument seems vulnerable to me on two counts. First, I think it is impossible for Weaver to lose God's active purpose in Jesus' death. Secondly, from the side of humanity, the cosmic battle as the form or story within narrative *Christus Victor* still utilizes the currency and language of violence, even if the means of triumph are nonviolent. For example, it is possible to gain comfort for violence from the narrative of the book of Revelation, as not a few have. In other words, it is not that easy to escape from the generative power or grammar of violence in culture. There has to be something deeper going on than simply a tactical change of story (from divine to human violence), if we are truly to transform a violent human universe.

Hans Boersma's *Violence, Hospitality and the Cross* has emerged as an important attempt to vindicate the traditional models of atonement, including a critique of Weaver. This book is a subtle interweaving of motifs, producing a many-sided discussion of violence and the cross. What makes it particularly relevant is the way it incorporates postmodern thinking on what is termed pure or absolute hospitality, from the work of Jacques Derrida, and on violence from that of René Girard. I want to turn to Boersma as a necessary foil in a discussion dominated by nonviolent thinking, but before I do I need also to delineate the work of other scholars, in order to round out as much as possible an understanding of what is at stake.

Sharon Baker's doctoral dissertation, *By Grace?: An "Economy" of Atonement* Southern Methodist University, May 2006) is a decisive attempt to break from economic versions of atonement, dominated of course by the satisfaction theory ("satisfaction" belongs to the essence of exchange, as the essence of payment: unless you pay me what you owe me I can never be "satisfied"). The final destination of her work is a concept of sheer forgiveness, uncontaminated by any payment of debt, quid pro quo, settlement of accounts etc. prior to its actual event. God forgives without payment because that is the nature of forgiveness. Helping her to reach this destination is the work of John D. Caputo, himself indebted to Jacques Derrida. Caputo makes forgiveness unnegotiated and unnegotiable and Sharon turns frequently to his lapidary descriptions. For example, she says, "Forgiveness remains the most amazing gift of all that disturbs our sense of a law and order. Indeed, forgiveness is the coin of the realm in the kingdom of God. 'Forgiveness is the gift in which [we] *give away* the debt" owed to us. When Jesus for-*gave*, he gave out of his substance, in excess, without a demand for a return or payback that balances the heavenly books. In fact, the whole of Christianity turns on the gift, on forgiveness, on notions of forgiving and forgetting. In forgiving we give away our credits, unconditionally, beyond the cycle of vengeance, retribution and debt-paying. 'The gift is a give-away. *Le don* is inseparable from *le par-don*. As the gift must not be a secret calculation of a way to get a return for oneself, so it must not encumber the other with a debt. Whatever debts, whatever guilt, the other incurs must be forgiven.'"[3]

Here is a clear point of arrival. However, on the way Sharon deals extensively with Thomas Aquinas, the angelic doctor or, alternately, a grim giant on the pathway! She comments on his doctrines of contingency and free will, divine causality, foreknowledge, providence, evil, salvation etc. etc. While she shows the places in the *Summa* where Aquinas insists on the efficacy of Christ's love in the passion, she equally demonstrates that Aquinas preserves the logic of ransom, satisfaction, payment and punishment. She concludes: "Consequently, even though Aquinas uses the language of forgiveness, God does not truly pardon sin; God receives compensation for sin so that sin is wiped out and forgiveness is unnecessary." (134)

Now, I include this tension—between her conclusions, and a significant teacher of the tradition—because the very same thing is at play in Boersma, and also paradoxically present, in virtue of its complete absence, in Weaver! This tension with the tradition throws into relief what I see as the core issue in these discussions and one that can only be resolved by allowing anthropology and not metaphysics as our first philosophy, our primary method of thought. The issue is this: the moment you attempt to see things from a God's-eye perspective, working everything out in eternal essential terms, of causality, will, necessity, and yet contingency, then you are involved in hopeless contradictions, between grace and freedom, eternity and history, judgment and mercy, law and love etc. etc. etc. But if you start from anthropology you know at once that all our thought is infected by violence, including our structuring of the universe into heaven and earth, gods and humans, good and bad, essence and existence, and even before and after, past and future. A succinct way of stating all this is to reformulate Sartre's famous epigram, recognizing violence in so many ways as a metonym for human existence: "violence comes before essence."

Once you understand that then you will begin radically to distrust any

3. Sharon Baker, 187, quoting Caputo, *Weakness of God: A Theology of the Event* (Bloomington, IL: Indiana University Press, 2006), 210, 232, and *The Prayers and Tears of Jacques Derrida: Religion Without Religion* (Bloomington, IL: Indiana University Press, 1997), 178, 227.

eternal formulations that the tradition has made, including those of Aquinas, and turn instead for meaning to the singular interruption in the midst of time that is the gospel of Jesus. So when Sharon shifts from Aquinas to Caputo, from economy to forgiveness, we know at once we are in the presence of something utterly new, a reshaping of the human cosmos itself. The crucial difference is that this re-shaping is taking place from within and in our lived experience, rather than somehow being orchestrated by a systematic meta- physics from outside, from above. It is the difference between Plato escaping from his cave and rising up to the philosophical form of forms, the pure heav- enly light, which those who learn from him can also possess, between this and Jesus entering the tomb in order to fill its depths with life, which those who learn from him will know also in the depth of their humanity.

One way of dealing with the discrepancy between forgiveness and the metaphysical tradition is to lose the rigor of any one model or concept and dissolve into a multiplicity. In terms of atonement doctrine this would mean a plurality of images and versions, and in the New Testament a "mélange of voices" as Mark Baker and Joe Green describe it in their book *Recovering the Scandal of the Cross, Atonement in New Testament and Contemporary Contexts*. As the title suggests they also continue the approach of plurality in the modern world, seeing the atonement through a variety of interpreters. The approach of multiplicity or plurality is also what I take to be the central method of Tom Finger and Peter Schmiechen. While this approach has the benefit of blunting the edge of violence in God and deflecting the necessity of economy, it fails I believe to respond to the depth of the postmodern crisis. In other words, no matter the plurality we invoke the challenge of violence will continually get worse until we confront it on the level of anthropology, which is really to confront it on the level of the New Testament and divine revelation.

The postmodern situation rather than characterized by a host of Cartesian subjects, each with their own personal metaphysics, is much more a matter of the future or coming of the other, *l'avenir de l'autre,* the messianic as Derrida calls it. Liberal modernity has been replaced by the secret yet absolute rela- tionship we have to each other. Boersma recognizes this as itself a Christian idea, beginning his work with the image of God's pure or absolute hospitality and rehearsing the thought of Levinas and Derrida as a kind of echo of this divine hospitality. Then similar to Sharon Baker he invokes a major figure of the tradition and seeks somehow to be faithful to the teacher's theology. The figure here is Calvin, notorious for such an absolute concept of God's will that it becomes an intense form of violence. Boersma recognizes this and seeks to reframe Calvin in a less terrible way. He is not entirely successful, and I think deliberately so. For in the overall text of his book, perhaps not fully acknowledged, I think that what is truly at stake in his reading of Calvin is not double predestination but God's determinative and unconditional move in Christ to bring us into his absolute hospitality. This is what provides the power of the book, and paradoxically he cannot give up Calvin for that reason.

I also think this gracious subtext in *Violence, Hospitality and the Cross*, is the same one underlying Sharon Baker's break from Aquinas, and it implies also the resolution of Boersma's severe critique of Weaver. The key difference in Boersma's Calvin from Sharon Baker's Aquinas was that Calvin, as a premier creative thinker of the Reformation, had moved closer to a sovereign, unmerited, noneconomic grace of God than the more Aristotelian and feudal Aquinas ever could, and he is, therefore, at a radical level coherent with pure hospitality. The resolution with Weaver then comes at the level of Weaver's complete rejection of violence in God's salvific work in Christ, a gesture of pure hospitality in sympathy with a radicalized Calvin! What I'm claiming in essence is that our contemporary situation of its own power is wearing away the old metaphysical discourse—deconstructing it—and letting emerge in its place the unconditional message of absolute hospitality. In my own terms in *Cross Purposes*, I called this message abyssal compassion, and the general anthropological shift in the collapse of metaphysics and the human demand for hospitality I have named here as the recreation of the humans space. The contemporary emergence of these changes, as a real transformation of the human cultural environment, is what allows me to read Boersma in this strong fashion.

Boersma critiques Weaver, using a univocal concept of violence (Girard liberates us from this); claiming he abandons the broad Christian tradition; claiming he forfeits divine intentionality.

Boersma criticizes Weaver for lacking any divine intentionality in his doctrine of atonement. Boersma in contrast is top heavy with divine intentionality. He starts his book with a quote from Cyril of Jerusalem: God "stretched out his hands on the cross, that he might embrace the ends of the world; for this Golgotha is the very center of the earth."[4] With this initial trope Boersma makes the cross the act of God himself and seals the meaning of the book as an essay on absolute hospitality. His subsequent treatment of Calvin seems to belie this, but it does not overwhelm Cyril's headline words. Boersma describes Calvin's concept of double predestination—the destiny of the elect to eternal happiness and the reprobate to eternal pain, an idea that already belonged to the right wing of the Augustinian tradition. There it was

4. Hans Boersma, *Violence, Hospitality and the Cross, Reappropriating The Atonement Tradition* (Grand Rapids, Michigan: Baker Academic, 2004), 25.

modified or camouflaged by the whole economic apparatus of medieval piety, for in Calvin it attained a much more central relief in the Reformation insistence on teaching and the word. In respect then of this central relief Boersma comments, "the cross can easily be overshadowed by our belief in predestination. When this happens, divine violence overtakes and eliminates divine hospitality."[5] And yet Boersma also says, "An important function of the doctrine of election is precisely to safeguard the hospitality of God. Divine election is God's determination to extend his grace, so it is the sovereignty of *grace* that Calvin is concerned with when he discussed predestination. The doctrine of predestination exalts, for Calvin, the mercy of God who accepts alienated strangers into fellowship with him and so brings them into his eternal home."[6]

From a strict logical point of view, however, the matter is settled by the explicit doctrine of God's eternal, ahistorical will for each individual, bliss for some, torture for others. This is God's "secret will" and it contrasts with God's "signified will" which is that all should be saved.[7] It is not that God is schizophrenic and has two wills (or so Boersma argues), but that the secret will is eternal and the revealed will is accommodated to our humanity, presumably to motivate us to live virtuously in real time, including, we may infer, those who will not ultimately be saved.[8] But then, of course, eternal meaning triumphs over the temporal every time, and so Boersma aptly comments, "The hidden will takes precedence over the revealed will. Violence trumps hospitality."[9] The issue becomes more fraught still when we read that a consequence of the secret will of God was the possibility the effect of the atonement was limited to the elect only: in other words Christ did not die for all. Calvin does not seem to have said this explicitly, but according to Boersma he seems to have thought it.[10]

At this point Boersma has reached an aporia between his initial announcement of divine hospitality and the absolute inversion to which it has led. It seems impossible to save this material from a sense of the most brutal, arbitrary violence—violence in the very heart of God as Boersma names it. For this reason it is at least important to be aware of this element in the Christian

---

5. Ibid., 54

6. Ibid., 55, Boersma's italics.

7. Ibid., 67, Calvin comments that God "desires all men to be saved" explaining 2 Peter 3.9, from *The Epistle of Paul the Apostle to the Hebrews and the First and Second Epistles of St. Peter,* trans. William B. Johnson, ed. David W. Torrance and Thomas F. Torrance (Grand Rapids: Eerdmans, 1963), 364.

8. *Violence, Hospitality and the Cross*, 60 & n.25, 58. n.18.

9. Ibid., 62

10. Ibid., 67

tradition, to know to what extremes the co-option of the gospel by generative human violence has led. The gospel has been read within a controlling metaphysics of eternity and time, and then very specifically in situations like 16th century Europe and contemporary North America, all riven by lethal political tensions. We should at least be grateful to Boersma for examining Calvin's theology as a question of violence and so letting us see clearly his disastrous metaphysics, with evident social and political consequences waiting in the wings for their cue.

Boersma, however, definitely does not want to leave it there and he embarks on an attempt to present a more temperate view. He rehearses Israel's story from the Old Testament and argues that, in concrete terms, election and reprobation had an historical and instrumental character. He talks, for example, about the war of invasion against the Canaanites, and for our purposes this can stand for any number of instances of biblical violence. "Precisely because God's hospitality takes place within a history that is already marred by human violence, his hospitality cannot be pure or universal in character. God's hospitality is concerned to put an end to human sin and violence, Giving universal, unconditional affirmation would mean that God would let human violence run amok."[11] Here is the nub of the argument: God may extend absolute hospitality but in concrete historical circumstances this must also include boundaries that are violently enforced. We are in the real world of unredeemed lives and hearts; you can't simply let it run over you and so allow the gesture of hospitality itself to be obliterated. Not surprisingly this refers also to Christ. "(T)o insist on 'pure hospitality" in an impure world would mean to give it over to the forces of inhospitality and violence. Put provocatively, God's hospitality in Christ needs an edge of violence to ensure the welcome of all humanity and all creation."[12] Or, put provocatively another way, political necessity arms the nonviolence of Christ, producing the inversion of God's hospitality. Indeed, once you admit that edge of violence all the old violent models of atonement, including ransom and satisfaction, demand their place at the table. And Boersma finds it for them, reintroducing them under the general heading of Irenaeus' "recapitulation." Because Christ sums up all things, he does so in terms of the theological tradition too, enacting in fact all the major atonement narratives from Irenaeus and Origen, through Abelard, and of course Anselm.

The mention here of "pure hospitality" is a reference back to Derrida and the review Boersma made of this concept at the outset of the book. It awakens the thread that weaves through the book like the classic subordinate part-

11. Ibid., 84
12. Ibid., 93

ner in Derrida's own theory of binaries in writing, the pairs of opposites out of which the text "constructs" its truth. By lifting up and revealing this hierarchical and subordinating effect the text is made at once to "deconstruct" itself. "Pure hospitality" is the subordinate partner to "the necessary violence of boundaries" in *Violence, Hospitality and the Cross*. By differentiating and deferring "pure hospitality," either to the cross, or the indefinite future of the eschaton, Boersma constructs his book. But then an amazing series of blocked pathways results: just as Calvin's thought of double predestination blocks the path of absolute divine hospitality, so the necessity of boundaries blocks the thought of pure hospitality. And the most pure thought of the divine, the hospitality of the cross, is validated in human historical terms by an atheist philosopher, but denied precisely in those historical terms by a Christian theologian. Derrida has always said that deconstruction is the opening to the other, whoever that might be, stranger, enemy, the devil himself. But because Christianity is about excluding the devil then Boersma refuses pure hospitality. He thus complains:

> Derrida's notion of "pure hospitality" is in itself a valuable notion. The problem is not with the idea as such. Christians have always affirmed that God is love or pure hospitality. The difficulty with Derrida's unconditional hospitality is that it is the logical outcome of his loss of God of a determinate religion. There is for Derrida no God who at some point will usher in the eschatological messianic future and deal with all violence that we have witnessed and participated in throughout our lives. It as though the lack of transcendent warrant for human hospitality (i.e. the God of the cross and the resurrection) creates a utopian impatience in Derrida that insists we introduce pure hospitality here and now. What is tragic about this insistence is Derrida's awareness that this hospitality remains an impossibility.[13]

This is a stunning piece of theological writing. Pure hospitality is not Derrida's idea, it belongs to Christians. Yet because Derrida is not Christian (or perhaps at least not a faithful Jew) he is actually the one who really, really wishes there was factual hospitality in the earth. Meanwhile those who hold belief in the cross and resurrection (sic!) are the ones who can comfortably defer it, put it off, indefinitely. And those who actually believe in impossible things (cross and resurrection) can dismiss his restless, urgent, human search, his "prayers and tears," as the old story of tragedy, because they understand their own belief as "transcendent warrant." Even so does Christian theology offend against itself because of its redefinition of the gospel as timeless metaphysics.

Derrida does not see the essentialized future of Christian metaphysics, what is called the eschaton, rather he sees the coming of the other now. It

13. Ibid., 36

is never fully realized, but it's clear, precisely because he is talking about the cultural and anthropological opening of language and meaning, and also about an historical "messianicity," that it is always to do with the real world. This indeed is the heart of Caputo and Sharon Baker's argument, that forgiveness is an event now. Boersma defers the coming of the Messiah into an idealized future, but in the very way his book is structured his thought is also part of the coming that Derrida talks about. The pure hospitality of the cross leaks into every page and breaks through the boundaries he himself invokes. He is right, therefore, both in principle and in the work of his text to critique Weaver for the latter's apparent absence of divine intention in his version of atonement. But by the same token of the coming of the other, in and through the cross of Christ, that divine intention is also obliquely present in Weaver,

Weaver of course calls on the resurrection as part of the triumph of God over the powers of oppression, and it's hard to conceive such a transcendent event without divine intentionality. Certainly in the gospels Jesus has a conviction of divine vindication following the necessity that he suffer and die. And in respect of the historical Jesus it seems to me implausible that such an extraordinary figure would go to his death without some willed, future, divinely authored meaning. But, again in respect of Weaver's overall text, I think the determining theme of nonviolence is itself an event of divine intentionality. And, once more the same as with Boersma, this is not an abstract eternal intentionality, but the concrete in-breaking of God's hospitality, his absolute nonviolent compassion, in the human scene here and now. It is God's bringing to birth of a new creation.

Boersma uses the classic word for this, Irenaeus' recapitulation, which he translates reconstitution. Weaver, from his side, is absolutely right to say Boersma uses this as camoflauge for violence, as an ahistorical way of sneaking back into theology the discredited themes of substitutionary atonement. Irenaeus never gives systematic development to this concept, but he does seem to use it to show Jesus repeating and reversing tropes from human history. And what would stand in greater need to reverse than generative violence, with its power to bring death and a false structuring of human life? So in fact Irenaeus says, "That which he appeared, that he also was: God recapitulating in Himself the ancient creation, in order that He might slay sin and destroy the power of death, and give life to men."[14] Yes, here is the violence of *Christus Victor*, but the hermeneutic core is not the rhetoric of combat but the goal, which is the overcoming of death falsely structured in creation. Girard has taught us that as far as human culture is concerned

14. *Cross Purposes*, 64

this structuring has come about through mimetic rivalry and violence which produces the actual human world. And what I have emphasized is the way this old world is collapsing under the pressure of the gospel, and that this sea-change is illustrated by the general themes of postmodernism, including the end of metaphysics. Thus recapitulation or reconstitution goes hand in had with deconstruction or de-constitution. When Boersma, in commenting on Girard, accuses him of ontologizing violence he has completely missed the gospel dynamic that we are in the midst of: it is not a matter of turning violence into being, but showing that the very being that we thought that was just there, was in fact being, is constituted out of violence. Girard does not ontologize violence. He and most of postmodern philosophy dissolve being into its constituent violence, and this in fact is the work of Christ. This is what it means, in the words of Irenaeus, to "slay sin and destroy the power of death." It is to expose the constitution of the human world for what it is, thereby to bring it to an end, and in the very same breath to offer it a totally new constitution.

For Weaver this is nonviolence. For me it is abyssal compassion. For Mark Baker, Schmiechen and Finger it is telling a different and a new story. For Derrida and Sharon Baker it is pure hospitality and forgiveness. In every case it is a breaking away from the closed order of the past, from the giants of the tradition, locked in their metaphysical dreams, into the radically new thing that only Christ brings. Here then is a dynamic version of atonement that is not exchange but creation, not legalism but poetry, not eternity but time, not violence but bringing to birth. It is the absolute nonviolence of Genesis chapter one and the acute violence of the passion rolled inseparably, transformatively, mysteriously into one. As Jesus said, "When a woman is in labor, she is in anguish because her hour has arrived; but when she has given birth to a child, she no longer remembers the pain because of her joy that a child has been born into the world." (John 16.21). I say that the birth pangs are upon us, indeed we are ten centimeters dilated!

Chapter Eighteen

RETAINING AND RECLAIMING THE DIVINE: IDENTIFICATION AND THE RECAPITULATION OF PEACE IN ST. IRENAEUS OF LYONS' ATONEMENT NARRATIVE

by Andrew P. Klager

The nonviolence of Christ is a notable yet typically undervalued coalescing element unifying the components of St. Irenaeus' atonement narrative, commonly understood as recapitulation.[1] This nonviolence is of course contextually and circumstantially stimulated, and in particular originates from anthropogonic notions of humanity's incompetence on the one side, while stimulating obedience and empowerment of the Church on the other. Irenaeus' atonement theology, therefore, functions as a narrative precisely because it chronicles a redemption *exemplum* from the (1) Edenic state of *shalom* and inchoate humanity to (2) the Incarnate Christ's nonviolent instruction, example and usurpation of death in order that (3) humanity might assimilate this same recapitulation of peace for itself.[2] Irenaeus' atonement narrative

---

1. St. Irenaeus' theory of recapitulation is well known. For instance, J.G. Davies claims, "His [Irenaeus] key concept may be summed up in the word 'recapitulation.'" J.G. Davies, The Early Christian Church: A History of its First Five Centuries (New York: Doubleday, 1967), 127. Justo L. Gonzalez states that for St. Irenaeus, "Jesus is the 'second Adam' because of his life, death, and resurrection a new humanity has been created, and in all his actions Jesus has corrected what was corrected because of sin." Justo L. González, *The Story of Christianity*, vol. 1 (San Francisco: HarperCollins, 1984), 70. Stuart G. Hall states, "Using a term borrowed from Paul (*anakephalaiosasthai*, Eph. 1:10), Irenaeus says repeatedly that Jesus Christ recapitulated ('summed up afresh') the career of Adam. ... He did this by coming in the flesh like Adam, and living through the years of a human life, triumphant always over the temptations of Satan. So he goes over the ground again, does well what was badly done before, and sums up the whole purpose of mankind's existence." Stuart G. Hall, *Doctrine and Practice in the Early Church* (Grand Rapids, MI: Eerdmans, 1991), 66. J.N.D. Kelly affirms this and says, "The key-conception, which Irenaeus employs to explain this is 'recapitulation' (ἀνακεφαλαίωσις), which he borrows from St. Paul's description of the divine purpose as being 'to sum up all things in Christ.'" J.N.D. Kelly, *Early Christian Doctrines* (New York: HarperCollins, 1978), 172. Kenneth Latourette asserts, "Jesus as man at every stage of his life, by what is known as *recapitulation*, or 'summing up', perfectly fulfilled what God had intended man and His entire creation to be." Kenneth Scott Latourette, *A History of Christianity*, vol. 1 (Peabody, MA: Prince Press, 2003), 143. Philip Schaff states that Christ "renewed or recapitulated the struggle of Adam with Satan, but defeated the seducer, and thereby liberated man from his thraldom." Philip Schaff, *History of the Christian Church*, vol. 2 (Peabody, MA: Hendrickson, 2002)

2. Schaff advances a similar tripartite division of Eden, Christ and the Church: "Redemption comprises the taking away of sin by the perfect obedience of Christ; the

is therefore decidedly teleological in that the end is of the utmost concern and is regulated by certain requisite obligations. Incidentally, the aforementioned outline is reflected also in the organization of this essay in an effort to illuminate the unmistakable presence of *identification*[3] in Irenaeus' atonement theology. Collateral strands of identification oscillate mutually between the Incarnate Christ and the latently deified human. The former identifies with humanity by becoming man and leaving himself vulnerable to the same socio-political oppression and exploitation humanity endures recurrently, while simultaneously *retaining his divinity* – this is to say, maintaining his obligation to the kingdom of God. Alternatively, humanity identifies with Christ by submitting to his nonviolent instruction and by participating in the kingdom of God, or *reclaiming the divine*, all within the threat of self-preserving impulses which one must learn to curtail in the face of socio-political opposition. The union of human and divine on both sides of identification are meant to rectify the ominous circumstances inherited by humanity on account of Adam's apostatical contagion.

Christ's *inculcation* and *capacitation* of humanity are the two antidotes designed to neutralize the latter's prideful self-interests and undermine death's tyrannical reign. Christ's teachings and nonviolent precedent function as a paragon of selflessness and altruism, an alternative which is consistent with the kingdom of God but is in opposition to the prideful and self-preserving impulses that are intrinsic to the created being by virtue of its autonomous existence and the compulsion to prolong this existence. Furthermore, Christ's victory over death enables humanity to follow Christ's way of suffering as an alternative to fighting back, while also providing solidarity and support to those who perennially confront socio-political opposition.

Methodologically, this assessment of Irenaeus' atonement theology will centre on his use of Christ's nonviolence as a mechanism for illuminating the various components of his atonement narrative. Although very real, Christ's nonviolence will then function as the agency through which I will interpret Irenaeus' atonement theory. Conversely, the components of Irenaeus' atonement theology will each bear out the significance of nonviolence in his thought, and in particular as it relates to humanity's redemption. This method, of course, runs the risk of overemphasizing an element, that of Christ's and the Church's nonviolence, which is perhaps less prominent in Irenaeus'

destruction of death by victory over the devil; and the communication of a new divine life to man." Philip Schaff, *History of the Christian Church*, 587.

3. Kelly uses this term in a representative description of Irenaeus' view of atonement: "Because He is identified with the human race at every phase of its existence, He restores fellowship with God to all, perfecting man according to God's image and likeness." J.N.D. Kelly, *Early Christian Doctrines*, 173.

writings than an essay such as this might give the impression. I acknowledge the *caveat* against such intemperance and trust that my readers will do the same by permitting the disclosure of an often neglected characteristic of Irenaeus' atonement theology, while, in addition to its overt exposition, remaining aware of its often allusive and cryptic yet pervasive expression throughout Irenaeus' writings.[4] Nonviolence is therefore a suitable foil by which one may gain insight into the import of Adam's apostasy, while also allowing revelation into the restoration of humanity through the reciprocal identification of Christ to humanity and *vice versa*.

Significantly, to surmise that this essay is just as concerned with theology as it is with the exposition of intellectual history, and in particular that of Irenaeus, is not entirely unwarranted. In keeping with Herbert Butterfield's contention that "religious thought is inextricably involved in historical thought,"[5] this essay will not shy away from discussing the theological implications inherent in Irenaeus' thought. The theological discussions in this essay are particularly cognizant of contemporary scholarship that questions the role of violence in atonement theology,[6] and deal specifically with its concern regarding penal substitutionary models that appear to facilitate the

4. It should be noted, however, that Irenaeus by no means avoids overt descriptions of Christ's nonviolence: cf. St. Irenaeus of Lyons, *Adversus Haereses* [*AH*] 2.20.3.; *AH* 3.16.9.; *AH* 3.18.4-5.; *AH* 4.28.3.; *AH* 4.34.4. (especially); *AH* 5.1.1.; *Epid.* 34. It is these explicit references to Christ's nonviolence and that of the Church that permits investigation into its significance for his atonement narrative as a whole. Unless otherwise indicated, all Latin references to St. Irenaeus' *Adversus Haereses* are from William Wigan Harvey, ed., *Sancti Irenaei Libros Quinque Adversus Haereses* (Cantabrigiae: Typis Academicis, 1857), while the divisions are from René Massuet, *Patroloigia Graeca*; all English translations are from Alexander Roberts and James Donaldson, eds., *Ante-Nicene Fathers: The Writings of the Fathers Down to A.D. 325*, vol. 1 (Peabody, MA: Hendrickson, 2004); all references to *Epideixis* [*Epid.*] are taken from the English translation, Armitage Robinson, trans., *St. Irenaeus: The Demonstration of the Apostolic Preaching* (New York: Macmillan, 1920).

5. Herbert Butterfield, *Christianity and History* (New York: Scribner's, 1950), 3. Significant to Irenaeus' distinctly narrative and teleological atonement theology, Butterfield also observes, "History must be a matter of considerable concern to Christians in so far as religion in this way represents the attempt to engage oneself with the whole problem of human destiny" (2).

6. See, for instance, Anthony W. Bartlett, *Cross Purposes: The Violent Grammar of Christian Atonement* (Harrisburg, PA: Trinity 2001); David Cone, *God of the Oppressed* (Maryknoll, NY: Orbis Books, 1997); John Driver, *Understanding the Atonement for the Mission of the Church* (Scottdale, PA: Herald, 1986); Raymund Schwager, *Jesus in the Drama of Salvation* (New York: Crossroad, 1999); J. Denny Weaver, *The Nonviolent Atonement* (Grand Rapids, MI: Eerdman's, 2001); Delores S. Williams, *Sisters in the Wilderness: The Challenge of Womanist God-Talk* (Maryknoll, NY: Orbis Books, 1993); James G. Williams, *The Bible, Violence and the Sacred: Liberation from the Myth of Sanctioned Violence* (Valley Forge, PA: Trinity, 1995); Walter Wink, *Engaging the Powers: Discernment and Resistance in a World of Domination* (Minneapolis: Fortress, 1984).

perpetuation of human violence by way of imitation and mimetic ratification.[7] It is hoped that the typicality[8] and authority of Irenaeus' careful exposition of the Incarnate Christ's redemptive efforts and procedure will generate more scholarly discussions on the patristic witness of nonviolence in atonement theology, not only with respect to the nature of God's wrath, Christ's passion and the Church's re-enactment of the same, but also with an awareness of the precursory anthropogonic imputations.

I. ADAMIC INCOMPETENCE AND THE VIOLENCE OF DEATH:

Central to St. Irenaeus' atonement narrative is the matter of human freedom and culpability in reference to Adam's apostasy. At issue is what Irenaeus understands the meaning of *freedom* to be and what effect this definition might have on whether or not Adam, and subsequent humanity, is to blame for his apostatical miscue. As with the forthcoming discussion on Irenaeus' conception of wrath and propitiation, the notion of freedom ought not be evaluated etymologically but instead philologically, this is to say, by allowing the literary context decide its meaning.[9] Therefore, the oft-cited notion of (1) Adam and Eve as *νήπιοι*[10] will also be analyzed contextually as will Irenaeus' perception of (2) humanity's creaturehood and (3) death's tyranny over subsequent humanity as violence; this tripartite regulation of human freedom will then be followed by a more comprehensive examination of human culpability within the context of the polemical function of God's wrath in Irenaeus' writings and his designation of 'propitiation' as humanity's ontological alignment with the Incarnate Christ.

---

7. This is in reference to René Girard's well known theory of mimetic violence, which draws upon an anthropological assessment of victimization in archaic religion definitively portrayed in René Girard, *Violence and the Sacred*, Patrick Gregory, trans. (Baltimore: John Hopkins University Press, 1977).

8. Gustaf Aulén is, I think, correct when he contends, "It is true that we do not find in [Irenaeus] the brilliant style of Tertullian, the philosophical erudition of Clement or Origen, or the religious depth of Augustine. Yet of all the Fathers there is not one who is more thoroughly representative and typical, or who did more to fix the lines on which Christian thought was to move for centuries after his day." Gustaf Aulén, *Christus Victor: An Historical Study of the Three Main Types of the Idea of the Atonement*, A. G. Herbert, trans. (New York: MacMillan, 1986), 16-17.

9. Matthew Steenberg makes the same assertion with regard to our immediate discussion of Adam and Eve as *νήπιοι* (infants): "Too much emphasis, however, must not be laid upon the intricacies of the vocabulary, which in any case is often conjectural due to the complex manuscript and translation history of the corpus. But giving due acknowledgement to the problems posed by this history, the importance of context in any case greatly outweighs that of terminology." M.C. Steenburg, "Children in Paradise: Adam and Eve as 'Infants' in Irenaeus of Lyons," *Journal of Early Christian Studies* 12, no. 1 (Spring 2004): 6.

10. "infants" or "infantile".

A. Initial and Subsequent Humanity's Disobedience

The origin of humanity, and the implications of its essential dissimilarity to that of the Uncreated or divine substance, occupies much of Irenaeus' atonement theology. Indeed, as Matthew Steenberg observes, "Scholars have long understood the anthropogonic discussion of Irenaeus of Lyons to be central to his whole conception of both the divine-human economy and the ultimate salvation of humankind."[11] Solely for purposes of precision, using medieval scholastic terminology borrowed from antecedent Aristotelian metaphysics, an evaluation of the origin of humanity in reference to Adam's apostasy and the ensuing tyranny of death must recognize an alteration in humanity's *quidditas*, or in metaphysics its *hypokeimenon*, or underlying and essential substance, what St. Irenaeus refers to as *substantia* or *οὐσία*.[12] For Irenaeus, humanity was constrained by imperfection naturally by virtue of its creaturehood and corporeality. Humanity was therefore impeded from the beginning, its apostasy a consequential occurrence due specifically to its created rather than Uncreated origin and *οὐσία*.[13] The modification to humanity's substance incurred by its infantile and creaturely disobedience implies a loss of divinity,[14] a loss which is further

---

11. M.C. Steenberg, "Children in Paradise: Adam and Eve as 'Infants' in Irenaeus of Lyons," 1.

12. Aristotle used the Greek variation *οὐσία*, which, as a Greek writer, was used also by St. Irenaeus. In philosophy, the *quiddity* of a person or thing refers to its essence or substance as opposed to its *haecciety* or properties, and is therefore a beneficial distinction to use within the context of Irenaeus' own thought. This is an important concept in Irenaeus' thought as it impacts his understanding of the image and likeness of God in humanity, the incarnation and resultant deification of humanity. Accordingly, St. Irenaeus declares, "He shows that all are from one essence [*"ex una substantia esse omnia"* or *"ἐκ μιᾶς οὐσίας εἶναι πάντα"*], that is, Abraham, and Moses, and the prophets, and also the Lord Himself, who rose from the dead, in whom many believe who are of the circumcision, who do also hear Moses and the prophets announcing the coming of the Son of God. But those who scoff [at the truth] assert that these men were from another essence, and they do not know the first-begotten from the dead." *AH* 4.2.4.; Cf. *AH* 4.36.1. For Irenaeus' understanding of *οὐσία* in his eschatology, Cf. *AH* 2.36.1.; in reference to Irenaeus' rudimentary apophaticism and the essence of God, Cf. *AH* 3.24.2.; *AH* 2.6.1.; in reference to the Incarnate Christ's essential union with God, Cf. *AH* 3.21.4.

13. "For the Uncreated is perfect, that is, God. Now it was necessary that man should in the first instance be created." *AH* 4.38.3.

14. "And then, again, this Word was manifested when the Word of God was made man, assimilating Himself to man, and man to Himself, so that by means of his resemblance to the Son, man might become precious to the Father. For in times long past, it was *said* that man was created after the image of God [*imaginem Dei*], but it was not [actually] *shown*; for the Word was as yet invisible, after whose image man was created, Wherefore also he did easily lose the similitude [*Propter hoc autem et similitudinem facile amisit*]. When, however, the Word of God became flesh, He confirmed both these: for He both showed forth the image truly, since He became Himself what was His image; and He re-established the similitude after a sure manner [*et similitudinem firmans*

maintained and encouraged by the tyranny of death.[15]

Adam and Eve as Infants:

In particular, it is the creation of Adam and Eve as infants that portends the impending apostasy, while it is also a notion that challenges the understanding of God's wrath as a genuine and imminent punishment intended for a deserving humanity. The two primary passages from Irenaeus' only complete extant works that illuminate his notion concerning the infantility of Adam and Eve are *AH* 4.38.1 and *Epid.* 14. The most comprehensive treatment of Adam and Eve's infant creation is M. C. Steenberg, "Children in Paradise: Adam and Eve as 'Infants' in Irenaeus of Lyons," *Journal of Early Christian Studies* 12, no. 1 (Spring 2004): 1-22.[16] Various other de-contextualized, yet no less accurate, conjectures as to what is implied by Irenaeus' designation of Adam and Eve as created infants, although usually only mentioned in passing, also exist; John I. Hochban believes St. Irenaeus' understanding of Adam and Eve as infants implies "a spiritual childhood or immaturity, in the sense that at the beginning Adam had not attained the full degree of perfection of which he was capable."[17] Affirming the claim above regarding humanity's created state and the Uncreated οὐσία, but specifically in reference to humanity's initial infantility, J.N.D. Kelly maintains, "Being a creature, Adam was necessarily far removed from the divine perfection and incorruptibility; an infinite distance divided him from God. In paradise, therefore, he was morally,

---

restituit], by assimilating man to the invisible Father through means of the visible Word." *AH* 5.16.2.

15. While accentuating the function of the Word become man, St. Irenaeus often vouches for humanity "who had been drawn by sin into bondage, but was held by death, so that sin should be destroyed by man [*ut peccatum ab homine interficeretur*], and man should go forth from death." *AH* 3.18.7.

16. Steenburg observes that this concept in Irenaeus' thought has not been addressed adequately. Other than Steenberg's study, the only other comprehensive insight into the notion of Adam and Eve as infants is the fourth chapter in Ysabel de Andia, *Homo vivens: Incorruptibilité et divinisation de l'homme selon Irénée de Lyon* (Paris: Etudes Augustiniennes, 1986), 127-145. Steenberg comments further on available studies: "Iain M. MacKenzie, *Irenaeus's Demonstration of the Apostolic Preaching: A Theological Commentary and Translation* (Aldershot, England: Ashgate, 2002), 116–17, describes the creation of Adam and Eve as children as 'one of the idiosyncrasies of Irenaeus' but never examines the issue further. More extensive treatment of the concept is given in John Behr, *Asceticism and Anthropology in Irenaeus and Clement* (Oxford: Oxford University Press, 2000), 43, 110, and later at 135–36 when he compares the theme in Clement and Irenaeus; but it is mentioned rather than explained, since in neither instance is it the focus of Behr's work. His quotations from Clement do show, however, that the notion of childhood was not limited solely to Irenaeus" (2: note 3).

17. John I. Hochban, "St. Irenaeus on the Atonement," *Theological Studies* 7, no. 4 (December 1946): 529.

spiritually and intellectually a child."[18] Christopher A. Hall also gives brief mention of Adam and Eve as infants,[19] while Stuart G. Hall recognizes as well that, for Irenaeus, "from the start man was juvenile."[20]

Matthew Steenberg's study, however, still has the most to offer our discussion of human freedom and culpability. Steenberg alleges that indeed, in its rudimentary form, Adam and Eve's infantility should be taken "at face value" retaining its "basic, physiological meaning."[21] But he points out also that the term νήπιος is not a pejorative and should in no way present a derogatory image of humanity since Adam and Eve's infantility is an ineluctable consequence of their corporeality.[22] While a purely physical understanding of humanity's original infantility in the thought of Irenaeus does not undermine the aforementioned challenge regarding human culpability, Steenberg's further suggestion that "Irenaeus' literalism need not and does not abolish altogether a more symbolic scope to his discussion" accentuates the vulnerability of attempts at assigning blame to humanity for its apostasy. If careful study of the literary context endorses, which it indeed seems to, Steenberg's assertion that "such passages as *Epid.* 14 and *AH* 3.23.5 can, indeed, be taken metaphorically for a 'childlikeness' in the mental state of an Adam and Eve of any physical age,"[23] this unique concept of Irenaeus' anthropogony alters significantly the purpose of God's wrath, the definition of human freedom and the affirmation of human culpability in the rest of his thought. Ultimately, Steenberg, I think correctly, acknowledges an alliance or mutual dependence between the physicality and metaphorical description of humanity's initial infantility: "The imperfection and 'infancy' of Adam are seen not as pure synonyms, but rather his 'infancy' is in fact logically antecedent to his imperfection."[24] Consequently, the challenge against distortions to the authentic definition of human freedom and the function of discussions surrounding theistic wrath in Irenaeus' atonement narrative as well as the prudence of blaming an essentially impotent and frustrated humanity is compounded by the inevitably imperfect creaturehood of humanity.

---

18. J.N.D. Kelly, *Early Christian Doctrines*, 171.
19. Christopher A. Hall, *Learning Theology with the Church Fathers* (Downers Grove, IL: InterVarsity, 2002), 126.
20. Stuart G. Hall, *Doctrine and Practice in the Early Church*, 65.
21. M.C. Steenberg, "Children in Paradise: Adam and Eve as 'Infants' in Irenaeus of Lyons," 7.
22. *Ibid.* 5.
23. *Ibid.* 11.
24. *Ibid.* 17. Steenberg elsewhere states, "νηπιος is not simply a title given in description of such attributes but rather is the root and cause of their presence in Adam's person."

Initial Humanity's Creaturehood and Existential Self-Preservation:

In particular, as a created being whose very existence congenitally ensures the specific characteristics of resolute continuance and autonomy, humanity must contend with impulses of self-preservation and pride.[25] The need to persist in one's existence, however, is also contingent on humanity's inherent dependence on time in the corporeal realm. But this self-preserving impulse is intuitive for one's survival as an autonomous created being whose existence advances in tandem with the trajectory of time.[26] Unfortunately, Adam's self-preserving impulses and prideful negligence, although intrinsic to his creaturehood and ultimately unavoidable,[27] led to his disobedience. The inclination towards self-preservation is a direct result of Adam's "essential imperfection..., an imperfection which arises from the very fact of his creaturehood."[28] As a corporeal being contingent on the progression of time, it is natural to do what is necessary to keep oneself alive, which for an imperfect and infantile being implies the neglect of others. The emphasis, however, must be placed on the ineluctability of this mutual interplay between creaturehood and self-preservation.[29] Accordingly, St. Irenaeus declares in opposition to those who question God's objectives,

> If, however, any one say, "What then? Could not God have exhibited man as perfect from beginning [*perfectum fecisse hominem*]?" let him know that, inasmuch as God is indeed always the same and unbegotten as respects Himself, all things are possible to Him. But created things must be inferior to Him who created them, from the very fact of their later origin; for it was not possible for things recently created to have been uncreated. But inasmuch as they are not uncreated, for this very reason do they come short of the perfect [*Propter quod autem non sunt infecta, propter hoc et ideo deficiunt a perfecto*]. Because, as these things are of later date, so are they infantile

25. *Epid.* 15.
26. "For Irenaeus time is logically posterior to (though actually simultaneous with) matter and dependent upon it: it is material existence that connects a given being to the progression of time, while spiritual beings (e.g. the angels) have no such physical composition and thus no time-bound existence." M.C. Steenberg, "Children in Paradise: Adam and Eve as 'Infants' in Irenaeus of Lyons," 18.
27. "Irenaeus' mention of the inferiority of created things to the uncreated and their unaccustomed and unexercised discipline is not a disparaging criticism: it is his precise point that such lack of perfection is entirely expected and natural in human beings, for it is the only possible state into which might arrive a newborn humanity." *Ibid.* 6-7.
28. John I. Hochban, "St. Irenaeus on the Atonement," 534.
29. "*AH* 4.38 suggests, in fact, that God created an imperfect Adam not solely because it was His desire at a later time to confer upon him a proper perfection, but because Adam *could not have been created into any other state than the imperfect*, specifically as a consequence of his status as created being." M.C. Steenberg, "Children in Paradise: Adam and Eve as 'Infants' in Irenaeus of Lyons," 17.

[*infantilia* or *νήπια*]; so are they unaccustomed to, and unexercised in, perfect discipline [*et inexercitata ad perfectam disciplinam*].[30]

The imperfection that originates in humanity's creaturehood and infantility is also the source of disobedience, and Adam's vulnerability in particular, in the face of the devil's deception. Christopher A. Hall remarks, "Adam and Eve, more from immaturity than anything else, succumbed to the devil's lures from 'want of care no doubt.' They lacked the maturity to recognize fully the danger before them, and disaster was the result."[31] St. Irenaeus elaborates that Adam "was disobedient to God, being led astray by the angel who, for the great gifts of God which He had given to man, was envious and jealous of him, and both brought himself to nought and made man sinful, persuading him to disobey the commandment of God."[32] Significantly, this disobedience to God and submission to the devil demonstrates that Adam did "entertain selfish imaginings of pride in opposition to God,"[33] and therefore succumbed to the self-preserving impulses intrinsic to his creaturehood and infantility, indeed his very existence.

Consequently, since such behaviour is natural, it requires instruction to alleviate future disobedience; only through the inculcation of humanity will it learn the composition of the kingdom of God and its opposition to self-preservation, an impulse of initial necessity but ultimately incompatible with kingdom priorities.[34] The antithesis to self-preservation is a concern for

---

30. *AH* 4.38.1. St. Irenaeus later also asserts, "God had power at the beginning to grant perfection to man; but as the latter was only recently created, he could not possibly have received it, or even if he had received it, could he have contained it, or containing it, could he have retained it." *AH* 4.38.2.

31. Christopher A. Hall, *Learning Theology with the Church Fathers*, 128. Stuart G. Hall also states that it is Adam's juvenile state that accounts for how he was "easily deceived." Stuart G. Hall, *Doctrine and Practice in the Early Church*, 65. Even Hans Boersma, who does not acknowledge the authority or typicality of Irenaeus' atonement theology enough, nor does he account for the problem of human culpability adequately, asserts, "Satan has abused Adam and Eve's moral immaturity." Hans Boersma, *Violence, Hospitality and the Cross: Reappropriating the Atonement Tradition* (Grand Rapids, MI: Baker Academic, 2004), 188. A later section of this essay, *The Wrath of God*, will address Boersma's shortcomings with respect to his adherence to the penal substitutionary atonement theory (see in particular notes 78 and 93).

32. *Epid.* 16.

33. *Epid.* 15.

34. "For all these do not contain or imply an opposition to and an overturning of the [precepts] of the past, as Marcion's followers do strenuously maintain; but [they exhibit] a fulfilling and an extension of them, as He does Himself declare: 'Unless your righteousness shall exceed that of the scribes and Pharisees, ye shall not enter into the kingdom of heaven [*regnum cœlorum*].' For what meant the excess referred to? In the first place, [we must] believe not only in the Father, but also in His Son now revealed; for He it is who leads man into fellowship and unity with God [*Primo quidem non tantum in Patrem, sed et in Filium ejus jam manifestatum credere; hic est enim, qui in communio-*

surrounding people and therefore presupposes a selfless and altruistic precedence. The perfect expression of such selflessness is nonviolence in the face
of threat of injury, a nonviolence manifested superlatively in Christ's passion as the operational inversion of Adam's apostatical facilitation of death's
violent reign over subsequent humanity. Initial humanity's infantility, the
nascent and immature state in which all humanity shares, and subsequent
humanity's subversion to the tyranny of death therefore requires instruction
so that it may eventually reclaim the divinity it forfeited through disobedience. Instruction is the method for illustrating precisely what the kingdom
of God looks like. St. Irenaeus elaborates on the contradistinction between
humanity's imperfect existence, an existence that humanity intuitively allows
to persist through self-preservation and pride, and Christ's selfless execution:
"The Almighty God of all ... who has granted existence to all [*quique omnibus
ut sint praestitit*]... [is] ... looking forward to the time when [humanity] shall
become like Him who died for him [*qui pro eo mortuus est*]" by "assigning
[humanity] as [His own] imitator to God [*imitatorem eum assignans Deo*]."[35]
Christ's death is the definitive instruction against humanity's self-preserving
impulses, as the nonviolence inherent to martyrdom demonstrates the reluc-
tance to fight back and the acquiescence in letting oneself forego her or his
existence instead of the existences of those who are inflicting the injury.

This instruction is again contingent on humanity's requisite dependence
on the progression of time and the limitations of corporeality. The novelty of
humanity's infancy necessitates its ignorance. And humanity's dependence on
time again illuminates how little one can understand concurrently with how

---

nem et unitatem Dei hominem ducit.]." *AH* 4.13.1.

35. *AH* 3.20.2. This reference to humanity's existence is perhaps too obscure to draw
any significant conclusions in isolation. However, in his polemics against the Platonic
affirmation of the pre-existence of the soul and metempsychosis [*AH* 2.33.2], St. Irenaeus does elsewhere discuss the "*essent*" of all creation and the significance of the
"*initio*" of the "*animabus, et de spiritibus*" and the life conferred on it and, significantly,
its inherent dissimilarity to the unbegotten: cf. *AH* 2.34. *passim*. St. Irenaeus also readily
acknowledges the deficiency inherent in humanity's very existence, a deficiency that
requires restoration and salvation: "God having predestined that the first man should
be of an animal nature, with this view, that he might be saved by the spiritual One. For
inasmuch as He had a pre-existence as a saving Being, it was necessary that what might
be saved should also be called into existence, in order that the Being who saves should
not exist in vain [*praedestinante Deo primum animalem hominem, videlicet ut a spiritali
salvaretur. Cum enim praeexisteret salvans, oportebat et quod salvaretur fieri, uti non
vacuum sit salvans*]." *AH* 3.22.3. Generally, Irenaeus indeed understands the infantility,
immaturity and corporeality of humanity, all of which sum up humanity's very existence
and are especially epitomized in Adam and Eve, as producing a situation that naturally
lends itself to impulses of self-preservation, impulses that are abated by the instruction
intrinsic to Christ's selfless and altruistic, nonviolent confrontation with socio-political
opposition as well as the central commandment of Christ to love one's enemies and pray
for one's persecutors: cf. *AH* 3.18.5.

little time has progressed.[36] Therefore, the inchoateness of Adam and Eve as infants, a beginning in which all humanity shares, facilitates such ignorance. Inception indelibly suggests unfamiliarity and incognizance, which, in turn, entails the need for instruction. In reference to Adam and Eve as "immature children" in Irenaeus' thought, Chadwick elaborates, "The history of salvation is a progressive education, in which God has brought humanity forward step by step in a long process culminating in the incarnation of the divine Word."[37] This sentiment is in direct agreement with St. Irenaeus' description:

> For as it certainly is in the power of a mother to give strong food to her infant, [but she does not do so], as the child is not yet able to receive more substantial nourishment; so also it was possible for God Himself to have made man perfect from the first, but man could not receive this [perfection], being as yet an infant [*infans enim fuit*]. And for this cause our Lord in these last times, when He had summed up [*recapitulans*] all things into Himself, came to us, not as He might have come, but as we were capable of beholding Him [*sed quomodo illum nos videre poteramus*]. He might easily have come to us in His immortal glory, but in that case we could never have endured the greatness of the glory; and therefore it was that He, who was the perfect bread of the Father, offered Himself to us as milk, [because we were] as infants [*infantibus*].[38]

The implications of Christ's incarnation, teachings, recapitulation and nonviolent resolve in the face of execution and socio-political oppression in general will receive its due consideration in a later section;[39] for our current discussion, however, it is important only to acknowledge the cumulative nature of Irenaeus' soteriology, and therein, the ignorance of humanity at its inception.[40] The language in this passage is particularly significant in that it lends itself to interpretations addressing the identification motif that is so essential to Irenaeus' theory of recapitulation. In an act of humility, therefore, God "*hominem ejus adventus*," so that humanity might equally be enabled to "*manducare et bibere Verbum Dei*" and be infected with the "*Spiritus Patris*."[41]

---

36. Steenberg makes this point as well: "*AH* 4.38 reinforces such an assertion with its own stress upon the fact of newly formed humanity's inability to receive full knowledge of or appropriation to God. Man's materiality is, in this sense, a preventative limitation: it is materiality that binds him to time and time that restricts the capabilities of his knowledge and receptivity of his body." M.C. Steenberg, "Children in Paradise: Adam and Eve as 'Infants' in Irenaeus of Lyons," 20.

37. Henry Chadwick, *The Early Church*, 80-81.

38. *AH* 4.38.1.

39. See the sections *The Incarnation as Pedagogue* and *Christ's Martyrdom and the Recapitulation of Peace* of this essay.

40. "It was necessary for man to be first created; and having been created, to grow; and having grown, to become mature; and having become mature, to multiply; and having multiplied, to grow strong; and having grown strong, to be glorified; and having been glorified, to see his Lord." *AH* 4.38.3.

41. *AH* 4.38.1.

Death's Violent Dominion Over Humanity:

If Adam and Eve's incipience and imperfection necessitate exposure to the kingdom of God through instruction, the tyranny of death over humanity requires the capacitation or empowerment of its subjects in conjunction with their emancipation. The presence and function of death occupies a prominent place in Irenaeus' atonement narrative, and makes its conspicuous entrance in the first segment of Irenaeus' tripartite atonement narrative, that of the Edenic state of *shalom*. It is notably this entrance which casts further doubt on the validity of human culpability, not only that of Adam but also the liability of subsequent humanity. If death maintains violent dominion over humanity on account of the latter's initial incompetence, how could God's wrath, as it is commonly understood, reasonably be intended for this same humanity and eventually redirected onto his Son? This is where an evaluation of Irenaeus' unique recapitulatory exposition of the subtext to God's strategy and objectives can serve to align current manifold atonement postulations with the more theologically collaborative understanding of the character of God, that of compassion and his willing the restoration rather than annihilation of all he created, of all he deems good.

The issue of Adam's confrontation with death must first be addressed, however. To designate death as "violence" is not inappropriate when considering Irenaeus' description of its ambition.[42] Within a compelling elucidation of Christ's nonviolent resolve through which he reclaims all of humanity as his own, St. Irenaeus describes the apostasy that had "obtained dominion over us at the beginning, when it insatiably snatched away what was not its own."[43] And in so doing, death altered the composition of humanity's essence and affiliation with the kingdom of God and restricted access to the divine. Steenberg tells us that for Irenaeus, "Adam 'possessed' likeness to God, but with respect to the fullness of his likeness he possessed it potentially."[44] An oscillating regulation and incapacitation exists where Adam did not possess the perfection in substance, or *οὐσία*, as that of the incarnated Word, and consequently became restricted further by facilitating death's dominion over humanity.[45] It is this situation that will eventually be eradicated through the

---

42. Hans Boersma acknowledges the association between violence and death in Irenaeus' thought, particularly in how God's hospitality reaches out to humanity's situation, "even to violence and death itself." Hans Boersma, *Violence, Hospitality and the Cross: Reappropriating the Atonement Tradition*, 187.

43. *AH* 5.1.1.

44. M.C. Steenberg, "Children in Paradise: Adam and Eve as 'Infants' in Irenaeus of Lyons," 14.

45. Cf. *AH* 4.38.4.

deification of humanity[46] as affected by the instruction of the incarnation and martyrdom of Christ, as well as the defeat of death itself. It is the capacitation of humanity that permits or empowers one to adhere to the instruction immanent in the incarnation as pedagogue.

However, death did not manipulate and restrain Adam alone since it was through his disobedience, his impulses of self-preservation, that he imperiled subsequent humanity's welfare by exposing it to the violence of death.[47] St. Irenaeus accordingly declares, "For as by the disobedience of the one man who was originally moulded from virgin soil, the many were made sinners [*peccatores facti sunt multi*], and forfeited life."[48] He further describes how humanity "had been led into captivity [*captivitatem*]" by apostasy,[49] which "tyrannized over us unjustly, and, though we were by nature the property of the omnipotent God, alienated us contrary to nature [*alienavit nos contra naturam*], rendering us its own disciples."[50] Again, this demonstrates the origin of humanity's essential dissimilarity to that of God, the loss of divinity. It is apostasy or death that 'alienated us contrary to nature' thus initiating the necessity of empowerment and the need to reclaim the divine. Identifying the origin of such substantial dissonance, the difference in οὐσία between humanity and God, itself requires instruction. During the time of Moses, it is therefore the law that testifies "of sin that it is a sinner," which did "truly take away his (death's) kingdom, showing that he was no king, but a robber; and it revealed him as a murderer [*homicidam*]."[51] But it is the Incarnate

---

46. Cf. *AH* 3.18.1.; *AH* 3.18.7; *AH* 4.33.4.; *AH* 5. *preafatio*. More will be said about this in the later section, *The Ontology of Nonviolence: Deification as Capacitation* (see note 192 in particular).

47. St. Irenaeus discusses the "generation subject to death [*mortis generationem*]" in *AH* 4.33.4. and the "*novam generationem*," that is, the Church, "which flows from the virgin through faith." Kelly states, "The original Adam, by his disobedience, introduced the principle of sin and death." He further asserts that "sin entailed consequence for the whole race; Irenaeus has no doubt that the first man's disobedience is the source of the general sinfulness and mortality of mankind, as also of their enslavement to the Devil. What Adam lost, all lost in him." J.N.D. Kelly, *Early Christian Doctrines*, 173, 171.

48. *AH* 3.18.7.

49. It must be noted that Irenaeus does not distinguish between sin or apostasy and death. Gustav Aulén states that a "close association of sin and death is specially characteristic of [Irenaeus]," and by way of Bulgarian theologian Stephen Zankow's insights, asserts that the separation of the two is an innovation of Western theologians, whereas patristic witness envisages that "empirically one is not separated from the other; where sin is, there is death also, and *vice versa*." Gustaf Aulén, *Christus Victor: An Historical Study of the Three Main Types of the Idea of the Atonement*, 23, as quoted in Stephen Zankow, *Das orthodoxe Christentum des Ostens*. Quoted from the English translation, *The Orthodox Eastern Church*, by Donald A. Lowrie (London, 1929), 49-50.

50. *AH* 5.1.1.

51. *AH* 3.18.7.

Christ specifically who fulfils the law[52] by perfectly embodying the kingdom of God in human form and whose function is the inculcation of humanity for embracing nonviolence in opposition to death's murderous compulsion. This violent description of death is therefore accentuated when compared to the peaceable kingdom of God as embodied in the Incarnate Christ. In reference to David's sin which the prophet Nathan had exposed, St. Irenaeus indeed makes this connection: "He [David] sung a penitential psalm, waiting for the coming of the Lord, who washes and makes clean the man who had been fast bound with [the chain of] sin," after which Solomon "announced the peace about to come upon the nations [*adventuram pacem gentibus annuntiabat*], and prefigured the kingdom of Christ [*Christi regnum*]."[53] Evidently, Irenaeus acknowledges a theological reality that many Western theologians neglect in their adoption of the Anselmian and later Reformed penal substitutionary atonement theories, but a reality that is of critical importance when evaluating the veracity of claims concerning God's wrath against a humanity that does not warrant punitive infliction but instead only restoration and reconciliation back to God.

B. The Human Condition and God's Response to the Inevitability of Apostasy

As mentioned earlier, to understand the genuine definition and function of terms such as blame, freedom, wrath and propitiation in St. Irenaeus' writings, etymology becomes less reliable where analysis within their literary contexts accounts for misgivings with respect to its translation and transmission history.[54] It is prudent, however, to deal with these themes within the context of the prevailing atonement motif in Western Christianity, that of penal substitution. This discussion will also function as a transition between the preceding evaluation of Adam's apostasy and the forthcoming treatment of *identification* in Irenaeus' atonement theology as per Christ's incarnation and nonviolent confrontation with socio-political oppression and its remedial effects on the aforementioned apostasy for the Church. Of particular interest, however, is the element of nonviolence immanent in Christ's identification with humanity and *vice versa*; using nonviolence as a foil will invariably expose the shortcomings of penal substitutionary models.

---

52. *AH* 5.21.3. Here, St. Irenaeus indicates that "Christ bears witness" to "that God who also gave the law."
53. *AH* 4.27.1.
54. See note 9 above.

Human Culpability:

We have already identified the three sources of Irenaeus' rejection of unqualified human culpability as Adam and Eve's (1) infantility and (2) creaturely existence and the (3) tyranny of death over initial and subsequent humanity. It is within this situation that doubt is cast over the validity of God's wrath as an authentic threat to humanity; this also accounts for Irenaeus' consistency on the matter. If Adam and Eve were created as infants, whether physically, cognitively or metaphorically, they would have lacked the capacity to avoid sin, a competency of which they were devoid congenitally by virtue of their infantile and created state. Is it then logical to blame humanity for its apostasy and consequentially impose on it punitive measures in the form of God's wrath, a wrath supposedly intended for this same exonerated humanity but ultimately redirected on his Son? St. Irenaeus says *no* and is clear that God "took compassion on man" precisely because Adam's apostasy occurred "through want of care no doubt [*negligenter quidem*]," and accordingly assigns blame "[on the part of another]."[55] Henry Chadwick observes, "It was natural that mistakes were made by the frail and immature children who were Adam and Eve,"[56] while Stuart G. Hall maintains that Adam's "disobedience over the tree in Eden was little more than an accident."[57] This sentiment indeed concurs with St. Irenaeus' own contention that Adam and Eve had "an innocent and childlike mind,"[58] and was consequently incapable of recognizing the repercussions of disobedience. Irenaeus therefore is not introducing a problem, as it may appear to those faithful to theology resonant with penal substitutionary atonement theories, but a *solution* concerning the origin of sin. Apostasy is not something for which humanity must receive its due punishment, but an opportunity for restoration and reconciliation back to

---

55. *AH* 4.40.3. The context clearly indicates that "another" refers to the devil or enemy [ἐχθρός]. The translator takes the liberty of assigning blame for the wicked deed on the devil since the Greek translation from the two ancient *Catenae Patrum*, in opposition to the Latin translation, indicates that it is the one who sows the tares [ἐπισπείραντα], that is, the devil or enemy [*inimicus* or ἐχθρός], rather than the tares [ζιζάνιον] themselves, who causes the transgression: William Wigan Harvey, ed., *Sancti Irenaei Libros Quinque Adversus Haereses*, vol. 2., 303, note 2. Indeed, Irenaeus immediately indicates that God had compassion [*miseratus*] on humanity instead of banishing them from God's presence, as he does with the one who sows the tares.

56. Henry Chadwick, *The Early Church* (New York: Penguin Books, 1993), 80. Chadwick is also correct when he declares, "He [Irenaeus] grants from the start that there is imperfection in the world, but it is like the blunders made by a growing child, and the purpose of our existence is the making of character by the mastery of difficulties and temptations" (81).

57. Stuart G. Hall, *Doctrine and Practice in the Early Church*, 65.

58. *Epid.* 14.

God. Once again, Steenberg suggests, "The doctrine...offers a cogent explanation for why sin would ever have entered into Paradise, for why Adam and Eve would have followed the deceitful leadings of the serpent—an issue that is always of some tension in conceptions of a fully perfect creation in the Garden."[59] The responsibility for Adam's apostasy does not therefore lie with humanity as such, although human freedom does permit escape from sinful inclinations, but with its created state of incompetence, an incompetence that hardly warrants vindictive penalization.

Adam's confrontation with temptation also exposed his self-preserving impulses and pride, impulses that can be alleviated by aligning oneself with the nonviolent instruction inherent in Christ's confrontation with the temptation to fight back and preserve his own existence. These existential impulses, however, occur naturally for the purpose of eventual and inevitable maturation and assimilation with the perfection of Christ's nonviolent resolve. Here, St. Irenaeus introduces the incarnational function that illuminates how ignorance and spiritual infirmity absolves humanity of responsibility for its apostatic blunder: "It is not right that we should lay blame [*imputare*] upon those who sinned before Christ's coming. For 'all men come short of the glory of God,' and are not justified of themselves, but by the advent of the Lord."[60] Humanity, therefore, is not an object of blame and neither is it susceptible to chastisement as an expression of retributive justice. Instead, justice is envisaged as the restoration of humanity back to God, the renovation of the likeness of God in humanity,[61] through instruction and empowerment, or the deposition of death's tyrannical reign and the nonviolent didactic mechanism therewith.

Accordingly, humanity's elicited role in the incurrence of apostasy simply cannot justify the infliction of God's wrath, "For at the first Adam became a vessel in his (Satan's) possession, whom he did also hold under his power, that is by bringing sin on him iniquitously [*inique*], and under colour of immortality entailing death upon him."[62] Logically, if humanity "had fallen into captivity" against its own volition, God would not perceive any motivation for exposing them to his wrath, but would instead deliver them from the power "that held them in bondage."[63] Irenaeus seems to differentiate between the presage or *threat* of God's wrath and actual *subjection*

---

59. M.C. Steenberg, "Children in Paradise: Adam and Eve as 'Infants' in Irenaeus of Lyons," 21-22.
60. *AH* 4.27.2.
61. Cf. *AH* 3.22.1.; *AH* 3.23.1-2.; *AH* 4.preface.4.; *AH* 4.37.7.; *AH* 5.11.2.; *AH* 5.16. *passim.* See also note 192.
62. *AH* 3.23.1.
63. *AH* 5.21.3. As quoted in Gustaf Aulén, *Christus Victor: An Historical Study of the Three Main Types of the Idea of the Atonement*, 34.

to God's wrath. Irenaeus is unequivocal in his implication of God in mercy[64] rather than wrath; it is the extension of mercy that *actually does happen* and is therefore the only real response God offers to the situation, whereas Irenaeus' mention of God's wrath is purely polemical on account of its non-actualization. One may rightly surmise that penal substitution models are conceived and manufactured based on hearsay. However, for St. Irenaeus, since humanity "could not be saved by their own instrumentality," he correspondingly demonstrates clearly that "salvation is not from us, but from God."[65] Moreover, the situation of apostasy and God's merciful response was envisaged from the beginning as a mode of conferring divinity and perfection on humanity: "Long-suffering therefore was God, when man became a defaulter, as foreseeing [*praevidens*] that victory which should be granted to him through the Word."[66] This is why Christ, while gaining access to death for his eventual victory, even forgave his executioners, the violence of whom epitomizes the repercussions of apostasy, and in his forgiveness "the long-suffering, patience, compassion, and goodness of Christ are exhibited, since He both suffered, and did Himself exculpate those who had maltreated Him [*et ipse excusaret eos qui se male tractassent*]."[67] Here, St. Irenaeus is clearly dissociating violence from God who instead loves "the human race to such a degree, that He even prayed for those putting Him to death."[68] At the advent of Christ, perfection was embodied for the first time for human consumption, perfection that patently separates itself from violence, which means that God, at the precise time of the atonement through the Incarnate Word, cannot be implicated in the violence for which he is revealing an alternative for the first time as an integral characteristic, even the nucleus, of the kingdom of God, namely nonviolence. Forgiveness, and in the face of socio-political opposition, nonviolence is the new measure.

---

64. St. Irenaeus contends, "For He bound the strong man, and set free the weak, and endowed His own handiwork with salvation, by destroying sin. For He is a most holy and merciful Lord, and loves the human race [*alligavit enim fortem, et solvit infirmos, et salutem donavit plasmati suo, destruens peccatum. Est enim piissimus et misericors Dominus, et amans humanum genus*]." *AH* 3.18.6.; cf. *AH* 3.20.2.

65. *AH* 3.20.3.

66. *AH* 3.20.1. González also makes this claim with respect to Irenaeus' understanding of the function of the incarnation: "The incarnation of God in Jesus Christ is not the result of sin. On the contrary, God's initial purpose included being united with mankind." Justo L. González, *The Story of Christianity*, vol. 1, 70.

67. *AH* 3.18.5.

68. *AH* 3.18.5.

Human Freedom:

Although Christ anticipated the apostasy from which humanity might eventually reclaim the divine, St. Irenaeus is clear that this in no way implies that human freedom is compromised. On the contrary, it is his intention to show how God restores humanity's freedom from the tyranny of death, and instead of using coercion[69] redeems what is rightfully his "by means of persuasion,"[70] as exhibited in his use of instruction and empowerment, both of which are invitational in nature rather than coercive. The means by which humanity may reclaim the divine is placed within their reach, but the responsibility lies with them,[71] which of course preserves their freedom. The above circumstances surrounding Christ's execution demonstrate his concern for human freedom. Much like in Ivan Karamazov's poem, "The Grand inquisitor," in Fyodor Dostoevsky's *The Brothers Karamazov*, where "Christ will not even censure the Inquisitor"[72] but instead "approaches the old man in silence and calmly kisses him on his bloodless ninety-year-old lips,"[73] Christ, as did Dostoevsky, "exalted freedom at any cost, including suffering,"[74] indeed even his own suffering.

This freedom, however, must not be confused with the kind of volitional intentionality where one has the capacity to choose God dispassionately and unencumbered. The facility for choosing God is dependent on one's *exposure* to divine instruction and empowerment without which God's victory over death and the instructive properties of his incarnation become ineffectual.[75] For Irenaeus, human freedom denotes the capacity to go either way; this is precisely why God so desires to emancipate humanity from the manipulation of death, while simultaneously resolving not to use coercion[76] himself but

---

69. St. Irenaeus states that God "seeks to turn us away from [the sin of] unbelief against Him, without, however, in any way coercing us [*non tamen de violentia cogens*]." *AH* 4.37.3.

70. *AH* 5.1.1. "*...sed secundum suadelam...*"

71. Christopher A. Hall asserts, "God will not, Irenaeus insists, compel us to believe or obey." Christopher A. Hall, *Learning Theology with the Church Fathers*, 124.

72. Ralph E. Matlaw, "Introduction" in *Notes From Underground: The Grand Inquisitor*, By Fyodor Dostoevsky (New York: E.P. Dutton, 1960), xxii.

73. Fyodor Dostoevsky, *The Karamazov Brothers*, translated by Ignat Avsey (New York: Oxford University Press, 1998), 329.

74. Ralph E. Matlaw, "Introduction" in *Notes From Underground: The Grand Inquisitor*, By Fyodor Dostoevsky (New York: E. P. Dutton, 1960), xxi.

75. In the same way, Hall contends that for Irenaeus, "Part of God's good creative plan is that human beings be given the *opportunity* to recognize and pursue goodness freely" (emphasis added). Christopher A. Hall, *Learning Theology with the Church Fathers*, 125.

76. St. Irenaeus insists that "there is no coercion with God [*vis enim a Deo non fit*], but a good will [*bona sententia*] [towards us] is present with him continually." *AH*

only persuasion, that is, instruction and empowerment, both of which summon obedience rather than demand it. This is also why St. Irenaeus believes that *empirically* humanity must gain an understanding of the repercussions of implicating oneself in either good or evil:

> And learning by experience that it is an evil thing which deprives him of life, that is, disobedience to God, may never attempt it at all, but that, knowing that what preserves his life, namely, obedience to God, is good, he may diligently keep it with earnestness. ... But how, if he had no knowledge of the contrary, could he have had instruction [*Disciplinam*] in that which is good? ... So also does the mind, receiving through the experience [*experimentum*] of both the knowledge of what is good, become more tenacious in its preservation, by acting in its obedience to God.[77]

It is this freedom along with death's delinquency and God's desire for humanity to be restored and reconciled rather than annihilated that brings into question the genuineness of threats of God's wrath, particularly as it occurs in penal substitutionary interpretations of Christ's atoning work.

The Wrath of God:

Irenaeus is quite consistent in his management of the issues surrounding the subject of violence, as is corroborated in his perception of God's wrath. In appealing to a 'hermeneutic of the character of God,' so to speak, Irenaeus takes seriously typical theological assertions of the victimhood of initial humanity, the advent of Christ as embodying perfection and the liability of death for the dawn of apostasy. Consequently, Irenaeus' exploration of the function of God's wrath,[78] discussions which admittedly are not infrequent,

---

4.37.1. It should be noted that Hochban, I think more accurately, interprets "coercion" [*vis*] as "violence" instead of "coercion": John I. Hochban, "St. Irenaeus on the Atonement," 530. Regardless, after insisting, perhaps paradoxically when compared to other statements absolving humanity from any apostatical responsibility, that humanity does "receive condign punishment [*meritam poenam percipient*]," and this "with justice [*juste*]," St. Irenaeus sheds some light on the function of such *poenam* at the end of the chapter as "bringing of man to perfection [*perfectionem*], for his edification [*aedifica-tionem*]...and that man may finally be brought to maturity at some future time [*et tandem aliquando maturus fiat homo*]," a much more restorative *telos* contrastive to a mere crude elimination.

77. *AH* 4.39.1.

78. The issue of God's wrath is a significant point of contention between those who, like J. Denny Weaver, envisage a nonviolent atonement and those who adhere to a penal substitution model [In order to allow Weaver to speak for himself, I will merely direct the reader to J. Denny Weaver's chapter in this book. See also a more comprehensive version of Weaver's narrative *Christus Victor* atonement model in J. Denny Weaver, *The Nonviolent Atonement* (Grand Rapids, MI: Eerdman's, 2001)]. Discussions of God's wrath in atonement theology must by necessity venture into the territory of defining violence itself. Weaver's contention that violence in atonement theology overlooks Black and Womanist struggles and interpretations of the atonement is indeed pragmatic, but

seems to imply a strong polemical objective. The failure of God's wrath to materialize against humanity specifically during the atonement events

so is Boersma's attempt to justify violence as a characteristic of God by his ad hoc use of contextual theological issues [See chapter five of J. Denny Weaver, *Anabaptist Theology in Face of Postmodernity*, C. Henry Smith Series, vol. 2 (Telford, PA: Pandora Press, 2000), 121-146.]. Boersma believes that theological discussions surrounding God and violence are similar to theodicean discussions that attempt to absolve God from any association with the existence of evil as a particularly pragmatic attempt to reconcile the character of God with the existence of suffering: Hans Boersma, *Violence, Hospitality and the Cross: Reappropriating the Atonement Tradition* (Grand Rapids, MI: Baker Academic, 2004), 43. However, Boersma, like any theologian who accepts at least some, or a nuanced version of, violence as part of God's redemptive plan, is also pragmatic in his attempt to justify violence. He makes the untenable claim, in agreement with Levinas and Derrida, that "in our world it is, strictly speaking, impossible to extend hospitality without at the same time also engaging in some violence" (48). Although he is referring to Derrida's tenuous definition of violence as including the inability to respond to the infinite number of situations needing attention (35), it is still an attempt to advocate violence for the sake of doing what *works* rather than what is *right*, however much violence always ultimately fails – for someone. Boersma does not entertain the notion that Jesus extended hospitality while at the same time avoiding violence, and that we too can avoid 'engaging in some form of violence' by instead *receiving* violence on ourselves. Of course, if Boersma is using the aforementioned Derridian interpretation of violence, it also implicates Jesus in the same, which renders it either *not* violence or else authorized and permitted of the Church. This then becomes merely an issue of semantics as it is with Boersma's interaction with Weaver's view of violence. While Boersma contends that interfering with a suicide, participating in economic boycotts and strikes is implicating oneself in violence, Weaver does not (46-47). However, both agree that such action is permitted and ultimately beneficial. If this is violence, then Boersma, Weaver and Jesus are violent. But if the opposite is true, not one of the three advocates or participates in violence. In the end, Boersma, in saying that God is implicated in violence, really says nothing at all, an evaluation of Boersma's work shared also by S. Mark Heim who suggests, "the work is somewhat marred by a rather elliptical pattern of argument. ... Nowhere is there a full and clear answer given to the problem implicit in the entire project: how exactly is God exercising violence in the crucifixion of Jesus and how (and why) is God exercising it against Jesus?" S. Mark Heim, "Cross Purposes: Rethinking the Death of Jesus," *Christian Century* 122, no. 6 (March 22, 2005): 25. Ultimately, Boersma regretably seems to take the easy road when he declares, "For the sake of consistency I think we should refer to all such acts of damage or injury (including the morally acceptable ones) as violence" [Hans Boersma, Violence, Hospitality and the Cross: Reappropriating the Atonement Tradition (Grand Rapids, MI: Baker Academic, 2004), 47.], an unfortunate response given that, as John Howard Yoder states it, "Neither 'power' nor 'violence' is a univocal, unidimensional something varying only in terms of more or less; each varies in quality, in depth, in direction, in wholeness." John Howard Yoder, "Jesus and Power," *Ecumenical Review* 25, no. 4 (October 1973): 454. In his attempt to define violence, Boersma seems to miss the implications of the kingdom of God inherent in the notion of *nonviolence*. Humanity's nonviolence is an imitation of and ontological affiliation with the incarnated and crucified Christ and is the result of remaining receptive to his instruction and empowerment; it is an identification with Christ subsequent to his identification with humanity which supersedes any definition of violence. Yoder states it this way, "When He *calls* and *enables* us to love our enemies, neither the meaning nor the power of that call is dependent on how we define 'violence'" (emphasis added). John Howard Yoder, "Jesus and Power," 454.

simultaneous with and after the incarnation portends such suspicion.[79] If the view in penal substitution is that God's wrath is an external instrument of his justice in response to humanity's apostasy but nevertheless fails to actually occur, then the claim that God is obligated to implicate himself in violence for the redemption of humanity loses all credibility. Of course, an adherent to the penal substitutionary model will say that God redirected his wrath from humanity and onto his Son. But if humanity, as a victim of the tyranny of death and its own creaturely incompetence, does not warrant the infliction of God's wrath, how authentic is this wrath in the first place? Irenaeus answers this question in his designation of God's wrath towards humanity as primarily polemical, the internalization of God's justice in the incarnation as God *in* Christ and the identification of the real culprit as death, itself defeated by virtue of the incarnation. Indeed, St. Irenaeus declares, "For in God there is no violence [*vis*]"[80] and identifies wrath itself as an "*opera carnis*,"[81] engaged in by those who "are without the Spirit, which bring death [upon their doers]."[82] It seems possible that given the general theological context of Irenaeus' understanding of atonement, he is employing the notion of God's wrath, in addition to its evident use in scripture, as an easily relatable mechanism by which humanity is instructed as to what is evil and exhorted through godly counsel, a polemical instrument whose *telos* is the restoration of humankind. St. Irenaeus discusses God's wrath within the context of the prophets who

> used to exhort men to what was good, to act justly and to work righteousness, as I have so largely demonstrated, because it is in our power to do so, and because by excessive negligence we might become forgetful, and thus stand in need of that good counsel which the good God has given us to know by means of the prophets."[83]

79. Since God revealed the kingdom of God incrementally from his covenant adoption of Abraham, he concurrently permitted violence temporarily as he did, for instance, divorce (see Mt. 19:3-9 and corresponding references, Dt. 24:1-4; Mt. 5:31-32). In fact, any of Jesus' 'You have heard it said...' statements would fit into this category. As it is with violence, God, as one who must toil within the limitations of matter and time within which humanity also endures, cannot instruct his creation concerning the composition of the kingdom of God all at once, but instead piece by piece over the course of time. The incarnation is the climax and it is here that God must embody and teach perfection and expect the same from humanity. However, this enacted wrath of God portrayed in the Old Testament has a polemical or didactic function for Irenaeus when applied to a teleological understanding of humanity, that is, humanity from beginning to *end*, and carries significance for the import of the incarnation as the embodiment of that which God had been revealing only incrementally up until then. This, of course, renders suspicious penal substitutionary accounts of the atonement, an event they contend occurred by means of God's violence during the incarnation: cf. *AH* 4.10.1.; *Epid.* 25, 27, 43-85.
80. *AH* 4.37.1. As quoted in John I. Hochban, "St. Irenaeus on the Atonement," 530.
81. *AH* 5.11.1. In reference to Gal. 5:19-21.
82. *AH* 5.11.2.
83. *AH* 4.37.2.

This prophetic role inherent to God's wrath demonstrates

> the independent will of man, and at the same time the counsel which God conveys to him, by which He exhorts us to submit ourselves to Him, and seeks to turn us away from [the sin of] unbelief against Him, without, however, in any way coercing us."[84]

It seems that Irenaeus is concerned, as was Paul, that in his own verification of death as the object of blame, humanity might feel inclined to exercise its freedom inappropriately. It is no wonder then that St. Irenaeus would invoke Paul, who says,

> 'All things are lawful to me, but all things are not expedient;' referring both to the liberty of man, in which respect, 'all things are lawful,' God exercising no compulsion in regard to him; and [by the expression] 'not expedient' pointing out that we 'should not use our liberty as a cloak of maliciousness,' for this is not expedient.[85]

After a lengthy elucidation of God's wrath and its function, St. Irenaeus must once again admit:

> God has displayed long-suffering [*magnanimitatem praestante*] in the case of man's apostasy; while man has been instructed [*erudito*] by means of it ... God thus determining all things before hand for the bringing of man to perfection, for his edification [*praefiniente Deo omnia ad hominis perfectionem, et ad aedificationem*], and for the revelation of His dispensations, that goodness may both be made apparent, and righteousness perfected, and that the Church may be fashioned after the image of His Son [*Ecclesia ad figuram imaginis Filii ejus coaptetur*].[86]

The image of God's Son is essential for accomplishing his redemptive objectives, and the incarnation is therefore pivotal – quite literally.

Irenaeus evokes the incarnation as the turning point in his atonement narrative and is the initial concern of the second segment in his tripartite theory of recapitulation. For now, however, it is important to evaluate only how the incarnation alters the function of God's wrath in Irenaeus' atonement theology. First, there is the issue of wrath as external punishment, which was initially the fate of humanity but ultimately redirected onto the Son of God. For adherents of penal substitution, mention of the incarnation in relation to the atonement seems somewhat incongruous, but for Irenaeus the incarnation is indispensable. S. Mark Heim comments with respect to the substitutionary view of the atonement, "Such a view has never been prominent in the Eastern Christian Church, and it was not the dominant view in the Western Church

---

84. *AH* 4.37.3. Reconciling the notion of God's wrath with his refusal to act coercively is an anomaly in and of itself. Acknowledging the sole function of God's latent wrath as *polemical* resolves such enigmatic language that Irenaeus seems to employ at times.

85. *AH* 4.37.4.

86. *AH* 4.37.7.

for the first half of its history."[87] This no doubt is the result of substitutionary models not taking serious enough the incarnation, the nucleus of Eastern and patristic soteriology. But this view indeed prevails in the Western Church today and is espoused by theologians who no doubt study Irenaeus' view of the atonement and other such Eastern or patristic expositions on the atonement, but nevertheless curiously find less authority in them compared to the Anselmian view proposed in his long-standing explication on the subject *Cur Deus Homo* written in 1098 C.E. Notwithstanding the Western Church's evident snub of Eastern and patristic perceptions and nuances of the atonement, in Irenaeus' view, "There is no trace of the cleavage between Incarnation and Atonement which appears in Anselm."[88] And despite Anselm's attempt at demonstrating the association between the two, as is evident from the title of his work on the subject, the implications he and subsequent proponents such as Aquinas and Calvin draw from the incarnation's role in atonement theology are quite rudimentary and are implicated in juridical transactions quite foreign to the more holistic theistic notions of *shalom*, restoration, reconciliation, forgiveness and their effect ontologically on the process of deification, *theopoiesis* and *theosis*. Substitution lacks an ontology of redemption, and it is for this reason that Irenaeus is unwilling to abandon the incarnation as the mechanism whereby humanity reclaims the divine. But the incarnation also renders suspect the notion of *external* wrath in addition to the proposition of wrath as such. In an effort to counteract the nebulous claims of Gnosticism and those promulgating the docetic rejection of Christ's physical suffering and eventually the incarnation itself, St. Irenaeus insists "that in Jesus God Himself suffered for men." Accordingly, he supplies the description of

> one God the Father, and one Christ Jesus, who came by means of the whole dispensational arrangements [connected with Him], and gathered together all things in Himself. But in every respect, too, He is man, the formation of God [*In omnibus autem est et homo plasmatio Dei*]; and thus He took up man into Himself, the invisible becoming visible, the incomprehensible being made comprehensible, the impassible becoming capable of suffering [*et impassibilis passibilis*].[89]

As was demonstrated above, Irenaeus envisages God's wrath as polemical on account of its notable absence or inability to actually materialize and because of its imprudence considering humanity's ingenuousness. But the substitution model does affirm God's wrath in its redirection onto the Son, however

---

87. S. Mark Heim, "Cross Purposes: Rethinking the Death of Jesus," 20.
88. Gustaf Aulén, *Christus Victor: An Historical Study of the Three Main Types of the Idea of the Atonement*, 21. Aulén continues, "Incarnation and atoning work are...set in the closest possible relation to one another; both belong to one scheme" (32-33).
89. *AH* 3.16.6.; cf. *AH* 3.20.4.

precarious the actual existence of this wrath is. Nonetheless, if it is indeed the case that God is actually *in* Christ restoring and reconciling humanity and all creation unto himself, how can God's wrath be *externally* directed away from humanity and towards his Son? The answer, of course, is that it cannot. God's self-donation implies that he cannot kill his Son as a propitiation for humanity's apostasy considering God resides *in* Christ for the purpose of ontologically altering humanity's οὐσια rather than "judiciously" destroying it; this is precisely why patristic instincts avoided the more negligent penal substitutionary interpretation that systemically undermines the centrality of the incarnation.

But an even more glaring discrepancy exists when attempting to reconcile penal substitution models with Irenaeus' own atonement narrative; Irenaeus is clear that the incarnation, as the fulcrum in his atonement chronology, is the anthropological embodiment of divine perfection, the kingdom of God personified.[90] He is equally clear that this perfection includes nonviolence, which is also affirmed by God and is expected of humanity.[91] How then can God be implicated in violence in his strategy for redeeming humanity, when simultaneously introducing and manifesting the nonviolence of the kingdom of God in the same Son he kills? It is as if God, as he who animates and indeed is the Incarnate Christ, instructs humanity in the way of nonviolence by refusing to fight back during his confrontation with socio-political opposition, while at precisely the same juncture in the atonement narrative he uses violence to redeem humanity by killing the nonviolent Son within whom he himself resides. Essentially, if Irenaeus were to anachronistically submit to the claims of penal substitutionary atonement, the resulting model would include God violently killing his own nonviolent self in an effort to demonstrate the

---

90. Boersma observes, "Irenaeus regards the incarnation as the climax of God's progressive self-revelation, something the Bishop of Lyons traces throughout the Old Testament." Hans Boersma, "Eschatological Justice and the Cross: Violence and Penal Substitution," *Theology Today* 60, no. 2 (July 2003): 197. Cf. *AH* 4.10.1.; *Epid.* 25, 27, 43-85. Accordingly, Irenaeus contends, "It is not right that we should lay blame upon those who sinned before Christ's coming. For 'all men come short of the glory of God,' and are not justified of themselves, but by the advent of the Lord." *AH* 4.27.2.

91. Interestingly, Boersma here, like in other descriptions, interprets Irenaeus correctly, but for one reason or another decides not to take him seriously as an authority in atonement theology. Nevertheless, he accurately observes, "The incarnation serves the victory of Christ over Satan and reveals to human beings what the Father is like, so that by imitating the Word, people may be restored to the image and likeness of God." Hans Boersma, "Eschatological Justice and the Cross: Violence and Penal Substitution," 195. Hochban also comments, "Christ underwent the passion to bring us to the knowledge of the Father." John I. Hochban, "St. Irenaeus on the Atonement," 546-547. And Latourette states that Irenaeus viewed Christ's recapitulation as "perfectly [fulfilling] what God had intended man and His entire creation to be." Kenneth Scott Latourette, *A History of Christianity*, vol. 1, 143. Cf. *AH* 2.20.3.; *AH* 3.18.7.; *AH* 5.1.1.

importance of nonviolence to the humanity he wishes to redeem – through violence. St. Irenaeus' response to docetic claims rejecting Christ's humanity as an illusion and therefore his physical suffering, can easily be transposed into a discussion concerning God's ostensible wrath:

> This also does likewise meet [the case] of those who maintain that He suffered only in appearance. For if He did not truly suffer, no thanks to Him, since there was no suffering at all; and when we shall actually begin to suffer, He will seem as *leading us astray*, exhorting us to endure buffeting, and to turn the other cheek, if He did not Himself before us in reality suffer the same; and as *He misled them* by seeming to them what He was not, so does He also mislead us, by exhorting us to endure what He did not endure Himself. [In that case] we shall be even above the Master, because we suffer and sustain what our Master never bore or endured. But as our Lord is alone truly Master, so the Son of God is truly good and patient, the Word of God the Father having been made the Son of man [*Verbum Dei Patris Filius Hominis factus*].[92]

It is noteworthy that Irenaeus assimilates the nonviolence of Christ and the Church with 'the Father [*Patris*] having been made the Son of man.' Contrary to penal substitutionary interpretations, the nonviolence of the *Verbum Dei* necessitates the nonviolence of the *Patris*. Moreover, if one were to supplant docetic claims with allegations that God used violence to accomplish the redemption of humanity, it would also seem as if he were 'leading us astray, exhorting us to endure buffeting, and to turn the other cheek,' if alternatively God by his own actions seems to advocate retributive and therefore violent measures to incite justice in his desire to destroy humanity and ultimately kill his own Son.[93] Irenaeus' last two statements, however, clearly indicate that

---

92. *AH* 3.18.6. Here, and in the last statement especially, Irenaeus is illuminating a strong identification motif in his atonement narrative.

93. Again Boersma interprets Irenaeus correctly, but with much difficulty tries to demonstrate how God's "self-donation" actually supports the penal substitutionary model. He admits that the incarnation "means for Irenaeus that God suffers on the cross," but again does not take Irenaeus' proposition seriously enough and proceeds to show how such an arrangement enhances penal substitution so that in the end it really is not penal substitution at all! Boersma states that Irenaeus' emphasis on the incarnation "counters the notion that penal substitution is God's unjust infliction of suffering on an innocent third party" and claims that Irenaeus' system shows that penal substitution does not "[glorify] suffering" or "[perpetuate] victimization" since humanity is not commanded to imitate God in everything. This last point is true, but as John Howard Yoder states, "There is thus but one realm in which the concept of imitation holds–but there it holds in every strand of the New Testament literature and all the more strikingly by virtue of the absence of parallels in other realms. This is at the point of the concrete social meaning of the cross in its relation to enmity and power. Servanthood replaces dominion, forgiveness absorbs hostility. Thus – and only thus – are we bound by New Testament thought to 'be like Jesus.'" John Howard Yoder, *The Politics of Jesus: Vicit Agnus Noster* (Grand Rapids, MI: Eerdmans, 1994), 131. To the extent that the Church fails to imitate Christ's servanthood, it imitates the alternative, that of retribution. The point is not that, as Boersma warns against, God is inviting humanity to imitate his ostensible vio-

the Father and the Son both, through their accumulative nonviolent resolve, endure suffering and expect the same from humanity. Irenaeus is reminding us that the advent of the Incarnate Christ means that God's piecemeal instructive measures up until that point are now made complete in the Word made flesh *for* the flesh to learn what it means to affiliate oneself with the Word, that is, for humanity to reclaim the divine. It is at this point in the atonement narrative that God must embody the kingdom of God perfectly, which must and indeed does include nonviolence.[94] Irenaeus constructs this idea of Christ's incarnational perfection in nonviolence within the context of his confrontation with Marcionist claims which sought to separate the "violent" God of the Old Testament, what Marcion referred to as the *demiurge*, from the nonviolent *Logos*, the New Testament God of Jesus, who accomplishes his work in humility and patience.[95] J.N.D. Kelly claims that one of Irenaeus' favourite themes

> is that the law of Moses and the grace of the New Testament, both adapted to different sets of conditions, were bestowed by one and the same God for the benefit of the human race. If the Old Testament legislation appears less perfect than the New, this is because mankind has to undergo a progressive development, and the old law was designed for its earlier stages.[96]

lence, but that the Christians would and indeed do imitate this unfortunate *interpretation* regardless. By virtue of this regrettable reality, an emphasis on the imitation of Christ's servanthood must be advanced and endorsed on account of the Church's occasional propensity for the contrary. Besides this, however, Boersma either brushes aside clear elements of penal substitution such as God's external wrath and that his wrath is very real since such elements are incompatible with the incarnation and the nonviolence therein, or he attempts to paint Irenaeus' atonement narrative with a substitutionary brush so that in the end the incarnation and nonviolence of Irenaeus are ignored, and he emerges as a great champion of penal substitution. Ultimately, Boersma fails with his elliptical arguments and attempt to alter Irenaeus' atonement narrative so that when convenient it is either not substitutionary or else not Irenaeus' own understanding of atonement: Hans Boersma, "Eschatological Justice and the Cross: Violence and Penal Substitution," 198. It should be noted also, Willard Swartley also discusses Christ as "self-donation" as Boersma does, but instead of awkwardly forcing such language into a penal substitutionary interpretation of the atonement, Swartley describes self-donation as Christ's obedience to the kingdom of God rather than submission to God's wrath: "Jesus taught so clearly the way of the cross, self-denial, humble service, and readiness to give up all for the kingdom." Willard M. Swartley, *Covenant of Peace: The Missing Peace in New Testament Theology and Ethics*, (Grand Rapids, MI: Eerdman's, 2006), 119.

94. See note 79 above.

95. For instance, Latourette observes that "He [Marcion] noted that the God of the Old Testament...[was]...a God of battles, rejoiced in bloodshed and was vindictive." Kenneth Scott Latourette, *A History of Christianity*, vol. 1, 126. Cf. *AH* 1.27.2.

96. J.N.D. Kelly, *Early Christian Doctrines*, 68. In relation to the infantility of humanity, Steenberg also declares, "the doctrine of the creation of man as 'child' assists Irenaeus greatly and has much to offer a Christian anthropology and soteriology. It provides the means, readily employed by Irenaeus, to address the question—which has plagued subsequent centuries of Christian thought—why God would wait so long to become

Kelly further claims that Irenaeus acknowledged, "The prophets had full cognizance of all the incidents of the incarnation, and were fully apprised of the Saviour's teaching and passion."[97] The temporary imperfection and future incarnational perfection were therefore an accepted state of affairs, both God's violence and nonviolence of which figure prominently in the equation. It is also particularly interesting that Irenaeus alters the Marcionist perception of God's wrath in the Old Testament rather than manipulate the nonviolent element of the Incarnate Christ illustrated in the New.

Perhaps the element in Irenaeus' atonement narrative that best challenges the notion of God's wrath is his insistence that God is determined to destroy *not* humanity nor his Son, but the origin of evil itself, the power of death. Christopher A. Hall comments, "The fault, though, seems to Irenaeus to be more the devil's than humanity's. ...The humans who succumbed to this temptation...God has treated with compassion. In a surprising and redemptive reversal, God has turned the enmity of the devil back upon the evil one."[98] St. Irenaeus is unequivocal on this point; in fact, it is the devil who tries to implicate humanity in the decadent deed, an attempt that God acknowledges and condemns:

> But He took compassion upon man, who, through want of care no doubt, but still wickedly [on the part of another], became involved in disobedience; and He turned the enmity by which [the devil] had designed to make [man] the enemy of God, against the author of it, by removing His own anger from man, turning it in another direction, and sending it instead upon the serpent [*auferens quidem suam, quae erat adversus hominem, inimicitiam; retorquens autem illam, et remittens illam in serpentem*].[99]

This is significant for the simple fact that the wrath of God is now given a justifiable destination. The tyranny of death will eventually come to an end allowing humanity to align itself ontologically with the Incarnate Christ, thus initiating the restoration of the kingdom of God here on earth—true justice.

---

incarnate in Christ; for the necessity of human growth mandates that a period of history pass before the arrival of such an event." M.C. Steenberg, "Children in Paradise: Adam and Eve as 'Infants' in Irenaeus of Lyons," 21. Cf. *AH* 4.13; 14; 48.

97. *Ibid.* Cf. *AH* 1.10.1.; *AH* 4.33.12.

98. Christopher A. Hall, *Learning Theology with the Church Fathers*, 128.

99. *AH* 4.40.3. To understand why the translator implicated "another" in the wicked disobedience, see note 55 above. Using quite militaristic language (see the section *Nonviolence and Chrisus Victor* later on in this essay), St. Irenaeus additionally declares, "He effected the consummation [restoration], and declared war on our enemy, and crushed him who in the beginning had led us captive in Adam." *AH* 5.20.2.

The Propitiation of God's "Wrath":

Irenaeus' allusions to propitiation, although infrequent, must be addressed in order to further challenge the propriety of penal substitutionary atonement models. It is here that the substitutionary motif's dependence on non-theistic retributive notions of justice is perhaps most glaring. Whereas substitution seeks justice by appeasing God forensically and conferentially by means of violent retribution, Irenaeus envisages justice holistically and ontologically as appeasing God by destroying death and restoring to him what is rightfully his, that is, all of creation – including humanity. In this fashion, justice is restorative rather than retributive;[100] God is appeased since his creation is transformed into that which he desires it to be, while humanity also receives justice by its new-found capacity for ontological affiliation with the Incarnate Christ. The thoroughly incarnational language St. Irenaeus employs demonstrates humanity's capacity for ontologically identifying with Christ: "How shall man pass into God, unless God has [first] passed into man [*Et quemadmodum homo transiet in Deum, si non Deus in hominem!*]?" [101] It is specifically the incarnation that Irenaeus is concerned about with regard to the atonement, and it is his confrontation with docetic claims of "Christ's laughter"[102] that Irenaeus feels inclined to defend the humanity and physicality of Christ. In this interpretation of the sacrifice of Isaac, which St. Irenaeus provides, Basilides contends,

> Unto the nations belonging to them it [the intellect] appeared on earth as a man, and he performed deeds of power. Hence he did not suffer. Rather, a certain Simon of Cyrene was forced to bear his cross for him, and it was he who was ignorantly and erroneously crucified, being transformed by the other, so that he was taken for Jesus; while Jesus, for his part, assumed the form of Simon and stood by, laughing at them [*irrisisse eos*].[103]

Therefore, when St. Irenaeus speaks of Christ "taking up the cross as Isaac

---

100. For more on restorative justice, cf. Moule and Northey in this book.

101. *AH* 4.33.4. St. Irenaeus also identifies the importance of the incarnation, so that humanity might become "*particeps fieri incorruptibilitatis.*" *AH* 3.18.7.; cf. *AH* 5.17.1.

102. For an intriguing fuller exposition of the relationship between the docetic rejection of Christ's physical suffering and Isaac as a *typos* or *figura* of Christ, see Guy G. Stroumsa, "Christ's Laughter: Docetic Origins Reconsidered," *Journal of Early Christian Studies* 12, no. 3 (Fall 2004): 267-288. In this essay, Stroumsa argues from patristic witness and the influence of Philo of Alexandria, particularly on Clement and Origen, that, as understood from the etymology of Isaac's name *yzhaq* ("he will laugh"), docetic interpretations of Isaac's *akedah* (binding) provided in Gen. 22 demonstrate that Christ almost suffered but not quite, and instead stood to the side "laughing" as Simon of Cyrene died in his stead.

103. *AH* 1.24.4. As quoted in *Ibid.* 273.

did the wood,"[104] he intends only to accentuate Christ's humanity, suffering and obedience as the mechanism for defeating death and deifying humanity, both for the stimulation of their own obedience in the face of this unique docetic interpretation.[105] Irenaeus must be read in light of the specific purpose for which he was writing; in this instance, Irenaeus maintains Christ's affiliation with Isaac where Basilides does the same but interprets it to mean that Christ did not actually physically suffer, but instead stood off to the side while Simon of Cyrene (the ram) is executed in his stead. It no doubt would have been a temptation to affiliate Christ with the ram, as substitutionary models do, in an attempt to demonstrate that he did indeed suffer physically, but Irenaeus resolved to stay true to the patristic consensus in preserving Isaac as a *typos* or *figura* of Christ. It is imperative, however, not to overlook Irenaeus' objective in defending Christ's humanity alone, and therefore to avoid drawing conclusions based on presuppositions rather than the passage itself and its historical and christologically anthropological context.

Boersma, however, attempts to embroil Irenaeus' use of propitiation, this time in the face of the aforementioned Marcionist claims regarding the dissonance between the Old Testament God (*demiurge*) and that of the Incarnate Christ, with characteristics of substitutionary atonement not found in the *Christus Victor* and moral influence motifs.[106] Boersma's unsuccessful attempt, however, neglects that St. Irenaeus' use of propitiation in this instance again mediates ontological ramifications of the incarnation that publicize the kingdom of God such as "cleansing the lepers" and "healing the sick," while Christ's suffering does not appease God through any punitive or juridical transaction, but instead for the purpose that humanity "might return without fear to his own inheritance."[107] Humanity has been acquitted of any wrongdoing, but it is the Word become flesh that allows him access to death

104. *AH* 4.5.4.

105. Hochban states, "Others, as Marcion and his followers, proposed a more radical solution, asserting that Christ was a completely celestial being, a revelation of the good God of the New Testament, who appeared suddenly on this earth in the reign of Tiberius, without the antecedent indignity of human birth; he appeared, indeed, in the form of a man, but His body was a mere illusion. Again, in conformity with there contempt of matter, the Gnostics maintained that man's body, being a material substance, was incapable of salvation. In light of these fundamental Gnostic positions we may, therefore, readily understand the importance which St. Irenaeus attaches to the demonstration of the true humanity of the Saviour and the unity of His person. We may likewise understand the reason for his strong vindication of the participation of the flesh in the fruits of the redemption." John I. Hochban, "St. Irenaeus on the Atonement," 526. Cf. *AH* 1.27.2. re: Marcionist allegations of Christ's body as an illusion: "*Jesum...in hominis forma manifestatum...*"

106. Hans Boersma, "Eschatological Justice and the Cross: Violence and Penal Substitution," 195.

107. *AH* 4.8.2. As quoted in *Ibid.*

so that it may be vanquished[108] thus enabling humanity access to the divine; this is propitiation, and this appeases God by balancing the economy of creation and restoring once again the initial state of *shalom*, of which humanity's ontological restoration is an integral signal. St. Irenaeus summarizes the implications of Christ's humanity thus: "If, not having been made flesh, He did appear as if flesh, His work was not a true one. But what He did appear, that He also was: God recapitulated in Himself the ancient formation of man, that He might kill sin, deprive death of its power, and vivify man [*Deus, hominis antiquam plasmationem in se recapitulans, ut occideret quidem peccatum, evacuaret autem mortem, et vivificaret hominem*]."[109]

That Irenaeus wishes to accentuate Christ's humanity in order to authorize and designate propitiation as the elimination of death and the procedure for restoring humanity corroborates with Aulén's contention that "the statement which is sometimes made, that Irenaeus is here propounding a 'juridical' doctrine of Atonement, shows a complete misconception of his meaning."[110] Reading back into history is of course a very risky venture. Irenaeus' notion of justice parallels patristic notions of ontological soteriology and is analogous to the Hebraic notion of *shalom*. Boersma's understanding of justice to include punitive measures against the offender to satisfy the victim's dignity is quite foreign to Irenaeus as it lacks any restoration on both sides. For Irenaeus, justice is essentially the reinstitution of the kingdom of God; if the offender is eliminated, she or he is excluded from this restoration, which would undermine Irenaeus' perception of justice. Furthermore, if the measure taken to satisfy the victim merely means reprimanding the offender proportionate to her or his transgression, the victim does not receive the healing or restoration required for incorporation into the kingdom of God. Irenaeus acknowledges justice to include eliminating the impediment that prevents humanity access to the divine. By freeing humanity from the tyranny of apostasy and death, justice is actualized not only because humanity is exonerated from the consequences of a situation it could not have avoided, but also because humanity is now receptive to restorative measures. Significantly, Aulén claims that Irenaeus "regards sin organically,"[111] and although he believes the devil does

---

108. Cf. *AH* 3.20.4. St. Irenaeus clearly states with regard to the relationship between the humanity of Christ and the defeat of death, "Those, therefore, who assert that He appeared putatively, and was neither born in the flesh nor truly made man, are as yet under the old condemnation, holding out patronage to sin; for, by their showing, death has not been vanquished." *AH* 3.18.7.

109. *AH* 3.18.7.

110. Gustaf Aulén, *Christus Victor: An Historical Study of the Three Main Types of the Idea of the Atonement*, 27.

111. *Ibid.* 23.

have "in some sense an objective existence,"[112] he also understands that sin, death and the devil "may be said to be in some measure personified."[113] Ultimately, St. Irenaeus refers to sin, death and the devil as "objective powers"[114] rather than objective beings. This is noteworthy since the exclusion of death from the kingdom of God does not entail violence or injustice, not only because such an inclusion would spoil the kingdom's equilibrium, but also because death is not a animate or sentient entity. It instead functions as the barrier between humanity's regrettable affiliation with apostasy and its access to the divine, or participation in the kingdom of God. In the end, therefore, St. Irenaeus advances a binary perception of justice:

> Justly [*juste*] indeed is he led captive, who had led men unjustly into bondage [*qui hominem injuste captivum duxerat*]; while man, who had been led captive in times past, was rescued from the grasp of his possessor, according to the tender mercy of God the Father [*extractus est a possessoris potestate, secundum misericordiam Dei Patris*], who had compassion [*miseratus*] on His own handiwork, and gave it to salvation, restoring [*redintegrans*] it by means of the Word – that is, by Christ.[115]

Therefore, (1) death is dissolved to (2) ensure humanity entrance to the divine, that is, complete ontological restoration.

II. CHRIST'S IDENTIFICATION WITH HUMANITY *WHILE* RETAINING THE DIVINE:

The advent of Christ, his recapitulation, his obedience to kingdom expectations even unto death, and his eventual defeat of death is the progressive arrangement with which St. Irenaeus demonstrates Christ's identification with humanity.[116] It is this identification that atones for humanity's apostasy by affecting their ontology so that through instruction and empowerment humanity might identify with Christ. A common strand running throughout the entire process of redemption is nonviolence and the recapitualtion of peace, if not the epitomizing characteristic of the kingdom of God, at least an indispensable one. The chronology of Irenaeus' atonement narrative until now has involved death's

---

112. *Ibid.* 26.
113. *Ibid.* 20.
114. *Ibid.* 20.
115. *AH* 5.21.3.
116. Affirming the atoning function of Christ's life in its entirety, Aulén then observes, "Assuredly, then, the death of Christ holds a central place in Irenaeus' thought. But, we must add at once, it is not the death in isolation; it is the death seen in connection, on the one hand, with the life-work of Christ as a whole, and on the other with the Resurrection and the Ascension" Gustaf Aulén, *Christus Victor: An Historical Study of the Three Main Types of the Idea of the Atonement*, 31.

implication of humanity in apostasy and God's methodical and arduous attempt to re-educate humanity in the composition and requirements of the kingdom of God. The second segment of this narrative opens with the advent of the Word become flesh, the re-education of humanity made complete in one man who in all things simultaneously and unwaveringly retains the divine.

The Incarnation as Pedagogue:[117]

S. Mark Heim asks in his explication of Boersma's own christological inter-pretation of the parable of the prodigal son (Luke 15:11-32), "What if God had gone into the far country to find the unrepentant child rather than wait-ing at home? What kind of hospitality would that be?"[118] Boersma himself correctly declares, "God's hospitality does not nullify human freedom. The father's embrace does not force itself in tyrannical fashion on a son who has no choice but to endure the father's imposition of his love."[119] This is a verity already affirmed above. But Boersma's elucidation of the par-able of the prodigal son makes the claim that God would not 'journey into the far country,' as this act would compromise human freedom. However, although avoiding personal subscription to this notion, Boersma makes the additional claim regarding Irenaeus' own thought that "God's hospitality is redemptive not merely insofar as God waits for humanity's homecoming but insofar as God himself journeys into the far country."[120] This is the essence of the incarnation; God discloses himself in human form *for* humans and identifies with humanity's onerous situation in the process.[121] St. Irenaeus appropriately affirms, "He is man, the formation of God; and thus He took man into Himself, the invisible becoming visible [*invisibilis visibilis factus*], the incomprehensible being made comprehensible, the impassible becom-ing capable of suffering."[122] Until Christ's advent, God had been revealed piecemeal, but in Christ, God has identified with humanity for the sake of

---

117. Boersma uses this term in reference to William P. Loewe's interpretation of Ire-naeus' understanding of Adam and Eve as infants who therefore need to be instructed in the ways of the kingdom by the Incarnate Christ. Hans Boersma, *Violence, Hospitality and the Cross: Reappropriating the Atonement Tradition*, 127.

118. S. Mark Heim, "Cross Purposes: Rethinking the Death of Jesus," 24.

119. Hans Boersma, *Violence, Hospitality and the Cross: Reappropriating the Atone-ment Tradition*, 26.

120. *Ibid.* 187.

121. Christopher A. Hall declares, "In the wonder of the incarnation, Irenaeus believes, the Word has genuinely come into our world, taking on all that we are, so that in Christ we might become all we were created to be." Christopher A. Hall, *Learning Theology with the Church Fathers*, 130.

122. *AH* 3.16.6.

imparting perfect and complete instruction[123] for the first time; God is essentially revealing what it means to be human and divine concomitantly in an effort to also demonstrate what it looks like when a human compels the divine to dominate over the flesh.[124] According to Chadwick, Irenaeus views "the history of salvation [as] a progressive education, in which God has brought humanity forward step by step in a long process culminating in the incarnation of the divine Word."[125] This description, of course, is meant to illuminate Christ's function as the turning point[126] in this process of re-education for, as St. Irenaeus declares, "In no other way could we have learned [*discere*] the things of God, unless our Master, existing as the Word, had become man [*Verbum exsistens, homo factus fuisset*]. For no other being had the power of revealing to us the things of the Father, except His own proper Word."[127] Specifically, however, Irenaeus intends to accentuate the kingdom of God, as it is this holistic domain of renewal and *shalom* in which Irenaeus envisages

123. The Latin translation of St. Irenaeus' works uses the term *erudito* [*AH* 4.37.7.] to illuminate Christ's role of instructing, educating or teaching humanity: "God has displayed long-suffering in the case of man's apostasy; while man has been instructed [*erudito*] by means of it." The Latin term *disciplinam* [*AH* 4.39.1.] is also used: "...instruction [*disciplinam*] in that which is good." Irenaeus also discusses the function of knowledge and learning for eventually partaking of incorruptibility: "This, therefore, was the [object of the] long-suffering of God, that man, passing through all things, and acquiring the knowledge [*agnitionem*] of moral discipline, then attaining to the resurrection from the dead, and learning [*discens*] by experience what is the source of his deliverance [*liberatus*], may always live in a state of gratitude to the Lord, having obtained from Him the gift of incorruptibility [*incorruptelae*]." *AH* 3.20.2.

124. St. Irenaeus describes this notion clearly when he asserts, "Into this paradise the Lord has introduced those who obey His call, 'summing up in Himself all things which are in heaven, and which are on earth;' but the things in heaven are spiritual, while those on earth constitute the dispensation in human nature (*secundum hominem est dispositio*). These things, therefore, He recapitulated in Himself: by uniting man to the Spirit, and causing the Spirit to dwell in man [*adunans hominem spiritui, et spiritum collocans in homine*], He is Himself made the head of the Spirit, and gives the Spirit to be the head of man: for through Him (the Spirit) we see, and hear, and speak [*per illum enim videmus, et audimus, et loquimur*]." *AH* 5.20.2. Steenberg demonstrates the progressive nature of this process in reference to Adam and Even as infants: "Irenaeus' whole soteriology begins here: it is for the growth of the child, Adam, that the Son of God becomes incarnate and shows forth the adult, the full image, that the child is to become." M.C. Steenberg, "Children in Paradise: Adam and Eve as 'Infants' in Irenaeus of Lyons," 22. And elsewhere he states, "This full humanity, the whole and complete man, is for Irenaeus unequivocally the person of Jesus Christ. It is He who is the true image of God into which humanity was created and in whom all other human persons may come to their own full maturity" (16).

125. Henry Chadwick, *The Early Church*, 80-81.

126. St. Irenaeus observes that there is "one Christ Jesus our Lord who came in fulfillment [*veniens per*] of God's comprehensive design [*universam dispositionem*] and consummates [*recapitulans*] all things in himself." *AH* 3.16.6.; cf. *Epid.* 56.

127. *AH* 5.1.1.; cf. *AH* 4.5.1.

humanity participating.[128] With respect to humanity's responsibility, reclaiming the divine *is* participating in the kingdom of God. At this point, however, Christ is functioning paradigmatically only,[129] while the capacitation or empowerment coincides with his victory over death further along in Irenaeus' atonement narrative.[130] Assuredly, Christ will identify with humanity by exemplifying the nonviolence of the kingdom of God in the face of socio-political oppression and therefore ultimately gaining access to death for its eventual defeat, which will in turn permit humanity access to the divine so we too can imitate Christ's nonviolence and participate in the kingdom of God.

The element of nonviolence in the incarnation is often omitted from interpretations of Irenaeus, but it is an essential component for understanding Irenaeus' entire atonement narrative. While detecting the significance of Christ's emergence on earth in relation to the restoration of peace, St. Irenaeus claims:

> From the Lord's advent [*Domini autem adventu*], the new covenant which brings back peace [*pacem reconcilians*], and the law which gives life, has gone forth over the whole earth, as the prophets said: 'For out of Zion shall go forth the law, and the word of the Lord from Jerusalem; and He shall rebuke many people; and they shall break down their swords into ploughshares, and their spears into pruning-hooks, and they shall no longer learn to fight [*et concident gladios suos in aratra, et lanceas suas in falces, et jam non discent pugnare*].'[131]

Irenaeus is truly convinced that this shift towards nonviolence has literally

---

128. In reference to God's interaction with Abraham, St. Irenaeus states that it is God "who introduces, through Jesus Christ, Abraham to the kingdom of heaven [*regno coelorum*], and his seed, that is, the Church." *AH* 4.8.1.

129. Boersma describes Christ from Irenaeus' perspective as a "model of obedience." Hans Boersma, *Violence, Hospitality and the Cross: Reappropriating the Atonement Tradition*, 126.

130. St. Irenaeus succinctly asserts, "Unless man had been joined to God, he could never have become a partaker of incorruptibility." *AH* 3.18.7. Irenaeus, showing signs of Abelard's moral influence atonement theory, describes the association between instruction and empowerment: "This, therefore, was the [object of the] long-suffering of God, that man, passing through all things, and acquiring the knowledge of moral discipline, then attaining to the resurrection from the dead, and learning by experience what is the source of his deliverance, may always live in a state of gratitude to the Lord, having obtained from Him the gift of incorruptibility, that he might love Him the more; for 'he to whom more is forgiven, [loves] more.'" *AH* 3.20.2. Aulén also elucidates this connection between Christ's instruction and empowerment, but with respect to Christ's victory over death: "His preaching and teaching are expressly regarded in the same light; the teaching by which we 'learn to know the Father' forms an element in Christ's victory over the powers of darkness."

131. *AH* 4.34.4.

occurred in the Church, or the *novam generationem*,[132] and in fact uses it to parry accusations by Marcion that a dissonance exists between the God of the Old Testament and that of the New. In an interesting analogy, St. Irenaeus associates the plough, where "the wood has been joined on to the iron," with the incarnation since the "Word, having been firmly united to flesh,"[133] exhibits a union for the sake of nonviolence, as the materials used to fabricate the plough also seek to do. The incarnation is indispensable for disseminating the message of nonviolence and at the same time affecting humanity for participating in the same. For Irenaeus, nonviolence is not a peripheral concern, but instead an essential element of the kingdom of God, that which encapsulates the comprehensiveness of kingdom obligations.

Christ's Martyrdom and the Recapitulation of Peace:

Adam's installment of death's tyrannical reign incurred violence on subsequent humanity and it is this situation that Christ intended to eradicate through the nonviolence intrinsic to the kingdom of God. Irenaeus is clear on this point,[134] but the implications for the Church are even more far-reaching. Within the context of describing Christ as "perfect in all things,"[135] St. Irenaeus further elucidates how Christ rescued humanity from apostasy's clutches and redeemed "from it His own property." However, this he did "not by violent means,"[136] as contrasted with apostasy's tyrannical rule,

---

132. *AH* 4.33.4.

133. *AH* 4.34.4. "*...lignum copulatum ferro ... firmum Verbum adunitum carni.*" William W. Harvey also detects this analogous relationship and equates the "union of two substances in its composition," that of the Word and Jesus, with a similar union of the "iron of the share and the wood of the beam," and therein, it appears, associates the nonviolence of the plough with that of Christ's teachings and example: William Wigan Harvey, ed., *Sancti Irenaei Libros Quinque Adversus Haereses*, vol. 2 (Cantabrigiae: Typis Academicis, 1857), 272: note 8.

134. Even Boersma, who recognizes a place for violence in God's redemptive plan, acknowledges the overt nonviolence of Irenaeus' atonement theology: "An additional intriguing element of Irenaeus' understating of the Christus victor theme is that he believes Christ gained the victory through nonviolent means." Boersma also comments that Irenaeus "overemphasizes the nonviolence of the atonement." Hans Boersma, *Violence, Hospitality and the Cross: Reappropriating the Atonement Tradition*, 189.

135. *AH* 5.1.1. Significantly, this same expression ["*perfectus in omnibus*"] is used elsewhere by St. Irenaeus who immediately afterward describes this perfection of Christ as *not* striking back in return or threatening retaliation when he endured violence [*AH* 3.16.9.].

136. St. Irenaeus here uses the Latin form *vi* and further down, *vim*, which denotes a sense of force, strength and power, as contrasted with *violentum*, which implies vehemence and impetuousness, and which Irenaeus uses in *AH* 4.37.7. in reference to Mt. 11:12 and the importance of the kingdom of God and the earnestness with which those who so desire may claim it as their own (as evident in his reference to 1 Cor. 9:24-27 immediately thereafter). This reference to Christ's nonviolence no doubt relates more

but instead "by means of persuasion, as became a God of counsel, who does not use violent means to obtain what He desires." Moreover, this nonviolence was demonstrated in Christ's redemption of humanity "through His own blood."[137] Although the context suggests that Irenaeus is illuminating Christ's nonviolence in an effort not to impair or defile humanity's freedom, it is nevertheless a reflection of Jesus' irenic and non-belligerent character which Irenaeus discusses elsewhere specifically within the context of Christ' passion.[138]

It is imperative to establish at the outset that martyrdom and suffering implies or is analogous with nonviolence for the sake of the kingdom of God; by choosing to suffer, one is concurrently choosing not to fight back, that is, engage in violence.[139] St. Irenaeus discusses God's attempt to diffuse the potentially violent situation between Cain and his brother, Abel, by instructing Cain to "be at rest," after which St. Irenaeus observes, "Now what else is it to 'be at rest' than to forego purposed violence [*impetu*]?"[140] Concurrently, St. Irenaeus declares:

> Jesus Christ, the Son of God, is one and the same, who did by suffering reconcile us to God [*qui per passionem reconciliavit nos Deo*], and rose from the dead; who is at the right hand of the Father, and perfect in all things; 'who, when He was buffeted, struck not in return; who, when He suffered, threatened not;' and when He underwent tyranny, He prayed His Father that He would forgive those who had crucified Him [*qui cum vapularet, non qui repercutiebat; qui cum pateretur, non est minatus, et cum tyrannidem pateretur, rogabat Patrem ut ignosceret his qui se crucifixerant*].[141]

And specifically through Christ's restraint and nonviolent resolve, "He did Himself bring in salvation."[142] Christ's passion is therefore the instrument by

---

to his refusal to use coercion as the apostasy had, and therefore his desire to preserve humanity's freedom. However, the language Irenaeus uses in this passage is too similar to other passages where Irenaeus describes Christ's physical nonviolence, his refusal to fight back (See, for instance, note 135 above and the references in note 138 below).

137. "*qui est perfectus in omnibus...ea quae sunt sua redimens ab ea, non cum vi, ... sed secundum suadelam, quemadmodum decebat Deum suadentem, et non vim inferentem, accipere quae vellet.*" *AH* 5.1.1.

138. Cf. *AH* 3.16.9.; *AH* 3.18.4-5.; *AH* 4.28.3.; *AH* 4.34.4.; *Epid.* 34.

139. With reference to Christ's decision not to fight back, Douglass asserts, "The logic of non-violence is the logic of crucifixion..." James W. Douglass, *The Nonviolent Cross: A Theology of Revolution and Peace*, 71.

140. *AH* 4.18.3. The Latin translation of Irenaeus' understanding here uses the term *quiesce*, for what in English translates as, 'be at rest,' which could also be translated, 'be at peace,' 'keep neutral' or 'keep calm'. The antithetical Latin term used here, *impetu*, implies an attack or assault and is therefore a pertinent description of the violent option with which one is provided in the face of socio-political oppression or occupation, the option that Christ rejects.

141. *AH* 3.16.9. cf. *Epid.* 34.

142. *Ibid.*

which humanity is reconciled to God: "*qui per passionem reconciliavit nos Deo.*"[143] This understanding of Christ's nonviolence affects humanity's status, as it demonstrates the demarcation of the kingdom of God: those who incriminate themselves through participating in violence belong to a different kingdom. St. Irenaeus accordingly observes, "The death of the Lord is the condemnation of those who fastened Him to the cross, and who did not believe His advent, but the salvation of those who believe in Him."[144] In reference to those who subjected Christ to violence, whom he identifies as the Pharisees and scribes, St. Irenaeus cites the words of Jeremiah and Isaiah: "For Jeremiah says, 'Behold, neither [their] eyes nor [their] heart are good; but [they are turned] to [their] covetousness, and to shed innocent blood, and for injustice, and for man-slaying, that [they may] do it.' And again Isaiah [says], '[You] have taken counsel, but not of Me; and made covenants, [but] not by My Spirit.'"[145] In similar character, St. Irenaeus is aware of the implications in Christ's rebuke of Peter, who evidently believed that a violent uprising would establish the kingdom of God:

'He began to show to His disciples, how that He must go unto Jerusalem, and suffer many things of the priests, and be rejected, and crucified, and rise again the third day.' ... Then He rebuked Peter, who imagined that He was the Christ as the generality of men supposed [that the Christ should be], and was averse to the idea of His suffering [*secundum opinionem hominum putanti eum esse Christum, et passionem ejus aversanti*].[146]

But, in agreement with Irenaeus' assessment above, James Douglass observes, "suffering" is the "reversal of violence."[147]

It is this suffering, particularly as is was exemplified in the cross, that is the sign of Christ's government in opposition to all those that dominated the earth before his appearance.[148] Utilizing the messianic prophecy from

143. *Ibid.*
144. *AH* 4.28.3.
145. *AH* 4.18.3.
146. *AH* 3.18.4. This is an important theme for Yoder as well who contrasts Jesus' nonviolence with the tactics of the insurrectionists: "Whereas Mark simply names Barabbas, and Matthew calls him simply, 'a notorious prisoner,' Luke tells us twice that he was imprisoned for insurrection and emphasizes the ironic tragedy of the trade: 'He released the man who had been thrown into prison for insurrection and murder, whom they asked for: but Jesus he delivered up to their will.' The story ends with both the inscription on the cross and the mockery of the soldiers focused upon his kingship and his not saving himself. Jesus was thus traded for a Zealot leader and put to death as 'King of the Jews'." John Howard Yoder, *The Politics of Jesus: Vicit Agnus Noster*, 48-49.
147. James W. Douglass, *The Nonviolent Cross: A Theology of Revolution and Peace* (New York: MacMillan, 1968), 290.
148. Boersma states, "Only by radically limiting Christ's redemptive role to his life (so that his life becomes an example to us) or by absolutely dissociating God from any

Isaiah concerning Christ's advent,[149] St. Irenaeus affirms the kingdom of God's "peace and health," for "Great is his rule, and of his peace there is no bound," but then aligns the kingdom of peace with the suffering of Christ in his confrontation with earthly kingdoms, *"Whose government is upon his shoulder*, the cross is in a figure declared, on which He was nailed back. For that which was and is a reproach to Him, and for His sake to us, even the cross, this same is, says he, His *government*, being a sign of His kingdom."[150] If Irenaeus identifies suffering and the nonviolence therein as a 'sign of

role in the cross (turning the crucifixion into a solely human act) can we somehow avoid dealing with the difficulty of divine violence." Hans Boersma, *Violence, Hospitality and the Cross: Reappropriating the Atonement Tradition*, 41. However, Boersma, although not advocating his own suggestion, is actually on the right track (and of course he knows he is insinuating current nonviolent opinion on the matter). Irenaeus' emphasis on the recapitulation of Christ and the incarnation is not so much limiting his 'redemptive role to his life' as much as he is emphasizing that which many contemporary theologians, including Boersma, seem to undervalue. However, more pertinent to our discussion concerning the dissonance between the kingdom of God and earthly governments is the notion that Christ's crucifixion was solely a human act. Boersma elsewhere contends, "That the cross is the church's central symbol is unlikely to be disputed. Whether this symbol is positive or negative, however, is a question that tends to generate more discussion." Hans Boersma, "Eschatological Justice and the Cross: Violence and Penal Substitution," 186. However, this is a false dichotomy. The cross is positive because of its redemptive power, however its atonement function may be interpreted. But it cannot be repudiated that "the 'cross' of Jesus was a political punishment," and it is the underestimation of the significance of this fact that impairs any New Testament hermeneutic. John Howard Yoder, *The Politics of Jesus: Vicit Agnus Noster*, 125. The cross exhibited the violence of those who executed the nonviolent Word made flesh. This is a negative thing, and the Church's continued embroilment in violence only accentuates its negativity. Swartley's interaction with Christopher Marshall and J. Denny Weaver demonstrates what is often missed by those who diminish the significance of the socio-political element in Christ's execution: "I agree with Marshall that Weaver is correct in saying that the cause of Jesus' death lies with the powers of evil manifest in human violence but wrong in denying that God has anything to do with Jesus' death on the cross." Willard M. Swartley, *Covenant of Peace: The Missing Peace in New Testament Theology and Ethics*, 193: note 7. This, I think, is a misinterpretation of Weaver's thought. Although Weaver does indeed emphasize the socio-political element of Christ's execution, he does not neglect the positive function of the cross as the method by which Christ persists in the narrative *Christus Victor* for the purpose of defeating death, freeing humanity and capacitating it for union with Christ. Within this structure, the cross has both a negative and positive constituent but should nevertheless not suffer the disconnect from its socio-political implications and the violent vs. nonviolent imputations therein.

149. Isaiah 9:6-7.

150. *Epid.* 56. Huebner contrasts Christ's implicating life in his own suffering with the priorities of the Roman empire and this in light of Pionius' martyrdom, an event readily known by Irenaeus: "In Christ both life and death as they are commonly understood are thoroughly reconceived and reordered. And such a different understanding could not but appear completely irrational and nonsensical to the 'cultured' Roman world, a world that prided itself on the strength of its knowledge and power." Chris K. Huebner, "Between Victory and Victimhood: Reflections on Culture and Martyrdom," 229-230.

[Christ's] kingdom,' it is vital to ascertain its significance for the atonement, both theologically and historically, and in particular for humanity's resulting transformation and its implications for deciding whether to identify with the blood *from* Christ's hands or the blood *on* Caesar's.

It is this either-or situation that renders Boersma's assessment that "in our world it is, strictly speaking, impossible to extend hospitality without at the same time also engaging in some violence"[151] all the more troubling. Boersma does not consider the option of *receiving* violence, and therein preserving one's affiliation with the kingdom of God. As Ray Gingerich observes, "If we hold to a violent God, in the name of justice, as being the one to rectify all things, we deny the way of the nonviolent cross of Jesus as being the revelation of God and the harbinger of God's new humanity."[152] But as a new humanity, the Church is obligated to *be* the Church, or the "*novam generationem,*"[153] and invite as many people as possible to enter into this same nonviolent domain of renewal. Otherwise, the only option we are left with is establishing the kingdom of God through force, however counterintuitive such an endeavour might be. Suffering and nonviolence, however, "is a testimony to a vision of life in which identity is not understood as a thing to be seized but rather a gift that can only be properly received in the absence of a drive to control."[154] And this 'drive to control' through fighting back represents a choice against Christ's government of nonviolence. Leo Tolstoy, who admittedly denies "the atonement by blood,"[155] nevertheless summarizes the

151. Hans Boersma, *Violence, Hospitality and the Cross: Reappropriating the Atonement Tradition*, 48. As noted earlier, Boersma is here referring to Levinas and Derrida's tenuous definition of violence to include a single person neglecting to address every issue in the world that needs someone's attention. However, Boersma's punitive understanding of justice affirms that he sees no way around incurring violence on at least one party, that of the offender, or the enemy Jesus calls us to love and therefore restore or heal along with the victim.

152. Ray Gingerich, "Reimaging Power: Toward a Theology of Nonviolence." In *Peace and Justice Shall Embrace: Power and Theopolitics in the Bible*, Ted Grimsrud and Lorne L. Johns, eds. (Scottdale, PA: Herald, 1999), 194.

153. *AH* 4.33.4.

154. Chris K. Huebner, "Between Victory and Victimhood: Reflections on Culture and Martyrdom," 235. Similarly, in reference to the 'Cain instinct' St. Irenaeus declares, "When Cain was by no means at rest, He [said] to him: 'To [you] shall be his desire, and [you shall] rule over him.' Thus did He in like manner speak to Pilate: '[You should] have no power at all against Me, unless it were given [you] from above;' God always giving up the righteous one [in this life to suffering], that he, having been tested by what he suffered and endured, may [at last] be accepted; but that the evildoer, being judged by the actions he has performed, may be rejected." *AH* 4.18.3.

155. Leo Tolstoy, *The Kingdom of God is Within You*, Translated by Constance Garnett (Lincoln, NE: University of Nebraska Press, 1984), 38. Tolstoy also admits to "not recognizing the Trinity, the redemption, and the immortality of the soul" (31). Tolstoy also says that the statements that "Jesus is also God the Son, who created all before

decision, and it is indeed a soteriological one, humanity must confront. In his exposition on the *Catechism of Non-resistance* by Adin Ballou, Tolstoy succinctly relates the choice placed before humanity, and in the process endorses the pedagogical half of Irenaeus' atonement narrative:

> Q. But if that is the true meaning of the rule of non-resistance, can it always be put into practice?
>
> A. It can be put into practice like every virtue enjoined by the law of God. A virtue cannot be practiced in all circumstances without self-sacrifice, privation, suffering, and in extreme cases loss of life itself. *But he who esteems life more than fulfilling the will of God is already dead to the only true life. Trying to save his life he loses it. Besides, generally speaking, where non-resistance costs the sacrifice of a single life of some material welfare, resistance costs a thousand such sacrifices.*
>
> Non-resistance is salvation; Resistance is ruin."
>
> Q. But so long as only a few act thus, what will happen to them?
>
> A. If only one man acted thus, and all the rest agreed to crucify him, would it not be nobler for him to die in the glory of non-resisting love, praying for his enemies, than to live to wear the crown of Caesar stained with the blood of the slain? (emphasis added)[156]

This is the didactic implications of Irenaeus' emphasis on nonviolence; by illuminating the nonviolence of Christ's confrontation with socio-political oppression and occupation, Irenaeus wishes to implicate humanity in the same, thus imploring them to participate in the kingdom of God, for there the divine resides and there the Church is required to be. Klaus Wengst summarizes this notion well:

> Jesus' own career led to suffering and death, and if one so wishes, one may note his failure. So was his way illusionary, because he did not calculate human behaviour wisely enough? But, were the Zealots more realistic in thinking that they had to counter the military power of Rome with equally military counter-violence? Was the peace-party [those who were more optimistic about the *pax romana* as demonstrating authentic peace] more realistic when it reconciled itself with the situation as a result of its assessment of the balance of power? It could be shown that Jesus saw the

---

time was; that this God came down upon the earth to atone for Adam's sin; that he rose again…had a certain meaning for men at that time [fourth century], but for men of today they have no meaning whatever" (38). Although unintentional, Tolstoy's understanding of the first half of the atonement, that of the inculcation of humanity and in particular that of his nonviolence, must not be overlooked.

156. Leo Tolstoy, *The Kingdom of God is Within You*, 14-15.

balance of power very clearly, but that he trusted the power of the kingdom of God even more. And he did not think that he had to help on this power by his own violent means. If hope for the kingdom of God is an illusion, then the way of Jesus was also an illusion. His disciples did not think that. The Easter experience, the faith that God did not abandon Jesus to failure in death, led them to resume Jesus' way and practice discipleship as a community.[157]

The Church is to itself embody the same nonviolence as Christ and invite others to do the same; in fact, to do otherwise is to infringe on the human freedom so vital to Irenaeus' atonement narrative. He therefore rejects attempts, although current among professed Christians, at rendering compatible the desire to preserve one's existence in the face of enmity and the desire to participate in the kingdom of God at the expense of 'a thousand such sacrifices.'

The desire to preserve one's existence, of course, alludes to Adam's apostasy in the beginning. It is Christ's obedient recapitulation[158] that relieves humanity of the tyranny of death inaugurated by Adam's self-preserving and prideful apostatic decision.[159] St. Irenaeus correspondingly states:

> Therefore does the Lord profess Himself to be the Son of man, comprising in Himself that original man out of whom the woman was fashioned [*ex quo ea quæ secundum mulierem est plasmatio facta est*], in order that, as our species went down to death

157. Klaus Wengst, *Pax Romana and the Peace of Jesus Christ* (Philadelphia, PA: Fortress Press, 1987), 71-72. Cf. *AH* 3.18.4-5.

158. Christ's recapitulation of Adam's apostasy through obedience is widely known. St. Irenaeus uses the term *recapitulans* ("recapitulation," *AH* 5.21.1.; "recapitulated," *AH* 3.18.7.; "recapitulating," *AH* 3.21.10.), *recapitulatus* ("summed up," *AH* 3.22.3.; "sums up," *AH* 3.21.9.; "summed everything up," *AH* 5.21.1.) and *recapitulationis* ("recapitulation," *AH* 3.21.10.).

159. The image of Christ restoring Adam despite the immeasurable destruction induced by his apostatical decision is, I think, most poignantly illustrated in the apocryphal *Gospel of Nicodemus*: "And the Lord stretched out His hand, and said: Come to me, all my saints, who have my image and likeness. Do you, who have been condemned through the tree and the devil and death, now see the devil and death condemned through the tree? Immediately all the saints were brought together under the hand of the Lord. And the Lord, holding Adam by the right hand, said to him: Peace be to thee, with all thy children, my righteous ones! And Adam fell down at the knees of the Lord, and with tearful entreaty praying, said with a loud voice: I will extol Thee, O Lord; for Thou hast lifted me up, and hast not made my foes to rejoice over me. O Lord God, I cried unto Thee, and Thou hast healed me. O Lord, Thou hast brought out my soul from the powers below; Thou hast saved me from them that go down into the pit. ... And the Lord, stretching forth His hand, made the sign of the cross upon Adam and upon all His saints; and holding Adam by the right hand, went up from the powers below: and all the saints followed Him. ... And the Lord, holding the hand of Adam, delivered him to Michael the archangel: and all the saints followed Michael the archangel, and he led them all into the glorious grace of paradise." "Gospel of Nicodemus: Part II: Christ's descent into Hell," Alexander Roberts and James Donaldson, eds., *Ante-Nicene Fathers: The Writings of the Fathers Down to A.D. 325*, vol. 8 (Peabody, MA: Hendrickson, 2004), 451-452.

[*descendit in mortem genus nostrum*] through a vanquished man, so we may ascend to life again through a victorious one; and as through a man death received the palm [of victory] against us [*et quemadmodum accipiamus palmam mors per hominem adversus nos*], so again by a man we may receive the palm against death.[160]

Christ's recapitulation epitomizes his identification with humanity and consists of a selfless concern for his oppressors exhibited in his own suffering as a response to Adam's self-preserving disregard for the consequences of his apostasy for subsequent humanity. This dynamic renders James Douglass' description of suffering as the "reversal of violence"[161] all the more meaningful. The identification motif in St. Irenaeus' notion of Christ's recapitulation is unmistakable:

> He was made an infant for infants, sanctifying infancy; a child among children, sanctifying childhood, and setting an example of filial affection, of righteousness and of obedience; a young man among young men, becoming an example to them, and sanctifying them to the Lord. So also he was a grown man among the older men, that he might be a perfect teacher for all, not merely in respect of revelation of the truth, but also with respect to this stage of life, sanctifying the older men, and becoming an example to them also. And thus he came even to death, that he might be 'the first born form the dead, having the pre-eminence among all, the Author of Life, who goes before all and shows the way.[162]

Christ's recapitulation is God's strategy for depriving death of its illegitimate reign and instructing humanity in the selfless, altruistic method by which this reversal can be accomplished for all humanity. Since from the above passage it is evident that St. Irenaeus understands Christ's recapitulation as an attempt to ontologically restore each stage of life, or sanctify infancy,

---

160. *AH* 5.21.1.; cf. *AH* 3.22.3.

161. James W. Douglass, *The Nonviolent Cross: A Theology of Revolution and Peace*, 290.

162. *AH* 2.22.4. An interesting interplay exists between instruction and empowerment in this passage; with reference to infancy [*infantibus*], the pre-eminence lies with empowerment or sanctification [*sanctificans*] with no mention of instruction at all; as a child [*parvulis*], Christ sanctified [*sanctificans*] that particular stage of life and was additionally an example [*exemplum*] for children; for young men [*juvenibus*] instruction and empowerment switch positions and Christ as an example [*exemplum*] contains more weight as it is the first item mentioned, no doubt because the intellectual capacity of young men has increased since infancy, after which sanctification [*sanctificans Domino*] is mentioned almost in passing; for older men [*senioribus*], even more emphasis is placed on Christ as the "perfect teacher" [*perfectus magister*] of the revelation of truth [*expositionem veritatis*] and instruction for that particular stage of life [*secundum aetatem*], after which sanctification [*sanctificans*] is again mentioned but this time with Christ as example [*exemplum*], again demonstrating the increasing weight placed in instruction; the final act of recapitulation, that of Christ's death [*mortem*], now places equal emphasis on Christ as the "Author of Life" [*princeps vitae*] who additionally "shows the way" [*proir omnium, et praecedens omnes*].

childhood, young men, older men and even death, a clear objective of Christ's recapitulation is to capacitate humanity "in order that man might be able [*potuit*] to receive Him."[163] Success is attained in this regard pending Christ's victory over death, his identification with humanity of which permits him access to death, this is to say, as a human, Christ is capable of suffering and dying;[164] it is only *in* death that death can be conquered.

To meet this condition, Christ must cancel the self-preserving and violent disobedience of Adam with his own selfless, nonviolent *obedientiam*.[165] This obedience is significant because it reveals the precise obligations of the kingdom of God and therefore functions as a conduit for humanity's obedience. Christ was obedient not in the sense that he allowed his Father to kill him, as penal substitutionary models espouse, but because he aligned his response to his political execution with what the kingdom of God expected of him. While not downplaying how burdensome such a decision is, Christ was nevertheless obedient insofar as he complied with what was natural to him and therefore *retained* the divine in the face of socio-political oppression; humanity conversely functions within the context of socio-political oppression by necessity, but aspires to *reclaim* the divine in the face of kingdom obligations through the same obedience typified by Christ. Irenaeus' use of recapitulation to illustrate the atonement narrative, therefore, perfectly suggests the implications of identification. Within this mutually sustainable relationship,

---

163. *AH* 4.38.2.

164. "The Word existed in the beginning with God and through him all things were made. He was always present with the human race, and in the last times, according to the time appointed by the Father, he has been united with his own handiwork and made man, capable of suffering [*unitum suo plasmati, passibilem hominem factum*]." *AH* 3.18.1. Also, in reference to the devil's tyranny, Irenaeus declares, "The Word of God, however, the Maker of all things, conquered him by means of human nature... [*per hominem vincens eum*]" *AH* 5.24.4.

165. "...for He was man contending for the fathers, and through obedience doing away with disobedience completely [*erat enim homo pro patribus certans, et per obedientiam, inobedientiam persolvens*]." *AH* 3.18.6. "For as by one man's disobedience sin entered, and death obtained [a place] through sin; so also by the obedience [*obedientam*] of one man, righteousness having been introduced, shall cause life to fructify in those persons who in times past were dead." *AH* 3.21.10. St. Irenaeus also speaks of obedience with a more submissive nuance when he indicates that Christ, as a child, was "setting an example of filial affection, of righteousness and of obedience [*subjectionis*]." *AH* 2.22.4. Hochban unequivocally declares, "When St. Irenaeus considers the life of Christ in general, it is summed up in the word 'obedience.'" John I. Hochban, "St. Irenaeus on the Atonement," 543. Aulén also affirms the emphasis on obedience in Irenaeus' thought: "It is remarkable what great weight he [Irenaeus] attaches to the obedience of Christ throughout His life on earth. He shows how the disobedience of the one man, which inaugurated the reign of sin, is answered by the One Man who brought life. By His obedience Christ 'recapitulated' and annulled the disobedience. The obedience is the means of His triumph." Gustaf Aulén, *Christus Victor: An Historical Study of the Three Main Types of the Idea of the Atonement*, 29.

the kingdom of God and the socio-political kingdoms of this world function as barometers of allegiance and, according to Irenaeus, divinity.[166] Christ's obedience to the kingdom of God, although not at all pleasant when placed within a socio-political context, is natural; humanity's obedience to socio-political manipulation is also natural by virtue of their proximity. As Christ did what was *un*natural, by subjecting himself to socio-political oppression and suffering, humanity is invited to also do what is *un*natural in practice, that is, subject itself to the obligations of the kingdom of God by reclaiming the divine. This is the function of identification in Irenaeus' atonement narrative.

Nonviolence is at the centre of identification since Christ is forced to respond to socio-political oppression in his identification with humanity, while humanity is invited to emulate the nonviolence associated with the kingdom of God as an expression of their identification with Christ. By using the Edenic tree as a prototype, St. Irenaeus discloses the significance of nonviolence in Christ's obedient recapitulation as a response to Adam's disobedience:

> The trespass which came by the tree was undone by the tree of obedience, when, hearkening unto God, the Son of man was nailed to the tree; thereby putting away the knowledge of evil and bringing in and establishing the knowledge of good: how evil it is to disobey God, even as hearkening unto God is good. And for this cause the Word spake by Isaiah the prophet, announcing beforehand that which was to come—for therefore are they prophets, because they proclaim what is to come: by

---

166. Cf. *Epid.* 56. It must be noted, however, that St. Irenaeus indeed affirms the function of earthly government as long as they "conduct themselves in a quiet manner, so that under the fear of human rule men may not eat each other up like fishes." But it is only when "considered from this point of view" that earthly rulers may be acknowledged as "God's ministers, serving for this very purpose." Moreover, Irenaeus insists that it is only because humanity "did not acknowledge the fear of God" that God permitted human rule "in order that, being subjected to the authority of men, and kept under restraint by their laws, they might attain to some degree of justice, and exercise mutual forbearance through dread of the sword suspended full in their view." *AH* 5.24.2-3. The deficiency of this arrangement is very evident from Irenaeus' description, and the sword is used only to instill a fear that ideally should have resulted from God's authority alone. In fact, upon reading the passage carefully, there seems to be the idea that the sword exists in order to demonstrate to humanity how deleterious it can be in order to invoke its prohibition among Christ's followers. Of course, in the latter half of the second century, Christianity was predominantly opposed to any participation in violence from capital punishment and infanticide to militaristic campaigns; for more on this subject, see such seminal works as John Driver, *How Christians Made Peace with War: Early Christian Understandings of War*, Peace and Justice Series, vol. 2 (Kitchener, ON: Herald Press, 1988); John Helgeland, Robert J. Daly and J. Patout Burns, *Christians and the Military: The Early Experience*, Edited by Robert J. Daly (Philadelphia, Fortress Press, 1985); and Jean-Michel Hornus, *It is Not Lawful for Me to Fight: Early Christian Attitudes Toward War, Violence, and the State*, Translated by Alan Kreider and Oliver Coburn (Kitchener, ON: Herald Press, 1980).

him then spake the Word thus: *I refuse not, nor gainsay: I gave my back to scourging, and my cheeks to smiting; and my face I turned not away from the shame of spitting.* So then by the obedience wherewith He obeyed *even unto death*, hanging on the tree, He put away the old disobedience which was wrought in the tree.[167]

More than his nuance of the Edenic tree as a place of violence, Irenaeus clearly illustrates the implications of the executioner's tree as a place of nonviolent obedience on the part of the oppressed, as is implied by the juxtaposition between the 'knowledge of good' and Christ's decision to endure 'scourging' instead of fighting back. Irenaeus is particularly interested in demonstrating Christ's retrieval of the pre-apostatical state of *shalom* of which Adam obliterated through his disobedience; while discussing "those who are unaccustomed to fighting, but when smitten, offer also the other cheek," St. Irenaeus further affirms:

> In Him is that declaration borne out; since it is He Himself who has made the plough, and introduced the pruning-hook, that is, the first semination of man, which was the creation exhibited in Adam [*hominis primam seminationem quae fuit secundum Adam plasmatio*], and the gathering in of the produce in the last times by the Word; and, for this reason, since He joined the beginning to the end, and is the Lord of both [*et propter hoc quod initium fini conjungebat, et utrorumque Dominus exsistens*].[168]

Irenaeus seems convinced that the nonviolence perpetuated through Christ's confrontation with socio-political opposition and initiated 'in the first semination of man' was a precondition of humanity's inception and residence in the garden, a dominant characteristic that could only be subdued by its antithesis, namely Adamic violence. St. Irenaeus further enhances this claim by linking the plough with Christ's execution: "He has finally displayed the plough, in that the wood has been joined on to the iron, and has thus cleansed His land; because the Word, having been firmly united to flesh, and in its mechanism fixed with pins, has reclaimed the savage earth [*et habitu taleis confixus emundavit sylvestrem terram*]."[169] Although the context verifies such an interpretation regardless, William W. Harvey nevertheless also contends that the expression 'fixed with pins ("*taleæ*")'

---

167. *Epid.* 34. Incidentally, Irenaeus often demonstrates the idea of Christ's identification with humanity by referring to him as the "Son of man," as he does in this passage and as is of course scripturally common. Philip Schaff also picks up on the tree motif as a symbol of Adam's disobedience and Christ's nonviolent obedience, "This obedience completed itself in the suffering and death on the tree of the cross, and thus blotted out the disobedience which the first Adam had committed on the tree of knowledge." Philip Schaff, *History of the Christian Church*, vol. 2 (Peabody, MA: Hendrickson, 2002), 587.
168. *AH* 4.34.4.
169. *Ibid.*

alludes to the ἦλοι (nails) of the cross.[170]

However, if this assessment is found wanting, as both René Massuet and John Ernest Grabe contend,[171] Irenaeus is nevertheless clear concerning the association between Christ's recapitulation and nonviolence when he incorporates all humanity between Adam and Christ and accordingly feels entitled to involve Abel. Concurrently, Christ "figured forth the pruning-hook by means of Abel,"[172] who is himself a "witness of fidelity"[173] to the nonviolence of the cross in contrast to "the impotent Cain instinct of the executioner."[174] As an instrument of peace in contrast to its former use, both Abel and Christ, like the plough and pruning hook, are instruments of peace in contrast to Adam's self-preserving violence. Irenaeus extends Christ's nonviolence, however, even to the battleground upon which death is vanquished by means of his faithfulness to divine expectations through nonviolent obedience, which in turn permitted humanity release from the tyranny of death as exhibited in Christ' resurrection. Therefore, Christ's "obedience is the means of His triumph."[175]

Nonviolence and Christus Victor:

Whereas the narrative exhibiting the composition of Christ's life and teachings, including especially the nonviolence of his confrontation with sociopolitical opposition, supplies a didactic element to Irenaeus' atonement theology, it is his use of *Christus Victor* which allows humanity to procure its own emancipation from the tyranny of death and therefore consummate union with Christ. Where Christ's passion *enjoins* humanity to imitate his

---

170. *Ibid.* When referring to, "*et habitu taleis confixus emundavit sylvestrem terram*," Harvey contends, "I do not hesitate to restore this word; *talis* is written in all but the Voss. MS., which has *tali*; Grabe adopting the former, Massuet the latter reading, but neither gives a sufficient, if any sense. … These *taleæ* being also the correlatives of the ἦλοι of the Passion."

171. See note 170 above.

172. *AH* 4.34.4.

173. John Howard Yoder, *The Politics of Jesus: Vicit Agnus Noster*, 125. Yoder points to Heb. 11:1-12:5, which describes examples of fidelity from Abel to the prophets where "'Faith' or 'fidelity' in each case meant the readiness to obey amid suffering, trusting God for a not yet discernable vindication."

174. James W. Douglass, *The Nonviolent Cross: A Theology of Revolution and Peace*, 291. In this same manner, St. Irenaeus compares those who executed Jesus, whom he identifies as the Pharisees and scribes, with Cain: "For while they [the Pharisees and scribes] were thought to offer correctly so far as outward appearance went, they had in themselves jealousy slew the Just One, slighting the counsel of the Word, as did also Cain. For [God] said to him, 'Be at rest;' but he did not assent. Now what else is it to 'be at rest' than to forego purposed violence?" *AH* 4.18.3.

175. Gustaf Aulén, *Christus Victor: An Historical Study of the Three Main Types of the Idea of the Atonement*, 29.

selflessness, humility and love, Christ's victory over death *enables* humanity to labour towards ontological affiliation with the Word, both elements
of which atone for humanity's apostasy and propitiate God by becoming
what he desires his creation to *be*. The incarnation is again front and centre
in this liberating initiative, an element that Aulén laments is largely absent
from Latin interpretations of the atonement.[176] The incarnation, however, is
a necessity for the defeat of death, for "how shall man pass into God, unless
God has [first] passed into man?"[177] The incarnation is also significant as it
demonstrates Christ's identification with humanity for the sake of its emancipation. The two are inseparable in St. Irenaeus' thought; humanity cannot
enjoy freedom if Christ does not first identify with humanity: "For it behoved
Him who was to destroy sin, and redeem man under the power of death,
that He should Himself be made that very same thing which he was, that is,
man."[178] As noted earlier, Christ's incarnation is significant also since his
carnal composition facilitates access to death on behalf of humanity "who
had been drawn by sin into bondage, but was held by death, so that sin should
be destroyed by man [*ut peccatum ab homine interficeretur*], and man should
go forth from death."[179] Inasmuch as Christ had engendered humanity's freedom from the tyranny of death, he can shift focus toward the restoration and
reconciliation of his creation. Since through Christ's victory over death he
"endowed His own handiwork with salvation,"[180] his mission was therefore
twofold, to eliminate death and vivify humanity: "*Ut occideret quidem peccatum, evacuaret autem mortem, et vivificaret hominem.*"[181]

For Irenaeus, however, this liberation and revivification of humanity
remains congruent with his emphasis on nonviolence to accomplish atonement objectives. Although St. Irenaeus' designation of Christ as nonviolent

---

176. "The Latin doctrine always involves an opposition, expressed or implied, between
the Incarnation and the work of Christ. But the opposition becomes meaningless as soon
as the 'classic' idea of the Atonement receives due consideration; for it is in this type of
view the Incarnation and the Atonement always stand in the closest relationship to one
another." Gustaf Aulén, *Christus Victor: An Historical Study of the Three Main Types of
the Idea of the Atonement*, 19.

177. *AH* 4.33.4. "*quemadmodem homo transiet in Deum, si non Deus in hominem?*"
Cf. *AH* 5.1.1.; *AH* 5.21.3.; *AH* 5.24.4.

178. *AH* 3.18.7.

179. *Ibid.* In essence, discussions regarding Christ's access to death are merely stating
the obvious, that "obedience is the means of His triumph." Gustaf Aulén, *Christus Victor: An Historical Study of the Three Main Types of the Idea of the Atonement*, 29. Aulén
elsewhere illuminates the relationship between Christ's life, and therefore his teachings
and example, and his victory over death: "Also His preaching and teaching are expressly
regarded in the same light; the teaching by which we 'learn to know the Father' forms an
element in Christ's victory over the powers of darkness" (30).

180. *AH* 3.18.6.

181. *AH* 3.18.7.

in the latter's attempt to "redeem from [apostasy] His own property," is juxtaposed with the mechanism of the cross and Christ's suffering,[182] it is also declared within the context of his victory over the injustices of apostasy. Indeed, even Boersma, although apparently stopping short of endorsing Irenaeus' restraint, admits, "There may seem to be a violent edge to Irenaeus' vocabulary here. But he immediately deals with this apprehension: whereas apostasy used deception and violence whereby 'it insatiably snatched what was not its own,' God uses 'persuasion' instead of 'violent means' and does not infringe on 'justice.'"[183] In keeping with the discussion above regarding Irenaeus' perception of the devil as merely death and apostasy personified, Boersma agrees that Irenaeus "does not push the battle imagery to extremes: respectful of human freedom and unwilling to take recourse to some kind of violent encounter between Jesus and Satan, Irenaeus interprets the battle by means of other metaphors."[184] This is evident by the language St. Irenaeus decides to use where Christ "did righteously turn against that apostasy"[185] for "the destruction of death."[186] Irenaeus indeed views that which ensnares humanity as a power or force, and therefore avoids the more elaborate descriptions of the cosmic battle between Christ and Satan common in posterior patristic writings on the atonement. This is significant for consistency's sake particularly as it complies with the second and third segments of Irenaeus' atonement narrative. For indeed, Christ's nonviolence, both in the socio-political sphere and the cosmic realm, stimulates a nonviolent response from humanity in its subsequent attempt to identify with Christ.

III. HUMANITY'S IDENTIFICATION WITH CHRIST *THROUGH* RECLAIMING THE DIVINE:

The recapitulation of Christ does not end with the Word made flesh, but continues in the flesh made divine.[187] Through the deification and obedience of humanity, St. Irenaeus insists that Christ's nonviolence finds permanency in the Church, even during his own second-century era. In reference to Mt. 10:37ff. and Mk. 8:34ff.; 10:39-40 and their descriptions of suffering as a

---

182. "Since the Lord thus redeemed us through His own blood..." *AH* 5.1.1.
183. Hans Boersma, *Violence, Hospitality and the Cross: Reappropriating the Atonement Tradition*, 188.
184. *Ibid.* 189.
185. *AH* 5.1.1.
186. *Epid.* 86.
187. Or, as Aulén states it, "The Recapitulation does not end with the triumph of Christ over the enemies which held him in bondage; it continues in the work of the Spirit in the church." Gustaf Aulén, *Christus Victor: An Historical Study of the Three Main Types of the Idea of the Atonement*, 22.

condition for salvation, Yoder contends, "It points not to a special elite moral vocation for Jesus or for a spiritual elite, but to a condition for salvation. This is one of the places where the 'Disciple/follow' and the 'Imitate/partake' language complexes overlap. To follow after Christ is not simply to learn from him, but also to share in his destiny."[188] Yoder's use of the terms "follow" and "partake" reflect Irenaeus' own emphasis on instruction and empowerment respectively, which translate into obedience and deification when actualized in the Church. With respect to Christ's passion, St. Irenaeus accordingly declares,

> The Lord suffered that He might bring back those who have wandered from the Father, back to knowledge and to His fellowship [*Dominus autem passus est, ut eos qui erraverunt a Patre, ad agnitionem, et juxta eum adduceret*]. ...the Lord, having suffered, and bestowing the knowledge of the Father, conferred on us salvation [*conferens, salutem donavit*]. ...Our Lord also by His passion destroyed death, and dispersed error, and put an end to corruption, and destroyed ignorance, while He manifested life and revealed truth, and bestowed the gift of incorruption.[189]

It is particularly interesting to note how St. Irenaeus oscillates between the effects of Christ's instruction and empowerment, the former of which 'dispersed error,' 'destroyed ignorance' and 'revealed truth,' and the latter of which 'destroyed death,' 'put an end to corruption,' 'manifested life' and 'bestowed the gift of *incorruptionem*.' This reciprocal significance placed on both the inculcation and capacitation of humanity illuminates specifically the effects of Christ's passion and suffering on his Church. Humanity is invited to ontologically affiliate itself with Christ, which in turn functions as the impetus for obedience, although obedience too galvanizes humanity's deification. In this fashion, humanity reclaims the divine.

The Ontology of Nonviolence: Deification as Capacitation

The ontological or metaphysical method by which humanity responds to Christ's incarnation is deification, the identification with Christ whereby humanity reclaims the divine. Irenaeus affirms this relationship between the incarnation and deification, giving reference specifically to the erosion of the likeness of God in humanity since Adam's apostasy. Writing against accusations that Jesus was created in time, which necessitates a beginning and therefore his temporary non-existence,[190] St. Irenaeus declares:

> I have shown that the Son of God did not then begin to exist, being with the Father

---

188. John Howard Yoder, *The Politics of Jesus: Vicit Agnus Noster*, 124.
189. *AH* 2.20.3.
190. Cf. *AH* 4.6. *passim.*

from the beginning; but when He became incarnate, and was made man [*sed quando incarnatus est, et homo factus*], He commenced afresh the long line of human beings, and furnished us, in a brief, comprehensive manner, with salvation [*salutem*]; so that what we had lost in Adam—namely, to be according to the image and likeness of God [*secundum imaginem et similitudinem esse Dei*]—that we might recover [*reciperemus*] in Christ Jesus.[191]

This passage, especially the last statement, summarizes what is meant by humanity *reclaiming the divine*.[192] The reference to Adam, however, is particularly significant, since it portrays the correlation between *existence* and *essence*. As was established in our earlier discussion, it is by virtue of Adam's

---

191. *AH* 3.18.1.

192. To *reclaim the divine* is to renew the likeness and similitude of God within oneself by means of the image in an effort to restore that which was abandoned by virtue of Adam's apostasy: "...that the Church may be fashioned after the image of His Son." *AH* 4.37.7.; "And then, again, this Word was manifested when the Word of God was made man, assimilating Himself to man, and man to Himself, so that by means of his resemblance to the Son, man might become precious to the Father. For in times long past, it was *said* that man was created after the image of God [*imaginem Dei*], but it was not [actually] *shown*; for the Word was as yet invisible, after whose image man was created, wherefore also he did easily lose the similitude [*Propter hoc autem et similitudinem facile amisit*]. When, however, the Word of God became flesh, He confirmed both these: for He both showed forth the image truly, since He became Himself what was His image; and He re-established the similitude after a sure manner [*et similitudinem firmans restituit*], by assimilating man to the invisible Father through means of the visible Word." *AH* 5.16.2.; connecting this ambition to the Edenic ideal, St. Irenaeus declares, "The Church has been planted as a garden in this world [*Plantata est enim Ecclesia Paradisus in hoc mundo*]." *AH* 5.20.2. St. Irenaeus is quite clear that to do so implies partaking of divinity by passing into God: "... human nature of promotion into God [*hominem ab ea ascensione quae est ad Dominum*] ... that man, having been taken into the Word, and receiving the adoption, might become the son of God [*commixtus Verbo Dei, et adoptionem percipiens fiat filius Dei*]." *AH* 3.19.1.; "How shall man pass into God, unless God has [first] passed into man? [*Et quemadmodum homo transiet in Deum, si non Deus in hominem?*]." *AH* 4.33.4.; "...we have not been made gods from the beginning, but at first merely men, then at length gods. [*Nos enim imputamus ei, quoniam non ab initio Dii facti sumus, sed primo quidem homines, tunc demum Dii.*]." *AH* 4.38.4.; "These things, therefore, He recapitulated in Himself: by uniting man to the Spirit, and causing the Spirit to dwell in man [*Haec igitur in semetipsum recapitulatus est, adunans hominem spiritui, et spiritum collocans in homine*]." *AH* 5.20.2. Often, St. Irenaeus will designate the deification of a human as the restoration of *incorruptelam* and *immortalitatem*: "For it was for this end that the Word of God was made man, and He who was the Son of God became the Son of man, that man, having been taken into the Word, and receiving the adoption, might become the son of God. For by no other means could we have attained to incorruptibility and immortality, unless we had been united to incorruptibility and immortality [*nisi adunati fuissemus incorruptelae et immortalitati*]." *AH* 3.19.1.; "... He also established fallen man by His own strength, and recalled him to incorruption [*sed et corruptum hominem firmavit robore suo, et in incorruptionem revocavit*]." *AH* 2.20.3.; "And unless man had been joined to God, he could never have become a partaker of incorruptibility [*Et nisi homo conjunctus fuisset Deo, non potuisset particeps fieri incorruptibilitatis*]." *AH* 3.18.7.; "...having obtained from Him the gift of incorruptibility [*incorruptelae*]." *AH* 3.20.2.

very existence that he must succumb to impulses of self-preservation in order to maintain this existence. However, Adam's self-preserving pride has fragmented subsequent humanity's essence whereby death regulates and curtails humanity's substantial affinity with the Word made flesh and restricts access to the divine, which impedes restoration. Therefore, both the perceived need to preserve one's existence at all costs, including the termination of existences of those who threaten one's own existence, must be abated through instruction, namely the visibility of Christ's selfless martyrdom in the face of violent subjugation. Moreover, one must be endowed with the capacity for receiving such instruction and ultimately enacting obedience; therewith, humanity is released from the violence of death, which Adam had unleashed through incompetence, for the purpose of deification and the capacity for obedience.

At the risk of oversimplifying an incredibly complex metaphysical issue, a philosophical rationale may nevertheless help to clarify the relationship between *existence* and *essence*, Adam's self-preservation and the violence of death, Christ's selfless nonviolence and his victory over death, and humanity's obedience and deification. Similarly, as definitions of metaphysical terms are notoriously as multifarious as the philosophers who employ them, it is also best to allow St. Irenaeus' own thought dictate their definitions. In reference to the notion of *quidditas*, as per the medieval distinction between essence and existence, the capacity for humanity to obey Christ is an ontological question concerning its essence, what in metaphysics is referred to as *hypokeimenon*, or substratum. Irenaeus is concerned about the alteration of humanity's essence, or *substantia* or οὐσια,[193] as it is directed by one's existence, or *esse*.[194] Because Irenaeus dissolves the distinction between deification and obedience, perhaps it is best to similarly reject the distinction between the *essence* and *accidents* of a thing or person as per George Santayana's metaphysical designation of "what-ness." Humanity's "what-ness," its essence, is therefore distinct from a person's "is-ness," or existence, as differentiated from *is* as an indicator of identity or predication; the former corresponds to death's ability to alter the *substantia* or "what-ness" of humanity, while the latter concerns Adam's self-preservation, the

---

193. See note 12 above.

194. The Latin translation of Ireaneus uses the term *esse* and in particular, *inchoavit esse*, or "begin to have existence," to designate existence, a person's "is-ness." See, for instance, Irenaeus' address of allegations by Marcion, Valentinus, Basilides, Carpocrates and Simon that the Word had a beginning in the person of Jesus only at his advent on earth during the reign of Tiberius: *AH* 4.6. *passim*. In particular, Irenaeus uses the expression *inchoavit esse* to introduce such Gnostic claims concerning the Incarnate Christ's beginning to exist: *AH* 4.6.2.

characteristic that maintains his *esse* or "is-ness". Therefore, an evaluation of Jean-Paul Sartre's famous existential mantra, *existence precedes essence*,[195] is an appropriate foil with which Irenaeus' atonement narrative can be juxtaposed. Sartre is here inverting the Aristotelian claim concerning the *telos* of one's essence. Although Sartre's naturalistic existentialism advocates the precedence of existence to subjectively determine the flux in one's essence, Aristotle understood the potentiality (*dynamis*) of the eventual actuality (*entelecheia*) of the essence (*ousia – οὐσία*) to maintain ascendancy over existence. Aristotle's concern for the *telos* of a thing or person's essence is therefore more congruous with Irenaeus' concern for the deification of humanity as the means by which a person may imitate Christ as compared to Sartre's more cynical and naturalistic assessment of *existence* and *essence*. Irenaeus would in all likelihood have accepted Sartre's conviction concerning existence as descriptively accurate to some extent, but seems to have favoured Aristotle's teleological supposition as patently *prescriptively* authentic. In opposition to the arbitrariness of Sartre's existentialist theory of essential flux, deification entails and represents the objective or *telos* of a person's essence, the likeness of God maintained potentially in humanity throughout history but ultimately overlooked due to death's despotism. In the end, the preservation of Adam's existence is supplanted by Christ's selfless, nonviolent concern for others' existences rather than his own, a perspective subsequently maintained through the deification and obedience of the Church.

The issue of nonviolence concerns a person's ontology since "sin had no dominion over the spirit, but over man,"[196] and therefore impedes corporeality's *access* to the spirit or the divine, the likeness of God, and humanity's proficiency for obedience to Christ's nonviolent precedent. Irenaeus could be interpreted here as repudiating the notion of death's jurisdiction over the likeness of God in humanity. However, the context seems to suggest otherwise, but only if the potentiality of deification is acknowledged first. It appears that Irenaeus intends to preserve the subsistence of the image of God from the beginning, while his concern for even the physical salvation of humanity implies that sin dominates humanity to the extent that it restricts

---

195. Jean-Paul Sartre, "L'existentialisme est un humanisme," Philip Mairet, trans., In Walter Kaufmann, ed. *Existentialism from Dostoevsky to Sartre* (New York: Meridian, 1975), 349. Sartre further explains this assertion: "What do we mean by saying that existence precedes essence? We mean that man first of all exists, encounters himself, surges up in the world – and defines himself afterwards. If man as the existentialist sees him is [*sic*] not definable, it is because to begin with he is nothing. He will not be anything until later, and then he will be what he makes of himself. Thus there is no human nature, because there is no God to have a conception of it. Man simply is."
196. *AH* 3.18.7. "*non enim Spiritui dominabatur peccatum, sed homini.*"

a person's access to the likeness of God; it forbids humanity the capacity to reclaim the divine. To eliminate this barrier between corporeal humanity and the spirit or divine, Christ "recapitulated in Himself: by uniting man to the Spirit, and causing the Spirit to dwell in man [*adunans hominem spiritui, et spiritum collocans in homine*]. He is Himself made the head of the Spirit, and gives the Spirit to be the head of man: for through Him (the Spirit) we see, and hear, and speak [*per illum (Spiritus) enim videmus, et audimus, et loqui-mur*]."[197] St. Irenaeus insists that the Word is responsible for granting human-ity the power to endure suffering, while violent, self-preserving alternatives may prove more enticing.[198] God grants the "power to receive the Father," so that a person "shall become like Him who *died* for him" (emphasis added).[199] Reflecting the oscillating nature of deification and obedience, St. Irenaeus further states that the Father's law and humanity's imitation of or obedience to Christ permits them to "*videndum Deum.*"[200] An alteration to a person's essence as deification will therefore supplant the inveterate self-preserving impulses intrinsic to one's very existence and exchange them for the selfless, altruistic suffering of Christ.

Douglass appropriately contends, "Suffering itself is evil, the result of sin. Love seeks union and community, not suffering," and further states that Christ's way of suffering and love "has been divinized. By becoming man God has sacramentalized man's suffering so that man might become God through the cost of love. Love is the Power, but a Power incarnate on the cross."[201] This is true also of Irenaeus' view of the atonement; as with Christ's suffering, the succeeding generation suffers not only because it has been capacitated for obedience, but also for the purpose of restoring its oppressors. Whereas penal substitutionary models mimic Western juridical transactions in an effort to restore "peace" and manufacture "justice" *for one side only*, that of the winning side, Irenaeus' emphasis on nonviolence in the atonement acknowledges the dignity of the losing side, or that of our enemy. When considering Irenaeus' allusion to Cain's murder of Abel as a paradigm motivating Christ's recapitulation of peace through nonviolence,[202] Doug-lass' observations regarding the "Cain instinct" rings true also:

---

197. *AH* 5.20.2.

198. "If, however, He [the Word] was Himself not to suffer, but should fly away from Jesus, why did He exhort His disciples to take up the cross and follow Him,—that cross which these men represent Him as not having taken up, but [speak of Him] as having relinquished the dispensation of suffering." *AH* 3.18.5.; cf. *AH* 2.22.4.

199. *AH* 3.20.2.

200. *Ibid.*

201. James W. Douglass, *The Nonviolent Cross: A Theology of Revolution and Peace*, 290.

202. Cf. *AH* 4.18.3.; *AH* 4.34.4.

Our search for the roots of the Cain instinct in man brings us finally to the murder of the man-God, whose loving acceptance of his murderers, on the other hand, is the power capable of redeeming the Cain instinct. The cross is at once both death and life to mankind. After man's rejection of the Incarnation, God has re-saved him by his transformation, in and through the Resurrection, of the most awful crime in history. …The form of man's rejection of Christ—the cross—has made necessary each man's reacceptance of Christ in terms of an existential commitment to the same cross *from the other side.…* The cross has two sides, violent and suffering, and to accept Christ each man must pass over from the first to the second, thus entering into Christ's suffering acceptance of man in his violence to him. …The Cain instinct can be redeemed from the side of man only through a reversal of the cross which is its source.[203]

The basis for redeeming the Cain instinct is the subscription to a restorative rather than punitive model of justice demonstrated best when Christ "included the outsider and the enemy in His liberating concern."[204] Irenaeus' consideration of Christ's nonviolence implies such a concern.

It is particularly an issue of human freedom where again Dostoevsky's "Grand Inquisitor" becomes all the more relevant when one considers Christ's identification with those who endured the merciless and egregious horrors of the Inquisition in sixteenth-century Seville, Spain. Much like Irenaeus' combined concern for human freedom and Christ's identification with humanity within this perceivably arbitrary arrangement, Ivan Karamazov interprets Christ's unwillingness to admonish the Grand Inquisitor as an interminable desire to uphold the independence and impunity of humanity's inner impulses. However, the sixteenth-century setting of Ivan's poem adds to the intrigue and helps illustrate the identification motif current in Irenaeus' atonement theology. Similar to Christ's visitation to the sixteenth-century during the horrors of the Spanish Inquisition, Christ abidingly identifies with the martyr who endures the same nonviolent suffering as his own. In this way, J. Denny Weaver's caveat against interpretations of the atonement that unwittingly trivialise the inequity and exploitation of oppressed demographics through undue glorification of subversion and martyrdom is relevant. Ivan Karamazov's poem illustrates Irenaeus' notion that Christ's initiation of humanity's deification is not an endorsement of inevitable violence and oppression, but is instead the method by which Christ empowers humanity not only for cognizant obedience but also for psychosomatic obedience, this is to say, the emotional and spiritual fortitude for enduring inevitable suffering. As Boersma observes, "Because Irenaeus emphasizes the true humanity and obedience of Christ in the face of temptation, he can combine

203. James W. Douglass, *The Nonviolent Cross: A Theology of Revolution and Peace*, 226.
204. John Howard Yoder, "Jesus and Power," 450.

the cosmic struggle with the human struggle here on earth."[205] Regrettably, Boersma's vindication of penal functionality obscures the restorative characteristics inherent in Christ's identification *with* humanity, but also *for* the Cain instinct redeemed through the alternative Abel nonviolent resolve.[206] As Yoder remarks, "The point is not the prohibition of violence as such but rather the dignity, the personhood, even of the enemy."[207] Correspondingly, Irenaeus acknowledges the freedom even of Christ's executioners and the violent oppressors of the Church; rather than eliminate that which is not compatible with the desired outcome, like Ivan's Grand Inquisitor sought to do, Irenaeus' emphasis on Christ's nonviolence demonstrates his propensity for restorative justice in opposition to penal impetuousness. Christ's two primary initiatives, that of instruction and empowerment, implies an invitation to reclaim the divine, and an invitation to nonviolence. It also insinuates the requirement that the Church *be* the Church first and foremost, which includes uncompromising nonviolence, while allowing the rest of humanity the opportunity to *be* the same.

The Cognizance of Nonviolence: Obedience to the Kingdom of God

Whereas the defeat of death functions as the impetus for humanity's inclination towards obedience, it is obedience to the kingdom of God itself that illustrates humanity's identification with Christ. Humanity is naturally incorporated into the context and manipulation of the kingdoms and empires of this world, and Christ's incarnation portends his compliance and identification with humanity's socio-economic suffering therein. Christ, however, as the Son of God, is naturally and intuitively obedient to the kingdom of God,

205. Hans Boersma, *Violence, Hospitality and the Cross: Reappropriating the Atonement Tradition*, 189.

206. With respect to the failure of punitive measures to correct violence, Boersma criticises Walter Wink's suggestion that "violence can never stop violence because its very success leads others to imitate it." Walter Wink, *Engaging the Powers: Discernment and Resistance in a World of Domination* (Minneapolis: Fortress, 1984). As quoted and discussed in Hans Boersma, *Violence, Hospitality and the Cross: Reappropriating the Atonement Tradition*, 46. It is unclear how Boersma accounts for this and René Girard's theory of mimetic violence, except to say that he cannot account for the latter's cultural anthropology, and in particular his insistence that "violence lies at the origin of human culture" (137), on which his theory of the secular scapegoat mechanism to explain religious atonement and sacrificial motifs are based. Notwithstanding his disagreement with both Wink and Girard, Boersma's endorsement of penal or juridical measures to restore peace fails to account for the subsistence of violence, or the Cain instinct. Instead of redeeming or transforming violence into the pursuit of *shalom*, Boersma seems content to allow the Church to participate in punitive, and therefore retributive, actions that create a winning and a losing side, the former of which invites violent imitation based on its success, which of course creates a proportionate number of losing sides.

207. John Howard Yoder, "Jesus and Power," 450.

and it is humanity's obedience to this same kingdom that typifies their identification with Christ. It is the integration of the kingdom of God and the kingdoms of this world specifically that accounts for humanity and Christ's internal struggles respectively. Christ must suffer a violent execution because he *retained* the divine within the context of an earthly empire that rejected him, while humanity must suffer because it is invited to *reclaim* the divine in its confrontation with the socio-political opposition to which it is already accustomed. Both scenarios demand nonviolence if Christ and humanity wish to obediently affiliate themselves with the kingdom of God. In acknowledgement of the didactic element to the atonement in Irenaeus, Boersma asserts, "Despite his strenuous opposition to Gnostic soteriology, Irenaeus is unwilling to abandon knowledge as lying at the heart of redemption."[208] Reverting back to our earlier discussion on the incarnation, St. Irenaeus therefore confirms that humanity could not have learned the

> things of the Father...than by seeing our Teacher, and hearing His voice with our own ears [*nisi magistrum nostrum videntes, et per auditum nostrum vocem ejus percipientes*], that, having become imitators [*imitatores*] of His works as well as doers [*factores*] of His words, we may have communion [*communionem*] with Him, receiving increase [*augmentum accipientes*] from the perfect One, and from Him who is prior to all creation.[209]

Of particular interest is the juxtaposition between St. Irenaeus' description of Christ's pedagogical influence and his redemption of humanity "by his own blood," yet significantly "not by violent means."[210] Accordingly, Irenaeus expresses a similar symbiosis between the nonviolent objectives of Christ and his Church to that of Douglass' suggestion that "nonviolence is humanly demanded because it is Christically demanded."[211] By virtue of the effects of Christ's incarnation, St. Irenaeus declares, "It is right that He being made visible, should set upon all things visible the sharing of His cross, that He

208. Hans Boersma, *Violence, Hospitality and the Cross: Reappropriating the Atonement Tradition*, 127.
209. *AH* 5.1.1. To this, Boersma affirms, "Irenaeus clearly connects Christ's role as our teacher to his role as our model. Christ is our teacher who requires our imitation." Hans Boersma, *Violence, Hospitality and the Cross: Reappropriating the Atonement Tradition*, 129.
210. *AH* 5.1.1. "*...sanguine suo rationabiliter redimens nos...non cum vi.*"
211. James W. Douglass, *The Nonviolent Cross: A Theology of Revolution and Peace*, 211. Elsewhere, Douglass contends, "The words of Gandhi reassert themselves, 'Living Christ means a living Cross, without it life is a living death,' and find their foundation in Jesus' statement of what it means to follow him. For a faith in Christ is not possible without the symbol and demanding reality that sums up a Christocentric life: 'If any man would come after me, let him deny himself and take up his cross and follow me.'"

might show His operation on visible things through a visible form."[212] Immanent in the visibility of Christ's nonviolent capitulation on the cross, which is permitted by his incarnation, is the responsibility of humanity to see, perceive and emulate this same nonviolence through the same obedience to the same kingdom of God.

Since Christ spoke openly about his impending suffering and the responsibility of his disciples to fulfil the same mandate when confronted by the threat of violence, the obligation to suffer as Christ suffered was widely known as an indication of one's ontological affiliation with the Word who truly did suffer as well. Irenaeus' encounter with allegations that the *Logos* and Jesus are separate beings prompted him to confirm that the Word "did not speak of any other cross, but of the suffering which He should Himself undergo first, and His disciples afterwards [*post deinde discipuli ejus*]" who are required to "strive to follow the footprints of the Lord's passion, having become martyrs of the suffering One."[213] And this obedience of the Church is feasible, St. Irenaeus continues, for the reason that "the Word of God, who said to us, 'Love your enemies, and pray for those that hate you,' Himself did this very thing upon the cross."[214] Convinced that the nonviolence of Christ's suffering had transferred to the behaviour of the persecuted Gallican Church within his own second-century context, St. Irenaeus defends the prophetic witness, particularly in reference to Isa. 2:3-4 and Mic. 4:2-3, against Marcionist accusations regarding the *demiurge's* influence before the advent of Christ, and accordingly maintains,

> If therefore another law and word, going forth from Jerusalem, brought in such a [reign of] peace [*pacem*] among the Gentiles which received it (the word), and convinced, through them, many a nation of its folly, then [only] it appears that the prophets spake of some other person. But if the law of liberty, that is, the word of God, preached by the apostles (who went forth from Jerusalem) throughout all the earth, caused such a change in the state of things, that these [nations] did form the swords and war-lances into ploughshares, and changed them into pruning-hooks for reaping the corn, [that is], into instruments used for peaceful purposes [*organa pacifica demutaverint*], and that they are now unaccustomed to fighting [*nesciunt pugnare*], but when smitten, offer also the other cheek, then the prophets have not spoken these things of any other person, but of Him who effected them [*non de aliquo alio prophetae dixerunt haec, sed de eo qui fecit ea*].[215]

For Irenaeus, therefore, the validity of the interdependence between the God

---

212. *Epid.* 34.
213. *AH* 3.18.5. "*...conantur vestigia assequi passionis Domini, passibilis martyres facti.*"
214. *Ibid.*
215. *AH* 4.34.4.

of the Old Testament and the Word made flesh is profoundly dependent on Christ's nonviolence and that of the following generation. Where it may be common to argue for God's advocacy of violence, St. Irenaeus in fact employs such logic of Old and New Testament unity to discourage violence, as the former projected towards the suffering of Christ. The Church is indeed the gathering "of a righteous race of men," whose nonviolent mandate was initiated "beforehand in Abel, [was] also previously declared by the prophets, but [was] accomplished in the Lord's person; and the same [is still true] with regard to us, the body following the example of the Head."[216] As Christ retained the divine by obediently complying with kingdom requirements, the Church, if it is to *be* the Church, must similarly reclaim the divine and ratify the nonviolent obligations of the kingdom of God.

IV. CONCLUSION

St. Irenaeus' view of the atonement simulates the narrative of a play. Each act contributes unique elements that explicate the function of identification and nonviolence in Irenaeus' atonement theology. The anthropogonic and anthropological questions of the first act, in addition to those queries concerning God's wrath and method of conciliation, illustrates the seemingly dire situation for which Christ's identification with humanity must take account. The second act opens with the optimism inherent in 'God with us,' and demonstrates Christ's identification with humanity through his incarnation, confrontation with temptation and socio-political oppression, inevitable execution and usurpation of death's throne. The final act records humanity's response to an invitation to participate in the kingdom of God by identifying with Christ, and in particular his nonviolent resolve. With his suggestive discussions surrounding the polemics of God's wrath and the more glaring notions of Adam and Eve's infantility and incompetence and the liability of death in the initiation of apostasy, Irenaeus' view of the atonement only tacitly encroaches on contemporary discussions surrounding God's redirection of his violence toward his Son, and the juridical exchange therein. Where Irenaeus makes an important contribution is with respect to the Incarnate Christ's nonviolence and its implications for the Father's capacity for violence *at the time of the atonement*. As Christ is the personification of the kingdom of God, he has a didactic responsibility to the humanity with whom he is now identifying, which significantly cannot involve violence by virtue of its contrariety to kingdom obligations. It is therefore counterintuitive to appease God through any use of violence,

216. *Ibid.* "*...consequente corpore suum caput.*"

whether suicidal, insurrectionary or cosmic, at the juncture in the atonement chronology when perfection is manifested both in the Son and for his Church. Irenaeus, therefore, understands the atonement for humanity's apostasy to consist of restoration rather than penal retribution. Atonement is humanity's comprehensive identification with Christ whose objective is the reinstatement of *shalom*, and this through his own identification with humanity by means of incarnational instruction, nonviolent obedience and victory over death.

Chapter Nineteen

JURIDICAL JUSTIFICATION THEOLOGY
AND A STATEMENT OF THE ORTHODOX TEACHING

by Dr. Kharalambos Anstall

Prologue: A Survey of the Western Juridical Justification Theology of Redemption and an Orthodox Refutation and a Statement of the Orthodox Teaching.

The One, Holy, Orthodox Catholic and Apostolic Church has functioned as a vibrant living organism and a regenerating force since entering the world at Pentecost with complete catholicity (fulness) to form the new, redeemed Israel under the guidance of the Holy Spirit. From earliest Orthodox memory, the Church has striven to realize and describe the process of mankind's salvation as a human/divine experience. In this context, she regards Christ's agonized death on the Cross to redeem humanity's collective sins "from ages to ages" as the paramount expression of unconditional love and magnanimity in all of recorded human history. When representing this extraordinary event to ordinary human beings, the Church employs terminology based on imagery from many diverse origins, reflecting both individual and collective activities in the context of humanity's "fallen" state. She can scarcely do otherwise. By using theological language that depicts actions common to all members of the human family, the Church seeks to help us better understand Christ's mission in a modern idiom. In so doing, she must always be prepared to subject that imagery to careful scrutiny and appropriate cleansing, both from rationalized interpretations and from explanations smacking of individualism; otherwise, such imagery may be deemed too self-oriented and confining for referencing to the whole human family. Integral to the Church's use of verbal imagery in characterizing God's relationship with mankind is its anticipated role in helping to restore humanity's loving communion with Him, which defined its pre-fallen condition. The Church knows that, unless we are renewed spiritually, our full human destiny cannot be realized.

Within various human societies, Western usage of terms such as "adoption," "atonement," "ransom," "redemption" and "justification" generally have categorical, legalistic meanings and applications. The Orthodox Church utilizes some contemporary terms when necessary, but her purpose in doing so is to re-define such terms through the sanctifying action of divine grace.

By this exposure, the Church hopes to lead mankind to a better understanding of the Crucifixion as a supreme, all-encompassing sacrifice, one made voluntarily by our Saviour in co-suffering love to re-establish the potentiality for our salvation and reunion with God. The Church's ultimate goal for all Christians is a fuller comprehension of the entire divinization process *(theosis)*, which comprises the quintessential dynamics of human salvation.

On the Unity of Human Nature

Crucial to this entire process, however, is our prerequisite development of a fully-evolved Christian conscience, an important aspect of which is our formation of a Christ-like perspective concerning the popular notion of "race." Racial prejudice has always derived from pernicious perceptions of inequality, most frequently engendered by man's irrationality and fear, usually fuelled by ignorance. Since, in point of fact, God created not "human races" but a single race[1] in which the one human species *(homo sapiens)* comprises a complex array of genetic variations, the disparagement of any particular clonal variance remains a human tragedy that defies all reason. Conflicts have continued to arise and fester in our troubled contemporary world between various ethnic (and even physical) subdivisions of mankind, just as they plagued most of humanity throughout its previous fallen history. It is imperative for the Christian ethos that the artificiality of all arbitrary human subdivisions be discerned, particularly when they imply racial differences indicative of subjective devaluations. Although human beings often differ markedly in many aspects, including both physiological and superficial characteristics, such as skin colour, these mutational disparities are merely an indication that human evolution has been variously influenced by environment, mitigating climactic conditions, and degree of isolation and mobility, among other factors. Despite the presence of ethnic, creedal and "colour" variances that may often give rise to widely diversified cultural expressions, Holy Scripture informs us that all of humanity is created uniquely in the likeness and image of God, whose universal love knows no discrimination.

Through the union of fallen man with the Holy Trinity (and, by extension, with all members of the human race),[2] the existential autonomy of the individual is effectively renounced. Since the ultimate disposition of humanity, in relation to God, cannot be considered until we fully accede to the commonality and equality of both our origin and our imperfect human nature, our

1. Gen. 1:25-27 and Jn. 15:12-13.
2. Anstall H. in: *Aspects of Theosis: Purification and Sanctification of the Human Intellect.* Robinson, *J* (ed). Synaxis Press, Dewdney, B.C., 1995, pp 21-24.

progression toward eternal life is entirely dependent upon our commanded obedience to God's ordinance - that we love one another unconditionally, just as He loves us. The Gospel informs us that human beings are the primary creation and icon of God[3] and, as such, *all* are equal members of His extended human family. Thus, it becomes our inherent Christian obligation and responsibility to extend in Christ-like fashion charity, mercy and forgiveness to *all* mankind, without harbouring any preconceptions, judgments or condemnation. Unless we do this, we cannot hope to return to the loving embrace of our Creator and Saviour. More will be said about the restorative process involving fallen humanity as we proceed with our thesis. But first, to gain an understanding of where we started in the "Christianizing" process and where we are now, let us first review the respective theological histories of the church in the East and in the West.

Centuries before the time of Christ and also throughout the development of Christianity, the quite disparate cultures of East and West (Greece and Rome), owing to pronounced differences in origin, aspirations and respective contributions to civilization, consistently manifested aspects of politics, ideology, military objectives and societal achievements that were fundamentally opposed to one another in *"weltanschaung"* (world view).

Emergent Theology

The emergent theology[4] of the West, based originally on the teachings of Tertullian (ca. 160-220) and his promotion of Stoic and Aristotelian philosophies, espoused rationalistic logic supportive of the viewpoint that mankind was largely "political" in nature.[5]

In Alexandria, some of the Christian writers drew theological inspiration from Platonic principles of thought, which advocated a transcending physical desire in pursuit of a more idealized spiritual reality. The most renowned of these were Clement of Alexandria, a semi-Platonist allegorist and the neo-Platonist Origen. They are not considered to be Church fathers in the Orthodox world, but both Roman Catholics and Protestants list these two Platonists as fathers of their respective Church bodies. This Alexandrian neo-Platonism was introduced to the West by Augustine of Hippo, whose

---

3. Gen. 1:25-27.
4. I had not intended this as a reference to the Western theory of the development of doctrine, but the atonement theory was a major key in the establishment of the principle of the development of doctrine *for* both Roman Catholics and later Protestants. The Orthodox Church does not accept the principle of the "development of doctrine."
5. For an interesting discussion of this matter see *The Evidence of Things Unseen,* by Archbishop Lazar Puhalo (Synaxis Press, Dewdney, BC, Canada, 1996).

theology was deeply and broadly influenced by the pagan neo-Platonist philosopher Plotinus.

Some of these early Christian theologians (such as Origen in the 3rd century and Augustine of Hippo in the 5th), although prolific in their writings and generally brilliant in their evocations on various ecclesial subjects, nevertheless were sporadically in grievous error on important points of doctrine and these were challenged in the East. In the West, these spiritual distortions went unchecked. Most of them were the product of Augustine, among them the idea of "Original Sin,"[6] The Gnostic idea of "Good" and "Evil" as two equal adversaries, and the *filioque* (which was among his many errors concerning the doctrine of the Trinity). These errors and many others began to dominate the spiritual and ecclesial climate of the Roman see, and created a corrupt way of thinking about theology, which resulted in further distortions. Augustine's corruption of the Symbol of Faith (the "Creed") with the concept of *filioque* created a radical error in the Trinitarian doctrine by changing both the procession of the Holy Spirit and, in essence, the fundamental action of the Trinity, in such a way that the very essence of the doctrine was destroyed and replaced by a concept of duality (Father and Son together, and the Holy Spirit as an emanation of both). These events dramatically focused the divergences which had long been developing in attitudes, structure and the essence of divine worship, and thereafter the chasm continued widening between West and East.

Then, in the 8th century, semi-barbaric Franks under their king, Charlemagne, took control of Rome. Utilizing its bishops to establish a new Western Empire, Charlemagne was crowned the Roman emperor in 800, although the Roman Empire still stood at Constantinople. In the 9th century, problems experienced during the parallel and competing reigns of Photios the Great, Patriarch of Constantinople (810-95), and Nicholas I, Bishop of Rome, reached epic proportions: the repeated interchanges of Photios and Ignatios as Patriarchs of Constantinople; the forceful assertion by Rome of papal authority over the most prestigious Eastern Patriarchate; the heavily opposed unilateral introduction by Rome of the *filioque* and a patent politicalisation of the Roman See with quite clear Caesaro-Papism, were brilliantly refuted by Saint Photios the Great in his encyclical of 867. A subsequent council was convened in Constantinople (869-70). In fact, this is the actual date of the schism, for Rome anathematized Photios. The Orthodox Church never accepted the legitimacy of this event, and the name of Saint Photios the Great

---

6. For an outstanding refutation of this heresy, see Romanides, John, *On The Ancestral Sin,* Tr. Dr George Gabriel (Zypheros Press, NJ. 2001).

became synonymous in time with the stand of the Orthodox Church against various papal incursions and the expansion of Rome's inflexible and uncompromising ecclesiastical policy of universalism.

During the murderous 12th century, the juridical theology of Augustine, reinforced and extended in the West by Anselm, Archbishop of Canterbury, was reaffirmed by Thomas Aquinas and the Spanish Jesuits who followed. Once certain heretical Augustinian postulations and other doctrinal aberrations had become firmly cemented into the fabric of Roman Catholicism, the Latin Church acquired a more-or-less regional universality. Three centuries later (1545-1563), its hierarchical stamp of approval was finally granted by the Council of Trent.

In the East, the Divine Liturgy and doctrines, dogma, ecclesiastical structure and unbroken apostolic succession of the Orthodox Church have remained in all its fulness, in conformity with the precedents established by the disciples under the leadership of the apostles. This in itself serves as ample testimony to the timeless authority of Jesus Christ. In contrast, in the West, the principal dogmas of the Roman Catholic Church were in a state of flux and uncertainty. They increasingly reflected a juridical concept of human redemption and of man's entire relationship with God. This was largely accomplished by reinterpreting the nature of Christ's death on the Cross; a reinterpretation informed by the heretical doctrine of "Original Sin," and quite at odds with the traditional doctrine of the Christian faith.

Scripture reminds us that juridical doctrine, upheld by certain Pharisees during Christ's time, were explicit targets of His denunciation. While quite foreign to the Christian Church before Montanus and Tertullian, they were later developed and advocated by Augustine and Anselm, as we have already noted. As a result of this heretical theology, the fall of Adam and Eve, and all subsequent human sins were progressively seen as constituting a severe and exceedingly grave insult to the honour and dignity of God.

It is especially noteworthy that the history of this juridical notion corresponds quite closely with the evolution and development of feudalism and feudal ideas of fealty and suzerainty, which were reinforced in the West through a reappraisal of the value and honour of humanity within the context of an aristocratic model.

Feudal aristocracy (patently a misnomer) developed positions of power and regional influence primarily through its judicious application of various forms of banditry. It was also a system that fostered a sort of childish romanticism, exalting "honour" as a kind of mystical acceptance of personal prowess, based upon the exercise of violence and scarcely-disguised brutality. In many areas, governance was reduced to a regional monarchical presence. When enforced by tyranny and pride, this form of rule was often punctuated by savage bouts of internecine strife and wanton destruction which resulted in great injury to the common people. Apart from the wholesale slaughter of local populations and the greed-driven violence, the feudal code of honour demanded fulfillment of certain expiatory rituals deemed appropriate to the degree of insult or injury visited upon rank, honour or majesty. Such punishment was inflicted irrespective of the origin of a particular insult. For instance, since effrontery to the honour of a knight could not be adequately expiated by the mere slaughter of a peasant, "atonement" was required by one of similar rank to satisfy the original office: a knight for a knight or a king for a king.[7]

By applying the simplistic concept of feudal/legalistic justice *(quid pro quo;* "evening the score") to determine human destiny and ultimate salvation, objective Western rationalists took the juridical concept one step further and arrived at a truly amazing theological conclusion, creating yet another heresy: Adam's sinful progeny henceforth would be uniformly lodged for a period of time in "purgatory" before a final fate in heaven was determined; this was to satisfy Adam's initial insult to the majesty and honour of God (as defined by the Augustinian tradition). The arbitrary time period for purgatory could be redeemed or reduced by fortuitous intervention, such as a hefty payoff to the Church. It may be concluded that this interim sentencing came from the diseased imagination of sadistic, arrogantly self-righteous religious fanatics much more interested in controlling the activities of their parishioners than in helping them to grow in spiritual truth and strength toward divinization and eventual salvation; and it proved to be an enormous source of revenue for the Roman Catholic Church.

According to juridical principles of theology, Adam's fall and its carry-over effect on humankind simply could not be atoned for by the suffering of any one person or combination of persons, nor even of the terrible suffering that millions do endure, nor even by the suffering of all humanity together, despite the ramifications of time spent in purgatory. With such a concept of the immensity and severity of humanity's collective offences before God, many Western theologians reasoned that appropriate redemption would obviously have to be bought and paid for by an atoning act of divine *feudal equivalency.* Thus they concluded that the allegedly wrathful, vengeful God of the Old Testament would require, in obedient satisfaction, the agony and death of His only-begotten Son, Jesus Christ, as a blood money *(wergild)* to redeem collective humanity before a reconciliation with God and all the rest of

---

7. Kelly, A. *Eleanor of Aquitaine and the Four Kings.* Random House, N.Y, 1950 and Azkoul, M. *Augustine of Hippo - an Orthodox Christian Perspective.* Synaxis Press, Dewdney, B.C., 1994, pp 26-30.

creation could be considered. It required, as in feudal law, the death of some-one equal to the offended overlord—God.

In the Orthodox Church, one finds that God is still implicitly perceived as the embodiment of love and mercy, a concept once held also by the Roman Church before the early centuries of shared tradition were altogether scrapped. Mindful of this once-mutual understanding, one is moved to question what sort of love would require a supposedly adoring father to demand the agony, torment, and bloody sacrifice of his only son to accomplish the fulfillment of his own selfish satisfaction. God as love and God as sacrificer, under such cir-cumstances and for such a reason, are clearly antithetical. It is therefore easy to understand why, in the holy tradition of the historic Church, this entire teaching is considered to be theological nonsense. It may also be construed as blasphemy against Christian teaching since prideful self-satisfaction at the expense of the "nearest and dearest" of our Creator seems unarguably to be a pernicious prerequisite for the reconciliation and salvation of the human race. To invalidate such heretical doctrine, we will offer a reasonable, legitimate Orthodox perception of the Incarnation, Crucifixion and Resurrection. This is the perception of the Gospel, of the Apostles, of the Apostolic Church.

The Incarnation: The Central Event in the History of Redemption

The prologue to the Gospel of Saint John the Theologian[8] explicitly spells out the principal and central event of human history–indeed, the entire his-tory of created being–which culminated in the most singularly important statement for all generations of true Christians, *"And the Word was made flesh and dwelt among us."* These words express the great *cri de coeur*–the ecstatic shout of joy–which has reverberated down the long corridors of time in an undiminished and wondrous Orthodox proclamation of our faith, our hope and our love. Here, the revelation of, God to mankind is made manifest in its fullness, wherein our eternal life through salvation becomes a vibrant reality.

The dark shadow of death is driven away by a new effulgence of uncreated light. All of creation, formerly submerged since the Fall in a black slough of despondence, rouses and shakes itself in the warmth and golden illumination of a new beginning–a virtual regeneration of life through loving communion with God.

In the first chapter of Genesis we are told, *"In the beginning, God created the heavens and the earth."* There is an extraordinary parallel to this passage

8. Jn. 1:1-14.

in the prologue to the Gospel of Saint John, where the Incarnate One is once more revealed to us in His uniqueness.[9] We are informed here again that *"In the beginning was the Word, and the Word was with God, and the Word was God."* The execution of the work of creation is identified in John, particularly with the activity of the Word, and a little later with the incarnate Christ in whom *"the Word was made flesh,"* a statement which forms the centre of genuine Christian belief. While Jesus Christ is known as the "Word of God" *(Logos)*, when associated with the person of the "Divine *Logos"* He actually acquires a perfected human nature in addition to His divine nature by putting on human flesh like a garment and simultaneously acquiring a human soul. Now we have a unique Being - one displaying both divine and human natures but without commingling or confusion Who establishes between God and man a perfect though asymmetrical union, the asymmetry merely reflecting the infinitude of God and the finitude of humanity. The two natures, however, remain clear and distinct: while the divinity of God is still undiminished, humanity, on the other hand, is perfected. In the God-man born to the *Theotokos,* we do not have a Divine/human hybrid in which an anthropomorphic demiurge is generated but, instead, One who is perfect God and perfect man at one and the same time. The patristic term *"the anthropos"* describes the simultaneous but clear, distinct and uncomingled presence of both Divine and human natures within one being. While the infinite, Divine majesty of the only begotten Son is uncircumscribable, Christ chooses voluntarily to become circumscribed. The old (first) Adam is thereby replaced through the Incarnation by the new (second) Adam in a recapitulation of human nature, and thus becomes deified.

It is essential, from the Christian perspective, to view the first Adam in his physical existence of pristine human innocence before the fall. Having been given free will to continue his immortal existence[10] in communion with God throughout eternity, he elected instead to ignore God's warning to avoid *"the fruit of the tree of knowledge of good and evil."* By inappropriately responding to diabolic temptation, Adam foolishly substituted his own human reason and desire for God's wisdom and guarantee of immortality.[11] Once choosing independence from God, he promptly fell into the forewarned predicament, *"If you eat that fruit you will surely*

---

9. Gen. 1:1-10, Jn. 1:1-14.

10. That is, the immortality which is a gift of God's grace. Man did not have immortality by nature.

11. Man is immortal by grace, not by nature. No aspect of man is immortal by nature, contrary to the heretical teaching that proclaims man to have an immortal soul trapped in a mortal body. Nor does the soul of man have a separate "subtle body" in the Gnostic sense, that it can operate fully without the body. Some of the fathers referred to angels and the human soul as having a subtle

'die.'' Through Adam's willful, selfish and myopic rejection of God he triggered a fundamental change in human nature: man was transformed into a creature of arrogantly chosen biological independence, immediately facing the challenge of material survival. No longer a creature in communion with the Creator, his potential for eternal life was exchanged for the mortal certainty of death and the age-old struggle for physical survival against insurmountable odds. In essence, Adam's fateful choice undermined forever the fate of his progeny, who thereafter acquired "coats of skin," an allusion to Adam's acquisition of corruptibility and lost innocence. Adam's "missing of the mark" *(hamartia),* caused by yielding to demonic temptation, produced a world consigned to everlasting confusion and perpetual sin (a constant missing of the mark). From this new "fallen" reality came mortal man's unlimited propensity to dominate his world as an individual now characterized by selfish preoccupations and limited thought, both for others and for the world itself.

Ultimately, the Second Adam would come as Jesus Christ, the God-man who would radically change forever all ramifications of this catastrophe. The Incarnation, in effect, offered humanity an opportunity to achieve the ultimate perfection of human nature through reconciliation with the Creator. Although the body of Christ resembled that of other men, the presence of His divine nature within the framework of His humanity guaranteed its perfection and purity even while the outward appearance of ordinary manhood was maintained. Once again we are reminded: Christ did *not* take unto Himself "fallen" human nature. The true status of Christ's humanity - the expression of glory which was His from all eternity, was made manifest at His transfiguration, when *"His face did shine as the sun, and his raiment was white as the light."* We are also assured by the voice (of the Father) *"out of the cloud, which said, 'This is my beloved Son, In whom I am well pleased; hear ye Him.'"*[12]

Although Scripture informs us that the Lord revealed Himself in the fullness of His eternal glory on Mt. Tabor, we must realize that for Christ to have appeared thus on an everyday basis would have defeated the purpose of His mission,[13] which was to redeem mankind's collective alienation, once and for all eternity. Since we were made perishable by Adam's fall from grace,

materiality, thus distinguishing the created spirits from the perfect spirit of *God.* To suggest, however, as Seraphim rose and others have, that this means a "subtle body" in the Gnostic sense of the so-called "aerial toll-house" myth is clearly heretical.

12. Mt. 17:1-8.

13. See St Antony Metropolitan of Kiev, *"Why Christ did not call Himself God,"* in *Collected Essays of St Antony, Metropolitan of Kiev* (Synaxis Press, 1996).

our human mortality and eternal bondage to the lord of this world (Satan) through wrong choices could not be overcome by a mere act of our human will. Man is not immortal by nature and he could in no way overcome the power of death.[14] In order to accomplish a recapitulation it was first necessary for Him to share the daily woes and anguish of ordinary human beings even while He Himself remained in a perfected state. Only by His incarnation as the second Person of the Holy Trinity, wherein He *"put on the flesh"* of humanity while still God, could He overcome human mortality, defeating death by (His) death in a single, magnificent display of co-suffering love. In Christ, the Expected One has come, the Anointed One, the Messiah of Israel: *"The Word was made flesh"* ('ο Λογοσ σαρ εγενατο), Word who, in the beginning, *"was with God and was God."* And, through His glorious Resurrection, He extended the potential for eternal life to all of humanity.[15]

"The life of man is hid with Christ in God."[16]

The great Paschal Hymn of the Orthodox Church says it all precisely:

"Christ is risen from the dead,
Trampling down death by death,
And to those in the tombs bestowing lift."

Although two millennia of Holy Scripture and Orthodox Tradition have consistently taught us why Christ/God became man, we must always be reminded that, while He created us in His image and urges us through loving communion to acquire His similitude, He did *not* create an automaton, a mindless creature subject only to external control. Instead, He created us with intellect *(nous)* and free will *(thelema),* unrestricted and always capable of voluntarily rejecting His love. He also gave us a great gift, that of reason—which is ours to use as we elect—for good or evil purposes. He utterly respects the decisions we make and will not interfere with them. Our eternal destiny is our responsibility alone to choose.

To Orthodox Christians throughout the world the holy Cross remains *"from ages unto ages"* a symbol of life eternal through Christ's exquisite sacrifice. In no way does it symbolize death nor does it imply an act of atonement for everlasting human guilt. Rather, the Cross and Resurrection represent for all mankind the same potential for "sonship" with God that is enjoyed eternally by Christ. His perfected example of how a human life should be lived has

---

14. The heretical teaching that man's soul is naturally immortal is based on the teachings of Plato and Plotinus, not on Scripture or any Christian teaching.

15. *Orthodox Paschal Hymn.*

16. Col. 3:3.

profoundly illustrated for mankind the need to live righteously in unrelenting faith through *synergeia* (cooperation) with God. By the gift of Divine grace mankind has been given the opportunity to achieve immortality through deification:

> *"That in the ages to come He might show the exceeding riches of His grace in His kindness toward us through Christ Jesus. For by grace are ye saved through faith; and that not of yourselves; it is the gift of God: Not of works, lest any man should boast"* (Eph. 2:7-9).

For Orthodox Christians, who follow faithfully the Word of God and choose to live righteously, biological death is not a gloomy finality but merely the gateway to a new and timeless existence in loving communion with the Holy Trinity, made possible only by Christ's saving work on the Cross. Scripture assures us that, after death, we enter into a state of spiritual rest until His Second Coming, when we will be raised, not as some disembodied ethereal entity—or as a ridiculous anthropomorph in a nightshirt, sporting wings and forever playing a harp—but instead, as a resurrected body reunited with our soul. We also know that, with eternal salvation, we may forever enjoy a filial relationship (an adopted sonship) with the Father, by which we may eventually pass from glory to glory.[17]

Deification implies a voluntary reciprocity between God and man - an extension to God of human love and desire *(eros),* and the consequent return of God's salvific Jove *(Divine eros)* to His human creation. While we have been taught through Christ's example that human transfiguration, salvation and adoption can result from a certain emptying out *(kenosis)* of Divine love, we also realize that these aspects of divinization are not automatic. As already inferred, Divine love is freely offered but never forced upon mankind and, furthermore, may be voluntarily accepted or rejected by each human recipient, acting individually and independently of the Creator. Since human freedom is never abolished or suspended by Divine *fiat,* Divine compulsion plays no part in the process of man's *theosis.* Therefore, for the moment, we merely draw attention to the importance of taking certain voluntary actions in order to establish a co-working relationship *(synergeia)* with God.[18] Man's deification through *theosis* must be a dynamic process - personal and intensely intimate - a synergy between God and man which allows each to play an interactive role with the other.[19] The initiation of this "mystical" relationship implies neither a magnanimous unilateral gesture by a potentate nor a grov-

---

17. St. Gregory of Nyssa, PG 44, 30.

18. *The Defense of the Holy Hesychasts* 1:34 and St. Dionysios the Areopagite *Concerning the Divine Names* 4, 7.

19. Anstall H. in: *Aspects of Theosis: Purification and Sanctification of the Human Intellect.* Robinson, J (ed). Synaxis Press, Dewdney, B.C., 1995, pp 21-24.

elling obsequiousness by man but, instead, a relationship where, in strength and dignity, both partners—Divine and human alike—play definitive parts in a mutual, all-embracing love for one another. This is a point of engagement which requires some emphasis from the outset since, as we have already indicated, the Orthodox explanation of this process differs substantially from doctrines of salvation espoused by the feudalistic Latin Church and certain fundamentalist Western churches as well.

Negative Results of Juridicalism

We believe that Roman Catholicism, under a long succession of Popes pretending to the status of "Vicar" of Christ, has progressively disaffected Western aspects of spiritual understanding, especially those deriving from fundamentalist interpretations of Christianity, characterized by egocentric moralizing. Occasionally, there have been frightening consequences. While most mainline Protestant sects have been vigorously opposed to Rome's moralistic inflexibility and feudalistic severity, certain fundamentalist Protestant organizations have evolved their own panoply of creedal doctrines and covenants "with Christ" which have been variously damaging to the human soul. In fact, a dazzling smorgasbord of confused quasi-Christian theologies now exists in the West, often typified by out-of-context Biblical quotations and egregiously off-base misinterpretations of Scripture. All told, there are many thousands of varying (often contrary) Protestantized facsimiles of "Christian truth," often characterized by an amorphous ethos. While some of these sects trace their historic roots back to the Reformation, many more have since emerged as the inevitable offshoots of socio-political dissidence and rebellion against the status quo. Western society and the inevitable consequences of secularization have also produced various para-Christian cults that fall loosely within the framework of Protestantism, but often take on psychologically damaging authoritarian doctrinal practices and organizational infrastructures, often resembling those of Rome, sometimes worse.

An alarming by-product of fundamentalist moral fascism in the West is the wide range of carefully shrouded-from-the-public abuses (mental, emotional, physical, pharmaceutical, sexual, financial, even occultic in nature); these frequently evolve from institutions of extremely pietistic religiosity. Whenever far-right Fundamentalism empowers pseudo-religious institutions, fanaticism tends to proliferate within the fringe elements of such organizations, often triggering irrational, sporadic violence and other mysterious forms of nefarious conduct. All too often, as Scripture has warned, the origin of human religiosity and its attendant follies is promoted by false prophets who materialize false christs through deceitful teachings evolving from spurious misinterpretations of biblical Scripture. In any case, the disparate problems resulting from para-Christian cultism represent a shocking testimony to the theological schizophrenia and disturbances directly or indirectly attributable to the re-emergence of heresies whose origins date back to the early Christian period or to Roman authoritarianism dominant since the Great Schism and the diabolic mysticism of the Middle Ages. Tragically, somewhere in between all of these soul-destroying religious movements which guilefully use and abuse the Holy Bible, many despairing human beings ultimately have become lost in the cracks of spiritual confusion. Even sadder, a goodly number of these people are quite innocently caught up in these movements under the misguided conclusion that they are, in fact, practising "Christians" who are working diligently toward their "salvation."

Whenever legalism, authoritarianism and self-righteous judgmentalism are controlling aspects of religious leadership, fear and guilt are generally the underlying results.

Gospel misinterpretations and/or politicized messages, spawned by egocentric leaders who have personal control agendas, frequently translate (either directly or indirectly) into spiritual abuse of their unwitting brethren. The usual by-product of such religions is a sort of "celestial police state" forever lurking in the shadows, gleefully and often maliciously recording every human action, thereby creating the perceived or actual threat of spiritual abuse. Under such punitive conditions of worship, the pluses generally are counted as "merits" toward one's eventual salvation and the minuses as "demerits" toward condemnation; a spiritual imprisonment of the soul roughly analogous to a penal system of rule.

Under the baleful god of the collective fundamentalist religions of the West, the themes of human salvation and redemption have proved to be highly amenable to the worldly agendas of money-making corporate empires, slickly and successfully masquerading under religious pretences, usually for non-taxable profiteering at the expense of their innocent followers. The age-old guilt/control syndrome is masterfully put to work by such institutions under a brilliantly wrapped package of fraudulent, empty promises to loyal supporters, who work endlessly and selflessly in good faith to "earn" their salvation. Their efforts are generally energized by innocent religious zeal. The cultures that promote cultism and fundamentalism often are characterized by poor educational systems which promote tunnel vision, resulting in the culture's failure to develop independent, critical thinking skills in its people. Cradle-to-adult brain washing programs, whether purposeful or accidental, are often quite sophisticated in their design and implementation, and an inevitable paucity of historical perspective results in the people who evolve to "maturity" within such confining societies. Inevitably, "blind faith" and spiritual pride emerge as hallmarks of decades (or even centuries) of limited diversity, narrow educational parameters and highly judgmental socio-religious experience.

In the moralistic settings of certain secular religions of Western society, salvation is often seen as entirely dependent upon a "balance sheet" which indicates more "good" than "bad" whether interpreted as attitude, faith or works, or even national patriotism, as in the case of us Americans. This is the religious system of attitudes that has effectively undergirded the fundamentalism of Western juridical/justification theologies since the emergence of Roman Catholicism, and the Reformation which followed.

The original Christian notion of sin as "missing the mark" *(hamartia)* has been changed in secular juridical theologies to reflect, instead, an oblique consideration of all sin as exclusively constituting some egregious legal transgression, for which a form of punishment (atonement) is due. Unfortunately, the faithful who subscribe to this form of abject spiritual bankruptcy labour under the suspicion that any act transgressing (wholly or partially) some arbitrary legal criterion of morality is beyond simple apology and resolution to "do better" next time. Thus, moralistic religiosity is effectively transformed into a morass of guilt and fear on the part of the innocent believer since what really constitutes the given transgression, and what degree of appropriate punishment will be due, generally is left unclear in the mind of the perpetrator.

Often, the control mechanisms of soul imprisonment, employed by ruling authorities who presumptuously preside over the eternal salvation of their followers, form the root cause of a panoply of serious mental, emotional and physical breakdowns, characteristic of repressive/suppressive religious organisations. We must, unfortunately, include some of the contemporary "elders" in the Orthodox Church to be in this sphere.

While often espousing strong "family values," secularized societies typically produce a significant percentage of dysfunctional members and sometimes bizarre, even violent societal manifestations. These can usually be traced to the fear/guilt syndrome engendered by enforced, rigid adherence to self-serving schemes for progressive religious, financial and corporate control, quite often cultic in origin. Often, it is incumbent upon church members to be at all times in strict compliance with humanly contrived secret ordinances—usually Gnostic and/or Masonic in design, which are falsely represented as being, in and of themselves, the primary means to eternal salvation. Most tragically, the combination of these impositions, as we have already remarked, creates spiritual pride in active, obedient members and their consequent indifference to the true message of the Gospel of Christ. Good works, as St. Paul indicated, spring from the love of God and one's fellow human beings. They are by-products of solid Christian faith, evolving quite naturally through righteous thoughts and conduct, quite contrary to the forced actions of those who suffer from out-of-context Biblical referencing, doctrinal mis-interpretations, and other acts of spiritual malfeasance arbitrarily contrived to support doctrines of salvation that inevitably destroy one's soul and any hope for communion with God in humility and repentance. The tragic result of misguided religious doctrines is that the souls of those who eventually summon the courage to leave the controlling organizations which promote them frequently are so damaged spiritually and emotionally, and so uni-versally distrustful, that they are practically incapable of conversion to true Christianity.

It is this writer's observation that certain juridical justification tradi-tions, especially fundamentalist/evangelical movements, deliberately cul-tivate gloom in the expressions and general demeanor of their followers, particularly in public situations where the outward signs of an individual's exemplary moral character are patronizingly and pietistically manifested. In unhappy fact, one finds precisely the same manifestation among sects within the Orthodox Church that are under the influence of Augustinian Scholasti-cism. The public conversation, speeches and prayers of such "moral" persons tend to be liberally salted with pietistic expressions. It is noteworthy that the continual practice of religiosity (pietism)—or popular righteousness—gener-ally results in the induction of arrogance and obnoxious spiritual pride (pre-viously alluded to), a process which, because it is absolutely inimical to the development and nurturing of a healthy personality, is often psychologically as well as spiritually destructive in its consequences.

Egocentric gestures are designed to create an impression of holiness that may be entirely counterfeit, and victims of this misbegotten practice often attempt to assuage the guilt they are induced to feel through a retributive orientation, often leading to serious mental imbalances and acts of des-peration. The reactionary Right-wing fringe of contemporary America's "Christian Coalition" has its own particular brand of public moralizing (which sounds alarmingly fascist at times). Saint Antony Khrapovitsky succinctly observed regarding egocentric guilt in general, "Who needs it anyway?"[20]

In humble contrast to the highly polished moralistic trappings of many Western-style para-Christian institutions, the Orthodox tradition of Christi-

20. Khrapovitsky, Saint Antony. *The Moral Idea of the Main Dogmas of the Faith.* Synaxis Press, Dewdney, B.C., 1988, pp 91-99.

anity offers up a very simple, age-old gesture of humility and sacred reverence before God: the "Sign of the Cross." A symbol *par excellence* in widespread usage among believing Christians (a term used in its ancient sense) on all continents, it is not merely a reminder of the passion of Christ, as has often been the case in the Latin tradition, nor is its use intended to recall for us the "blood-money" construed to have been paid for the ransom of human souls, a false perception already exposed. Orthodox Christians use the sign to seal their bodies or to express blessings for people, places, things or actions; in fact, it represents the willing renunciation of self, a rejection of individual self-sufficiency, and a profound awareness of the necessity for personal cooperation and communion with God.

God as Love

"He who does not love does not know God, for God is love."
"God is love, and he who abides in love abides in God, and God in him."
"Beloved, let us love one another, for love is of God,
and everyone who loves is born of God and knows God."[21]

This is the apt instruction in the Gospel According to Saint John (the Theologian) on the subject of how love is righteously manifested in all of its aspects. Here, he equates Divinity with love: he who loves knows God and is within God as God is within him. Therefore, to be godlike we must love not only God, who already is love, but we must also love one another as He loves us.

We know from Scripture that Christ entered the world, not in self-aggrandizement, with the pomp and majesty of a potentate but as a poor and humble man who straight away began a recapitulation of the human experience. Entirely of His own free will, He took upon Himself the same risks, privations and vulnerabilities as fallen humanity to injury, ridicule, poverty and shame, even unto His agonizing Death upon the Cross. In this ultimate act of co-suffering love and self-sacrifice, He exercised no judgmentalism and manifested no pride, only utter humility and the profoundest compassion for humanity. Here in our humble Saviour, Whose life was lived in complete rectitude, without error or sin, is the summation of how our lives were intended by God to be lived. Christ's attitude toward all of humanity is reflected in His unconditional love. That the Son of God—He by whom all that exists in the universe came into being out of nothing—had cause to enter His own created order in total humility to suffer, die and rise again, for the reconstruction of the human race and for all of creation (thereby extending to each of us the

---

21. 1 Jn.4:8; 1 Jn.4:16; 1 Jn.4:7.

potential for eternal life), exceeds the comprehension of fallen humanity. And, that this shameful Divine-human *kenosis* was required to save us from our own selfish inequities calls forth from us floods of tears, utter anguish and sorrow for His suffering. Simultaneously, however, we first ourselves experiencing an offsetting sense of limitless joy that, in His infinite mercy, compassion and love, He elected to descend to our level and beyond to endure for our redemption the depths of lowliness, the insults, anguish of rejection, venomous hatreds and agonizing, violent and humiliating death. What is so shocking to the Orthodox Christian mind is how and why certain secular religionists in the juridical West nevertheless can persist in the perception of such a God as somehow cruel, capricious, judgmental and vindictive. Such a depiction is oxymoronic and almost beyond comprehension. We see it as not only tragically mistaken theology but, at worst, as outright blasphemy. That such theological nonsense is still held by some Fundamentalists to be "accurately interpreted" from Scripture, irrespective of the glaring inconsistencies and conflicts of such thought, is stupefying. The proliferation of centuries of spiritual confusion, abuse, unnecessary human suffering and desolation are an obvious consequence.

Let us once again reflect on Saint John's assurance that God is love, a premise that is indeed integral to Orthodox Christian theology:

> *"I say unto you, that likewise there will be more joy in Heaven over one sinner who repents than ninety-nine just men who need no repentance. Or what woman, having ten silver coins, if she lose one coin, does not light a lamp and sweep the house, and seek diligently after the lost coin? And when she has found it; she calls her friends and neighbours saying, 'rejoice with me, for I have found that which was lost.'"*22

Here, in our loving God, is a presence to whom all creatures are precious— not a sparrow falling but that He is fully aware of it. It can be truly said that the God of love is eternally present to answer our knock on His door for help. We know that He forgives all - and that His mercy is boundless. He utterly respects our personhood and does not force Himself upon us. Thus He plays no part in the infliction of punishment, most especially not eternal punishment. In the final analysis of Orthodox theology, damnation consists entirely in the voluntary rejection of God by us. We have the Gospel, the Prophets, the Apostles, the Martyrs, the Fathers, and the Mystical Body of Christ (the Church) with which we can choose to associate or from which we can elect to walk away. The choice of acceptance or rejection of His love (in all of its manifestations) is ours alone to make, purely by voluntary exercise of our

---

22. Lk.15:7-9.

God-given free will. Yet, despite our often contrary and wayward decisions, we are *never* rejected by the God of love; He merely awaits with infinite patience and mercy our remorse, contrition, eventual humility, repentance and, most importantly, our determination to return to His loving care.

Damnation, then, is seen by Orthodox Christians solely as the inevitable consequence of our expressed desire to renounce and reject God. Simply postulated, condemnation to hell is always self-inflicted. We do not consider the fires of hell to be material flames but rather a burning inversion of the radiant light of Divine love, once wilfully spurned and rejected. Hatred of God and rejection of His love are entirely human choices. To think contrarily, thereby entering into negativism and inversion, is a particularly pernicious deceit of the devil - the father of lies.

Theosis versus Satisfaction

One of the most pernicious effects of the juridical/justification theology of human rationalism upon our perception of reality and our human inter-relationship with God is the adverse, mitigating effect it has upon the process of *theosis,* the mechanism of deification by which human beings may progressively acquire a "likeness" to Him. A juridical outlook, representing God as conceived in largely human philosophical terms - not as the personification of love but as a tyrant bent upon the administration of justice - offers little compassion for or cognizance of personhood.

In the Orthodox Tradition, a person voluntarily enters into a cooperative relationship with God, extending his love to the Saviour and praying to receive God's love similarly unto himself, while keeping the commandments of God and endeavouring to accomplish the true path of Christ within limits of his capability. The faithful in Christ enter into a relationship of intense intimacy of personal and reciprocal love; an exercise of passion which, by passion, overcomes passion and leads the soul to rest through dispassion, to "the peace which passeth all understanding."

In the juridical tradition of Western Fundamentalists, *theosis* as an operative concept is largely incomprehensible and meaningless. In fact, it might even be considered blasphemous whereas, in reality, as the holy fathers reassure us, it constitutes the most sublime experience available to us.[23] While the Orthodox Christian sees in *theosis* a potential actualization of the entire salvific process, to the Western secularist, the reciprocity of Divine *eros*

23. St. Nicholas Kavasilas. *The Life in Christ,* 1, 2; Lk.15:1-9.

with human *eras* is virtually an unknown activity, essentially denied by the theological processes of juridical moralism, theoretically based upon the accumulation of "good" attributes and performances which, as previously described, can be quantitatively and numerically offset, quite arbitrarily, by a collection of "bad" (unacceptable) performances. In such a seesaw system of religious thought, one's ultimate fate apparently is entirely dependent upon the so-called good deeds eventually outweighing the bad ones. The "aerial toll-house myth," which is roughly analogous to "celestial bingo," is precisely such a legal fiction/myth designed as a fear control mechanism. It is advocated in the Orthodox Church exclusively by those of an Augustinian neo-Gnostic bent, and is patently silly.

The Gospel plainly informs us that, if we fall into sin, we are guilty and are called to contrition and repentance in full humility before our Saviour. In this sense, He is our "personal God." The Gospel does not imply that the number of good or bad deeds, in a purely arithmetical or quantitative appraisal of total performance, arbitrarily defined as "goodness" or "badness," determines our final destiny. It is implicit, however, that we comprehend the inescapable fact that we are all sinners since we are all in a fallen state. Whatever form our sins take they are sins nonetheless, and any sin demands personal action (in Greek, it is called *"metanoia,"* which is understood as "changing our perspective and our direction) to avoid its repetition in the future. This is what is meant by repentance, and we can never repent enough.

At the height of juridical folly in the Middle Ages, acts of penance (a Latin term in opposition to the Orthodox Christian concept of repentance)[24] included both self-flagellation and flagellation of others (typically, sadomasochistic acts), trekking for miles over stony roads on bare knees (with what physical results may be imagined), the wearing of hair shirts or sackcloth garments impregnated with ashes, and diverse other unseemly and injurious extravagances. These penitent actions did nothing but violate the integrity of the human body, the temple of the Holy Spirit given to us by God to maintain in health and freshness. Of course, such garish penances and legalistic renunciations of supposed sin are in keeping with a belief system founded on penal legalism and fully supportive of a theology of vengeance and punishment. While a wrathful god may be thought to appreciate such things, a capricious god may equally derive from them sadistic pleasure and choose to ignore them. On balance, any theology producing a juridical view of God

---

24. There is no such thing as "penance" in the Orthodox Church although the term has been borrowed from Roman Catholicism. Penance means "punishment," and indicates self-efforts to satisfy God's justice in order to obtain absolution. There is no relationship whatsoever between "penance" and *metanoia,* no is there any relationship between "absolution" and "forgiveness."

as a vengeful potentate is blasphemous and insulting to the Word of God contained throughout Holy Scripture. Juridical arguments for penance and satisfaction in connection with salvation are a sacrilegious view of Divinity.

In the Orthodox Faith, *metanoia* implies a changing of one's mind and an altering of one's behaviour to avoid again falling for the blandishments of the devil and yielding to inimical temptation. Eastern tradition tends to be rather more effective in its methods of correction than the extravagant penances observed in the West which, as we have already reviewed, fail by their aggrandizement of judgmental, arrogant self-righteousness and condemnation. We may validly conclude from this discussion that many Western forms of quasi-Christian theology constitute temptations in two directions: either sacrilegious acceptance of the given (faulty) belief system, or rejection of such a system of beliefs, which may undermine faith in God altogether.

Epilogue

As previously asserted, the juridical justification theology of secular Fundamentalism (whether Western or Eastern, for that matter) is intrinsically hostile to the process of divinization. Unfortunately, the notion of *theosis* is scarcely comprehended by many Western theologians since their collective conception of human destiny is primarily based either upon a system of merits and demerits, numerically considered and evaluated that Christ satisfied God's justice by being tortured and executed in our place (or, usually, a combination of both). The sacrilegious "aerial toll-house myth" is just such a juridical blasphemy - not to mention being in radical contradiction of Divine Scripture.

Redemption is necessarily an extension of the notion of salvation, rather than the end result of earned merits, just penance paid, satisfying God's needs or an arbitrary fee charged and paid for at some "tollgate" to Heaven. Once again, as we understand Scripture from the Orthodox perspective, the "cost" of human salvation cannot in any way be paid by man. The grace of God flows freely to those who seek and righteously desire it, regardless of the numeric proliferation of good works performed. As stated earlier in the text, such works flow naturally from the righteous and charitable acts of any person who truly believes in God. In and of themselves, however, as the New Testament reminds us, they cannot "earn" or "win" our salvation. Works are not counted for that purpose since Christ, our Saviour, does not compare pluses against minuses in the granting of salvation; He was not our scapegoat in death but is our final arbiter *for* life everlasting. Eternal damnation can only result *from* humanity ignoring and discrediting Christ's unconditional act of redemptive sacrifice *for* our collective sins on earth. By exercising our *free* will in unrighteous ways and inverting God's love, we reject our Saviour's offer of salvation and, in so doing, we seal our own fate - an everlasting torment of supreme self-deprivation, wherein we meander alone, unaided and unloving, throughout' an eternity of self-imposed misery.

In essence, an Orthodox conscience leads us to conclude that a life lived in self-righteous, worldly judgmentalism and condemnation of our fellow man (hallmarks of spiritual pride) is plainly self-condemning in its inferences. Active pursuit of any juridical theology based on self-justification makes eternal isolation *from* God entirely probable. While spiritual truth and the potential *for* communion with God lie within each human heart and soul, the choice of direction is entirely ours alone to make.

Acquisition of the Holy Spirit versus "spirituality" or "spiritualism," and piety versus "pietism" are aspects in opposition to one another. The choices we make lie within the exercise of human intellect. "Blind faith" is a self-imposed human blindfold spawned by foolish dependency upon external influences, entirely of earthly origin.

God gave us *free* will, intellect and the ability to reason expressly *for* the purpose of avoiding blind faith in false prophets and false teachers. Those Christians who have carefully read Holy Scripture know these warnings well. We are given special human faculties of intellect and reason that we may seek knowledge and gain wisdom by which to make wise and righteous choices. "Seek, and ye shall find;" "Knock, and the door shall be opened."[25] If we ask God in humility and faith *for* truth, having absolute trust in His guidance and therefore not fearing where His truth may lead us, we will avoid the pitfalls of heresy and false doctrine. *Theosis* is only possible through absolute, unswerving faith and trust in our Saviour and Lord, Jesus Christ, Who died *for* all our sins, "from ages unto ages," so that we might have salvation in His eternal kingdom.

25. 2 Cor.5:17, 18. See St. Gregory of Nyssa, PG 45,93.

Chapter Twenty

DIVINIZATION, THE CHURCH AND PROPHETIC POLITICS IN OUR POST 9-11 WORLD

by Ronald S. Dart

The mystery of Pentecost is as important as the mystery of the Redemption. The redeeming work of Christ is an indispensable precondition of the deifying work of the Holy Spirit.

Vladimir Lossky
In the Image and Likeness of God

The charity of Christ in the Eucharist, seizing upon the best natural instincts of the human soul, elevates and divinizes them, uniting men to one another in a charity and peace which this world can never give.

Thomas Merton
The Living Bread (p. xviii)

Both the Scriptures and the Fathers attest to the truth of deification as the teaching of the church from the beginning, universally confessed even if not universally expounded.

Michael Azkoul
Ye Are Gods: Salvation According to the Latin Fathers (p.2)

I. Into the Dark Forest

Why did Jesus the Christ come to earth, and why should we be drawn to and interested in such a coming? Many has been the sage and enlightened one that has spoken and lived with much wisdom and insight. Why was the presence of Christ in creation, the advent of Christ in the incarnation and the life of Christ in the one, holy, catholic and apostolic church of such importance?

There have been many a missive and tome written on the reasons for the incarnation of Christ, and, within the Christian theological tradition, ideas and theories about both the incarnation and atonement abound. The journey into the meaning of the atonement can be seen and understood in different ways, and much hinges on how the life, death and resurrection of Christ are interpreted by theologians and the church.

The dialogue within the Christian tradition about the significance of atonement theology does walk us into a dark forest. There are rays of light that often illuminate certain perspectives, but tribes do gather in different parts of the forest and often claim their read of the atonement is the best and finest.

Needless to say, such shafts of light through thick branches and denser leaf cover tend to obscure yet reveal. The light above the forest and under the blue canopy is much brighter and fuller, of course, but for those who dwell in the shadows and tree cover of the forest, much is missing and only limited light finds its way through.

The task before us is to find our way out of the forest of atonement tribalism to the high peaks and lofty summits of a fuller understanding of why Christ came to this fragile earth, our island home. It is this more comprehensive understanding of the atonement that will awaken and illuminate for us the nature of our faith journey. We need not, in short, get mired in one-dimensional and single-vision interpretations of the reasons for Christ with us. Sadly so, this has happened in the Christian tradition, and such different reads of the atonement have divided and separated people of equal commitment. What, then, are some of the theories of the atonement, what is the nature and content of the different perspectives, and is it possible to see each theory as but a pointer to a higher and fuller view of why Christ came and is ever with us?

We do need, also, to desperately discern what the integration of deification and prophetic politics means in both our post 9-11 world and the intense culture wars that beset us in the public square in a daily way and manner. If we shy away from linking theology and earth-bound politics, we can slip into a more sophisticated notion of Gnosticism. And, as Canadians, what does it mean to think through and live these issues on the doorsteps of the largest empire in world history?

II. *Violence, Hospitality, and the Cross*:
Reappropriating the Atonement Tradition

The publication in 2004, by Hans Boersma, of *Violence, Hospitality, and the Cross: Reappropriating the Atonement Tradition*, did much to stir and galvanize a rethink about ideas of the atonement. Tribes, denominations and clans had settled into their favoured read of the atonement, and most refused to budge or move. Models were converted into absolutes that dared not nor could not be questioned or doubted. Idols had come to replace ikons, and the fuller redemptive message of Christ had become lost in thinned-out versions of the atonement.

Hans Boersma, to his critical and reflective credit, opened up the discussion again in a fuller and more thoughtful way. It is always best to hear and heed the time-tried message of the Classical Christian Tradition before jumping on the bandwagon of limited and reductionistic versions of the faith. Boersma does just this in his turn to the Christian tradition. There is much

of good in *Violence, Hospitality, and the Cross*, and there are some limitations, and to these we now turn. We will need to hike beyond Boersma in our
understanding of the atonement, but we do need to pass through the wider
gate he has opened for us.

Violence, Hospitality, and the Cross is divided into four sections: 1) The
Divine face of Hospitality, 2) The Cruciform Face of Hospitality, 3) The
Public Face of Hospitality, and 4) Epilogue. There is no doubt that Boersma
is grappling, in an honest and searching way, with the tension between the
welcoming and generous, gracious and hospitible God of the *Bible* and the
obstinate and persistent reality of exclusion, violence and brutality in the
same book.

How, then, do hospitality and violence, inclusion and exclusion dwell
together in one house and family? Are these not inconsistent and contradictory positions? Some think they are. Boersma sends out many probes to ponder the problem in more depth.

'The Divine Face of Hospitality' approaches the dilemma without flinch-
ing. Boersma emerges from a Reformed and Calvinist positions, he has many
a concern with aspects of Calvinism, but he is also concerned about the way
a soft liberal left attempts to snap the tension between hospitality/inclusion
and violence/exclusion. 'The Divine Face of Hospitality' opens up, in all its
fullness, the problems faced when hospitality as a divine virtue is held high in
the *Bible*. There is no doubt that Boersma is walking the extra mile to engage
both Calvin and Calvinists, yet step beyond both.

The main course of *Violence, Hospitality, and the Cross* is 'The Cruciform face of Hospitality'. This is where Boersma turns to the various ideas
about the atonement to assist him in understanding the hospitality-violence
tension. The genius of this section of the book is the way Boersma highlights
three facts: there are various notions of the atonement, each should be seen as
a suggestive metaphor, each metaphor should be seen as pointing towards a
greater mystery. Boersma, in short, relativizes ideas about the atonement. He
points out, in thoughtful detail, that each metaphor has both a certain appeal
and limitation. The metaphor and model approach to the atonement broadens
out, in a healthy manner, ways of understanding why Christ took on the form
of a human and came to this earth, our fragile home.

The atonement as moral influence, the atonement and mimetic violence,
punishment and the atonement and the *Christus Victor* tradition of Gustav
Aulen are held high, examined, welcomed, and yet each, in their own way,
found wanting when day is done. Such an approach, though, does not exhaust
ways of approaching or understanding the atonement. It is to Boersma's
credit that he turns to Irenaeus (and his notion of recapitulation) to fill out
lower, more limited and lesser views of the atonement. There is a richness

and fullness to the recapitulation notion of the atonement, and Irenaeus has thought through this deeper meaning in much detail. It is to the tradition of Irenaeus that Boersma finds some of the finest insights on the atonement. Yes, there are some truths in the moral influence, penal/juridical, *Christus Victor* and mimetic traditions and interpretations of the atonement, but Irenaeus, for Boersma, tells the tale in the best and finest way.

'The Public Face of Hospitality' is more applied and touches on the church and issues of public justice. This is a much shorter section, and needs more thought and pondering, but, in many ways, this need not detain nor worry the reader. The burden of *Violence, Hospitality, and the Cross* is to highlight how many Christians have gone astray with one-dimensional views of the atonement and call them back to a fuller view of why Christ came, how he is with us now and what the drama will look like when the curtain of time is pulled back in the escaton.

The 'Epilogue' points in directions that need greater fleshing out, but, in many ways, add yet more to the meaning of the atonement. The 'Epilogue' is only a few pages, but in these pages Boersma touches on the end of violence, eschatology and deification. It is too bad the notion of deification was brought in so late in the discussion, and equally problematic that the notion of the end of violence is equated with eschatology and deification. Many would argue, of course, that the coming of Christ brought an end to violence, and those that are one in Christ and the one, holy, catholic and apostolic Church must be, if not committed pacifists, then peacemakers. It would have been fruitful if Boersma had unpacked some of his final reflections of deification, eschatology and the end of violence in a more challenging manner. This might have illuminated much about the meaning and significance of the atonement not really dealt with in the moral influence, mimetic, substitutionary, *Christus Victor* and recapitulation traditions of the atonement.

There is no doubt that *Violence, Hospitality, and the Cross* is a groundbreaking book. It should be absorbed and internalized by all interested in the meaning of the atonement. The limitation, and it is an important one, is the way Boersma never truly unpacks or understands the meaning of deification as the final end and destination of the atonement. Also, deification is not something that occurs on the far side of history and time. The mystical and contemplative traditions of the church have consistently pointed out that if we are united to Christ, we participate in the very substance and nature of God. We are, in fact, raised up to the Divine level, and such a raising up and transformation, metamorphosis and conversion is at the heart and core of the atonement.

It is a long stretch and journey for a thoughtful Calvinist to reach the mystical notion of deification, but, to Boersma's credit, he was inching in such a direction by the end of *Violence, Hospitality, and the Cross*. The idea of divinization/deification can certainly be found in the writings of Irenaeus, and it might have helped if Boersma had trekked this trail more. If we ever hope to get a fuller notion of deification and the atonement, it is best and wisest to turn to the mystical theologians of the Orthodox tradition. They, more than most, have attempted to understand the meaning of the atonement from the perspective of our deified life in Christ and the Church. It is to the Orthodox tradition we now turn to get a feel and fix for notions of the atonement tradition that add to, yet go beyond, the many fine insights in *Violence, Hospitality, and the Cross*.

III. Mystical Theology and Deification:
Vladimir Lossky and Michael Azkoul

Vladimir Lossky was one of the most important Orthodox theologians of the 20th century. George Florovsky was the only other Orthodox mystical theologian equal to Lossky in the 1950s-1960s. The publication of *The Mystical Theology of the Eastern Church* (1944) and *The Vision of God* (1961) made it clear that Lossky was a writer that needed to be heard. His doctoral dissertation on Meister Eckhart (with a foreward by Etienne Gilson) has a depth, solidity and substance to it that cannot be doubted. It takes the curious and thoughtful to places that many modern commentators on Eckhart do not go. The crown jewel of Lossky's publications is *In the Image and Likeness of God* (1974). The many fine essays in this compact volume make it more than clear why Lossky still speaks to us.

Lossky's thinking emerged at a time when there was a growing interest in the Christian patristic tradition. There is a depth and breadth in such a tradition that still sorely needs to be mined, and we can be grateful that such an interest still remains. Lossky stated quite clearly, in his article 'Redemption and Deification' (*In the Image and Likeness of God*) this truth:

> In the West, the theological thought of our day is making a great effort to return to the patristic sources of the first centuries—particularly to the Greek Fathers—in order to incorporate them into a catholic synthesis. Not only Post-Tridentine theology, but also Medieval scholasticism, with all its philosophical richness, nowadays appears theologically inadequate. A powerful effort is being made to put back into use the notion of the Church as the body of Christ, as a new creature recapitulated by Christ, a nature or a body having the Risen Christ as her Head. (Section 3)

Lossky and Florovsky were front and centre in the turn to the patristics in the 1950s-1960s. Such pioneers have done much to mentor and guide the West to forgotten Alpine pastures and white-capped peaks of faith. The interest has continued to deepen in our time, but such a turn has rarely, in the Western interest in the Fathers, seriously mined the meaning of the atonement and deification. This is an issue that Lossky held front and centre. 'Redemption and Deification' approaches the topic in an insightful and incisive manner.

'Redemption and Deification' highlights how and why some aspects of the Western theological tradition have gone astray by being overly committed to and uncritical of Anselm's view of the atonement. Lossky brings the larger debate into focus by saying this: "After the constricted horizons of an exclusively juridical theology, we find in the Fathers an extremely rich idea of redemption."

And what is this 'rich idea of redemption'? Simply put, it is this. In Christ, the body of Christ, the Church, is raised up to the Divine level. 'God made Himself man, that man might become God'. Or, to follow the lead of St. Peter: 'we partake of the divine nature' by being in Christ. This is a high view of the atonement and redemption. This is more than the juridical, moral influence, Christus Victor or mimetic tradition can offer. Ireneaus stands very much in such a fuller line and lineage.

The notion of deification is not, though, merely about the individual becoming divinized in Christ. The process of deification takes place within the life of the unified and united Church. Just as Father, Son, and Spirit are One, so, to the degree the Church participates in such a divine unity, those in the body of Christ are deified. It is hard in our era and time to make such a point clear. We live in period of time in which the Church is fragmented and divided at a formal and material level, hence the corporate notion of deification is lost and at a fading distance for many. It is impossible when reading Lossky to miss the fact that deification is both linked to our new life in Christ, and such a new life is lived in the corporate reality of Christ's Divine body, the Church. Most of 'Redemption and Deification' makes this telling point again and again.

The strength and appeal of Lossky's thinking and 'Redemption and Deification' is the way he makes it abundantly clear that our new life in Christ cannot be fully lived unless we are united in the body of Christ in a spiritual, formal and material way. Redemption and Unity in the Church cannot be separated. This is not an individualist view of either the atonement or redemption. This is a mystical theology that views deification as a corporate reality.

Lossky should be applauded and warmly welcomed for his many fine insights. He has moved the meaning about the atonement beyond a limited view that has often dominated the West. He has pointed out that deification is also connected to life in Christ's historic and corporate body, the Church.

Lossky does err, though, when he fails to flesh out the social, political, cultural and economic meaning of deification. There is virtually little or no discussion in Lossky of the political, public and prophetic nature and implications of deification and divinization. This is a serious and substantive flaw and weakness that needs to be noted, and it is a problem that can be found again and again within the Orthodox clan that holds high the notion of deification.

Michael Azkoul, like Lossky, has done much from within the Orthodox tradition to hold high the notion of deification. Azkoul has filled out areas in such a terrain that Lossky has missed or not fully developed. *Justification, the Path to Theosis* (1993), and, more importantly, *Ye Are Gods: Salvation According to the Latin Fathers* (2002), walks the reader into areas that are often missed in the discussion of deification. Azkoul makes three important points that need to be acknowledged.

First, he argues, in 'Deification in the Scriptures' (*Ye Are Gods*), that the notion of divinization is not only drawn from the much-quoted passage from Peter. Azkoul asks this question: 'Lacking the second epistle of St. Peter and its famous verse, would the Church and her Fathers nonetheless have taught deification?' (p. 6). Azkoul's answer to such a question is a firm Yes. There is no doubt that deification is taught in the Scriptures, hence such an idea is not an invention of Greek theologians taken in by Greek philosophers or those who came from the mystery religions of the ancient world. Azkoul, in a meticulous and careful way, makes it clear that deification can be clearly found in the Scriptures. The Orthodox tradition did not invent this. In fact, they are being the truest to the Scriptures by protecting this high notion of redemption and the atonement. It is the West that has shrunk and thinned out the larger epic tale and deeper meaning of Christ's incarnation.

Second, there are those who, falsely so, assume the Orthodox tradition holds to the position of deification and the Western tradition (Roman Catholic and Protestant) turn their backs on such a view. This again is not the case, and Azkoul points out the hard facts that cannot be denied. It is true, of course, that Protestant Christianity has little or no view of deification and significant portions of Medieval and post-Reformation Roman Catholic thought have veered away from the notion of deification, but this has not always been the case. Just as Lossky had suggested that the turn to the patristics was occurring in his time, Azkoul walks the interested to the Latin Fathers of the patristic era to make it clear that they held to a notion of deification, also. It is just simply untrue that the Eastern fathers were for deification and the Latin Fathers were either opposed to it or ignored it. 'The Latin Fathers' (*Ye Are Gods*) visits many of the Western Fathers and, in hearing them, makes it clear they had a committed understanding of divinization. Few of the Latin fathers are missed by Azkoul: Clement, Hippolytus, Cyprian, Hilary, Ambrose, Jerome, Niceta,

Paulinus, Maximus, Peter, Leo and Gregory are called forth and called up to give their views of the atonement, redemption and deification, and each and all reinforce and agree with the Eastern Fathers. Therefore, the Scriptures and the Fathers of the West and East agree that deification is the goal and end, purpose and meaning of the atonement.

Azkoul makes it clear that this cannot be missed in a careful and honest reading of the Scriptures and the Fathers (West and East).

Third, Azkoul, reflecting an Orthodox perspective on Augustine, tends to see Augustine as an aberration and distortion within the Latin tradition. Needless to say, Azkoul has not come to such a conclusion in a light or flippant way. He has pondered the writings of Augustine for many years, and in much depth and detail. *The Influence of Augustine of Hippo on the Orthodox Church* (1990) and *Augustine of Hippo: An Orthodox Christian Perspective* (1994) take Augustine to task for a variety of failings. 'Augustine: A Departure' (*Ye Are Gods*) hikes the same path. Azkoul recognizes that Augustine does have an understanding of deification, but he questions the sources, content and implications of his understanding. Azkoul is right to raise hard questions about Augustine (many in the West don't do this, and this is problematic for a variety of reasons), but, I fear, Azkoul, in reacting to Augustinian hagiography or moderate Augustinian criticism tends to be overly critical of Augustine. He misses the more complex and nuanced thinking of Augustine and his notion of deification, redemption and the atonement. A careful read of *Augustine* (1994), by the well-known Canadian Augustinian scholar, John Rist, might make for a better and more moderate read of Augustine. *Augustine of Hippo: A Biography* (1967), by Peter Brown, could be used also to offset some of Azkoul's more extreme yet insightful reactions to Augustine.

There is no doubt that Azkoul has done much good in clarifying how the notion of deification can be found in the Scriptures and the Latin Fathers. Azkoul tends to be rather questionable in three areas, though: first, his interpretation of Augustine needs to be read with some caution and a critical eye: second, Azkoul tends to have a rather negative, simplistic and reductionist understanding of Greek thought. Plato and Aristotle had much depth, wisdom and insight to them, and this why the mystical theology of the early church was indebted to some of the fine insights and reflections of Plato and Aristotle. The reasons the early church turned to Greek philosophical thought is carefully and meticulously unpacked by Andrew Louth in *The Origins of the Christian Mystical Tradition: From Plato to Denys* (1981). *Discerning the Mystery: An Essay on the Nature of Theology* (1983), by Louth, should also be read as a corrective to Azkoul. Azkoul tends to equate the Platonism of Plotinus with Classical Greek philosophy, and he then dismisses much of the Classical tradition; in this he sorely errs.

There are greater depths to Plato than Azkoul has plumbed. Third, Azkoul, like Lossky before him, never unpacks and enfleshes the meaning of deification in the area of public, political and prophetic life. This is a serious flaw and weakness in his thinking on deification, the atonement and the meaning of redemption in Christ and the Church.

There are some fine Anglican theologians that have pondered the meaning of Christ, the Church, deification and the public and the political implications of such a vision. I will, briefly, deal with two such mystical theologians: A.M. Allchin and Archbishop Rowan Williams.

IV. The Anglican Tradition and Deification:
A.M. Allchin and Rowan Williams

I had published, about a decade ago, a small article: 'The Oxford Movement and the Politics of Deification' (*Fellowship Papers:* Winter 1996-1997). This missive was my initial attempt to probe and examine, within the Anglican tradition, the relationship between ideas of the atonement, redemption, Christ, the Church, deification and prophetic politics. I was somewhat surprised at the time that few had attempted to think through and live forth the integration of deification and public and political life. 'The Oxford Movement and the Politics of Deification' was a pointer in such a direction. Much was probed in the essay. A few more probes have been sent out in this article.

The Anglican tradition, like the Orthodox and Roman Catholic, is a tradition that holds high the centrality of the Scriptures, as interpreted by the Fathers in the Latin West and Greek East. The Creeds and Councils embody and reflect the conclusions of such thinking, and mystical theology wins the day at a much deeper and more informed level. I find, amongst many today that are turning to 'The Great Tradition', a weak understanding of the genius of the Anglican way. Many who turn to 'The Great Tradition' seem to think, wrongly so, that there are only two choices: Orthodox or Roman Catholic. The Anglican tradition is as old as the Orthodox and Roman Catholic traditions, and it is as committed as these traditions are to the Scriptures as interpreted by the Fathers in the Latin West and Greek East. The Creeds and Councils are duly honoured. This being so, the idea of Christ, the Church and deification are part and parcel of the Anglican tradition, also. A.M. Allchin and Rowan Williams, more than Lossky and Azkoul, have written about the public and the political dimensions of deification, and to Allchin and Williams we now turn.

It is significant to note that A.M. Allchin dedicated *The Kingdom of Love and Knowledge: The Encounter between Orthodoxy and the West* (1979) to 'Vladimir Lossky, theologian: 8 June 1903 – 7 February 1958', and the final article in *The Kingdom of Love and Knowledge* is 'Vladimir Lossky'. Interestingly enough, the present Archbishop of Canterbury, Rowan Williams, did his graduate thesis on Lossky. Allchin, in a timely footnote, said this:

> It is greatly to be hoped that Dr. Rowan Williams's masterly thesis on the theology of Lossky, which can be consulted in the Bodleian Library in Oxford, will soon be published. It would greatly enlarge our understanding of the Russian theological tradition. (p. 205)

The Anglican tradition, from which A.M. Allchin and Archbishop Rowan Williams come, has a profound respect and commitment to the Classical patristic Tradition in which Lossky and Florovsky dipped their buckets deep. The encounter between Anglicans and the Orthodox has been a rich and fruitful experience, and Allchin and Williams have participated in this interaction in a meaningful manner.

There are, though, distinct ways in which Williams and Allchin have translated and interpreted the meaning and significance of deification. Both men have sought to understand what the notion of divinization means—publicly and politically—to of those on the faith journey. There is much more of a wholistic, whole and truly holy understanding of deification in Williams and Allchin than we find in Lossky and Azkoul.

Allchin was, at one time, the chairman of the Council of the Fellowship of St. Alban and St. Sergius, an Anglican/Orthodox ecumenical group. *Sobornost* was the flagship magazine for such an ecumenical endeavor, and Allchin and Williams were quite involved with the work. The major difference, though, between the Anglicans and the Orthodox was the way those like Allchin and Williams attempted to make sense of deification in the public world of politics, economics and social concerns.

The Kingdom of Love and Knowledge concludes with a chapter, 'F.D. Maurice' and 'Evelyn Underhill'. Both Maurice and Underhill integrated the mystical and political. Maurice was often seen as an early Christian socialist and Underhill was quite committed to the peace movement. Allchin's chapter, 'Trinity and Incarnation in the Anglican Tradition', clearly draws together the tight knit relationship between the Trinity, the welcome fact of the incarnation, deification and issues of justice and peace. 'Trinity and Incarnation in the Anglican Tradition' is a fine primer and introduction on the way Anglicans have exquisitely threaded together the deeper purpose of the incarnation, a more earthbound and grounded notion of deification and the larger issues of concern for the human condition.

Allchin and Williams both contributed to *Essays Catholic and Radical*. This excellent collection of essays draws together, yet once again, an organic and applied perspective on Christ, the Church, deification and justice. Just as

Father, Son and Spirit are One, so the vision of the deified Church is to be one in God and one in an integrated view of all that is good and meaningful in life and the world. *Essays Catholic and Radical* makes it quite clear how deep the roots of change go, and the fruit that can emerge when a catholic vision is wed to radical politics. Such an integrative approach brings together aspects of the faith that are often kept separate. A fine friend of Allchin's and William's was Kenneth Leech. Leech was quite involved in the bringing together of *Essays Catholic and Radical*, and he has summed up the deeper and more public/prophetic meaning of deification in *Subversive Orthodoxy: Traditional Faith and Radical Commitment* (1992). Again, we can see how an older and more integrated notion of Christ, the Church and public responsibility can merge and unite both a catholic and radical perspective, be thoroughly orthodox yet completely radical.

I introduced this paper with a quote from Merton. Merton's view of the atonement was also about divinization, and the liturgy and sacraments, for Merton offered the attentive and receptive the living bread of the Divine.

Merton's position (being sensitive to the best of the Classical Christian notion of divinization) on the contemplative dimensions of deification is best spelled out in *The Inner Experience: Notes on Contemplation*. Merton, though, never separated the divinizing work of God through the sacraments and life itself, from public responsibility. Kenneth Leech, in his fine pamphlet, *Thomas Merton: Theologian of Resistance* (1993), makes this quite clear. Many of Merton's most important writings in the 1960s were focused on issues of justice and peace. A whole and holy vision dominates the day yet once again. The atonement, deification and prophetic politics are linked and at one.

The way Allchin, Williams, Merton and Leech, in their different ways, have brought together deification and prophetic politics within the time-tried Anglican and Roman Catholic traditions does move them a significant step beyond the more limited approach of Boersma, Lossky and Azkoul. There is a breadth and depth, a wholeness and fullness to Allchin, Williams, Leech and Merton that does not emerge or appear in the more restricted approach to deification and the meaning of the atonement in Lossky and Azkoul; this does need to be noted.

There are questions that do need to be addressed to Leech, Williams, Merton and Allchin, though. Has their more integrated approach to deification truly dealt with the more complex philosophical questions in our ethical culture wars? Or, has such an approach merely integrated in principle, but not in practice, the troubling ethical problems we face as each button issue comes our inevitable way? And, we also need to ponder how injustice must be faced and dealt with. Is it through protest actions or advocacy groups? What about the role of formal political parties? What role does non-government organizations, inter-government organizations, government-assistance organizations and liberation groups play in bringing about justice and peace? There is a worrisome sense that Allchin, Williams, Merton and Leech have not really probed the meaning of deification at a deeper practical and theoretical level when it comes to thinking through and acting upon the tough ethical questions we face. This does need to be done, and done in a more demanding manner. Is this what the radical catholic movement of John Milbank, Catherine Pickstock and clan are doing these days? Such a movement has not yet, in a substantive way, raised the issues of serious political party engagement.

Leech, in *Thomas Merton: Theologian of Resistance*, pointed out that he thought that Merton was a thoughtful 'social critic', but he was not a 'social activist'. This is true, of course. But, do we need more than social critics or social activists? Protest and advocacy activism have a place, but do such approaches truly deal with the larger means by which political change is brought about? Social criticism and protest and advocacy activism are important and needed yet limited. What is the relationship between deification and substantive political action in and through political parties? This is a question that is rarely dealt with by those who hold high the importance of the atonement and deification. Why, we might ask, is this the case?

How do we, in an age of bitter and intense culture wars, articulate an ethical vision that transcends the tribalism of the political left, right and sensible centre? Where and when is the political right right and when wrong and inconsistent? When and where is the left right and when is it inconsistent? When is the sensible centre neither sensible nor of the centre? If we do not ask these sorts of questions, Christians, in one form or another, will be taken captive by the subtle and not so subtle spirit of our age.

I must frankly admit, in my ponderings over the years, I have found few that integrate the notion of deification in a substantive and well thought through way, with contemporary ethical and political issues. Fewer still transcend the clan-like nature of the culture wars and less still have done this within the unique Canadian context. This, it seems to me, is the challenge for Canadians who are committed to drawing water from their own wells. These sorts of questions do need to be pondered and thought through, but as this essay is winding down, I do need to conclude with one more reflection.

V. The Beatitudes and Deification

The nature of an acorn is to become a tall and stately oak tree. A sunflower seed will produce an attractive sunflower that will track the light and warmth of the sun. A colt will become a horse, a calf a cow. The nature of an eagle is to soar under the blue canopy, and the nature of a dolphin is to swim with joy in the water. The nature of a mountain goat is to dwell amongst the white crags and rock ridges, and the nature of the birds in spring is to produce young ones. We know what the nature of a thing is by how faithfully and naturally it moves from its innate and implicit potential to its fulfillment, in an explicit, developmental and unfolding way.

What does the deified and divinized life look like, and what is its nature?

How can we tell when we have the genuine and authentic thing? Are there markings and cairns along the path that make it plain we are on the right trail to the summit of our new being in Christ? I have found it somewhat interesting over the years, as I have read and pondered a variety of books and articles on the meaning of deification, that few authors bring together the intricate and intimate relationship between the Beatitudes and deification. Scripture and the Fathers are often used, but rare is the writer on deification that highlights how our new nature in Christ and the Church can be best understood by the leading light of the Beatitudes.

The fact that this connection is rarely made does need to be challenged. The fact that the Beatitudes, more than any other Biblical texts, justify the meaning of deification must be pondered. What is about the Beatitudes that point the way to deification?

Most translations of the Beatitudes begin with 'Blessed are those who' or 'Happy are those who'. This seems to miss the meaning of the Greek word that is translated as 'Blessed' or 'Happy'. What is the Greek word used, and what is its deeper and older meaning? The Greek word used is *makarios*. The root of *makarios* is *makar*. What do *makar* and *makarios* mean in Greek? William Barclay and Jim Forest provide excellent guidance in this area.

Barclay suggests in his interpretation/translation of *makarios* this insightful truth: The word blessed which is used in each of the beatitudes is a very special word. It is the Greek word *makarios*. *Makarios* is the word which specially describes the gods. If then, *makarios*, in Greek myth, is the word used to describe the gods, Jesus is pointing in a direction often missed by many translations of the Beatitudes. Jim Forest, a member of the Orthodox Tradition, chair of the Orthodox Peace Network, and former friend of Thomas Merton, penned a fine book on the Beatitudes. *The Ladder of the Beatitudes* (1999) walks the interested reader beyond the suggestive insights of William Barclay. Forest has these illuminating insights:

> In Classsical Greek *makar* was associated with the immortal gods. *Kari* means 'fate' or 'death', but with the negative prefix *ma* the word means 'being deathless, no longer subject to fate', a condition both inaccessible and longed for by mortals. It was because of their immortality that the gods, the *hoi Makarioi*, were the blessed ones. (p.20)

A few lines later in *The Ladder of the Beatitudes*, Forest, quoting from Archimandrite Ephrem, says this:

> The Greek *makar* starts life as precisely something which the gods are ... In Christian use, *makarios* came to mean sharing in the life of God. (p.20)

The language of deification and divinization is often drawn from the Greek words *theosis* or *apotheosis*. The primary text used by many Orthodox to justify deification is 2 Peter 1:4: 'whereby it is given to us exceeding great and precious promises: that by these you might be partakers of the divine nature'. What does it mean to be a partaker of the 'divine nature' in both a mystical and contemplative manner? And, are the Beatitudes a better place to turn to for the vision of deification than 2 Peter? Second Peter has been the cornerstone text, whereas the Beatitudes have been ignored.

There is no doubt that the Beatitudes, and the language of *makarios* and *makar*, do point the way to being as the gods. The transformative journey that the Beatitudes point out for us (a way-mark deep into the inner life and a corresponding journey into the prophetic calling of justice/peace-makers) is the divine path of becoming like God. The fact that the Church has often not known what to do with the Beatitudes, as faithfully reflected in Clarence Bauman's, *The Sermon on the Mount: The Modern Quest for its Meaning* (1985), should alert us to some telling signals.

It was and is these omissions that drew me to write a missive on the Beatitudes a couple of years ago. *The Beatitudes: When Mountain Meets Valley* (2005) deals with the fact that the nature of the redeemed and deified should embody and incarnate the Beatitudes. I attempted in a chapter in *The Beatitudes* ('Blessedness and Deification') to explain how we have often mistranslated *makarios*, and what a deeper translation might mean.

Conclusion

There is no doubt we have been in a dark forest for many years in our understanding of the atonement. The time has surely come when we must leave the shade and shadow and enter the mountains and open vistas. *Violence, Hospitality, and the Cross: Reappropriating the Atonement Tradition* brings us into a fine and spacious clearing. The uphill trek is before us, and peaks draw us ever onward. The thinking about deification by such Orthodox theologians as Lossky and Azkoul bring us to the alpine meadows with their rich flora and fauna. Anglican theologians such as ·
Allchin and Williams lead us yet higher, ever closer to the summit of the meaning of deification and prophetic politics. The Beatitudes take us to

the ethical Everest and K2 of deification. The task, as ever, is to know how to trek to such peaks yet return to the valley. Such is the challenge of those who seek to understand the highest and fullest meaning of the atonement and redemption as deification in Christ and the one, holy, catholic and apostolic church.

We must always be wary, though, of trading in one reductionistic theory of the atonement for another. We might be bidding adieu to the ransom or juridical theory of the atonement as the dominant metaphors (gratefully so), but we must also shy away from reducing the atonement to either a Girardian read or a pacifist/nonviolent interpretation of the atonement. Our divinized life in Christ, the one, holy, catholic and apostolic church and the world is much more subtle and nuanced than any one-dimensional understanding of the atonement. Let us live with the mystery, and be gracious with those who miss the comprehensive epic vision that cannot be easily netted nor reduced to a simple formula and explanation.

Fiat Lux

Permissions

Scripture Index